Contents – Text

W9-AUO-493

2 Contents – Text

Contents – Maps

MAP INDEX

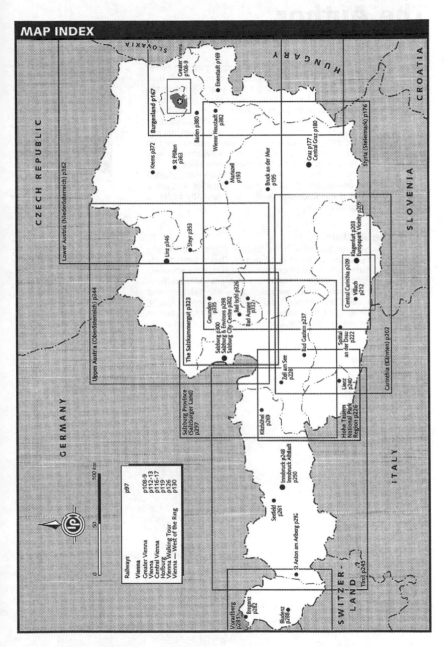

SLOVAKIA

HUNGARY

CROATIA

CZECH REPUBLIC

Greater Vienna p108-9

Burgenland p167

Eisenstadt p169

Krems p372

St Pölten p363

Baden p380

Wiener Neustadt p382

Mariazell p193

Bruck an der Mur p195

Graz p177 Central Graz p180

Styria (Steiermark) p176

Lower Austria (Niederösterreich) p362

SLOVENIA

Linz p346

Steyr p353

Upper Austria (Oberösterreich) p344

Klagenfurt p203 Europapark Vicinity p205

The Salzkammergut p323

Gmunden p335

Bad Ischl p326

Bad Aussee p332

Salzburg p300 Salzburg & Environs p298 Salzburg City Centre p302

Central Carinthia p209

Villach p212

Bad Gastein p237

Spittal an der Drau p222

Carinthia (Kärnten) p202

Salzburg Province (Salzburger Land) p297

Zell am See p228

Lienz p240

Kitzbühel p269

Hohe Tauern National Park Region p226

GERMANY

Innsbruck p248 Innsbruck Altstadt p250

Seefeld p261

St Anton am Arlberg p295

ITALY

Tirol p245

Vorarlberg p281

Bregenz p282

Bludenz p288

SWITZERLAND

0   50   100 km

The Author

Mark Honan

After a university degree in philosophy opened up a glittering career as an office clerk, Mark soon decided that there was more to life than form filing and data entry. He set off on a two year trip round the world, armed with a backpack and a vague intent to sell travel stories and pictures upon his return to England. Astonishingly, this barely formed plan succeeded and Mark became the travel correspondent for a London-based magazine. He toured Europe in a camper van, mailing back articles and gathering the experience that would later enable him to contribute to the 1st edition of Lonely Planet's *Western Europe*. Mark has been writing regularly for Lonely Planet ever since.

He has written Lonely Planet guidebooks to *Switzerland*, *Austria* and *Vienna*, and worked on updated editions of guides to *Central America*, *Mexico* and the *Solomon Islands*. He is currently updating part of the *India* guidebook.

From the Author

Thanks to everyone connected with the Austrian tourist industry who responded to my numerous and diverse inquiries. That includes the efficient staff at many local tourist offices around Austria, but particularly Marion and Ingrid at ANTO in London, and Maria Altendorfer in Salzburg. Peter Kuhn also helped me get to grips with Salzburg, and Irmgard Lauria and Franz Schubert did likewise in Vienna. Finally, many thanks to Dragica Stojanović for finding my moneybelt in Salzburg, thereby ensuring that my final research trip didn't start in disaster.

This Book

Mark Honan researched and wrote the first edition of *Austria* and updated this second edition.

From the Publisher

This edition of *Austria* was produced in Lonely Planet's London office. David Rathborne coordinated the editing with invaluable assistance from Paul Bloomfield and Christine Stroyan. Paul, David, Tim Ryder and Dorinda Talbot proofread the book. David Wenk coordinated the mapping and design, assisted by Michelle Lewis, Angie Watts and Sara Yorke. The cover was designed by Dale Buckton and Nicky Castle drew the illustrations. Sara Yorke designed the colour pages with photographs supplied by Lonely Planet Images and the Austrian National Tourist Office (ANTO), London. Lisa Ball, Wendy Bashford and Sandra Dartnell provided additional research and the air travel information was updated by Simon Calder. Thanks to Leonie Mugavin for her help with the health section, to Quentin Frayne for the language section, to Chris Klep, Richard Nebesky and Nick Tapp for their comments on the Walking & Skiing special section and to Marion Telsnig of ANTO in London for fielding numerous inquiries. Thanks also to Katrina Browning, Michelle Lewis, Cathy Lanigan and Katharine Leck for their extraordinary patience, advice and assistance.

Thanks

Many thanks to the following travellers who used the last edition and wrote to us with helpful hints, advice and interesting anecdotes:

Mel, Kostas Alexopoulos, Suzi Asmus, Nina & Moshe Berant, Elaine Boeshe, Leslie Clark, Brigette Clarke, Adam Coyle, Heidi Dawn, Lars Dicht, Graham Elliott, Kathryn Fleming, Iain Franklin, Kathryn Godfrey, Bob Greiner, Erich Gutsjahr, Keith A Havas, Eric Hempsall, Tea Die Henrich, Lee-Anne & Matthew Horsfall, Rachel Hursthouse, Sue Jeffery, Richard Lloyd, Ian McAllister, Megan McGregor, Paul Miller, Luisella Mori, Caroline Newhouse, WD Pennycook, Wilco Pruysers, Peter Richmond, Claire Rosenbaum, Matt Salmon, Michel Schinz, Jason Smith, Lisa Spratling, Louise Stanley, Rakefet & Gil Stav, Mary Steer, Jenny Stewart, Peggy Storniolo, Ann Sy, E Thomas, Dr C Tiligada, Remi Tourtet, Glenn Townend, Brendan Vargas, Astrid van der Vlugt, Scott Wayne, John Whitten, Per Wickenberg, Kate Wilford, Theo Wilhelm, Dr Michael L Wyzan, Lea Zore.

Foreword

ABOUT LONELY PLANET GUIDEBOOKS

The story begins with a classic travel adventure: Tony and Maureen Wheeler's 1972 journey across Europe and Asia to Australia. Useful information about the overland trail did not exist at that time, so Tony and Maureen published the first Lonely Planet guidebook to meet a growing need.

From a kitchen table, then from a tiny office in Melbourne (Australia), Lonely Planet has become the largest independent travel publisher in the world, an international company with offices in Melbourne, Oakland (USA), London (UK) and Paris (France).

Today Lonely Planet guidebooks cover the globe. There is an ever-growing list of books and there's information in a variety of forms and media. Some things haven't changed. The main aim is still to help make it possible for adventurous travellers to get out there – to explore and better understand the world.

At Lonely Planet we believe travellers can make a positive contribution to the countries they visit – if they respect their host communities and spend their money wisely. Since 1986 a percentage of the income from each book has been donated to aid projects and human rights campaigns.

Updates Lonely Planet thoroughly updates each guidebook as often as possible. This usually means there are around two years between editions, although for more unusual or more stable destinations the gap can be longer. Check the imprint page (following the colour map at the beginning of the book) for publication dates.

Between editions up-to-date information is available in two free newsletters – the paper *Planet Talk* and email *Comet* (to subscribe, contact any Lonely Planet office) – and on our Web site at www.lonelyplanet.com. The *Upgrades* section of the Web site covers a number of important and volatile destinations and is regularly updated by Lonely Planet authors. *Scoop* covers news and current affairs relevant to travellers. And, lastly, the *Thorn Tree* bulletin board, and *Postcards* section of the site carry unverified, but fascinating, reports from travellers.

Correspondence The process of creating new editions begins with the letters, postcards and emails received from travellers. This correspondence often includes suggestions, criticisms and comments about the current editions. Interesting excerpts are immediately passed on via newsletters and the Web site, and everything goes to our authors to be verified when they're researching on the road. We're keen to get more feedback from organisations or individuals who represent communities visited by travellers.

Lonely Planet gathers information for everyone who's curious about the planet – and especially for those who explore it first-hand. Through guidebooks, phrasebooks, activity guides, maps, literature, newsletters, image library, TV series and Web site we act as an information exchange for a worldwide community of travellers.

Research Authors aim to gather sufficient practical information to enable travellers to make informed choices and to make the mechanics of a journey run smoothly. They also research historical and cultural background to help enrich the travel experience and allow travellers to understand and respond appropriately to cultural and environmental issues.

Authors don't stay in every hotel because that would mean spending a couple of months in each medium-sized city and, no, they don't eat at every restaurant because that would mean stretching belts beyond capacity. They do visit hotels and restaurants to check standards and prices, but feedback based on readers' direct experiences can be very helpful.

Many of our authors work undercover, others aren't so secretive. None of them accept freebies in exchange for positive write-ups. And none of our guidebooks contain any advertising.

Production Authors submit their raw manuscripts and maps to offices in Australia, USA, UK or France. Editors and cartographers – all experienced travellers themselves – then begin the process of assembling the pieces. When the book finally hits the shops some things are already out of date, we start getting feedback from readers, and the process begins again ...

WARNING & REQUEST

Things change – prices go up, schedules change, good places go bad and bad places go bankrupt – nothing stays the same. So, if you find things better or worse, recently opened or long since closed, please tell us and help make the next edition even more accurate and useful. We genuinely value all the feedback we receive. Julie Young coordinates a well-travelled team that reads and acknowledges every letter, postcard and email and ensures that every morsel of information finds its way to the appropriate authors, editors and cartographers for verification.

Everyone who writes to us will find their name in the next edition of the appropriate guidebook. They will also receive the latest issue of *Planet Talk*, our quarterly printed newsletter, or *Comet*, our monthly email newsletter. Subscriptions to both newsletters are free. The very best contributions will be rewarded with a free guidebook.

Excerpts from your correspondence may appear in new editions of Lonely Planet guidebooks, the Lonely Planet Web site, *Planet Talk* or *Comet*, so please let us know if you *don't* want your letter published or your name acknowledged.

Send all correspondence to the Lonely Planet office closest to you:

Australia: PO Box 617, Hawthorn, Victoria 3122
UK: 10A Spring Place, London NW5 3BH
USA: 150 Linden St, Oakland CA 94607
France: 1 rue du Dahomey, Paris 75011

Or email us at: talk2us@lonelyplanet.com.au

For news, views and updates see our Web site: www.lonelyplanet.com

HOW TO USE A LONELY PLANET GUIDEBOOK

The best way to use a Lonely Planet guidebook is any way you choose. At Lonely Planet we believe the most memorable travel experiences are often those that are unexpected, and the finest discoveries are those you make yourself. Guidebooks are not intended to be used as if they provide a detailed set of infallible instructions!

Contents All Lonely Planet guidebooks follow the same format. The Facts about the Country chapter or section gives background information ranging from history to weather. Facts for the Visitor gives practical information on issues like visas and health. Getting There & Away gives a brief starting point for researching travel to and from the destination. Getting Around gives an overview of the transport options when you arrive.

The peculiar demands of each destination determine how subsequent chapters are broken up, but some things remain constant. We always start with background, then proceed to sights, places to stay, places to eat, entertainment, getting there and away, and getting around information – in that order.

Heading Hierarchy Lonely Planet headings are used in a strict hierarchical structure that can be visualised as a set of Russian dolls. Each heading (and its following text) is encompassed by any preceding heading that is higher on the hierarchical ladder.

Entry Points We do not assume guidebooks will be read from beginning to end, but that people will dip into them. The traditional entry points are the list of contents and the index. In addition, however, there is a complete list of maps and an index map illustrating map coverage.

There's also a colour map that shows highlights. These highlights are dealt with in greater detail in the Facts for the Visitor chapter, along with planning questions and suggested itineraries. Each chapter covering a geographical region begins with a locator map and another list of highlights. Once you find something of interest in a list of highlights, turn to the index.

Maps Maps play a crucial role in Lonely Planet guidebooks and include a huge amount of information. A legend is printed on the back page. We seek to have complete consistency between maps and text, and to have every important place in the text captured on a map. Map key numbers usually start in the top left corner.

Although inclusion in a guidebook usually implies a recommendation we cannot list every good place. Exclusion does not necessarily imply criticism. In fact there are a number of reasons why we might exclude a place – sometimes it is simply inappropriate to encourage an influx of travellers.

Introduction

Austria is terrific as a year-round holiday destination. Much of the country is dominated by the soaring magnificence of the Alps, and this magical mountain landscape has relaxed chalet villages, first-rate winter sport resorts, isolated hiking trails, traditional Alpine festivals and much more.

The cities have plenty to engage visitors, not least world-class museums and art collections. Vienna is the capital, hub of the country's unrivalled musical tradition and home to some of the most impressive architecture in Europe. Baroque music, art and architecture reached their peaks in Salzburg, Mozart's birthplace. Innsbruck is stunningly situated, with snow-capped peaks a backdrop to its fascinating historic buildings.

Throughout Austria you'll find that the rhythm of normal daily life has a musical beat. Important music festivals, especially those featuring classical music, fill the calendar. There's also an extensive variety of outdoor activities, ranging from lounging on lakeside beaches to paragliding from mountains. It hardly needs adding that you can enjoy a spot of skiing, too. An efficient tourist industry, good transport, charming hotels and atmospheric restaurants make it easy and pleasurable just to be in Austria.

This is a country that has something for everybody, and for all budgets. It costs nothing to walk amid the stupendous Alpine scenery, to cycle along the castle-strewn and vineyard-terraced Wachau stretch of the Danube River, or to admire the exuberant décor of the many Baroque churches. It costs nothing to wander around imperial Vienna and enjoy the colourful street artists, or to gaze in awe at the lavish façades of the grandiose public buildings. And it costs nothing to appreciate the wonder of Salzburg's many superb church spires. Sure, it costs something to get there and stay there, but you'll find it's a cost well worth paying.

Facts about Austria

HISTORY

The Danube Valley was populated during the Palaeolithic Age, as proved by the discovery there of a 25,000-year-old statuette, the *Venus of Willendorf*. In 1991 the body of a late Stone Age man was discovered in a glacier in the Ötztal Alps (see the boxed text 'Entombed in Ice' in the Tirol chapter). When the Romans arrived in the 1st century BC, there were already Celtic settlements in the Danube Valley, the result of migrations east from Gaul some 500 years earlier. Celts had also long been mining salt in Hallstatt and trading along the north-south Alpine trading routes. The Romans established settlements from Brigantium (Bregenz) to Carnuntum (Petronell), 40km east of a military camp known as Vindobona (Vienna). The Danube River, known to the Romans as Danuvius, marked the northern border of the empire and served to discourage advances by Germanic tribes from the north.

By the 5th century, the Roman Empire had collapsed and the Romans were forced south by invading tribes. The importance of the Danube Valley as an east-west crossing meant successive waves of tribes and armies tried to gain control of the region. Before and after the Roman withdrawal came the Teutons, Slavs, Huns, Goths, Franks, Bavarians, Avars and Magyars. In the 7th century the Bavarians controlled territory between the eastern Alps and the Wienerwald (Vienna Woods). Meanwhile, the Slavs were encroaching on the region from the south-east.

Charlemagne

Charlemagne, the king of the Franks and eventually Holy Roman Emperor, brushed aside all opposition and established a territory in the Danube Valley known as the Ostmark (Eastern March) in 803. This was west of Vienna and bordered by the rivers Enns, Raab and Drau. Upon his death in 814 the Carolingian empire was divided into three parts, and the Magyars overran the Ostmark in determined invasions.

Otto I (the Great), controller of the eastern portion of Charlemagne's old empire, defeated the Hungarians at Augsburg and re-established the Ostmark in 955. Seven years later Pope John XII crowned Otto as Holy Roman Emperor of the German princes. In 996 the Ostmark was first referred to as Ostarrichi, which is a clear forerunner of the modern German word Österreich (Austria), meaning eastern empire.

The Babenbergs

Leopold von Babenberg, a descendant of a noble Bavarian family, became the margrave (German noble ranked above count) of the Ostmark in 976. The Babenbergs gradually extended their sphere of influence and, during the 11th century, Vienna and most of modern-day Lower Austria fell into their hands; in 1192 they also acquired Styria and much of Upper Austria. This was a period of trade and prosperity for the region. In 1156 the Holy Roman Emperor, Friedrich Barbarossa, elevated the territory to that of a duchy. In the same year the Babenbergs, under Duke Heinrich II, established their permanent residence in Vienna.

In 1246 Duke Friedrich II was killed in a battle with the Hungarians over the Austro-Hungarian border. He left no heirs, which allowed the Bohemian king Ottokar II to move in and take control. Ottokar held sway over a huge area (stretching all the way from the Sudeten, on the northern border of the present-day Czech Republic, to the Adriatic Sea) and refused to swear allegiance to the new Holy Roman Emperor, Rudolf of Habsburg. His pride was costly: Ottokar died in a battle against his powerful adversary at Marchfeld in 1278. Rudolf granted his two sons the fiefdoms of Austria and Styria in 1282; and thus began the rule of one of the most powerful dynasties in

European history. The Habsburgs were to retain the reins of power right up to the 20th century.

The Habsburg Dynasty

The Habsburgs initially suffered a few reversals (including some humiliating defeats by the Swiss) but managed to consolidate their position: Carinthia and Carniola were annexed in 1335, followed by Tirol in 1363. Rudolf IV (ruled 1358 to 1365) went as far as to forge some documents (the *Privilegium maius*) to elevate his status to that of an archduke. He also laid the foundation stone of Stephansdom (St Stephen's Cathedral) in Vienna and founded the University of Vienna. These acts helped to placate the wealthy Viennese families, whose privileges had been reduced in the previous century.

In 1453 Friedrich III managed to genuinely acquire the status that was faked by Rudolf IV and was crowned Holy Roman Emperor. Furthermore, he persuaded Pope Paul II to raise the status of Vienna to that of a bishopric in 1469. Friedrich's ambition knew few bounds. His motto was AEIOU, usually interpreted to mean *Austria Est Imperare Orbi Universo*, though some scholars stake a claim for *Alles Erdreich Ist Österreich Untertan*, or even *Austria Erit In Orbe Ultima*. If the exact wording is in dispute, the meaning isn't, because either way it expressed the view that the whole world was Austria's empire. To try to prove this, Friedrich waged war against King Matthias Corvinus of Hungary, who occupied Vienna (1485-90). He also made no friend of the Archbishop of Salzburg, who sided with his opponents. Salzburg was a powerful ecclesiastical principality until the 19th century.

Friedrich instigated the famous and extremely successful Habsburg policy of acquiring new territories through politically motivated marriages. The intermarriage policy had a genetic side effect, albeit discreetly played down in official portraits: the distended lower jaw and lip became a family trait. In 1477 Friedrich's son, Maximilian, gained control of Burgundy and the Netherlands by marriage to Maria of Burgundy. Maximilian's eldest son, Philip, was married to the infanta of Spain in 1496. Philip's son Charles eventually gained most from this. He became Charles I of Spain in 1516 (which included control of vast overseas territories) and Charles V of the Holy Roman Empire in 1519.

Charles' acquisitions were too diverse for one person to rule effectively and he handed over the Austrian territories to his younger brother Ferdinand I in 1521. Ferdinand also inherited Hungary and Bohemia through his marriage to Anna Jagiello after her brother, King Lewis II, died in battle in 1526.

The Turkish Threat

Ferdinand became preoccupied with protecting his territories from the incursions of the Turks, who were rampant under the leadership of Süleyman the Magnificent, sultan of the Ottoman Empire; Styria was particularly vulnerable. The Turks overran the Balkans, and killed Lewis II in their conquest of Hungary. In 1529 the Turks reached Vienna, but their 18 day siege of the city foundered with the onset of an early winter. They withdrew but continued to be a powerful force, and it was this threat that prompted Ferdinand to move his court to Vienna in 1533, the first Habsburg to reside in the city permanently. This move increased the city's prestige.

In 1556 Charles abdicated as emperor and Ferdinand was crowned in his place. Charles' remaining territory was inherited by his son, Philip II, finalising the split in the Habsburg line. In 1571 Maximilian II granted religious freedom to his subjects, upon which the vast majority of Austrians turned to Protestantism. In 1576, Maximilian's grandson, Rudolf II, became emperor and embraced the Counter-Reformation; much of the country reverted to Catholicism – not always without coercion. The problem of religious intolerance was the cause of the Thirty Years' War which started in 1618 and had a devastating effect on the whole of Central Europe. In 1645 a

The Turks & Vienna

The Ottoman Empire viewed Vienna as 'the city of the golden apple', but it wasn't *Apfelstrudel* they were after in their two great sieges. The first, in 1529, was undertaken by Süleyman the Magnificent, but the 18 day endeavour was not sufficient to break the resolve of the city. The Turkish sultan subsequently died at the siege of Szigetvár, yet his death was kept secret for several days in an attempt to preserve the morale of the army. The subterfuge worked for a while. Messengers were led into the presence of the embalmed body which was placed in a seated position on the throne. They then unknowingly relayed their news to the corpse. The lack of the slightest acknowledgment of the sultan towards his minions was interpreted as regal impassiveness.

At the head of the Turkish siege of 1683 was the general Kara Mustapha. Amid the 25,000 tents of the Ottoman army that surrounded Vienna he installed his 1500 concubines, guarded by 700 black eunuchs. Their luxurious quarters contained gushing fountains and regal baths, all set up in haste but with great opulence.

Again, it was all to no avail – perhaps the concubines proved too much of a distraction. Whatever the reason, Mustapha failed to put garrisons on Kahlenberg and was surprised by a swift attack from Charles of Lorraine heading a German army and supported by a Polish army led by King Sobieski. Mustapha was pursued from the battlefield and defeated once again, at Gran. At Belgrade he was met by the emissary of the sultan, Mehmed IV. The price of failure was death, and Mustapha meekly accepted his fate. When the Austrian imperial army conquered Belgrade in 1718 the grand vizier's head was dug up and brought back to Vienna in triumph, where it is preserved (but no longer exhibited) in the Historisches Museum der Stadt Wien.

Protestant Swedish army marched to within sight of Vienna but did not attack. Peace was finally achieved in 1648 and, through the Treaty of Westphalia, Austria lost some territory to France.

For much of the rest of the century, Austria was preoccupied with halting the advance of the Turks into Europe. Vienna, already depleted by a severe epidemic of bubonic plague, found itself in 1683 again under Turkish siege (see the boxed text 'The Turks & Vienna'). The Viennese were close to capitulation when they were rescued by a Christian force of German and Polish soldiers. Combined forces subsequently swept the Turks to the south-eastern edge of Europe. The removal of the Turkish threat saw a proliferation of Baroque building in many cities. Under the musical emperor, Leopold I, Vienna became a magnet for musicians and composers.

Years of Reform

The death of Charles II, the last of the Spanish line of the Habsburgs, saw Austria become involved in the War of the Spanish Succession (1701-14). At its conclusion Charles VI, the Austrian emperor, was left with only minor Spanish possessions (such as the Low Countries and parts of Italy). Charles then turned to the problem of ensuring his daughter, Maria Theresa, would succeed him as he had no male heirs. To this end he drew up the Pragmatic Sanction, signed jointly by all the main European powers, and Maria Theresa duly ascended the Habsburg throne in 1740. However, to ensure she stayed there it was necessary to win the War of the Austrian Succession (1740-48).

Maria Theresa, aided by Britain and the Netherlands, had to fight off three rivals to the throne, including the elector of Bavaria.

Prussia took advantage of the Europe-wide conflict to wrest control of Silesia from Austria, which it retained in the ensuing peace. In the Seven Years' War (1756-63) the European powers changed alliances. Austria, now opposed by Britain, sought without success to regain Silesia from Prussia.

Maria Theresa's rule lasted 40 years, and is generally acknowledged as a golden era, in which Austria developed as a modern state. Centralised control was established, along with a civil service. The army and economy were reformed and a public education system was introduced. Vienna's reputation as a centre for music grew apace.

Maria Theresa's son, Joseph II, who ruled from 1780 to 1790 (he was also jointly in charge from 1765), was an even more zealous reformer. He issued an edict of tolerance for all faiths, secularised religious properties and abolished serfdom. Yet Joseph moved too fast for the general population and was ultimately forced to rescind some of his measures.

The ideas of the Enlightenment influenced Maria Theresa in her reform of state structures.

Crumbling Empire

The rise of Napoleon proved to be a major threat to the Habsburg empire. He inflicted major defeats on Austria in 1803, 1805 and 1809. Franz II, the grandson of Maria Theresa, had taken up the Austrian crown in 1804 and was forced by Napoleon in 1806 to relinquish the German crown and the title of Holy Roman Emperor. The cost of the war caused state bankruptcy and a currency collapse in 1811.

European conflict dragged on until the Congress of Vienna in 1814-15, in which Austria and its capital regained some measure of pride. The proceedings were dominated by the Austrian foreign minister, Klemens von Metternich. Austria was left with control of the German Confederation until forced to relinquish it in the Austro-Prussian War in 1866. Thereafter Austria had no place in the new German empire unified by Otto von Bismarck in 1871.

On the home front, all was not well in post-Congress Vienna. The arts and culture as pursued by the middle class flourished in the Biedermeier period, but the general populace had a harder time. Metternich had established a police state and removed civil rights. Coupled with poor wages and housing, this led to revolution in Vienna in March 1848. The war minister was hanged from a lamppost, Metternich was ousted and Emperor Ferdinand I abdicated. The subsequent liberal interlude was brief, though, and the army helped to reimpose an absolute monarchy. The new emperor, Franz Josef I (1830-1916), a nephew of Ferdinand, was just 18 years old.

Technical innovations led to an improvement in Austria's economic situation. Franz Josef became leader of the dual Austro-Hungarian monarchy, created in 1867 by the *Ausgleich* (compromise), which was Austria's response to defeat by Prussia the previous year. Common defence, foreign and economic policies ensued but unity was not complete, because two parliaments remained. Another period of prosperity began, which particularly benefited Vienna.

The Emperor & the Minister

France declared war on Austria in 1792 and enjoyed significant victories in northern Italy. However, it was Napoleon, French emperor from 1804, who inflicted the heaviest defeats on Franz II and his subjects. In 1805 Austria joined a coalition with Britain and Russia to try to restore the French monarchy. Within a year Austria was defeated at Ulm, Vienna was taken and Austro-Russian forces were defeated at Austerlitz. Under the Treaty of Pressburg in December 1805, Austria lost territory to both France and Bavaria.

Napoleon was at the peak of his power in 1809 when Austria joined another coalition with Britain. An Austrian defeat at Wagram in the same year led to the Treaty of Vienna, by which Austria lost more land. Also in 1809, Klemens von Metternich (1773-1859) was appointed Austria's foreign minister. A hereditary prince, Metternich was something of a reactionary who supported the monarchy and the status quo and sought to suppress liberal and egalitarian forces. He was instrumental in arranging the marriage of Franz II's daughter, Marie Louise, to Napoleon in 1810. The marriage was meant to buy peace with France, yet it wasn't long before Metternich helped to create the decisive coalition that engineered Napoleon's downfall at Waterloo in 1815.

Universal suffrage was introduced in Austro-Hungarian lands in 1906.

Peace in Europe had been maintained by a complex series of alliances (Austria-Hungary was linked to the German empire and Italy through the secret Triple Alliance), but that peace was wrecked in 1914 when Franz Josef's nephew and heir to the Austrian throne, Franz Ferdinand, was assassinated in Sarajevo on 28 June. A month later Austria-Hungary declared war on Serbia and WWI began.

The Republic

In 1916 Franz Josef died and his successor, Charles I, abdicated at the conclusion of the war in 1918. The Republic of Austria was created on 12 November 1918, marking the end of the centuries-old Habsburg dynasty and the right of the monarchy to participate in government. Under the peace treaty signed by the Allied powers on 10 September 1919, the Republic's planned union with Germany was prohibited, and it was forced to recognise the independent states of Czechoslovakia, Poland, Hungary and Yugoslavia. Previously, these countries, along with Romania and Bulgaria, had been largely under the control of the Habsburgs.

The loss of so much land caused severe economic difficulties in Austria – the new states declined to supply vital raw materials to their old ruler – and many urban families were soon on the verge of famine. By the mid-1920s, however, the federal government had stabilised the currency and established new trading relations.

The Rise of Fascism

After WWI, Vienna's socialist city government embarked on a programme of enlightened social policies. The rest of the country, however, was firmly under the sway of the conservative federal government, causing great tensions between the capital and the state. These tensions were heightened in July 1927, when right-wing extremists were acquitted of an assassination charge (a dubious decision which was widely seen as politically motivated) and the Justizpalast (Palace of Justice) in Vienna was torched by demonstrators. Police fired on the crowd and 86 people were killed.

Political and social tensions, such as the polarisation of political factions and rising unemployment, coupled with a worldwide economic crisis, gave the federal chancellor, Engelbert Dolfuss, an opportunity in 1933 to establish an authoritarian regime. In February 1934 civil war between the left and right-wing factions erupted, with hundreds of people killed over four days. The right wing proved victorious. In July the outlawed Nazis (National Socialists) assassinated Dolfuss. His successor, Kurt von Schuschnigg, couldn't stand up to increased threats from Germany. In 1938 he capitulated and included Nazis in his government.

On 11 March 1938 German troops marched into Austria and encountered little resistance. Adolf Hitler, a native of Austria who had departed Vienna decades before as a failed and disgruntled artist, returned to the city in triumph and held a huge rally at Heldenplatz. Austria was incorporated into the German Reich under the *Anschluss* (joining) on 13 March. A national referendum in April supported this union.

The arrival of the Nazis had a devastating effect on Austrian Jews, though many non-Jewish liberals and intellectuals also fled the Nazi regime. Representing 10% of Vienna's population, the Jews had enjoyed full civil rights. However, after May 1938, Germany's Nuremberg Racial Laws were applicable in Austria, leading to Jews being stripped of many of those rights. They were excluded from some professions and universities, and were forced to wear the yellow Star of David. Vienna's Jewish community was rocked by racial violence on the night of 9 November 1938, when their shops were looted and all but one of the temples burnt down. Many Jews fled the country, but about 60,000 were sent to concentration camps, where all but 2000 perished.

Austria was part of Germany's war machine during WWII. The government was a puppet of the German Nazis, and Austrians were conscripted into the German army. However, there were undercurrents of resistance to Germany: 100,000 Austrians were imprisoned for political reasons and 2700 resistance fighters were executed. Allied bombing was particularly heavy in Vienna in the last two years of the war and most major public buildings were damaged or destroyed, as were about 86,000 homes. As the war neared its end, Allied troops overran Austria from east and west. The Soviets reached Vienna first, entering the city on 11 April 1945.

Post-WWII

Austria was declared independent again on 27 April and a provisional federal government established under Karl Renner. The country was restored to its 1937 frontiers and occupied by the victorious Allies – the USA, the Soviet Union, the UK and France. The country was divided into four zones, one for each occupying power. Vienna, within the Soviet zone, was itself divided into four zones, with control of the city centre alternating between the four powers on a monthly basis. The situation in Austria and Vienna was very similar to that in Germany and Berlin; the Soviet zones in the latter were eventually sealed off, but Austria remained united because its postwar communists (unlike those in Germany's Soviet sector) failed to gain electoral support.

Delays caused by frosting relations between the superpowers ensured that the Allied occupation dragged on for 10 years. It was a tough time for Austria's people; the black market dominated the flow of goods and the rebuilding of national monuments was slow and expensive. On 15 May 1955 the Austrian State Treaty was ratified, with Austria proclaiming its permanent neutrality. The Allied forces withdrew, and in December 1955 Austria joined the United Nations. As the capital of a neutral country bordering the Warsaw Pact countries, Vienna attracted spies and diplomats in the Cold War years. Kennedy and Khrushchev met there in 1961, as did Carter and Brezhnev in 1979.

Austria's international image suffered when former secretary-general of the United Nations, Kurt Waldheim, was elected as president in 1986, even though it was revealed that he had served as a lieutenant in a German *Wehrmacht* unit implicated in WWII war crimes. There was no specific evidence against Waldheim but several countries barred him from making state visits. Strangely, Waldheim virtually ignored his three years military service in his biography, *In the Eye of the Storm*, published in 1985. A further, if rather belated, recognition of Austria's less than spotless WWII record came with Chancellor Franz Vranitzky's admission in 1993 that Austrians were 'willing servants of Nazism'.

In 1992, Waldheim was succeeded by Thomas Klestil; like Waldheim, he was a candidate of the right-wing Austrian People's Party (ÖVP). Klestil easily won a second term in April 1998. In the federal government, the Social Democrats have enjoyed sole or coalition power (with the ÖVP) since the 1970s.

In the postwar years Austria has worked hard to overcome economic difficulties. In 1972 it established a free trade treaty with the European Union (EU, then known as the EEC), and full membership was applied for in July 1989. Terms were agreed early in 1994 and the Austrian people endorsed their country's entry into the EU in the referendum of 12 June 1994; a resounding 66.4% were in favour. Austria formally joined the EU on 1 January 1995. Since then, many Austrians have been rather ambivalent about the advantages of EU membership.

GEOGRAPHY

Austria occupies an area of 83,855 sq km, extending for 560km from west to east, and 280km from north to south. The Alps are a dominating feature of the country. Two-thirds of Austria is mountainous, with three ranges running west to east and forcing most east-west travel into clearly defined channels.

The Northern Limestone Alps, on the border with Germany, reach nearly 3000m and extend eastwards, almost as far as the Wienerwald. The valley of the Inn River separates them from the High or Central Alps, which form the highest peaks in Austria, by. Many of the ridges in the Central Alps are topped by glaciers and most of the peaks are above 3000m. North-south travel across this natural barrier is limited to a handful of high passes and road tunnels. The Grossglockner is the highest peak at 3797m. The Southern Limestone Alps, which include the Karawanken range, form a natural barrier along the border with Italy and Slovenia.

Away from the mountains, the mighty Danube (Donau) River is the country's most famous natural feature. The Salzach River joins the Inn River near Braunau, which in turn joins the Danube at Passau, on the German border. The main rivers in the south-east are the Mur and the Drau. Lakes are numerous, particularly in the Salzkammergut region and Carinthia. Neusiedler See (Lake Neusiedl), in the east, is Central Europe's largest steppe lake. In the west, Austria has a small share (along with Germany and Switzerland) of Bodensee (Lake Constance), through which the Rhine River flows.

The most fertile land is in the Danube Valley; cultivation is intensive and 90% of Austria's food is home-grown. North of the Danube the land is mostly flattish and forested. Burgenland is also relatively flat, as is the area south-east of Graz. Lower Austria, Burgenland and Styria are the most important wine-growing regions.

CLIMATE

Austria lies within the Central European climatic zone, though the eastern part of the country has what is called a Continental Pannonian climate, characterised by a mean temperature in July above 19°C and annual rainfall usually less than 80cm. Austria's average rainfall is 71cm per year, with the west of the country receiving significantly higher levels. Mountains tend to draw the clouds, though the Alpine valleys often escape much of the downfall.

Visitors need to be prepared for a range of temperatures depending on altitude – the higher, the colder – but the sun is also very intense at high elevations, which receive more sunshine in autumn and winter than the Alpine valleys. The *Föhn* is a hot, dry

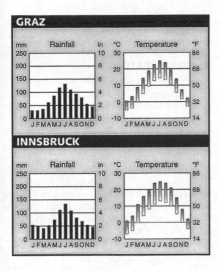

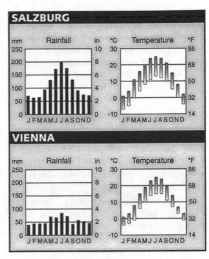

wind which sweeps down from the mountains, mainly in early spring and autumn, and can be rather uncomfortable for some people.

Average maximum temperatures in Vienna are: January 1°C, April 15°C, July 25°C and October 14°C. Average minimum temperatures are lower by about 10°C (summer) to 4°C (winter). Temperatures in Salzburg and Innsbruck are similar to those in Vienna, except that winter is a few degrees cooler.

On 11 August 1999 there will be a total eclipse of the sun, visible from a corridor of land running east-west across Europe and passing through Austria approximately between Vienna and Graz.

ECOLOGY & ENVIRONMENT

Austrians are well informed about environmental issues and the country has signed up to various international agreements intended to reduce pollution and preserve natural resources. Austria actually exceeds EU environmental dictates in many regards. Mountains have a fragile ecosystem and environmental measures to protect these areas have been in place in Austria for

many years, yet Austria has experienced some forest degradation caused by air and soil pollution.

Measures introduced to protect the environment range from banning leaded petrol to setting up an 'Eco Fund' to promote natural forms of energy, such as wind and solar power. In a 1978 referendum, Austrians voted against developing a nuclear power industry, prompting the federal Nuclear Prohibition Law later that year. Vienna's Spittelau incinerator has one of the lowest emission levels of any incinerator worldwide. Environmentally-friendly trams are a feature of many cities. Bicycles are another popular way to get around – there's even free bike rental in Vienna (see the Vienna Getting Around section).

Recycling is well established. Austrians diligently separate tin cans, paper and plastic from their refuse, for recycling. This isn't dictated by conscience: they are compelled to do so by law. In addition, hazardous materials such as aerosol cans must be put aside and are collected twice-yearly by municipal authorities. Recycling bins are a common sight in city streets. Glass containers (especially beer bottles) often have a return value, and some super-markets have an automatic bottle-returning area (*Flaschen Rücknahme*). It's all very efficient. You put your bottle into the recess, press a button and the machine works out what type it is and the appropriate return value. Then out pops a credit note for use against the rest of your shopping.

In Tirol, look for hotels bearing a sign reading 'Umweltsiegel Tirol – Wirtschaften mit Natur'. This means that the establishment has met various environmental standards, such as not providing a breakfast consisting of wasteful, individually packaged ingredients.

Visitors should endeavour to show the landscape and the environment the same respect that the Austrians do. In particular, you must not litter the countryside, and especially the Alpine regions, with non-biodegradable materials.

FLORA & FAUNA

Nearly half of Austria (46%) is forested. At low altitudes oak and beech are common. At higher elevations conifers such as pine, spruce and larch predominate. At around 2200m trees yield to Alpine meadows. Beyond 3000m, only mosses and lichens cling to the stark crags.

Alpine flowers add a palette of colour to the high pastures from about June to September and have adapted to cope with harsh conditions: long roots counter harsh winds, bright colours (a result of strong ultraviolet light) attract the few insects, and hairs and specially developed leaf shapes protect

Marmot Society

The marmot is a type of rodent seen in the mountains, particularly in the Tirol Alps. It generally lives in colonies comprising about two dozen animals. Members mark out the group's territory using pungent secretions from their cheeks. They all take part in lookout duty, watching not only for predators but also for unfamiliar marmots, which they will attack. Sentries raise themselves on their hind legs to better scan the surrounding area. The warning cry they give upon spotting a predator (such as a fox or golden eagle) is recognised by the chamois, which shares the same enemies.

For living quarters, the marmot builds a complex network of burrows which may have up to 100 exits. The marmot has powerful claws to aid digging and, although it can use its four limbs together, a burrow usually takes several generations to finish. The marmot sleeps on beds of dried grass, which it regularly cleans out and replaces.

Its long hibernation (concluding in April) leaves only five months to complete the breeding cycle and replenish energy for the next hibernation; these monogamous creatures therefore start mating soon after emerging in spring. The young are born blind and stay underground for the first four weeks of life. Once on the surface, they must quickly acquire the family smell (to be recognised as part of the group) and learn the warning cries. The marmot commonly feeds on grass and plants.

The edelweiss, *Leontopodium alpinum*, as celebrated in song in *The Sound of Music*.

against frost and dehydration. Orchids, edelweiss, dandelions and poppies all survive at higher altitudes. Edelweiss is found on rocks and in crevices, and has white, star-shaped flowers. Although one of Austria's most famous Alpine plants, it actually originated in central Asia. Most Alpine flowers are protected species and should not be picked.

The fauna of the lowlands is typical for Central Europe, though Neusiedler See is a unique sanctuary for numerous species of bird. In Alpine regions, the ibex (a mountain goat with huge curved horns) was under threat but is now breeding again. The ibex can master the art of leaping around mountains from the day it is born. In July it may migrate to an elevation of 3000m or more. The chamois (a small antelope) doesn't go quite so high, but it's equally at home scampering around on mountainsides. It can leap 4m vertically and its hooves have rubbery soles and rigid outer rims – ideal for maintaining a good grip on loose rocks. The chamois is more often seen than the ibex; they have similar habits and tend to rest in the noon heat. The marmot, a chunky rodent related to the squirrel, is also indigenous to the Alps. Butterflies are numerous in the Alpine meadows.

GOVERNMENT & POLITICS

The head of state is the president, who is chosen by the electorate for a six year term. The chancellor, appointed by the president, is the head of the federal government and the most influential political figure. Franz Vranitzky, chancellor since 1986, resigned in January 1997 and was succeeded by Victor Klima.

The country is divided into nine federal provinces (*Bundesländer*), each of which has its own head of government (*Landeshauptmann*) and a provincial assembly (*Landtag*). As well as being Austria's capital, Vienna has been a federal province in its own right since 1922. The term of office for each Landtag is four or five years, depending upon the province. Each has a degree of autonomy over local issues and elects representatives to the Federal Council (*Bundesrat*), the upper house of the national legislative body. The lower house, the National Council (*Nationalrat*), is elected every four years in a vote by citizens over the age of 18.

In national politics, the 1970s saw the dominance of the Socialist Party, now called the Social Democrats (SPÖ). In the 1990 election, the SPÖ formed a ruling coalition with the Austrian People's Party (ÖVP). This coalition retained power in the general elections of October 1994 and October 1995, though both parties won fewer seats than in 1990.

Despite the fact that the largest party in the coalition is left-wing, Austria has been perceived from abroad as retaining a sneaking affection for fascism. Such a view gained ground with the casual acceptance by Austrians of former president Waldheim and his murky past. The far-right Freedom Party (FPÖ) has made huge gains in the 1990s under the leadership of the personable but ruthless populist, Jörg Haider, who stands on an anti-immigration, anti-EU, anti-foreigner platform. He has raised the party's support from 4% to around 30%, edging it ahead of the ÖVP as Austria's second-largest party. The FPÖ's support is strongest in Carinthia, the province where

Haider was formerly governor. He had been forced out of office after he praised the employment policy of Hitler's Nazis. Haider has been softening his tone of late, and seems to have his eyes set on becoming chancellor after the 1999 election.

ECONOMY

Austria has a strong economy, with unemployment under 7% and inflation under 2%. It easily met the criteria necessary for EU economic and monetary union, and will be among the first wave of nations adopting the euro as the national currency. Austrian citizens enjoy wide-ranging welfare services including free education and health care, and a benign pensions and housing policy.

Industries controlled by government or the big banks have been a feature of life in postwar Austria. In common with much of Europe, the federal government recently embarked on a programme of privatisation; however, the nationalised sector remains significant, especially in Vienna where the city government still has fingers in many economic pies. The national economy is bolstered by a large contingent of foreign labour, particularly from Eastern Europe. Guest workers, mostly poorly paid, account for about 8.5% of the workforce.

Production in labour-intensive manufacturing industries was developed after WWII and now accounts for 75% of Austria's exports. Machinery, metallurgical products and textiles are particularly important. Linz is one of Austria's main iron and steel centres, feeding from iron ore mined at Eisenerz. Austria is relatively poor in natural resources and deposits of oil and natural gas are supplemented by hydroelectric power and imported coal. Forestry and agriculture together employ about 5% of the population. The country's cosseted farmers lost some of their protection with Austria's entry into the EU, but have responded well to the challenge posed by the EU open market. However, some prices (such as for dairy products) have not dropped as much as economists predicted.

Austria generally has a trade deficit in visible earnings, which is offset by income from tourism. This industry is hugely important for the whole country, but particularly for Tirol, where there are around 70 overnight tourist stays per local inhabitant each year. One-third of Tirol's private farms list providing tourist accommodation as their primary or secondary source of income. However, earnings from tourism have declined since the early 1990s. Austria is increasingly gearing itself towards big-spending tourists, with a rise in the number of four and five star hotels and a fall in those with one or two stars. The majority of visitors are Germans and Germany is also Austria's largest trading partner.

POPULATION & PEOPLE

Austria has a population of about eight million; Vienna accounts for 1.64 million, followed by Graz (with 245,000), Linz (203,000), Salzburg (144,000) and Innsbruck (120,000). On average, there are 95 inhabitants per sq km. Native Austrians are mostly of Germanic origin. Vienna and the south-east have the most ethnic diversity: industrial expansion in the late 19th century brought an influx of European migrants, particularly from the Czech-speaking parts of the former Habsburg empire.

In May 1993 about 600,000 foreigners were living legally in the country, mostly Turks, Poles, Germans, Slovaks and Czechs, plus 65,000 war refugees from the former Yugoslavia. In September 1992 a survey established that the public perception of the greatest threat to the country was being 'overrun by waves of refugees' (voiced by an incredible 38% of respondents). Given such sentiments, it's not surprising that the federal government has tightened up immigration controls considerably, and immigration now approximately matches emigration. Yet Austria still has a problem with illegal immigrants from Eastern Europe, and significantly increased the number of border guards in 1997.

National service is compulsory for male

Austrians (six months plus two months at a later time), though they may opt out of the military in favour of civil service duties. Women are not conscripted and cannot even volunteer to join the armed services.

EDUCATION

Austrian citizens are among the best educated in the world. The schooling system is uniform throughout the country. Children have nine years of compulsory education, from age six to 15. At age 10 children embark on either a basic secondary education (at a *Hauptschule*) or an extended secondary education (at a *Gymnasium*). The former lasts four years, and leads to a one year technical course or extended vocational training. Gymnasium pupils may also opt for vocational training after four years, or they can graduate at age 18 and try to win a university place.

Austria has 12 universities and six fine arts colleges, offering places for over 200,000 students. A university education, like schooling, is free for Austrians. Over 10% of students are foreigners, though they are usually charged tuition fees.

SCIENCE & PHILOSOPHY

Salzburg-born Christian Johann Doppler (1803-53), physicist and mathematician, demonstrated that wavelengths of light and sound shorten relative to the observer as objects approach, and lengthen as they move away. This explains why the siren pitch alters as a police car or ambulance speeds past. Known as the Doppler Effect, this principle has been used to demonstrate that other galaxies are moving further away from ours, and that the universe is therefore expanding.

The Wiener Kreis (Vienna Circle) was a group of philosophers centred on the University of Vienna in the 1920s and 1930s. The term logical positivism was coined to describe their views. They owed an initial debt to the work of the Austrian philosopher and scientist Ernst Mach (whose name lives on as a measure of the speed of a body in relation to the speed of sound). The Wiener Kreis formulated the verifiability principle, which sought to find meaning in phenomena by the method of its verification. Mathematics and pure logic were meaningful by virtue of being tautological, but, in order to be meaningful, anything not tautological had to be empirically verifiable; hence the laws of science were meaningful, whereas metaphysical questions (such as 'is there a God?') were not. Many members emigrated when the Nazis arrived in 1938. The movement remained influential, though it lost some of its appeal when philosophers couldn't agree whether the verifiability principle itself should be subject to empirical verification.

Sir Karl Popper (1902-94) was loosely connected with the Wiener Kreis, but mainly in a critical capacity. He was born in Vienna and lived and worked there until he also emigrated rather than face the Nazis. He had an impact on the way the nature of scientific enquiry was understood. Popper stated that the hallmark of science is falsifiability rather than verifiability, which was bad news for the credibility of the logical positivists and their verifiability principle. He pointed out that general scientific laws could never be logically proved to apply all the time, they could only be disproved if and when contrary data became manifest. Scientific laws are therefore accepted until they are seen to require revision (as in the way that Newtonian physics was refined by Einstein), thus leading to the advancement of scientific endeavour. Popper was also known for his work in the field of social and political philosophy.

Ludwig Wittgenstein (1889-1951) made a significant impact with his philosophical writings, not least on the Vienna Circle. He was born in Vienna and died in Cambridge, England, where he spent the latter part of his career as a research fellow at the university. Much of his output was concerned with the scope and limitations of language. His *Tractatus* was an adamant treatise ordered as a series of logical statements. By analysing language using language he ended up in the paradoxical situation of having to say what he admitted could only be shown. Nevertheless, Wittgenstein was so convinced that this work had achieved all that it was possible for such a text to do, that he believed it effectively heralded an end to philosophical enquiry. He retreated to the obscurity of a teaching post in rural Austria but later came out of retirement and proceeded to all but contradict his earlier work. His new theories were less rigid and attempted to illuminate the inventiveness of language. Wittgenstein has been hailed as one of the most influential 20th century philosophers, yet in his personal life he cut a rather lonely figure. One of his great fears was that his writings would be destroyed by fire (only the *Tractatus* was published in his lifetime), and he obsessively stored these in a fireproof safe.

Sigmund Freud (1856-1939), the founder of psychoanalysis, had a love-hate relationship with Vienna, the city where he lived and worked for most of his life. He too fled the Nazis in 1938. Freud believed the repression of infantile sexuality was the cause of neurosis in adult life. Central to his treatments was getting the patient to recognise unconscious conflicts. Early on he employed hypnosis to uncover these conflicts, but later abandoned hypnosis in favour of free association and the study of symbolism in dreams. *The Interpretation of Dreams* (1900) was his first major work.

Sigmund Freud

Sigmund Freud was born in Freiberg, Moravia, on 6 May 1856. Three years later his father, a Jewish wool merchant, relocated the family to the Leopoldstadt quarter of Vienna. Freud was educated in Vienna and graduated as a Doctor of Medicine in 1881 (his degree took three years longer to complete than was usual, as he spent much of his time engaged in neurological research that wasn't part of the curriculum). In 1886 he set up his first office as a neurologist at 01, Rathausstrasse 7, and later that year married Martha Bernays, who went on to bear him six children. In 1891 he moved his practice to 09, Berggasse 19. He first came up with the term 'psychoanalysis' in 1896.

Although many academics and physicians were hostile towards his published works, Freud was able to gather round him a core of pupils and followers who would meet in his waiting room on Wednesday evenings. Among their number was the Swiss psychologist Carl Jung, who later severed his links with the group (in 1914) because of personal differences with Freud. In 1923 Freud was diagnosed as having cancer of the palate, an affliction that caused him great pain and forced him to undergo surgery over 30 times. The illness prompted him to largely withdraw from public life; his daughter, Anna (a child psychiatrist), often appeared in his stead at meetings and conventions.

The arrival of the Nazis in 1938 instigated a mass evacuation by many of Vienna's Jews. Freud was allowed to emigrate to London on 4 June, accompanied by Anna. The rest of his children also managed to escape, but other family members weren't so fortunate – four of his elderly sisters were detained in the city and finally killed in a concentration camp in 1941. Freud breathed his last in London on 23 September 1939.

His final psychoanalytical work was *The Ego and the Id* (1923), advancing a new theory in which the tensions between the id (basic urges), the ego (the conscious personality) and the superego (idealised ingrained precepts) were explored. Although Freud's views have always been attacked, his legacy to the 20th century remains enormous. A mental landscape of Oedipus complexes, phallic objects and Freudian slips are only a few of the manifestations. Generations of patients supine on couches are another.

ARTS

See the special section 'Austria's Architecture' between pages 31 and 33 for information about the wealth of remarkable buildings found in Austria.

Music

Above all other artistic pursuits, Austria is known for music. Composers throughout Europe were drawn to Austria, and especially Vienna, in the 18th and 19th centuries by the willingness of the Habsburgs to patronise this medium. In fact many of the royal family were themselves gifted musicians – Leopold I was a composer, and Charles VI (violin), Maria Theresa (double bass) and Joseph II (harpsichord and cello) were all players. The various forms of classical music – symphony, concerto, sonata, opera and operetta – were explored and developed by the most eminent exponents of the day.

As early as the 12th century, Vienna was known for its troubadours (*Minnesänger*) and strolling musicians. In 1498 Maximilian I relocated the court orchestra from Innsbruck to Vienna. Opera originated in Italy around 1600 but it was in Vienna that it attained its apotheosis. The genre was reformed by Christoph Willibald von Gluck (1714-87) who married the music to a more dramatic format (as in *Orpheus & Eurydice* and *Alceste*).

Classicism Opera was taken to further heights by the great Wolfgang Amadeus Mozart (1756-91), who succeeded Gluck as court composer (albeit at less than half of the former's salary!) in 1787. Mozart achieved a fusion of Germanic and Italianate styles (his librettos were first in Italian and later, innovatively, in German). Pundits consider Mozart's greatest Italian operas to be *The Marriage of Figaro* (1786), *Don Giovanni* (1787) and *Così fan Tutte* (1790); in each case the librettist was Italian writer Lorenzo da Ponte. Mozart's *The Magic Flute* (1791) was a direct precursor of the German opera of the 19th century. (See also the boxed text 'Musical Mozartistry' in the Salzburg chapter.)

Mozart's mentor was Josef Haydn (1732-1809), the dominant musical figure of the 18th century. Haydn has been credited with ushering in the classicist era in Viennese music. He spent 38 years as musical director for the Esterházy family in nearby Eisenstadt. He wrote two great oratorios, *The Creation* (1798) and *The Seasons* (1801), as well as concertos, symphonies, operas, Masses and sonatas. (See also the boxed text 'Haydn Seek' in the Burgenland chapter.)

Ludwig van Beethoven (1770-1827) was born in Bonn (Germany) and moved to Vienna at the age of 21 to study under Haydn, although he was already a virtuoso pianist. He stayed in the city up to the time of his death, living at as many as 80 addresses. He was greatly inspired by the Viennese countryside (an influence evident in the *Pastoral Symphony* of 1808, among others). Among his piano sonatas, overtures and concertos are the opera *Fidelio* and the *Ninth Symphony* (concluding with the majestic *Ode to Joy*). Beethoven began to lose his hearing at the age of 30, understandably a cause of deep depression to him, and was profoundly deaf while composing some of his major works.

Franz Schubert (1797-1828), a native of Vienna, was responsible for giving the ancient German *lieder* (lyrical song) tradition a new lease of life, creating a craze for what became known as 'Schubertiade' musical evenings.

The Waltz The waltz originated in Vienna at the beginning of the 19th century and went down a storm at the Congress of Vienna. The early masters of this genre were Johann Strauss the Elder (1804-49), who also composed the *Radetzky March*, and Josef Lanner (1801-43).

The man who really made this form his own was Johann Strauss the Younger (1825-99), composer of 400 waltzes. Young Strauss became a musician against the wishes of Strauss senior (who had experienced years of struggle) and set up a rival orchestra to his father's. He composed Austria's unofficial anthem, the *Blue Danube* (1867), and *Tales from the Vienna Woods* (1868).

This joyful if lightweight style became so popular that more 'serious' composers began to feel somewhat disenfranchised. The operetta form became equally fashionable. The younger Strauss proved also to be a master of this style, especially with his eternally popular *Die Fledermaus* (1874) and *The Gipsy Baron* (1885). Franz Lehár (1870-1948) was another notable operetta composer, renowned for *Die lustige Witwe* (The Merry Widow).

Other 19th Century Composers Anton Bruckner (1824-96) was raised in Upper Austria and was long associated with the abbey in St Florian. He settled in Vienna on his appointment as organist to the court in 1868. Bruckner is known for dramatically intense symphonies and church music. Hugo Wolf (1860-1903) rivalled Schubert in lieder composition, though he later went insane.

In the late 19th century Austria was still attracting musicians and composers from elsewhere in Europe: Johannes Brahms (1833-97) and Gustav Mahler (1860-1911) were both German. Brahms greatly enjoyed Vienna's village atmosphere and said it had a positive effect on his work, which was of the classical-Romantic tradition. Mahler is known mainly for his nine symphonies, and was director of the Vienna Court Opera from 1897 to 1907. Richard Strauss (1864-

1949) was also German, and was drawn more to Salzburg than Vienna.

The New School Vienna's musical eminence continued in the 20th century with the innovative work of Arnold Schönberg (1874-1951), who founded what has been dubbed the 'New School' of Vienna. Schönberg developed theories on 12 tone composition, yet some of his earlier work (such as *Pieces for the Piano op. 11* composed in 1909) went completely beyond the bounds of tonality. The most influential of his pupils were Alban Berg (1885-1935) and Anton von Webern (1883-1945), who both explored the 12 tone technique. Schönberg was also a competent artist.

Music Today The wine taverns (*Heurigen*) in Vienna have a musical tradition all their own, with the songs often expressing very maudlin themes. Known as *Schrammelmusik*, it is usually played by musicians wielding a combination of violin, accordion, guitar and clarinet. In the field of rock and pop Austria has made little impact (unless you count the briefly emergent and now deceased Falco), though both Vienna and Graz have a thriving jazz scene, and Vienna was home to Joe Zawinul of Weather Report.

Today, Austrian orchestras, such as the Vienna Philharmonic, have a worldwide reputation, and institutions such as the Vienna Boys' Choir, the Staatsoper (State Opera), the Musikverein and the Konzerthaus are unrivalled. Salzburg and Graz are also major music centres and all three cities host important annual music festivals. Linz has the International Bruckner Festival, Feldkirch its Schubertiade festival, and Innsbruck its Early Music concerts. The Bregenz festival is famous for productions performed on a floating stage on Bodensee. A visit to some sort of musical event is an essential part of any trip to Austria.

Literature

The outstanding Austrian work of the Middle Ages was the *Nibelungenlied* (Song of the Nibelungs), written around 1200 by an unknown hand. This epic poem told a tale of passion, faithfulness and revenge in the Burgundian court at Worms. Its themes were adapted by Richard Wagner in his *The Ring of the Nibelungen* operatic series.

The first great figure in the modern era was the playwright Franz Grillparzer (1791-1872). He anticipated Freudian themes in his plays, which are still performed at the Burgtheater in Vienna. Other influential playwrights whose works still regularly get an airing are Johann Nestroy (1801-62), known for his satirical farces, and Ferdinand Raimaund, the 19th century author of *Der Alpenkönig und der Menschenfeind* (The King of the Alps and the Misanthrope). Adalbert Stifter (1805-68) is credited as being the seminal influence in the development of an Austrian prose style.

Austria's literary tradition really took off around the turn of the century, when the Vienna Secessionists and Sigmund Freud were creating waves. Influential writers who emerged at this time included Arthur Schnitzler, Hugo von Hofmannsthal, Karl Kraus and the poet Georg Trakl. Kraus' apocalyptic drama *Die letzten Tage der Menschheit* (The Last Days of Mankind) employed a combination of reports, interviews and press extracts to tell its tale – a very innovative style for its time. Kraus (1874-1936) had previously founded *Die Fackel* (The Torch), a critical literary periodical. The poet Peter Altenberg produced a body of work depicting the bohemian lifestyle of Vienna.

Robert Musil was a major 20th century writer, but he only achieved international recognition after his death. He was born in Klagenfurt in 1880 and died in poverty in Geneva in 1942, with his great literary achievement, *Der Mann ohne Eigenschaften* (The Man Without Qualities), still unfinished. Fortunately, enough of this work was completed for it to fill three volumes (English translation available) and reveal a fascinating portrait of the collapsing Austro-Hungarian monarchy.

Another important figure in the 20th century was Heimito von Doderer (1896-1966). He grew up in Vienna and first achieved recognition with his novel *Die Strudlhofstiege* (The Strudlhof Staircase). His magnum opus was *Die Dämonen* (The Demons), an epic fictional depiction of the end of the monarchy and the first years of the Austrian Republic. It looks at all strata of society and is published in English in three volumes.

The Wiener Gruppe (Vienna Group) was formed in the 1950s by HC Artmann. Its members incorporated surrealism and Dadaism in their sound compositions, textual montages, and Actionist happenings. (See also the boxed text 'Art through Action' in the Vienna chapter.) Public outrage and police intervention were a regular accompaniment to their meetings. The group's activities came to an end in 1964 when Konrad Bayer, its most influential member, committed suicide.

Thomas Bernhard (1931-89) was born in Holland but grew up and lived in Austria. He was obsessed with negative themes such as disintegration and death but in later works, such as *Cutting Timber*, he turned to polemic attacks against social conventions and institutions. His novels are seamless (no chapters or paragraphs, few full stops) and seemingly repetitive, but surprisingly readable once you get into them. He also wrote plays and short stories. Bernhard was influenced by Ludwig Wittgenstein's writings, and even wrote an autobiographical novel about his friendship with the philosopher's nephew. Both *Cutting Timber* and *Wittgenstein's Nephew* are published in English translations.

Austria's best known living writer is Peter Handke (born 1942). His output encompasses innovative and introspective prose works (*The Left-Handed Woman*) and stylistic plays (*The Hour When We Knew Nothing of Each Other*).

Contemporary female writers include the provocative novelist Elfriede Jelinek, who dispenses with direct speech and indulges in strange flights of fancy, but is worth persevering with. Translations of her novels *The*

Piano Teacher, Lust and *Women as Lovers* have been succesfully published in paperback. Friederike Mayröcker, a prominent contemporary poet and author of *Phantom Fan* and *Farewells*, has been described as 'the avant-garde's bird of paradise'.

Painting

Examples of Gothic church art in Austria are best seen in the Middle Ages collection at the Orangery in Vienna's Unteres Belvedere. Early Renaissance art is represented in Austria by the Danube School, which combined landscapes and religious motifs; notable exponents included Rueland Frueauf the Younger, Wolf Huber, Max Reichlich and Lukas Cranach.

Johann Michael Rottmayr and Daniel Gran were Baroque artists responsible for many church frescoes and Franz Anton Maulbertsch was an important canvas painter, who combined mastery of colour and light with intensity of expression.

The leading Biedermeier painters were Georg Ferdinand Waldmüller and Friedrich Gauermann, who captured the age in portraits, landscapes and period scenes. Some of Waldmüller's evocative if idealised peasant scenes can be seen in the Historisches Museum der Stadt Wien and the Oberes Belvedere, both in Vienna. Rudolf von Alt was an exponent of watercolour. Another Biedermeier artist was Moritz Michael Daffinger, who appears on the AS20 note.

Prominent painters of the historicist period included August von Pettenkofen and Hans Makart (1840-84). The age of expressionism was anticipated by Anton Romako (1832-89).

Egon Schiele (1890-1918) and Oskar Kokoschka (1886-1980) were important exponents of Viennese expressionism. The work of these Austrian painters is best viewed in the Oberes Belvedere; the Egon Schiele museum in Tulln, Lower Austria, is also worth a visit.

Gustav Klimt is possibly the most famous Austrian painter. For details of his life, see the boxed text in the Vienna chapter.

Sculpture & Design

The development of sculpture has reflected the changes in architectural styles over the years. The *Verdun Altar* in Klosterneuburg abbey in Lower Austria dates from the Romanesque period. Austria has some beautiful Gothic altars carved using limewood: the best known can be seen in St Wolfgang, and was the work of Michael Pacher (1440-98) – see also the boxed text 'Pacher's Religious Art' in the Salzkammergut chapter.

The best Renaissance sculpture is the tomb of Maximilian in Innsbruck's Hofkirche. The same church has impressive statues in bronze, including several by that master of all trades, Albrecht Dürer.

The fountain by George Raphael Donner in Vienna's Neuer Markt, and Balthasar Permoser's statue of Prince Eugene in the Unteres Belvedere are fine examples of Baroque sculpture. Baroque even extended to funeral caskets, as created by Balthasar Moll for Maria Theresa and Francis I. All of these are in Vienna, but the Baroque style is evident throughout the country.

Neoclassical sculpture is typified by the equestrian statue of Emperor Joseph II in Josefsplatz in Vienna's Hofburg. Salzburg has several distinctive equine fountains in its old town centre.

The Biedermeier period was strongly represented in furniture, examples of which can be seen in Vienna's Museum für angewandte Kunst (Museum of Applied Art). After Biedermeier, the technique of bending wood in furniture, particularly in the backs of chairs, became popular. The bentwood chair has since became known as the Viennese chair.

In 1903 the Wiener Werkstätte (Vienna Workshops) were founded. The artisans involved created a range of high-quality, if expensive, household products, as well as garments and jewellery. Aesthetic considerations were given priority over practicality, resulting in some highly distinctive styles, such as Josef Hoffmann's silver tea service (displayed in the Museum für angewandte Kunst). Another key figure involved in the

Wiener Werkstätte was Hoffman's co-founder Kolo Moser (1868-1918).

Cinema

Austrian endeavours in the film industry go mostly unnoticed outside the German-speaking world, with a few exceptions. The director Fritz Lang (1890-1976) was responsible for the innovative science fiction silent film *Metropolis* (1926), and *M* (1931) starring Peter Lorre. Fred Zinnemann (*From Here to Eternity, High Noon*) was Austrian born. Klaus Maria Brandauer is a well-known actor and the star of a number of films including *Mephisto* (1980); and of course there's ex-Mr Universe Arnold Schwarzenegger, whose bulk fills the screen in action epics such as *The Terminator* (1985), *Total Recall* (1990) and *True Lies* (1994), as well as in other, more light-hearted films.

Theatre

Austria's tradition in the theatre was bolstered by the quality of operas and operettas produced in the golden age of music. In addition to these forms, Greek drama, avant-garde, mime, comedy, farce and other theatrical genres are regularly performed. Vienna is home to the four federal theatres and opera houses – the Staatsoper, Volksoper, Akademietheater and Burgtheater. The Burgtheater is one of the premier venues in the German-speaking world. Vienna also has a number of municipal theatres and there are major theatres in all of the provincial capital cities.

SOCIETY & CONDUCT
Traditional Culture

The people in Alpine areas often live up to the Austrian stereotype. Women can still be seen in the *Dirndl*, a full, pleated skirt with tight bodice, worn with traditional apron, bonnet, and blouse with short, puffed sleeves. The men, meanwhile, are anything but self-conscious in collarless loden jackets, green hats, wide braces and shorts or knee breeches. Although such clothes are worn on a daily basis in out-of-the-way places, as a tourist you're more likely to see them during celebrations and processions.

In early summer, hardy herders climb to Alpine pastures with their cattle and live in summer huts while tending their herds. They gradually descend to village level as the grassland is grazed. Both the departure and the return is a cause for celebration and processions. The cattle wear heavy bells and decorated headdresses.

Rural ritual retains a foothold in the consciousness of Alpine village folk, and finds exuberant expression in the many festivals scattered through the year. These often act out ancient traditions, such as welcoming the spring with painted masks and the ringing of bells. Yodelling and playing the alphorn are also part of the tradition. Alpine wrestling, where the object is to pin both your opponent's shoulders to the ground at the same time, is another festival event.

Dos & Don'ts

It is customary to greet people with the salute *Grüss Gott* and to say *Auf Wiedersehen* when departing. This applies to shop assistants, café staff and the like. Not greeting someone will be taken as a personal affront. When being introduced to someone it is usual to shake hands, likewise when you take your leave. This applies even in younger, informal company.

At a meal, Austrians dining together normally raise their glasses and say *Prost* before taking their first sip of wine; look people in the eye while you're doing it – some may consider you insincere otherwise. Similarly, there will be a signal before people start to eat, such as the exchange of a *Guten Appetit*.

Some older Viennese still cling to the language and etiquette of the old empire, known as *Kaiserdeutsch* or *Schönbrunndeutsch*. This can be seen as pompous or charming depending upon your point of view; it may manifest itself at introductions, with men addressing women as *Gnädige Frau* (gracious lady) and formally adding *Küss die Hand* (I kiss your hand), perhaps backing this up by actually performing the act or clicking the heels together. Formal titles should also be used (*Herr* for men and *Frau* for women).

Men would be advised to wear a jacket and tie when dining in some of the top restaurants mentioned in this book. Austrians tend to dress up when going to the opera or theatre, so the wearing of jeans and running shoes (trainers) by foreigners at such events is tolerated but rather frowned upon. You will find conservative behaviour exhibited in various other ways too, such as in the rigid respect for the 'don't walk' red figure on traffic lights; even if there's no traffic anywhere in sight, people will obediently wait for the lights to change (in theory you could be fined about AS100 if the police spot you jaywalking).

On the beach, nude bathing is usually limited to restricted areas (look for a sign saying FKK), but topless bathing is common in many parts. Women should be wary of taking their tops off as a matter of course. The rule is, if nobody else seems to be doing it, don't. It is no problem for men to wear shorts away from the beach.

RELIGION

Religion plays an important part in the lives of many Austrians. In the countryside you'll often see small roadside shrines decorated with fresh flowers. Freedom of religion is guaranteed under the constitution. Even the religious rights of children are protected: up to age 10 their religious affiliation is in the hands of parents, yet from age 10 to 12 the child must be consulted about their preferred religion, and from age 12 to 14 a change of religion cannot be imposed upon any child. Upon reaching 14, children have full independence to choose their own faith.

The national census of 1991 revealed that 78% of the population is Roman Catholic, 5% Protestant and 9% non-denominational.

Nearly 5% of Austrians belong to other religious groups and the rest of the population declined to reveal their affiliation. The majority of Austria's Protestants live in Burgenland and Carinthia.

LANGUAGE

The national language of Austria is German, though for a small country there are a surprising number of regional accents and dialects. This is due in part to the isolating influence of high mountain ranges, causing language to evolve differently in different communities. Austrians will probably tell you that they have difficulty understanding the accents of compatriots from other regions; indeed, the dialect spoken in Vorarlberg is much closer to Schwyzertütsch (Swiss-German, a language all but incomprehensible to most non-Swiss people) than it is to standard Hochdeutsch (High German).

In some areas of the country, a significant minority may have a different first language to German. In Burgenland about 25,000 people speak Croatian, and in Carinthia about 20,000 people speak Slovene.

Fortunately for visitors, Austrians can switch from their own dialect to High German when necessary, and many speak some English. Young people are usually quite fluent in English. As might be expected, English is more widely spoken in cities and tourist areas than in out-of-the-way rural districts. Staff at tourist and train information offices almost invariably speak English; hotel receptionists and restaurant waiters usually do as well, especially in the more upmarket establishments. As with all countries you visit, any attempts to communicate with the people in their native tongue will be appreciated, so some knowledge of German will definitely be an asset. (For some helpful phrases and vocabulary see the Language chapter later in this book.)

AUSTRIA'S ARCHITECTURE

Little is known of pre-Romanesque architecture in Austria, although significant Roman ruins (built between the 1st and 5th centuries AD) can be seen at sites such as Petronell and Magdalensberg. The latter site is particularly interesting as features of pre-Roman Celtic culture can be seen in the remains of the Romano-Celtic town.

Romanesque

The Romanesque style in Austria was almost entirely sacred and flourished along with the Babenberg dynasty between 976 and 1246. This period saw cathedrals and abbeys constructed throughout the country. The exteriors of Romanesque churches are characterised by thick walls, closely spaced columns and heavy, rounded arches, as well as the use of statues and reliefs on the portals and apses. This use of sculpture was continued inside the buildings in representations of the Crucifixion and the lives of saints.

Romanesque buildings have generally been extended and modified using later architectural styles. One of the purest examples of the Romanesque style is the Gurk Dom (cathedral) in Carinthia. It has not only retained its Romanesque shape, but also has fine Romanesque sculptures and frescoes. Schloss Porcia in Spittal an der Drau is also Romanesque in style.

Inset: The west wing portal of the Augustinian abbey at St Florian, Upper Austria, features fine Baroque sculpture (photograph by Mark Honan).

Right: While the main structure of Carinthia's Gurk cathedral was built between 1140 and 1200, the distinctive onion domes were added in the 17th century.

Gothic

This style was popular from the 13th to 16th centuries, originating in France and reaching Austria as the Habsburg dynasty came to power. It was made possible by engineering advances that permitted thinner walls and (in churches) taller, more delicate columns and great expanses of stained glass. Distinctive features include pointed arches and ribbed ceiling vaults, external flying buttresses to support the walls, and elaborately carved doorway columns.

In the 15th century, Austria was the site of some of the grandest architectural experimentation, and the use of stained glass windows enhanced some of the finest sacred buildings ever constructed. The most impressive Gothic structure in Austria is Vienna's Stephansdom. Its three naves of equal height are typical of the Gothic style in Austria. Secular Gothic buildings include the Goldenes Dachl in Innsbruck, the Kornmesserhaus in Bruck an der Mur and the Brummerlhaus in Steyr.

Renaissance

The 16th century saw a new enthusiasm for classical forms and an obsession with grace and symmetry. As the Habsburg empire emerged as a major power, the nobility and increasingly prosperous middle class had palaces, mansions and houses built by Italian architects, who combined Italian and Austrian influences. Generally, though, Renaissance architecture had little impact in Austria except in Salzburg.

One of the hallmarks of the era was the arcade courtyard, and a supreme example of this can be seen at Schloss Schallaburg in Lower Austria. Another typically Renaissance device was the creation of sgraffito façades, in which two layers of different colours are applied and a design scratched in the top layer revealing the colour of the layer beneath. Gmünd in Carinthia has houses displaying this technique.

Baroque

This resplendent, triumphal style is closely associated with the rebuilding (and the reimposition of Catholicism) in Austria after the Thirty Years' War. The emperor, the nobility and the church were all responsible for the profusion of buildings in this style, which featured marble columns, emotive sculpture and painting, and rich, gilded ornamentation to produce extravagant and awe-inspiring interiors.

Learning from the Italian model, Graz-born Johann Bernhard Fischer von Erlach (1656-1723) developed a national style called Austrian Baroque. This mirrored the exuberant ornamentation of Italian Baroque but gave it a specifically Austrian treatment through dynamic combinations of colour coupled with irregular or undulating outlines.

Among the many outstanding examples of Baroque in Austria are Fischer von Erlach's Kollegienkirche in Salzburg and his Karlskirche in Vienna, Johann Lukas von Hildebrandt's Schloss Belvedere, also in Vienna, and Jakob Prandtauer's Stift Melk in Lower Austria.

Top: Magnificent Gothic spires surround the multicoloured chevron design on the roof of Vienna's Stephansdom.

Middle: Terracotta arches at Schloss Schallaburg near Melk perfectly illustrate the Renaissance use of decorative motifs.

Bottom: Architect Jakob Prandtauer called together the most notable Baroque artists to create the spectacular Stift Melk over a period of almost 40 years.

Top: Rococo architecture often incorporated Chinese elements, as seen here in the *Blauer Chinesicher Salon* (Blue Chinese Salon) of Schloss Schönbrunn, Vienna.

Middle: Grecian, as in the Athena fountain at the *Parlament*, and Flemish Gothic, illustrated by the arcaded courtyard of the *Rathaus*, were two of the styles employed in Vienna during the period of historicism.

Bottom: Friedensreich Hundertwasser rigorously applied his modernist principles when designing the controversial Hundertwasserhaus.

Rococo

In Austria, this style was the product of a combination of Italian Baroque and French Rococo. Although spectacular, it is essentially late, over-the-top Baroque; florid, elaborate and 'lightweight'.

Rococo became popular with architects in the late 18th century and was a great favourite of Empress Maria Theresa. She chose this fussy style for most of the rooms of Schloss Schönbrunn when she commissioned Nicolas Pacassi to renovate it in 1744. Austrian rococo is sometimes referred to as late-Baroque Theresien style.

Historicism

The revival of old architectural styles became popular after the 1848 revolution. Neoclassicism favoured grand colonnades and pediments, and often huge and simple symmetrical buildings. The Technical University in Vienna is a good example of this.

In the second half of the 19th century, historicism took hold. This is seen principally in Vienna's Ringstrasse developments on the site of the old city walls instigated by Franz Josef I's imperial decree of 1857. The Ringstrasse demonstrates a great diversity of retrograde styles, including French Gothic (Votivkirche), Flemish Gothic (Rathaus), Grecian (Parlament), French Renaissance (Staatsoper) and Florentine Renaissance (Museum für angewandte Kunst).

Modern

The end of the 19th century saw the emergence of Art Nouveau (Jugendstil), a sensuous and decorative style of art and architecture that spread through much of Europe. In Vienna the style flowered with the founding of the Secession movement in 1897. Otto Wagner (1841-1918), designer of the Postsparkasse (Post Office Savings Bank) and the Kirche am Steinhof, was one of the leading architects in the field. In the early 20th century, Wagner led the movement towards a style in which the more sinuous and decorative features of Art Nouveau became subservient to functional considerations both in design and building materials. Adolf Loos (1870-1933) was even more important in moving towards a new functionalism. He was a bitter critic of the Ringstrasse buildings, yet also became quickly disillusioned with the ornamentation in Secessionist buildings.

The dominance of the Social Democrats in the Vienna city government of the new Republic (from 1918) gave rise to a number of municipal building projects, not least the massive Karl-Marx-Hof apartment complex. Postwar architecture was mostly utilitarian. More recently some strange multicoloured, haphazard-looking structures have been erected in Vienna, the work of the maverick artist and architect, Friedensreich Hundertwasser (see the boxed text 'Peace Empire & a Hundred Waters' in the Vienna chapter). Austria's premier postmodern architect is Hans Hollein, designer of the Haas Haus in Vienna.

Facts for the Visitor

SUGGESTED ITINERARIES

Depending on the length of your stay, you might want to see and do the following things:

One week
Spend four days in Vienna, two days in Salzburg and one day visiting the Salzkammergut lakes.

Two weeks
Spend five days in Vienna, three days in Salzburg (with a day trip to the Werfen ice caves and fortress), two days at the Salzkammergut lakes, two days in Innsbruck and two days at a Tirolean Alpine resort, say St Anton or Kitzbühel.

One month
Visit the same places as in the two week scenario but at a more leisurely pace, possibly including a Danube cruise. After Tirol add a tour of the south, taking in Lienz, Klagenfurt and Graz.

Two months
Expand the one month itinerary by spending time at Bregenz before heading to the south. While in the south, explore Carinthia's lakes and Styria's wine trails.

PLANNING
When to Go

Summer sightseeing and winter sports make Austria a year-round destination. When to go depends on what you want to do or see. See the 'Festivals of Austria' boxed text and the Public Holidays & Special Events section later in this chapter for seasonal events, and study the climate charts in Facts about Austria to determine what the weather will be like at any particular time of year.

The summer high season is in July and August, when crowds will be bigger and prices higher. But this isn't necessarily the best time to visit Austria – it can be uncomfortably hot in the cities and many famous institutions close down, among them the opera, the Spanish Riding School

and the Vienna Boys' Choir. Consequently, June and September are also busy months for tourism. During the winter you'll find things less crowded in the cities and the hotel prices lower (except over Christmas and Easter), but it can get very cold. Consider visiting in spring or autumn as a good compromise.

Winter sports are in full swing from mid-December to late March, with the high season over Christmas, New Year and in February. The length of the skiing season depends on the altitude of the resort – virtual year-round skiing is possible on glaciers. Alpine resorts are very quiet from late April to early June, and in November and early December; at these times some bars, restaurants and hotels close down. Spring in the Alps is in June, when the Alpine flowers start coating the mountains with colour.

Maps

Freytag & Berndt of Vienna has the most comprehensive coverage of the country. It publishes good town maps (1:10,000 to 1:25,000 scale) and has a *Wanderkarte* series for walkers, mostly on a 1:50,000 scale. Motorists should consider buying its *Strassen & Städte* road atlas. This covers Europe (1:350,000), Austria (1:250,000) and 29 Austrian towns. Extremely detailed walking maps are produced by the Austrian Alpine Club, on a scale of 1:25,000. Michelin maps are also of a high standard. Bikeline maps cost AS79 and are recommended for those travelling round the country by bicycle; eight maps (1:200,000 or 1:150,000) cover the whole country.

For getting around cities, maps provided by tourist offices, in conjunction with the maps in this book, are generally adequate. These are usually free, but where there's a charge – in Salzburg, for instance – you can probably make do with the hotel map instead.

Highlights

Vienna and Salzburg are Austria's most rewarding cities, followed by Innsbruck and Graz. Be sure to spend time at a traditional coffee house and a wine tavern (*Heuriger* or *Buschenschank*). Make sure you pay a visit to the opera or some other musical event. Take in the chaos and clutter of Vienna's flea market at the Naschmarkt. Spend some time in the Alps; perhaps take a Danube River cruise. Visit the ice caves at Werfen or Dachstein. For skiing and glitz, head for Kitzbühel or Lech, or for a less elitist skiing ambience, try St Anton. The following should help you prioritise your time.

Churches & Abbeys
Stephansdom, in Vienna, is *the* Gothic church in Austria. The abbeys at Melk and St Florian are perfect examples of Baroque architecture. Friedensreich Hundertwasser's unusual and idiosyncratic design for the St Barbara Kirche in Bärnbach is unique. See the winged high altar in St Wolfgang's pilgrimage church, and the statues and mausoleum in Innsbruck's Hofkirche.

Museums & Galleries
The Kunsthistorisches Museum in Vienna is best for art; the Haus der Natur, Salzburg, is best for natural history. For something a little more bizarre, try the Josephinium, the medical museum in Vienna. For ancient armaments, go to the Landeszeughaus in Graz. Austrian art can be viewed in Schloss Belvedere, Vienna.

Palaces
In Vienna, enjoy Schloss Schönbrunn for its grounds and Baroque rooms, and the Hofburg for its grand scale and many museum collections. In Salzburg, see Schloss Mirabell for its gardens and Schloss Hellbrunn for its water fountains. Also visit Schloss Eggenberg in Graz and Schloss Ambras in Innsbruck.

Picturesque Views
Take in the Nordkette peaks from Innsbruck's Maria Theresien Strasse, Friesach's castles from near the town moat, Steyr at the confluence of its two rivers, Ehrenhausen's Marktplatz, and Burg Hochosterwitz with its spiralling defences. Don't miss Salzburg's domes from the Salzach, and the panorama from Festung Hohensalzburg. Also view Graz from the Schlossberg, and admire the Schlossberg and Landhaus from the Landeszeughaus.

Marvel at the unfolding magnificence of the Grossglockner Road. Linger over the view back to Krimml from the top of Krimml Falls. Expansive mountain vistas are part of the package at all ski resorts.

What to Bring

Pack as lightly as you can. Anything you forget to bring you can easily buy in Austria. Allow for colder weather in winter and at high altitudes (several layers of thin clothing are better than one thick one). Even if they prefer to dress informally, men will need proper shoes (not trainers or running shoes), smart trousers (not jeans) and a tie to get into casinos and maybe some nightclubs; this is also the accepted attire for top restaurants and trips to the opera. Dressing smartly helps when dealing with officials such as police or customs officers.

Whether to take a suitcase or a backpack is a matter of personal choice. If you're travelling by car it doesn't really matter what you take, but a backpack is better if you plan to do much walking. Unfortunately, it doesn't offer too much protection for your valuables; the straps tend to get caught on things and some airlines may refuse to be responsible if the pack is damaged or broken into. Travelpacks are a nifty combination of backpack and shoulder bag, where the backpack straps zip away inside the pack. When city sightseeing, a small daypack is better than a shoulder bag for deterring bag snatchers.

A money belt worn around your waist beneath your clothes is probably one of the safest ways of carrying important documents such as your passport and travellers cheques on your person. Some people prefer a pouch attached to a string and worn round the neck, concealed beneath a shirt or jumper. Leather belts with secret compartments are also available from travel goods suppliers. A padlock (and chain) is useful for locking your bag to a train or bus luggage rack, and may also be needed to secure a youth hostel locker. Swiss Army knives are among the most versatile pocket knives available; get one with at least a bottle opener and corkscrew.

Other items that might be useful include a compass, a flashlight (torch), an alarm clock (or watch alarm), an adapter plug for electrical appliances, a universal bath/sink plug (sometimes a film canister will do the job), sunglasses, clothes pegs and string (for an emergency clothesline). A few hostels charge extra for sheets so you may save money if you have your own. If you take a water bottle you won't have to keep buying expensive drinks when sightseeing. Consider also acquiring a cup water heater to make your own hot beverages. A supply of passport photos is useful for visa or travel pass applications. Condoms, tampons and sanitary towels are widely available in Austria.

Compile a packing list before you leave home, and don't forget wet-weather gear. Pack a few plastic carrier bags: they can help keep your clothes separate, clean and dry. Tag your luggage both inside and out with your name and address.

TOURIST OFFICES
Local Tourist Offices
These are efficient and helpful. They may be called a number of different things in German, depending on the place – *Fremdenverkehrsverband*, *Kurort*, *Verkehrsamt*, *Kurverein*, *Tourismusbüro* or *Kurverwaltung* – but they can always be identified by a white 'i' on a green background.

In addition, each province has its own tourist board, though some of these are geared more to handling written or telephone inquiries than dealing with personal callers. In this book their addresses are included at the beginning of each chapter. Sometimes there are regional offices that promote a designated area, such as the Salzkammergut tourist board in Bad Ischl.

Any town or village that tourists are likely to visit will have a centrally situated tourist office, and at least one of the staff will speak English. Most offices have an accommodation-finding service, often charging no commission. Maps are always available and usually free. Staff can answer a range of inquiries, ranging from where and when to attend religious services for different denominations, to where to find vegetarian food.

Some local offices hold brochures on other localities, allowing you to stock up information in advance. If you're empty-handed and arrive somewhere too late in the day to get to the tourist office, try asking in the railway ticket office, as staff often hold a supply of hotel lists or city maps. Top hotels usually have a supply of useful brochures in the foyer.

Tourist Offices Abroad
The Austrian National Tourist Office (ANTO) has branches in many countries; sometimes its functions are taken care of by the Austrian Trade Commission. Make contact by telephone or letter in the first instance – most offices prefer to send

information rather than accept personal callers. ANTO offices abroad include:

Australia
(☎ 02-9299 3621, fax 9299 3808,
email oewsyd@world.net)
1st floor, 36 Carrington St, Sydney, NSW 2000

Canada
(☎ 416-967 3381, fax 967 4101,
email anto.tor@sympatico.ca)
2 Bloor St East, Suite 3330, Toronto, Ontario M4W 1A8

Czech Republic
Österreich Werbung
(☎ 2-26 85 18, fax 26 67 16,
email oewprag@traveller.cz)
Krakovská 7, CR-12543 Prague 1

Germany
Österreich Information
(☎ 089-66 67 10, fax 66 67 12 01,
email oewmuc@mail.isar.net)
Postfach 1231, D-82019 Munich

Hungary
Osztrák Nemzeti Idegenforgalmi Képviselet
(☎ 1-351 11 91, fax 351 11 95,
email oewbud@hungary.net)
Rippl Rónai utca 4, H-1068 Budapest

Ireland
(☎ 01-283 0488, fax 283 0531,
email ahstdub@indigo.ie)
Eirc Merrion Hall, Strand Rd, Sandymount, PO Box 2506, Dublin 4

Italy
Austria Turismo
(☎ 02-467 51 91, fax 439 90 176,
email oewmil@oewmil.inet.it)
Casella Postale No 1255, I-20121 Milan

South Africa
(☎ 11-442 7235, fax 788 2367,
email oewjnb@cis.co.za)
Cradock Heights, 2nd floor, 21 Cradock Ave, Rosebank, 2196 Johannesburg

Switzerland
Österreich Werbung
(☎ 01-451 15 51, fax 451 11 80,
email oewzrh@access.ch)
Zweierstrasse 146, Postfach, CH-8036 Zürich

UK
(☎ 0171-629 0461, fax 499 6038; after 23 April 2000 ☎ 020-7629 0461, fax 7499 6038, email oewlon@easynet.co.uk)
14 Cork St, London W1X 1PF

USA
(☎ 212-944 6880, fax 730 4568,
email antonyc@ibm.net)

PO Box 1142, New York, NY 10108-1142;
(☎ 310-477 2038, fax 477 5141,
email antolax@ix.net.com)
11601 Wilshire Blvd, Suite 2480, Los Angeles, CA 90025

There are also tourist offices in Amsterdam, Brussels, Paris, Madrid, Copenhagen, Stockholm and Tokyo. New Zealanders can get information from the Austrian consulate in Wellington (see the Austrian Embassies & Consulates section later in this chapter).

VISAS & DOCUMENTS
Visas
Visas are not required by the vast majority of nationalities, including those from the EU, the USA, Canada, Australia and New Zealand. Visitors may stay a maximum of three months (six months for Japanese) although passports rarely receive an entry stamp. If you need to stay longer, simply leave the country and re-enter. Travellers from the EU and Switzerland may stay as long as they like, though if they are taking up residency they should register with the local police within five days of arrival. Any other nationals seeking residency should apply in advance in their home country.

South Africans and travellers from some Arab and Third World countries (such as Kenya, Nigeria, Egypt and Saudi Arabia) require a visa, which is valid for up to three months; the procedure varies depending upon the nationality – some nationals may be required to show a return ticket. Visa extensions are not possible: you will need to leave the country and reapply.

There are no border controls between EU nations signed up to the Schengen Agreement, namely Austria, Belgium, France, Germany, Italy, Luxembourg, the Netherlands, Portugal and Spain. Greece was expected to ratify the agreement in 1998 and Denmark, Finland and Sweden should have entered into the agreement by 1999. Once you've entered one of these countries, you don't need a passport to move between them. Similarly, a visa valid for any of them ought to be valid for them all, but double-check with the relevant embassy.

Visa and passport requirements are subject to change, so always double-check before travelling. As a precaution against loss or theft, keep a separate record of document numbers or, better still, photocopy key pages. Ensure your passport is valid until well after you plan to end your trip; if it's not, renew it before you depart. Once you start travelling, carry your passport at all times and guard it carefully. Austrians are required to carry personal identification, and you too will need to be able to prove your identify.

Travel Insurance

Good travel insurance is essential. You should inquire about claims procedures, especially in the event that medical treatment is required as a few insurers require notification *before* treatment is received to confirm that they will meet the claim – tricky in an emergency situation. Other things to look for are whether the policy covers sports such as skiing and mountaineering, and whether ambulances, helicopter rescue or emergency repatriation are included.

Driving Licence & Permits

Proof of ownership of a private vehicle (the Vehicle Registration Document for British-registered cars) should always be carried when touring Europe. A British or other Western European driving licence is acceptable for driving throughout Europe. If you have any other type of licence you should obtain an International Driving Permit (IDP) from an automobile association.

See the Motorway Tax section in the Getting Around chapter for details of that payment.

Student & Youth Cards

An International Student Identity Card (ISIC) can get the holder all sorts of discounts on admission prices, air and international train tickets, and even some ski passes. In Austria, student discounts sometimes only apply to those under 27 years of age. If you're under 26 years old but not a student, you can apply for a Federation of International Youth Travel Organisations (FIYTO) card; this is not so useful, but may work for reductions in place of an ISIC.

Both cards will be issued by student unions and by most youth-oriented travel agents in your home country. Within Austria, contact offices of the Österreichisches Komitee für Internationalen Studienaustausch (ÖKISTA; email info@oekista .co.at). This travel agency specialises in student and budget fares, and issues ISIC cards for a AS70 fee, if you can prove your student status. ÖKISTA has branches in Vienna, Graz, Linz, Innsbruck and Salzburg – see the relevant city sections for details.

Other Documents

Hostelling International (HI) membership is required to stay in youth hostels; it's cheaper to join in your home country, rather than paying for the guest stamp in Austria.

EMBASSIES & CONSULATES
Austrian Embassies & Consulates

The foreign ministry Web site (www.bmaa .gv.at) has all Austrian embassy addresses as well as other travel information. The Austrian embassy's site in the UK (www .austria.org.uk) is linked to it. Austrian embassies include:

Australia
   (☎ 02-6295 1376, fax 6239 6751)
   12 Talbot St, Forrest, Canberra, ACT 2603
Canada
   (☎ 613-789 1444, fax 789 3431)
   445 Wilbrod St, Ottawa, Ontario K1N 6M7
Ireland
   (☎ 01-269 4577, fax 283 0860)
   15 Ailesbury Court Apartments, 93 Ailesbury Rd, Dublin 4
New Zealand
   (☎ 04-801 9709, fax 385 4642)
   22-4 Garrett St, Wellington (consulate only) – does not issue visas or passports; contact the embassy in Australia for these services
UK
   (☎ 0171-235 3731, fax 235 8025; after 23 April 2000 ☎ 020-7235 3731, fax 7235 8025)
   18 Belgrave Mews West, London SW1 8HU

USA
(☎ 202-895 6700, fax 895 6750)
3524 International Court NW, Washington, DC
20008

Foreign Embassies & Consulates in Austria

It's important to realise what your own embassy – the embassy of the country of which you are a citizen – can and can't do to help you if you get into trouble.

Generally speaking, it won't be much help in emergencies if the trouble you're in is remotely your own fault. Remember that you are bound by the laws of the country you are in. Your embassy will not be sympathetic if you end up in jail as a result of committing a crime locally, even if such actions are legal in your own country.

In genuine emergencies you might get some assistance, but only if other channels have been exhausted. For example, if you need to get home urgently, a free ticket home is exceedingly unlikely – the embassy would expect you to have insurance. If you have all your money and documents stolen, it might assist with getting a new passport, but a loan for onward travel is out of the question.

Some embassies used to keep letters for travellers or have a small reading room with newspapers from home, but these days the mail holding service has usually been stopped, and if newspapers are provided they are often out of date.

For a complete listing of embassies and consulates, look in the telephone book under *Botschaften* (embassies) or *Konsulate* (consulates). Details for consulates in Vienna are the same as for the embassies unless indicated. Double-check visa requirements if you plan to make excursions to neighbouring countries such as Hungary, the Czech Republic or Slovakia.

Embassies are in Vienna only; other towns may have a consulate. Addresses include:

Vienna

Australia
(☎ 512 85 80) 04, Mattiellistrasse 2-4

Canada
(☎ 531 38-3000) 01, Laurenzerberg 2
Czech Republic
(☎ 894 31 11) 14, Penzingerstrasse 11-13
France
Embassy: (☎ 505 47 47-0) 04, Techniker-strasse 2
Consulate: (☎ 535 62 09) 01, Wipplinger Strasse 24-26
Germany
(☎ 711 54-0) 03, Metternichgasse 3
Hungary
(☎ 533 26 31) 01, Bankgasse 4-6
Ireland
(☎ 715 42 46-0) 03, Landstrasser Hauptstrasse 2, Hilton Center
Italy
Embassy: (☎ 712 51 21-0) 03, Rennweg 27
Consulate: (☎ 713 56 71) 03, Ungarngasse 43
Japan
(☎ 501 71-0) 04, Argentinierstrasse 21
New Zealand
The New Zealand embassy (☎ 0228-22 80 70) in Bonn, Germany, has responsibility for Austria; in Vienna there's only an honorary consul (☎ 318 85 05)
Slovakia
(☎ 318 90 55) 19, Armbrustergasse 24
Slovenia
(☎ 586 13 04-0) 01, Nibelungengasse 13
Switzerland
(☎ 795 05-0) 03, Prinz Eugen Strasse 7
UK
Embassy: (☎ 716 13-0) 03, Jaurèsgasse 12
Consulate: (☎ 714 61 17) 03, Jaurèsgasse 10
USA
Embassy: (☎ 313 39) 09, Boltzmanngasse 16
Consulate: (☎ 313 39) 01, Gartenbauprome-nade 2

Graz

Italy
(☎ 81 79 17) Conrad von Hötzendorfstrasse 8
Slovenia
(☎ 80 76 51) Stempfergasse 3/2
UK
(☎ 82 61 05) Schmiedgasse 10

Innsbruck

Germany
(☎ 596 65) Adamgasse 5
Italy
(☎ 58 13 33) Conradstrasse 9
Switzerland
(☎ 53 70-500) Karl Kapferer Strasse 5

UK
   (☎ 58 83 20) Matthias Schmid Strasse 12/I

Klagenfurt
Hungary
   (☎ 50 41 41) Pierlstrasse 33
Slovenia
   (☎ 54 15 0) Radetzkystrasse 26

Salzburg
Czech Republic
   (☎ 87 96 24) Bergerbräuhofstrasse 27
Germany
   (☎ 84 15 91) Bürgerspitalplatz 1/II
Italy
   (☎ 87 83 01) Bergstrasse 22/IV
Switzerland
   (☎ 62 25 30) Alpenstrasse 85
UK
   (☎ 84 81 33) Alter Markt 4
USA
   (☎ 84 97 77) Alter Markt 1/3

CUSTOMS

For duty-free purchases, anybody aged 17 or over may bring into Austria 200 cigarettes or 50 cigars or 250g of tobacco, plus 2L of wine and 1L of spirits. Note that duty-free shopping within the EU is scheduled to be abolished in July 1999. No duty is payable on items brought in for personal or professional use, nor on gifts or souvenirs up to the value of AS2400 for air passengers, or AS1000 if arriving by road from the Czech Republic, Hungary, Slovakia or Slovenia.

You may import much larger quantities of duty-paid alcohol and tobacco bought in high-street shops in other EU countries providing they are for personal use and that you do not intend to sell the goods for profit. The amounts that officially constitute personal use are 800 cigarettes (or 200 cigars or 1kg of tobacco), 10L of spirits, 90L of wine and 110L of beer.

MONEY
Currency

The Austrian Schilling (AS, or *ÖS* in German) is a fully convertible, stable currency. There are 100 Groschen to the Schilling. Banknotes come in denominations of AS20, AS50, AS100, AS500, AS1000 and AS5000. There are coins to the value of one, five, 10, 25, 50, 100 and 500 Schillings, and for two five, 10 and 50 Groschen. There is no limit on the amount of Austrian currency that can be imported or exported.

Austria will participate in the establishment of a single European currency on 1 January 1999, at which point the exchange rate of the Schilling against the euro (the unit of the new currency) will be irrevocably fixed for non-cash transactions such as cheques, credit cards and electronic transfers. By 1 January 2002, euro notes and coins will be circulated and bank accounts will operate in euros. The Schilling will cease to be legal tender on 1 July 2002.

Exchange Rates

country	unit		schilling
Australia	A$1	=	AS7.10
Canada	C$1	=	AS7.93
Czech Republic	Kcs10	=	AS3.84
euro	€1	=	AS13.82
France	1FF	=	AS2.10
Germany	DM1	=	AS7.04
Hungary	Ft100	=	AS5.43
Italy	L1000	=	AS7.13
Japan	¥100	=	AS8.85
New Zealand	NZ$1	=	AS6.08
Slovakia	Sk10	=	AS3.43
Slovenia	SIT100	=	AS7.47
Switzerland	Sfr1	=	AS8.52
UK	UK£1	=	AS19.98
USA	US$1	=	AS11.93

Exchanging Money

Changing foreign currency is not a problem. It's also easy to acquire cash in US dollars or Deutschmarks, which may be useful if you're travelling on to Eastern Europe. Exchange rates vary a little between banks. It pays to shop around, not only for the best exchange rates but also for the lowest commission charges. Changing cash attracts a negligible commission but the exchange rate is sometimes marginally lower than for travellers cheques.

Who's on the Money

The choice of people honoured on banknotes is sometimes quite revealing about a society. Yet something that is so familiar is often barely looked at; many Austrians couldn't tell you which famous personalities appear on their currency.

Occupying a modest place on the AS20 note is Moritz Michael Daffinger (1790-1849), a Biedermeier artist and designer in the applied arts field; his image is backed with the Albertina graphic arts collection, which houses some of his work. Sigmund Freud (1856-1939), psychoanalyst supreme, stares pensively out from the AS50 note; on the reverse is the Josephinium, the Museum of Medical History. The AS100 note is the domain of the statesman and academic Eugen Böhm-Bawerk (1851-1914), who from 1911 to 1914 was president of the Academy of Sciences, which appears on the back. Occupying pride of place on the AS5000 note (rather ironically, for a man who died a pauper) is Wolfgang Amadeus Mozart (1756-91); on the reverse is the Staatsoper, where many of his operas are staged.

Until recently, the Art Nouveau architect Otto Wagner (1841-1918) appeared on the AS500 note, and Nobel Prize-winning physicist Erwin Schrödinger (1887-1961) resided on the AS1000 note. These were replaced in 1997 by a AS500 note bearing Rosa Mayreder (1858-1938), artist and women's rights activist, and a AS1000 note portraying Karl Landsteiner (1868-1943), Nobel prize-winner in medicine.

Commentators questioned the need to issue new notes just a few years before the Schilling was due to be scrapped in favour of the euro, but at least the new issue means there's a female figure to be found in the nation's pockets.

Austrian banks are open Monday to Friday from 8 or 9 am to 3 pm, with late opening on Thursday until 5.30 pm; smaller branches close between 12.30 and 1.30 pm. All except the smallest train stations have extended hours for currency exchange at ticket counters or exchange offices. Branch post offices can exchange money up to 5 pm on weekdays and on Saturday morning. Some main post offices in cities have longer hours for exchange.

American Express (Amex) offices have slightly unfavourable exchange rates but the lowest commission charges – starting at AS10 for cash and between AS25 and AS40 for travellers cheques; no commission applies on Amex's own travellers cheques. The post office charges nothing for cash and AS80 for cheques. Exchange counters at train stations charge about AS30 for cash and a minimum of AS65 for cheques. Banks typically charge AS100 or more. Avoid changing a lot of low-value cheques

as commission costs will be higher. Big hotels also change money, but rates are invariably poor.

Cash Avoid carrying large amounts of cash, but it's worthwhile having some with you on arrival. Towards the end of your trip, try not to change more than you think you'll need, as you will lose out if you have to reconvert the excess. Banks rarely accept coins in currencies other than their own, so spend your last coins before departure.

Travellers Cheques All major travellers cheques are equally widely accepted, though you may want to use American Express, Visa or Thomas Cook because of their 'instant replacement' policies. A record of the cheque numbers and the initial purchase details is vital when it comes to replacing lost cheques. Without this, you may well find that 'instant' is a very long time indeed. You should also keep a record of which cheques you have cashed. Keep these details separate from the cheques.

Buy cheques in your home currency (as long as it's freely convertible and stable), because if you buy too many in Schillings you'll lose on the 'spread' of the exchange rate when cashing in the excess back home.

Credit Cards & ATMs Visa, EuroCard and MasterCard (Access in the UK) are equally welcome, although a surprising number of shops and restaurants refuse to accept credit cards. The same applies to American Express and Diners Club charge cards. Plush shops, hotels and restaurants will accept credit cards. Train tickets can be bought by credit card in main stations. You can also use a debit (EDC) card.

Credit cards allow you to get cash advances at most banks. In Austria, automated teller machines (ATMs) are known as Bankomats. They are extremely common and are accessible 24 hours a day. Even villages should have at least one machine: look for the sign showing blue and green horizontal stripes. ATMs are linked up internationally and have English instructions. You'll need to know your personal identification number (PIN) to get instant cash advances. You can usually withdraw up to AS2500 at each transaction with Visa or MasterCard, or AS5000 with EuroCard. However, getting cash advances with cards issued in Australia is sometimes a problem, so check with your bank before departure. Fees may work out lower than using travellers cheques, and the currency conversion rate will be better. There's no charge at the ATM end, but your credit card company will usually charge a 1.5% or 2.5% fee on the total withdrawn. You can avoid the monthly interest charged on your credit card account (due from the day of withdrawal) by leaving your account in credit at the start of your holiday. You may even earn interest on this credit balance.

International Transfers International transfer of funds is rarely as straightforward as it should be – getting a cash advance

with a credit card might be a better option (see the Credit Cards & ATMs section). Things will go more smoothly if you nominate a large bank in a major city to receive the funds, instead of an out-of-the-way branch. There are always charges made by the sending bank – a telegraphic transfer (with a charge of around US$30) is usually more expensive than an International Money Order (IMO). You sometimes need to allow up to two weeks for transfers. The 'Swift' system (electronic transfer of funds) within Europe can take just a few hours, but from the UK you should allow two to three days.

You can also transfer money through American Express or Thomas Cook. There's no charge at the Austrian end to receive an American Express Moneygram. US nationals can also use Western Union but there may not be a convenient collection office.

Other Methods Eurocheques are the most popular form of guaranteed personal cheque and are available from most European banks. They're a convenient way to organise your money if you're a European or have time to set up a European bank account (it takes at least two weeks for the cheques to arrive). But it can be an expensive system to use, with the issuing bank charging both a joining fee and an annual fee.

Another way to organise your money in Europe is to use the giro system, which operates through post office accounts. Contact your post office for details. If you're staying in Austria for several months or making repeat trips, it might be worth opening an Austrian post office account. There are no fees and you will earn a small amount of interest.

Costs

Vienna is averagely expensive for a western capital. Other Austrian cities and tourist resorts tend to be slightly cheaper, and less-visited towns or rural places are cheaper still. A survey conducted by the Union

Bank of Switzerland in 1997 rated Vienna as the 19th most expensive city in the world, excluding rent (London was 9th, New York was 14th, Sydney was 20th and Toronto was 36th).

In tourist areas, budget travellers can get by on about AS450 per day if they camp or stay in hostels, hitchhike (or have previously bought a rail pass), stick to student cafés, cheap lunch specials or self-catering, and only have the occasional alcoholic drink. Staying in a cheap pension and dispensing with self-catering will push costs up to about AS800 a day – add AS150 for a room with private shower/WC. To stay in a mid-range hotel, have a moderate lunch and a decent dinner, have some money to spend on evening entertainment and not be too concerned about how expensive a cup of coffee is, a daily allowance of about AS1500 would be needed. These estimates don't include extras like souvenirs, postage, tours or admission fees. Churches have free entry; museums occasionally do, but AS20 to AS60 is more usual. Other admission fees may be up to AS100. Transport must be allowed for, too. For instance, taking cable cars in the mountains can add significantly to costs. Off the beaten track, the main saving will be from lower accommodation prices.

Note that children pay lower prices; students and senior citizens often do, too.

Tipping & Bargaining

Hotel and restaurant bills include a service charge, but hotel porters and cleaning staff usually expect something for their services. How much you leave depends on the type of place and the quality of the service. It is also customary to tip in restaurants and cafés. Round up small bills and add an extra 5 to 10% to larger ones: except in plush places, simply say the total amount you want them to take when you hand over the money (it's not usual to leave the tip on the table). Taxi fares do not include tips and the driver will expect around 10% extra. Tour guides, cloakroom attendants and hair-

dressers are also usually tipped by a similar amount.

Prices are fixed in shops, but it can't hurt to ask for 'a discount for cash' if you're making several purchases. Bargain hard in flea markets. In theory, hotel prices are not negotiable; in practice, you can often haggle for a better rate in the low season or if you're staying more than a few days.

Taxes & Refunds

Value-added tax in Austria (*Mehrwertsteuer* or MWST) is set at 20% for most goods. Prices are always displayed inclusive of all taxes; in hotels and restaurants service charges are usually included.

All non-EU tourists are entitled to a refund of the MWST on purchases over AS1000. To claim the tax, a U34 form or tax-free cheque and envelope must be completed by the shop at the time of purchase, and then stamped by border officials when you leave the EU. The airports at Vienna, Salzburg, Innsbruck, Linz and Graz have a counter for payment of instant refunds, but you can only claim these if you're not leaving Austria for another EU country. There are also counters at two of Vienna's train stations (Westbahnhof and Südbahnhof) and at major border crossings. The refund is best claimed as you leave the EU; otherwise you will have to track down an international refund office or claim by post from your home country.

Before making a purchase, ensure the shop has the required paperwork; some places display a 'Tax Free for Tourists' sticker. Also confirm the value of the refund; it's usually advertised as 13% (which is the refund of the 20% standard rate of VAT after various commissions have been taken), though it may vary for certain categories of goods.

POST & COMMUNICATIONS
Post

Post office hours vary: typical hours are Monday to Friday from 8 am to noon and 2 to 6 pm (currency exchange only till 5 pm) and Saturday from 8 to 11 am; main post offices may stay open until any time between 7 and 9 pm (see the Information sections of the various chapters). A few main post offices in big cities are open 24 hours. Some post offices have photocopiers, though those in copy shops or universities are cheaper.

Sending Mail Postcards and letters within Austria cost AS6.50 and AS7 respectively. Letters (up to 20g) cost AS7/6.50 priority/non-priority to Europe and AS13/7.50 to other destinations. Stamps are available in tobacconist shops (*Tabak*) as well as post offices. The normal weight limit for letter post (*Briefsendung*) is 2kg, which costs AS260/125 priority/non-priority to Europe and AS450/135 to elsewhere. Up to 5kg of printed matter, such as books and brochures, can be sent at a reduced rate. Airmail takes about four days to the UK, seven days to the USA and about 10 days to Australasia. By surface mail (*Erdwegpakete*) you can send packages up to 20kg. EMS is a special (and expensive) express service for national or international mail weighing up to 20kg.

Receiving Mail Poste restante is *Postlagernde Briefe* in German, though you can use either term when addressing letters. Mail can be sent care of any post office and is held for a month; a passport must be shown to collect. Ask people who are sending you letters to write your surname in capitals and underline it. *Postamt* means post office: this, together with the post code, street name and town, will be sufficient to ensure mail ends up at the correct post office. Get in the habit of crossing sevens in the continental style when addressing mail (and get others to do likewise), as it reduces the possibility of mail being misdirected and eventually returned to sender or despatched to the recycling bin.

American Express (see Money earlier in this chapter) will also hold mail for 30 days for customers who have its charge card or travellers cheques.

Telephone

The Austrian telephone network is being upgraded to a digital system, which has resulted in many changed telephone numbers. This process had mostly been completed by the time this book went to press, but you'll still come across a few numbers that have changed since publication.

Telecommunications were liberalised in Austria in 1998, with the former monopoly supplier, Post & Telecom Austria, facing competition for the first time, so expect a shake-up of services. Telephone calls are expensive. At present there are four tariff periods for local and national calls. In descending price order, they are: Monday to Friday from 8 am to noon and Monday to Thursday from 1 pm to 4 pm; Monday to Thursday from noon to 1 pm and 4 to 6 pm and Friday from noon to 6 pm; Monday to Friday from 6 to 8 am and 6 to 8 pm, and weekends and holidays from 6 am to 8 pm; and every night from 8 pm to 6 am. There are also three distance rates: over 200km, between 50km and 200km and up to 50km. The rate per minute for a local call is AS0.59 at night or AS1.47 on weekday mornings, and for a call over 200km it is AS1.68 and AS5.60, respectively. It costs a minimum of AS2 for connection in a public phonebox, or AS1.40 in the special booths in post offices where you pay for your call at the counter.

You may still come across the odd old-style telephone where you need to press the red button when the dialled party answers (though you still have to feed the money in first). Be wary of using telephones in hotels, as they are two or three times more expensive than using a public phonebox. You can save money and avoid messing around with change by buying a phonecard (*Telefon-Wertkarte*) from a post office, tobacconist or train station ticket office. For AS48 you get AS50 worth of calls and for AS95 and AS190 you get AS100 and AS200 worth of calls, respectively.

Special Numbers Any call with a 0660 prefix is a free or local-rate number. Calls to

Telephone Numbers Explained

Austria's telephone system is being upgraded and some numbers have yet to be changed. If the number has recently been replaced, you'll get a recorded message, in German, telling you to dial ☎ 1611 or 1619 or to check the phone book.

Note that telephone numbers for the same town may not always have the same number of digits: the reason for this is that some telephone numbers have an individual line, others a party line, and sometimes numbers are listed with an extension that you can dial direct. This is relevant for reading phone numbers listed in the telephone book. If, for example, you see the number 123 45 67 ... -0, the 0 signifies that the number has extensions. Whether you dial the 0 at the end or not, you will (with a few exceptions) get through to that subscriber's main telephone reception. If you know the extension number of the person you want to speak to, dial that instead of the 0 and you'll get straight through to them.

Fax numbers are often an extension of the main number, and it's fairly common to see them listed only by their extension, sometimes following the letters DW (an abbreviation for *Durchwahl*, indicating 'extension'). In this book, any telephone extensions are separated from the main number by a hyphen, and fax extensions are shown only by a hyphen and the extension number. This means you have to dial the main number first to reach it. If there's no hyphen, it's the full fax number that's shown.

If you get the rising three-bleep signal it means you've dialled an invalid number. Check the phone book or call ☎ 1611 for directory assistance. Patience is called for as it's nearly always engaged. Getting the fast beeps means it's engaged and you'll have to try again later. If you get the recorded message, hang on as you're now in the queue and will speak to a human being eventually. If the frustration of constant failure gives you sleepless nights, try calling in the early hours when you'll have more success.

a mobile phone (a 'handy' to use the Austrian vernacular) are more expensive, and begin with 0663 or 0664. Premium rate numbers, in ascending order of price, are 0457, 0450, 0459 and 0458.

Emergency For urgent service you should call the following:

Ambulance	☎ 144
Doctor (out of hours)	☎ 141
Police	☎ 133
Fire	☎ 122

International Calls For the directory of international telephone numbers, dial ☎ 1612 for Germany, ☎ 1613 for the rest of Europe, and ☎ 1614 for outside Europe. To direct-dial abroad, first telephone the overseas access code (00), then the appropriate country code, then the relevant area code (minus the initial 0 if there is one), and finally the subscriber number. If direct dialling is not possible, call ☎ 09 for the international operator; as with the information lines, you may have to wait a while to be connected. For calling to Austria from abroad, the country code is 43.

For international calls there are two rates: the normal rate is from 8 am to 6 pm, Monday to Friday except holidays, and the cheap rate is at all other times. At normal/cheap rate, telephone calls from Austria cost about AS10/7.50 per minute to the UK, AS10.50/9.50 to the USA, AS17/14 to Australia, and AS20/17.50 to New Zealand or South Africa.

To reverse the charge (call collect), you need to dial ☎ 09; this is only possible to some countries, such as the USA, Canada

London Calling

London phone numbers and area codes are changing. This book quotes the existing numbers and also provides the new numbers. Existing inner London numbers in the range 0171 xxx xxxx will become 020 7xxx xxxx and existing outer London numbers in the range 0181 xxx xxxx will become 020 8xxx xxxx. From 1 June 1999 the new numbers can be dialled (you must use the new area code). The new numbers will operate in parallel with the old numbers until 22 April 2000. As of 23 April 2000 the new numbers only can be dialled.

The UK will also be introducing new numbers and area codes at the same times for Belfast, Cardiff, Coventry, Portsmouth and Southampton.

and Ireland. To other countries you have to dial an international access number and still pay AS1 per minute, even though it's a reverse-charge call. You may prefer to do this anyway, as the operator will speak the language of that country. Some of the numbers are:

Australia	☎ 022 903 061
Canada	☎ 022 903 013
New Zealand	☎ 022 903 064
UK BT	☎ 022 903 044
UK Mercury	☎ 022 903 441
USA AT&T	☎ 022 903 011
USA Sprint	☎ 022 903 014

Fax & Telegram

Luxury hotels will offer fax services but it's cheaper to use the facilities at the post office. To fax from the post office costs AS12 for 10 pages plus the cost of the telephone time; to receive faxes costs just the AS12. Some hotels *may* let you receive a fax free of charge.

Telegrams can also be sent from main post offices but they're very expensive. To Europe it's AS7.30 per word plus AS50, and even each word of the address is charged for! Telexes can be sent from the Telegraphenzentralstation (☎ 534 160) at 01, Börseplatz, Vienna, but you need an Austrian telephone account.

Email & Internet Access

Email is a good way to keep in touch with folks back home. Various servers (www .hotmail.com, www.lycos.com and www .yahoo.com, for example) can supply you with a free email account.

Internet use is, as yet, not as widespread in Austria as in other western European countries. Nevertheless, there is public Internet access in most big cities (Vienna, Salzburg, Graz and Innsbruck). See under Information in the relevant city sections for details of Internet cafés and prices. If you have your own laptop and modem, you can usually plug into the pay-at-the-counter phones in post offices. This is not always possible with the phone systems at hotels.

INTERNET RESOURCES

The World Wide Web is a rich resource for travellers. You can research your trip, hunt down bargain air fares, book hotels, check on weather conditions or chat with locals and other travellers about the best places to visit (or avoid!).

There's no better place to start your Internet explorations than the Lonely Planet Web site (www.lonelyplanet.com). Here you'll find succinct summaries on travelling to most places on earth, postcards from other travellers and the Thorn Tree bulletin board, where you can ask questions before you go or dispense advice when you get back. You can also find travel news and updates to many of our most popular guidebooks, and the subWWWay section links you to the most useful travel resources elsewhere on the Web.

Many Austrian organisations now have a Web page, including the Vienna Tourist Board (info.wien.at) and the Austrian National Tourist Office (austria-tourism.at). For details aimed at the English-speaking community in Vienna there's www.austria guide.com/info, which includes links to other online publications.

For travel information, look at the Web sites of Austrian Federal Railways (www .oebb.at) and Lauda Air (www.laudaair .com), among others. Searching the Internet using the keyword 'Austria' will yield lots of other interesting information.

BOOKS

A great deal has been written about Austria, and especially Vienna. Some bookshops in Austrian cities stock English-language titles, though they will cost more in Schillings than a direct currency conversion of the cover price would indicate. Most books are published in different editions by different publishers in different countries. As a result, a book might be a hardcover rarity in one country while it's readily available in paperback in another. Fortunately, bookshops and libraries search by title or author, so they should be best placed to advise you on the availability of the following titles.

Lonely Planet

For more detail on Vienna, including colour maps, turn to the *Vienna* city guide. Austria is also covered in the *Western Europe* and *Central Europe* guides; each has a companion phrasebook.

Guidebooks

A useful volume for walkers is *Mountain Walking in Austria* by Cecil Davies. It's periodically updated.

For an enthusiastic assessment of a variety of restaurants, turn to *Eating Out in Austria* by Gretel Beer. The detailed glossary of culinary terms is especially useful. The tongue-in-cheek *Xenophobe's Guide to the Austrians* contains some amusing and revealing insights into Austrian people and society.

Once in Vienna, *Falter's Best of Vienna* (AS45) is worth looking at. It's a locally available seasonal magazine giving over 250 useful and up-to-date recommendations

for eating, drinking, shopping and entertainment. Some categories are typically quirky and playful; past highlights include best wall to lean against, best workers' *Beisl* (pub) with a parrot, best U-Bahn (underground) station clock, and best wild boar farm in the city. The same publisher releases an annual guide solely dedicated to eating, *Wien, wie es isst* (AS165). Both of these publications are in German only, which is a pity for monolinguists, as Falter is known for its witty wordplay.

History & Politics

Steven Beller's *Vienna and the Jews* is concerned specifically with the years 1867 to 1938. You could also try *Austria, Empire and Republic* by Barbara Jelavich. *A History of the Habsburg Empire 1526-1918* is a large tome by Robert A Kann. Two books available in Austria are *A Brief Survey of Austrian History* and *Music and Musicians in Vienna*, both by Richard Rickett.

General

A number of books deal with Austria from the slant of its musical heritage. *Mozart and the Enlightenment* by Nicholas Till is a scholarly work placing Mozart in historical context, with detailed analysis of his operatic works. *Mozart and Vienna* by HC Robbins Landon focuses on the Vienna years, and successfully evokes the city of the time by quoting extensively from a contemporary work, *Sketch of Vienna* by Johann Pezzl. *Mozart – his Character, his Work* by Alfred Einstein has a self-explanatory title, as does *Gustav Mahler – Memories and Letters* by Alma Mahler. *Freud's Women* by Lisa Appignanesi & John Forrester is a large volume that offers an insight into the psychoanalyst. There's also *The Life and Work of Sigmund Freud* by Ernest Jones.

The Third Man is Graham Greene's famous Viennese spy story. John Irving's *Setting Free the Bears* is a fine tale about a plan to release the animals from Vienna's zoo. The zoo plot takes place in 1967, yet the book is also very evocative of life in Austria before, during and after WWII. Irving's *The Hotel New Hampshire* is also partially set in Vienna, and offers an interesting perspective on the city. *Invisible Architecture* is a collection of three stories by Steven Kelly. The architecture in question is more to do with the make-up of the Viennese soul than the buildings in the city.

Mozart and the Wolf Gang by Anthony Burgess is a learned and enjoyable celestial fantasy in which the great composers discourse on music and Mozart. *The Strange Case of Mademoiselle P* by Brian O'Doherty is a story about an attempted medical cure in Maria Theresa's Vienna. It's based on a real incident and gives an insight into the petty power struggles in the imperial court, though it does rather peter out at the end.

The Salzburg Tales by Christina Stead is a Canterbury Tales-like novel in which gatherers at the Salzburg Festival in the 1930s tell each other stories. It has some good character sketches but, apart from its setting, sheds little light on Austria.

See the Literature section in the Facts about Austria chapter for examples of fiction by Austrian authors.

FILMS

The most famous film on Vienna is *The Third Man* – see the boxed text in the Vienna chapter for more on this. Equally renowned is *The Sound of Music*, set in and around Salzburg.

CD ROMS

CD ROMs of interest include an alternative guide to Vienna in English and German (☎ 01-212 50 31, email g.handler@magnet .at), for AS480, and an extensive guide to Schloss Belvedere (AS498).

There is also a complete listing of Austrian telephone numbers and at least two Austrian route planners on CD ROM.

NEWSPAPERS & MAGAZINES

English-language newspapers are widely available in Austrian cities, usually on the same day they're published (in Vienna) or the following day. Prices are between AS20 and AS40. The first to hit the stands each day are the *Financial Times* and the *International Herald Tribune*. *USA Today*, *Time*, *Newsweek* and most British newspapers are easy to find. There are Buch and Presse shops in several of the larger train stations: they stock many newspapers and magazines from around the world.

Of the several German-language daily newspapers available, the magazine-size *Neue Kronen Zeitung* (AS8) has the largest circulation; the tabloid-size *Die Presse* adopts a more serious approach. *Austria Today* is a monthly national newspaper in English (AS25), with several informative sections and a listing of cultural events. *Vienna Reporter*, another English-language monthly (AS25), includes features, reviews of Vienna's restaurants and pubs, and a summary of the month's news.

Austrian newspapers are often dispensed from bags attached to pavement posts, and rely on the honesty of readers to pay for the copies they take. Foreign-language titles are only available from newsstands or pavement vendors.

RADIO & TV

As yet Austria has no commercial TV stations, and commercial radio only started up in the last few years.

State-run national radio channels are Ö1 (87.8 and 92 FM), giving a cultural diet of music, literature and science; Ö2 (89.9 and 95.3 FM), broadcasting local and regional news and programmes; and Ö3 (99.9 FM), offering progressive entertainment and topical information. The above frequencies are all for Vienna: they'll be different in other parts of the country.

Blue Danube Radio is a news and music station, mostly in English but with some French programmes. News is broadcast at 30 minutes past the hour in German and English (sometimes also in French). At 1 pm it has a 'What's on in Vienna' segment. In some parts of the country you pick the station up on a different frequency, but it's usually somewhere between 100 and 104 FM. In Vienna it's on 103.8 FM.

The two state-run national TV channels are ÖRF1 and ÖRF2. But many homes (and good hotels) have satellite or cable and can pick up a whole host of TV channels from Germany and elsewhere, including MTV, Eurosport, CNN (the 24 hour news network) and NBC (an American general entertainment channel). Local newspapers and events magazines give a full listing of programmes.

VIDEO SYSTEMS

Videos in Austria use the PAL image registration system, as in the UK and Australia. This is not compatible with the NTSC system used in the USA, Canada and Japan.

PHOTOGRAPHY & VIDEO

There are no special restrictions on what you can or cannot photograph, though as in many other countries, some art galleries and museums insist you leave your camera in the cloakroom. Don't use a camera flash at the opera, theatre or similar events; it's very distracting for the performers, whether they're humans or Lipizzaner stallions.

Photography in snow can be tricky. The bright whiteness of snow can dominate a picture and cause the subject to be underexposed (dark and dull on the photograph). Some cameras will allow you to compensate for this.

Film & Equipment

Film is widely available and reasonably priced, though you'll find prices a little higher than in Germany and Switzerland. Note that the price of slide film (*Diafilm*) often excludes mounting (*Rahmung*) and sometimes processing (*Entwicklung*) too. Alternatively, there may be a coupon for processing that is valid only in Austria (check before buying).

The Niedermeyer chain store is one of the cheapest places to buy film: a 36-exposure roll costs AS50 for Kodak Gold 100 and AS149 for Kodachrome 64 (including processing but not mounting).

Niedermeyer also has its own make of film, which is much cheaper. Its main rival in price and range is Hartlauer Optik, which has a 'lowest price' guarantee for cameras and equipment; however, this doesn't apply to film or developing, where Niedermeyer has better prices. However, developing is still pricey: at Niedermeyer, photo processing (9cm by 13cm) costs AS35 plus AS2.90 per picture for the three day service; express service is a shocking AS7.90 per print. Both chains have a good range of cameras and lenses, for which prices are comparable to elsewhere in Europe.

TIME

Austrians use the 24 hour clock when writing times, rather than dividing the day up into am and pm. Austrian time is GMT/UTC plus one hour. If it's noon in Vienna it is 6 am in New York and Toronto, 3 am in San Francisco, 9 pm in Sydney and 11 pm in Auckland. Clocks go forward one hour on the last Saturday night in March and back again on the last Saturday night in October.

Note that in German *halb* is used to indicate the half hour before the hour referred to, hence *halb acht* means 7.30, not 8.30.

ELECTRICITY

The current is 220V, 50Hz AC. Sockets are the round two-pin type standard throughout most of Continental Europe. US and Canadian appliances need a transformer if they don't have built-in voltage adjustment.

WEIGHTS & MEASURES

The metric system is used. Like other continental Europeans, Austrians indicate decimals with commas and thousands with points (full stops). You will sometimes see meat and cheese priced per *dag*, which is an abbreviation referring to 10g (to ask for this quantity say 'deca').

LAUNDRY

Look for *Wäscherei* for self-service (*Selbstbedienung*) or service washes (which are only slightly more expensive). The minimum charge is around AS100 to wash and dry a 5kg load. Many youth hostels have cheaper laundry facilities, and most good hotels have an expensive laundry service, based on a price per item.

TOILETS

Toilet cubicles in some places, including many train stations, are attended or coin-operated; either way, expect to pay around AS5 (you can avoid the station charge by using the train toilets instead), though men's urinals are usually free. There are many public toilets to be found: *Damen* means women and *Herren* means men. Toilets in restaurants, museums and galleries are unattended and free to use.

HEALTH

No immunisations are required for entry to Austria, unless you're coming from an infected area (in which case you'll need to show an International Health Certificate). However, get a tetanus jab before you travel, and you may want to get protection against encephalitis (see Ticks later in this section).

Medical Services

There is a charge for hospital treatment and doctor consultations, so some form of medical insurance is advised (cover provided by normal travel insurance would be sufficient). EU nationals can get free emergency medical treatment, though payment must still be made for the actual medication used, and also for most non-urgent treatment. Inquire before leaving home about the documentation required. In Austria British citizens only need to show a British passport to take advantage of reciprocal health agreements. However, in other European countries British people normally need to show an E111 form (available from the DSS), so it's worth getting one if you're travelling through Europe. The regional health insurance office (*Gebietskranken-kasse*) will know which other countries have reciprocal agreements with Austria

(the USA, Canada, Australia and New Zealand don't), but it's wise to establish this with your own health department before you leave home. These regional offices also provide a health insurance scheme voucher for obtaining medical or dental treatment under reciprocal arrangements (in an emergency situation go straight to the hospital). If you go to a private hospital and the treatment is more expensive than it would be in a public hospital, you'll have to pay the difference (even if you're covered under a reciprocal arrangement). The following are contact details for Gebietskrankenkasse in major cities:

Vienna
  (☎ 01-601 220) 10, Wienerbergstrasse 15-19
Graz
  (☎ 0316-80 35-0) Josef Pongratz Platz 1
Innsbruck
  (☎ 0512-59 15-0) Klara Pölt Weg 2
Salzburg
  (☎ 0662-88 89-0) Faberstrasse 19-23

Chemist shops (*Apotheken*) are open normal shop hours, though in some places they operate an out-of-hours service in rotation. Check at your hotel or in the local paper for details of the rota.

Pre-Departure Preparations

Make sure you have health insurance; see under Travel Insurance in the Visas & Documents section earlier in this chapter.

Medical Kit A small, straightforward medical kit is a wise thing to carry. See the Medical Kit Check List for suggestions. All the items in the list can be bought in Austria.

An effective local product for clearing up blisters is *Hirschtalg* (Stag Fat). If you wear glasses, take a spare pair and your prescription. If you're taking medication, bring prescriptions with the generic rather than the brand name, and take a letter from your doctor to show you legally use the medication. Keep the medication in its original container. If you're carrying a syringe for some reason, have a note from your doctor to explain why you're doing so.

A Medic Alert tag is a good idea if your medical condition is not always easily recognisable (such as heart trouble, diabetes, asthma, allergic reactions to antibiotics).

Basic Rules

Austria is a healthy place and if you're healthy when you arrive, there's no reason why you should experience any particular health problems. Even street snack stands have adequate sanitary standards. Try to avoid food that has been cooked and left to go cold (which might happen in some self-service places) and keep your diet varied.

Tap water is perfectly drinkable (except in the rare instance when you come across a sign announcing 'Kein Trinkwasser'). Beware of natural water, even crystal-clear Alpine streams, and take a water bottle on long walking trips. If you need to resort to natural water, it should be boiled for 10 minutes; remember that at high altitude water boils at a lower temperature, so germs are less likely to be killed. Iodine is very effective in purifying water and is available in tablet form (such as Potable Aqua), but follow the directions carefully and remember that too much iodine can be harmful.

Potential Hazards

Altitude Sickness The higher you go, the thinner the air and the easier you need to take things (and the quicker you get drunk!). Older people and those with high blood pressure have an increased reaction to altitude. Acute Mountain Sickness (AMS) occurs at high altitude and can be fatal. However, AMS is only a risk above 3000m, so in Austria it may affect mountaineers, but is unlikely to be a danger for walkers or skiers.

Headaches, nausea, dry coughs, insomnia, dizziness, breathlessness and loss of appetite are all signs to heed. Mild altitude problems will generally abate after a day or so, but if the symptoms persist or become worse the only treatment is to descend – even 500m can help.

Medical Kit Check List

Following is a list of items you should consider including in your medical kit – consult your phamacist for brands available in your country.

☐ **Aspirin** or **paracetamol** (acetaminophen in the US) – for pain or fever.

☐ **Antihistamine** – for allergies, such as hay fever; to ease the itch from insect bites or stings; and to prevent motion sickness.

☐ **Antibiotics** – consider including these if you're travelling well off the beaten track; see your doctor, as they must be prescribed, and carry the prescription with you.

☐ **Loperamide** or **diphenoxylate** – 'blockers' for diarrhoea; **prochlorperazine** or **metaclopramide** for nausea and vomiting.

☐ **Rehydration mixture** – to prevent dehydration, eg due to severe diarrhoea; particularly important when travelling with children.

☐ **Insect repellent, sunscreen, lip balm** and **eye drops.**

☐ **Calamine lotion, sting relief spray** or **aloe vera** – to ease irritation from sunburn and insect bites or stings.

☐ **Antifungal cream** or **powder** – for fungal skin infections and thrush.

☐ **Antiseptic** (such as povidone-iodine) – for cuts and grazes.

☐ **Bandages, Band-Aids (plasters)** and other wound dressings.

☐ **Water purification tablets** or **iodine.**

☐ **Scissors, tweezers** and a **thermometer** (note that mercury thermometers are prohibited by airlines).

☐ **Cold** and **flu tablets, throat lozenges** and **nasal decongestant.**

☐ **Multivitamins** – consider for long trips, when dietary vitamin intake may be inadequate.

Animal & Snake Bites Rabies is now rare in Europe, but you should still be wary of making contact with stray dogs or other mammals. Any bite, scratch or even lick from a mammal should be cleaned immediately and thoroughly.

Austria is home to several types of snake, a couple of which can deliver a nasty, although not fatal, bite. Snakes are more prevalent in the mountains. Wear suitable boots when walking through undergrowth, don't put your hands into holes and crevices, and be careful when collecting firewood.

Hypothermia If you are trekking at high altitudes or in a cool, wet environment, be prepared: take waterproof clothing, even if the weather looks fine. Hypothermia occurs when the body loses heat faster than it can produce it and the core temperature of the body falls. It is surprisingly easy to progress from very cold to dangerously cold due to a combination of wind, wet clothing, fatigue and hunger, even if the air temperature is above freezing point. It is best to dress in layers, and wear a hat (a lot of heat is lost through the head). A strong, waterproof outer layer is essential, as keeping dry is vital. Carry basic supplies, including food that contains simple sugars to generate heat quickly, and lots of fluid to drink.

Symptoms of hypothermia are exhaustion, numb skin (particularly on the toes and fingers), shivering, slurred speech, irrational or violent behaviour, lethargy, stumbling, dizzy spells, muscle cramps and violent bursts of energy. Irrationality may manifest itself in the form of sufferers claiming they are warm and trying to take off their clothes.

To treat hypothermia (in the absence of professional medical help), first get the patient out of the wind and/or rain, remove their clothing if it's wet and replace it with dry, warm clothing. Give them hot liquids – not alcohol – and some high-kilojoule, easily digestible food. This should be enough for the early stages of hypothermia, but if it has gone further, it may be neces-

sary to place victims in warm sleeping bags and get in with them. Do not rub victims or remove their wet clothes in the wind. If possible, place the sufferer in a warm (but not hot) bath.

Sexually Transmitted Diseases (STDs) While abstinence is the only infallible method of avoiding STDs, using condoms is also effective. Gonorrhoea and syphilis are the most common of these diseases: sores, blisters or rashes around the genitals, discharges, and pain when urinating are common symptoms. Symptoms may be less marked or not observed at all in women. Syphilis symptoms eventually disappear completely but the disease continues and can cause severe problems in later years. The treatment of gonorrhoea and syphilis is by antibiotics.

The most dangerous STD is of course AIDS (Acquired Immune Deficiency Syndrome), which is caused by HIV (Human Immunodeficiency Virus). HIV can also be spread by dirty needles, acupuncture, tattooing and body piercing.

Sunburn On water, ice, snow or sand, and at higher altitudes, you can get sunburnt surprisingly quickly, even through cloud. Use a sunscreen and take extra care to cover areas that don't normally see sun, such as your feet. A hat provides added protection, and it may be a good idea to use zinc cream or some other barrier cream for your nose and lips. Calamine lotion is good to ease mild sunburn.

Sunglasses eliminate potential damage from reflected glare from water, ice or snow, but make sure they're treated to absorb ultraviolet radiation – if not, they'll actually do more harm than good.

Ticks Ticks might be a problem in forested areas and occasionally even in urban situations. They're usually found below 1200m in undergrowth at the forest edge or beside walking tracks. A very small proportion are carriers of bacterial and viral encephalitis, which may become serious if not detected early. Both types of encephalitis initially appear with influenza-like symptoms, and can affect the skin, nervous system, muscles or heart, often causing headaches and sore joints. In rare instances, encephalitis can be fatal. If you plan to spend a lot of time in forested areas, get an encephalitis immunisation before you leave. You'll see warnings about this hazard in many Austrian train stations.

The tick embeds its head in the host's skin in order to suck its blood. While a good insect repellent will often stop ticks from biting, some medical authorities now strongly discourage using oil, alcohol or the heat of a flame to persuade ticks to let go, as this may actually release encephalitis pathogens into the bloodstream. Instead, grab the insect's head with a pair of tweezers then pull the tick out slowly without levering or twisting the hand. Pharmacies may be able to sell you a special instrument for this purpose.

WOMEN TRAVELLERS

In cities, Austrian women enjoy equal status and opportunity with men, though in conservative, rural parts of the country some males still consider that a woman's proper place is in the home.

Female travellers should experience no special problems. Fortunately, physical attacks and verbal harassment are less common than in many other countries. However, normal caution should be exercised when alone or in unfamiliar situations (which obviously occur quite often when travelling). Some Austrian trains have a special section for women travelling alone – inquire in advance.

Organisations

Cities usually have a women's centre (*Frauenzentrum*) and/or telephone helplines. In Vienna, for example, there is the Frauenotruf (☎ 01-71 71 9), an emergency, 24 hour hotline for reporting rape and sexual violence, and the Frauentelefon (☎ 01-408 70 66), for non-urgent problems.

GAY & LESBIAN TRAVELLERS

This book lists some contact addresses and gay and lesbian venues – in Vienna, for instance – and you will be able to get more information from the following Web sites: Vienna Nights Gay Guide vienna.gay.at; Vienna Gay Guide www.gayguide.at; and Gay Austria www.gay.at. The national gay magazine, *Connect*, also produces the free *Gay Map of Vienna*.

The *Spartacus International Gay Guide*, published by Bruno Gmünder (Berlin), is a good international directory of gay entertainment venues worldwide (mainly for men). Lesbians can turn to *Places of Interest for Women* (Ferrari Publications).

Though not as liberal as places like Berlin or Amsterdam, Vienna is reasonably tolerant towards gays and lesbians, more so than the rest of Austria. Recently two of the three federal statutes concerning homosexuality were repealed: these had banned gay meetings and the promotion of homosexuality. The third statute relates to the age of consent, which is 18 for sex between gay men, in contrast with only 14 for heterosexual sex. This inequality will be contested in the European courts. There is no corresponding statute covering lesbian sex, as the legislators apparently thought it would be impossible to distinguish between full sex and the intimate mutual washing of bodily parts. While lesbians welcome the lack of legislation, they see this as a typical (male) denial of female sexuality.

Organisations

The Homosexualle Initiative (HOSI) is a national organisation with a branch in many towns – see the Gay & Lesbian sections under Information in the Vienna and Salzburg chapters. Cities generally have other gay or lesbian organisations as well.

DISABLED TRAVELLERS

If you have a physical disability, get in touch with your national support organisation at home (preferably the travel officer if there is one). They often have complete libraries devoted to travel, and can put you in touch with travel agents who specialise in tours for the disabled, or provide useful advice on independent travel.

Within Austria, hotels with three stars and above invariably have a lift (elevator) as well as stairs. More basic places often don't have a lift. Wheelchair ramps are reasonably widespread in cities. Disabled people may get reductions in admission prices (look for the word *Behinderte*) and travel tickets; for example, there is a 50% reduction on regional travel passes in Vorarlberg.

Local tourist offices have information on disabled access, parking (free in blue zones with the international disabled sticker), toilets, specialised shops and other matters. The Vienna office has the very detailed *Wien für Gäste mit Handicaps*. The Salzburg office also has good information.

Organisations

The British-based Royal Association for Disability and Rehabilitation (RADAR; ☎ 0171-250 3222; after 23 April 2000 ☎ 020-7250 3222) has some information about travel abroad, but perhaps a more useful organisation is the Holiday Care Service (☎ 01293-774535), 2nd floor, Imperial Buildings, Victoria Rd, Horley, Surrey RH6 6PZ. This charity has information sheets on several countries, including Austria; send stamps to cover return postage.

The city of Vienna runs an advice centre for disabled people, the Behindertenberatungsstelle (☎ 01-531 14-85350), 01, Schottenring 24. The Österreichische Arbeitsgemeinschaft für Rehabilitation (☎ 01-513 15 33, fax -150), 01, Stubenring 2, is an umbrella organisation for disabled associations and services.

The Österreichischer Zivilinvalidenverband (☎ 0662-451 044-0), Haunspergstrasse 39, Salzburg, looks after the needs of disabled people.

SENIOR TRAVELLERS

Senior travellers are entitled to many discounts on the cost of such things as public transport and museum admission, provided they show proof of age. The minimum qualifying age for Austrians is 65 for men, and 60 for women. If the requisite age is lower in your own country, you *may* be able to persuade the Austrian official to give you a discount at that lower age.

In your home country, you may be entitled to all sorts of interesting travel packages and discounts (on car hire, for instance) through organisations and travel agents that cater for senior travellers. Start hunting at your local senior citizens' advice bureau.

Organisations

The Vienna-based Senioren-Servicetelefon (☎ 01-4000-8580) can give information on reductions for seniors, plus travel, cultural and leisure-time tips; it's staffed on weekdays from 8 am to 4 pm.

TRAVEL WITH CHILDREN

Successful travel with young children can require some special effort. Don't try to overdo things; even for adults, packing too much into the time available can cause problems. And make sure your activities include the children as well; for instance, in Klagenfurt balance a tour of the museums with a trip to the Minimundus miniature park. Include children in the trip planning: if they have helped to work out where you will be going, they will be much more interested when they get there. See Lonely Planet's *Travel with Children* by Maureen Wheeler for more information.

There are sometimes special events and festivals for children. Local tourist offices will be able to supply details. Entry prices are usually reduced for children. In Vienna, during school holidays, children travel free on public transport and get free entry to municipal swimming pools.

DANGERS & ANNOYANCES
Theft

Crime rates in Austria are low by international standards but you should always be security-conscious – you're never more

Avalanche Warning

Modern safety precautions mean that the days of entire villages being buried by snow have passed, but the dangers of avalanches should not be underestimated. Each year, up to 200 people are killed by avalanches in the Alps.

Problems usually originate on slopes high above the prepared ski runs. Accordingly, mountain resorts now have series of crisscross metal barriers built high on the peaks to prevent snow slips. In addition, helicopter teams routinely drop explosive devices in the mountains to cause controlled slides and prevent the dangerous build-up of snow. Resorts also have a system involving flags or flashing lights to warn skiers of the likelihood of avalanches, and up-to-date reports on weather conditions are always available.

Despite these measures, skiers cannot afford to be complacent. Avalanche warnings should be heeded and local advice sought before detouring from prepared runs. If skiers are buried in an avalanche snowfall, chances of rescue are improved if they carry an avalanche transceiver, a radio that transmits and receives a 457kHz signal. These cost around UK£160. A more expensive precaution (but of debatable value) is an ABS air balloon rucksack.

vulnerable to theft than when travelling. Be wary of leaving valuables in hotel rooms. Staff will look after expensive items if you ask them, even in hostels. Don't leave valuables in cars – especially overnight. Beware of pickpockets (who thrive in crowds) and snatch-thieves (a daypack is more secure than a shoulder bag). Carry your own padlock for hostel lockers. Use a moneybelt and keep some emergency money hidden away from your main stash.

Generally, keep your wits about you, and be suspicious of anything that seems out of the ordinary, even unlikely offers of help. Sadly, other travellers are sometimes the people you most have to guard against.

In the event of theft or loss, get a police report – this will be necessary for you to claim on your travel insurance. Your consulate should be able to help if you're left in a desperate situation.

Other Concerns

Austrian train stations can be a haunt of drunks and vagrants. The problem has lessened now that many stations are locked for a few hours at night, to stop people sleeping there.

Always treat drugs with a great deal of caution. Don't ever think about trying to carry drugs across the border. Dope (cannabis) is illegal but still available if you look hard enough.

There is some anti-racial feeling in areas with high immigrant populations, such as Vienna and Carinthia. It's mostly directed towards Eastern Europeans and Turks, but rarely erupts into violent incidents.

Take care if you're mountaineering or embarking on a long-distance walk. Make sure somebody knows where you're going and when you can be expected back.

LEGAL MATTERS

Austria offers the level of civil and legal rights you would expect of any industrialised western nation. If you are arrested, the police must inform you of your rights in a language that you understand.

In Austria, legal offences are divided into two categories: criminal (*Gerichtdelikt*) and administrative (*Verwaltungsübertretung*). If you are suspected of having committed a criminal offence (such as assault or theft) you can be detained for a maximum of 48 hours before you are committed for trial. If you are arrested for a less serious, administrative offence, such as being drunk and disorderly or committing a breach of the peace, you will be released within 24 hours.

Drunken driving is an administrative matter, even if you have an accident.

However, if someone is hurt in the accident it becomes a criminal offence. Possession of a controlled drug is usually a criminal offence but if, for example, you have a small amount of dope that is considered to be for personal use only (there's no hard and fast rule on quantity) you may merely be cautioned and released without being charged. Possession of a large amount of dope (around 300g) or dealing (especially to children) could result in a five year prison term. Prostitution is legal provided prostitutes are registered and have obtained a permit.

If you are arrested, you have the right to make one phone call to 'a person in your confidence' within Austria, and another to inform legal counsel. If you can't afford legal representation, you can apply to the judge in writing for legal aid.

Free advice is given on social and legal matters in some towns, for example in the Bürgerdienst in each of Vienna's districts (addresses are in the phone book). As a foreigner, your best bet when encountering legal problems is to contact your national consulate in the first instance.

BUSINESS HOURS

Most shops are open Monday to Friday from 8 am to between 6 and 7.30 pm, and on Saturday from 8 am to between 1 and 5 pm. Shops that close at 1 pm on Saturday might stay open later only on the first Saturday of the month, known as *Langersamstag* (long Saturday) or *Einkaufsamstag* (shopping Saturday). Shops close for up to two hours at noon (except in big cities), and sometimes on Wednesday afternoon too.

PUBLIC HOLIDAYS & SPECIAL EVENTS

Public holidays are:

New Year's Day
  1 January
Epiphany (Heilige Drei Könige)
  6 January
Easter Monday (Ostermontag)
Labour Day
  1 May

Ascension Day (Christihimmelfahrt)
  40 days after Easter
Whit Monday (Pfingstmontag)
Corpus Christi (Fronleichnam)
Assumption (Maria Himmelfahrt)
  15 August
National Day
  26 October
All Saints' Day (Allerheiligen)
  1 November
Immaculate Conception (Mariä Empfängnis)
  8 December
Christmas Day (Weihnachten)
  25 December
St Stephen's Day (Stephanitag)
  26 December

Some businesses also close on Good Friday.

See the boxed text 'Festivals of Austria' for information on a selection of Austria's many and varied festivals and special events.

ACTIVITIES

Alpine mountains and lakes provide a superb setting for outdoor sports. See the Walking & Skiing special section (pages 59 to 70) for more information about these activities.

In addition to the sports mentioned below, golf, tennis and horse-riding are widely pursued; see individual chapter entries for details of regional centres. Cycling is also extremely popular: see the Getting Around chapter.

Aerial Sports

Mountains are great for paragliding and hang-gliding. Both activities are popular, especially paragliding, for which the equipment is more portable. Many resorts have places where you can hire the gear, get tuition, or simply go as a passenger on a flight. Ballooning is also taking off, despite the high costs.

Water Sports

Austria's lakes offer equally good sporting facilities as its mountains. Water-skiing, sailing and windsurfing are common on most lakes and courses are usually available. The Österreichischer Segel-Verband (Austrian Sailing Federation; ☎ 587 86 88,

Festivals of Austria

Most festivals and cultural events are small-scale local affairs, so it's worth checking with local tourist offices. The Austrian National Tourist Office compiles a list of annual and one-off events taking place in Austria. The cycle of music festivals throughout the country is almost unceasing. Religious holidays provide an opportunity to stage colourful processions. Corpus Christi (the second Thursday after Whitsun) brings carnivals, including some held on lakes in the Salzkammergut. National Day on 26 October inspires various events, often accompanied by much patriotic flag-waving.

More details of specific events are given in the text, but a selection of the annual highlights are:

January
New Year concerts
Lavish balls in Vienna (continues into
   February)

February
Fasching (Shrovetide Carnival) week in
   early February

March or April
Easter Festival in Salzburg

May
Maypole dances on 1 May
Gauderfest in Zell am Ziller
Vienna Festival of arts and music (continues
   into June)

June
Midsummer night's celebrations on
   21 June
Donauinselfest in Vienna (last weekend in
   June)
Schubertiade (Schubert Festival) in
   Feldkirch

July & August
Summer of Music Festival in Vienna
Salzburg Festival

September
Trade Fairs, especially in Vienna, Graz and
   Innsbruck
Bruckner Festival in Linz

October
Viennale Film Festival in Vienna
Autumn Festival in Styria
Cattle Roundup in Alpine areas
Wine Harvest celebrations in Burgenland
   and Lower Austria

November
St Martin's Day on 11 November (goose
   eating, Heuriger wine)
Modern Vienna Festival

December
St Nicholas Day parades on 5-6 December
Christmas markets in Vienna, Salzburg,
   Innsbruck and elsewhere

And Now for Something Completely Different ...

The Giant Chocolate Festival (Bludenz, Vorarlberg, 11 July)
Indulge in some hedonistic gorging on one of Austria's specialities: chocolate. The emphasis is on kids; children living in or visiting the area are encouraged to participate in the games and competitions on offer. Thankfully everyone gets to sample the delights, so it's well worth a visit. One thousand kilograms of the stuff is given away in prizes, with the overall winner taking home their weight in chocolate.

continued over

Festivals of Austria

Lederhosen Meeting (Windischgarsten, 50km south of Linz, 1-3 August)
Fun and general merriment is to be had at the annual Lederhosen Meeting in Windischgarsten. Legend has it that the raucous dancing derives from ancient pagan fertility rituals. Apparently all the slapping and smacking mimicked the workers in the ice-fringed Alps who used similar actions to stimulate their circulation. Coats and gloves can have the same effect, but this seems like more fun.

Festival Rauchkuchldumpling (St Johann, Tirol, 28 September)
Sample some of the 20,000 dumplings prepared by one of the 18 chefs who line the streets of St Johann at the waist-expanding Dumpling Festival. Those attempting to discover the recipes for this traditional dish will be hard pressed to persuade the makers to reveal their arcane knowledge – the exact ingredients are often closely guarded secrets. The proof of the dumpling will have to be in the eating.

Perchtenlaufen (Tirol & Salzburg regions, 6 January)
Cross-dressing, outlandish apparel and heathen rituals accompany one of the most curious festivals in Austria. The Perchtenlaufen festival heralds the end of the harsh winter, and is supposed to promote good fortune and a prosperous harvest for the forthcoming year. Thousands of people line the streets for one of the most famous events in Pongau which rotates annually between the towns of Altenmarkt (1999), Bischofshofen, (2000), St Johann (2001) and Bad Gastein (2002). Menfolk waltz precariously through the streets crowned with elaborate headdresses, which can weigh anything up to 50kg. Adorned in bright, mirrored costumes to scare off evil spirits, they are accompanied by a gaggle of other masked misfits, ranging from birch-wielding goodly spirits, mischievous devils and young men masquerading as women (females traditionally are not allowed to participate in the parade). Festive revelry prevails throughout.

1040 Vienna. Carinthia and Salzkammergut are good regions for water sports. Although you can swim for free in some places, many lakeside beaches charge a moderate entrance fee (generally around AS20 to AS70 per day). Anglers should contact the local tourist office to obtain a fishing permit valid for lakes and rivers. Rafting is another popular activity on rivers. Paddleboats or pedalos (*Tretboote*), rowing boats (*Ruderboote*) and motorboats (*Motorboote* or *Elektroboote*) can usually be hired at lakeside resorts.

WALKING
& SKIING
IN
AUSTRIA

WALKING

INFORMATION

Walking is popular with Austrians and visitors alike. Thousands of kilometres of trails allow you to explore the Alps. En route there are regular direction signs, and paths may also be indicated by red-white-red stripes on a convenient tree trunk. The practice of marking mountain trails according to their difficulty has started in Tirol and is becoming more widespread. Paths are colour-coded according to the skiing system: blue for easy, red for moderate (fairly narrow and steep), and black for difficult (only for the physically fit, some climbing may be required).

Most tourist offices have free or cheap maps of walking routes. The best trails are away from the towns and in the hills. If you can afford it, take a cable car to get you started.

Tirol has more opportunities than anywhere else in Austria for mountain climbing. Be sure to consult local information phone numbers about weather conditions and avalanche warnings before you set out, and prepare yourself adequately. The Kaisergebirge mountains in northern Tirol are a favourite with mountaineers, although other areas such as the Ziller Valley are also popular.

The *Walking Guide Tirol*, available free from the Austrian National Tourist Office or the Tirol regional office, contains contact addresses for mountain guides and mountaineering schools in the province, as well as details of Alpine huts and walking trails.

The Österreichischer Alpenverein (ÖAV, Austrian Alpine Club) caters for both walkers and mountaineers. Adult membership costs an initial AS70 plus AS530 per year, with substantial discounts for students and people aged under 25 or over 60. ÖAV members pay half-price at Alpine huts and get other benefits, including insurance. The ÖAV head office (☎ 0512-58 78 28, fax 58 88 42) is at Wilhelm Greil Strasse 15, A-6010 Innsbruck. At the same address is its mountaineering school, the Bergsteigerschule (☎ 0512-595 47 34, fax 57 55 28). This offers various mountain touring programmes for members, mostly in the summer.

Alpine Huts

[011 - 43 - 512 - 58 -88- 42
  (country) ↑ INNSBRUCK]

There are 500 of these in the eastern Alps, and most are maintained by the ÖAV. Huts are at altitudes of between 900 and 2700m and may be used by the general public. Meals or cooking facilities are often available. Bed prices for non-members are typically AS250 in a double or AS180 in a dormitory. Members of the ÖAV or an affiliated club pay half-price and have priority. Contact the ÖAV or local tourist office for lists of huts and to make bookings.

Previous Page & Inset: One of the joys of Alpine walking is waking up to glorious mountain scenery (photograph by Chris Mellor).

MOUNTAIN SAFETY & EMERGENCIES

First a sobering statistic: during some summers, fatalities involving walkers account for almost 50% of all deaths resulting from 'mountain recreations accidents'. The remainder lose their lives pursuing more obviously dangerous activities – mainly roped mountaineering, rock-climbing, and paragliding. Unlike other mountain sports, however, where the objective risks are higher, most walker deaths are directly attributable to tiredness, carelessness and inadequate clothing or footwear. A fall resulting from sliding on grass, autumn leaves, scree or iced-over paths is a common hazard. Watch out for black ice. In high Alpine routes avalanches and rockfall can be a problem, never leave the marked route and if you get lost turn back immediately. Study the weather forecast before you go. In mountain regions weather patterns change dramatically so take appropriate clothing and good walking shoes. Make sure you have enough carbohydrate rich food for the day (including emergency rations) and at least 1L of water per person to avoid dehydration. Increase the length and altitude of your walks gradually, until you are acclimatised to the vast Alpine scale. It's hard to get lost in Austria, where all paths are well signposted.

Where possible don't walk in the mountains alone. Two is considered the minimum number for safe mountain walking, and having at least one additional person in the party will mean someone can stay with an injured walker while the other seeks help. Properly inform a responsible person, such as a family member, hut warden or hotel receptionist, of your plans, and avoid altering your specified route. Under no circumstances should you leave the marked trails in foggy conditions. With some care, most walking routes can be followed in fog, but otherwise wait by the path until visibility is clear enough to proceed.

The standard Alpine distress signal is six whistles, six calls, six smoke puffs – that is, six of whatever sign you can make – followed by a pause equalling the length of time taken by the calls before repeating the signal again. Some walkers even take their mobile phones with them. Mountain rescue in the Alps is very efficient but extremely expensive, so make sure you have insurance.

Mountaineering is a potentially dangerous activity, and you should never climb on your own or without proper equipment.

Although the author and publisher have done their utmost to ensure the accuracy of all information in this guide, they cannot accept any responsibility for any loss, injury or inconvenience sustained by people using this book. They cannot guarantee that the tracks and routes described here have not become impassable for any reason in the interval between research and publication.

The fact that a trip or area is described in this guidebook does not mean that it is safe for you and your walking party. You are ultimately responsible for judging your own capabilities in the light of the conditions you encounter.

CONSIDERATIONS FOR RESPONSIBLE WALKING

The popularity of walking is placing great pressure on the natural environment. Please consider the following tips when walking and help preserve Austria's ecology and beauty.

Trail Etiquette

Walking is a very casual affair of course, but observing a few simple rules of etiquette will keep you in good stead with other walkers.

Except on very busy routes, it's considered impolite not to greet others you pass along the trail – see the Language chapter for a few expressions. The custom on narrow paths is that ascending walkers have right of way over those descending.

Always leave farm gates as you find them. In summer low-voltage electric fences are set up to control livestock on the open Alpine pastures; where an electric fence crosses a path, it usually has a hook that can be easily unfastened to allow walkers to pass through without getting zapped.

Don't pick Alpine wild flowers – they really do look lovelier on the mountainsides. Animal watchers should approach wildlife with discretion. Moving too close will unnerve wild animals, distracting them from their vital summer activity of putting on fat for the long Alpine winter.

Rubbish

- Carry out all your rubbish. If you've carried it in you can carry it out. Don't overlook those easily forgotten items, such as silver paper, orange peel, cigarette butts and plastic wrappers. Empty packaging weighs very little anyway and should be stored in a dedicated rubbish bag. Make an effort to carry out rubbish left by others.
- Never bury your rubbish: digging disturbs soil and ground cover and encourages erosion. Buried rubbish will more than likely be dug up by animals, who may be injured or poisoned by it. It may also take years to decompose, especially at high altitudes.
- Minimise the waste you must carry out by taking minimal packaging and taking no more food than you will actually need. If you can't buy in bulk, unpack small-portion packages and combine their contents in one container before your trip. Take reusable containers or stuff sacks.
- Don't rely on bought water in plastic bottles. Disposal of these bottles is creating a major problem in the world. Use iodine drops or purification tablets instead.
- Sanitary napkins, tampons and condoms should also be carried out despite the inconvenience. They burn and decompose poorly.

Human Waste Disposal

- Contamination of water sources by human faeces can lead to the transmission of hepatitis, typhoid and intestinal parasites such as *Giardia*, amoebae and roundworms. It can cause severe health risks to members of your party, to local residents and to wildlife.
- Where there is a toilet, please use it.
- Where there is none, bury your waste. Dig a small hole 15cm deep and at least 100m from any watercourse. Consider carrying a light-weight trowel for this purpose. Cover the waste with soil and a rock. Use toilet paper sparingly and bury that too. In snow, dig down to the soil; otherwise your waste will be exposed when the snow melts.
- If the area is inhabited, ask locals if they have any concerns about your chosen toilet site.

Washing

- Don't use detergents or toothpaste in or near watercourses, even if they are biodegradable.
- For personal washing, use biodegradable soap and a water container (or even a lightweight, portable basin) at least 50m away from the watercourse. Disperse the waste-water widely to allow the soil to filter it fully before it finally makes it back to the watercourse.
- Wash cooking utensils 50m from watercourses using a scourer, sand or snow instead of detergent.

Erosion

- Mountain slopes and hill-sides, especially at high altitudes, are prone to erosion. It is important to stick to existing tracks and avoid short cuts that bypass a switch-back. If you blaze a new trail straight down a slope, it will turn into a watercourse with the next heavy rainfall and eventually cause soil loss and deep scarring.

Right: Alpine flora such as the snow gentian or Schneenzian (*Gentiana nivalis*) abound in the Austrian mountains.

- If a well used track passes through a mud patch, walk through the mud: walking around the edge will increase the size of the patch.
- Avoid removing the plant life that keeps topsoils in place.

RECOGNISED WALKS

The following is a selection of the many recognised walks in Austria. For detailed maps and further information on each of these and other walks, see the brochures available from Austrian National Tourist Offices. Ensure you have full directions, sufficient provisions and an adequate map before you set off on these walks.

Neusiedler See (Burgenland)

This walk from Illmitz follows cycle paths and minor roads on flat ground throughout and is suitable for everyone. Over the course of 16km (four to five hours) you'll encounter lakes and reed beds which are a haven for wildlife. Bring your binoculars to observe the lofty antics of the migrating geese, ducks and waders that visit the region each spring. Storks nesting on rooftops are a common sight in Illmitz.

Map: Freytag & Berndt, *Neusiedler See, Rust & Seewinkel*, 1:50,000

Gamlitz (Styria)

Starting at Gamlitz, follow waymarked route 3. This 17km (five hour) walk explores the farm tracks, footpaths and country lanes snaking through this vineyard region. The gentle hills make walking fairly easy going.

Map: Kompass Wanderkarte 217, *Südsteirisches Weinland*, 1:35,000

Hermagor (Carinthia)

Exploring the water-carved gorge, cut deep into the Karnische Alpen, this 13km route is a good family walk. Although the waterfalls and pools make for some stunning scenery, watch out for the gorge path which can be slippery in places. Allow 5½ hours if you leave from Hermagor or 4½ hours if you park at the gorge entrance.

Map: Kompass Wanderkarte *Gailtaler Alpen-Karnische Alpen*, 1:50,000

Nassfeld Pass (Carinthia)

You will need to be fit and have a head for heights to complete this 12km (5½ hour) walk on the high mountain ridge of Sonnenalpe Nassfeld, which marks the border between Austria and Italy. The terrain varies from gentle pasture to boulder slopes. Some rock hopping is involved. Look for the indigo-blue bell-flower of the protected *Wulfenia Carinthiaca* in the meadows from June to August.

Map: Kompass Wanderkarte, *Gailtaler Alpen-Karnische Alpen*, 1:50,000

Hundstein (Hohe Tauern National Park)

One of the best things about a multi-day walk is spending the night in a mountain hut to experience the magic of an Alpine sunset and

Top: The routes around the Stubaital are some of the most popular with walkers in Austria.

Middle: Alpine huts provide a great base from which to explore the surrounding mountainscapes.

Bottom: The 230km-long Inn Valley is the perfect place to really get away from it all.

Top: As well as providing fine skiing opportunities, Kitzbühel retains the look of a 9th century town.

Middle: Ski instructors showing how it's done on powder snow.

Bottom: Lech is not just a great place to ski; it also has a fascinating geological structure.

sunrise. From Thumersbach, fit walkers should cover the 21km in two days, with breathtaking views of the Königssee, a fjord-like lake, and pastures of Alpine flowers in early summer. The waymarked routes use good trails and forest paths including a stretch of minor road.

Map: Freytag & Berndt WK382, *Zell am See, Kapurn, Saalbach*, 1:50,000

Ötztaler Alpen (Tirol)

The mountain scenery of the Ötztaler Alpen is among the best in Austria, making this 18km, two day walk well worth the effort for fit and experienced hill walkers. Starting at the Gepatschhaus, at the southern end of the Gepatsch reservoir in the Kaunertal, well-signed paths mark the route. Some rock hopping is involved and you have to overcome a steep snow slope from the Ölgrupen Joch. One of the best parts of this walk is the view after an overnight stay in an Alpine hut.

Map: Kompass Wanderkarte 43, *Ötztaler Alpen*, 1:50,000

Stubaier Alpen (Tirol)

Starting at Neustift/Neder in the Stubaital, you will need to have at least seven to nine days to enjoy this 120km walk as well as a good level of fitness to tread the well-marked route of the Stubaier Höhenweg. The huts along the way are as varied as the stunning views, although all are warm and comfortable. Every section involves battling at least one pass, and many sections have fixed wire ropes to assist with difficult steps. Snow patches are possible even in late summer.

Map: Kompass Wanderkarte 83, *Stubaier Alpen – Serleskamm*, 1:50,000

Innsbruck (Tirol)

From Maria Theresien Strasse in Innsbruck, this 9km walk explores the best of the old town before climbing the vast Nordkette mountains to expose stunning views of the town below. Footpaths and minor roads make for easy walking, although there are some steep ascents. For fit walkers, the route should take three to four hours.

Map: Freytag & Berndt WK333, *Innsbruck und Umgebung*, 1:25,000

Matrei (Tirol)

Exploring the region's valleys, this 15km walk is good if low cloud is obscuring the panoramic mountain views. The pathway walking is gentle, although the uphill forest track can be slightly arduous and sometimes overgrown. There is some interesting architecture along the route including the delicate whitewashed chapel at Hinteregg and the Romanesque church of St Nikolaus with its 13th and 14th century frescoes. Leaving from Matrei, allow five hours for this stroll.

Map: Kompass Wanderkarte 48, *Kals am Grossglockner*, 1:50,000

Bielerhöhe (Vorarlberg)

Starting at the road-pass linking the Montafon and Paznaun valley via the Silvretta Hochalpenstrasse, this 13km walk passes lakes, deep pools and mountains. The best time to visit is early summer when carpets of alpine flowers flourish on the hills. Taking about five to six hours, the terrain is fairly gentle, although you will need good walking boots. The first descent from Radsattel can be tricky and there may be patches of snow on the route.

Map: Kompass Wanderkarte 41, *Sivlretta Verwallgruppe*, 1:50,000

Tennengebirge (Salzburg Province)

For fit walkers, this 21km walk covers the high pasture of the Tennengebirge, the area used for the opening sequence of *The Sound of Music*. The town of Werfen, overlooked by Werfen castle, is the start of an idyllic seven to eight hour walk through beautiful meadows, forest and farmland. The Eisriesenwelt Caves, the largest ice caves in the world, are nearby.

Map: Tennengebirge Wanderkarte, *Werfen, Pfarrwerfen, Werfenweng*, 1:35,000, available from the Werfen tourist office.

Katrin (Upper Austria)

Take the cable car from the spa town of Bad Ischl to the Katrin upper cable car station to reach the start of this 11.5km route. Some of the more precarious segments of this walk, where the vegetation gives way to bare rocky ridges, have fixed ropes to assist walkers, who will need a good head for heights. The tough descent is made more bearable by the excellent views of lakes and valleys below. Allow 4½ hours.

Map: Kompass Wanderkarte 20, *Dachstein, Südliches Salzkammergut*, 1:50,000

Hallstatt (Upper Austria)

Starting at the Steeg-Gosau railway station, most of this 16km clockwise circuit of the Hallstätter See is easy going, although the ascent of a long flight of steps on leaving Hallstatt can be taxing. Hallstatt is one of the most beautiful and historic villages in Austria, so make sure you have time to explore the village before setting off on the return leg.

Map: Kompass Wanderkarte 20, *Dachstein, Südliches Salzkammergut*, 1:50,000

Eisenstein (Lower Austria)

Starting in Türnitz, the well-marked footpaths and farm tracks lead to the summit of the Eisenstein, with panoramic views of the town below. The 13km walk should take about five hours, passing isolated farms, old windmills and Eistenstein's famous trout streams.

Map: *Wanderkarte Türnitz*, 1:25,000, available from Fremdenverkehrsverein Türnitz.

SKIING

This book is not a skiing guide. It does contain plenty of skiing information, but Austria has hundreds of top-notch ski resorts and no attempt has been made to cover them exhaustively. Don't assume the skiing is not good in a resort if it is not mentioned here. Rather, ski resorts have been selected if good skiing is allied to fame, scenery and general attractions. For a detailed assessment of resorts based primarily on skiing criteria, consult a specialist book or magazine, such as the UK's *The Good Ski Guide*. More information on ski resorts can be provided by the Austrian National Tourist Office and the resort tourist offices, most of which have Web sites now.

Austria has gentle nursery slopes in picturesque surroundings to inspire any first time skier, as well as world-class serious terrain at resorts such as St Anton am Arlberg and Kitzbühel to satisfy the slickest of professionals. Access to the slopes is easy, with most of the main areas accessible from major towns such as Salzburg and Innsbruck. Many resorts offer regional passes, such as Sportwelt in Salzburg province or Skiwelt in Tirol, allowing free access to hundreds of different pistes in the district.

INFORMATION
Costs, Passes & Seasons

Skiing for tourists is reasonable value, and generally cheaper than in neighbouring Switzerland. Ski passes cover the cost of specified mountain transport, including ski buses between the ski areas. Pass prices for little-known places may be as little as half that charged in the jet-set resorts such as Kitzbühel. Vorarlberg and especially Tirol are the most popular areas, but there is also skiing in Salzburg province, Upper Austria and Carinthia. Ski passes are available from ski lifts and usually from buses to the lifts, and also occasionally from tourist offices. Equipment can always be hired at resorts. You may initially get some strange looks if you ask to buy ex-rental stock, but great bargains can be picked up this way.

Ski coupons for ski lifts can sometimes be bought, but usually there are general passes available for complete or half days. Count on around AS250 to AS470 for a one day ski pass, with substantial reductions for longer-term passes. The skiing season starts in December and last well into April in the higher resorts. At the beginning and end of the season, and sometimes in January, ski passes may be available at a reduced rate as this is the low season. The slopes get the biggest crowds at Christmas/New Year and February. Mid-April to June and late October to mid-December fall between the summer and winter seasons in mountain resorts. Some cable cars will be closed for

Inset: Whatever your level of skiing ability, Austria will have something for you (photograph by Mark Honan).

maintenance and many hotels and restaurants will be shut, but you'll avoid the crowds and find prices at their lowest. Year-round skiing is possible at several glaciers, such as the Stubai Glacier near Innsbruck.

Rental prices for skis, stocks and shoes, are around AS290 per day for downhill and AS160 for cross-country. The rate per day will decrease if the equipment is hired for longer periods. Telemark skis can be hired but are not always easy to find.

Ski Schools

There are numerous schools where you can learn to ski – Tirol province alone has 1600 registered ski instructors. All the ski resorts listed in this book have at least one ski school and you can join a group class or pay for individual tuition on a per-lesson basis. It shouldn't be necessary to arrange these in advance. The ski school in Obertraun, a fairly low-profile resort, costs AS1300 for five days tuition (AS450 per hour for individual tuition). In contrast, the ski school in upmarket Lech charges AS1590 for five days.

Snowboarding & Cross-Country Skiing

Snowboarding, the Alpine equivalent of surfing, is popular in Austria. Boards can be hired from ski shops. Cross-country skiing (*Langlauf*) is also extremely popular, and is the cheapest form of skiing: it's not necessary to buy lift passes in order to reach the trails and the slender cross-country skis are generally cheaper to hire than the sturdier downhill version.

DANGERS & ANNOYANCES

Despite precautions such as expensive anti-avalanche fences and tunnels, avalanches pose a very real danger in snowbound areas. Each year many people die as a result of these disasters, and whole valleys can be cut off for days. All avalanche-warning signs should be strictly obeyed, whether they are along roads or on ski slopes. They are there for a reason. (For further information, see the boxed text 'Avalanche Warning' in the Facts for the Visitor chapter.)

If you go skiing it is essential that you are covered by a health insurance policy as medical costs are expensive and accident rates are high. Not all travel insurance policies cover activities such as skiing, so make certain that your policy does.

Although the author and publisher have done their utmost to ensure the accuracy of all information in this guide, they cannot accept any responsibility for any loss, injury or inconvenience sustained by people using this book.

The fact that a resort is described in this guidebook does not mean that it is safe for you and your skiing party. You are ultimately responsible for judging your own capabilities in the light of the conditions you encounter.

SOME RESORTS AT A GLANCE

The following is a selection of a few of the differing skiing highlights to be found in Austria. Six-day ski passes are quoted at high season rates; check with local tourist offices for details.

Saalbach/Hinterglemm (Salzburg Province)

This lively resort just north of the Hohe Tauern mountain chain has excellent skiing for all standards. Fifty-eight lifts take you to 200km of prepared runs. Good snow conditions last from December to the end of March and a six day adult pass costs AS1980.

Altitude range: 1003-2100m

Schladming (Styria)

Part of the Dachstein Tauern region, the resort offers 14 lifts to 16 pistes from beginner to advanced levels. A special ski pass allows access to 241 pistes in the region. A six day adult pass costs AS1930. The season runs from December to April. In summer, passes are available to ski the Dachstein Glacier.

Altitude range: 750-1894m

Innsbruck (Tirol)

This attractive Olympic centre and capital of Tirol is the gateway to five main ski areas as well as the Stubai Glacier, which offers year-round skiing. All resorts are connected by skibus, and a skipass gives access to 51 pistes of varying difficulty. A six day adult pass costs AS1780 and the season runs from December to April.

Altitude range: 575-2334m

Right: Look, no skis! There's more than one way of getting down a mountain.

Ischgl (Tirol)

Ischgl lies in the Paznaun Valley, and 42 lifts will take you to what is hailed Austria's best skiing area. A six day adult pass costs AS2510 and gives access to 66 runs throughout the valley, including Samnaun in Switzerland. The season runs from December to April.
  Altitude range: 1400-2872m

Kirchberg (Tirol)

Kirchberg offers access to the same slopes as Kitzbühel but with less queuing and less expense The village offers 16 lifts to 14 pistes, while a ski pass will link you to 328 slopes in the area. A six day adult pass costs AS1890, with the season lasting from December to March.
  Altitude range: 860-1934m

Kitzbühel (Tirol)

The medieval town of Kitzbühel, one of Austria's most famous resorts, is the gateway to some excellent intermediate and advanced ski slopes. The area offers 60 lifts to reach 160km of pistes. Ski passes giving access to 328 pistes in the region are also available. In high season a six day pass costs AS1890. The season lasts from December to April.
  Altitude range: 800-2000m

Söll (Tirol)

Once notorious for its après-ski scene, Söll has been transformed to re-capture some of its Tirolean grace. With 12 lifts to 16 pistes, the real charm of Söll is its proximity to Skiwelt, one of Austria's largest ski areas: a ski pass allows access to 328 pistes. The season runs from December to April, and a six day adult pass costs AS1800 in peak season.
  Altitude range: 720-1829m

Lech (Vorarlberg)

The rich, royal and infamous who frequent this resort lend to its air of exclusivity. Most of the 54 runs, accessible by 34 lifts, are relatively gentle, although there is some trickier off-piste terrain. Lech is linked by lifts to the nearby resort of Zürs, and both have buses to St Anton am Arlberg. You can get a ski pass to all three resorts. The season lasts from December until March, with a six day pass costing AS2330.
  Altitude range: 1450-2444m

St Anton am Arlberg (Vorarlberg)

Resting between Vorarlberg and Tirol, St Anton am Arlberg is as dynamic as other resorts nearby but less elitist. Popular with advanced skiers, the resort offers 85 lifts to 260km of prepared pistes and 185km of deep-snow descents plus a vibrant après-ski scene. The season runs from November to mid-April and a six day pass will cost you AS2330.
  Altitude range: 1304-2811m

COURSES

In addition to activity-based holidays and schools for specific sports, Austria offers the chance to learn new practical skills or academic disciplines. A variety of institutions in the cities offer a host of courses, either on an intensive full-time basis or as evening courses. Inquire at tourist offices for details. The most relevant for visitors are likely to be German-language classes. Language schools are included in the sections on Vienna, Salzburg and Innsbruck.

WORK

Since January 1993 EU nationals have been able to obtain work in Austria without needing a work permit, though as prospective residents they need to register with the police within five days of arrival. They can also contact the Aufenthaltsbehörde (Residence Authority) office in towns, or the Gemeindeamt (Council office) in smaller places. The Austrian embassy in your home country will have more information, and the Bundesministerium für Arbeit und Soziales (☎ 01-711 00), 01, Stubenring 1, Vienna, may also be helpful.

Non-EU nationals need both a work permit and a residency permit, and would find it pretty hard to get either, though if they are undertaking seasonal work for up to six months they do not require a residence permit. Inquire (in German) about job possibilities via the Arbeitsmarktservice für Wien (☎ 01-515 25), Weihburggasse 30, A-1011 Vienna. The work permit would need to be applied for by your employer in Austria. Applications for residence permits must be applied for via the Austrian embassy in your home country. In theory a residence permit might be granted without a pre-arranged work permit, but you would need sufficient funds, confirmed accommodation in Austria, and perhaps some form of Austrian sponsorship. A Volunteer Work Permit may be fairly easy to get; the drawback is that with this sort of permit you're not supposed to earn anything. Employers face big fines if they're caught employing workers illegally.

In ski resorts there are often vacancies in snow clearing, chalet cleaning, restaurants and ski equipment shops. These will often involve working unsociable hours. Language skills are particularly crucial for any type of work in service industries. Your best chance of finding work is to start writing or asking around early – in summer for winter work and in winter for summer work. Try to get it all organised before places close for the off season. Some people do get lucky by arriving right at the beginning of the season and asking around. Although it is beyond their brief, tourist offices may be able to help you find work.

In October, grape-pickers are usually required in the wine-growing regions. Street theatre and general busking is not uncommon in Austria and may make you a few Schillings if you have the required skills. Buskers are occasionally moved on by the police – ask about local regulations before you start up. Also inquire about the relevant permits before trying to sell goods at flea markets.

One publication worth looking at is the fortnightly *Rolling Pin International* (AS35). This magazine has articles in German and English and carries employment advertisements (mostly for jobs in the hotel industry) from around the world. By far the biggest section is for jobs in Austria. It should be available in most countries, but if you have difficulty finding a copy, contact the head office (☎ 0316-811 277, email office@rollingpin.at), PO Box 44, A-8016 Graz. The principle of equal opportunity doesn't seem to apply: many jobs specify females only.

Useful books include *Working in Ski Resorts – Europe & North America* by Victoria Pybus, *Work Your Way Around the World* by Susan Griffith and *The Au Pair and Nanny's Guide to Working Abroad* by Susan Griffith & Sharon Legg; all are published in the UK by Vacation Work.

ACCOMMODATION

Accommodation is classified and graded in an efficient system, according to the type of establishment and level of comfort. Tourist offices invariably have extensive information on nearly all available accommodation, including prices and on-site amenities. Often the office will find and book rooms for little or no commission. They tend not to deal with the very cheapest places, but this service could save you a lot of time and effort, especially in somewhere like Vienna, where finding a place to stay can be a problem.

In Austria there has been a general move towards providing higher quality accommodation at higher prices. Rooms where guests have to use hall showers are gradually being upgraded and fitted with private showers. This makes life more difficult for budget travellers, who increasingly will have to rely on hostels.

It's wise to book ahead at all times, but reservations are definitely recommended in July and August and at Christmas and Easter. If the need for a flexible itinerary prevents you from making reservations a long way in advance, a telephone call the day before is better than nothing. However, some places will not accept telephone reservations. Confirmed reservations in writing are binding on either side and compensation may be claimed if you do not take a reserved room or if a reserved room is unavailable.

Breakfast is included in hostel, pension and hotel prices listed in this book, unless stated otherwise. Prices quoted here are high-season prices. In mountain resorts these can be up to double the prices charged in the low season (May and November, which fall between the summer and winter seasons). In towns, the difference may be as little as 10%, or even nothing in budget places.

Camping

Austria has over 400 camp sites, which offer a range of facilities such as washing machines, electricity connection, on-site shops and occasionally cooking facilities. Camping Gaz canisters are widely available. Camp sites are often scenically situated in an out-of-the-way place by a river or lake – fine if you're exploring the countryside but inconvenient if you want to sightsee in a town. For this reason, and because of the extra gear required, camping is more viable if you have your own transport. Sites charge from AS35 to AS70 per person, plus the same again for a tent and for a car, though a few have a system of charging an all-inclusive rate for a site. For budget solo travellers, hostelling doesn't work out much more expensive.

Some sites are open all year but the majority close in the winter. If demand is low in spring and autumn, some camp sites shut even though their literature says they are open, so telephone ahead to check during these periods. In peak season, camp sites may be full unless you reserve, although higher prices may then apply.

The Österreichischer Camping Club (Austrian Camping Club; ☎ 01-711 99-1272), Schubertring 1-3, A-1010 Vienna, sells camping guides. Annual membership costs AS300 and includes a camping carnet (for reduced site fees).

Free camping in camper vans is OK in Autobahn rest areas and alongside other roads, as long as you're not causing an obstruction (in tents, however, it's illegal). Note that it's prohibited in urban and protected rural areas, and you may not set up camping equipment outside the van. However, Tirol is very strict and even people in camper vans have been moved on. Collect all your rubbish and dispose of it responsibly. Check with the owners of private land – they may allow you to camp, either for free or for a small charge.

Alpine Huts

There are 500 of these in the Eastern Alps, and most are maintained by the Österreichische Alpenverein (ÖAV; Austrian Alpine Club). See the Walking & Skiing special section (pages 59 to 70) for details of these.

Hostels

Hostels are no longer specifically aimed at young people, although most people who stay in them are young. Noisy school groups can sometimes disrupt the peace of such places. Facilities in hostels are improving: four to six-bed dorms with private shower/WC are common, and some places have double rooms or family rooms. Some hostels, such as that in Graz, are even aiming for a 'youth hotel' concept: providing cheap dorm beds and also added services such as longer reception opening hours, on-site shops and pre-made beds. In all hostels, having to do chores is a thing of the past, but the annoying habit of locking the doors during the day (usually from 9 am to 5 pm) still persists in many places. Only rarely can you check in before 5 pm. Night-time curfews can often be avoided by getting a key, or there may be an electronic key-code system.

Austria has over 100 hostels affiliated with Hostelling International (HI), plus a smattering of privately owned hostels. Membership cards are always required except in a few private hostels. It's cheaper to become a member in your home country than to wait till you get to Austria. Non-members pay a surcharge of AS40 per night for a guest card (*Gästekarte*); after six nights the guest card counts as a full membership card. Most hostels accept reservations by telephone, and some are part of the worldwide computer reservations system. A few hostels will make your reservation for your next hostel via fax, for a small fee. Dormitory prices range from AS110 to AS200 per night.

The word for youth hostel in German is *Jugendherberge*, though *Jugendgästehaus* or other titles may be used instead.

Austria has two hostel organisations. Hostels that are affiliated to the worldwide HI network are linked to one or the other; which one they are linked to is something of a historical legacy and makes no difference to how the hostels are run. Either head office in Vienna can give information on all HI hostels. The Österreichischer Jugendherbergsverband (☎ 01-533 53 53, fax 535 08 61, email oejhv-zentrale@eejhv.or.at) is at 01, Schottenring 28, and has a travel service. The Österreichischer Jugendherbergswerk (☎ 01-533 18 33, fax -33, email oejhw@oejhw.or.at) is at 01, Helfersdorferstrasse 4, and has a travel arm called Supertramp (☎ 01-533 51 37, email supertramp@supertramp.co.at).

Cheap dormitory-style accommodation is sometimes available in ski resorts even if there is no hostel. Look for *Touristenlager* or *Massenlager*; unfortunately, such accommodation might only be offered to pre-booked groups.

Hotels & Pensions

Hotels and pensions are rated from one to five stars depending on the facilities they offer. However, as the criteria are different you can't assume that a three star pension is equivalent to a three star hotel. Pensions tend to be smaller than hotels, and usually provide a more personal service and less standardised fixtures and fittings. Pensions generally offer a better size and quality of room for the price than hotels. Where they can't usually compete is in back-up services, such as room service and laundry, and in on-site facilities, such as private car parking, bars and restaurants. If none of that matters to you, stick with the pensions.

With very few exceptions, rooms in hotels and pensions are clean and adequately appointed. In tourist areas, expect to pay a minimum of around AS280/500 for a single/double with hall shower or AS350/600 with private shower. In less-visited places the cost may be as much as AS50 per person lower. Prices quoted here are for the main high season, which means summer prices except in ski resorts. In the low season, prices should be noticeably lower, though in cities the difference will be less marked.

If business is slow, mid-range and top-end hotels (and to a lesser extent pensions) may be willing to negotiate on prices. It's always worth asking for a special deal as prices can come down quite substantially. Some places will also offer special weekend rates, or two nights for the price of one. Even in budget places, ask for a special price if you're planning to stay for more than a few days. Credit cards are rarely accepted by cheaper places.

In low-budget accommodation, a room advertised as having a private shower may mean that it has a shower cubicle rather than a proper en suite bathroom. Where there is a telephone in the room it's usually direct-dial, but this will still be more expensive than using a public telephone. TVs are increasingly hooked up to satellite or cable (especially in places with three stars and above), which is a definite plus over TVs that only get the two national channels. Rooms that have a TV generally also have a mini-bar; prices will be comparable to ordinary bar prices in mid-range accommodation, but quite expensive in upmarket places.

Many hotels and pensions have rooms with three or more beds, or can place a fold-up bed in the room for a child; ask at the establishment. Smaller places with two stars or less tend not to have a lift (elevator); most other places do. Some old Viennese apartment blocks have a lift that needs to be operated by a key, which the pension will give you.

Usually, meals are available, either for guests only or, more often, in a public restaurant on-site. A pension that supplies breakfast only is known as a *Frühstückspension*; the hotel equivalent is *Hotel-Garni*. Other hotels and pensions will offer the option of paying for half or even full board. In budget places, breakfast is basic, unsually consisting of only a drink, bread rolls, butter, cheese spread and jam. As you pay more, breakfast gets better: in two star places it's usually 'extended' (*erweitert*), and in places with three stars or more it could take the form of a help-yourself buffet. A typical buffet will include the standard breakfast, plus cereals, juices and a selection of cold meats and cheeses. In five star and some four star places, you can also expect hot food, such as egg, sausage and bacon.

Student Residences

Studentenheime are available to tourists from 1 July to 30 September while students are on holiday. During university terms the kitchen and dining room on each floor are open, but when they're used as seasonal hotels these useful facilities generally

Spa Resorts

Indulgence by the rich and famous in Austria's spa towns have made these resorts some of the most famous in Europe. In an attempt to rid himself of deafness, Beethoven was a regular visitor to Baden, while Princess Sophie proclaimed that the waters of Bad Ischl were a boost to her fertility. The popularity of the treatments has led to the rise of over 100 spa resorts scattered across the country.

The validity of the benefits is a topic of heated debate throughout the medical profession. Sufferers from a variety of conditions ranging from eye diseases to poisoning have hailed the curative properties of the spa as miraculous. Different resorts often promote specialised benefits: the water of Bad Deutsch-Altenburg is rich in sulphur, a substance supposedly beneficial for the relief of spine and joint complaints, and Bad Ischl's abundance of salts is said to alleviate rheumatism. For a list of condition-specific resorts, contact the Austrian National Tourist Office.

Of course, you don't need an ailment in order to enjoy the luxury of a spa treatment. Everything seems to be on offer, from traditional massage to high-tech aroma-light therapy. While the debate rages on, there can be no denying that the stress-relieving qualities of a long hot soak can work wonders for the body and soul.

remain locked. Rooms are perfectly OK but nothing fancy; some have a private shower/WC. Expect single beds (though beds may be placed together in double rooms), a work desk and a wardrobe. The widest selection is in Vienna, but look for them also in Graz, Salzburg and Innsbruck. Prices are likely to range from AS170 (without breakfast) to AS500 (including breakfast).

Other Accommodation

Self-catering holiday apartments (*Ferienwohnungen*) are very common in mountain resorts, though it is often necessary to book these well in advance. In the UK, for competitive rental deals inquire at Interhome (☎ 0181-891 1294; after 23 April 2000 ☎ 020-8891 1294), who have a Web site at www.interhome.co.uk. You may sometimes come across hotels which have self-contained apartment rooms.

A cheap and widely available option, particularly in more rural areas, is to take a room in a private house (AS130 to AS280 per person) or a farmhouse (*Bauernhof*). In either case, look for signs saying *Zimmer frei* or *Privat Zimmer*.

A *Gasthaus* or *Gasthof* is a small-scale country inn. In these places you may not be able to check in on a day that the restaurant is closed for its rest day (*Ruhetag*). You should phone ahead to check; somebody is normally there in the morning to organise breakfast for the guests.

In many resorts (not so often in cities) a guest card (*Gästekarte*) is issued to people who stay overnight. The card may offer useful discounts on things such as cable cars and admission prices. Check with the tourist office if you're not offered one at your resort accommodation – even camp sites and youth hostels should be included in these schemes. The guest card system is often financed by a resort tax (not payable for children), which may be anything from AS6 to AS25 per night, depending upon the place and type of accommodation. Prices quoted in accommodation lists are usually inclusive of such taxes.

FOOD

The main meal is taken at noon, whether in a restaurant, café or tavern. Many places have a set dish (*Tagesteller*) or menu (*Tagesmenu* or *Mittagsmenu*): a lunch menu with soup might cost as little as AS60. Occasionally Tagesmenus are also available in the evening. Chinese restaurants are particularly good value for set menus, and the food is generally reliable. There are around 700 Chinese restaurants in Austria, and around 1000 pizzerias. Wine taverns (called *Heurigen* or *Buschenschenken*) are fairly inexpensive places to eat, and are an Austrian institution, particularly in the suburbs of Vienna.

The cheapest deal around for sit-down food is in university restaurants (*Mensas*). Those mentioned in this book are open to everyone, though they usually only serve weekday lunches and may be closed during university holidays. Expect to find two or three different daily specials, including a vegetarian choice. Students may be able to get a discount of AS4 or so if they show an ISIC card. Mensas are good places to meet students (who usually speak English well) and find out about the 'in' places round town.

The main train stations all have several options for a cheap meal. Branches of Wienerwald offer unremarkable but reasonably priced chicken dishes, either on an eat-in or takeaway basis. Nordsee is its fishy equivalent. Self-service places are usually the cheapest and are often indicated by *SB* (*Selbstbedienung*).

For expensive dining, five star hotels invariably have a gourmet restaurant. The more expensive restaurants usually add a cover charge (*Gedeck*), typically around AS25 at lunch and AS45 in the evening. In restaurants without a cover charge, the bread (*Gebäck*) that appears on the table usually costs extra – if in doubt, ask.

If you just want to fill up with fast food, there's usually somewhere you can do this. A McDonald's awaits in every town, but sausage stands (*Würstel Stände*) selling various sausages with bread are more

A Culinary Institution

The *Würstel Stand* (sausage stand) is a familiar Austrian institution and may sell up to a dozen types of sausage. Each comes with a chunk of bread and a big dollop of mustard (*Senf*) – which can be sweet (*süss* or *Kremser Senf*) or hot (*scharf*). Tomato ketchup and mayonnaise can be requested. The thinner sausages are served two at a time, except in the less expensive 'hot dog' version, when a single sausage is placed in a bread stick.

Types of sausage include: the *Frankfurter*, a standard thin, boiled sausage; the *Bratwurst*, a fat, fried sausage; and *Burenwurst*, the boiled equivalent of Bratwurst. *Debreziner* is a thin, spicy sausage from Hungary. *Currywurst* is Burenwurst with a curry flavour, and *Käsekrainer* is a sausage infused with cheese. *Tiroler Wurst* is a smoked sausage. In Vienna, if you want to surprise and perhaps impress the server, use the following slang to ask for a Burenwurst with sweet mustard and a crust of bread: 'A Hasse mit an Síassn und an Scherzl, bitte'. But you probably won't get it – crusts are reserved for regular customers.

authentically Austrian, as are the schnitzel chains Eurosnack and Schnitzelhaus. Deli shops sometimes offer hot food, such as spit-roasted chicken (an Austrian favourite). Occasionally they have tables so you can eat on the premises.

Be wary of public holidays: restaurants that have a rest day (*Ruhetag*) often close on these days as well. Although inns and restaurants often stay open till 11 pm or midnight, the kitchen is rarely open beyond 9 or 9.30 pm (except in pizzerias and Chinese restaurants).

Self-Catering

If you plan on self-catering, Hofer is perhaps the cheapest of the several national supermarket chains, while Julius Meinl is more expensive. With the exception of a few outlets in or around train stations in big cities, food shops are not open after 7.30 pm or on Sunday. Those that do open outside these hours are often much more expensive.

Austrian Cuisine

Traditional Austrian food is generally quite heavy and hearty with meat strongly emphasised. In some parts of Austria vegetarians will have a fairly tough time finding varied meals. Even so, many places now offer at least one vegetarian dish, and there has been a noticeable move towards providing light, healthy meals, such as a *Fitnessteller*, especially in summer. Kosher restaurants are few and far between.

Jause is a light meal, served between normal eating times. You may come across regional variations in the German spellings used below.

Soup is the standard starter to a meal, particularly with a menu of the day. *Markknödelsuppe* is a clear bone marrow soup with dumplings. *Frittatensuppe* is a clear soup with shreds of pancake.

Dumplings (*Knödel*) are an element of many meals, and can appear in soups and desserts as well as main courses. They may be made of a variety of ingredients, such as liver (*Leberknödel*) or bread (*Semmelknödel*).

Nockerln (sometimes called *Spätzle*, especially in the west) is small home-made pasta with a similar taste to Knödel. *Nudeln* is normally flat pasta (like tagliatelle), except when it's tiny noodles in a soup. In Carinthia, pasta is made into balls and combined with cheese (*Käsnudeln*). *Käsnocken*, *Kässpätzle* and *Käsnödel* are variations on a similar theme.

Potato will usually appear as French fries (*Pommes*, pronounced 'Pom-es'), boiled (*Kartoffel*), roasted (*Bratkartoffel*) or as *Geröstete*, sliced small and sautéed. *Erdapfel* is another word for potato.

Meat & Fish *Wiener Schnitzel* is Vienna's best known culinary concoction, but it's consumed everywhere, not just in Vienna. It's a cutlet covered in a coating of egg and breadcrumbs and fried. The cutlet is either veal (*Kalb*) or, less expensively, pork (*Schwein*); occasionally there are variations, such as turkey (*Puter*).

Goulash (*Gulasch*) is also very popular. It's a stew with a rich sauce flavoured with paprika. Paprika pops up in various other dishes too, though note that *Gefüllte Paprika* will be a bell pepper (capsicum) stuffed with rice and meat.

Chicken may be called variously *Huhn* (hen), *Geflügel* (poultry) or *Hähnchen* (small chicken) and is usually fried (*Backhuhn*) or roasted (*Brathuhn*). A great variety of sausage (*Wurst*) is available, and not only at the takeaway stands. Beef (*Rindfleisch*), lamb (*Lammfleisch*) and liver (*Leber*) are mainstays of many menus. *Kümmelfleisch* is pork stew, flavoured with cumin. *Krenfleisch* is pork with horseradish. *Tafelspitz* is boiled beef, often served with *Apfelkren* (apple and horseradish sauce).

Austrians are fond of eating bits of beasts that some other nations ignore. *Beuschel* may be translated on menus as 'calf's lights'. It's thin slices of calf's lungs and heart in a thick sauce, usually served with a bread dumpling. It's quite tasty. Really. *Tiroler Bauernschmaus* is a selection of meats served with sauerkraut, potatoes and dumplings.

Common fish are trout (*Forelle*), pike (*Hecht*), pike-perch (*Fogosch*) and carp (*Karpfen*). *Saibling* is a local freshwater fish, similar to trout.

Desserts & Cakes The most famous Austrian dessert is the *Strudel*, baked dough filled with a variety of fruits – usually apple (*Apfel*) with a few raisins and cinnamon. The Salzburg speciality, *Salzburger Nockerl*, is a fluffy baked pudding made from eggs, flour and sugar. Pancakes are another popular dessert and come in various flavours, such as *Moosbeernocken* (blueberry pancakes). *Germknödel* are sour dough dumplings. *Mohr im Hemd* is chocolate pudding with chocolate sauce. *Pofesen* is stuffed fritters.

Austria, and especially Vienna, is renowned for excellent pastries and cakes, which are very effective at transferring bulk from your money belt to your waistline. *Guglhupf* is a cake shaped like a volcano.

DRINKS
Nonalcoholic Drinks

Coffee is the preferred hot beverage rather than tea, though both are expensive in cafés and restaurants. Coffee houses (known as *Kaffeehäuse* or *Café Konditoreien*) are an established part of Austrian life, particularly in Vienna. Strong Turkish coffee is popular. Linger over a cup (from AS22) and read the free newspapers. Mineral or soda water is widely available, though tap water is fine to drink. Apple juice (*Apfelsaft*) is also popular. *Almdudler* is a soft drink found all over Austria; it's a sort of cross between ginger ale and lemonade.

Alcoholic Drinks

Austrian wine comes in various categories that designate quality and legal requirements in the production, starting with the humble *Tafelwein*, through to *Landwein*, *Qualitätswein* and *Prädikatswein*; the latter two have subgroups. In restaurants, wine bought by the carafe or glass will be the cheapest choice. In autumn the whole country goes mad for *Sturm*, Heuriger wine in its semi-fermented state. See the boxed text 'Drink & Be Merry' in the Vienna chapter for more on wine and wine taverns.

Austria is also known for its beer; some well known varieties include Gösser, Schwechater, Stiegl and Zipfer. It is usually a light, golden colour (*hell*), though you can sometimes get a dark (*dunkel*) version too. In places where both types are on draught you can ask for a *Mischbiere*, a palatable mix of the two. *Weizenbier* or *Weissbier* (wheat/white beer) has a distinctive taste. It can be light or dark, clear or cloudy, and is sometimes served with a slice of lemon

Coffee Treats

Legend insists that coffee beans were left behind by the fleeing Turks in 1683, and it was this happy accident that resulted in today's plethora of coffee establishments. Vienna's first coffee house opened in 1685, but it could have been emulating successful establishments already opened in Venice (1647 – the first in Europe), Oxford (1650), London (1652), Paris (1660) and Hamburg (1677), rather than having anything to do with the Turks.

Austrian coffee consumption was modest in the ensuing centuries, and it was only after WWII that it really took hold among the population at large. Austrians now drink more coffee than any other beverage, gulping down 221L per person per year (next in line comes beer at 120L, followed by milk at 104L, soft drinks at 84L, mineral water at 76L, black tea at 39L and wine at 33L). Only Finland, Sweden and Denmark consume more coffee per person.

In traditional coffee houses, especially in Vienna, you'll come across various coffee-based drinks:

Mocca (sometimes spelled *Mokka*) or *Schwarzer* – black coffee
Brauner – black but served with a tiny jug of milk
Kapuziner – with a little milk and perhaps a sprinkling of grated chocolate
Melange – served with milk, and maybe whipped cream too
Einspänner – with whipped cream, served in a glass
Masagran (or *Mazagran*) – cold coffee with ice and Maraschino liqueur
Wiener Eiskaffee – cold coffee with vanilla ice cream and whipped cream

Waiters normally speak English and can tell you about any specialities available. In particular, various combinations of alcohol may be added to give such concoctions as *Mozart* coffee (with Mozart liqueur), *Fiaker* (with rum), *Mocca gespritzt* (with cognac) and *Maria Theresa* (with orange liqueur). Some people find the basic coffee too strong, so there's the option of asking for a *Verlängerter* (lengthened), a *Brauner* weakened with hot water. Traditional places will serve the coffee on a silver tray and with a glass of water. Some types of coffee are offered in small (*kleine*) or large (*grosse*) portions. According to an old Viennese tradition, if the waiter fails to give you the bill after three requests you can walk out without paying (three requests in rapid succession don't count!).

---

straddling the glass rim. Draught beer (*vom Fass*) comes in a either a 0.5L or a 0.3L glass. In Vienna and some other parts of eastern Austria these are called respectively a *Krügerl* (sometimes spelled *Krügel*) and a *Seidel*. Elsewhere these will simply be *Grosse* (big) or *Kleine* (small). A small beer may also be called a *Glas* (glass). A *Pfiff* is 0.125L. *Radler* is a mix of beer and lemonade.

Austria produces several types of rum. *Obstler* is a spirit created from a mixture of fruits. *Schnaps* is also a popular spirit.

ENTERTAINMENT

Late opening is common in the cities, and in Vienna you can party all night long. It isn't hard to find bars or taverns featuring traditional or rock music. Some are listed under the Entertainment heading in city sections. Many ski resorts, such as St Anton, have a lively *après ski* environment.

Some cinemas show films in their original language. When this is the case, it should be stated on advertising posters: look for *OF* (*Original Fassung*) or *OV* (*Original Version*). *OmU* (*Original mit*

Untertiteln) means the film is in the original language with subtitles.

The main season for opera, theatre and concerts is September to June. Cheap, standing-room tickets are often available shortly before performances begin and they represent excellent value. Once inside, those standing tie a scarf to the rails or balcony to reserve their place when they go to the bar. If you're really on a budget, bear in mind you can often get into these places free after the first interval.

Casinos

Gamblers can indulge at a dozen casinos around the country, including ones in Vienna, Graz, Linz, Innsbruck and Salzburg. Stakes for blackjack, roulette and other games are from AS50 (AS100 after 9 pm) up to much more than you can probably afford. There's no entry fee and you need to show identification to get in. To get you started on the gambling road, you only need to pay AS260 for your first AS300-worth of chips (these are a different colour, so you can't just cash them in and walk out!). Smart dress is required for the gaming tables. A collared shirt, a tie (in winter) and jacket are required. Jackets and ties can sometimes be hired for a refundable deposit. Usual opening hours are from 3 pm to 3 am. There may be a slot-machine section without a dress code.

SPECTATOR SPORTS

Football is a major spectator sport. The country's top teams are based in Vienna, Salzburg and Graz, though there are numerous teams competing in professional or semi-professional leagues across the country. Crowd hooliganism is not generally a problem at the big games, and tickets are usually available at the venue on match day. ATP tennis events are held in Vienna, St Pölten and Kitzbühel.

Skiing is of course a big draw in winter, with World Cup ski races held annually in mountain regions. The most important skiing event outside the Olympics is the biennial Alpine Skiing World Champion-

The Iron Man & The Herminator

Austria has witnessed some amazing feats of determination and resilience from two of the country's top sporting heroes.

Thomas Muster, Austria's top clay-court tennis player, had his kneecap crushed by a drunk driver, just hours after a stunning win at the 1989 Lipton Championship semi-final in Florida. He didn't make the final and, in fact, the resulting damage to the joint made it doubtful he would play tennis again. However, he showed massive courage in undertaking a gruelling rehabilitation programme, which entailed on-court training while strapped to an osteopathic bench. He went on to become world number 1 and in the process earned the nickname 'The Iron Man'.

The somewhat bumbling and chaotic side of skier Hermann Maier has led to him being likened to Superman's human alter ego, Clark Kent. However, in the 1998 Nagano Olympics, Maier showed the amazing toughness and resilience he had gained as a bricklayer and which characterises his all-or-nothing skiing style. During the men's downhill competition, he misjudged a difficult curve, got too close to a gate, somersaulted 30m through the air, bounced over a fence and crashed through two safety nets before finally coming to rest. Austria held its breath as the man known as 'The Herminator' got to his feet, dusted himself down and waved at the crowd. He went on to win two gold medals in the next six days.

ships. This will be held in St Anton in 2001 (contact the St Anton tourist office for details).

SHOPPING

Local crafts such as textiles, pottery, wood-carvings, wrought-iron work and painted glassware make popular souvenirs.

Unfortunately, shopping in Austria is not cheap. *Heimatwerk* is the official retail outlet for goods adhering to certain standards. There's one in each major city (see the various city sections for details).

For special reductions, look for signs saying *Aktion*. Top Viennese hotels dispense a free *Shopping in Vienna* booklet detailing all sorts of shopping outlets. Graz and Salzburg each have their own version.

Getting There & Away

Travel within most of the European Union, whether by air, rail or car, has been made easier following the Schengen Agreement, first signed in 1997, which abolished border controls between participating states (see Visas & Documents in the Facts for the Visitor chapter). Border controls still exist when travelling to/from the UK.

AIR

Air travel is the quickest, easiest and sometimes cheapest means of transcontinental travel. If you're visiting Austria from outside Europe, it may be cheaper to fly to a European 'gateway' city and travel on from there: Munich, for example, is only two hours by train from Salzburg. There are some great fares available on certain routes thanks to serious competition between the airlines. Students, people aged under 26 and senior citizens often qualify for excellent deals.

Don't forget to arrange travel insurance (see Visas & Documents). Paying for your ticket with a credit card may offer limited travel accident cover, but this is no replacement for an adequate insurance policy. However, paying by credit card can give you a degree of protection against the company going bankrupt, as does buying a ticket from a bonded agent, such as one covered by the Air Transport Operators Licence scheme in the UK.

Airports & Airlines

The main air transport hub is Vienna's airport (Flughafen Wien Schwechat), which handles over eight million passengers a year; more people travel to/from London than any other city. It has all the facilities expected of a major airport, such as tourist information, money exchange counters (with high commission rates) and car rental. See the Getting Around section in the Vienna chapter for information on transport from the airport to the city.

Other Austrian airports which handle international flights are at Graz, Innsbruck, Klagenfurt, Linz and Salzburg. From these airports you can get scheduled or charter

Lauda Air Takes Off

Austria's Niki Lauda, three-times Formula 1 racing world champion, founded Lauda Air in 1979. It initially operated only as a charter airline with Lauda himself, a trained pilot, often taking the controls. In 1985 a long battle to operate scheduled flights began. Partial approval was given in 1987, and Lauda's first scheduled flight took off in May 1987.

Lauda Air's struggle to establish itself was made all the harder by the attitude of the state-owned Austrian Airlines. It halved air fares on certain routes, denigrated the fledgling airline in the press and was often uncooperative in air traffic rights negotiations. It took another three years of intensive political and public pressure (greatly aided by Lauda's status as a national hero) before the airline finally received a worldwide concession to operate scheduled flights in August 1990. Ironically, Austrian Airlines has since purchased a 36% stake in Lauda Air.

Lauda Air currently flies to Europe, the USA, Asia and Australia in aircraft named after such well known figures as Johann Strauss, Enzo Ferrari, James Dean and Bob Marley. Lauda Air's innovative style has seen it introduce quality in-flight meals (supplied by the gourmet Viennese restaurant DO & CO), jeans as part of the staff uniform, and in-flight gambling on the Vienna-Australia route.

Air Travel Glossary

Baggage Allowance This will be written on your ticket and usually includes one item of about 20kg to go in the hold, plus one item of hand luggage.

Bucket Shops These are travel agencies specialising in discounted airline tickets.

Bumped Just because you have a confirmed seat doesn't mean you're going to get on the plane (see Overbooking).

Cancellation Penalties If you have to cancel or change a discounted ticket, there are often heavy penalties involved; most travel insurance policies cover you for such occurrences as illness or car breakdown on the way to the airport. Some airlines impose penalties on regular tickets as well, particularly against 'no-show' passengers.

Check-In Airlines ask you to check in a certain time ahead of the flight departure (usually one to two hours on international flights). If you fail to check in on time and the flight is overbooked, the airline can cancel your booking and give your seat to somebody else.

Confirmation Having a ticket written out with the flight and date you want doesn't mean you have a seat until the agent has checked with the airline that your status is 'OK' or confirmed. Meanwhile you could just be 'on request'.

Courier Fares Businesses often need to send urgent documents or freight securely and quickly. Courier companies hire people to accompany the package through customs and, in return, offer a discount ticket which is sometimes a phenomenal bargain. In effect, what the companies do is ship their freight as your luggage on regular commercial flights. This is a legitimate operation, but there are two shortcomings – the short turnaround time of the ticket (usually not longer than a month) and the limitation on your luggage allowance. You may have to surrender all your allowance and take only carry-on luggage.

Full Fares Airlines traditionally offer 1st class (coded F), business class (coded J) and economy class (coded Y) tickets. These days there are so many promotional and discounted fares available that few passengers pay full economy fare.

ITX An ITX, or 'independent inclusive tour excursion', is often available on tickets to popular holiday destinations. Officially it's a package deal combined with hotel accommodation, but many agents will sell you one of these for the flight only and give you phoney hotel vouchers in the unlikely event that you're challenged at the airport.

Lost Tickets If you lose your airline ticket an airline will usually treat it like a travellers cheque and, after inquiries, issue you with another one. Legally, however, an airline is entitled to treat it like cash and if you lose it then it's gone forever. Take good care of your tickets.

MCO An MCO, or 'miscellaneous charge order', is a voucher that looks like an airline ticket but carries no destination or date. It can be exchanged through any International Association of Travel Agents (IATA) airline for a ticket on a specific flight. It's a useful alternative to an onward ticket in those countries that demand one.

No-Shows No-shows are passengers who fail to show up for their flight. Full-fare passengers who fail to turn up are sometimes entitled to travel on a later flight. The rest are penalised (see Cancellation Penalties).

Air Travel Glossary

On Request This is an unconfirmed booking for a flight.

Onward Tickets An entry requirement for many countries is that you have a ticket out of the country. If you're unsure of your next move, the easiest solution is to buy the cheapest onward ticket to a neighbouring country or a ticket from a reliable airline which can later be refunded if you do not use it.

Open Jaw Tickets These are return tickets where you fly out to one place but return from another. If available, this can save you backtracking to your arrival point.

Overbooking Airlines hate to fly empty seats and since every flight has some passengers who fail to show up, airlines often book more passengers than they have seats. Usually no-shows allow enough room for excess passengers, but occasionally somebody gets bumped onto the next available flight. It's most likely to be the passengers who check in late.

Point-to-Point Tickets These are discount tickets that can be bought on some routes in return for passengers waiving their rights to a stopover.

Promotional Fares These are officially discounted fares, available from travel agencies or direct from the airline.

Reconfirmation At least 72 hours prior to departure time of an onward or return flight, most airlines require you to contact them to 'reconfirm' that you intend to be on the flight. If you don't do this the airline can delete your name from the passenger list and you could lose your seat. Find out if your airline requires reconfirmation.

Restrictions Discounted tickets often have various restrictions on them – such as needing to be paid for in advance and incurring a penalty to be altered. Others are restrictions on the minimum and maximum period you must be away, such as a minimum of 14 days or a maximum of one year.

Round-the-World Tickets RTW tickets give you a limited period (usually a year) in which to circumnavigate the globe. You can go anywhere the carrying airlines go, as long as you don't backtrack. The number of stopovers or total number of separate flights is decided before you set off and they usually cost a bit more than a basic return flight.

Stand-by This is a discounted ticket where you only fly if there is a seat free at the last moment. Stand-by fares are usually available only on domestic routes.

Transferred Tickets Airline tickets cannot be transferred from one person to another. Travellers sometimes try to sell the return half of their ticket, but officials can ask you to prove that you are the person named on the ticket. This is less likely to happen on domestic flights, but on an international flight tickets are compared with passports.

Travel Agencies Travel agencies vary widely. Some simply handle tours, while others handle everything from tours and tickets to car rental and hotel bookings. If you just want a cheap ticket, your best bet may be a bucket shop.

Travel Periods Ticket prices vary with the time of year. There is a low (off-peak) season and a high (peak) season, and often a low-shoulder season and a high-shoulder season as well. Usually the fare depends on your outward flight – if you depart in the high season and return in the low season, you pay the high-season fare.

flights to a few European destinations, and there are transfer flights to and from Vienna for intercontinental passengers.

Austrian Airlines (☎ airport area code + 1789) is the national carrier and has the most extensive services to Vienna. It operates several daily nonstop flights to/from all major European transport centres, such as Amsterdam, Berlin, Frankfurt, Paris, London and Zürich, as well as to many other cities worldwide. Its subsidiary Tyrolean Airways (☎ 017111-11 11) operates domestic routes as well as some international services.

Lauda Air is another home-grown airline; ☎ 0660-6655 is its toll-free number accessible within Austria for reservations and information. Originally set up to compete with Austrian Airlines, the two are now linked and 'code-share' on many flights.

Buying Tickets

World aviation has never been so competitive, making air travel better value than ever. But you have to research the options carefully to make sure you get the best deal

Some airlines now sell discounted tickets direct to the customer, and it's worth contacting airlines anyway for information on routes and timetables. Sometimes, there is nothing to be gained by going direct to the airline – specialist discount agents often offer fares that are lower and/or carry fewer conditions than the airline's published prices. You can expect to be offered a wider range of options than a single airline would provide. And, at worst, you will just end up paying the official airline fare.

The exception to this rule is the new breed of 'no-frills' carriers, which mostly sell direct. At the time of writing none of the leading players (easyJet and Go of Britain, Ryanair of Ireland and Virgin Express of Belgium) had established links to Austria, but Vienna is sure to be on the wish-lists of several of them.

Unlike the 'full-service' airlines, the no-frills carriers often make one-way tickets available at half the return fare – meaning that it is easy to stitch together an open-jaw

itinerary where you fly in to one city and out of another. Regular airlines may offer open-jaws, particularly if you are flying in from outside Europe.

Round-the-World (RTW) tickets are another possibility, and are comparable in price to an ordinary return long-haul ticket. RTWs start at about UK£800, A$1800 or US$1300 depending on the season, and can be valid for up to a year. Special conditions might be attached to such tickets (such as you can't backtrack on a route). Also beware of cancellation penalties for these and other tickets.

Courier fares, where you get cheap passage in return for accompanying an urgent package through customs, offer very low prices but there are usually special restrictions attached and demand for couriers is decreasing in this electronic age.

You may find that the cheapest flights are being advertised by obscure agencies. Most such firms are honest and solvent, but there are some rogue fly-by-night outfits around. If you feel suspicious about a firm, it's best to steer clear, or only pay a deposit before you get your ticket, then ring the airline to confirm that you are actually booked on the flight before you pay the balance. Established outfits, such as those mentioned in this book, offer more security and are almost as competitive as you can get.

The cheapest deals are only available at certain times of the year or on weekdays, and fares are particularly subject to change. Always ask about the route: the cheapest tickets may involve an inconvenient stopover. Don't take schedules for granted, either: airlines usually change their schedules twice a year, at the end of March and the end of October. The Internet is a useful resource for checking air fares: many travel agents and airlines have a Web page.

Travellers with Special Needs

Airlines can often make special arrangements for travellers if they're warned early enough, such as wheelchair assistance at airports or vegetarian meals on the flight. Children under two years travel for 10% of the standard fare (or free on some airlines) as long as they don't occupy a seat. They don't get a baggage allowance. 'Skycots', baby food and nappies should be provided by the airline if requested in advance. Children aged two and 12 can usually occupy a seat for half to two-thirds of the full fare, and do get a baggage allowance.

Departure Tax

There is no departure tax to pay at the airport when flying out of Austria. Austria has a 'passenger service tax' (sometimes called a 'security tax') of around AS140 but this is included in the airline ticket price. Note that travel agents sometimes initially quote fares without taxes to make their fares seem lower.

The UK

London is one of the world's major centres for buying discounted air tickets, and it ought to cost less to fly to Austria than to go by train. Cheap fares appear in the weekend national papers and, in London, in *Time Out*, the *Evening Standard* and *TNT* (a free magazine available from bins at underground stations). The main carriers between the UK and Austria are Austrian Airlines (☎ 0171-434 7300; after 23 April 2000 ☎ 020-7434 7300, a number it shares with Swissair); British Airways (☎ 0345 222 111); and Lauda Air (☎ 0800 767 737). All of them fly several times daily from London Heathrow, though Austrian and Lauda share their flights. BA and Lauda fly daily from London Gatwick, Lauda also operates from Manchester.

The lowest return fare at most times of year from London to Vienna is around UK£150, slightly more from Manchester. Most of the good discount agents are in London. Reliable sources of cheap flights between the UK and continental Europe include Hamilton Travel (☎ 0171-344 3344; after 23 April 2000 ☎ 020-7344 3344) and Trailfinders (☎ 0171-937 5400; after 23 April 2000 ☎ 020-7937 5400).

For travellers under 26 years or students, fares may be even lower and conditions less restrictive – for example, the standard 'Saturday night minimum stay' rule may be waived. The two leading agencies in the UK are Usit Campus (☎ 0171-730 3402; after 23 April 2000 ☎ 020-7730 3402) and STA Travel (☎ 0171-361 6161; after 23 April 2000 ☎ 020-7361 6161), both of which have branches across Britain and sell tickets to all travellers but cater especially to young people and students.

There are also some travel agents that focus specifically on Austria. One such is Mondial Travel (☎ 0181-777 7000; after 23 April 2000 ☎ 020-8777 7000), 32 Links Rd, West Wickham, Kent BR4 0QW, which can arrange fly/drive deals. See Organised Tours at the end of this chapter for other outlets.

Continental Europe

Across Europe many travel agents have ties with STA Travel, where cheap tickets can be purchased and STA-issued tickets can be altered (usually for a US$25 fee). Outlets in major cities include: Voyages Wasteels (☎ 1-43 43 46 10), 2 rue Michel Chasles, Paris; STA Travel (☎ 069-43 01 91), Berger Strasse 118, Frankfurt; and ISYTS (☎ 01-322 1267), 1st floor, 11 Nikis St, Syntagma Square, Athens. There are no travel agents in Austria currently linked with STA.

In continental Europe, Athens is a recognised centre for cheap flights: check the many travel agents in the backstreets between Syntagma and Omonia squares. As well as ISYTS, try Magic Bus (☎ 01-323 7471), Filellinon 20, for discounted air fares, or Consolas Travel (☎ 01-323 2812) next door.

Amsterdam also has a good reputation as a source of cheap fares: try Budget Air (☎ 020-627 12 51), Rokin 34; Flyworld/Grand Travel (☎ 020-657 00 00, fax 648 04 77), Wallaardt Sacrestraat 262; or the student agency, NBBS (☎ 020-624 09 89), Rokin 38.

Vienna has excellent connections to and from Eastern Europe, including Bucharest, Kiev, Moscow, St Petersburg, Vilnius and Warsaw. Austrian Airlines has extensive direct services to these and other places. Lauda Air has at least one daily flight to Vienna from Munich.

The USA

The North Atlantic is the world's busiest long-haul air corridor: the *New York Times*, *LA Times, Chicago Tribune* and *San Francisco Examiner* all produce weekly travel sections in which you'll find numerous travel agents' ads. Non-stop flights from the USA to Austria are relatively rare; the main ones are Atlanta-Vienna on Delta and New York JFK-Vienna on Austrian Airlines. Fares for these are likely to be high – around US$1000 return for the cheapest and most restrictive ticket. A much wider range of departure points, and lower fares, is available on airlines that stop in third countries en route: Air France via Paris, BA via London and Lufthansa via Frankfurt are the main ones. Fares from the east coast may be available for as little as US$600, while flights from the west coast start around the US$900 mark.

Council Travel (☎ 800-226 8624) and STA Travel (☎ 800-777 0112) sell discounted tickets from numerous outlets across the USA. STA branches include those in San Francisco (☎ 415-391 8407) and New York (☎ 212-627 3111). One-way fares can be very cheap on a stand-by basis. Airhitch (☎ 800-326 2009, email airhitch@ netcom.com) specialises in this sort of thing and can get you from the east/west coast to Europe, one way, for US$159/239; their Web site is at www.airhitch.org. For courier flights, try Now Voyager (☎ 212-431 1616) in New York.

Canada

There are currently no direct flights between Canada and Austria, so travelling via another European city with airlines such as Lufthansa or KLM is the most likely option. From Montreal or Toronto, the minimum fare is around C$1000; from Calgary, Edmonton or Vancouver, it's around C$1250.Check ads in the Toronto *Globe & Mail*, the *Toronto Star* and the

Vancouver Province. Look for the budget agency Travel CUTS (☎ 888-838 2887, toll free). Its head office (☎ 416-977 2185) is at 187 College St, Toronto M5T 1P7, or check out its Web site www.travelcuts.com. For courier fares, contact FB On Board Courier Services on ☎ 514-631 2677 in Montreal, or ☎ 604-278 1266 in Vancouver.

Australia & New Zealand

Check the travel agents' ads in the Yellow Pages, and the Saturday travel sections of the *Sydney Morning Herald* and the Melbourne *Age*. STA Travel and Flight Centres International are major dealers in cheap air fares. STA has offices at 224 Faraday St, Carlton, Melbourne (☎ 03-9349 2411); 24-30 Springfield Ave, Kings Cross, Sydney (☎ 02-9368 1111); and 10 High St, Auckland (☎ 09-366 6673). Flight Centres International has a toll free number in Australia: ☎ 131 600. They also have offices all over Australia and New Zealand, including 19 Bourke St, Melbourne (☎ 03-9650 2899, fax 9650 3751) and 205-225 Queen St, Auckland (☎ 09-309 6171).

From Australia to Vienna, Lauda Air (☎ 1800-642 438) operates the only direct flight (via Kuala Lumpur), with departures from Sydney on most days; expect to pay around A$2500/2000 in high/low season. There are many options for travelling to Vienna via Asia in the low season. BA (in association with Qantas), Swissair, Thai Airways International and Singapore Airlines all offer good deals.

From New Zealand, there are no direct flights to Austria. Most of the cheaper fares to Europe are via Asia. A return flight to Vienna with Singapore Airlines (via Singapore) costs around NZ$2700/2400 in high/low season. Going via the USA is equally feasible, or consider buying a RTW ticket.

Africa

Austrian Airlines flies direct to Vienna, usually three times a week, from Cairo and Johannesburg. Another option from Africa is to fly to another European point, such as

Frankfurt, Paris, London or Zurich, and transfer from there. Nairobi has some of the best prices thanks to keen competition between bucket shops; a typical one-way/return fare to London would be about US$550/800.

Several West African countries, such as Burkina Faso, Gambia and especially Morocco, offer cheap charter flights to France and Germany. From Cairo, the best option might be to take a flight to Athens, then a budget bus or train from there.

Asia

Singapore and Bangkok are the best places in Asia to buy discounted air tickets. It's worth shopping around and asking the advice of other travellers before buying a ticket, as some bucket shops are unreliable. STA has branches in Bangkok, Tokyo, Singapore, Hong Kong and Kuala Lumpur.

Mumbai and Delhi are the air transport hubs of India with many cheap options. Try Student Travel Information Centre (☎ 332 7582) in the Imperial Hotel, Janpath, Delhi.

There are direct flights to Vienna from Beijing, Ho Chi Minh City, Hong Kong, Kuala Lumpur, Shanghai, Singapore, Taipei and Tokyo.

LAND
Bus

Buses are generally cheaper but slower and less comfortable than trains. Europe's biggest network of international buses is provided by a group of bus companies operating under the name Eurolines.

Addresses for Eurolines include:

Eurolines
   (☎ 1-43 54 11 99) 55 Rue Saint Jacques, Paris
Deutsche Touring
   (☎ 069-790 32 40) Am Romerhof 17, Frankfurt
Eurolines Nederland
   (☎ 020-627 51 51) Rokin 10, Amsterdam
Eurolines Italy
   (☎ 06-44 04 00 9) Ciconvallazione Nonentana 574, Lato Stazione Tiburtina, Rome
Eurolines UK
   (☎ 0990-143 219) 52 Grosvenor Gardens, London SW1

Eurolines in Austria is Blaguss Reisen (☎ 01-712 04 53), based in Vienna's international Autobusbahnhof (bus station), Landstrasser Hauptstrasse 1/B, next to Wien Mitte train station. Eurolines tickets must be purchased in person from the Blaguss Eurolines counters, not from the Blaguss hut, though you can make reservations by telephone. There are bus connections across Western and Eastern Europe, with reduced prices (of 10% or more, depending on the operator) for people aged under 26 and over 60. Eurolines buses to/from London (Victoria coach station) depart six days a week (daily in summer); the trip takes 22 hours and costs around UK£80/120 for a one-way/return adult fare (about UK£10 more in July, August and pre-Christmas).

Eurolines buses to Budapest depart from Wien Mitte several times daily, starting at 7 am (3½ hours). The fare is AS310 one way or AS440 return. Thre are also direct buses from Vienna airport to Budapest. Buses run every two hours or so to Bratislava, also departing from Wien Mitte, travelling via the airport and Hainburg. The fare from Vienna is AS110/200 one way/return, but it would work out cheaper to buy the return leg in Bratislava.

Columbus (☎ 01-534 11-123), 01, Dr Karl Lueger Ring 8, runs buses to Prague (sometimes continuing to Karlsbad), leaving Vienna from 01, Rathausplatz 5 at 8 am Monday to Thursday and Saturday, and at 2 pm on Friday and Sunday (AS325; five hours). Coming from Prague, buses leave at 9 am Monday to Thursday, and at 2 pm Friday to Sunday.

If you want to visit several countries by bus, try Busabout (☎ 0181-784 2816; after 23 April 2000 ☎ 020-8784 2816, email bus about.info@virgin.net, Web site www.busabout.com). This UK-based alternative to Eurolines has buses travelling set routes across Europe, and you can jump on and off as many times as you like within a given period. For the northern zone it costs UK£129/149/159 for one/two/four months (UK£119/129/139 for students). Tickets can be bought direct or from agents such as Usit Campus or STA. European passes are also available from Eurolines UK: they're more flexible but more expensive, from UK£159/199 for young people/adults for 30 days.

Train

Trains are a popular, convenient and relatively environment-friendly way to travel. They are also comfortable, reasonably frequent, and can be good places to meet other travellers.

Stories about train passengers being gassed or drugged and then robbed occasionally surface, though bag-snatching is more of a worry. Sensible security measures include not letting your bags out of your sight (or at least chaining them to the luggage rack) and locking compartment doors overnight.

European Rail Passes

European rail passes make train travel affordable but, unless you want to explore other countries, it may work out cheaper to pay the normal fare to Austria then use a national rail pass to explore the country (see the Rail Passes section in the Getting Around chapter). Reservation costs (and most supplements) are not covered by rail passes, and pass holders must always carry their passport on the train for identification. Buying a circular ticket, such as the **Explorer** tickets sold under the name Eurotrain, might be a viable alternative to a full rail pass.

Treat rail passes as if they were cash, as replacement can be difficult or expensive, and always study the terms and conditions. European seniors can buy a Rail Europe Senior Card, entitling the holder to reductions on European train fares.

Eurailpass

This pass can only be bought by residents of non-European countries. Eurailpasses are valid for unlimited travel on national railways and some private lines in Austria, Belgium, Denmark, Finland, France (including Monaco), Germany, Greece, Hungary, Ireland, Italy, Luxembourg, the Netherlands, Norway, Portugal, Spain, Sweden and Switzerland (including Liechtenstein). The UK is not covered. The pass is also valid for free or discounted travel on various international ferries and national lake/river steamers.

There are several different types of pass. The standard **Eurailpass** costs from US$538 for 15 days up to US$1512 for three months. The **Flexipass** costs US$634 for 10 days travel or US$836 for 15 days travel, to be taken on any chosen days within a two month period. These passes are available in 1st class only. Two people travelling together can save around 15% each by buying 'saver' versions (child fares available).

The **Youthpass**, for travellers aged 26 or under, is valid for unlimited 2nd class travel within a given time period, ranging from 15 days (US$376) up to three months (US$1059). The **Youth Flexipass**, also for 2nd class, is valid for freely chosen days within a two month period: 10 days for US$444 or 15 days for US$585.

There's also a Euraildrive Pass.

Europass

This gives a number of freely chosen days of unlimited travel within two months in France, Germany, Italy, Spain and Switzerland. The youth/adult fare starts at US$216/326 for 5 days of travel, or US$261/386 including Austria, which is an 'associate' country to the scheme. Extra rail days can be purchased for US$29/42 each (to a maximum of 15 days).

The *Thomas Cook European Timetable* is the trainophile's bible, giving a complete listing of train schedules, supplements and reservations information. It is updated monthly and is available from Thomas Cook outlets. In the USA, call ☎ 800-367 7984.

UK & Continental Europe Austria benefits from its central location within Europe by having excellent rail connections to all important destinations. Vienna is one of the main rail hubs in central Europe; for details of the main train stations and the routes they serve see the Getting There & Away section in the Vienna chapter. There are four trains each day from Vienna's Südbahnhof to Bratislava; the journey takes 70 minutes. Elsewhere in Austria, Salzburg has trains at least every hour to/from Munich (AS272)

European Rail Passes

There is a **Eurail and Europass Aid Office** (☎ 5800-335 98) in Vienna's Westbahnhof, open Monday to Saturday from 9 am to 4 pm.

Inter-Rail Pass
Inter-Rail passes are available in Europe to people who have been resident there for at least six months. The standard Inter-Rail pass is for travellers aged under 26, though older people can get the Inter-Rail 26+ version. The pass divides Europe into eight zones (A to H); Austria is in zone C, along with Denmark, Germany and Switzerland. The standard/26+ fare for any one zone is UK£159/229, valid for 22 days. To purchase a pass covering two/three/all zones (valid one month) costs UK£209/229/259, or UK£279/309/349 for the 26+ version.

The all-zone (global) pass would take you everywhere covered by Eurail, plus Bulgaria, Croatia, Czech Republic, Macedonia, Morocco, Poland, Romania, Slovakia, Slovenia, Turkey and Yugoslavia. As with Eurail, the pass gives discounts or free travel on some ferry, ship and steamer routes.

Euro-Domino Pass
There is a Euro-Domino pass (called a **Freedom pass** in Britain) for each of the countries covered by the Inter-Rail pass, except for Macedonia. Adults (travelling 1st or 2nd class) and young people (under 26 years) can opt for three, five, or 10 chosen days of travel within a month. The Domino pass for Austria is a viable alternative to buying one of Austria's national rail passes. For three/five/10 days travel in 2nd class it costs UK£96/105/176 for adults and UK£76/79/139 for those aged under 26.

Austrian Flexipass
This is a similar to the Austrian Domino Pass, but costs less. It may be marketed simply as an Austrian Railpass, and is only available to non-Europeans. It allows three travel days in 15 for US$98 (US$145 in 1st class). Extra days (five maximum) can be purchased for US$15 (US$21) each.

European East Pass
This is sold in North America and Australia, and is valid for train travel in Austria, the Czech Republic, Hungary, Poland and Slovakia. The cost is US$185 for five days travel in one month; extra travel days (five maximum) cost US$22 each.

with onward connections north. Express services to Italy go via Innsbruck or Villach. From Villach there are trains going south-east. Trains to Slovenia go through Graz or Villach.

Paris, Amsterdam, Munich and Milan are also important cities for rail connections. From the UK, the main route is through the Channel Tunnel from London Waterloo to Brussels. You must change trains there, and possibly also in Cologne, Frankfurt or Munich. The fastest journey time is about 16 hours. Services are run by the Eurostar passenger train service (☎ 0990-186 186) or the Eurotunnel vehicle-carrying service (☎ 0990-353 535). These operators do not sell tickets to Vienna, but Rail Europe (0990-848 848), part of French Railways, arranges rail travel between the UK and many European countries, including Austria. The lowest adult fare is likely to be around UK£120/200 one-way/return.

Travellers aged under 26 can pick up Billet International de Jeunesse (BIJ) tickets, which cut fares by up to 50%. Various agents in Europe issue BIJ tickets, including Wasteels (☎ 0171-834 7066; after 23 April 2000 ☎ 020-7834 7066) in London's Victoria railway station and Voyages Wasteels (☎ 1-43 43 46 10) at 2 rue Michel Chasles, Paris. Rail Europe (☎ 0990-848 848) sells BIJ tickets and rail passes. It has London offices at 179 Piccadilly and in Victoria railway station.

Express trains can be identified by the symbols EC (EuroCity, serving international routes) or IC (InterCity, serving national routes). The French TGV and the German ICE trains are even faster. Supplements can apply on fast trains and international trains, and it is a good idea (sometimes obligatory) to make seat reservations for peak times and on certain lines. Overnight trips usually offer a choice of couchette (around US$28) or a more expensive sleeper. Long-distance trains have a dining car or snacks available. Reserving IC or EC train seats in 2nd class within Austria costs AS30; in 1st class, it's free. In Austria you can sometimes pick up cheap fares on international return tickets valid for less than four days.

The Orient Express is an old-style private train that serves European routes. It passes through Austria: inquire at travel agents.

Asia The direct train from Vienna to Moscow takes 47 hours (AS1392, plus AS410 for a sleeper). From there you can choose from four different trains for onwards eastern travel. Three of them (the trans-Siberian, trans-Mongolian and trans-Manchurian) follow the same route to/from Moscow across Siberia but have different eastern railheads. The fourth, the trans-Kazakhstan, runs between Moscow and Ürümqi (north-western China) across central Asia. Prices can vary enormously, depending on where you buy the ticket and what is included, but you won't save money compared with flying. If you have time (between six and nine days minimum) train travel is an interesting option, but only really worthwhile if you want to stop off and explore China and Russia on the way through. Possibilities for overland travel to/from Asia, whether by train, bus or private vehicle, should become more widespread as tourism expands in the region.

Car & Motorcycle

Getting to Austria by road is simple as there are fast and well-maintained motorways through all surrounding countries. German autobahns have no tolls or speed limits, whereas those in France (autoroute) and Italy (autostrada) have both. Switzerland levies a one-off charge of Sfr40 (about US$25) for using its motorways. The Czech Republic and Slovakia also impose a motorway charge, as does Austria (see Motorway Tax & Tunnel Tolls in the Getting Around chapter).

Driving is on the right throughout continental Europe, and priority is usually given to traffic approaching from the right. Road signs are generally standard throughout Europe. Be aware that Europeans are particularly strict on drink-driving laws. The blood-alcohol concentration (BAC) limit when driving is between 0.05 and 0.08%, but in some areas (Eastern Europe, Scandinavia) it can be 0%. For more on motoring regulations within Austria, see the Car & Motorcycle section of the Getting Around chapter.

By road into Austria there are numerous entry points from Germany, the Czech Republic, Slovakia, Hungary, Slovenia, Italy and Switzerland. The only other country that borders Austria, Liechtenstein, is so small that it has just one border crossing point, near Feldkirch in Austria. The presence of the Alps limits options for approaching Tirol from the south (Switzerland and Italy). All main border crossing points are open 24 hours. Those served by minor roads are open from around 6 or 8 am until 8 or 10 pm. The *Facts and Sights* map, available at Austrian National Tourist Offices, indicates which are major and which are minor border crossings. Remember that there are no border controls to/from Germany and Italy, thanks to the Schengen Agreement.

To avoid a long drive to Austria, consider putting your car on a motorail service run by national railways: many head south from Calais and Paris. German Rail has services to Brussels to Salzburg costs about UK£340/560 for one way/return in the low season for a car and two adults, including a couchette.

Paperwork & Preparations See Driving Licence & Permits in the Facts for the Visitor chapter for information on those documents.

Third-party motor insurance is a minimum requirement in Europe: get proof of this in the form of a Green Card, issued by your insurers. Also ask for a 'European Accident Statement' form. Taking out a European breakdown assistance policy, such as the AA Five Star Service or the RAC Eurocover Motoring Assistance, is a good investment.

Every vehicle travelling across an international border should display a nationality plate of its country of registration. A warning triangle, to be used in the event of breakdown, is compulsory almost everywhere (including Austria). Recommended accessories are a first-aid kit (compulsory in Austria, Slovenia, Croatia, Yugoslavia and Greece), a spare bulb kit and a fire extinguisher. In the UK, contact the RAC (☎ 0800-550055) or the AA (☎ 0990-500600) for more information.

The RAC publishes its annual *Motoring in Europe*, giving an excellent summary of regulations in each country, including parking rules. Motoring organisations in other countries have similar publications.

If you're a member of an automobile association, ask about free reciprocal benefits offered by affiliated organisations in Europe.

Camper Van Travelling in a camper van can be a surprisingly economical option for budget travellers, as it can take care of eating, sleeping and travelling in one convenient package. London is a good place to buy: look in *TNT* magazine and *Loot* newspaper, or go to the van market on Market Rd, London N7. Expect to spend at least UK£2000 (US$3200). The most common camper van is the VW based on the 1600cc or 2000cc Transporter, and spare parts are widely available in Europe. Discreet free camping, such as in autobahn rest areas, is rarely a problem, and is actually permitted in most places in Austria, Germany and Switzerland.

A drawback with camper vans is that they're expensive to buy in spring and hard to sell in autumn. A car and tent might do just as well instead.

Motorcycle Touring Europe and Austria are ideal for motorcycle touring, with winding roads of good quality, stunning scenery to stimulate the senses, and an active motorcycling scene. The wearing of crash helmets for motorcyclists and passengers is compulsory everywhere in Europe. Austria, Belgium, France, Germany, Luxembourg, Portugal, Spain, Scandinavia and most countries in Eastern Europe require motorcyclists to use headlights during the day; in other countries it is recommended.

Fuel Leaded petrol is no longer available in Austria, but Super Plus has a special additive which allows it to be used for engines taking leaded petrol. Prices per litre are about AS12 for Super Plus, marginally more than for unleaded petrol, and AS9 for diesel. Plan to arrive in the country with a full or empty tank depending on where you're coming from: petrol is cheaper in the Czech Republic, Slovakia and Hungary, similarly priced in Germany and Switzerland, and more expensive in Italy.

Bicycle

This is one of the best ways to travel in terms of your bank balance, your health, and the environment, but it does require a high level of commitment to see it through.

Starting from the UK, consider joining the Cyclists' Touring Club (CTC; ☎ 01483-417 217, email cycling@ctc.org.uk), Cotterell House, 69 Meadrow, Godalming, Surrey GU7 3HS. It can supply information to members on cycling conditions in Europe, as well as detailed routes, itineraries, maps and specialised insurance. Membership costs UK£25 per annum, UK£12.50 for students and people aged under 18, or UK£16.50 for seniors.

If coming from farther afield, bikes can be carried by aeroplane, but check with the carrier in advance, preferably before buying your ticket. To take it as a normal piece of luggage you may need to remove the pedals or turn the handlebars sideways, but beware of possible excess baggage costs.

A primary consideration on long cycling trips is to travel light, but you should take a few tools and spare parts, including a puncture repair kit and a spare inner tube. Panniers are essential to balance your possessions on either side of the bike frame. A bike helmet is also a very good idea, as is a sturdy bike lock. Seasoned cyclists can average 80km a day but there's no point overdoing it. The slower you travel, the more locals you're likely to meet.

Bicycles are not allowed on European motorways – not that you would want to use those tedious bits of concrete anyway. Stick to small roads or dedicated bike tracks where possible. If you get weary of pedalling or simply want to skip a boring section, you can put your feet up on the train. On slower trains, bikes can usually be taken on board as luggage, subject to a small supplementary fee. Fast trains (IC, EC etc) can rarely accommodate bikes: they might need to be sent as registered luggage and may end up on a different train from the one you take. (One solution is to semi-dismantle your bike, shove it in a bag or sack and take it on a train as hand luggage.) British trains are outside the European luggage registration scheme, except for Eurostar. In Austria, it costs AS140 to send a bike as international luggage.

Hitching

See the Getting Around chapter for advice about hitching.

Ferry tickets for vehicles sometimes include a full load of passengers, so hitchers may be able to secure a free passage by hitching before cars board the boat. This also applies to Eurotunnel through the Channel Tunnel.

A safer way to hitch is to arrange a lift through an organisation, such as Allostop-Provoya in France and Mitfahrzentralen in Germany. You could also scan university notice boards. Vienna has a Mitfahrzentrale – see the Getting There & Away section in the Vienna chapter.

SEA

If you're interested in taking the adventurous option of leaving Europe as a paying passenger on a freighter, contact Frachtschiff Reisen (☎ 01-587 34 11), an English-speaking agent in Vienna. Trips can involve anything from five to 100 days at sea.

RIVER

Since the early 1990s the Danube has been connected to the Rhine by the Main-Danube canal in Germany. The MS *Swiss Pearl* does 12-day cruises along this route, from Amsterdam to Vienna, between June and mid-September. It departs monthly in each direction. In Britain, bookings can be made through Noble Caledonia (☎ 0171-409 0376; after 23 April 2000 ☎ 020-7409 0376); deck prices start at UK£1780. In the USA, you can book through Uniworld (☎ 800-733 7820).

Several companies run services along the Austrian stretch of the Danube. From Vienna, fast hydrofoils travel eastwards to Bratislava and Budapest. The trip to Bratislava (once daily, Wednesday to Sunday, between 1 May and late October) costs AS230 one way and AS350 return. It takes 1½ hours downstream (Vienna to Bratislava), 1¾ hours upstream. To Budapest costs AS750 one way, AS1100 return and takes at least 5½ hours; there's one daily departure from early April to early November (two daily from early July to early September). Bookings can be made in Vienna through Mahart Tours (☎ 01-7292-161), 02, Handelskai 265, or DDSG Blue Danube (☎ 01-588 80-0, fax -440, email ddsg.blue.danube@telecom.at), 01, Friedrichstrasse 7. Hydrofoils are more expensive than the bus or the train, but make a pleasant change if you can afford them.

Various steamers ply the Danube to the west of Vienna. Several operators run boats on the Lower Austria section of the Danube – see the Danube Valley section in the Lower Austria chapter for details. Boats also go between Linz and Passau, on the German border: see the Linz section in the Upper Austria chapter.

ORGANISED TOURS

For tailor-made tours, see your travel agent or look under Special Interests in the small ads in newspaper travel pages. Various packages are available with a musical theme. Austrian Holidays (☎ 0171-434 7399, fax 434 7393; after 23 April 2000 ☎ 020-7434 7399, fax 7434 7393), 10 Wardour St, London W1V 4BQ, can offer flight-only deals or construct holidays

based around tourist sights, winter sights or the opera. Austria Travel (☎ 0171-222 2430, fax 233 0293; after 23 April 2000 ☎ 020-7222 2430, fax 7233 0293), 46 Queen Anne's Gate, London SW1H 9AU, has competitive air fares, and sells city breaks with excursions included; discounts often apply for members of the linked Anglo-Austrian society (☎ 0171-222 0366; after 23 April 2000 ☎ 020-7222 0366) which organises lectures and musical events relating to Austria.

There are also bus tours based on hotel or camping accommodation. London-based operators include Acacia (☎ 0171-937 3028; after 23 April 2000 ☎ 020-7937 3028, email acacia@afrika.demon.co.uk); Contiki (☎ 0181-290 6422; after 23 April 2000 ☎ 020-8290 6422, email travel@contiki.co.uk) and Top Deck (☎ 0171 370 4555; after 23 April 2000 ☎ 020-7370 4555, email s+m.topdeck@dial.pipex.com). They all have representatives in North America, Australia and New Zealand.

For people aged over 50, Saga Holidays (☎ 0800-300500), Saga Building, Middelburg Square, Folkestone, Kent CT20 1AZ, offers holidays ranging from cheap coach tours to luxury cruises (and also arranges cheap travel insurance). Saga operates in the USA as Saga International Holidays (☎ 800-343 0273), 222 Berkeley St, Boston, MA 02116, and in Australia as Saga Holidays Australasia (☎ 02-9957 4266), Level One, 110 Pacific Highway, North Sydney.

WARNING

The information in this chapter is particularly vulnerable to change: prices for international travel are volatile, routes are introduced and cancelled, schedules change, special deals come and go, and rules and visa requirements are amended. Airlines and governments seem to take a perverse pleasure in making price structures and regulations as complicated as possible. You should check directly with the airline or a travel agent to make sure you understand how a fare (and any ticket you buy) works. In addition, the travel industry is highly competitive and there are many lurks and perks.

The upshot of this is that you should get opinions, quotes and advice from as many airlines and travel agents as possible before you part with your hard-earned cash. The details given in this chapter should be regarded as pointers and are not a substitute for your own careful, up-to-date research.

Getting Around

Transport systems in Austria are highly developed and generally very efficient, and reliable information is usually available in English. For detailed planning, consider buying an annual timetable (*Fahrplan*). The rail timetable, available from train stations, costs AS100 and includes details of the more important ferry and cable car services. The bus timetable is produced in two volumes. Information staff in train stations will look up specific information from these guides for you, or there may be a copy for you to look through.

Most provinces (such as Carinthia, Styria, Tirol and Vorarlberg) have an integrated transport system offering day passes covering regional zones, and you can choose between bus or train travel on the same ticket. These passes can often save you money compared with buying standard single tickets, so always inquire about this option before you buy. Day passes for city transport often give a one-zone discount on regional travel.

AIR

Domestic flights are operated by Tyrolean Airways, which is partially owned by Austrian Airlines. There are several flights a day from Vienna to Graz, Klagenfurt and Innsbruck, and at least two a day to Salzburg and Linz. Austrian Airlines is a sales agent for Tyrolean Airlines. Rheintalflug (☎ 0222-7007-6911, email see wald@rheintalflug.vol.at) flies daily from Vienna to Altenrhein (Switzerland), with free bus transfers to/from Bregenz in Vorarlberg. The fare starts at AS2990 one way. Check schedules as they vary according to the season.

The price of tickets means that getting around by air is not a viable option for most people. The air fare between Vienna and Klagenfurt, for example, is AS1740 one way. The flying time is 55 minutes, and on top of this you have check-in time and the hassle of getting to and from each airport. In comparison, the train takes 4½ hours and costs AS430 for a one-way ticket.

BUS

The Bundesbus (federal bus) network is primarily a backup to the rail service, more used for reaching out-of-the-way places and local destinations than for long-distance travel. Rail routes are sometimes duplicated by bus services, but buses really come into their own in the more inaccessible mountainous regions. Some of the ski resorts in Tirol and Vorarlberg, for example, can only be reached by Bundesbus or by private transport.

Bundesbuses are painted either yellow or orange, and are run by the post office (Postbus) or the rail network (Bahnbus). As far as the traveller is concerned, there's no real difference between the two types: in this book buses are simply called Bundesbus throughout. The buses are clean and punctual, and usually depart from outside train stations.

Bus fares are comparable in price to train fares; however, unlike with the train, you can't buy a long-distance ticket and make stopoffs en route. It's possible to make advance reservations on some routes, but on others you can only buy tickets from the drivers. Neither European nor Austrian rail passes are valid on Bundesbuses. Austrian citizens can get some excellent deals on buses, with reduced prices for senior citizens and families.

Fahrpläne BundesBus booklets are often available free of charge from bus station offices, major post offices and sometimes local or regional tourist offices as well. The booklets are updated each year in late May and cover provinces or specific regions. Telephone numbers for information about bus services include ☎ 0660-51 88 and ☎ 0660-80 20; all calls will be charged at the local rate.

TRAIN

Austrian trains are comfortable, clean and reasonably frequent. The country is well covered by the state network, with only a few private lines. Eurail and Inter-Rail passes (see the boxed text 'European Rail Passes' in the Getting There & Away chapter) are valid on the former; inquire before embarking on the latter. The state network is at least as efficient as most other European national rail systems, especially considering such obstacles as the Alps. However, Österreichischen Bundesbahnen (ÖBB; Austrian Federal Railways) does suffer in comparison with its Swiss neighbour, the Schweizerische Bundesbahnen (SBB), which encounters similar terrain and manages to run trains as if they were quartz watches on wheels. Austrian trains are often on time, but delays of five to 15 minutes are not uncommon. Think twice before you schedule very tight transport connections.

The German for train station is *Bahnhof* (abbreviated *Bf*); the main train station is the *Hauptbahnhof* (abbreviated *Hbf*). Some small rural stations are unstaffed, and at these you should either buy the ticket from a platform dispenser or, more usually, on the train. Such stations are indicated on timetables, either by 'Hu' or a special symbol. All reasonably-sized stations have facilities for exchanging foreign currency or travellers cheques. Stations almost always make some provision for luggage storage, either at a staffed counter (usually AS30 per piece), or in 24-hour luggage lockers for AS20 (large enough for one backpack) or AS30 (two backpacks). Newer digital lockers may cost up to AS40, and some stations have lockers for skis. Luggage can be dispatched between Austrian stations for AS90 per piece (up to 25kg). This service covers transporting bicycles – see the Bicycle section later in this chapter for more details.

Many stations have information centres where the staff speak English. Pick up the free booklet *Austria By Train* at station information offices; it tells you everything about travelling by rail, including special tickets, reservations and contact numbers. *Die Bahn im Griff* is a more detailed version in German.

Platforms at train stations (*Bahnsteig*) are divided into zones A, B and sometimes C: take care as a small rural train may be already waiting at one end while you're vainly waiting at the other for it to arrive. Usually you only realise when the train's pulling out (it's happened to me more than once). Even if you board the correct train, make sure you sit in the correct carriage, as trains occasionally split en route. Diagram boards on the platforms show the carriage order (1st or 2nd class, dining car etc) of IC and EC trains. Separate yellow posters in stations list arrivals (*Ankunft*) and departures (*Abfahrt*).

Rail Passes

The following passes can be purchased from travel agents or rail network offices, either inside or outside Austria.

The Bundes-Netzkarte is the national rail pass, valid on all state railways, including rack (cogwheel) railways; it also entitles the holder to a discount of 50% on Bodensee ferries and 25% on Wolfgangsee ferries and the Schafbergbahn. It is valid for one month and costs AS5900 for 1st class, AS4300 2nd class. It's the best deal if you're travelling extensively and intensively.

The Österreich Puzzle is not particularly puzzling – it's a kind of more flexible, regional Netzkarte which divides the country into four zones – north, south, east and west. You can buy a pass for each zone for AS1090 (AS660 if aged under 26), giving you four days unlimited travel in a 10 day period. First class costs 50% more. This pass is no longer promoted, so it may soon be discontinued. Zone areas overlap, so you can cover the whole country without actually needing to buy the east zone. West covers Vorarlberg, Tirol, East Tirol and Salzburg province. South covers Salzburg province, East Tirol, Carinthia and Styria. East covers Styria, Burgenland, Vienna and Lower Austria. North covers Upper and Lower Austria, Vienna and Burgenland.

RAILWAYS

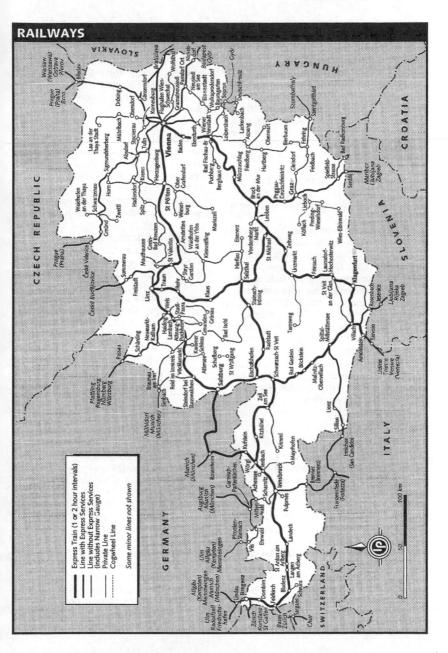

If you want to take your time exploring the country another pass, the Kilometer-bank, may be the best deal. It is valid for a year and allows up to six people to travel on journeys over 51km. You can use the pass for shorter trips, but you'll still be charged 51km per person. The maximum amount that can be debited per person on one trip is 600km; if your journey is longer that that, the rest is free. The ticket inspector on the train debits the number of kilometres used on each trip from your pass. Each kilometre in 1st class is debited as 1.5km. The cost is AS2500 for 2000km, AS3720 for 3000km, and AS6150 for 5000km. These prices represent a discount of about 10% on normal fares.

The Vorteilscard (photo required) is valid for half-price travel, and costs AS1190 for one year. The Grüne Bank (Green Bank) is like a debit card for the rail system and avoids the need to queue for tickets. The ticket inspector will debit your card once you're on the train. It costs AS2000 and can be used on trips of over 51km. Strecken-karten are passes giving hefty discounts on repeat fares for a specific trip, mostly of interest to commuters.

Private train companies in Austria accept Austrian rail passes (though the Achensee-bahn accepts only the Bundes-Netzkarte and the Österreich Puzzle).

Types of Train

The type and speed of a train can be identified by its prefix. EC (EuroCity), IC (InterCity) and SC (SuperCity) are all express trains, stopping only at major stations. They usually have a dining car where food and drink prices are quite reasonable. EN (EuroNight) is an international night train, with sleeping cars and couchettes. E (*Eilzug*: literally, hurry train) is a fast train which stops at some smaller stations. D Zug trains are medium fast. Slow, local trains have no letter prefix and stop everywhere. On small local trains serving relatively isolated routes, there may be a button to press to request the train to stop (as on buses). Trains have smoking and nonsmoking com-partments, though Vienna's S-Bahn trains are nonsmoking only.

Long-distance express trains always provide the choice of travelling in 1st or 2nd class, though some local services are 2nd class only. Second class is comfortable enough but 1st class is roomier and less crowded.

Reservations

Reserving train seats in 2nd class within Austria costs AS30 for most express services; in 1st class, reservations are free. If you haven't reserved a seat, check before you sit whether your intended seat has been reserved by someone else down the line.

Tickets & Costs

Austrian train fares are expensive (such as AS164 for 100km, AS280 for 200km) but the cost can be reduced by the rail passes mentioned earlier. There's also a variety of discount tickets available, especially for youth groups. There's also the City Star Austria ticket, which is a return ticket for anywhere within Austria (excluding some private rail lines) for AS1190; a maximum of four extra passengers travelling the same route pay AS590 each. It is valid for day trains from Monday to Thursday and on Saturday, and on all night trains.

Fares for children aged six to 15 are half-price; younger kids travel free if they don't take up a seat. Small pets (in suitable containers) travel free; larger pets go half-price.

Tickets can be purchased on the train but they cost AS30 extra (unless you board at an unstaffed station or the ticket machine is out of order). In this book, the fares quoted are always those for 2nd class. Credit cards are accepted at over 130 stations; Euro-cheque cards and cheques are accepted at all stations.

Ordinary return tickets for journeys of 101km or more each way are valid for two months. You can break your journey as often as you like, but you should tell the conductor so your ticket can be suitably endorsed. This is worth doing, as longer trips cost less per kilometre. Single journeys of

101km or more can also be broken up: these are valid for four days. One-way tickets for journeys of 100km or under are valid for only one day, and the journey can't be broken up. A return fare is usually the equivalent price of two one-way tickets.

Reduced rail fares on both national and international routes are sometimes available for those aged under 26: wave your passport and ask. In the larger towns, train information can be obtained from ☎ 1717.

CAR & MOTORCYCLE

Rural driving is an enjoyable experience in Austria. Roads are well maintained, well signposted and generally not too congested. Compared with train and bus travel, private transport gives more flexibility (such as the opportunity to stop when you want to admire that Alpine view), but it does tend to isolate you to some extent from local people and other travellers. The use of cars is often discouraged in city centres; consider ditching your trusty chariot and relying on public transport.

The fastest roads round the country are Autobahns, identified on maps by national 'A' numbers or pan-European 'E' numbers (both are usually given in this book). These are subject to a general motorway tax (see that section later in this chapter). Their course is often shadowed by alternative fast routes (*Schnellstrassen* or *Bundesstrassen*). These principal routes are as direct as the terrain will allow, sometimes using tunnels to maintain their straight lines. In the mountains, you can opt instead for smaller, slower roads that wind over mountain passes. These can add many minutes and kilometres to your journey but are much more scenic. Some minor passes are blocked by snow from November to May.

Road Distances (km)

	Bad Ischl	Bregenz	Bruck an der Mur	Eisenstadt	Graz	Innsbruck	Kitzbühel	Klagenfurt	Krems	Kufstein	Landeck	Lienz	Linz	Salzburg	St Pölten	Vienna	Villach	Wiener Neustadt
Bad Ischl	---																	
Bregenz	432	---																
Bruck an der Mur	170	577	---															
Eisenstadt	297	704	127	---														
Graz	193	600	54	175	---													
Innsbruck	239	193	384	511	407	---												
Kitzbühel	191	300	275	469	400	113	---											
Klagenfurt	245	510	145	298	133	322	264	---										
Krems	222	626	175	132	229	433	372	320	---									
Kufstein	161	271	331	460	356	78	37	286	355	---								
Landeck	316	117	461	588	484	77	186	394	510	155	---							
Lienz	232	424	266	393	277	178	94	144	432	142	248	---						
Linz	103	507	190	246	237	314	247	253	145	236	391	359	---					
Salzburg	58	374	228	362	264	181	129	223	257	103	258	180	138	---				
St Pölten	206	610	140	123	194	417	356	285	32	339	494	416	129	241	---			
Vienna	266	670	145	50	191	477	420	316	79	399	554	411	189	301	66	---		
Villach	250	486	178	335	170	287	226	37	353	251	370	109	330	188	318	353	---	
Wiener Neustadt	268	675	98	31	146	482	441	267	137	431	559	364	237	339	114	302	53	---

Carrying snow chains in winter is highly recommended and may be compulsory in some areas.

Cars can be transported by motorail trains (*Autoreisezüge*). Vienna is linked by a daily motorail service to Feldkirch, Innsbruck, Salzburg and Villach. A daily motorail goes from Graz to Innsbruck and Feldkirch. Around 180 Austrian train stations offer Park and Ride facilities (free or cheap parking while you continue your journey by train). In rural areas, petrol stations may close on Sunday. See the Car & Motorcycle section of the Getting There & Away chapter for more details on fuel.

Road Rules

The minimum driving age is 18, both for Austrians and foreigners. Like the rest of continental Europe, Austrians drive on the right-hand side of the road. Speed limits are 50km/h in towns, 130km/h on autobahns and 100km/h on other roads. Cars towing a caravan or trailer are limited to 100km/h on autobahns. Seatbelts must be used, if fitted in the car, and children aged under 12 should have a special seat or restraint.

Motorcyclists and their passengers must wear a helmet, and dipped lights must be used in daytime. Motorcyclists should also carry a first-aid kit, though apparently the police rarely enforce this regulation. Car drivers must carry a first-aid kit and a warning triangle.

Austrian police have the authority to impose fines of up to AS500 for various traffic offences. These can be paid on the spot (ask for a receipt) or within two weeks. The penalty for drink-driving (over 0.05% BAC, or blood-alcohol concentration) is a hefty on-the-spot fine and confiscation of your driving licence.

Give priority to vehicles coming from the right. On mountain roads, buses have priority; otherwise, priority lies with the vehicle which would find it most difficult to stop (generally the one facing downhill). Drive in low gear on steep downhill stretches – as a rule of thumb, use the same gear downhill as you did uphill.

Austrian road signs generally conform to recognised international standards. Triangular signs with a red border indicate dangers, and circular signs with a red border illustrate prohibitions. A sign with a crisscrossed white tyre on a blue circular background means that snow chains are compulsory. *Umleitung* is the German for 'diversion', though in Austria you may see the word *Ausweiche* instead. On maps or signs, look for the Austrian word *Maut*, which indicates a toll booth.

Trams are a common feature in Austrian cities; take care if you've never driven among them before. Trams always have priority and no matter how much you might swear, they're never going to deviate from their tracks just to suit you. Vehicles should wait behind while trams are slowing down for passenger stops.

Motorway Tax & Tunnel Tolls

A general charge for using Austrian motorways was introduced in 1997. The annual fee for the required display disc is AS550 for cars (below 3.5 tonnes) and AS220 for motorcycles. Fortunately, unlike in neighbouring Switzerland, tourists have the option of buying shorter-term passes. The weekly disc costs AS70 for cars and motorcycles and is actually valid for up to 10 days: from Friday until midnight two Sundays hence. The two monthly disc, which is valid for consecutive calendar months, costs AS150 for cars and AS80 for motorcycles.

In addition to the motorway tax, some mountain roads and tunnels levy a toll. Toll roads and Alpine passes are mentioned in this book when relevant, but not all are covered. The useful *Facts and Sights*, a free brochure from the Austrian National Tourist Office (ANTO), has a serviceable country map and lists all toll roads and prices, and all Alpine passes and their altitudes. For more detailed information, consult a motoring organisation. Though the motorway tax doesn't cover the toll fee for other roads and tunnels, it does give a 15% discount on some of them.

Urban Parking

Most town centres have a designated *Kurzparkzone* (short-term parking zone), which means that on-street parking is limited to a maximum of 1½ or three hours (depending upon the place) between specified times. These are known as blue zones because of their blue markings; a parking voucher (*Parkschein*) should be purchased from a Tabak shop or pavement dispenser and displayed on the windscreen. Sometimes blue zone parking is free, but you should get a clock indicator from a Tabak shop or a police station to show the time at which you first parked. Outside the specified hours there are no parking restrictions in blue zones.

On some streets stopping may be prohibited altogether (marked by a circular blue sign with a red border and red cross) or only permitted for 10 minutes (a circular blue sign with a red border and single diagonal line – a *Halten* area). Plaques under the sign will state any exceptions or specific conditions (for example, the Halten sign may also be marked as a Kurzparkzone, allowing 1½ or three hours parking). Motorcycles cannot be parked on the pavement.

Parking tickets incur a fine of AS300 if you pay within two weeks. Don't assume you can get away with it if you're due to leave the country, as Austria has reciprocal agreements with some countries for the collection of such debts. Don't risk getting towed, as you'll find it expensive (at least AS1000) and inconvenient to retrieve your car or motorcycle.

Motoring Organisations

The main national motoring organisation is the Österreichischer Automobil, Motorrad und Touring Club, or ÖAMTC (☎ 01-711 99-0), Schubertring 1-3, A-1010 Vienna. For 24 hour emergency assistance within Austria, dial ☎ 120. The ÖAMTC has many affiliations with motoring clubs worldwide and members of these clubs do not have to pay for assistance (ask your club before leaving home). If you're not entitled to free assistance, call-out charges are AS1066 during the day or AS1366 from 10 pm to 6 am. The ÖAMTC also offers ordinary travel agency services.

The other national motoring club, the Auto, Motor und Radfahrerbund Österreichs (ARBÖ; ☎ 01-891 21), 15, Mariahilfer Strasse 180, A-1150 Vienna, offers 24 hour emergency assistance on ☎ 123. Unfortunately it does not have any international reciprocal agreements for free assistance, so anyone not a member of ARBÖ would have to pay. Call-out charges are similar to those of ÖAMTC.

Both of these organisations have branches throughout Austria.

Rental

For the lowest rates, organise car rental before departure. Holiday Autos (☎ 0990-300400) in the UK charges UK£199 for its lowest category car for one week, including airport surcharge, unlimited mileage and collision-damage waiver, and has a lowest price guarantee. It has branches in Europe and its USA office is Kemwel Holiday Autos (☎ 800-678 0678) in Harrison, New York.

Within Austria, shop around to get the best deal; sometimes the same company may have two or more different rates – *Lokal Tarif*, *City Tarif*, *Hotel Tarif* and so on – plus you can pay by the kilometre or go for unlimited rates. Also, there are lower-priced deals for weekend rental, which usually (but not always) runs from noon Friday to 9 am Monday. The following prices include 20% VAT (known as MWST in Austria).

Of the multinationals, Europcar (☎ 01-799 61 76, email europcar@telecom.at) usually has the best unlimited-kilometre rates, starting at AS596 per day. However, it's worth comparing the prices of all the operators as there might be attractive one-off deals. Avis (☎ 0660-87 57, local call rate), for example, sometimes has a real bargain: subject to availability, it can provide an Opel Corsa or VW Polo for only AS440 per 24 hours, all inclusive (note that you can't book this deal in advance).

The cheapest category weekend rates (including 1000km mileage) for the other multinational rental companies are: Hertz (☎ 0660-5162, local call rate) at AS1180; ARAC/Eurodollar (☎ 01-869 37 06-33) at AS1188; and Budget (☎ 07242-777 74) at AS1387. A recent arrival in Austria is the German company Sixt (☎ 01743-600 600) which usually offers competitive rates. Buchbinder (☎ 01-717 50-0) has about 100 outlets in Austria, but its prices are generally fairly high.

All of these companies have branches in main cities and may also have an airport office (though prices are 12% higher than in city offices). Local rental agencies often have cheaper rates than the multinationals; the local tourist office will have details.

The minimum age for renting small cars is 19, for prestige models it is 25, and driving licences must have been held for a year or sometimes more. All companies offer a collision damage waiver for an additional charge (Avis is the cheapest, starting at AS246 per day). Personal accident insurance is an optional extra and may not be necessary if you or your passengers hold travel insurance. Add AS8.40 per day for road tax. Be sure to inquire about all terms and conditions before commencing a rental: Hertz, for example, has a surcharge of AS60 per day for drivers aged under 25. Pay attention to the make of cars on offer, too: most companies place an Opel Corsa within the cheapest category, but Europcar puts it in the next group up.

Note also that some rental companies will not allow you to drive the car outside Austria (or will add a surcharge); you may find this inconvenient going to/from Tirol as some routes pass into Germany or Italy.

If you're planning a long trip, leasing a car instead of renting might work out cheaper. This can be done through large car sales outlets in your home country; the head offices of car manufacturing companies can supply details.

For information on hiring a motorcycle see under Car & Motorcycle in the Getting Around section of the Vienna chapter.

Purchase

Car prices are slightly higher than in Germany and Italy. All Austrian-registered cars must undergo an annual technical inspection. Numberplates are issued to the owner, so whether you buy new or second-hand, the vehicle will come without plates. If you sell a vehicle, you remove the plates and return them to the motor registration office (or transfer them to your new car).

Importing a vehicle into Austria is a tedious bureaucratic process, and all newly registered cars must be fitted with a catalytic converter.

BICYCLE

Cycling is a popular activity in Austria, and most regional tourist boards have brochures on cycling facilities and routes within their region. In Vienna, Argus is an organisation which provides information for cyclists; for more details, see the Information section in the Vienna chapter.

Separate bike tracks are common (in cities, make sure you're walking on the footpath, not the bike path). The Danube cycling trail is something of a Holy Grail for cyclists, though there are many other excellent bike routes in the country. Most are close to bodies of water, where there are fewer hills to contend with.

Bicycles can be hired from over 120 train stations and returned to any other station with a rental office (there's a AS45 charge if you don't return it to the same one). You'll need to show a passport or other photo ID to rent a bike. The rate for a normal bike (called a city bike) is AS150 per day, or AS90 if you can show a train ticket valid for that day (or for arrival at that station after 3 pm the previous day). Mountain bikes, where available, cost AS160/200 per day with/without a train ticket. Rental for one week costs AS200/360 (AS720/900 for mountain bikes). Rental periods operate per calendar day, not per 24 hours. Some stations have a half-day rate (AS70/120 for city bikes with/without a ticket).

Within Austria, you can take your bike with you on slower trains, on special 'Rad

Tramper' trains along the Danube and on the Fahrradbus round Neusiedler See. A bicycle ticket (transferable) valid on trains costs AS40 per day, AS90 per week and AS270 per month. There is a fixed fare of AS140 for transporting a bike as registered luggage on a train (not necessarily the same train as you travel on). This may be the only option on fast trains, though a few also now allow you to accompany your machine (reservation required, plus the bike ticket).

HITCHING

Hitching is never entirely safe in any country in the world, and we don't recommend it. Travellers who to hitch should understand they are taking a small but potentially serious risk. Hitchers will be safer if they travel in pairs and let someone know where they are planning to go.

Throughout Europe, hitching is illegal on motorways – stand on the slip roads, or approach drivers at petrol stations, border posts and truck stops. You can increase your chances of getting a lift by looking presentable and cheerful, and by making a cardboard sign indicating your intended destination in the local language. Showing a flag or some other indication of your country of origin can also help. Don't try to hitch from city centres: take public transport to suburban exit routes and hitch from there. Never hitch where drivers can't stop in good time or without causing an obstruction. Once you find a good spot, stay put and hope for the best. When it starts getting dark – forget it!

Hitching in Austria is patchy, but not too bad overall (though the route west from Salzburg to Munich was identified in a hitching guide as one of the most difficult spots in Europe to get a lift). It is illegal for minors under 16 years to hitch in Burgenland, Upper Austria, Styria and Vorarlberg.

WALKING

Many city centres are compact enough to enable major tourist sights to be seen on a walking tour, but walking really comes into

its own in rural areas. See the Walking & Skiing special section in the Facts for the Visitor chapter for further information and a selection of walks.

BOAT

Services along the Danube are slow and expensive scenic excursions rather than functional transport. Nevertheless, a boat ride is definitely worth it if you like lounging on deck and having the scenery come to you rather than the other way round. See the Danube Valley section in the Lower Austria chapter and the Linz section in the Upper Austria chapter for more details on Danube services. There are boat services on the larger lakes throughout the country. On some, such as Bodensee and Wörthersee, special day passes offer good deals.

MOUNTAIN TRANSPORT

Austria now has 3500 transport facilities in steep Alpine regions, compared with just 26 in 1945. These fall into five main categories. A funicular (*Standseilbahn*) is a pair of counter-balancing cars drawn by cables along an inclined track. A cable car (*Luftseilbahn*) is a cabin dramatically suspended from a cable high over a valley, with a twin that goes down when it goes up. A gondola (*Gondelbahn*) is a smaller version of a cable car except that it is hitched onto a continuously running cable once the passengers are inside. Nowadays the terms gondola and cable car are interchangeable and no distinction is made in this book. A cable chair (*Sesselbahn*) is likewise hitched onto a cable but is unenclosed. A ski lift (*Schlepplift*) is a T-bar hanging from a cable, on which the skiers hold or sit while their ski-clad feet slide along the snow. T-bars aren't as safe as modern cable cars (a careless skier could let go) and are being phased out.

LOCAL TRANSPORT

Buses cover urban areas efficiently and comprehensively, and in many larger cities they are supplemented by environmentally

Top Trips

Best Road Journey
- Wind up the Grossglockner Road (Hohe Tauern National Park)

Best Train Trips
- Follow the Inn and Rosanna rivers between Innsbruck and St Anton am Arlberg (Tirol)
- Absorb the scenery of the Gasteiner Tal on the journey between Schwarzach and Spittal (Hohe Tauern National Park & Carinthia)
- Chug up Europe's first Alpine railway between Semmering and Mürzzuschlag (Lower Austria)
- Climb above the Inn Valley from Innsbruck to Seefeld

Best Cogwheel Train Trips
- Haul up Schafberg (Salzkammergut)
- Gaze into the stark Breite Ries from Schneeberg (Lower Austria)

Best Cable Car Ascents
- Soar up to the Hafelekar belvedere (2334m) above Innsbruck (Tirol)
- Take the short cut to fine hikes on the Kitzbüheler Horn (1996m) by Kitzbühel (Tirol)
- Take in views of German and Swiss peaks from the mighty Zugspitze (2962m) near Erhwald (Tirol)
- Glide over the glacier on the Kitzsteinhorn (3203m) south of Zell am See (Hohe Tauern National Park)

friendly trams. Vienna also has an underground metro system which is great for getting round the city quickly but you don't get to sightsee as you go. Most towns have an integrated transport system (meaning you can switch between bus and tram routes on the same ticket) and offer excellent value one-day or 24-hour tickets (costing from AS20 to AS50). Weekly or three-day passes may be available too, as well as multi-trip tickets, which will work out cheaper than buying individual tickets for each journey. Tickets are usually transferable, so you can sell (or even give!) unused portions to other travellers.

Passes and multi-trip tickets are available in advance from Tabak shops, pavement dispensers, and occasionally tourist offices. They usually need to be validated upon first use in the machine on buses or trams. In some towns drivers will sell single tickets, but rarely the better value passes. Some-times drivers don't sell any tickets, so even single tickets must be bought in advance (in Linz, for example). Single tickets may be valid for one hour, 30 minutes, or a single journey, depending on the place. If you're a senior, at school in Austria, or travelling as a family, you may be eligible for reduced-price tickets in some towns.

Keep alert when you're about to get off a bus: if you haven't pressed the request button and there's nobody waiting at the bus stop, the driver will go right past.

On-the-spot fines of between AS400 and AS500 apply to people caught travelling without tickets. Depending on the inspector, you could have real problems if you aren't carrying enough cash to pay the fine at the time you're caught.

Public transport runs from about 5 or 6 am to midnight, though in smaller towns evening services may be patchy or finish for the night rather earlier.

Taxi

Taxis are metered and there are two elements to the fare: a flat fee plus a charge per kilometre. Owing to the good level of public transport, you're unlikely to need a taxi unless returning to your hotel particularly late at night. Taxis can usually be found waiting outside train stations and large hotels. There's usually a surcharge of approximately AS10 to AS30 for calling a radio taxi. Telephone numbers for radio taxis are given under Getting Around in the Graz, Innsbruck, Klagenfurt, Salzburg and Vienna sections.

ORGANISED TOURS

These vary from two-hour walks in a city centre to all-inclusive packages covering regional attractions. Arrangements can usually be made through tourist offices or local travel agents; details are given in the regional chapters. Sometimes you can pick up good deals on excursions via train and boat or bus. Look for brochures at train stations or inquire in train station travel offices. A brochure called *Erlebnis Bahn & Schiff,* available from train stations and some travel agents, details all sorts of trips by ferry and/or steam train.

Vienna

☎ 01 • pop 1.64 million • 156m

Vienna conjures up countless images: elaborate imperial palaces, coffee houses crammed with rich cakes and Baroque mirrors, angelic choirboys, Art Nouveau masterpieces, strutting Lipizzaner stallions, and many more. Its musical tradition is all-pervasive: the mighty Danube (Donau) River may slice through 2840km of Europe, from the Black Forest to the Black Sea, but it owes its fame largely to Vienna – thanks to the Strauss waltz, it will be forever pictured 'blue' in numerous minds.

Vienna has gradually cast off its image as a haunt for genteel old ladies. The somewhat staid delights of its historical heritage remain, yet it is also a city where you can party all night, if that's what you want. Mix together the music, the nightlife, the stunning architecture and some of the best museums in Europe, and you get a city fully deserving of a leisurely exploration.

HISTORY

Vindobona, the military camp established by the Romans in the 1st century AD, was in the heart of Vienna's current Innere Stadt (1st district). A civilian town sprang up outside the camp and flourished in the 3rd and 4th centuries. During this time a visiting Roman emperor, Probus, introduced vineyards to the hills of the Wienerwald (Vienna Woods).

After the departure of the Romans in the 5th century, 'Wenia' was mentioned in the annals of the archbishopric of Salzburg in 881, and it became an important staging post for armies travelling to and from the Crusades. The city continued to flourish as the seat of the Babenbergs, descendents of a noble Bavarian family, who granted Vienna its city charter in 1221.

The Babenbergs were succeeded by the Habsburgs. Although this dynasty was active in Vienna from the 13th century, the first of the Habsburgs to permanently reside

Highlights

- Admire Stephansdom's Gothic spire, the picture gallery of the Kunsthistoriches Museum and the Baroque splendour in the palaces of Schönbrunn and Belvedere

- Take a tour of the Ringstrasse by foot, tram, bicycle or fiacre

- Pick through the chaos and clutter of the Naschmarkt flea market

- Let street performers along Kärntner Strasse and Graben entertain you

- Have a night on the wine in a Heuriger or an evening of high culture in the Staatsoper

- Marvel at the bizarre waxworks in the Josephinium museum

in the city was Ferdinand I, who moved his court to Vienna in 1533. The music-loving Habsburgs helped Vienna become the music capital of Europe, especially during the 18th and 19th centuries.

Vienna developed apace under the Austro-Hungarian dual monarchy, created in 1867, and it hosted the World Fair in 1873. At the end of WWI, the Republic of Austria came into being and, in 1919, voting rights were extended to all Viennese adults. The Social Democrats (SPÖ) gained an absolute majority and embarked on an impressive series of social policies, particularly covering communal housing and health. Karl-Marx-Hof on Heiligenstädter Strasse, which originally contained 1325 apartments, is the best example of the municipal buildings created in this so-called 'Red Vienna' period. In 1934, after the socialists were defeated in the civil war, Vienna's city council was dissolved and all progressive policies instantly stopped. Democracy was not re-established in the city until after WWII.

In the coalition produced by the local election of October 1996, the SPÖ remained the largest party. The anti-EU, right-wing Freedom Party (FPÖ) won the next-highest vote. The assembly serves for a five year term.

Vienna's provincial assembly also functions as the city council (*Gemeinderat*). Likewise, the offices of provincial governor and mayor are united in the same person. The Rathaus (City Hall) is the seat of these offices.

ORIENTATION

Vienna occupies more than 400 sq km in the Danube Valley, with the hills of the Wienerwald beyond the suburbs to the north and west. The Danube River divides the city diagonally into two unequal parts. The old city centre and nearly all the tourist sights are south of the river, mostly in the Innere Stadt. This is encircled by the Ringstrasse, or Ring, a series of broad roads sporting sturdy public buildings. Circling the Ring at a distance of between 1.75km and 3km is a larger traffic artery, the Gürtel (literally belt), which is fed by the flow of vehicles from outlying autobahns.

The Danube runs down a long, straight channel, built between 1870 and 1875 to eliminate flooding. This was supplemented 100 years later by the building of a parallel channel, the New Danube (Neue Donau), creating a long, thin island between the two. This is known as the Donauinsel (Danube Island), and is now a recreation area. The Old Danube (Alte Donau), the remnant of

the original course of the river, forms a loop to the north of the New Danube. This loop encloses the Donaupark, beaches and water-sports centres. North and east of the Old Danube are relatively poor, residential districts.

In the Donaupark is the Vienna International Center (UNO City), where the international organisations are housed, including the most important base of the United Nations (UN) after New York and Geneva. UNO City has extraterritorial status – it's leased to the UN for AS1 a year – so take your passport when visiting. The park also contains the Austria Center Vienna, Austria's largest convention hall. Small trade fairs are held in UNO City, though the main centre for trade fairs is the exhibition centre (*Messegelände*) in the Prater, a large park to the east of the Innere Stadt.

Stephansdom (St Stephen's Cathedral), with its slender spire, is in the heart of the Innere Stadt and is Vienna's principal landmark. Leading south from Stephansplatz is Kärntner Strasse, an important pedestrian street that terminates at Karlsplatz, a major transport hub for the centre.

The majority of hotels, pensions, restaurants and bars are in the Innere Stadt or west of the centre between the Ringstrasse and the Gürtel.

Addresses

Vienna is divided into 23 districts (*Bezirke*), fanning out in approximate numerical order clockwise around the Innere Stadt. Take care when reading addresses. The number of a building within a street *follows* the street name. Any number *before* the street name denotes the district. The middle two digits of a postcode correspond to the district. Thus a postcode of 1010 means the place is in district one, and 1230 refers to district 23. Another thing to note is that the same street number may cover several adjoining buildings, so if you find that what you thought was going to be a pizza restaurant at Wienstrasse 4 is really a rubber fetish shop, check the buildings either side before

VIENNA

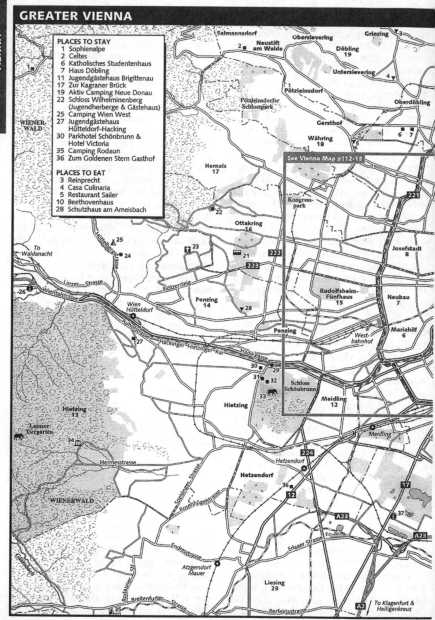

GREATER VIENNA

PLACES TO STAY
1 Sophienalpe
2 Celtes
6 Katholisches Studentenhaus
7 Haus Döbling
11 Jugendgästehaus Brigittenau
17 Zur Kagraner Brück
19 Aktiv Camping Neue Donau
22 Schloss Wilhelminenberg
   (Jugendherberge & Gästehaus)
25 Camping Wien West
27 Jugendgästehaus
   Hütteldorf-Hacking
30 Parkhotel Schönbrunn &
   Hotel Victoria
35 Camping Rodaun
36 Zum Goldenen Stern Gasthof

PLACES TO EAT
3 Reinprecht
4 Casa Culinaria
5 Restaurant Sailer
10 Beethovenhaus
28 Schutzhaus am Ameisbach

See Vienna Map p112-13

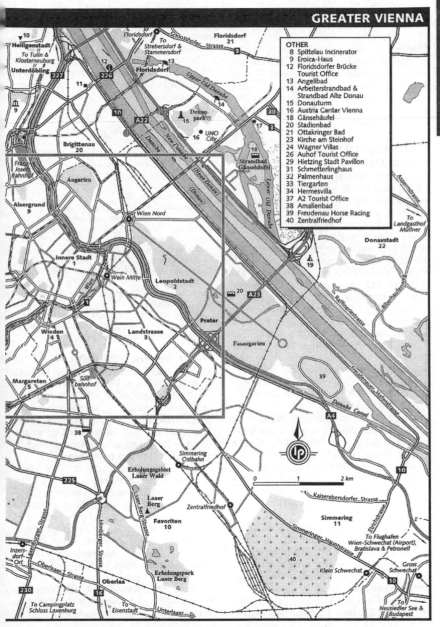

GREATER VIENNA

OTHER
8   Spittelau Incinerator
9   Eroica-Haus
12 Floridsdorfer Brücke
    Tourist Office
13 Angelibad
14 Arbeiterstrandbad &
    Strandbad Alte Donau
15 Donauturm
16 Austria Center Vienna
18 Gänsehäufel
20 Stadionbad
21 Ottakringer Bad
23 Kirche am Steinhof
24 Wagner Villas
26 Auhof Tourist Office
29 Hietzing Stadt Pavillon
31 Schmetterlinghaus
32 Palmenhaus
33 Tiergarten
34 Hermesvilla
37 A2 Tourist Office
38 Amalienbad
39 Freudenau Horse Racing
40 Zentralfriedhof

you resign yourself to a radical change of eating habits.

Maps

Freytag & Berndt (see under Bookshops) produces a variety of clear maps of Vienna, though the free map provided by the tourist office is sufficient for most purposes. This shows public transport routes, but doesn't have a street index.

INFORMATION
Tourist Offices

The main tourist office (☎ 513 88 92 or 513 40 15) is at 01, Kärntner Strasse 38. It is small and hectic but there is extensive free literature on hand, covering museums, events, architecture, hotels and restaurants. *Young Vienna Scene*, containing lots of useful information for all ages despite the title, and *Vienna Scene* are free and worth getting. The office is open daily from 9 am to 7 pm, and has a room-finding service (AS40 commission per reservation).

Vienna From A to Z (AS50) covers information on over 200 sights, and includes walking tour itineraries of the centre. The Vienna Card (AS180) includes a 72 hour travel pass (see Getting Around in this chapter) plus numerous benefits, particularly discounts on shopping and admission to attractions. Both are available from the tourist office and elsewhere.

Telephone inquiries, advance requests for brochures and more unusual matters are dealt with at the head office of the Vienna Tourist Board (☎ 211 14, fax 216 84 92, email inquiries@info.wien.at), Obere Augartenstrasse 40, A-1025 Wien. They aren't really prepared for personal callers. The office is open Monday to Friday from 8 am to 4 pm.

The Österreich Werbung, or Austria Information Office (☎ 588 66, fax -20, email oeinfo@oewien.via.at), 04, Margaretenstrasse 1, is open Monday to Friday from 10 am to 5 pm (6 pm on Thursday) and has information on the whole country.

Niederösterreich Touristik-Information (☎ 513 80 22, fax -30, email noe.tourist-info@ping.at), 01, Walfischgasse 6, is a section of a travel agency, providing information on Lower Austria. It's open Monday to Friday from 8 am to 6 pm.

Information and room reservations (AS40 commission per reservation) are also available in offices at various entry points to the city:

Airport
    Arrivals hall, open daily from 8.30 am to 9 pm
Train stations
    Westbahnhof (open daily from 7 am to 10 pm) and Südbahnhof (open daily from 6.30 am to 10 pm; open till 9 pm from 1 November to 30 April)
From the north by road
    Floridsdorfer Brücke (bridge) on the Donauinsel, open from 9 am to 7 pm (May to September)
From the south by road
    A2 autobahn exit Zentrum, Triester Strasse, open daily from 9 am to 7 pm (Easter to June, and October) and from 8 am to 10 pm (July to September)
From the west by road
    A1 autobahn exit Wien-Auhof, open daily from 8 am to 10 pm (Easter to October), from 9 am to 7 pm (November) and from 10 am to 6 pm (December to pre-Easter)

Other Information Offices

The city information office in the Rathaus is open Monday to Friday from 8 am to 6 pm. Phone inquiries (☎ 525 50) will also be answered on Saturday and Sunday from 8 am to 4 pm, as well as during office hours. The office provides information on social, cultural and practical matters, geared as much to residents as to tourists.

Jugend Info (Youth Info; ☎ 17 79, email jugendinfo.vie@blackbox.ping.at), 01, Dr Karl Renner Ring, in the below-ground Bellaria Passage, sells tickets for a variety of events at reduced rates for those aged between 14 and 26. There's plenty of information on rock concerts, city events, Internet facilities, language courses and much else. It's open Monday to Saturday from noon to 7 pm.

Argus (☎ 505 84 35), 04, Frankenberggasse 11, is an organisation promoting cycling, and provides maps and cycling information covering the whole of Austria. It's open Monday to Friday from 2 to 6 pm.

Money

There are banks and currency exchange offices all over the city, but compare commission rates before changing money. Exchange offices are open daily from 7 am to 10 pm in the Westbahnhof, and from 6.30 am to 10 pm (9 pm from 1 November to 31 March) in the Südbahnhof. Moneychangers at the airport charge at least AS110 commission, though the exchange rates are standard.

American Express (see the Travel Agencies section) charges from AS25 to AS40 commission for cashing non-Amex travellers cheques; Amex cheques are cashed free of charge. Cash exchanges attract a small commission on a sliding scale.

There are Bankomats at all main train stations, at the airport and at 200 branches of Bank Austria.

Post & Communications

The main post office (Hauptpost 1010) is at 01, Fleischmarkt 19. It's open 24 hours a day for collecting and sending mail, changing money, using the telephone and sending faxes. Only a few services (such as paying bills) are not available round the clock. There are also post offices open daily at Südbahnhof and Franz Josefs Bahnhof (both open 24 hours) and at Westbahnhof (closed between 1 and 4 am).

Branch post offices are open Monday to Friday from 8 am to noon and 2 to 6 pm, and on Saturday from 8 to 10 am (though district head offices close at noon on Saturday). They generally have a counter for changing money, but this closes at 5 pm on weekdays.

Email & Internet Access Vienna has about a dozen institutions offering public access to online services, including Café Stein (☎ 319 72 411), 09, Währinger Strasse 6, and the Virgin Megastore (☎ 581 05 00), 06, Mariahilfer Strasse 37-39; charges are around AS50 for 30 minutes access. The

Public Netbase (☎ 522 18 34, email office@t0.or.at), Museumsquartier, 07, Museumsplatz 1, has a couple of machines where you can surf for free; it's open on weekdays from 2 to 7 pm.

Internet and email services are also available at the Nationalbibliothek (National Library) in the Hofburg (email tief@grill .onb.ac.at) – see the Libraries section later in this chapter.

Travel Agencies

American Express (☎ 515 40, fax -777), 01, Kärntner Strasse 21-23, is open Monday to Friday from 9 am to 5.30 pm and on Saturday from 9.30 am to noon.

The ÖKISTA head office (☎ 401 48, fax -6290, email info@oekista.co.at), at 09, Garnisongasse 7, is open Monday to Friday from 9 am to 5.30 pm. There are other ÖKISTA offices at 09, Türkenstrasse 6 (☎ 401 48-7000) and 04, Karlsgasse 3 (☎ 505 01 28). ÖS Reisen (☎ 402 15 61), 01, Reichsratstrasse 13, is a linked agency.

Österreichisches Verkehrsbüro (☎ 588 00, fax 586 85 33), 01, Friedrichstrasse 7 and elsewhere, is a major national agency. Cedok (☎ 512 43 72, fax -85), 01, Parkring 10 (entry from Liebenberggasse), is a specialist agency for travel to the Czech Republic.

Bookshops

Many bookshops can be found on Wollzeile, near Stephansdom; Morawa (☎ 515 62) at No 11 is the biggest. The British Bookshop (☎ 512 19 45), 01, Weihburggasse 24-6, has the largest selection of English-language books. Shakespeare & Co Booksellers (☎ 535 50 53), 01, Sterngasse 2, is smaller but has some second-hand books. Freytag & Berndt (☎ 533 20 94), 01, Kohlmarkt 9, stocks a vast selection of maps, and sells English-language travel guides. Reiseladen (☎ 513 75 77), 01, Dominikanerbastei 4, and Reisebuchladen (☎ 317 33 84), 09, Kolingasse 6, both have a comprehensive selection of Lonely Planet guides and other travel books.

VIENNA

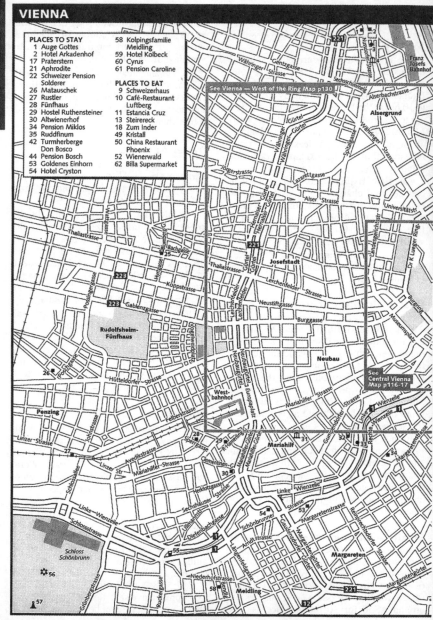

PLACES TO STAY
1 Auge Gottes
2 Hotel Arkadenhof
17 Praterstern
21 Aphrodite
22 Schweizer Pension Solderer
26 Matauschek
27 Rustler
28 Fünfhaus
29 Hostel Ruthensteiner
30 Altwienerhof
34 Pension Miklos
35 Ruddfinum
42 Turmherberge Don Bosco
44 Pension Bosch
53 Goldenes Einhorn
54 Hotel Cryston

58 Kolpingsfamilie Meidling
59 Hotel Kolbeck
60 Cyrus
61 Pension Caroline

PLACES TO EAT
9 Schweizerhaus
10 Café-Restaurant Luftberg
11 Estancia Cruz
13 Steirereck
18 Zum Inder
49 Kristall
50 China Restaurant Phoenix
52 Wienerwald
62 Billa Supermarket

See Vienna — West of the Ring Map p130

See Central Vienna Map p116-17

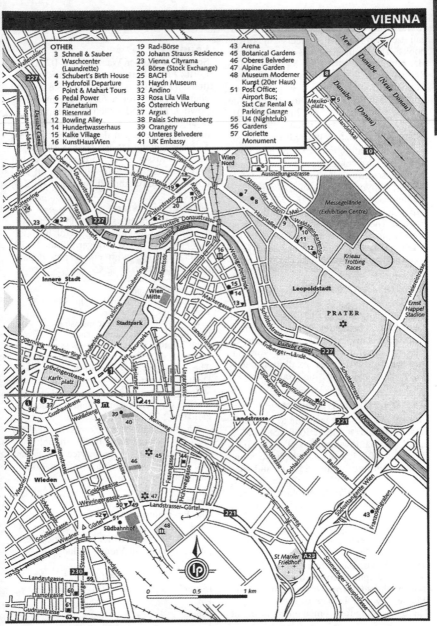

OTHER
3 Schnell & Sauber
   Waschcenter
   (Laundrette)
4 Schubert's Birth House
5 Hydrofoil Departure
   Point & Mahart Tours
6 Pedal Power
7 Planetarium
8 Riesenrad
12 Bowling Alley
14 Hundertwasserhaus
15 Kalke Village
16 KunstHausWien

19 Rad-Börse
20 Johann Strauss Residence
23 Vienna Cityrama
24 Börse (Stock Exchange)
25 BACH
31 Haydn Museum
32 Andino
33 Rosa Lila Villa
36 Österreich Werbung
37 Argus
38 Palais Schwarzenberg
39 Orangery
40 Unteres Belvedere
41 UK Embassy

43 Arena
45 Botanical Gardens
46 Oberes Belvedere
47 Alpine Garden
48 Museum Moderner
   Kunst (20er Haus)
51 Post Office;
   Airport Bus;
   Sixt Car Rental &
   Parking Garage
55 U4 (Nightclub)
56 Gardens
57 Gloriette
   Monument

Libraries

Libraries are dotted around Vienna. Anyone can use them but only residents can borrow books. The main branch is the Städtische Hauptbücherei (☎ 4000-84 551), 08, Skodagasse 20, open on Monday and Thursday from 10 am to 7.30 pm, and on Tuesday and Friday from 2 to 7.30 pm. The British Council (☎ 533 26 16-81), 01, Schenkenstrasse 4, has a library, with newspapers and magazines in English.

The Nationalbibliothek in the new wing of the Hofburg contains huge reference and lending sections plus collections of CD ROMs, papyrus and musical scores. The reading room upstairs has the *Times* newspaper and many other publications in English. The main part of the library is open Monday to Friday from 9 am to 7 pm (to 3.45 pm only from 1 July to 31 August) and on Saturday till 5 pm.

Cultural Centres

The Museumsquartier (☎ 523 58 81), 07, Museumsplatz 1, is in the former imperial barracks. It is being developed as a cultural centre and will be the base for dozens of different organisations. Already you can find museums, theatres, exhibitions, galleries, cafés and discussion groups.

Gay & Lesbian Travellers

Probably the best organisation to contact is Rosa Lila Villa (☎ 586 81 50, fax 587 17 78, email rosalila.tip@blackbox.at), 06, Linke Wienzeile 102. It provides telephone counselling, literature and advice and has information on what's on offer in the city. Pick up the *Gay City Map*, which lists gay-friendly hotels, shops, bars, cafés and clubs. It's open Monday to Friday from 5 to 8 pm. On the premises is Café Willendorf, open daily from 7 pm to 2 am (with good food till midnight). The Homosexualle Initiative (HOSI) Wien, 02, Novaragasse 40, also provides telephone counselling (☎ 216 66 04) on Thursday from 6 to 8 pm, and on Wednesday and Friday from 7 to 9 pm There's dancing for women only starting at 7 pm on Friday and it's open to visitors from 8 to 10 pm on Tuesday.

Laundry

Schnell & Sauber Waschcenter, 07, Urban Loritz Platz, Westbahnstrasse, has instructions in English, is open 24 hours a day and charges AS60 for a 6kg load, including powder, plus AS10 each for spinning and drying. There's another branch at 09, Nussdorfer Strasse (open daily till late). Miele Selbstbedienung (☎ 405 02 55), 08, Josefstädter Strasse 59, is more expensive, but dry cleaning is available. It's open till 7.30 pm on weekdays and till noon on Saturday.

Medical Services

Medical treatment is available at the Allgemeines Krankenhaus (general hospital; ☎ 404 00) at 09, Währinger Gürtel 18-20. Other hospitals with emergency departments include:

Hanusch-Krankenhaus
  (☎ 910 21) 14, Heinrich Collin Strasse 30
Krankenhaus Lainz
  (☎ 801 100) 13, Wolkerbergenstrasse 1
Lorenz Böhler Unfallkrankenhaus
  (☎ 331 100) 20, Donaueschingenstrasse 13

The Universitäts-Zahnklinik (University Dental Hospital; ☎ 401 81) is at 09, Währinger Strasse 25A. For recorded information on out-of-hours dental treatment, call ☎ 512 20 78.

Chemist shops or drugstores (*Apotheken*) are open normal shop hours, though they operate an out-of-hours service in rotation; dial ☎ 1550 for recorded information in German on which are open.

Emergency

The Frauenotruf (☎ 71 71 9) is a 24 hour emergency hotline for reporting rape and sexual violence. Other emergency telephone numbers in Vienna include:

Ambulance	☎ 144
Doctor	☎ 141
Fire	☎ 122
Police	☎ 133

The police headquarters for the Innere Stadt (☎ 313 470) is at 01, Deutschmeisterplatz 3; there are police stations at Stephansplatz and Karlsplatz U-Bahn stations.

Dangers & Annoyances

Vienna is a relatively safe city, but use common sense: avoid unlit streets and parks after dark. Drug addicts sometimes congregate in the Karlsplatz U-Bahn station near the Secession exit.

INNERE STADT
Stephansdom

The latticework spire of this Gothic masterpiece rises high above the city and is a focal point for visitors.

The cathedral was built on the site of a 12th century church, of which the surviving Riesentor (Giant's Gate, the main entrance) and the Heidentürme (Towers of the Heathens) are incorporated into the present building. Both are Romanesque in style; however, the church was rebuilt in Gothic style after 1359.

The dominating feature, the skeletal **Südturm**, or south tower, is nicknamed 'Steffl'. It stands 136.7m high and was completed in 1433 after 75 years of building work. Negotiating 343 steps will bring you to the viewing platform for an impressive panorama (AS25, open daily from 9 am to 5.30 pm). It was to be matched by a companion tower on the north side, but the imperial purse withered and the Gothic style went out of fashion, so the incomplete tower was topped off with a Renaissance cupola in 1579. Austria's largest bell, the **Pummerin** (boomer bell), was installed here in 1952; it weighs 21 tonnes. Admission to the north tower, which is accessible by lift, costs AS40. It's open daily from 8 am to 5 pm; from 9 am to 6 pm between 1 April and 30 September.

Interior walls and pillars are decorated with fine statues and side altars. The **stone pulpit**, fashioned in 1515 by Anton Pilgram, is a magnificent Gothic piece. The expressive faces of the four fathers of the church (the saints Augustine, Ambrose, Gregory and Jerome) are at the centre of the design, and Pilgram himself can be seen peering out from a window below. The Baroque **high altar** in the main chancel shows the stoning of St Stephen. The left chancel contains a winged altarpiece moved here from Wiener Neustadt and dating from 1447; the right chancel houses the red marble tomb of Friedrich III, which is Renaissance in style. Under his guidance the city became a bishopric (and the church a cathedral) in 1469.

Don't ignore the decorations and statues on the outside of the cathedral: at the rear the agony of the Crucifixion is well captured, although some irreverent souls attribute Christ's pained expression to toothache. A striking feature of the exterior is the glorious **tiled roof**, showing dazzling chevrons on one end and the Austrian eagle on the other; a good view can be had from Schulerstrasse.

The **Katakomben** (catacombs) in the cathedral are open daily, with tours approximately hourly between 10 am and 4.30 pm (AS40; English commentary if there's sufficient demand). The tour includes sights such as a mass grave of plague victims, a bone house, and rows of urns containing the internal organs of the Habsburgs. One privilege of being a Habsburg was to be dismembered and dispersed after death: their hearts are in the Augustinerkirche in the Hofburg (viewed by prior appointment only; ☎ 533 70 99 daily except Sunday) and the rest of their bits are in the Kaisergruft (see the entry later in this chapter).

Hofburg

The huge Hofburg (Imperial Palace) is an impressive repository of culture and heritage. The Habsburgs were based here for over six centuries, from the first emperor (Rudolf I in 1279) to the last (Charles I in 1918). During that time new sections were periodically added, including the early Baroque Leopold Wing, the 18th century Imperial Chancery Wing, the 16th century Amalia Wing and the Burgkapelle (Royal Chapel), which was commissioned by

VIENNA

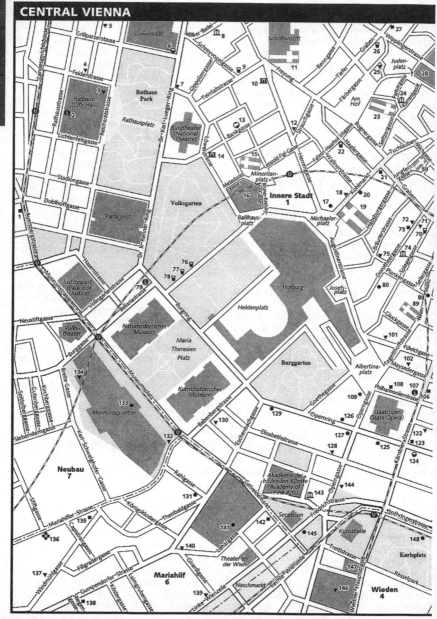

CENTRAL VIENNA

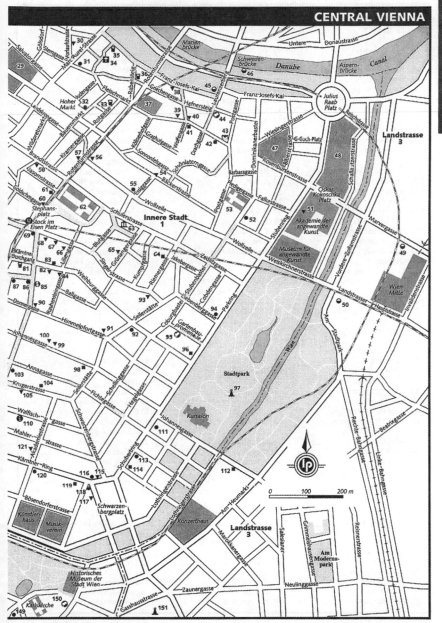

VIENNA

CENTRAL VIENNA

VIENNA

Friedrich III and refitted in Baroque style by Empress Maria Theresa. This is where the Vienna Boys' Choir sings Sunday Mass. The palace now houses the offices of the Austrian president.

The oldest part is the 13th century **Schweizerhof** (Swiss Courtyard), named after the Swiss guards who used to protect its precincts. The Renaissance Swiss gate dates from 1553. The courtyard adjoins a much larger courtyard, **In der Burg**, with a monument to Emperor Franz II at its centre. The buildings which surround it are from various eras.

Kaiserappartements The former Imperial Apartments are as opulent as you might expect, with fine furniture, hanging tapestries and bulbous crystal chandeliers. However, they don't match those in Schloss Schönbrunn (see later in this chapter). Rooms in this part of the palace were occupied by Franz Josef I and Empress Elisabeth. Entry costs AS70 for a guided tour in German (AS50 for students aged under 26) and it's open Monday to Saturday

from 8.30 am to noon and 12.30 to 4 pm, and on Sunday and holidays from 8.30 am to 12.30 pm. A combined ticket also covering the adjoining **Silberkammer** (Silver Treasury) of porcelain and tableware costs AS90 (AS60 students, AS45 children).

Schatzkammer The Imperial Treasury contains secular and ecclesiastical treasures of great value and splendour. The sheer wealth exhibited is staggering: Room 7 contains a 2860 carat Colombian emerald, a 416 carat balas ruby and a 492 carat aquamarine. The imperial crown (Room 11) dates from the 10th century; the private crown of Rudolf II (1602; Room 2) is a more delicate piece. Room 5 contains mementoes of Marie Louise, daughter of Franz II and wife of Napoleon. Room 8 contains two unusual objects formerly owned by Ferdinand I: a 75cm-wide bowl carved from a single piece of agate, and a narwhal tusk, 243cm long and once claimed to have been a unicorn horn.

The religious relics include fragments of the True Cross, one of the nails from the

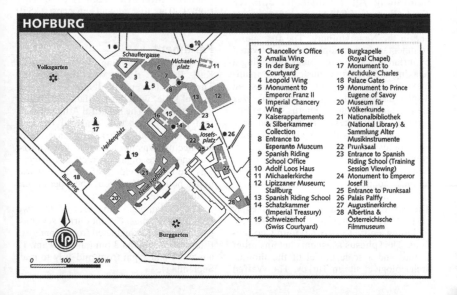

HOFBURG

1	Chancellor's Office
2	Amalia Wing
3	In der Burg Courtyard
4	Leopold Wing
5	Monument to Emperor Franz II
6	Imperial Chancery Wing
7	Kaiserappartements & Silberkammer Collection
8	Entrance to Esperanto Museum
9	Spanish Riding School Office
10	Adolf Loos Haus
11	Michaelerkirche
12	Lipizzaner Museum; Stallburg
13	Spanish Riding School
14	Schatzkammer (Imperial Treasury)
15	Schweizerhof (Swiss Courtyard)
16	Burgkapelle (Royal Chapel)
17	Monument to Archduke Charles
18	Palace Gates
19	Monument to Prince Eugene of Savoy
20	Museum für Völkerkunde
21	Nationalbibliothek (National Library) & Sammlung Alter Musikinstrumente
22	Prunksaal
23	Entrance to Spanish Riding School (Training Session Viewing)
24	Monument to Emperor Josef II
25	Entrance to Prunksaal
26	Palais Palffy
27	Augustinerkirche
28	Albertina & Österreichische Filmmuseum

0   100   200 m

Crucifixion, and one of the thorns from Christ's crown. Ecclesiastical vestments display delicate and skilled work.

Allow anything from 30 minutes to two hours to get around. Entry costs AS80 (students and seniors AS50) and includes a personal electronic guide; it's open daily except Tuesday from 10 am to 6 pm.

Prunksaal The Prunksaal (literally Magnificent Hall) is an archetypal Baroque structure was created by the Fischer von Erlachs (Johann and his son Josef) between 1723 and 1726. It was commissioned by Charles VI, whose statue stands under the central church-like dome, on which is a Daniel Gran fresco depicting the emperor's apotheosis. Leather-bound, scholarly books line the walls, and rare 15th century volumes stored in glass cabinets are opened to beautifully illustrated sections of text. The hall is open Monday to Saturday from 10 am to 4 pm, and on Sunday and holidays till 1 pm. Admission costs AS60 (students and seniors AS48). The entrance is on Josefsplatz.

Sammlung Alter Musikinstrumente The Collection of Old Musical Instruments is the best part of the three-museums-in-one in the Neue Hofburg. The free audio commentary (on headphones) is activated by infrared as you walk round, providing a relaxing and evocative musical accompaniment to the variety of instruments on display. Instruments of all shapes and sizes are to be found, including horns shaped like serpents, a mini keyboard disguised as a book, and violins with carved faces. Different rooms are dedicated to different composers, such as Haydn, Mozart and Beethoven, and contain instruments played by those notables.

The collection is open daily except Tuesday from 10 am to 4 pm, and entry costs AS30 (children and seniors AS15), including entry to two adjoining collections. The **Ephesus Museum** contains relief statues and a scale model of the famous archaeological site in Turkey. The **Waffen und Rüstungen** (Collection of Arms and Armour) dates mostly from the 15th and 16th centuries and houses some fine examples of ancient armour; note the bizarre pumpkin-shaped helmet from the 15th century.

Kaisergruft

The Imperial Burial Vault is beneath the Kapuzinerkirche (Church of the Capuchin Friars) on Neuer Markt. Its construction was instigated by Empress Anna (1557-1619), and her body and that of her husband, Emperor Matthias (1557-1619), were the first to be placed here. Since then, all but three of the Habsburg dynasty found their way here, the last being Empress Zita in 1989. The only non-Habsburg is the Countess Fuchs.

Fashion extends even to tombs: those in the vault range from the unadorned to the ostentatious. By far the most elaborate caskets are those portraying 18th century Baroque pomp, such as the huge double sarcophagus containing Maria Theresa and Franz I. The tomb of Charles VI has been expertly restored. Both were the work of Balthasar Moll. The vault is open daily from 9.30 am to 4 pm and entry costs AS30 (students and seniors AS20).

Parlament

The parliament building (1873-83), on Dr Karl Renner Ring, was designed by Theophil Hansen. It displays a Greek revival style, with huge pillars and figures lining the roof. The beautiful **Athena Fountain** at the front was sculpted by Karl Kundmann. Choosing a Grecian style of architecture was not a mere whim. Greece was the home of democracy and Athena was the Greek goddess of wisdom. It was hoped both qualities would be a permanent feature of Austrian politics.

The Parlament is the seat of the two federal assemblies. Except during sessions, guided tours are conducted from Monday to Friday at 11 am and 3 pm (also at 9 am, 10 am and 1 and 2 pm from mid-July to mid-September).

Otto Wagner

Along with Adolf Loos, Otto Wagner (1841-1918) was one of the most influential *fin de siècle* Viennese architects. He was trained in the classical tradition, and became a professor at the Akademie der bildenden Künste (Academy of Fine Arts). His early work was in keeping with his education, and he was responsible for some neo-Renaissance buildings along the Ringstrasse. But as the new century approached he developed an Art Nouveau style, with flowing lines and deco-

Stadt Pavillon, Karlsplatz, Vienna

rative motifs. Wagner joined the Secession in 1899 and attracted public criticism in the process, one of the reasons why his creative designs for Vienna's Historical Museum were never adopted. In 1905, Wagner, the painter Gustav Klimt and others split from the Secession. Wagner began to discard the more decorative aspects of his designs, concentrating instead on presenting the functional features of buildings in a creative way.

Am Hof

The Babenberg rulers of Vienna once had a fortress on Am Hof square before moving to the Hofburg, and there are also Roman ruins here. The **Kirche Am Hof**, on the southern side, is a Baroque adaptation of its fire-damaged Gothic predecessor. On the northern side, at No 10, is the former 16th century civic armoury. The **Mariensäule** (a column dedicated to the Virgin Mary) in the centre of the square was erected in 1667. **Judenplatz**, the old Jewish quarter, is to the north-east.

Ankeruhr

This picturesque Art Nouveau clock, mounted on the Anker insurance company's buildings at Hoher Markt 10-11, was created by Franz von Matsch in 1911. Over a 12 hour period, figures such as Josef Haydn and Maria Theresa slowly pass across the clock face – details of who's who are outlined on a plaque on the wall below. It draws crowds of tourists at noon when all the figures trundle past in turn, and organ music from the appropriate period is piped out. If you walk north under the clock you'll come across **Ruprechtskirche** (St Rupert's

Church), the oldest church in Vienna, built in the 11th century.

Postsparkasse

This celebrated building at Georg Coch Platz, the Post Office Savings Bank, was the work of Otto Wagner. The design and choice of materials were both innovative: inside, note the sci-fi aluminium heating ducts and the exposed stanchions – pared-down functionality *par excellence*. The main savings hall can be viewed Monday to Friday from 8 am to 3 pm, and on Thursday till 5.30 pm. Compare the modern appearance of the Postsparkasse with the classical looks of the **Kriegsministerium** (Imperial War Ministry) on Stubenring opposite; it was built around the same time (1909).

Kunsthistorisches Museum

The Museum of Fine Arts is one of the finest museums in Europe and should not be missed. The Habsburgs were great collectors and the huge extent of land under their control led to many important works of art being funnelled back to Vienna.

Rubens was appointed to the service of a Habsburg governor in Brussels, so it is not surprising that the museum has one of the best collections of his works. The collection of paintings by Pieter Brueghel the Elder is also unrivalled. The building itself has some delightful features. The murals between the arches above the stairs were created by three artists, including a young Klimt (northern wall), painted before he broke with classical tradition.

It's impossible to see the whole museum in one visit, so concentrate on specific areas. The coin collection is closed for renovation until about 1999. Guided tours in English depart at 3 pm (AS30) and provide an interesting analysis of a handful of main works. Written guides are also available on site. The museum is open Tuesday to Sunday from 10 am to 6 pm, with the picture gallery open till 9 pm on Thursday. Entry to the museum costs AS45 (students and seniors AS30) or AS100 (AS70) if, as is usual, there's a special exhibition (these sometimes cause some reorganisation of the permanent collection).

Ground Floor In the west wing is the Egyptian collection, including the burial chamber of Prince Kaninisut and the mummified remains of various animals. The Greek and Roman collection includes the Gemma Augustea cameo (displayed in Saal XV), made from onyx in 10 AD.

The east wing contains sculpture and decorative arts, covering a range of styles. There's some exquisite 17th century glassware and ornaments, and unbelievably lavish clocks from the 16th and 17th centuries (Saal XXXV and Saal XXXVII). The prime item in this wing (in Saal XXVII), is the gold salt cellar by Benvenuto Cellini, made for Francis I of France in 1543. It depicts two naked deities, the goddess of the earth and the god of the sea, and has tiny wheels within so it can be pushed easily around the table.

First Floor The Gemäldegalerie (picture gallery) on this floor is the most important part of the museum. Some rooms provide information cards in English giving a cri-

tique of particular works. In a slightly confusing system, this floor has smaller rooms (1-24) leading off from a series of interconnected halls (Saal I to Saal XV).

East Wing This wing is devoted to German, Dutch and Flemish paintings. Saal X is home to the Brueghel collection, amassed by Rudolf II. A recurrent theme in Brueghel the Elder's work is nature; see for instance *The Hunters in the Snow* (1565). Brueghel's peasant scenes, such as *The Battle Between Carnival and Lent* (1590), are also excellent.

The next gallery (Saal XI) displays the warm, larger-than-life scenes of Flemish Baroque, in vogue some 80 years after Brueghel. The motto in *The Feast of the Bean King* by Jacob Jordaens (1593-1678), to which the revellers are raising their glasses, translates as 'None resembles a fool more than the drunkard'.

Works by Albrecht Dürer (1471-1528) are displayed in Rooms 16 and 17. His brilliant mastery of colour is shown in *The Holy Trinity Surrounded by All Saints*, originally an altarpiece. The *Martyrdom of 10,000 Christians* is another fine work.

The paintings by the mannerist Giuseppe Archimboldo (1527-93) in Room 19 use a device well explored by Salvador Dalí – familiar objects arranged to appear as something else – the difference being that Archimboldo did it nearly 400 years earlier!

Peter Paul Rubens (1577-1640) synthesised northern European and Italian traditions. His dramatic Baroque scenes are displayed in Saal XIII, Saal XIV and Room 20. Note the open brushwork and diaphanous quality of the fur in the *Indefonso Altar*.

There are several self-portraits by Rembrandt in Saal XV. Vermeer's *The Allegory of Painting* (1665-66) is in Room 24. It's a strangely static scene of an artist in his studio, but one that transcends the mundane by its composition and use of light.

West Wing Saal I has some evocative works by Titian, a member of the Venetian school. In Room 2 hangs *The Three Philosophers* (1508), one of the few properly authenticated works by Giorgione, Room 4 contains Raphael's harmonious and idealised *Madonna in the Meadow* (1505). The triangular composition and the complementary colours are typical features of the Florentine high Renaissance. Compare this with Caravaggio's *Madonna of the Rosary* (1606) in Saal V, in which the supplicants' dirty feet are an example of the new realism in early Baroque. Caravaggio emphasises movement in this picture by a subtle deployment of light and shadow.

Tintoretto's *Susanna at her Bath* (1555) can be found in Saal III. It recreates the Old Testament tale and successfully portrays both serenity and implicit menace. Tintoretto employs several mannerist devices (contrasting light, extremes of facial features) to achieve his effect.

Saal VII contains paintings by Bernardo Bellotto (1721-80), Canaletto's nephew. He was commissioned by Maria Theresa to paint scenes of Vienna. Several are shown here, though some landscapes, such as the view from the Belvedere, are not faithful reproductions but have been creatively recomposed.

Room 10 houses portraits of the Habsburgs. Juan Carreño's portrait of Charles II of Spain shows the characteristic Habsburg jaw. Most of the young women in Diego Velázquez's royal portraits are wearing dresses broad enough to fit round a horse, but the artist still manages to make the subjects come to life.

Naturhistorisches Museum

The Museum of Natural History is the scientific counterpart of the Kunsthistorisches Museum. The building is just as grand but the exhibits aren't quite in the same league. Minerals, meteorites and animal remains are displayed in jars; zoology and anthropology are covered in detail and there's a children's corner. A replica of the 25,000-year-old statuette of the *Venus of Willendorf* is on display (see the boxed text in the Lower Austria chapter) and there are some good

dinosaur exhibits. The museum also has occasional special exhibitions. It's open daily except Tuesday from 9 am to 6 pm. In winter it's open only till 3 pm and the geological and palaeontological collections are closed. Entry costs AS30 (students AS15).

Museum für angewandte Kunst

The Museum of Applied Art (MAK), 01, Stubenring 5, was built in high Renaissance style in 1871. The **exhibition rooms** highlight different styles, such as Renaissance, Baroque, Oriental and Wiener Werkstätte. The layout of each room was the responsibility of a specific artist, and their reason for displaying the exhibits as they have done is explained. In the room by Barbara Bloom, Art Nouveau chairs are back-lit and presented behind translucent white screens. There's a Klimt frieze upstairs, and some interesting pieces in the 20th century Design & Architecture room (for example the cardboard chair by Frank Gehry).

In the basement is the **Study Collection**, which groups exhibits according to the type of materials used. There are some particularly good porcelain and glassware pieces, with casts showing how they're made. The museum (☎ 711 36) is open daily except Monday from 10 am to 6 pm (to 9 pm on Thursday). Entry costs AS90 (AS30 if there are no special exhibitions) for adults, AS45 (AS15) for students and seniors, or AS150 (AS50) for a family ticket. Entry is free on 14 April, 26 October and 4 November.

Akademie der bildenden Künste

The Academy of Fine Arts at 01, Schillerplatz 3 has a picture gallery, open on Tuesday, Thursday and Friday from 10 am to 2 pm, on Wednesday from 10 am to 1 pm and 3 to 6 pm, and at weekends from 9 am to 1 pm. Hieronymus Bosch's *The Last Judgement* altarpiece is the most impressive exhibit, though Flemish painters are well represented. Admission costs AS30 (students AS15). The building itself has an attractive façade (which was constructed between 1872 and 1876) and was designed by Theophil Hansen. It was this academy that turned down would-be artist Adolf Hitler, forcing him to find a new career. In front of the Academy is a statue of Schiller.

Secession Building

In 1897 the Vienna Secession movement was formed by 19 progressive artists breaking away from the conservative artistic establishment which met in the Künstlerhaus. Their aim was to present current trends in contemporary art and leave behind the historicism then in vogue. Among their number were Gustav Klimt, Josef Hoffman, Kolo Moser and Josef M Olbrich, a former student of Otto Wagner.

In 1898, Olbrich designed the movement's exhibition centre at 01, Friedrichstrasse 12. Its most striking feature is the enormous golden sphere (a 'golden cabbage head', according to some Viennese) rising from a turret on the roof. Above the door are highly distinctive mask-like faces with dangling serpents instead of earlobes. The motto above the entrance asserts: 'Der Zeit ihre Kunst, der Kunst ihre Freiheit' (To each time its art, to art its freedom). Could the unspoken implication be: to historicism its dustbin?

The 14th exhibition held in the building, in 1902, featured the famous *Beethoven Frieze* by Klimt. This 34m-long work was only supposed to be a temporary display, but has been painstakingly restored and is on view in the basement. The frieze, combining both dense and sparse images, shows willowy women with bounteous hair jostling for attention with a large gorilla, while slender figures float and a choir sings. Beethoven would no doubt be extremely surprised to learn that it is based on his Ninth Symphony.

The rest of this so-called 'temple of art' holds true to the original ideal of presenting contemporary art, though it may leave you wondering exactly where the altar is. 'Sometimes people just walk past the art, they think they're in empty rooms,' the lady at the desk once told me. You have been warned! It's open Tuesday to Friday from 10 am to 6 pm, and at weekends till 4 pm;

entry costs AS60 (students AS40). The Secession building also has an outside café.

Jüdische Museum

The Jewish Museum, 01, Dorotheergasse 11, documents the history of the Jews in Vienna, from the first settlements at Judenplatz in the 13th century to the present. Relations between the Jews and Viennese have not always been tranquil: Jews were expelled in 1420 (the 300 who remained were burned to death in 1421) and again in 1670. The darkest chapter came with the arrival of the Nazis in 1938 and the consequent curtailment of Jewish civil rights. Violence was unleashed on the night of 9 November 1938, known as the *Reichskristallnacht* (night of broken glass). All the synagogues in the city except for the Stadttempel (01, Seitenstettengasse 4) were destroyed and more than 7000 of Vienna's Jews were sent to concentration camps. There are now 12,000 Jews in the city, compared with 185,000 before 1938. The museum is open daily except Saturday from 10 am to 6 pm (9 pm Thursday) and admission costs AS70 (concessions AS40).

Lipizzaner Museum

This new museum at 01, Reitschulestrasse 2, by the Hofburg expounds on Lipizzaner stallions, the Spanische Reitschule (Spanish Riding School), and the Bundesgestüt Piber (stud farm). There's English text, but the content is a little thin. Windows allow a view directly into the stallion stables, albeit obscured by thick glass and fine mesh. Entry costs AS50 (concessions AS35) and it's open daily from 9 am to 6 pm.

Stadtpark

The city park lies on the eastern side of Parkring. It has a pond, winding walkways and several statues. The **Kursalon** at the south-western corner hosts waltz concerts in the afternoon and evening daily from April to late October. Nearby in the park is a golden statue of Johann Strauss under a white arch which will be familiar to many from tourist brochures.

VIENNA WALKING TOUR

This walk covers about 2.5km. Major sights are considered in greater detail in this chapter.

Kärntner Strasse

From the main tourist office, walk north up the pedestrian-only Kärntner Strasse, a walkway of plush shops, trees, café tables and street entertainers. Detour left down the short Donnergasse to look at the **Donnerbrunnen** (1739) in Neuer Markt. The four naked figures on this fountain (which were too revealing for Maria Theresa's taste) represent the four main tributaries of the Danube: the Enns, March, Traun and Ybbs. Across the square is the **Kapuzinerkirche** (Church of the Capuchin Friars) and the **Kaisergruft**. Back on Kärntner Strasse, detour left again down Kärntner Durchgang. Here you'll find the **American Bar** designed in 1908 by Adolf Loos, one of the prime exponents of a functional Art Nouveau style, though the façade here is somewhat garish. Next door is a strip club, Chez Nous. This was formerly the base for the art club of the Vienna Group; ironically, many of the group's performance art events also involved naked postures.

Stephansplatz to Michaelerplatz

From Kärntner Strasse, the street opens out into Stock im Eisen Platz. Adjacent to the western corner with Kärntner Strasse is a **nail-studded stump**. It is said that this tree trunk acquired its crude metal jacket in the 16th century from blacksmiths banging in a nail for luck when they left the city. Across the square is Stephansplatz and Vienna's prime landmark, **Stephansdom** (St Stephen's Cathedral). Facing it is the unashamedly modern **Haas Haus**, built by Hans Hollein and opened in 1990. Many Viennese were rather unhappy about this curving silver structure crowding their beloved cathedral, but tourists seem happy enough to snap the spindly reflections of Stephansdom's spire in its rectangular windows.

Leading north-west from Stock im Eisen Platz is the broad pedestrian thoroughfare of **Graben**, another plush shopping street. Like Kärntner Strasse and Stephansplatz, it's a fine place to linger, soak up the atmosphere, absorb the hubbub of voices and appreciate the musicianship of street artists. Graben is dominated by the knobbly outline of the **Pestsäule** (Plague Column), completed in 1693 to commemorate the 75,000 victims of the Black Death who perished in Vienna some 20 years earlier. Adolf Loos was busy in Graben, creating the Schneidersalon Knize at No 10 and, rather appropriately given his surname, the toilets nearby.

Turn left into Kohlmarkt, so named because charcoal was once sold here. At No 14 is one of the most famous of the Konditorei-style cafés

Inset: Look up to see the detail on the roof of Stephansdom (photograph by Jon Davison).

in Vienna, **Demel**. Just beyond is Michaelerplatz, with the dome of St Michael's gateway to the **Hofburg** towering above.

The so-called **Loos Haus** (the Goldman & Salatsch building; 1910) on Michaelerplatz is a typical example of the clean lines of Loos' work. However, Franz Josef hated it and described the windows, which lack lintels, as 'windows without eyebrows'. The excavations in the middle of the square are of Roman origin. **Michaelerkirche** (St Michael's Church) on the square betrays nearly five centuries of architectural styles, ranging from 1327 (Romanesque chancel) to 1792 (Baroque doorway angels).

Ringstrasse

Pass through St Michael's Gate and the courtyard to find yourself in Heldenplatz, with the vast curve of the **Neue Hofburg**, built between 1881 and 1908, on your left. Hitler addressed a rally here during his triumphant return to Vienna in 1938. Walk past the line of fiacres, noting the Gothic spire of the **Rathaus** (1873-83) rising above the trees to the right. Ahead, on the far side of the Ring, stand the rival identical twins, the **Naturhistorisches Museum** (1872-81) and the **Kunsthistorisches Museum** (1872-91). They were the work of Gottfried

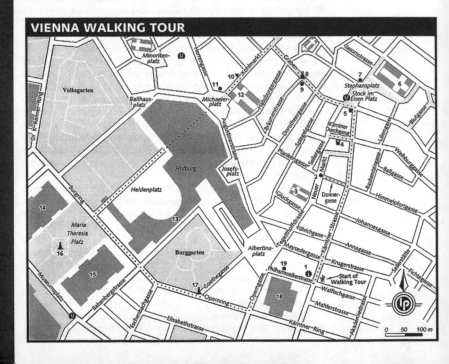

VIENNA WALKING TOUR

Semper, who designed the exteriors, and Karl von Hasenauer, who did the interiors. Between the museums is a large statue of Maria Theresa, surrounded by key figures of her reign. She sits regally, holding her right hand out, palm upwards, as if in an early version of the 'gimme five' greeting.

Emperor Franz Josef was largely responsible for the monumental architecture round the **Ringstrasse**. In 1857 he decided to tear down the redundant military fortifications and exercise grounds and replace them with grandiose public buildings in a variety of historical styles. Work began the following year and reached a peak in the 1870s. Ironically, the empire the buildings were supposed to glorify was lost after WWI. Plans for a grand walkway connecting the Hofburg and the museums, and for a companion wing to the Neue Hofburg, were shelved due to a lack of money and determination. A full tour of the Ringstrasse is recommended, or at least the section from the university to the Staatsoper (under 2km). Break up your walk by relaxing en route in the Volksgarten, with its many roses, or in the Rathauspark, featuring statues and fountains. The **Burggarten**, formerly reserved for the pleasure of the imperial family and high-ranking officials, contains statues of Mozart (erected 1896) and Franz Josef.

From the Hofburg, walk anticlockwise round the Ring, passing a vast statue of a seated Goethe, until you reach the **Staatsoper** (State Opera), built between 1861 and 1869. This may appear the equal of any other Ringstrasse edifice, but initial public reaction was so hostile that one of the designers, Eduard van der Nüll, committed suicide. The building was all but destroyed in WWII and reopened only in 1955. The opulent interior is best explored during the interval of a performance, though you can also take a guided tour for AS60 (students AS30, seniors AS45); schedules vary – see the timetable at the window on the Kärntner Strasse side.

At the north-western corner of the Staatsoper is **Albertinaplatz**. The south-eastern extremity of the Hofburg, containing the famous Albertina collection of graphic arts, is to the north. This is closed for long-term renovations, but part of the collection can be viewed at the Akademiehof, 01, Marktgasse 3 (entry AS45, concessions AS20; closed on Monday). On the square is a troubling work by sculptor and graphic artist Alfred Hrdlicka (born 1928), created in 1988. This series of pale block-like sculptures commemorates Jews and other victims of war and fascism. Some of the stone originally came from the Mauthausen concentration camp in Upper Austria.

Turn into Philharmonikerstrasse, passing between the Staatsoper and the **Hotel Sacher**, purveyor of a famous cake, the Sacher Torte. Sacher and Demel had a long-running dispute over who was the true creator of the authentic chocolate torte: the former was Metternich's cook, the latter was pastry cook to the Habsburgs.

Another few steps will bring you back to Kärntner Strasse, with the tourist office on your left.

1 Main Tourist Office
2 Donnerbrunnen
3 Kapuzinerkirche & Kaisergruft
4 American Bar
5 Nail-Studded Stump
6 Stephansdom
7 Haas Haus
8 Pestsäule (Plague Column)
9 Schneidersalon Knize
10 Demel
11 Loos Haus
12 Michaelerkirche
13 Neue Hofburg
14 Naturhistorisches Museum
15 Kunsthistorisches Museum
16 Statue of Maria Theresa
17 Statue of Goethe
18 Staatsoper
19 Hotel Sacher

OTHER DISTRICTS
Schloss Belvedere

This splendid Baroque palace was built for Prince Eugene of Savoy between 1714 and 1723, and was the work of Johann Lukas von Hildebrandt. The Unteres (Lower) Belvedere was Eugene's summer residence and the Oberes (Upper) Belvedere was used for banquets and other festivities. Running between the two is a long garden laid out in French style, lined with statues of sphinxes and other mythical beasts. Immediately east of this is the Botanical Gardens, which belongs to the university; admission to the Botanical Gardens is free. The Habsburgs were rather irked that Prince Eugene should have a residence to match the Hofburg, and the palace was eventually purchased by Maria Theresa.

Schloss Belvedere is now home to the **Österreichische Galerie** (Austrian Gallery); the Baroque section is in the Unteres Belvedere (entrance 04, Rennweg 6A; take tram No 71 from Schwarzenbergplatz) and 19th and 20th century art is displayed in the Oberes Belvedere (entrance 04, Prinz Eugen Strasse 27; take tram D from Schwarzenbergplatz). Opening hours are Tuesday to Sunday from 10 am to 5 pm; combined entry costs AS60 (you needn't

visit both on the same day), or AS30 for students and seniors.

Oberes Belvedere This houses the most important collection. Grand Baroque fixtures include Herculean figures and a fresco depicting the apotheosis of Prince Eugene. The 19th century section includes paintings from the Biedermeier period, including many paintings by Georg Waldmüller, and work by Hans Makart and Anton Romako which had an influenc on the Viennese Art Nouveau artists.

The 20th century section of the gallery contains the best exhibits. One of Gustav Klimt's best known and most intriguing works is *The Kiss* (1908), displayed here. Pundits disagree as to whether the kiss in question is proffered willingly or conceded under coercion. Some of Klimt's impressionistic landscapes are also here. (See also the boxed text 'Gustav Klimt' below.)

Egon Schiele produced intense, melancholic work, typified by the hypnotic and bulging eyes on the portrait of his friend, *Eduard Kosmack* (1910). Schiele's bold, brooding colours and unforgiving outlines are a contrast to Klimt's golden tapestries and idealised forms. He lived with one of Klimt's models for a while – but Schiele's

Gustav Klimt

Born in Baugarten, near Vienna, in 1862 Gustav Klimt was the leader and best known member of the Secession movement founded in 1897. The movement was born when a group of young artists revolted against the traditional art establishment and established their own journal (*Ver Sacrum*), exhibition forum (The Secession Hall) and unique modern style. The Secession artists worked in a highly decorative style. Klimt's famous painting *The Kiss* is typical of the rich ornamentation, vivid colour and floral motifs favoured by the Secession artists. His later pictures (such as the two portraits of Adele Bloch-Bauer) employ a harmonious but ostentatious use of background colour with much metallic gold and silver to evoke or symbolise the emotions of the main figures.

Klimt became the most celebrated artist in Vienna at the turn of the century. His works were renowned then, as now, for their sexuality and decadence. However, his *femmes fatales* exuded an eroticism and power too explicit for their time. Klimt was accused of ugliness, pornography and perverted excess. His response was typical; a work entitled *Goldfish* or *To My Critics*, portraying a voluptuous flame-haired maiden baring her bottom to the world.

unset on the Alte Burg, Heldenplatz, Vienna.

Ernst Fuchs' ornate Brunnerhaus, Vienna.

You can find everything from cheese to clothes and curios at Vienna's Naschmarkt.

Vienna's famous Ferris wheel.

Fiacre drivers in Heldenplatz, Vienna, awaiting the next fare.

Heldenplatz, Vienna, at dusk.

Peterskirche – the best Baroque interior in Vienna's Innere Stadt.

Café culture is a quintessential feature of life in Vienna.

Schloss Schönbrunn, Vienna's imperial summer residence, was once home to Napoleon.

portraits of her were much more explicit, bordering on the pornographic. *The Family* was Schiele's last work; he died of Egyptian flu in 1918, before he could put the finishing touches to the painting.

Other Austrian artists represented here include Herbert Boeckl, Anton Hanak, Arnulf Rainer and Fritz Wotruba. There are several examples of the work of the influential expressionist, Oskar Kokoschka. The gallery also displays some exhibits from non-Austrian artists such as Munch, Monet, Van Gogh, Renoir and Cézanne.

Unteres Belvedere The Baroque section offers some good statuary, such as the originals from Donner's Neuer Markt fountain (1738-39), and especially *The Apotheosis of Prince Eugene* (again!), this time fashioned in marble in 1721 by the Baroque sculptor Balthasar Permoser. Eugene was presumably experiencing delusions of grandeur by this time, for he commissioned the latter work himself; the artist, not to be outdone, depicted himself at the prince's feet. Paintings include portraits of Maria Theresa and Franz I. A whole room is devoted to the vibrant work of Franz Anton Maulbertsch (1724-96).

The **Orangery** houses a collection of Austrian medieval art comprising religious scenes, altarpieces and statues. There are several impressive works by Michael Pacher, who was influenced by both early art from the Low Countries and the early Renaissance of northern Italy.

Schloss Schönbrunn

This sumptuous Baroque palace is one of Vienna's most popular attractions. It's in Schönbrunn Park, in the 13th district, and can be reached on U-Bahn line No 4.

Leopold I commissioned Johann Bernhard Fischer von Erlach to build a luxurious summer palace where a 'beautiful fountain' (*schöner Brunnen*) had previously stood. The building was completed in 1700 but was nowhere near as grand as originally envisaged. Maria Theresa chose Nikolaus Pacassi to renovate and extend the palace between 1744 and 1749. The interior was fitted out in rococo style and had 2000 rooms as well as a chapel and a theatre. Like most imperial buildings associated with Maria Theresa, the exterior was painted a rich yellow, her favourite colour.

Napoleon lived in the palace in 1805 and 1809. In 1918 the last Habsburg emperor, Charles I, abdicated in the Blue Chinese Salon, after which the palace became the property of the new republic. In 1992 the palace administration was transferred to private hands.

The Palace The interior is suitably majestic, featuring frescoed ceilings, tapestries, crystal chandeliers and gilded ornaments. However, the endless stucco and gold twirls can seem overdone. Franz Josef evidently thought so too, for he ordered the rococo excesses stripped from his personal bedchamber in 1854.

The pinnacle of finery is reached in the **Grosse Galerie** (Great Gallery). Gilded scrolls, ceiling frescoes, chandeliers and huge crystal mirrors create the effect. Numerous lavish balls were held here, including one for the delegates to the Congress of Vienna (1814-15).

The **Spiegelsaal** (Mirror Room) is where Mozart, aged six, played his first royal concert in 1762 in the presence of Maria Theresa. Afterwards young Wolfgang leapt onto the lap of the empress and kissed her. The **Rundes Chinesisches Kabinett** (Round Chinese Kabinett) had a table that could be drawn up and down through the floor for serving food, so that servants need not enter during secret consultations. The **Millionenzimmer** (Million Gulden Room) has Persian miniatures set in rosewood panels in rocaille frames.

The interior of the palace can be visited daily between 8.30 am and 5 pm (4.30 pm from 1 November to 31 March). There are two self-guided tours, each including a personal audio guide in English. The Imperial Tour gives access to 22 rooms for AS90 (students under 26 AS80, children AS45); allow 45 to 60 minutes. The Grand Tour

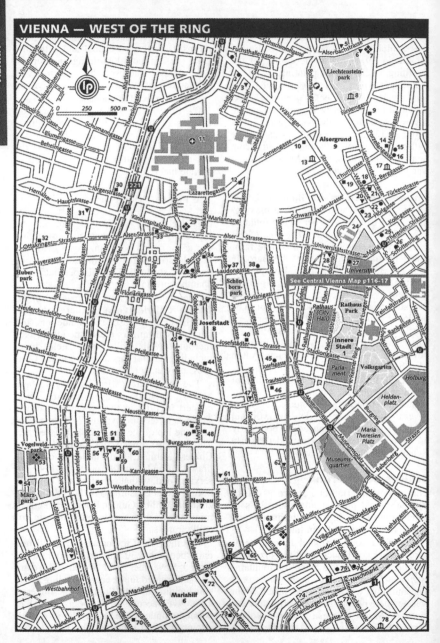

VIENNA — WEST OF THE RING

VIENNA – WEST OF THE RING

PLACES TO STAY		
9	Porzellaneum	
10	Hotel Atlanta	
12	Auer	
14	Pension Falstaff	
19	Hotel Am Schottenpoint	
30	Thüringer Hof	
32	Hotel Maté	
33	Pension Ani	
34	Hostel Zöhrer	
40	Theater-Hotel	
44	Hotel Avis; Gästehaus Pfeilgasse	
46	Pension Wild	
48	Believe It Or Not	
49	Jugendherberge Myrthengasse	
50	Jugendherberge Neustiftgasse	
51	Pension Atrium	
52	Panda Hostel and Lauria	
59	Alla Lenz	
65	Pension Esterházy	
69	Hotel Fürstenhof	
70	Hotel Westend	
73	Pension Kraml	

PLACES TO EAT
3 Vegi Rant
5 Feuervogel
6 Hofer Supermarket
20 Afro-Asiatisches Institut Mensa

28 University Mensa
31 Thai Haus
37 Laudon Stüberl
39 Tunnel Café & Bar
41 Fromme Helene
47 Hofer Supermarket
56 Burg-Keller
57 Gaunkerl
58 Mondo Supermarket
60 Ungar-Grill
61 Schnitzelwirt Schmidt
62 Amerlingbeisl
67 Beim Novak
68 Pulkautaler Weinhaus
72 Schnitzelhaus
77 Schnitzelhaus

OTHER
1 Volksoper
2 WUK
4 US Embassy
7 Niedermeyer (Store)
8 Museum Moderner Kunst (Palais Liechtenstein)
11 Allgemeines Krankenhaus (Hospital)
13 Josephinium (Museum of Medical History)
15 Fundus
16 International Theatre
17 Sigmund Freud Museum
18 Polizeifundamt (Lost Property)

21 Café Berg
22 ÖKISTA (Travel Agency)
23 Café Stein
24 Votivkirche
25 Reisebuchladen
26 Kino de France
27 University Library
29 Niedermeyer (Store)
35 Städtische Hauptbücherei (Library)
36 Mitfahrzentrale Josefstadt
38 Odyssee Mitwohnzentrale (Accommodation Agency) & Beislbar Geralala
42 Miele (Laundrette)
43 Chelsea
45 English Theatre
53 Lugner City (Shopping Centre)
54 Stadthalle
55 Schnell & Sauber Waschcenter (Laundrette)
63 Gerngross Department Store
64 Niedermeyer (Store)
66 Camera Club & Café Tralala
71 Flotten Center (Cinema)
74 Flohmarkt
75 Majolikahaus
76 Café Savoy
78 Schubert Commemorative Rooms

takes in 40 rooms and costs AS120 (students AS105, children AS60); allow up to 1½ hours. During the busy summer months you should buy your ticket for the tour straight away and then explore the gardens till your tour departs.

Wagenburg The Imperial Coach Collection on the western side of the palace includes both tiny children's wagons and great vehicles of state. The most ornate is the imperial coach of the court, built for Maria Theresa around 1765. This is an example of extreme Baroque on wheels, with fussy gold ornamentation and painted cherubs.

Allow 30 minutes to look round; it's open daily from 9 am to 6 pm, but between 1 November and 31 March it closes at 4 pm and all day Monday (entry AS30, students and seniors AS15).

Gardens The beautifully tended formal gardens, arranged in French style, are a symphony of colour in the summer. The extensive grounds contain Roman ruins (now the site of summer concerts), the **Neptunbrunnen** (Neptune Fountain, a riotous ensemble from Greek mythology), and the crowning glory on the hill, the **Gloriette** monument. The view from the monument towards the palace and Vienna is excellent, virtually as good as that from its roof, which is accessible from May to October (entry AS20). The palace grounds are open from 6 am until sunset.

On the western side of the grounds are the **Schmetterlinghaus** (Butterfly House) and the **Palmenhaus** (Palm House). Admission to either costs AS45 (AS30 for students under 29) or AS75 (AS45) for a combined ticket. In the latter, butterflies are enticed onto fake flowers sprayed with honey.

The attractively laid-out **Tiergarten** (zoo) is the oldest in the world, established in 1752. The once-cramped animal cages have now mostly been improved. Entry costs AS90 (seniors AS70, students under 29 AS40, children AS25). The zoo opens at 9 am and closes at 4.30 pm (November to January), 5 pm (February and October), 5.30 pm (March), 6 pm (April) or 6.30 pm (May to September). Feeding times vary for the different animals; sea lions dine at 10.30 am and 3.30 pm, lions have to wait until one hour before closing time.

Museums

Josephinium Also known as the Museum of Medical History, the Josephinium is at 09, Währinger Strasse 25, on the 1st floor of the right-hand wing. This small museum is fascinating, and a little bizarre. The prime exhibits are the wax specimen models of the human frame, created more than 200 years ago by Felice Fontana and Paolo Mascagni. They were used in the Academy of Medico-Surgery, set up by Joseph II in 1785 to improve the skills of army surgeons who lacked medical qualifications. These models, showing the make-up of the body under the skin, were intended to give the students a three-dimensional understanding of the organs, bones, veins and muscles. Three rooms of this gore will make you feel like you've wandered onto the set of a tacky horror movie. One strange touch is the necklace on the female model lying down in the first room. She's hardly dressed for a sophisticated night out, given that half her torso is missing.

The rest of the museum contains cases of arcane medical instruments, photos of past practitioners, accounts of unpleasant-looking operations, and some texts (one book is thoughtfully left open on a page dealing with the dissection of eyeballs).

Art through Action

Viennese Actionism spanned the years 1957-68 and was one of the most extreme of all modern art movements. It was linked to the Vienna Group and had its roots in abstract expressionism. Actionism sought access to the unconscious through the frenzy of an extreme and very direct art: the Actionists quickly moved from pouring paint over the canvas, which was then slashed with knives, to using bodies (live people, dead animals) as 'brushes', and using blood, excrement, eggs, mud and whatever else came to hand as 'paint'. The traditional canvas was soon dispensed with altogether. The artist's body became the canvas, the site of art became a deliberated event (the scripted action, staged both privately and publicly) and even merged with reality.

It was a short step from self-painting to inflicting wounds upon the body, and engaging in physical and psychological endurance tests. For 10 years the Action-ists scandalised the press and public, incited violence and panic – and got plenty of publicity. Often poetic, humorous and aggressive, the actions became increasingly politicised, addressing the sexual and social repression that pervaded the Austrian state. *Art in Revolution* (1968), the last Action to be realised in Vienna, resulted in six months hard labour all round.

Opening hours are Monday to Friday from 9 am to 3 pm (except public holidays) and entry is AS10 (free for students).

Museum Moderner Kunst The Museum of Modern Art, eventually to be moved to the Museumsquartier, is currently at two locations: Palais Liechtenstein, 09, Fürstengasse 1, and the modern exhibition space of the 20er Haus, 03, Arsenalstrasse 1. In the former, the Baroque setting provides a good contrast to the rooms devoted to various movements in 20th century art: expressionism, cubism, futurism, constructivism, surrealism, pop art, photorealism, and Viennese Actionism. Well known artists represented include Picasso, Klee, Warhol, Magritte, Ernst and Giacometti. There's a café, and entry to the grounds is from Alserbachstrasse, on the northern side.

The 20er Haus exhibits conceptual art, minimal art and installations ranging from about 1950 to the present. Both sites have sculpture gardens. Entry to each venue costs AS45 (concessions AS25) and a combined ticket costs AS60 (AS30) – you don't have to visit both on the same day. It's open from 10 am to 6 pm daily except Monday.

Sigmund Freud Museum This museum is at 09, Berggasse 19, in the apartments where Freud lived and worked from 1891 to 1938, when he fled the Nazis. It contains his furniture, possessions, letters, documents and photographs; very detailed notes in English illuminate the exhibits. Students and Freud freaks could spend a while here but most visitors will probably just skim through the three main rooms and wonder what on earth Freud wanted with a terra cotta votive offering of male genitals (exhibit 24). There's also a fairly dull home movie on Freud, narrated by his daughter, Anna. The museum is open daily from 9 am to 4 pm (6 pm in summer) and entry costs AS60 (concessions AS40).

Municipal Museums There are several municipal museums run by the City of Vienna. Entry to these is free before noon on Friday (except holidays).

The **Historisches Museum der Stadt Wien** (Historical Museum of the City of Vienna) is the best. It gives details on the development of Vienna from prehistory to the present day, and puts the city and its personalities in context. There are three floors of exhibits, including maps and plans, artefacts, paintings (by such artists as Klimt, Schiele and the Biedermeier painters) and reconstructed rooms from the homes of

Adolf Loos and Franz Grillparzer. Models show the development of the Ringstrasse, and there are also some good period photographs. The museum is at 04, Karlsplatz 5, by Karlskirche, and it's open daily except Monday from 9 am to 4.30 pm (entry AS50; students AS20).

The **Uhren Museum** (Clock Museum), 01, Schulhof 2, displays 1200 clocks and watches, ranging from 15th century pieces to a 1989 computerised clock. The **Hermesvilla** in the Lainzer Tiergarten (see Walking in the Activities section of this chapter) is a former hunting lodge. It features the private apartments of Franz Josef and Empress Elisabeth (entry AS50).

Several municipal museums are based in the former residences of the great composers, and generally contain assorted memorabilia and the furniture of their exalted former inhabitants. Most are open daily except Monday from 9 am to 12.15 pm and 1 to 4.30 pm. A visit may take up to 30 minutes. Entry to each of the following costs AS25 (students AS10):

Eroica-Haus
   19, Döblinger Hauptstrasse 92. This house was named after Beethoven's symphony No 3 which was written here.

Ludwig van Beethoven (1770-1827) came to Vienna at the age of 21 to study under Haydn.

Haydn Museum
06, Haydngasse 19. Haydn lived here for 12 years, during which he composed most of his oratorios *The Creation* and *The Seasons*. He died here in 1809. The museum also has rooms devoted to Brahms.

Johann Strauss Residence
02, Praterstrasse 54. Strauss composed *The Blue Danube* waltz here.

Mozart's Apartment (Figarohaus)
01, Domgasse 5. Mozart spent 2½ productive years here including the writing of *The Marriage of Figaro*.

Pasqualatihaus
01, Mölker Bastei 8. Beethoven lived on the 4th floor of this house from 1804-14.

Schubert Commemorative Rooms
04, Kettenbrückengasse 6. Schubert lived here briefly before his death in 1828. You can also see the house where he was born at 09, Nussdorfer Strasse 54.

Churches

Karlskirche St Charles' Church, south-east of Ressel Park at Karlsplatz, was built between 1716 and 1739 in fulfilment of a vow made by Charles VI at the end of the 1713 plague. It was designed by Johann Bernhard Fischer von Erlach, who began the construction, which was completed by his son, Josef. Although predominantly Baroque, it combines several architectural styles. The twin columns are modelled on Trajan's Column in Rome, and show scenes from the life of St Charles Borromeo (who succoured plague victims in Italy), to whom the church is dedicated. The huge oval dome is 72m high and its interior is graced by cloud-bound celestial beings painted by Johann Michael Rottmayr.

About 100m east of the church is Schwarzenbergplatz, site of the **Russian Monument**, a reminder that the Russians liberated Vienna at the end of WWII. In front of the monument is the Hochstrahlbrunnen fountain, and behind stands Palais Schwarzenberg, co-created by Johann Bernhard Fischer von Erlach and Johann Lukas von Hildebrandt.

Kirche am Steinhof This distinctive Art Nouveau church (1904-07) was the work of Otto Wagner. Kolo Moser chipped in with the mosaic windows. The design illustrates the victory of function over ornamentation prevalent in much of Wagner's work, even down to the sloping floor to drain cleaning water. It's about 6km west of the Innere Stadt at 14, Baumgartner Höhe 1, near the end of bus route No 48A. The church is in the grounds of the Psychiatrische Krankenhaus der Stadt Wien (Psychiatric Hospital of the City of Vienna). Unless taking a tour (see the Organised Tours section later in this chapter), the interior can only be seen on Saturday at 3 pm (entry AS40).

Less than 2km west of the church is Hüttelbergstrasse, where you'll find two **villas** designed by Wagner at Nos 26 and 28. The more unusual (No 26) was built in 1888 and is now the Ernst Fuchs private museum. In the gardens (visible from the road) are some interesting statues and ceramics, and the ornate Brunnenhaus created by Fuchs.

Votivkirche In 1853, Franz Josef survived an assassination attempt when a knife-wielding Hungarian failed to find the emperor's neck through his collar – reports suggested that a metal button deflected the blade. This church, at 09, Rooseveltplatz, was commissioned in thanks for his lucky escape. Heinrich von Ferstel designed this twin-towered Gothic construction, completed in 1879. It's open from 9 am to noon and 4 to 6.30 pm Tuesday to Saturday and from 9 am to noon on Sunday.

Cemeteries

The **Zentralfriedhof** (Central Cemetery), 11, Simmeringer Hauptstrasse 232-244, contains the memorial tombs of numerous famous composers including Beethoven, Brahms, Gluck, Schubert, and Schönberg. Mozart also has a monument here, but he was actually buried in an unmarked grave in **St Marxer Friedhof** (Cemetery of St Mark), 03, Leberstrasse 6-8. Many years after the true location had been forgotten, gravediggers cobbled together a poignant memorial from a broken pillar and a discarded stone angel. For the Marxer Friedhof, take tram No 71 to Landstrasser

Corpse Disposal, Viennese Style

It is said that nowhere are people so obsessed with death as in Vienna. Songs performed in wine taverns often deal with the subject, and the city has a unique museum dealing with coffins and the undertakers' craft (the Bestattungsmuseum). The country as a whole has the highest suicide rate in the world. Being able to afford a lavish funeral at death is a lifetime ambition for many Viennese. Joseph II caused outrage in the 1780s with his scheme to introduce false-bottomed, reusable coffins.

In 1784 the huge Zentralfriedhof (Central Cemetery) was opened, because there was simply no more space in the city cemeteries. To try to persuade the populace that their future dearly departed would rest better in this new location, they shipped the coffins of famous composers to the Zentralfriedhof, where they now rest together in group 32A. An unusual method was contemplated for transporting bodies to the suburban site: engineers drew up plans for a tube, many kilometres long, down which coffins would be fired using compressed air. However, the high cost of this scheme (one million florins) led to its abandonment.

At dawn, before the public are admitted to the Zentralfriedhof, special hunters are employed to shoot male pheasants, hares and wild rabbits. The reason is that these inconsiderate creatures have a tendency to eat or disturb the carefully arranged flowers around the graves. Meanwhile, you won't find any cemeteries for pets in Vienna. It is expressly forbidden to bury animals in the soil, as the high water table might be contaminated by seepage of chemicals used in inoculations and in putting the pets down. Pet cremations are now big business, although they are strictly controlled.

Hauptstrasse then follow the signs (a 10 minute walk).

From St Marxer Friedhof, take tram No 71 or 72 to the Zentralfriedhof's Tor (gate) 2 to visit the aforementioned composers' graves and those of post-war Austrian presidents. Behind the memorial church are simple plaques devoted to those who fell in the world wars. These contrast with to the ostentatious displays of wealth exhibited in the mausoleums of the rich, who couldn't take it with them but certainly tried. Most graves are neat and well tended, and gar-landed with fresh flowers, though the old Jewish section is a tangle of broken and lopsided headstones and unfettered undergrowth, a reminder that few relatives are around to maintain these graves.

Other Attractions

Donauturm The Donauturm (Danube Tower) is the tallest structure in Vienna. Two revolving restaurants (at heights of 170m and 160m) allow you to enjoy a fine panorama and you can watch the sun set behind the Wienerwald. Meals in the restaurants cost between AS75 and AS300. Entry costs AS65 (children AS45). The tower stands in the Donaupark.

Karlsplatz This open square, really a small park, straddles the 1st and 4th districts. At its northern edge of Resselpark sit Wagner's **Stadt Pavillons**, the station buildings for Vienna's first public transport system, built between 1893 and 1902. Wagner was in charge of the design of the metro lines, bridges and buildings. Here he incorporated floral designs and gold trim on a steel and marble structure. His Stadt Pavillon at Hietzing, on the outskirts of Vienna near Schönbrunn, is also worth a look.

Immediately north of Karlsplatz you can see two traditional Viennese buildings, the white **Künstlerhaus** and the rust and white **Musikverein** (1867-69).

KunstHausWien This art gallery at 03, Untere Weissgerberstrasse 13, looks like something out of a toyshop. It was designed by Friedensreich Hundertwasser, whose highly innovative buildings feature uneven floors, coloured ceramics, patchwork decoration, irregular corners and grass and trees on the roof.

The contents of the KunstHausWien are something of a tribute to Hundertwasser, presenting his paintings, graphics, tapestry, philosophy, ecology and architecture. Hundertwasser's quotes are everywhere, ranging from the profound to the cringeworthy ('Each raindrop is a kiss from heaven'). The gallery is open daily from 10 am to 7 pm and entry costs AS90 (concessions AS50). The same amount is charged for temporary exhibitions, and a combination ticket costs AS140 (AS100). Entry on Monday is half-price, unless it's a public holiday. There's a café round the back.

While you are in the area, walk down the road to see the **Hundertwasserhaus**, a block of residential flats designed by Hundertwasser on the corner of Löwengasse and Kegelgasse. It is now one of Vienna's most prestigious addresses, albeit council-owned rented accommodation. Opposite is the **Kalke Village**, also by Hundertwasser, created in an old Michelin factory. It contains a café, souvenir and art shops, and is open daily.

Linke Wienzeile This road runs southwest of the Secession building and into the

Peace Empire and a Hundred Waters

Friedensreich Hundertwasser was born Friedrich Stowasser on 15 December 1928. In 1943, 69 of his Jewish relatives on his mother's side were deported to Eastern Europe and killed.

In 1948, he spent three months at the Akademie der bildenden Künste (Academy of Fine Arts) in Vienna, and the following year adopted his new name, meaning 'peace empire' and 'a hundred waters'. Environmental themes were present even in his early work such as *People (Complement to Trees)* from 1950, now displayed in the KunstHausWien. His paintings employ vivid colours, metallic silver and spirals (sometimes reminiscent of Gustav Klimt's ornamental backgrounds).

Hundertwasser considers 'the straight line is Godless' and faithfully adheres to this principle in his building projects, proclaiming that his uneven floors 'become a symphony, a melody for the feet and bring back natural vibrations to man'. His belief is that cities should be more harmonious with nature: buildings should be semisubmerged under undulating meadows, homes should have 'tree tenants' that pay rent in environmental currency.

Hundertwasser has always seemed something of an oddity to the Viennese establishment. He complains that they won't allow him to put into practice his more radical building projects. Nevertheless, he was commissioned to recreate the façade of the Spittelau incinerator. This was opened in 1992; it's the most unindustrial-looking heating plant you'll ever see (it's just north of Franz Josefs Bahnhof: take U3 to Spittelau). Hundertwasser has stated that man is shielded from nature by three levels of insulation: cities, houses and clothes. He has tried to limit the effect of the first two levels with his building projects. His proposed solution to the third is to go naked (he did make a couple of public speeches in the nude in the 1960s).

Hundertwasser remains one of Vienna's most idiosyncratic inhabitants. Whether he's organising a campaign to retain Austria's traditional car number plates, designing postage stamps, redesigning national flags or simply painting pictures, he's always passionate, sometimes irritating and usually challenging.

6th district. Passing the Theater an der Wien, you soon reach two Art Nouveau buildings created by Otto Wagner. No 38 features a façade of golden medallions by Kolo Moser, railings created from metal leaves and a brace of jesters on the roof who look like they could be shouting abuse at the traditional buildings nearby. No 40 is known as the **Majolikahaus** (1899) because Wagner used majolica tiles to create the flowing floral motifs on the façade.

Volksprater East of the Innere Stadt, this large amusement park, also known as the Wurstelprater, is dominated by the giant **Riesenrad** (Ferris wheel) built in 1897. This achieved celluloid fame in *The Third Man* in the scene where Holly Martins confronts Harry Lime. The wheel is almost 65m high and weighs 430 tonnes. It rotates very slowly, allowing plenty of time to enjoy the view from the top. It operates as late as 11.40 pm in summer and rides cost AS50.

The amusement park contains all sorts of funfair rides costing from AS10 to AS50, but it's a great place simply to wander round and soak up the atmosphere. As you walk, you're liable to come across one of the colourful metal sculptures depicting humans caught up in strange hallucinogenic happenings. Look for them on Rondeau and Calafatti Platz.

ACTIVITIES

The best place to check for information on sporting facilities is the Sportamt (☎ 4000-84111), Ernst Happel Stadion, 02, Meiereistrasse 7. Municipal indoor and outdoor swimming pools (*Bäder*) are described in tourist office leaflets, or you can obtain information by calling ☎ 60112-8044 on weekdays from 7.30 am to 3.30 pm.

The Prater is an important location for participatory sports. It has tennis courts, a bowling alley at 02, Hauptallee 124, horse-riding, sports stadia and swimming pools. A more compact sports complex is the Stadthalle (☎ 98 100), 15, Vogelweidplatz 15, which has a swimming pool, ice rink and bowling alley.

Walking

To the west of the city, the rolling hills and marked trails of the Wienerwald are perfect for walking. The Prater also has a wood with walking trails. The *Wander bares Wien* leaflet, available from the Sportamt, shows trails close to the city and explains how to get to them. A good one in the north-west starts in Nussdorf (take tram D from the Ring) and reaches Kahlenberg, at an altitude of 484m, giving a fine view over the city. On your return to Nussdorf you can counteract all that exercise by imbibing a few drinks at a *Heuriger* (wine tavern). The round trip is an 11km walk; to save your legs try taking the Nussdorf-Kahlenberg 38A bus in one or both directions.

Another place in the Wienerwald to roam around is the Lainzer Tiergarten animal preserve, open between 8 am and dusk from February to November. To get there take Tram No 62 to Hermesstrasse and then bus No 60B to the terminal.

Swimming

Swimming pools are usually open daily. Entry costs about AS70, with reduced entry prices after midday and, in some places, further discounts after 4 pm. In the municipal pools, kids under six years get free entry; those aged between six and 15 get free entry during the summer holidays. Many pools are open-air and open only from May to mid-September, such as the Stadionbad (☎ 720 21 02), a large privately owned complex of pools in the Prater. Bus No 80B runs there from the U3 stop Schlachthausgasse. Some swimming baths also have sauna facilities (for which seniors get discounts). One such place is the Ottakringer Bad (☎ 914 81 06), 16, Johann Staud Strasse 11, which is open year-round.

There are free swimming spots with easy access to the water on both banks of the New Danube. Some of these, mostly near the edge of the city, are for nude bathing and are marked FKK (*Freikörperkultur*) on maps and signs.

Municipal bathing complexes line the Old Danube and are generally open from

May to September. A day ticket for these costs AS70 including a locker, or AS90 with a cabin (reductions after noon). Strandbad Alte Donau provides beaches on the Old Danube as well as separate outdoor swimming pools. Gänsehäufel, also city-owned, is the biggest bathing complex and has a nude section.

Sailing

The Old Danube is the favoured area for sailing. Hofbauer (☎ 219 34 30), 22, Obere Alte Donau, rents sailing boats and also has a branch on the New Danube at the Reichsbrücke bridge. Rowing on the river is also possible.

LANGUAGE COURSES

The tourist office's leaflet *Young Vienna Scene* lists many places offering German-language courses. ÖKISTA (☎ 401 48-8820, fax -8800, email german.course@ oekista.co.at), 09, Türkenstrasse 8, 1st floor, Door 11, offers standard/intensive courses beginning every Monday, with 20/30 lessons per week. It costs AS5200/7300 for a minimum of two weeks and thereafter AS1360/2200 per week, with a maximum of 15/six students per class. It also offers individual tuition.

The Internationales Kulturinstitut (☎ 586 73 21, fax 586 29 93), 01, Opernring 7, runs intensive courses (15 hours per week, AS4400 for four weeks; monthly starts) and evening classes (five hours per week, AS4400 for 10 weeks; starting in January, April and October). Inlingua Sprachschule (☎ 512 22 25, fax 512 94 99) is at 01, Neuer Markt 1. All three schools can arrange accommodation.

ORGANISED TOURS

Tourist guides conduct around 50 different walking tours, covering a range of themes. The monthly *Walks in Vienna* leaflet from the tourist office details all of these (indicating whether the commentaries are in English) and gives the various departure points. Tours last about 1½ hours and cost AS130 (AS65 for those under 18 years).

The Third Man Tour, conducted in English by Dr Brigitte Timmermann (☎ 774 89 01), departs at 4 pm, usually on a Friday; the tour doesn't run in July or August. The meeting place is the exit of the U4 station at Friedensbrücke, and ideally you should bring a torch and a tram ticket. The tour takes in all the main locations used in the film, including the underground sewers, home to 2.5 million rats, and Harry Lime's apartment at Josefsplatz.

Vienna Sightseeing Tours (☎ 712 46 83, fax 714 11 41, email vst@via.at), 03, Stelzhamergasse 4/11, offers a wide variety of tours in English with free hotel pick-up. Some city tours include performances of the Vienna Boys' Choir (AS640; three hours) or the Lipizzaner stallions (AS590; three or five hours). This is one way to see such performances when other tickets have sold out. Vienna Cityrama (☎ 534 13, fax -22), 01, Börsegasse 1, offers a similar programme and prices. Both companies have reductions for children aged 12 or under.

Reisebuchladen (☎ 317 33 84), 09, Kolingasse 6, conducts an alternative to the normal sightseeing tour, concentrating on 'Red Vienna' and Art Nouveau sights. It costs AS330 per person and the guide is not afraid to reveal uncomplimentary details about the city. Tours in English are possible, depending upon demand.

Boat tours of the Danube canal are provided from 1 May to late October by DDSG Blue Danube (☎ 588 80-0, email ddsg.blue .danube@telecom.at) and Donau Schiffahrt (☎ 715 15 25-20). DDSG's 90 minute tour goes from Schwedenplatz to Reichsbrücke (on the Danube River) and costs AS120. It also offers dinner/dance cruises.

Pedal Power (☎ 729 72 34, fax 729 72 35, email office@pedalpower.co.at), 02, Ausstellungsstrasse 3, conducts half-day bicycle tours from 1 May to 31 October. Tours cost AS280 (AS230 for students), or AS180 if you have your own bike. From May to October at weekends, 'old-time tram' tours depart from Karlsplatz (AS200, children AS70); for more information call ☎ 7909-440 26.

The Story behind the Story of *The Third Man*

'I had paid my last farewell to Harry a week ago, when his coffin was lowered into the frozen February ground, so that it was with incredulity that I saw him pass by, without a sign of recognition, among the host of strangers in the Strand.' Thus wrote Graham Greene on the back of an envelope. There it stayed, for many years, an idea without a context. Then Sir Alexander Korda asked him to write a film about the four power occupation of postwar Vienna. The film was to be directed by Carol Reed, who worked with Greene on an earlier film, *The Fallen Idol*.

So Greene now had an opening scene and a framework. He still needed a plot. He flew to Vienna in 1948 and roamed the bomb-damaged streets, searching with increasing desperation for inspiration. Nothing came to mind until, with his departure imminent, Greene had lunch with a British intelligence officer. The conversation proved more nourishing than the meal. The officer told him about the underground police who patrolled the huge network of sewers beneath the city. He also waxed lyrical on the subject of the black-market trade in penicillin, which the racketeers exploited with no regard for the consequences. Greene put the two ideas together and created his story.

Another chance encounter completed the picture. After filming one night, Carol Reed went drinking in the *Heurigen* area of Sievering. There he discovered Anton Karas playing a zither and was mesmerised by the hypnotic rhythms the instrument produced. Although Karas could neither read nor write music, Reed flew him to London where he recorded the soundtrack. The bouncing, staggering refrain that became Harry Lime's theme dominated the film, became a hit and earned Karas a fortune.

As a final twist of serendipity, the most memorable lines of dialogue came not from the measured pen of Greene but from the improvising tongue of Orson Welles as Harry Lime. They were delivered in front of the camera in the Prater, under the towering stanchions of the Ferris Wheel: 'In Italy for 30 years under the Borgias they had warfare, terror, murder, bloodshed – they produced Michelangelo, Leonardo da Vinci and the Renaissance. In Switzerland they had brotherly love, 500 years of democracy and peace, and what did that produce? The cuckoo clock. So long Holly.'

And in Vienna they had the ideal setting for a classic film.

SPECIAL EVENTS

No matter what time of year you visit Vienna, there will be something special happening – get the monthly booklet of events from the tourist office. Tickets for many events are available to personal callers at Wien Ticket (☎ 588 85) in the hut by the Staatsoper. They charge little or no commission; cash only.

On New Year's Eve various celebrations are arranged in the Innere Stadt, and one of the evening's musical events is relayed onto a giant screen at Stephansplatz. The Opera Ball at the Staatsoper is one of the most lavish of the 300 or so balls held in January and February.

The Vienna Festival (from mid-May to mid-June) has a wide-ranging arts programme and is considered the highlight of the year. Contact Wiener Festwochen (☎ 589 22-22, fax -49, email festwochen@festwochen.at), Lehárgasse 11, A-1060 Vienna, after December for details. At the end of June, look out for three days of free rock, jazz and folk concerts, plus general outdoor fun in the Donauinselfest.

Vienna's Summer of Music (from July to mid-August) fills an otherwise flat spot in the musical calendar, taking place at various venues around town. Contact KlangBoden (☎ 4000-8410), 01, Stadiongasse 9, after 1 June for tickets by credit card. Reduced student tickets go on sale at the various venues 10 minutes before the performance. In the first two weeks of July the Jazz Festival is held at the Staatsoper and the Volkstheater; contact the KlangBoden office for tickets.

The free open-air Opera Film Festival on Rathausplatz runs throughout July and August; hundreds of Viennese turn up in their best evening attire. In November and December the Wien Modern festival, features modern classical and avant-garde music, performed in the Musikverein and the Konzerthaus.

Vienna's traditional Christmas market (*Christkindlmarkt*) takes place in front of the Rathaus from mid-November to 24 December. Trees are decorated in the Rathaus park, and inside the Rathaus there are free concerts of seasonal music.

PLACES TO STAY

Vienna can be a nightmare for budget travellers. Even those who can afford a range of options may find their accommodation choice full, especially in the summer. Reserve in advance or at least inquire by telephone before you trek all over town. Reservations are especially recommended at Christmas and Easter and between June and October.

From July to September student residences are converted to seasonal hotels, giving a much-needed boost to the number of beds at the lower end of the market. A few rooms in private homes are on offer, mostly in the suburbs, but economic affluence over recent years has reduced the supply; expect a three day minimum stay.

Accommodation Agencies

Several agencies can help you find accommodation. Tourist offices (see the Facts for the Visitor chapter) charge a commission of AS40 per reservation, irrespective of the number of rooms being booked. They can

help to find private rooms but don't have lists to give out. They can also give you the useful *Jugendherbergen* pamphlet detailing youth hostels and camp sites, and a booklet of hotels and pensions, revised annually.

ÖKISTA (☎ 401 48), 09, Türkenstrasse 8, Door 11, charges AS150 to find hotel rooms (three star and above) for a minimum of three nights. For stays exceeding two weeks it can find a room in a family house from AS180 per night B&B (AS700 commission). The Odyssee Mitwohnzentrale (☎ 402 60 61, fax -11, email mitwohnzentrale@odyssee.vienna.at), 08, Laudongasse 8, can find private single/double rooms costing upwards of AS250/320, or apartments starting at AS6000 per month (AS4000 in summer). Commission is 24% of the rent for a minimum three day stay, but decreases for stays of over one month.

Another approach for those seeking longer term accommodation is to check university notice boards or scan the ads in the magazines *Bazar*, *Findegrube* and *Falter*, available at newsstands. Kolping-Gästehaus (see under Hotels & Pensions – Budget) has cheap monthly rates.

Choosing a Location

Staying within the Innere Stadt is convenient for the sights, although inevitably accommodation here is the most expensive in the city. Most hotels and pensions are between the Ring and the Gürtel; these are better value and still within easy striking distance of the centre. Places in the suburbs have the lowest prices but are less accessible; these are a more viable option if you're not too interested in late-night attractions in the city.

If you have a car, parking costs in the city centre can be high. A better option might be to find somewhere farther out where you can safely leave your car, and then rely on public transport. Even if you stay out late and have to take a taxi home, the taxi fare will still be less than a day's garage fees. Hotels outside the Innere Stadt with private garages charge from around AS100 to AS250 for 24 hours parking (about half the going rate in the Innere Stadt); the farther from the centre the place is, the cheaper it gets. Street parking is no problem in the suburbs.

Camping

Camping Wien West (☎ 914 23 14, fax 911 35 94; 14, Hüttelbergstrasse 80) is open all year except February. It costs AS67/37 per adult/tent, or AS73/42 in July and August. Four-bed bungalows are AS400 (AS440 in July and August). To get there, take U4 or the S-Bahn to Hütteldorf, then bus No 148 or 152. **Aktiv Camping Neue Donau** (☎/fax 202 40 10; 22, Am Kleehäufel) charges the same and is open from early May to mid-September. It's the closest camp site to the city centre and the only one east of the Danube. Take U1 to Kaisermühlen, then the No 91A bus.

Camping Rodaun (☎ 888 41 54; 23, An der Au 2) is open from late March to mid-November and charges AS65/55 per adult/tent. Take S1 or S2 to Liesing then bus No 60A. Beyond the city to the south is the largest site, **Campingplatz Schloss Laxenburg** (☎ 02236-713 33, Münchendorfer Strasse), which has a swimming pool and boat rental and costs AS63/35 per adult/tent, or AS69/40 in July and August, and is open from 1 April to 31 October.

Hostels

Near the Centre No hostels invade the imperial elegance of the Innere Stadt. The nearest are two linked HI **Jugendherbergen** (☎ 523 63 16, fax 523 58 49). One is at 07, Myrthengasse 7, the other is round the corner at 07, Neustiftgasse 85. Both are well run with newish facilities and helpful staff. All rooms have a private shower. Beds (each with a personal bedside light) cost AS165 in six- or four-bed dorms or AS195 in double rooms. Lunch or dinner costs AS60 and laundry is AS50 per load. Curfew is at 1 am. You can check in to either hostel at any time during the day at Myrthengasse; Neustiftgasse closes from 11.15 am to 3.45 pm. Telephone reservations are accepted and strongly advised.

Believe it or Not (☎ 526 46 58; 07, Apartment 14, Myrthengasse 10) is a small private hostel opposite the Myrthengasse hostel. There are no signs outside, except on the doorbell. It has a friendly atmosphere, but one room has triple-level bunks and can get hot in summer. Breakfast isn't provided so use the kitchen facilities instead. Beds are AS160 in summer or AS110 during winter. You get your own key so there's no curfew. **Panda Hostel** (☎ 524 78 88; 07, 3rd floor, Kaiserstrasse 77) has the same prices and a similar setup, with a TV in every room and at least 20 beds. It's linked to Lauria (see Hotels & Pensions – Budget later in this chapter).

Hostel Zöhrer (☎ 406 07 30, fax 408 04 09; 08, Skodagasse 26) is a private hostel close to the Ring, and is reasonable value. Dorm beds cost AS170 and doubles (bunk beds) are AS460, all with private shower. There's a kitchen, courtyard and own-key entry; reception is open from 7.30 am to 10 pm and there's no curfew.

Turmherberge Don Bosco (☎ 713 14 94; 03, Lechnerstrasse 12), south-east of the Ring in a church tower, has the cheapest beds in town; AS75 plus AS25 for sheets if required. However, the place hasn't been modernised since the 1950s – some rooms are cramped and have few lockers (no locks). There are only basic kitchen facilities and breakfast isn't provided. It has 50 beds and is open from 1 March to 31 November. Curfew is 11.45 pm; you can only check in before noon or after 5 pm (telephone reservations accepted).

Near Westbahnhof, **Hostel Ruthensteiner** (☎ 893 42 02, fax 893 27 96, email hostel.ruthensteiner@telecom.at; 15, Robert Hamerling Gasse 24), one block south of Mariahilfer Strasse, is open 24 hours a day. Beds in large dorms cost AS125 in summer or AS145 at other times. You need your own sheets, which can be bought for AS120. Sheets are provided in the smaller dorms, in which beds are AS169, and in the basic singles/doubles (AS245/470). Breakfast costs AS25 and there's a kitchen, a shady rear courtyard and Internet access.

VIENNA

The modern *Kolpingsfamilie Meidling* (☎ *813 54 87, fax 812 21 30; 12, Bendlgasse 10-12)* is near the Niederhofstrasse U6 stop, south of Westbahnhof. Beds cost from AS100 in eight to 10-bed dorms to AS155 in four-bed dorms. Dorms all have a private shower and some have a WC; the four-bed dorms have a balcony. There are lockers but no keys, and there's a patio round the back. Non-HI members pay AS20 extra, which is a bit cheeky as they don't stamp your guest card. Breakfast is AS45; sheets (if required) cost AS65. Curfew is at midnight, but reception is open 24 hours.

In the Suburbs *Jugendgästehaus Brigittenau* (☎ *332 82 94, fax 330 83 79; 20, Friedrich Engels Platz 24)* is a HI hostel with 334 beds, in a modern multistorey building a couple of minutes walk from the Danube (trams N, 31 and 33 stop outside). Beds in four-bed dorms cost AS165 and doubles with private shower are AS195 per person; dinners cost AS60 and there's a café, games room and garden. Reception is open 24 hours but curfew is at 1 am (later access may be possible).

Jugendgästehaus Hütteldorf-Hacking (☎ *877 02 63, fax 877 02 63-2, email jgh@ wigast.com; Schlossberggasse 8)* has beds in dorms of varying sizes for AS156 (AS30 surcharge for single occupancy) and a total of 271 beds. Meals are available and there are laundry facilities and a lounge. Curfew is at 11.45 pm but you can buy a key card (AS25) which will give you late entry; doors are locked from 9.30 am to 3 pm. This HI hostel is a long way from the centre of town, but only five minutes walk from both the U4 Hütteldorf station and the N49 nightbus route.

Schlossherberge am Wilhelminenberg (☎ *485 85 03-700, fax -702; 16, Savoyenstrasse 2)* has beds in dorms with shower/ WC for AS220, and doubles costAS500. Reception is open all day but the dorms are locked from 9 am to 2 pm. Curfew is at 11.45 pm, or a key card (AS25) allows late entry. The view includes Vienna and some vineyards but this HI hostel is a long way

from the centre: Bus Nos 46B and 146B link with city-bound trams J, 44 and 46.

Student Residences

These become seasonal hotels from 1 July to 30 September – see the Accommodation section in the Facts for the Visitor chapter. Most are outside the Innere Stadt.

Auge Gottes (☎ *319 44 88-10, fax -11; 09, Nussdorfer Strasse 75)* offers single/ double rooms with hall shower for AS270/ 470; doubles with private shower cost AS570 and triples/quads are AS630/840. *Auersperg* (☎ *406 23 40; 08, Auerspergstrasse 9)* is near the Ring and has 24 hour reception. Singles/doubles start at AS355/ 580, or AS500/820 with private shower/ WC. You can make advance reservations by calling ☎ 512 74 93 or faxing 512 19 68 during office hours.

At *Haus Döbling* (☎ *34 76 31, fax -25; 19, Gymnasiumstrasse 85)* all singles/ doubles have private shower and hall WC. 'Hostel service' costs AS270/340; 'hotel service' – including bathroom towels and bed-making – costs AS300/400. There are over 300 beds.

At *Gästehaus Pfeilgasse* (☎ *401 74, fax 401 76-20; 08, Pfeilgasse 4-6)* singles/ doubles/triples with hall shower and WC cost AS270/480/600. Reception (open 24 hours) is in Hotel Avis. *Katholisches Studentenhaus* (☎ *34 92 64; 19, Peter Jordan Strasse 29)* has singles/doubles with hall shower/WC for AS235/340, not including breakfast.

Music Academy (☎ *514 84-48, fax -49; 01, Johannesgasse 8)* has singles/doubles for AS410/740 or AS480/960 with private bath/WC; triples/quads are AS780/960. It's central, with 24 hour reception, and one apartment is available year round.

At *Porzellaneum* (☎ *317 72 82; 09, Porzellangasse 30)* singles or doubles with hall shower cost AS175 per person, without breakfast; reception is open 24 hours.

Ruddfinum (☎ *505 53 84; 04, Mayerhofgasse 3)* has singles/doubles/triples with hall shower for AS280/500/650. Reception is open 24 hours.

Hotels & Pensions – Budget

Near the Centre You'll find the entrance to *Kolping-Gästehaus* (☎ 587 56 31-119, fax 586 36 30; 06, Gumpendorfer Strasse 39) on Stiegengasse; singles with/without shower cost AS550/250. Doubles go for AS800 with shower, or AS940 with shower/WC; triples are also available. Rooms are OK, and there are kitchen facilities, but this is partially a student residence and feels like it. Book well ahead.

Auer (☎ 406 21 21, fax -4; 09, Lazarett-gasse 3) is friendly, pleasant and more Viennese in style. Singles/doubles with hall shower start at AS370/540; doubles with private shower cost AS610. Reception is on the 1st floor; there's no lift.

Pension Wild (☎ 406 51 74, fax 402 21 68; 08, Langegasse 10) is central and quieter than the name suggests. Singles/doubles/triples cost AS450/590/860; add AS100 per room for a private shower. It's run by an elderly Frau who speaks a quirky combination of English and German. Reception is open 24 hours and the kitchen on each floor is a bonus. A health centre offering massage and sauna shares the building.

Lauria (☎ 522 25 55; 07, 3rd floor, Kaiserstrasse 77) has clean, well decorated rooms, some with large pictorial scenes and homey touches; all have a TV, and there are communal kitchens (no breakfast provided). Doubles cost AS530 (AS480 with bunk beds), or AS700 with private shower. Triples (AS700) and quads (AS850) are also available, and there are some fully equipped apartments (AS1400/1600 for four/six people). There may be a two day minimum stay for reservations. Credit cards are accepted.

Hotel Westend (☎ 597 67 29, fax -27; 06, Fügergasse 3) is close to Westbahnhof and has reasonable singles/doubles for AS340/610 (AS390/730 with shower). Reception is open 24 hours.

Pension Kraml (☎ 587 85 88, fax 586 75 73; 06, Brauergasse 5) is small, friendly and family-run. It has single/double rooms for AS310/620 and large doubles with private shower for AS700, AS820 with shower/WC. There are also triples and family apartments.

Pension Miklos (☎ 587 51 61, fax 587 27 50; 05, Schönbrunner Strasse 41) is near the Naschmarkt and transport routes, and has simple singles with hall shower for AS250. Single/double rooms with private shower cost AS450/580; they're rather basic conversions from residential flats, but most are large, with a lounge area. Add AS35 per person for breakfast.

Pension Falstaff (☎ 317 91 86, fax -4; 09, Müllnergasse) has singles/doubles for AS370/620 (with an irksome fee of AS30 fee to use the hall shower) or AS490/740 with private shower. Prices are around AS100 lower in winter. The rooms are long but some are narrow; fittings are ageing but adequate. It's convenient for tram D to the Ring and Nussdorf.

Praterstern (☎ 214 01 23, fax 214 78 80, email 113052.3725@compuserve.com; 02, Mayergasse 6), east of the Ring, has singles/doubles for AS290/545. Rooms with private shower cost AS385/655, or AS425/685 with shower/WC. There are cheaper rates, excluding breakfast, in the low season. Some travellers have reported poor service here.

Close to the centre is *Quisisana* (☎ 587 71 55, fax 587 71 56-33; 06, Windmühl-gasse 6). Singles/doubles start at AS380/600 with shower, AS330/520 without. Rooms vary in size and quality but are generally good value.

Hotel Kolbeck (☎ 604 17 73, fax 602 94 86; 10, Laxenburger Strasse 19) is just ten minutes walk from Südbahnhof. Singles/doubles with hall shower cost AS400/750; with private shower/WC and cable TV they're AS600/1000. The patterned floor tiles in the corridor are typically Viennese. Reception is open 24 hours.

Down the road is *Cyrus* (☎/fax 604 42 88; 10, Laxenburger Strasse 14), offering a range of rooms, all with shower and cable TV. Singles cost from AS300 to AS450 and doubles are from AS500 to AS800, depending on the size, furnishings, and whether they have a private WC.

Nearby, and handy for local transport, is *Pension Caroline* (☎ *604 80 70, fax 602 77 67; 10, Gudrunstrasse 138)*. Attractive renovated singles/doubles with shower, WC and satellite TV cost AS520/820; it's on the 4th floor (there's a lift).

Pension Ani (☎ *408 10 60, fax 408 10 82; 09, Kinderspitalgasse 1)* charges from AS400/650 for single/double rooms with shower, cable TV and phone; bigger, pricier rooms have private WC. It's good value anyway, but rates seem to be negotiable, and the owner may give a discount to students and young people.

Pension Esterházy (☎ *587 51 59; 04, Nelkengasse 3)*, just off Mariahilfer Strasse, has decent-sized rooms (including many singles) costing AS320/490 without breakfast. Most rooms share shower/WC, but there are also some rooms which have private facilities.

Fünfhaus (☎ *892 35 45; 15, Sperrgasse 12)*, near Westbahnhof, has a range of rooms and prices; singles/doubles start from AS390/590, or AS470/680 with private shower. Breakfast costs AS35, and courtyard parking costs AS50 (English not spoken; closed in winter).

Pension Bosch (☎ *798 61 79, fax 799 17 18; 03, Keilgasse 13)* has singles/doubles for AS380/650 with hall showers, AS530/720 with private shower and AS600/860 with shower/WC. The rooms have personal touches, satellite TV, and old-fashioned furnishings. Reception is on the 1st floor (there's a lift).

Goldenes Einhorn (☎ *544 47 55; 05, Am Hundsturm 5)* is a small, simple place opposite a post office and an underground car park. Singles/doubles with hall shower start at AS270/480 without breakfast; doubles with shower cost AS520. Reception hours can be irregular so phone ahead; it's closed in February.

In the Suburbs *Zum Goldenen Stern Gasthof* (☎ *804 13 82; 12, Breitenfurter Strasse 94)*, south of Schloss Schönbrunn, has singles/doubles with hall shower for AS250/440, breakfast excluded. However,

it's very basic; too basic even to make it into the tourist office accommodation list. Bus 62A from Meidling goes there.

Matauschek (☎/fax *982 35 32; 14, Breitenseer Strasse 14)* is by the new Hütteldorfer Strasse U3 stop and has 25 fairly basic rooms. It costs AS330/560 for single/double rooms with hall shower, or AS620 for doubles with private shower. The simple restaurant is closed on Wednesday and Thursday.

Rustler (☎/fax *982 01 62; 14, Linzer Strasse 43)* is an efficiently run place close to the Schönbrunn U4 stop, or you can take tram No 52 from Westbahnhof. It has a pretty garden (with garden gnomes) and double glazing. Singles/doubles/triples cost AS330/600/810; add about AS160 per room for a private shower and the same again for a private WC. It's closed in winter, except over New Year.

Waldandacht (☎ *979 16 50; 14, Wurzbachtalgasse 23)* is as far as you can get into the Wienerwald without crossing into Lower Austria, and has 10 doubles with hall shower costing AS500. Take the S50 to Weidlingau-Wurzbachtal.

Hotels & Pensions – Mid-Range

Innere Stadt *Pension Nossek* (☎ *533 70 41, fax 535 36 46; 01, Graben 17)* is good value considering its ideal situation. Clean, comfortable singles (AS650 to AS800) and doubles (AS1100 to AS1500) are individually priced depending on the size, view and facilities. You have to book weeks ahead during high season. Around the corner, *Pension Aclon* (☎ *512 79 40-0, fax 513 87 51; 01, Dorotheergasse 6-8)* has rooms for AS520/880, or AS720/1220 with private shower.

Schweizer Pension Solderer (☎ *533 81 56, fax 535 64 69; 01, Heinrichsgasse 2)* is very clean and is run by Swiss sisters. It has singles/doubles costing from AS450/580 with hall shower, AS650/860 with private shower and AS700/980 with shower/WC. Most rooms have cable TV and ornamental ceramic stoves. There are street parking places for AS70.

Pension Am Operneck (☎ 512 93 10; 01, *Kärntner Strasse 47*), opposite the tourist office, has big singles/doubles with private shower/WC and TV for AS620/900. It's very popular, however, and is usually booked up months ahead.

Hotel Orient (☎ 533 73 07, fax 535 03 40; 01, *Tiefer Graben 30*) has a *fin-de-siècle* hallway and façade, and rooms are decked out in a variety of interesting styles. Some of the scenes from *The Third Man* were shot here. Single/double rooms with private shower start at AS700/850 and singles with hall shower (AS20 charge) cost AS450. Rooms are rented by the hour for discreet liaisons, but it's by no means a seedy place.

Hotel Post (☎ 51 583-0; 01, *Fleischmarkt 24*) has pricey singles/doubles with shower/WC costing AS900/1140; rooms without shower (from AS500/770) are a better deal.

Near the Centre *Alla Lenz* (☎ 523 69 89, fax -55; 07, *Halbgasse 3-5*) is an excellent top-of-the-range pension with a rooftop swimming pool (free to guests) and a garage next door (AS150 per day). Doubles start at AS980 (lower in winter and for stays of two nights or more) and have air-con, private shower/WC, telephone and cable TV. The singles (AS900) aren't such a good deal. Apartments are also available.

Nearby, *Pension Atrium* (☎ 523 31 14, fax -9; 07, *Burggasse 118*) has clean, renovated rooms with shower/WC and TV starting at AS590/720. It also has one apartment (AS980).

Altwienerhof (☎ 892 60 00, fax -8; 15, *Herklotzgasse 6*) is a small, family-run hotel offering good value, decent sized rooms, and a quality restaurant. Stylish singles/doubles with shower/WC, TV and phone cost AS700/1080.

Hotel Cryston (☎ 813 56 82, fax 812 37 01-70, email hotel.cryston@netway.at; 12, *Gaudenzdorfer Gürtel 63*) offers free private parking. Good singles/doubles with shower/WC, satellite TV and double glazing start at AS700/1180. Rooms costing

AS420/650 have a sink but don't have a TV, shower or WC. There's a AS10 charge to use the hall showers.

Hotel Fürstenhof (☎ 523 32 67, fax -26, email fuerst@ping.at; 07, *Neubaugürtel 4*), opposite Westbahnhof, is a typically Viennese family-run hotel. Rooms (with TV) cost AS880/1260 with shower/WC, or AS500/800 without.

Hotel Am Schottenpoint (☎ 310 87 87, fax -4, email schott@treangeli.at; 09, *Währinger Strasse 22*) has for its entrance a small stuccoed gallery, but the rest of the hotel is more modern in style. Singles/doubles cost AS980/1400, or AS890/1180 in winter.

In the Suburbs *Hotel Victoria* is next to the plush Parkhotel Schönbrunn (see Hotels – Top End) and has its reception there. It's an excellent deal because guests can use all of the top facilities at the Schönbrunn. Single/double rooms start at AS775/1100 and have shower/WC, TV and telephone; there are a few singles without shower, which start at AS455.

West of the city in the Wienerwald is *Sophienalpe* (☎ 486 24 32, fax 485 16 55 12, email sophienalpe@hotels.or.at; 14, *Sophienalpe 13*) which has an indoor swimming pool and a restaurant. There's no adequate public transport so you really need a car to stay here. Singles/doubles with private shower/WC cost from AS350/700. Note that it's closed in winter.

Schloss Wilhelminenberg (☎ 485 85 03, fax 485 48 76; 16, *Savoyenstrasse 2*) has a big garden, stately appearance and fine views. Prices start at AS850/1270 for rooms with very high ceilings, cable TV, shower and WC. Bus Nos 46B and 146B stop outside and link to city-bound trams J, 44 and 46. There's plenty of parking.

There are few options east of the Danube. One is *Landgasthof Müllner* (☎ 774 27 26, fax -21; 22, *Esslinger Hauptstrasse 82*); it's a small, good value place with free parking. Renovated singles/doubles with shower/WC and cable TV cost AS480/900. Phone ahead if arriving on Monday or Tuesday and after 3 pm on Sunday as the reception/ restaurant is closed. Take the U1 to Kagran, then bus No 26A for 20 minutes.

Just east of the Old Danube, five minutes walk from the U1 line, is the hotel and restaurant *Zur Kagraner Brück* (☎ 203 12 95; 22, Wagramer Strasse 52). It offers large single/double rooms with shower/WC for AS660/980. There's parking at the back.

Hotels – Top End

All rooms in this category should have, as a minimum, a private shower or bath and WC, cable TV, direct-dial telephone, radio, and minibar. These hotels will have all the facilities business visitors might require.

Innere Stadt The *Hotel am Schubertring* (☎ 717 02-0, fax 713 99 66; 01, Schubert-ring 11) is a good choice. Maze-like corridors lead to well-equipped single/double rooms (staring at AS1350/1850; less in winter) with Biedermeier or Art Nouveau furniture.

Hotel Austria (☎ 515 23, fax -506; 01, Am Fleischmarkt 20) is next to a quiet cul-de-sac. Rooms are good for the price, costing AS1160/1690 with private shower/ WC, or AS770/1110 without.

Appartement Pension Riemergasse (☎ 512 72 200, fax 513 77 78, email otto@ otto.co.at; 01, Riemergasse 8) can arrange parking for AS90 a day. Apartments have a kitchenette, cable TV and bath/WC. Prices are AS920/1960 for one/four people. There's also a range of other apartments; the largest sleeps up to seven people for AS4300. Breakfast costs AS66 each; credit cards are not accepted.

Hotel zur Wiener Staatsoper (☎ 513 12 74, fax -15; 01, Krugerstrasse 11) has an attractive stuccoed façade. Single/double rooms, costing AS1000/1400, are quiet and compact. Garage parking is discounted to AS160 per day.

The plain frontage of *Hotel Kaiserin Elisabeth* (☎ 515 26, fax -7; 01, Weih-burggasse 3) belies its pleasant interior and long history (Mozart stayed here). Nicely decorated rooms with bath/WC cost AS1450/2450, and there are a few smaller rooms for AS950/1900 with shower/WC.

Hotel am Stephansplatz (☎ 53 405-0, fax -711; 01, Stephansplatz 9) is the closest you can sleep to Stephansdom without building a nest in the belfry. Comfortable, sizeable singles/doubles cost AS1560/2360 or less.

Near the Centre *Hotel Maté* (☎ 404 55, fax -888; 17, Ottakringer Strasse 34-36) has four-star rooms but five-star facilities, with swimming pool, solarium, sauna and fitness room (all free for guests). Prices start at AS1080/1780, or AS960/1280 in winter.

Thüringer Hof (☎ 401 79, fax -600; 18, Jörgerstrasse 4-8) has rooms starting at AS850/1290, some very spacious. There's parking for AS50 and a rooftop terrace.

Hotel Arkadenhof (☎ 310 08 37, fax 310 76 86; 09, Viriotgasse 5) is a comfortable, stylish, small-scale hotel. Rooms have air-con and cost AS1380/1880 (AS200/300 less in winter). The *Theater-Hotel* (☎ 405 36 48, fax 405 14 06; 08, Josefstädter Strasse 22A) is a comparable but larger place, with an Art Nouveau aura. Rooms cost AS1600/ 2510, with reductions of 20% in winter.

Hotel Atlanta (☎ 405 12 30, fax 405 53 75; 09, Währinger Strasse 33) has reasonably spacious, often elegant rooms. Singles/ doubles/triples cost AS1020/1500/1800. From November to March prices are reduced by about AS200 per person.

Hotel-Pension Schneider (☎ 588 38-0, fax -212; 06, Getreidemarkt 5) is close to the Theater an der Wien, and in the lobby are displayed signed photos of actors and opera stars who have stayed here. Singles cost between AS880 and AS1380, doubles cost AS1700, and there are excellent self-contained two-person apartments for AS2180. Prices are lower in the winter.

Aphrodite (☎ 211 48, fax -15; 02, Prater-strasse 28) is a four star hotel with a unique extra: beauty treatments for both men and women (a three day programme costs AS4830). Rooms bedazzle with many mirrors so you can admire your progress, and there's a rooftop terrace, swimming pool, sauna and fitness room, all free for guests. Singles/doubles cost AS1650/2250.

In the Suburbs *Celtes (☎ 440 41 51, fax -116; 19, Schwedenplatz 3-4)* is in the Neustift am Walde Heurigen area (take bus No 35 from the centre). It's good value for a four star place at AS850/1400 for singles/doubles. There's a bar, garden and gym.

Parkhotel Schönbrunn (☎ 87 804, fax -3220; 13, Hietzinger Hauptstrasse 10-20) is easily accessible from the centre by U4 (get off at the Hietzing stop). Franz Josef himself partially funded its construction and considered it his guesthouse. The lobby and grand ballroom all have the majesty of a five star place, and the rooms surround a large garden with sun loungers, trees and grass. There's also a 12m swimming pool (free for guests), and entry to the fitness room and sauna costs AS140. Singles/doubles with bath/WC start at AS1385/1780, and there are a few cheaper, smaller singles. The best rooms are in the older, more expensive part of the building.

Hotels – Over the Top
Nearly all of Vienna's five-star hotels are within the Innere Stadt. Standard or 'economy' (something of a misnomer in this category) rooms are comfortable and have all of the expected fittings and facilities, but they're not necessarily much better than those in a good four star place; you're really paying the premium for the ambience, reputation, better service and the grandeur of the reception and lobby areas. All of these places offer 'superior' rooms and suites. Breakfast generally costs extra, but may be included in special, lower weekend rates.

At the *Hotel Sacher (☎ 51 456, fax -810, email hotel@sacher.com; 01, Philharmonikerstrasse 4)* elegance and tradition go hand in hand. Rooms with Baroque furnishings and genuine 19th century oil paintings start at AS2500/4200.

Hotel Imperial (☎ 501 10-0, fax -410; 01, Kärntner Ring 16) is a truly palatial, expensive period hotel with rooms from AS4200/5300. Similarly impressive is *Hotel Bristol (☎ 51 516-0; fax -550; 01, Kärntner Ring 1)*, where singles/doubles start at AS3500/5900.

The *Inter-Continental (☎ 711 22-0, fax 713 44 89, email vienna@interconti.com; 03, Johannesgasse 28)* has a huge stylish lobby and ballroom, and rooms starting at AS2850/3190 with traditional furnishings. The solarium, sauna and fitness room are free for guests.

Hotel Marriott (☎ 515 18-0, fax -6736; 01, Parkring 12A) has harmonious, galleried lobby shelters, shops, cafés and fake pink flamingos. Large, renovated rooms cost AS2800 (single or double), and the excellent hotel facilities, including a fitness room, sauna and 13m swimming pool, are free to guests.

PLACES TO EAT
Vienna has thousands of restaurants covering all budgets and all styles of cuisine. Coffee houses and Heurigen are almost defining elements of the city, and these are places where you can eat well. *Beisl* is a Viennese name for a small tavern or restaurant. If you haven't the time or money for a sit-down meal, there are many takeaway places, including Würstel stands, another Viennese institution; they provide a quick snack of sausage and bread from about AS20 to AS35.

Vienna has dozens of Chinese restaurants. These are generally reliable and most have a cheap weekday lunch menu. Branches of *Wienerwald* and *Nordsee* are also reliable and inexpensive stand-bys, as are the many pizzerias. The *Schnitzelhaus* chain is an excellent place for fast food, and prices are low at AS45 for a schnitzel with fries or potato salad, a schnitzel burger for AS25, and large cans of beer for AS22. There are nearly 30 branches round town, and all are open daily from 10 am to 10 pm.

Self-Service & Budget Restaurants
Innere Stadt If you only want a snack, try one of the *Würstel stands*. Alternatively,

you can choose from *Nordsee (01, Kärntner Strasse 25)* or *Schnitzelhaus (01, Krugerstrasse 6)*.

The *University Mensa (01, Universitätsstrasse 7)* serves dishes starting at a mere AS36. Take the lift to the 6th floor then walk up one storey. The café adjoining the Mensa has the same meals and longer hours (weekdays from 8 am to 6 pm), and it stays open over the summer.

Close by, the *Katholisches Studenthaus Mensa (01, Ebendorferstrasse 8)* is open Monday to Friday from 11.30 am to 2 pm (closed from August to mid-September). Main courses cost AS35 or AS44, and there's a salad buffet. At the *MAK Cafeteria (01, Oskar Kokoschka Platz 2)*, open weekdays from 9 am to 6 pm (3 pm on Friday), you can get cheap snacks and light meals. At the Akademie der bildenden Künste there's a small *Mensa (01, Schillerplatz 3)*, open on weekdays from 8.30 am to 7 pm (closed from July to September).

The most central university cafeteria is the *Music Academy Mensa (01, Johannesgasse 8)*. Lunches costing from AS48 are served Monday to Friday between 11 am and 2 pm (daily till 1.30 pm during the summer holidays), though you can also have coffee and snacks on weekdays from 7.30 am to 3 pm. Nearby at No 3 is *Zur Fischerin Capua*, with fishing trophies on the walls and weekday menus for around AS78; it's open until 6 pm. There are tables on the 1st floor above the bar area, which is open daily except Sunday lunchtime.

Trzesniewski (01, Dorotheergasse 1) is open Monday to Friday from 8.30 am to 7.30 pm and on Saturday from 9 am to 1 pm. It's a basic deli bar where you stand in line to choose your food from the counter. Open sandwiches with a variety of toppings are about AS9 each; they're tiny (two bites and they're gone), but this is a famous Viennese institution and you may want to sample a few, if only to emulate Kafka (he was a regular here). Beer comes in equally tiny *Pfiff* (0.125L) measures.

At *Rosenberger Markt Restaurant (01, Maysedergasse 2)* the downstairs buffet

offers a fine array of meats, drinks and desserts to enable you to create a meal for around AS100. If you really want to save Schillings, concentrate on the salad or vegetable buffet: people unashamedly pile a Stephansdom-shaped food tower on small plates (AS29) for a filling feast. It is open daily from 11 am to 11 pm, and has free lockers for your bags.

Restaurant Marché Movenpick (Kärntner Ring 5-7), in the Ringstrassen Galerien shopping complex, is almost the same as Rosenberger except the small salad or vegetable bowls are only AS26. Another good offer is the pizza for AS57, available most days; you can help yourself to a variety of toppings. It's open Monday to Saturday from 9 am to 11 pm, and on Sunday and holidays from 11 am to 11 pm.

Akakiko (01, Singerstrasse 4) serves sushi starting at AS20 per piece, or complete lunchboxes from AS88; it's open daily from 10.30 am to 10.30 pm.

Pizza Bizi (01, Rotenturmstrasse 4) is a convenient self-service place open daily from 11 am to 11.30 pm. Pasta with a choice of sauces costs AS65, pizzas are from AS60 to AS75 (or AS28 for a slice) and there are salad and vegetable buffets. There's a takeaway version on Franz Josefs Kai.

Brezel Gwölb (01, Ledererhof 9) offers Austrian food costing from AS80 to AS175 in a cobbled courtyard or an atmospheric, cellar-like interior. It's open daily from 11.30 am to 1 am.

China Restaurant Turandot (01, Vorlaufstrasse 2) is open daily. Three-course weekday lunch specials cost AS68, and there's an all-you-can-eat lunch buffet for AS79 (AS129 on weekends and weekday evenings). Weekday Chinese lunches start at only AS57 in *Restaurant Siam (01, Rotenturmstrasse 11)*.

Naschmarkt (01, Schottengasse 1 and 01, Schwarzenbergplatz 16) offers a good choice of buffet-style meals, including a three course lunch menu for AS67 (AS77 at weekends); it's open daily. An unconnected place at the corner of Ebendorferstrasse and Felderstrasse, also called *Naschmarkt*, has two parts. The self-service section has set menus for AS54 and AS59 and is open on weekdays from 11 am to 2 pm. The cosier *Stüberl* (small room), with outside tables, is open on weekdays from 6.30 am to 2.30 pm and serves similar food, plus breakfasts.

Restaurant Smutny (01, Elisabethstrasse 8) serves typical Viennese food in a room with wall tiles and colourful lightshades. Dishes are filling and reasonably priced (from AS80) and it's open daily from 10 am to midnight.

The North-West There are many cheap places to eat to the north and west of the university. The *Afro-Asiatisches Institut (AAI) (09, Türkenstrasse 3)* has a Mensa serving meals costing about AS45, and there's courtyard eating in the summer. It's open on weekdays from 11.30 am to 7 pm (1.30 pm from July to September). The café on the 1st floor is open daily and has copies of *Newsweek*.

Tunnel (☎ 405 34 65; 08, Florianigasse 39) is another student haunt, open daily from 9 am to 2 am. The food is satisfying and easy on the pocket. Breakfast costs AS29, lunch specials are AS45, spaghetti starts at AS38, big pizzas cost from AS60 and salads from AS20. Bottled beer starts at AS25 for 0.5L. Tunnel also has a cellar bar with live music (see the Entertainment section later in this chapter).

Vegi Rant (☎ 425 06 54; 09, Währinger Strasse 57) offers a three course daily vegetarian menu costing AS102, as well as dishes such as cheese schnitzel for AS79; it's open from 11.30 am to 2.30 pm Sunday to Friday. Next door is a health food shop.

Laudon Stüberl (08, Laudongasse 16) is open on weekdays from 9 am to 6 pm. Lunch menus (served till 3 pm) cost AS50 or AS58. A block east on Laudongasse is *Beislbar Geralala*, where similarly priced food is available till the early hours.

The South-West There are many *Würstel stands* in this area, but it's worth wandering down to the Ringstrasse end of Mariahilfer Strasse to choose between two cheap, adja-

cent ones engaged in cut-throat competition. The sign on one proclaims *mein Kunde ist König* (my customer is king); the other counters with *mein Kunde ist Kaiser* (my customer is emperor). The nearby Naschmarkt has plenty of places to eat, many on a Turkish theme; filling kebabs costing around AS35 are a popular for lunch.

The *Technical University Mensa (04, Resselgasse 7-9)* serves good weekday lunches (from 11 am to 2.30 pm) from only AS30 to AS55, with several choices. Once in the building, find the yellow area and go upstairs to the 1st floor. There are two *Schnitzelhaus* branches, one at 06, Otto Bauer Gasse 24, the other at 05, Kettenbrückengasse 19.

Schnitzelwirt Schmidt (☎ 523 37 71; 07, Neubaugasse 52) prides itself on its enormous schnitzel portions (from AS64). This informal, often hectic place is something of an institution among travellers; you really have to visit to see the size of these things. It offers many variations on the basic schnitzel: one can feed two people (they're used to supplying two plates!) or leftovers can be wrapped to take away. Extra garnishes cost around AS22 each. Opening hours are Monday to Friday from 10 am to 10 pm and Saturday from 10 am to 2.30 pm and 5 to 10 pm.

Gaunkerl (07, Kaiserstrasse 50) serves meals starting at about AS65; it's closed on Sunday. The décor in the front room creates the illusion that you're sitting outside, complete with glowing stars and witches on broomsticks flying overhead. The illusion becomes more convincing after a couple of beers. Around the corner is *Burg-Keller (07, Burggasse 115)*, a quiet, relaxing place with tasty Austrian cooking costing from AS65 to AS150. Weekday lunch specials are excellent value – three courses from about AS60. It's open daily from 10 am to midnight and has menus in English.

Amerlingbeisl (07, Stiftgasse 8) attracts mainly young people, both as an eating and a drinking venue; in summer people flock into the rear courtyard. Food costs from AS58 to AS115 and beer is AS36 a *Krügerl*

(0.5L glass). It's open daily from 9 am to 2 am. It's in the Spittelberg quarter, a historic area with restored Biedermeier houses, various interesting shops and bars, and plenty of tempting restaurants to seek out.

K & K Bierkanzlei (06, *Windmühlgasse 20*) is small, cheap and typically Viennese. Filling and straightforward daily menus cost from AS59. Opening hours are 8 am to 6 pm. There are many images of Franz Josef and Elisabeth – their faces even appear on the salt and pepper pots. *Pulkautaler Weinhaus (15, Felberstrasse 2)*, near Westbahnhof, is a simple place serving good food for between AS40 and AS115. There's a bar area with several different beers to try (about AS32 a Krügerl), and it's open daily from 9 am to 10 pm. It has English menus.

Schutzhaus am Ameisbach (14, Braillegasse 1), in the western suburbs, is great value, and has many tables in a large garden, plus a play area for kids. A popular choice is spare ribs: the full serving for AS140, including sauces and baked potato, will feed two (a half portion is AS80). Take bus No 51A from Hietzing to Braillegasse. It's open from 9 am (3 pm on Tuesday) to midnight (11 pm on Sunday); the kitchen closes at 9.30 pm (9 pm on Sunday). It's closed on Monday and in February.

The South There are several inexpensive places to eat on Wiedner Gürtel opposite Südbahnhof. These include a branch of *Wienerwald* for chicken dishes (open 8 am to 12.30 am daily) and *China Restaurant Phoenix*, where weekday lunch menus cost AS56. A few doors down at No 4 is *Kristall*, open daily from 7 am to 4 am. Meals start at about AS60 (English menu); the food is surprisingly good for the price and there's plenty of it.

The East Wien Mitte station has several places for cheap and quick eating, including an *Interspar* supermarket which has a self-service restaurant upstairs (meals AS50 to AS90; closes at 7 pm on weekdays and 5 pm on Saturday).

For Indian food, try *Zum Inder (02, Praterstrasse 57)* which is open daily. Weekday lunches start at just AS50.

Middle & Top-End Restaurants

Innere Stadt *La Crêperie* (☎ 512 56 87; 01, Grünangergasse 10) has various rooms with diverse and creative décor, ranging from arty odds and ends and ancient books to an imitation circus tent complete with clowns' faces. There's also outside seating during summer. It's open daily from 11.30 am to midnight. Meat and fish dishes cost from AS145 to AS245, beer is AS40 a Krügerl and wine is AS24 for 0.125L. If you stick to its speciality, crêpes, a light meal can be inexpensive. These are available with sweet or savoury fillings; the Florentine (AS98) is a good combination of spinach, ham, cheese and egg with a dollop of sour cream.

Zu den Drei Hacken (☎ 512 58 95; 01, Singerstrasse 28) is a down-to-earth place with outside tables and a small room devoted to Schubert (despite the anachronistic WWII radio). It serves typical Austrian food from around AS90 to AS220, and is open Monday to Saturday from 9 am to midnight.

Wrenkh (☎ 533 15 26; 01, Bauernmarkt 10) is a fairly upmarket vegetarian place, open until midnight daily except Sunday. Meticulously prepared dishes cost from AS88 to AS125, and a three course menu is AS175. It has a bar next door serving the same meals, and a simpler *Gasthaus (☎ 892 33 56; 15, Hollergasse 9)*.

Zum Weissen Rauchfangkehrer (☎ 512 34 71; 01, Weihburggasse 4) is open daily and provides a complete contrast, with many hunting trophies on the wall and partitioned booths. Meat specialities cost between AS100 and AS230 (plus a AS30 cover charge). There's live piano music nightly from 7 pm.

Griechenbeisl (☎ 533 19 77; 01, Fleischmarkt 11) is a famous old tavern once frequented by the likes of Beethoven, Schubert and Brahms. Choose from the many different vaulted rooms displaying hanging antlers, or sit in the plant-fringed front garden. Viennese main dishes cost from AS165 to AS230 and it's open daily from 11 am to 1 am.

Grotta Azzurra (☎ *586 10 44-0; 01, Babenburgerstrasse 5)* is open daily and does good Italian food, with most dishes costing over AS160 (plus AS35 cover charge). Try the popular antipasti buffet.

Wiener Rathauskeller (☎ *405 12 19; 01, Rathausplatz 1)* is in the Rathaus – the entrance is in the north-eastern corner. Enjoy the atmosphere in the arcaded *Rittersaal* (Knights' Hall) where the walls are covered with murals and floral designs; live harp music (after 7 pm; AS15 extra) adds to the ambience. Down the corridor, *Grinzinger Keller* is similar if barer; from 1 April to 31 October, Tuesday to Saturday, it puts on a dinner show for AS395, comprising music, waltzing and a three course meal. Otherwise, the same Viennese and international dishes (mostly above AS145) are offered in both halls (open 11.30 am to 3 pm and 6 to 11.30 pm, closed Sunday).

The busy *DO & CO* (☎ *535 39 69; 01, Stephansplatz 12)* in Haas Haus serves good food to match the good view. Superb international and oriental dishes cost around AS200. It is open daily from noon to 3 pm and 6 pm to midnight, and there's also a café-bar (open from 9 am to 2 am); book well ahead. DO & CO also has a restaurant (☎ 811 18) in Schloss Schönbrunn.

Zum Kuckuck (☎ *512 84 70; 01, Himmelpfortgasse 15)* is a tiny place with a vaulted ceiling. Viennese dishes cost from AS200; there are multi-course gourmet menus. The kitchen is open Monday to Friday from noon to 2 pm and 6 to 11 pm.

For Japanese food, try *Yugetsu Saryo* (☎ *512 27 20; 01, Führichgasse 10)*. On the ground floor is a sushi bar, and upstairs they'll cook the food in front of you on a large hotplate built into the table. Lunch menus start at AS120 but otherwise expect to pay over AS200 per person, plus drinks. Evening set menus start at AS320. The kitchen is open from noon to 2.30 pm and 6 pm to 11 pm (daily except Sunday).

Korso (☎ *515 16-546; 01, Mahlerstrasse 2)* features wood-panelled elegance and opulent chandeliers. Viennese and international specialities cost from AS290 to AS420 and there's a vast wine cellar. Its proximity to the opera prompts it to offer a light three course meal (AS630) for those who are replete with culture but depleted of cuisine. Opening hours are from noon to 3 pm and 7 pm to 1 am, though it's closed at lunchtime on Saturday, and on Sunday in July and August.

Drei Husaren (☎ *512 10 92-0; 01, Weihburggasse 4)* is in the same price range and is similarly formal and elegant, with soothing live piano music to aid digestion. There's a huge selection of excellent hors d'oeuvres, which are priced according to season and selection. This traditional Viennese restaurant is open daily from noon to 3 pm and 6 pm to midnight.

The North-West For Thai food, try *Thai Haus* (☎ *405 71 56; 17, Hernalser Hauptstrasse 21)*. Main courses cost from AS88 to AS195, plus AS18 to AS40 for garnishes like rice and noodles. All dishes can be mild or mouth-burning. It's open daily except Tuesday from 6 pm to midnight.

Fromme Helene (☎ *406 91 44; 08, Josefstädter Strasse 53)* is a small place with a cluttered salon look and good Viennese food. Midday dining is not too expensive (menus from AS75 with soup) though evening dishes cost over AS155. It's open on weekdays from 11 am to 2.30 pm and 6 pm to midnight, and on Saturday from 6 pm to midnight.

Restaurant Sailer (☎ *479 21 21-0; 18, Gersthofer Strasse 14)* serves traditional Viennese dishes for around AS180, but with refined touches. The quality and service are exceptional for the price. There's a garden, and a cellar area serving snacks, perhaps to musical accompaniment. It's open daily, as is *Casa Culinaria* (☎ *328 70 30; 19, Sieveringer Strasse 4)*, which is worth trying for upmarket Italian food.

Feuervogel (☎ *317 53 91; 09, Alserbachstrasse 21)* is a Russian restaurant that has been run by the same family of Ukrainians for over 75 years. The colourful décor matches the conversational gambits (in English) of the surviving generations. The food, costing from AS150 to AS635, is hearty rather than refined, but tasty nonetheless, and there's sometimes live music at the weekend. It's open from 6 pm to 2 am, but closed on Sunday and between mid-July and mid-August.

The South-West *Ungar-Grill (☎ 523 62 09; 07, Burggasse 97)* is a Hungarian restaurant with a patio area and live gypsy music every night. Fish, chicken, grills and other dishes cost between AS85 and AS180, and there's an AS11 cover charge. Opening hours are Monday to Saturday from 6 pm to midnight. Reserve ahead as it's popular with tour groups.

Glacisbeisl can be found in the middle of the Museumsquartier – it feels miles away from the city centre. Ascend the path to garden tables surrounded by trees, a trellis and vines. Vegetarian and traditional Austrian food are in the AS90 to AS225 range and it's open daily from 10 am to midnight.

Beim Novak (☎ 523 32 44; 07, Richtergasse 12) has traditional Austrian food (AS85 to AS255), a detailed English menu and attentive service. Speciality of the house is *Überbackene Fledermaus* (bat au gratin) for AS160. The 'bat wings' are actually cuts of beef. It's closed on Saturday evening, on Sunday, and from mid-July to mid-August.

The Hotel *Altwienerhof* (see Places to Stay earlier in this chapter) has an elegant restaurant serving quality French and international cuisine for around AS300. There's a huge wine cellar.

The South The *Vier Jahreszeiten Restaurant (☎ 711 22 140)*, in the Hotel Inter-Continental, is highly rated for gourmet food and also serves standard Viennese fare. The sumptuous lunch buffet costs AS490 and à la carte dishes cost from AS195 to AS325; a pianist plays in the evening. The restaurant closes at weekends.

The East *Schweizerhaus (02, Strasse des Ersten Mai 116)*, in the Prater, is famous for its roasted pork hocks (*Hintere Schweinsstelze*). A meal consists of a massive chunk of meat on the bone (about 750g minimum at AS182 per kilogram – eat alone and end up the size of two people), best served with mustard (AS5) and freshly grated horseradish (AS10). Chomping your way through vast slabs of pig smacks of medieval banqueting; it's certainly very tasty when washed down with draught Czech Budweiser. There are many outside tables but it gets incredibly busy. It's open daily from 10 am to 11 pm, mid-March to 31 October only. *Café-Restaurant Luftberg*, nearby on Walsteingarten Strasse, offers a similar meat feast.

Vegetarians will have better luck in the Prater at *Estancia Cruz (Hauptallee 08)*, a large place with many outside tables in a shady garden. Latin American food costs from AS76 to AS152, including many vegetarian choices. It's open daily from 11 am to 1 am.

Steirereck (☎ 713 31 68; 08, Rasumofskygasse 2) is gourmet territory; in fact, it's rated one of the best restaurants in Austria. Different parts of the restaurant have a different ambience, but it's pretty formal throughout – even the toilets are stylish! Tempting main courses all cost over AS300 (choose from delicacies such as lobster, rabbit, pigeon or venison) yet you still have to book days in advance for the evening. The three course lunch menu costs AS395; the multi-course evening menu is AS880, or AS1430 including wine. It's open from Monday to Friday.

Self-Catering

There are **supermarkets** scattered around the city. Outside normal shopping hours you can stock up with groceries at the main train stations, though prices are considerably higher (except in the Billa stores). **Westbahnhof** has a large shop (selling alcohol as well as food) in the main hall open daily from 6 am to 10.50 pm. The shops in **Südbahnhof** are only tiny kiosks, but they're open daily until late. Franz Josefs Bahnhof has a *Billa* supermarket open every day from 7 am to 7.30 pm. Wien Nord Bahnhof has a *Billa* with late opening (till 8 pm) on Friday, and several small provision shops open daily from 5.30 am to 9 pm. Wien Mitte has a large *Interspar* supermarket (open standard hours) and a reasonably sized store open daily from 5.30 am to 9.50 pm. The *Billa* supermarket in the airport is open daily from 7.30 am to 10 pm.

See the Shopping section in this chapter for information on markets.

Coffee Houses

The coffee house is an integral part of Viennese life. The story goes that the tradition started in the 17th century after retreating Turkish invaders left behind their supplies of coffee beans.

Small/large coffees cost about AS24/38. Although that's expensive, the custom is to take your time. Linger as long as you like and enjoy the atmosphere or read the café's newspapers – some places stock British and other foreign titles (saving you the AS30 it would cost to buy them). Traditional places will serve a glass of water with your coffee (see also the boxed text 'Coffee Treats' in the Facts for the Visitor chapter).

Coffee houses basically fall into two types, though the distinction is rather blurred nowadays. A *Kaffeehaus*, traditionally preferred by men, offers games such as chess and billiards, and serves wine, beer, spirits and light meals as well as coffee. The *Café Konditorei* attracts more women and typically has a salon look with rococo mouldings and painted glass. A variety of cakes and pastries is usually on offer.

Café Museum (01, Friedrichstrasse 6) is open daily from 8 am to midnight and has chess, newspapers and outside tables. The building was created by Adolf Loos in 1899 but has since been extensively renovated.

Café Bräunerhof (01, Stallburggasse 2) has British newspapers and free classical music on weekends and holidays from 3 to 6 pm. It's open on weekdays till 7.30 pm (8.30 pm in winter) and weekends till 6 pm.

Café Central (01, Herrengasse 14) has a fine ceiling and pillars, and piano music from 4 to 7 pm. Trotsky came here to play chess. Note the plaster patron near the door with the walrus moustache – a model of the poet Peter Altenberg. Opening hours are Monday to Saturday from 8 am to 10 pm.

Café Hawelka (01, Dorotheergasse 6) is another famous coffee house. At first glance it's hard to see what the attraction is: scruffy pictures and posters, brown-stained walls, smoky air, cramped tables. Then you see why – it's the people not the place; an ideal location for people-watching. The whole gamut of Viennese society comes here, from students to celebrities. It's also a traditional haunt for artists and writers. After 10 pm it gets really busy. You're constantly being shunted up to accommodate new arrivals at the table, the elderly organising Frau seizing on any momentarily vacant chair to reallocate it elsewhere – curtail those toilet visits! Café Hawelka is open from 8 am (4 pm on Sunday and holidays) to 2 am and it's closed on Tuesday.

Alt Wien (01, Bäckerstrasse 9) is a rather dark coffee house, with students and arty types. At night it becomes a lively drinking venue; beer is AS34 a Krügerl. Also known for its goulash (AS55/80 small/large), it's open daily from 10 am to 2 am.

After a hard night drinking or dancing, greet the dawn at *Café Drechsler (06, Linke Wienzeile 22)* where you'll rub shoulders with traders at the Naschmarkt. Opening hours are 3 am to 8 pm (6 pm on Saturday; closed on Sunday). There are billiard tables, and meals cost from AS55 to AS75.

The *Hotel Sacher Café (01, Philharmonikerstrasse 4)*, behind the Staatsoper, is a picture of opulence with chandeliers, battalions of waiters and rich, red walls and carpets. It's open from 6.30 am to 11.30 pm daily and is famous for its chocolate apricot cake, *Sacher Torte* (AS50 a slice). Its main rival in terms of torte is the elegant, equally expensive, mirrored environment of *Demel (01, Kohlmarkt 14)*. It's the archetypal Konditorei establishment, open daily from 10 am to 7 pm.

VIENNA

Hitler's Vienna

Born in Braunau am Inn, Upper Austria, in 1899, Adolf Hitler moved to Vienna when he was just 17. Six unsettled, unsuccessful, poverty-stricken years later he abandoned the city to make a name for himself in Germany. He later wrote in *Mein Kampf* that his Vienna years were 'a time of the greatest transformation which I have ever been through. From a weak citizen of the world I became a fanatical anti-Semite'. Hitler briefly returned to Vienna in 1938 at the head of the German army, to be greeted by enthusiastic crowds.

Although Vienna would be happy for the world to forget its association with Hitler, an increasing number of tourists are retracing the Vienna footsteps of the infamous fascist. He spent several years living in a small, dimly lit apartment at Stumpergasse 31, in the 6th district. It's a private block, but frequent visits by curious tourists have prompted plans to turn the apartment into a museum.

Hitler was a regular visitor to the opera and, despite his penury, preferred to pay extra to stand in sections that were barred to women. Café Sperl (see the Coffee Houses section in this chapter) is another address on the Hitler itinerary: here he would noisily express his views on race and other matters. Among his gripes was probably the fact that the nearby Akademie der bildenden Künste (Academy of Fine Arts) twice rejected an application by the would-be artist, dismissing his work as 'inadequate'. Although convinced that proper training would have made him into a very successful artist, these rejections made Hitler speculate to a friend that perhaps fate may have reserved for him 'some other purpose'.

Café Schwarzenberg (01, Kärntner Ring 17) has live piano music from Tuesday to Friday between 8 and 10 pm, and at weekends from 4 to 7 pm and 8 to 10 pm. It has outside tables and English newspapers, as does *Café Restaurant Landtmann (01, Dr Karl Lueger Ring 4)*. There's also Hitler's former haunt, *Café Sperl (06, Gumpendorfer Strasse 11)*, with the *Times* newspaper and billiard tables.

Heurigen

Heurigen (wine taverns) can be identified by a green wreath or branch (*Busch'n*) hanging over the door. Many have outside tables in large gardens or courtyards. Inside, they're fairly rustic and have an ambience all their own. Heurigen almost invariably serve food, which you select from hot and cold buffet counters; prices are generally reasonable. It's acceptable to bring your own food but this rarely happens nowadays.

Heurigen usually have a relaxed atmosphere which gets livelier as the mugs of wine – and customers – get drunk. Many feature traditional live music, perhaps ranging from a solo accordion player to a fully fledged oompah band; these can be a bit touristy but great fun nonetheless. The Viennese tend to prefer a music-free environment. Opening times are approximately 4 pm (before lunch on weekends) to 11 pm or midnight. In the less touristy regions some may close for several weeks at a time before reopening, and some are only open in the summer or from Thursday to Sunday.

The common measure for Heuriger wine is a *Viertel* (0.25L) in a glass mug, costing between AS25 and AS30, but you can also drink by the *Achterl* (0.125L). A Viertel Gespritzer costs between AS16 and AS20.

Heurigen are concentrated in the wine-growing suburbs to the north, south, west, and north-west of the city. Once you pick a region to explore, the best approach is to simply go where the spirit moves you (or to whichever places happen to be open at the time); taverns are very close together and it would be easy to visit several on the same evening.

City Heurigen *Esterházykeller (01, Haarhof 1, off Naglergasse)* is a busy wine cellar with cheap wine from AS23 for 0.25L. Meals and snacks are available and it's open daily from 11 am (4 pm weekends and holidays) to 11 pm.

St Urbani-Keller (☎ 533 91 02; 01, Am Hof 12) is expensive (AS38 a Viertel), though it does have live accordion music. It's open daily from 6 pm to midnight.

North-West This is the most well known region. The area most favoured by tourists is Grinzing (count the tour buses lined up outside at closing time), and this is probably the best area if you want live music and a lively atmosphere. However, bear in mind that this area is mostly eschewed as a tourist ghetto by Viennese. There are several good Heurigen in a row along Cobenzlgasse and Sandgasse, near the terminal of tram 38 (which starts at Schottentor on the Ring). *Reinprecht (19, Cobenzlgasse 22)* is a very large, lively, sing-along place.

From Grinzing, you can hop on the 38A bus to Heiligenstadt, where in 1817 Beethoven lived in the *Beethovenhaus (19, Pfarrplatz 3)*. This has a big hall with live music and many annexes. From Heiligenstadt it's just a few stops on tram D to Nussdorf, where a couple of Heurigen await right by the tram terminal. But don't just settle for these without exploring first; there are several others worth visiting along Kahlenberger Strasse.

Farther west are the areas of Sievering (terminal of bus No 39A) and Neustift am Walde (bus 35A). Both these buses link up with the No 38 tram route. Ottakring is a small but authentic Heurigen area a short walk west of the tram J terminal.

North The Heurigen here in the 21st district are less visited by tourists and are therefore more typically Viennese, catering to a regular clientele. They are also cheaper: a Viertel costs around AS22. Live music is not the norm. Stammersdorf (terminal of tram No 31) is Vienna's largest wine-growing district, producing about 30% of its wine. From the tram stop, walk north to Stammersdorfer Strasse, the next street running east-west. The western end of this street has many Heurigen. Two good ones are *Weinhof Wieninger* at No 78 and *Weingut Klager* at No 14.

Strebersdorf is at the terminal of tram No 32, or about a 30 minute walk west of Stammersdorf. The Heurigen are north of the tram terminal. *Weingut Schilling (21, Langenzersdorferstrasse 54)* has a good reputation for wine. It's closed during alternate months (January, March, and so on), when *Strauch* next door at No 50A is open. Another place is *Noschiel-Eckert (☎ 292 25 96; 21, Strebersdorfer Strasse 158)*.

South As in the north, tourists are less prevalent in the Heurigen in these districts. Mauer is in the south-west, at the edge of the Wienerwald. Take the U4 to Hietzing and then tram No 60 to Mauer Hauptplatz. Oberlaa is farther east. To get there, take the U1 to Reumannplatz, bus 66A or 67A to Wienerfeld, and then transfer to bus 17A. This runs along Oberlaaer Strasse where there are several Heurigen.

ENTERTAINMENT

The tourist office produces a monthly listing of concerts and other events; see also its *Vienna Scene* magazine. Publications worth referring to are the weekly magazines *City* (AS10) and *Falter* (AS28), as well as the Thursday edition of the *Neue Kronen*

Drink & Be Merry

The *Heuriger* (wine tavern) tradition in Vienna dates back to the Middle Ages, but in 1784 it was Joseph II who first officially granted producers the right to sell their wine directly from their own premises. It proved to be one of his more enduring reforms. These taverns are now one of Vienna's most popular institutions with visitors. The term Heuriger refers not only to the tavern itself but also to the year's new vintage, which officially comes of age on St Martin's Day (11 November). It continues to be Heuriger wine up to its first anniversary, at which time it is promoted (relegated?) to the status of *Alte* (old) wine. St Martin's Day is a day of much drinking and consumption of goose.

A *Buschenschank* is a type of Heuriger within the Vienna region that may only open for 300 days a year. It can only sell its own wine, either new or old, and must close when supplies have dried up. The term Buschenschank is protected. Not so Heuriger: taverns can use the term to describe themselves even if they buy in stocks from outside; in fact some don't even produce their own wine. Similar wine taverns are found in other wine-producing provinces, especially Lower Austria, Burgenland and Styria.

Austrian wine production is 80% white and 20% red. The most common variety (36%) is the dry white Grüner Veltliner; it also tends to be the cheapest on the wine list. Other common varieties are Riesling and Pinot Blanc. Sekt is a sparkling wine. Some of the young wines can be a little sharp, so it is common to mix them with 50% soda water, called a *Gespritzer* or *G'spritzer*. The correct salute when drinking a Heuriger wine is *Prost* (cheers). But Austrians can't wait for 11 November to drink the new vintage, and are prepared to consume it early, as unfermented must (*Most*), partially fermented (*Sturm*), or fully fermented but still cloudy (*Staubiger*); they taste a little like cider. The correct salute when drinking these versions is *Gesundheit* (health), perhaps in recognition of the risk taken by the palate.

Zeitung newspaper (AS8). Blue Danube Radio produces *What's on in Vienna*, broadcast in English daily at 1 pm.

Apart from bars and clubs, classical music still dominates Vienna. The programme of music events is never-ending, and as a visitor in the centre you'll continually be accosted by people in Mozart-era costume trying to sell you tickets for concerts or ballets. Even some of the buskers playing along Kärntner Strasse and Graben are classical musicians.

Bars & Clubs

Vienna has plenty of places for a night out and, unlike some other European capital cities, you don't have to spend a lot of money in nightclubs to drink until late. Venues are by no means limited to the Innere Stadt – dozens of small bars and cafés in the 6th, 7th, 8th and 9th districts stay busy until well after midnight.

Innere Stadt The best known area for a night out is around Ruprechtsplatz, Seitenstettengasse, Rabensteig and Salzgries. This compact area has been dubbed the *Bermuda-Dreieck* (Bermuda Triangle) as drinkers can disappear into the numerous pubs and clubs and apparently be lost to the world. *Krah Krah (01, Rabensteig 8)* has 50 different brands of beer (from about AS37 for 0.5L) and is open daily until 1 or 2 am.

Porgy & Bess (☎ 512 84 38; 01, Spiegelgasse 2) is a good jazz club. It's open on weekdays from 8 pm to 2 am and at weekends from 8 pm to 4 am (closed in summer). Entry costs AS120 or more, except on the Wednesday 'session nights', which cost AS30. Another place is *Jazzland (☎ 533 25*

75; 01, Franz-Josefs-Kai 29); entry costs from AS150. *P1 (01, Rotgasse 9)* is a disco that attracts a rather younger set (open till 4 or 5 am; closed on Sunday).

The Volksgarten has three venues appealing to a variety of tastes. The *Volksgarten Nightclub* plays different music on successive nights starting at about 10 pm: check the weekly listings newspapers for details. Entry costs AS100 or more. There's a garden bar (drinks from AS55) and the dance-floor roof can be opened to reveal the night sky.

Right next door is the *Tanz Volksgarten* venue where serene and somewhat restrained couples glide waltz-style across the open-air dance floor to 'evergreen' classics. Dancing is nightly throughout the summer and entry costs about AS55 unless there's a live concert, when it costs about AS140. Participants in these diverse places can gaze in disbelief at each other's antics through the window.

The third Volksgarten venue is the *Pavillon Café*, open daily from 11 am to 2 am. It has garden tables, a DJ and food. Beer costs AS39 for 0.5L. Entry is free except if you're going to one of the occasional 'unplugged' concerts or garden barbecues. It's closed from 1 October to 30 April.

Irish bars are currently trendy in Vienna. One of the best is *Molly Darcy's Irish Pub (01, Teinfaltstrasse 6)*, open daily from 11 am to 2 am (1 am on Sunday).

Other Districts *Tunnel* (see Places to Eat) has a cellar bar with live music nightly from 9 pm. Weekday entry costs from AS30; it's AS100 on weekends, but there are discounts for students. On Monday there's generally a free 'Jazzsession'.

Chelsea (08, Lechenfelder Gürtel 29-31) is open daily from 4 or 6 pm to 4 am. A DJ spins loud sounds (usually indie, sometimes house) and live bands play weekly, when there may be an entry charge. There's also English football via satellite.

Andino (☎ 587 61 25; 06, Münzwardeingasse 2) is a Latin American bar and restaurant with lively murals and meals for

under AS100, open daily from 6 pm to 2 am. Upstairs it has a venue where there's live music or theme parties, usually on Friday and Saturday; tickets cost from AS60 to AS140 (less if bought in advance).

Camera Club (07, Neubaugasse) by Mariahilfer Strasse, is a relaxed bar and disco featuring music (reggae to rock; no house/techno) and rock videos. It's open nightly from 9 pm to 4 am and there's a modest cover charge.

BACH (☎ 450 19 70; 16, Bachgasse 21) has different events depending upon the night, with live music (usually 'alternative' bands; entry from AS70 to AS150) and discos (anything from rave to 60s). Drink prices are reasonable and it's open from 8 pm until 2 or 4 am.

WUK (☎ 401 21; 09, Währinger Strasse 59) is an interesting venue offering a variety of events, including alternative bands, classical music, dance, theatre, children's events, political discussions and practical-skills workshops. It is subsidised by the government but pursues an independent course. Prices are not high; some events are even free. There's also a Beisl in the cobbled courtyard, open daily till 2 am.

Arena (☎ 798 85 95; 03, Baumgasse 80) is another good venue, centred in a former slaughterhouse. From May to September, headline rock, soul and reggae bands play on the outdoor stage (entry from AS250 to AS350), though in August this space becomes an outdoor cinema instead. All year, smaller bands play in one of two indoor halls (entry from AS100), and there's sometimes theatre, dance and discussions. Keep an ear open for the monthly all-night parties (about AS80) featuring techno or other music.

One of the best clubs in Vienna is *U4 (☎ 815 83 07; 12, Schönbrunner Strasse 222)*, open nightly, usually from 10 pm to 4 or 5 am. Drink prices aren't too bad, and there are two rooms and a slide show. Each night has a different style of music and attracts a different clientele. Friday (80s and 90s music; AS100) is a popular night. The Sunday 'Speak Easy' (AS50) revives 60s and 70s music; Thursday is gay night (AS70). Occasionally there are live bands.

Gay & Lesbian Venues

Some places popular with gays and lesbians are: *Café Berg (09, Berggasse 8)*, open daily from 10 am to 1 am; *Café Savoy (06, Linke Wienzeile 36)*, open on weekdays from 5 pm to 2 am and on Saturday from 9 am to 6 pm and 9 pm to 2 am; *Why Not? (01, Tiefer Graben 22)*, a bar/disco open on Friday and Saturday from 11 pm to 5 am, and on Sunday for cabaret and drag queens; and the *Eagle Bar (06, Blümelgasse 1)*, a men's bar with a mostly leather-clad crowd.

Opera

Productions in the *Staatsoper* are lavish affairs and shouldn't be missed. Seats cost anything from AS50 (restricted view) to AS2300. AS30 *Stehplatz* (standing-room) tickets put you in a good position at the back of the stalls, whereas those costing AS20 leave you high up at the rear of the gallery. The Viennese take their opera very seriously and dress up accordingly. Wander around the foyer and the refreshment rooms in the interval to fully appreciate the gold and crystal interior. There are no opera performances in July and August, but the venue may be used for other events.

The other main venue for opera is the *Volksoper (09, Währinger Strasse 78)*, close to the Gürtel and the U6 line. Operettas and musicals are included in its repertoire.

Cinemas

Entry prices start at AS70; Monday is known as *Kinomontag*, when all cinema seats cost AS70. A number of cinemas show films in the original language. The *Österreichische Filmmuseum (☎ 533 70 54-0; 01, Augustinerstrasse 1)* requires annual membership (AS180) and is closed from 1 July to 30 September. *Burg Kino (☎ 587 84 06; 01, Opernring 19)* has regular screenings of *The Third Man*. *Audimax HTU (☎ 588 01-5897; 06, Getreidemarkt 9)* is a lecture theatre in the Technical University and prices are lower than at conventional cinemas. There's a giant screen at *IMAX Filmtheater (☎ 894 01 01; 14, Mariahilfer Strasse 212)*.

Other cinemas include *De France (☎ 317 52 36; 01, Schottenring 5)*, *Filmcasino (☎ 587 90 62; 05, Margaretenstrasse 78)*, *Flotten Center (☎ 586 51 52; 06, Mariahilfer Strasse 85-87)* and *Top Kino (☎ 587 55 57; 06, Rahlgasse 1)*.

Classical Music

The Vienna Philharmonic Orchestra performs in the Grosser Saal (large hall) of the *Musikverein (☎ 505 81 90; 01, Bösendorferstrasse 12)*, which is said to have the best acoustics of any concert hall in Austria. The interior is appropriately lavish and can sometimes be visited on a guided tour. Standing-room tickets in the main hall cost AS50 but there are no student tickets. In the smaller Brahms Saal the cheapest tickets (AS60) have no view. The ticket office is open Monday to Friday from 9 am to 7.30 pm, and on Saturday from 9 am to 5 pm; it's closed during July and August.

Another major venue for classical and other music is the *Konzerthaus (☎ 712 12 11; 03, Lothringerstrasse 20)*, which has three separate halls. Student tickets (for those under 27 years with an ISIC card) are half-price. The Konzerthaus ticket office is open Monday to Friday from 9 am to 7.30 pm and on Saturday from 9 am to 1 pm. The Konzerthaus is closed during July and August except when it hosts Summer of Music events.

There are sometimes free concerts at the *Rathaus* or in one of the churches; check with the tourist office.

Vienna Boys' Choir Another famous institution, the Vienna Boys' Choir (Wiener Sängerknaben), is actually four separate choirs; duties are rotated between singing in Vienna, touring the world, resting, and perhaps even occasionally going to school. The choir was instigated in 1498 by Maximilian I and at one time numbered Haydn and Schubert in its ranks. The choir sings every Sunday (except during July and August) at 9.15 am in the *Burgkapelle* (Royal Chapel) in the Hofburg. Tickets for seats cost from AS60 (restricted view) to AS310 and must usually be booked weeks in advance. However, standing room is free. You should queue by 8.30 am to find a place inside, although you can get a flavour of what's going on from the TV in the foyer. Also interesting is the scrum afterwards when everybody struggles to photograph, and be photographed with, the serenely patient choir members.

The choir also sings a mixed programme of music in the *Konzerthaus* at 3.30 pm on Friday in May, June, September and October. Tickets cost from AS390 to AS430 and are available through *Reisebüro Mondial (☎ 588 04 141; 04, Faulmanngasse 4)*, quite near the Konzerthaus booking office.

Theatre

There are performances in English at the *English Theatre (☎ 402 82 84; 08, Josefsgasse 12)*, where tickets cost from AS180, and the smaller *International Theatre (☎ 319 62 72; 09, Porzellangasse 8)*, entrance on Müllnergasse, where entry costs AS220. At the latter, students (under 26) and seniors pay AS140. It closes for around five weeks at the beginning of August. There is a linked venue, *Fundus (09, Müllnergasse 6A)*.

Mime performances (generally avant-garde) are held at the *Serapionstheater im Odeon (☎ 214 55 62; 02, Taborstrasse 10)*.

If you can follow German, the best theatre to visit is the *Burgtheater (Dr Karl Lueger Ring)*, though there are plenty of other theatres, such as the nearby *Volkstheater (☎ 523 27 76)* to the north-west of the Museumsquartier. The *Theater an der Wien (☎ 588 30 265; 06, Linke Wienzeile 6)* usually puts on musicals (standing-room and student tickets are available).

Buying Opera/Theatre Tickets *Stehplatz* (standing-room) tickets costing from around AS20 go on sale 30 minutes before

performances at the *Staatsoper* and *Volksoper*, and one hour before the start of German-language productions in the *Burgtheater* and *Akademietheater*. Queue up at the venue concerned: for major productions you may have to allow two or three hours; for minor works, you can often get tickets with minimal queuing. There is a separate queue for same-day student tickets at these venues. They cost from AS50 for any seats left unsold, and are available to students under age 27 who can show university ID and an ISIC card. Buying cheap, restricted-view seats doesn't involve queuing.

The Bundestheaterkassen (☎ 514 44-2959; 01, Goethegasse 1) is the state ticket office. It doesn't charge commission and sells tickets for the four venues mentioned above. It closes in July until the last week in August. Tickets are available here in the month prior to the performance and credit cards are accepted (for September performances, apply in June); credit card bookings can also be made by telephone (☎ 513 15 13). For postal bookings at least three weeks in advance, apply to the Bundestheaterverband (☎ 514 44-2653, fax -2969) at the same address. You pay only after your reservations are confirmed.

Agents around town sell tickets for all sorts of venues, but beware of hefty commission rates (20 to 30%!). Wien Ticket (☎ 588 85) in the hut by the Oper is linked to the city government and charges negligible commission (0 to 6%; open from 10 am to 7 pm daily).

Spanische Reitschule

The Lipizzaner stallions which strut their stuff in the *Spanische Reitschule* (Spanish Riding School) are famous Viennese performers with a difference. The breed was imported from Spain by Maximilian II in 1562, and in 1580 a stud was established at Lipizza, now in Slovenia. They perform an equine ballet to a programme of classical music while the audience cranes to see from pillared balconies, and chandeliers shimmer above. Although they are born dark, the mature stallions are all snow-white and the riders wear traditional clothing. It's a long-established Viennese institution, truly reminiscent of the Habsburg era.

Performances are booked up months in advance: for tickets, write to the Spanische Reitschule, Michaelerplatz 1, A1010 Wien; fax 535 01 86; ticket agents charge an extra 20 to 30%. Otherwise, ask in the office about cancellations; cancelled tickets are sold around two hours before performances. You need to be pretty keen on horses to pay AS250 to AS900 for seats or AS200 for standing room, although a few of the tricks, such as seeing a stallion bounding along on only its hind legs like a demented kangaroo, do tend to stick in the mind.

Tickets to watch the horses train can be bought on the day (AS100) at gate No 2, Josefsplatz in the Hofburg. Training is from 10 am to noon, Tuesday to Saturday, mid-February to mid-December, except when they are on tour or in July and August when they go on their summer holidays (seriously!) to Lainzer Tiergarten. Queues are very long early in the day, but if you try at around 11 am most people have gone and you can get in fairly quickly – indicative of the fact that training is relatively dull except for isolated high points. On the half-hour you can sometimes see the stallions crossing between the school and the *Stallburg* (stables). For details of the Lipizzaner stud farm see the Piber & Köflach section of the Styria chapter.

Casino

Vienna's *casino* is opposite the tourist office in Kärntner Strasse. A dress code applies upstairs and jackets and ties can be hired at the counter. There's blackjack, roulette and other games from 3 pm to 3 am. Downstairs slot machines are open from 11 am to midnight (no dress code).

SPECTATOR SPORTS

As in any large city, plenty of sports are played. International and domestic soccer games are held at the Ernst Happel Stadion, 02, Meiereistrasse 7, in the Prater. The

Stadthalle (☎ 98 100), 15, Vogelweidplatz, hosts competitions ranging from an ATP tennis tournament (mid-October) to water polo. There is horse racing at Freudenau, 02, Rennbahnstrasse 65; call ☎ 728 95 31 for information. Also in the Prater, there are trotting races at Krieau.

Vienna's Spring Marathon is run (jogged, walked, abandoned – depending upon the fitness of the participants) in April or May. The route takes in Schönbrunn, the Ringstrasse and the Prater.

SHOPPING

Vienna is not a place for cheap shopping but does offer numerous elegant shops and quality products. Local specialities include porcelain, ceramics, wrought-iron work, handmade dolls and leather goods. *Shopping in Vienna* is a free guide, distributed in upmarket hotels.

Normal shopping hours are from 8 or 9 am to 6 pm on weekdays, and from 8 am to noon or 1 pm on Saturday, though some supermarkets and large stores stay open till 7.30 pm on weekdays and 5 pm on Saturday. *Bazar* and *Findegrube* are magazines available from pavement newsstands containing privately advertised items.

Shopping Centres

The main shopping streets in the Innere Stadt are the pedestrian-only thoroughfares of Kärntner Strasse, Graben and Kohlmarkt. Mainly upmarket and specialist shops are found here. Generally speaking, outside the Ring is where you'll find shops catering for those with shallower pockets. Mariahilfer Strasse is regarded as the best shopping street, particularly the stretch between the Ring and Westbahnhof, and has large department stores like Gerngross which aren't found in the central zone. Other prime shopping streets are Landstrasser Hauptstrasse, Favoritenstrasse and Alser Strasse.

The area near the church in Mexikoplatz is an interesting place to have a wander. It has many shops selling cheap electrical goods and watches, and is also known as a location for obtaining goods on the black

Interior designs by Franz Matsch and Gustav Klimt decorate Vienna's Burgtheater.

From March to August each year, storks return to the same nesting sites in Rust to rear their young.

JON DAVISON

AUSTRIAN NATIONAL TOURIST OFFICE, WIESENHOFER

Hundertwasser's idiosyncratic steeple, Bärnbach.

Decorative façade, Hauptplatz 18, Mariazell.

WWII memorial, one of the many thought-provoking pieces in the St Barbara Kirche, Bärnbach.

market. Various shady types may approach you on the pavement and offer foreign currency and other deals.

Niedermeyer has stores at various locations in the city; they're good places to look for hi-fi, radios, TVs, video and audio tapes, photographic equipment and computer hardware and software.

The Ringstrassen Galerien, along Kärntner Ring, is Vienna's most central covered shopping mall; there's also Lugner City, 15, Gablenzgasse, not far from the Gürtel. For major shopping expeditions, the Viennese head south of town to Shopping City Süd, marketed simply as SCS. It's said to be the biggest shopping centre in Europe, and is south of the city precincts at Vösendorf, near the junction of the A21 and A2. Take the free shuttle bus departing every 90 minutes during shopping hours from opposite the Staatsoper (near tram No 2 stop). Get a stamp in IKEA to get the return leg free. The Lokalbahn service to Baden, departing from opposite Hotel Bristol in Opernring, stops at SCS (every 15 minutes; fare AS34, or AS17 for those with a city travel card).

Markets

The biggest and best known market is the Naschmarkt, 06, Linke Wienzeile. It's a 'farmer's market', mainly consisting of meat, fruit and vegetable stalls, but there are some clothes and curios. Prices are said to get lower the farther from the Ring end you go. Opening times are Monday to Friday from 6 am to 6 pm, and Saturday from 6 am to 5 pm. The Naschmarkt is also a good place to eat cheaply in snack bars.

On Saturday a flea market (*Flohmarkt*) is tacked onto the south-western end, extending for several blocks. It's very atmospheric and shouldn't be missed, with goods piled up in apparent chaos on the walkway. You can find anything you want (and everything you don't want): books, clothes, records, ancient electrical goods, old postcards, ornaments, carpets ... you name it. I even saw a blow-up doll (second-hand, of course). Bargain for prices here.

There are also food markets to be found at 16, Brunnengasse between Thaliastrasse and Gaullachergasse, and also around the intersection of Landstrasser Hauptstrasse and Salmgasse.

Souvenirs & Crafts

There are various souvenir shops in the arcade which connects the old and new Hofburgs. These shops sell artefacts such as mugs, steins, dolls, petit point embroidery, porcelain Lipizzaner stallions and so on. Pawalata, 01, Kärntner Strasse 14, has lower prices than most souvenir shops, and also stocks lots of distinctive tableware from Gmunden.

The Augarten Porcelain Factory (☎ 512 14 94), 01, Stock im Eisen Platz and 06, Mariahilfer Strasse 99, produces a variety of gifts and ornaments, including Lipizzaners. Albin Denk, 01, Graben 13A, is a specialist outlet for porcelain and crystal.

Österreichische Werkstätten (☎ 512 24 18), a co-operative at 01, Kärntner Strasse 6 sells jewellery, handicrafts and ornaments in eye-catching designs. J & L Lobmeyer, at No 26, is well known for glassware, and has a small museum.

Art & Antiques

Selling works of art is big business; it's worthwhile having a look at the auctions in the state-owned Dorotheum (☎ 515 60), 01, Dorotheergasse 17. It was founded in 1707 by Joseph I and it's interesting to watch the proceedings even if you don't intend to buy anything. Lots can be inspected in advance and have the opening prices marked. If you do want to buy but haven't got the confidence to bid you can commission an agent to do it for you.

A range of objects is sold, not only expensive antiques but also relatively undistinguished household knick-knacks. Prices sometimes include VAT (MWST), which you may be able to claim back (see Taxes & Refunds in the Facts for the Visitor chapter). There are many antique shops and art galleries along Dorotheergasse and the surrounding streets.

GETTING THERE & AWAY
Air
Vienna is the main centre for international flights – see the Getting There & Away chapter. There are many airline offices on Opernring opposite the Staatsoper, and they can be found in the Gelbe Seiten telephone book under *Fluggesellschaften*. Offices include:

Aer Lingus
   (☎ 369 28 85) 19, Scheibengasse 12
Air Canada
   (☎ 712 46 08-412) 01, Schubertring 9
Air France
   (☎ 514 18-0) 01, Kärntner Strasse 49
Austrian Airlines
   (☎ 505 57 57-0) 01, Kärntner Ring 18
British Airways
   (☎ 505 76 91-0) 01, Kärntner Ring 10
Delta Airlines
   (☎ 512 66 46-0) 01, Kärntner Ring 17
Lauda Air
   (☎ 514 77 or freephone 0660-6655)
   01, Opernring 6
Lufthansa
   (☎ 599 11-240) 06, Mariahilfer Strasse 123
South African Airways
   (☎ 587 15 85-0) 01, Opernring 1/R
Swissair
   As for Austrian Airlines
TWA
   (☎ 587 68 680) 1 Opernring 1/R/742

Bus
National Bundesbuses arrive and depart from the Wien Mitte Autobusbahnhof (bus station) next to the train station. Many regional destinations are served; routes are displayed near the Bundesbus ticket counters. For information on international buses, see the Getting There & Away chapter.

Train
Vienna has excellent train connections to Europe and the rest of Austria. Check with information centres in train stations or telephone the 24 hour information line (☎ 1717) for the best way to go: not all destinations are exclusively served by one station and schedules are subject to change. All of the following stations (except Meidling) have lockers, currency exchange, Bankomats, and places to eat and buy provisions for your journey.

Westbahnhof This is one of the main entry points to Vienna. Trains to western and northern Europe and western Austria depart from Westbahnhof. Services head to Salzburg city approximately every hour (AS419; 3½ hours). Some of these services continue to Munich (five hours) and terminate in Paris Gare de l'Est (13½ hours). Two daytime trains run to Zürich (AS1126; nine hours) and there's a sleeper service departing at 9.25 pm (AS1074 plus a charge for a fold-down seat/couchette). A direct train goes to Bucharest (16 hours). The Athens service (AS1833, departs at 7 pm) requires two changes. Eight daily trains go to Budapest (AS368; three to four hours). Westbahnhof is also on U-Bahn lines U3 and U6, and many trams stop outside.

Südbahnhof This is the other main station, from which trains to Italy, the Czech Republic, Slovakia, Hungary and Poland depart. Direct trains to Rome (10 hours via Venice and Florence) leave at 7.30 am and 7.30 pm. Five trains a day go to Bratislava (AS94; one hour); four go to Prague (AS488; five hours), with two continuing to Berlin (10 hours). Trams D (to the Ring and Franz Josefs Bahnhof) and O (to Wien Mitte and Praterstern) stop outside. The quickest way to transfer to Westbahnhof is to take tram 18, or the S-Bahn to Meidling and then the U6. This takes about 20 minutes.

Franz Josefs Bahnhof This handles regional and local trains, including trains to Tulln, Krems and the Wachau region (see the Lower Austria chapter for details). It also has one daily train to Prague (AS432; 5½ hours). From outside, there's tram D (to the Ring) and tram No 5 (to Westbahnhof, via Kaiserstrasse) in one direction and Praterstern (Wien Nord) in the other.

Other Stations Wien Mitte is used for local trains, and is adjacent to the U3 stop at Landstrasse. Wien Nord handles local and regional trains, including the airport service which also stops at Wien Mitte. It's at the Praterstern stop on the U1. Praterstern is a hub for many tram routes. Meidling is a stop for most trains to/from Südbahnhof; it is linked to the Philadelphiabrücke stop on the U6.

Car & Motorcycle

Driving into Vienna is straightforward: the A1 from Linz and Salzburg and the A2 from Graz join the Gürtel ring road; the A4 from the airport leads directly to the Ring, and the A22 runs to the centre along the north bank of the Danube.

Rental Offices See the Getting Around chapter earlier in this book for a comparison of rental charges.

Avis
   (☎ 587 62 41) 01, Opernring 3-5
Budget
   (☎ 714 65 65) 03, Hilton Air Terminal
Europcar
   (☎ 799 61 76) 03, Park & Ride U3 Erdberg, Erdbergstrasse 202/1
Eurodollar (ARAC Autovermietung)
   (☎ 714 67 17) 01, Schubertring 9
Hertz
   (☎ 512 86 77, or ☎ 795 32 for the central reservations office) 01, Kärntner Ring 17

All of these companies have an airport office.

Motorcycles can be rented from 2 Rad-Börse (☎ 214 85 95), 02, Praterstern 47. Various Hondas are available, ranging from a 50cc scooter (AS390 plus AS1.50 per kilometre) to a Goldwing 1500cc (AS2990 plus AS6 per kilometre). These rates are for 24 hours and include 100 free kilometres. The weekend rates (from 5 pm Friday to 10 am Monday) include 200 free kilometres and are AS1390 and AS6990 respectively. Helmet hire costs AS100 a day.

Hitching

Before you start hitching, take public transport to the main traffic routes in the suburbs. Heading west from Vienna, the lay-by across the footbridge from the U4 Unter St Veit stop has been recommended.

Vienna has an agency that links up hitchers and drivers. Mitfahrzentrale Josefstadt (☎ 408 22 10), 08, Daungasse 1A, is open Monday to Friday from 10 am to 6 pm and on Saturday and Sunday from 11 am to 1 pm. Examples of fares are Klagenfurt AS190, Salzburg AS210, Innsbruck AS270, Munich AS310, Vorarlberg AS350, Frankfurt AS470, Cologne AS580 and Brussels AS720. Telephone to check availability before going to the office. Lifts across Austria tend to be limited, but there are usually lots of cars going into Germany. If you're offering a lift, visit the office in person. Drivers get paid the balance of the fees after the office takes its cut.

Boat

Steamers head west (mostly from Krems) and fast hydrofoils head east. See the Getting There & Away and Lower Austria chapters for details.

GETTING AROUND
To/From the Airport

Flughafen Wien Schwechat (☎ 7007; 7007-2233 for flight enquiries) is 19 km east of the city centre. The cheapest way to get to the airport is by S-Bahn on line S7. The fare is AS34, or AS17 if you have a city pass. Trains leave from Wien Nord, usually at three and 33 minutes past the hour, calling at Wien Mitte three minutes later. The trip takes about 35 minutes and the first/last trains depart at 5.03 am/9.33 pm. In the opposite direction, trains usually depart at 14 and 44 minutes past the hour, with the first/last service at 6.07 am/10.23 pm. (There are earlier trains in both directions on weekdays only.)

Buses run from the City Air Terminal at the Hotel Hilton to the airport every 20 or 30 minutes from 4.30 am (5 am in the opposite direction) to 12.30 am. From late March to late October buses also run hourly during the night. The 20 minute journey costs AS70/130 one way/return. Buses also run from Westbahnhof between 5.30 am and 11 pm, stopping at Südbahnhof after 15 minutes. The fare is also AS70/130 and departures are every 30 or 60 minutes. For more information on airport buses, phone ☎ 5800-2300.

If taking a taxi is the only option, expect to pay from around AS400 to AS450, comprising the metered fare plus a AS130 supplement for the driver's return trip to the city. Cityrama (☎ 534 13-13) offers airport transfers for up to four passengers for the fixed price of AS390.

Public Transport

Vienna has a comprehensive and unified public transport network that is one of the most efficient in Europe. Flat-fare tickets are valid for trams, buses, the U-Bahn (the underground metro system) and the S-Bahn (trains to the suburbs; Inter-Rail, Eurail and Austrian rail passes are also valid on these). Services are frequent, and you rarely have to wait more than five or 10 minutes for a vehicle to arrive. Public transport begins at around 5 or 6 am. Buses and trams usually stop running by midnight, though some S-Bahn and U-Bahn services may continue until 1 am.

Buses tend to cover a wider area than trams and always have a number followed by an 'A' or 'B'. These usually link to a tram number. Thus, bus 38A connects with tram 38, and bus 72A continues from the terminal of tram 72.

Night buses to all suburbs run every 30 minutes from 12.30 am to about 5 am. Most routes meet the Ringstrasse, generally at Schwedenplatz, Schottentor and the Staatsoper; the AS25 fare is not covered by daily passes.

Transport routes are shown on the free tourist office map. For a more detailed listing, buy a map (AS15) from a Vienna Line ticket office, which can be found in many U-Bahn stations. In addition, there are transport information offices at Karlsplatz, Stephansplatz and Westbahnhof (open Monday to Friday from 6.30 am to 6.30 pm and weekends and holidays from 8.30 am to 4 pm), and at Volkstheater,

Landstrasse, Philadelphiabrücke, Spittelau and Praterstern (open Monday to Friday from 7 am to 6.30 pm). For public transport information in German, call ☎ 7909-105.

Tickets & Passes Single tickets, valid for immediate use, cost AS20 from Verkehrverbund Ost-Region (VOR) ticket machines on trams and buses. Children aged between six and 15 travel half-price, or free on Sunday, public holidays and Vienna school holidays (photo ID necessary); younger children always travel free. Seniors are eligible for special tickets. VOR machines give change for certain bills only, so you need to check the instructions carefully.

Multiple tickets costing AS68/85 for four/five can be purchased from ticket offices, VOR ticket machines and Tabak shops, as can various travel passes. VOR machines in U-Bahn stations also sell single tickets for AS17. Each ticket must be validated in the blue boxes (inside buses and trams, beside U-Bahn escalators) at the beginning of the journey. There's a AS500 fine (plus the fare) for being caught without a valid ticket.

Daily city passes (*Stunden-Netzkarte*) are a good deal if you're doing extensive sightseeing. Costs are AS50 (valid for 24 hours from first use) and AS130 (valid for 72 hours). Validate the ticket before your first journey only. A multiple user pass, called an *Acht-TageStreifenkarte*, costs AS265 and is valid for eight freely chosen days, for example eight days for one person, one day for eight people, and so on. Validate the ticket once per day per person.

There are also two transferable passes: weekly (Monday to Sunday), costing AS142 and monthly (calendar month) for AS500. The yearly pass costing AS4700 is not transferable and a photo is required.

Car & Motorcycle

Taking public transport is an easier option than driving in the city centre. Irrespective of the complications created by one-way streets, you'll find it inconvenient or expensive to park in the centre. There are central underground parking garages by the Staatsoper on Kärntner Strasse and in front of the Rathaus. They are both open 24 hours a day and charge about AS40/450 per hour/ day. The one at Museumsplatz is cheaper, charging AS35 per hour (AS245 per day), and garages outside the Innere Stadt are cheaper still.

All of the Innere Stadt is a blue parking zone (except where parking is prohibited altogether), allowing a maximum of 1½ hours parking between 9 am and 7 pm from Monday to Friday. Vouchers (*Parkschein*) for parking on these streets cost AS6 per 30 minutes. Blue zones apply on weekdays from 9 am to 8 pm in the districts bordering the Ring. Farther out you can still find white zones with no time restrictions on parking.

Petrol stations can be found in the city (for instance in the Innere Stadt at Börsegasse and Schmerlingplatz) and some are self-service. Very late at night, you may find that the only stations open are near the autobahn exits. The ÖAMTC (☎ 711 99; fax 713 18 07) is at 01, Schubertring 1-3.

Taxi

Taxis are metered for city journeys. The flag fall starts at AS26 (AS27 on Sunday, holidays and from 11 pm to 6 am). The rate is then about AS14 per kilometre (AS16 on Sunday, holidays and at night) in AS2 increments, plus AS2 per 22 seconds of being stuck in traffic. The rate for trips outside the city borders is usually double but try negotiating. Taxis are found by train stations, top hotels, or can simply be flagged down in the street. There is a AS26 surcharge for

phoning a radio taxi; numbers include ☎ 31 300, ☎ 40 100, ☎ 60 160 and ☎ 81 400.

Bicycle

There are 480km of bicycle tracks in and around Vienna, including those along the banks of the Danube. Pick up the *Nützliche Tips für Radfahrer* booklet from the tourist office, showing circular bike tours. This also lists bike rental outfits (*Radverleih*). Bicycles can be rented at Westbahnhof, Südbahnhof, Wien Nord and Floridsdorf train stations; they can be returned up till midnight at Westbahnhof and Südbahnhof. Bikes can be carried on the S-Bahn and U-Bahn outside rush-hour times for half the adult fare.

In 1999 the city of Vienna is going to make 2000 bicycles available for free use. If this system works, the scheme will be continued in future years; inquire at the Rathaus or the tourist office for further details of the scheme.

Fiacre

More of a tourist novelty than a practical mode of transport, a fiacre (*Fiaker*) is a traditional-style open carriage drawn by a pair of horses. These charming vehicles can be found at Stephansplatz, Albertinaplatz and Heldenplatz at the Hofburg. Costing AS500 for a 20 minute trot, these horses must be among Vienna's richest inhabitants. Try to bargain for a lower fare before you set off. Drivers generally have a fairly good command of English and point out places of interest en route.

Burgenland

Burgenland is a province of tree-lined hills, vineyards and orchards. Wine production is particularly important for this agricultural region. Tasting the local wines, either over a meal or on an organised tour, is an extremely popular activity with visitors. The most interesting area for tourists is Neusiedler See and the resorts nearby.

History

Austria and Hungary contested ownership of this region for centuries. Hungary appeared to have won out when Austria's Ferdinand III relinquished it in 1647, yet Hungary itself became wholly or partially subservient to the Habsburgs in the ensuing years. Austria finally lost control of Hungary after WWI, but the German-speaking western region of Hungary went to Austria under the Treaty of St Germain concluded in 1919.

A further twist was to follow. The people of Sopron, the natural capital of the region, voted in 1921 to stay in Hungary. Some Austrians maintain that the Hungarian government manipulated the vote by importing extra Hungarian citizens on the day.

The new province was named Burgenland, not for its numerous castles, but for the 'burg' suffix of the old western Hungarian district names. Eisenstadt became the capital. Across the border, Sopron has meanwhile become little more than a shopping centre for Austrians seeking lower Hungarian prices.

Orientation

Burgenland occupies 3965 sq km and is one-third forested. Geschriebenstein, at a mere 884m, is the highest point; at 117m, Illmitz is Austria's lowest town. The province is home to 272,000 people, mostly living in the north. One-fifth of the area is owned by the Esterházys, one of the richest families in the country.

Highlights

- Visit the home of Haydn in Eisenstadt, the provincial capital

- Set sail on Neusiedler See, Central Europe's only steppe lake

- Explore the national park at Seewinkel, a haven for birdlife

- Sample the local wine in one of Rust's numerous *Buschenschenken* (wine taverns)

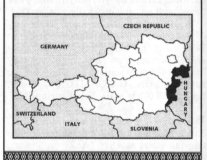

This Austrian province receives fewer foreign visitors than any other – just 638,000 overnight stays a year, only one-third of the number in Lower Austria, the next least-visited province. As a consequence there is less tourist literature available than one normally finds, and what is produced is sometimes only in German.

Information

The provincial tourist board is Burgenland Tourismus (☎ 02682-633 84-16, fax 633 84-20, email info@burgenland-tourism. co.at), Schloss Esterházy, A-7000 Eisenstadt. Personal callers are welcome (see the Eisenstadt Orientation & Information section for opening times); here you can pick up the *Strassenkarte*, a detailed map of

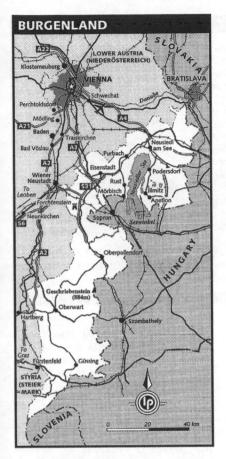

the province; bicycle routes, camp sites and other attractions are marked. The board's *Burgenland Weindegustationen* leaflet gives information on wine-tasting.

Eisenstadt

☎ 02682 • pop 12,500 • 181m

Eisenstadt received its town charter in 1373, and its status was enhanced in 1622 when it became the residence of the Ester-házys, a powerful Hungarian family. In 1648 Eisenstadt was granted the status of *Freistadt* (free city). It has been the provincial capital since 1925.

Eisenstadt really milks its connection with the seminal 18th century musician and composer Josef Haydn. 'Fascinating, not only for Josef Haydn', the town's tourist literature trumpets. Unfortunately, beyond the traces of Mozart's mentor, the sources of this fascination are somewhat elusive.

Orientation & Information

Eisenstadt lies 50km south of Vienna. To reach the town centre from the train station, walk straight ahead down Bahnstrasse for about 10 minutes until you get to the pedestrian-only Hauptstrasse, a street with cafés, shops and restaurants. Turn left for Schloss Esterházy, which houses the two tourist offices, Eisenstadt Tourismus (☎ 673 90) and the provincial office (☎ 633 84-16). Both are open daily from 9 am to 5 pm (closed weekends from 1 November to 31 March). Good free maps are available, as well as a brochure listing hotels, private rooms, and details of museum opening times and prices.

A post office and the Bundesbus ticket office and departure point are next to the Domkirche (cathedral) at Domplatz. The main post office (Postamt 7000) on Pfarrgasse is open on weekdays from 7 am to 6 pm, and on Saturday from 7 am to 1 pm.

Things to See & Do

Josef Haydn revealed that Eisenstadt was 'where I wish to live and to die'. He achieved the former, being a resident for 31 years, but it was in Vienna that he finally tinkled his last tune. He also rather carelessly neglected to give any directive about his preferred residence after death. His skull was stolen from a temporary grave shortly after he died in 1809, after which it ended up on display in a Viennese museum. The headless cadaver was subsequently returned to Eisenstadt (in 1932), but it wasn't until 1954 that the skull joined it.

Haydn's white marble tomb can now be seen in the **Bergkirche**. The church itself is

Haydn Seek

After several years of struggle as a freelance musician, Josef Haydn (1732-1809) achieved a degree of financial security in 1761 with his appointment as *Kapellmeister* (music director) to the Esterházys.

However, he had to work hard for his money. His duties included rehearsing and conducting the orchestra, performing as organist, violist and violinist, and generally coaching and controlling the singers and musicians under his charge (and many were as highly strung as their instruments). In addition, he had to compose various works for his employers' delectation, including 125 pieces of music featuring the baryton, a hybrid string instrument favoured by one of the princes.

Haydn married Maria Anna Keller in 1760, but the childless union was not a happy one – Maria had no love of music. During his lifetime Haydn composed 19 operas and operettas, 107 symphonies, 68 string quartets, 62 piano sonatas and 43 piano trios.

remarkable for the Kalvarienberg, a unique Calvary display; access is via a separate entrance to the rear of the church. Life-sized figures depict the Stations of the Cross in a series of suitably austere, dungeon-like rooms. It's open between 1 April and 31 October daily from 9 am to noon and 2 to 5 pm; entry costs AS25 (seniors AS20, students AS10) and includes the mausoleum.

Schloss Esterházy dates from the 14th century. It was restored initially in Baroque and later in classical style. The provincial government occupies two-thirds of the interior, and the rest can be visited by guided tour. Egotists will enjoy the multiple reflections in the mirrored corridor. The highlight is the frescoed **Haydn Hall**; its former marble floor was replaced by an aesthetically inferior but acoustically superior wooden floor (it's rated the second-best concert hall in Austria, after Vienna's Musikverein). The hall is where Haydn conducted the orchestra on a near nightly basis; he worked for the Esterházys in this

capacity from 1761 to 1790. There's also a new exhibition on the Esterházy family. The palace is open the same hours as the tourist offices, with the last tour departing at 4 pm. Entry costs AS50 (students/seniors AS30) for a 40 minute guided tour (sometimes in English, or ask for the English notes).

Haydn's former residence, **Haydnhaus**, Josef Haydn Gasse 21, is now a small museum containing unexciting Haydn memorabilia. It's open daily from Easter Sunday to 30 October; entry is AS20 (students/seniors AS10, families AS40). A combined ticket (AS40, students/seniors AS20) can be purchased to include admission to the **Landesmuseum**, Museumsgasse 5, which otherwise costs AS30 (students AS15, families AS60). The collection includes Roman mosaics, ancient artefacts, items relating to 20th century history (with some good period posters), wine-making equipment, and a Franz Liszt room, complete with a warty death mask of the

Hungarian composer. The Landesmuseum is open Tuesday to Sunday between 9 am and noon and 1 and 5 pm. The **Jüdisches Museum**, Unterbergstrasse 6, is primarily concerned with exhibitions concerning the Jewish religion. It's open daily except Monday from 10 am to 5 pm between 1 May and 31 October. Entry is AS30 (students AS20); temporary exhibitions cost the same again.

Special Events

Behind Schloss Esterházy is the large, relaxing Schlosspark, the setting for the Fest der 1000 Weine in late August.

A Haydn festival, the Haydntage, is staged from early to mid-September. Most events take place in the Haydn Hall or the Bergkirche. It's the high point in Eisenstadt's cultural calendar. For details contact the Haydnfestspiele Büro (☎ 618 66-0, fax

618 05), Schloss Esterházy. Free frolics take place during the EisenSTADTfest in early June.

Places to Stay

Eisenstadt has few hotels, but the staff at the tourist office can help to find rooms. There are even fewer private rooms available: *Toth Ewald (☎ 642 22, Vicedom 5)* off Domplatz has rooms with shower/WC for AS230 per person, including cooking facilities and a TV area. It's usually full with students, except in July and September.

Gasthof Kutsenits Ludwig (☎ 635 11, Mattersburger Strasse 30), south of the city centre, is OK if you have your own transport: singles/doubles cost AS250/400, or AS300/500 with shower/WC.

Das Sportliche Haus (☎ 623 26-12, fax -10, Hotterweg 67) near the city's football ground has rooms with shower/WC and

BURGENLAND

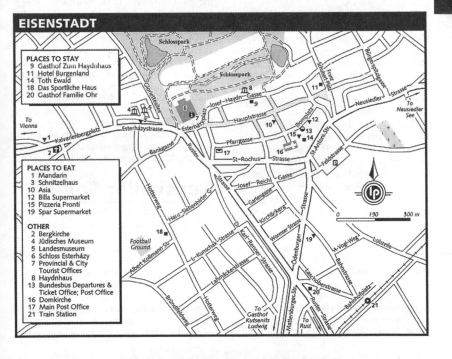

EISENSTADT

PLACES TO STAY
9 Gasthof Zum Haydnhaus
11 Hotel Burgenland
14 Toth Ewald
18 Das Sportliche Haus
20 Gasthof Familie Ohr

PLACES TO EAT
1 Mandarin
3 Schnitzelhaus
10 Asia
12 Billa Supermarket
15 Pizzeria Pronti
19 Spar Supermarket

OTHER
2 Bergkirche
4 Jüdisches Museum
5 Landesmuseum
6 Schloss Esterházy
7 Provincial & City Tourist Offices
8 Haydnhaus
13 Bundesbus Departures & Ticket Office; Post Office
16 Domkirche
17 Main Post Office
21 Train Station

cable TV for AS355/630. *Gasthof Zum Haydnhaus* (☎ *646 36, Josef Haydn Gasse 24)* is central but closed from Christmas to 31 January. All rooms have private shower/WC and cost AS400/600.

The only three star hotel is *Gasthof Familie Ohr* (☎ *624 60, fax -9, Ruster Strasse 51)*, west of the train station. Singles/doubles with shower/WC, cable TV and telephone cost from AS510/850.

Hotel Burgenland (☎ *696, fax 655 31, Franz Schubert Platz 1)* is the town's only four star place. Rooms have all requisite facilities and start at AS1150/1590. The indoor swimming pool and sauna are free for guests.

Places to Eat

On Domplatz is a *Billa* supermarket, open Monday to Friday from 8 am to 7 pm (till 7.30 pm on Friday) and Saturday from 7 am to 5 pm. There's also a *Spar* supermarket at Bahnstrasse 16-18.

For lunch, think Chinese: *Asia*, at Hauptstrasse 32 (entrance on Matthias Markhl Gasse), and *Mandarin (Wiener Strasse 2)* both have excellent three-course menus for about AS60. Evening meals start at around AS75 and both places are open daily. There's a branch of the fast-food chain *Schnitzelhaus* at Esterházystrasse 16, open daily till 10 pm.

Hidden away down Vicedom, off Domplatz, is *Pizzeria Pronti*, where small/big pizzas start at AS55/80. This place is also an American steakhouse: steak or rib portions start at AS60. It's closed on Monday.

The following are also worth trying; see Places to Stay for locations. *Gasthof Zum Haydnhaus* has a simple *Stube* with a vaulted dining area (open daily) and serves regional and Austrian dishes costing from AS65 to AS150. *Gasthof Familie Ohr* (closed Monday) is a little more expensive and offers a wide selection of meals, including Pannonian (west Hungarian) cooking. *Café-Restaurant Bienenkorb* in Hotel Burgenland is comfortable yet affordable, with Austrian and international dishes priced from AS95 to AS185. It's open daily.

Getting There & Away

Regular trains leave Vienna's Südbahnhof. There's a direct train leaving at 10.03 am daily (AS68; 66 minutes). At other times you have a choice of two routes but each involves a change: at Neusiedl am See (AS68; total journey time 80 minutes) or Wulkaprodersdorf (AS85; 68 minutes). Trains run every one or two hours by either route.

Buses to/from Vienna (AS85) take 70 minutes; they depart from Wien Mitte in the early morning and leave the Eisenstadt Bundesbus terminal mid-afternoon to early evening; there are about three buses per day in both directions. Wiener Neustadt is on the Vienna-Graz train route: buses from there take 30 minutes.

AROUND EISENSTADT
Burg Forchtenstein

About 20km south-west of Eisenstadt and 15km south-east of Wiener Neustadt, this is the best known of Burgenland's many castles. It is a large and imposing pile, topped by a circular tower and an onion dome. It was built in the 14th century and enlarged by the Esterházys in 1635, in whose hands it remains. The extensive arms and armour collection can be visited by guided tour (AS55, April to October, daily). Call ☎ 02626-812 12 for information.

Getting There & Away Forchtenstein is not on a railway line, though Bundesbuses run there at varying frequencies from both Eisenstadt and Wiener Neustadt.

Neusiedler See

Birdwatchers flock to Neusiedler See, the only steppe lake in Central Europe. It's ringed by a wetland area of reed beds, providing an ideal breeding ground for nearly 300 bird species. The Seewinkel area is the favoured site for ornithologists (see that section later in this chapter).

Neusiedler See is only 1 to 2m deep and there is no natural outlet, giving the water a slightly saline quality. The shallowness means the water warms quickly in summer.

Water sports are a big draw: boats and windsurfers are for hire at resorts around the lake, and there are many bathing beaches. Typical prices round the lake for boat hire per hour are: *Elektroboot* (motor boat) AS140, *Tretboot* (pedal boat) AS80, and *Segelboot* (sailing boat) AS140. Beaches are invariably cordoned off and a modest fee (about AS20) is charged for admission. Note that, even if you have your own windsurfer, you will have to pay a daily charge (from AS35 to AS50) to go windsurfing. Swimming is also possible in some of the Seewinkel lakes. Horse riding and fishing are other popular pursuits.

For ambitious cyclists, a cycle track winds all the way round the reed beds; you can make a full circuit of the lake but it'll take more than one day to do it. Remember to take your passport as the southern section is in Hungary. The boat services that cross the lake will carry bikes. In July and August (Sunday and holidays only) there's a special Fahrradbus that loops round the lake once a day between Mörbisch and Illmitz, via Neusiedl am See and all resorts in between.

In early September the national triathlon is held at Neusiedler See. Watch 500 people voluntarily put themselves through hell – 42km of running, 180km of cycling and 3.8km of swimming in under nine hours. You could even join the fun: contact the Podersdorf tourist office (see the Podersdorf section later in this chapter).

Neusiedler See is a place to be visited in summer; tourist trade is much reduced in the winter, when many hotels and restaurants close down. If you stay in the area, inquire about the Neusiedler See Gästekarte, provided by the local tourist office upon receipt of your accommodation slip. The ordinary Gästekarte (free) gives useful discounts, but the VIP Card (costing about AS20 per day) provides extra benefits, such as free entry to various beaches.

NEUSIEDL AM SEE
☎ 02167 • pop 5300 • 133m
Neusiedl is the region's main town and is easily accessible from Vienna. There's no real reason to base yourself here; the smaller places round the lake are preferable – they are closer to the lake, more scenic and more representative of the region.

Neusiedl has a tourist office (☎ 2229) in the Rathaus at Hauptplatz 1. The lake (where there's bathing and boating) is a 10 minute walk though the reed beds from the edge of town, or 20 minutes from Hauptplatz. Neusiedl also has a couple of museums, and the Tabor, a tiny ruin (free entry) with a view of the lake.

Staff at the tourist office will help you find somewhere to stay. The town has a HI *Jugendherberge* (☎/fax 2252, Herbergsgasse 1) which is open from March to November, but isn't central. It's 15 minutes walk from both the train station and the tourist office, and 30 minutes from the lake. Hostel beds are AS166 (AS144 for those aged under 19); sheets are AS17. Reception is open from 8 am to 2 pm and 5 to 10 pm.

Getting There & Away
Regular trains from Vienna's Südbahnhof take 50 minutes and cost AS68. Neusiedl train station is a 20 minute walk from the centre of town, or a AS17 bus ride. Occasional buses from the train station continue to the beach via Hauptplatz. Bundesbuses leave from outside the train station, though those to Seewinkel also stop at Hauptplatz.

For road access, the A4 from Vienna to Bratislava passes just north of the town.

RUST
☎ 02685 • pop 1700 • 121m
Rust, 14km east of Eisenstadt, is famous for storks and wine. Its name derives from *Rüster*, the German word for elm tree. The town's prosperity has been based on wine for centuries. In 1524 the emperor granted local vintners the right to display the letter 'R' on their wine barrels; corks today still bear this insignia.

Orientation & Information
Bundesbuses unload at the post office, 100m from Conradplatz, which leads to the town hall and Rathausplatz.

The tourist office (☎ 502, fax -10, email info@rust.or.at) is in the Rathaus; it has lists of hotels and private rooms, and staff can give details of wine-tasting venues. During the summer it's open Monday to Friday from 8 am to noon and 2 to 6 pm, Saturday from 9 am to noon and Sunday from 10 am to noon. From 1 October to 30 April, hours are weekdays only from 8 am to noon and 1 to 5 pm. There's a 24 hour accommodation notice board outside the office.

Things to See & Do

Rust's affluent past has left a legacy of attractive burghers' houses on and around the main squares. **Storks** descend on Rust from the end of March, rear their young, then fly to new pastures in late August. Many homes in the centre (particularly on Rathausplatz and Conradplatz) have a metal platform on the roof to entice storks to build a nest there. Preservation measures have been introduced to maintain the numbers of winged visitors, though in 1997 only six adult pairs reared their young in Rust. A good vantage point is attained from the tower of the **Katholische Kirche** at the southern end of Rathausplatz; entry costs AS10 (students AS5). The **Fischerkirche** at the other end of Rathausplatz is the oldest church in Rust (built between the 12th and 16th centuries).

Access to the **lake** and bathing facilities is 1.5km down the reed-fringed Seepromenade. Here you'll find a swimming pool (AS30 per day), schools for windsurfing and sailing, mini-golf, and motor boats, pedal boats and sailing boats for hire.

Places to Stay

Rust's *camping ground (☎ 595)* is near the lake. In the summer a pitch costs AS55 per adult, and AS44 each for a car and tent; in the shoulder seasons (April, September and October) prices are lower. There's a shop and a cheap restaurant.

The *Ruster Jugendgästehaus (☎ 591, fax -4)* opened in the summer of 1998; there's a kitchen and beds cost up to AS150.

It's open year-round but advance reservations are required.

Private rooms provide cheap beds: there are a couple of *Zimmer frei* places down Kraugartenweg. *Gästehaus Ruth (☎ 277)* is at Dr Ratz Gasse 1, off Weinberggasse. It has two singles and four doubles, all with shower, for AS260/440.

Pension Halwax (☎ 520, Oggauer Strasse 21) offers seven doubles with shower/WC for AS500; rooms are clean and fresh. Pensions with a swimming pool include *Alexander (☎ 302, fax -4, Dorfmeistergasse 21)*, charging AS425/640, and *Magdalenenhof (☎ 373, fax -4, Feldgasse 40)*, charging AS370/580.

Places to Eat

Create a picnic at the *ADEG* supermarket *(Oggauer Strasse 3)* to eat by the lake. It is open Monday to Friday from 7 am to noon and 3 to 6 pm, and Saturday from 7 am to noon.

For sit-down meals, look no farther than the many *Buschenschenken* (wine taverns) around town. Many have outside tables in attractive courtyards; staff at the tourist office can provide a list. A place with good food and wine is *Schandl (Hauptstrasse 20)*, open Wednesday to Monday from 4 pm to midnight. Meals cost from AS70 to AS135 and wine starts at AS22 for a *Viertel* (0.25L). Another possibility is *Haydn-Keller (Haydngasse 4)*, where the *Aal* (eel) is recommended.

Café Piano (Zum Alten Stadttor 1) is open daily from 11 am till the early hours. It has drinks, ice cream, light meals and outside tables. *Rathauskeller (Rathausplatz 1)* serves local specialities. It's open daily from 11.30 am, except Wednesday.

Getting There & Away

Buses run approximately hourly to/from Eisenstadt (AS34; 30 minutes). Services cease in the early evening. Rust receives many bicycle tourists, and several places in the centre rent bikes. Schiffahrt Gmeiner (☎ 493) sends boats across the lake to the shore near Illmitz (AS60).

MÖRBISCH

☎ 02685 • pop 2400

Six kilometres round the lake south of Rust, **Mörbisch** is just a couple of kilometres short of the Hungarian border. It's worth spending an hour or so here, enjoying the relaxed atmosphere and the quaint white-washed houses with hanging corn and flower-strewn balconies.

There's a tourist office (☎ 8430, fax -9) on the main street at Hauptstrasse 23. Staff can fill you in on the Seefestspiele, an important summer operetta festival (mid-July to late August), and on the lakeside facilities. Plenty of pensions and private rooms await if you decide to stay the night. As in Rust, several Buschenschenken (on Hauptstrasse and elsewhere) will happily fill you with food and wine.

Getting There & Away

By bus, the fare to Rust is AS17, though to/from Eisenstadt costs the same (AS34) as only going from Rust to Eisenstadt. South of Mörbisch, cyclists may cross into Hungary but there's no road through for cars. To cross the border, car drivers need to return almost to Eisenstadt and then take highway 16 to Sopron.

Between May and September, Dreschler (☎ 8820) sends frequent boats across the lake to Illmitz, and also conducts a daily circular tour.

SEEWINKEL

☎ 02175

Naturalists are particularly attracted to this area, a national park of grassland and wetland interspersed with myriad small lakes on the eastern shore of Neusiedler See. Tourist offices have information in English on the park and the species of bird that visit particular lakes, though for more detail on the nature reserve areas you should contact the Nationalparkhaus (☎ 3442-0, fax -4), Hauswiese, A-7142 Illmitz.

The protected areas cannot be directly accessed by visitors, so to really get into the **birdwatching** you need a pair of binoculars.

There are viewing stands along the way. The vineyards, reed beds, shimmering waters and constant bird calls make this an enchanting region for an excursion. Even if you're not an ornithologist, this is an excellent area to explore on foot or, especially, by bicycle.

There are no hills in the Seewinkel, so a cheaper, gearless bicycle from the rental places is all you need. Another option is to go by *Pferdewagen*, a carriage pulled by ponies: tours lasting 1½ hours cost about AS70 per person (carrying up to 19 people), or it's AS400 for two people on smaller carts.

The town of **Illmitz** is surrounded by the national park area and makes a good base. Staff at its tourist office (☎ 2383, fax 2303-22), at Obere Hauptplatz 2-4, can provide information on both the town and Seewinkel. There are lots of pensions and private rooms available in the town. Like Rust, Illmitz has some rooftop platforms to encourage storks to nest. The beach at Illmitz is 3km from the town. From there, Gangl (☎ 2158) has all types of boat for hire and runs several lake tours. In the summer it also sends hourly ferries across the lake to Mörbisch (AS60 one way or AS100 return; bikes carried free).

Another possible base is nearby **Apetlon** (☎ 2220 for the tourist office); Podersdorf is also convenient.

PODERSDORF

☎ 02177 • pop 2100 • 121m

Podersdorf, on the eastern shore, is the most popular holiday destination on the lake, receiving more visitors than anywhere else in Burgenland. The town owes this status to its position directly on the shore, made possible by the absence of reed beds in the immediate area.

Information

Staff at the tourist office (☎ 2227, fax 2170), Hauptstrasse 2, can help find accommodation. The office is open daily in summer, weekdays only in winter, and there's a computer screen in the entrance displaying room vacancies (this service is accessible daily until late evening). A *Tourismusbüro* (tourist office) is open during summer on Strandplatz.

Things to See & Do

Podersdorf offers the most convenient bathing opportunities on Neusiedler See, with a long grassy **beach** (AS20, free with VIP card and in winter) for swimming, boating and windsurfing. New beachside facilities (including mini-golf, volleyball, surf park), partly financed by the EU, will be open for the 1999 summer season.

The town is also within easy reach of the protected lakes in the Seewinkel area: the nearest, 5km to the south, are the Stinkersee lakes. Cyclists of all ages stream along the lakeside bike trail from the town. Bikes can be hired from various places in Podersdorf. Tauber (☎ 2204) on Strandplatz allows you to return machines up till 9 pm (a gearless bike is AS95 per day; AS85 with the VIP card).

Places to Stay & Eat

It's worth booking ahead in the high season, especially for the limited number of single rooms. In winter, many places close for a few months. Note that many guesthouses in the resort share the same family name.

The *camping ground* (☎/fax 2279) by the lake is open from 1 April to 30 October; a pitch costs AS80 per adult, AS52 for a tent and AS62 for a car.

Seestrasse, the street leading from the beach to Hauptstrasse, has many small places to stay. *Ettl* (☎ 2366) at No 46 has the advantage of offering guests free bicycles. Rooms with shower and WC cost AS220 per person. *Steiner* (☎ 2358), closer to the beach at No 89, has doubles with or without private shower for AS360, and a couple of singles (with hall shower) for AS200. It's actually a *Heuriger* (wine tavern), with cold buffets, wine for AS18 a Viertel, and a zither player strumming three or four nights a week – it can be a bit noisy here till about 11.30 pm.

Haus Pannonia (☎ 2245, Seezeile 20) is a three star place with 64 beds (only two singles) costing from AS320 to AS395 per person. It also has a sauna. Its restaurant serves dishes costing from AS70 to AS220.

There are various places to eat near the beach, most with outside tables. *Gasthof Kummer* (*Strandplatz*) has good food and low prices; it's open daily in summer, weekends only for the rest of the year. *Gasthaus Zum Heiligen Urban*, on the corner of Seestrasse and Neusiedler Strasse, has a small garden; the *Dorschfilet* (AS65), fish in batter with a generous portion of potatoes and salad is cheap but tasty. There's a *Spar* supermarket at Seestrasse 16.

Getting There & Away

Bundesbuses between Neusiedl am See and Podersdorf (AS34) run approximately hourly in both directions on weekdays but are infrequent at weekends; they continue to Illmitz and Apetlon. Ferries connect Podersdorf and Purbach on the western shore.

Styria

Occupying 16,387 sq km, Styria (Steiermark) is Austria's second-largest province and has a population of around 1.2 million. It encompasses mountain ranges, forested hills and green pastures. The main river, the Mur, flows through Graz, the provincial capital.

Graz is the major tourist attraction, but other places worth visiting in Styria include the pilgrimage site of Mariazell and the open-air museum at Stübing. The Lipizzaner stud farm at Piber and the St Barbara Kirche (church) at nearby Bärnbach combine to make an excellent day trip. Styria accounts for about 5% of Austria's wine production, and exploring the wine routes south of Graz is a popular excursion for those with their own transport. Styria extends as far as the Salzkammergut to the north-west, and this holiday region is dealt with in the Salzkammergut chapter.

History

When Duke Ottokar IV died without an heir in 1192, Styria passed to the Babenberg duke Leopold V as an inheritance. Control subsequently fell to King Ottokar II of Bohemia and then (in 1276) to the Habsburgs. In the next century the population grew, but there followed two centuries of local conflicts and invasions by the Turks and Hungarians. The year 1480 was particularly dire; it was known as the year of the 'Plagues of God' – the Turks, the Black Death and locusts all paid unwelcome visits. Exactly 200 years later one-quarter of the population of Graz was wiped out in a further epidemic of the Black Death.

The Turkish threat was removed after 1683 and the economy and infrastructure of the region developed. Then, in 1779, 1805 and 1809, it was the turn of the French to invade. After the Nazi occupation of WWII, the first Allied troops to liberate the area were from the Soviet Union, followed by the British, who occupied Graz until 1955.

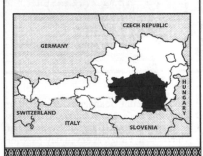

STYRIA

Orientation & Information

Styria is in south-eastern Austria and is bordered by Slovenia. Although Graz is the capital, Bruck an der Mur is the main railhead for the region. Styria is subdivided into various tourist regions, though information on the whole province is available to personal callers at the Graz city tourist office (see the Graz Information section). For information sent by post, contact the provincial tourist board: Steiermark Tourismus (☎ 0316-40 03-0, fax -10, email tourismus@steiermark.com), St Peter Hauptstrasse 243, A-8042 Graz.

STYRIA (STEIERMARK)

Landesmuseum Joanneum, founded in 1811, is Austria's oldest museum; exhibits are dispersed among 10 sites in Styria (eight of which are in Graz). A seven day pass for all sections costs AS200, and is available from any of the individual sites.

Getting Around

As in most other provinces, regional transport (including city transport) is integrated under a zonal ticketing system. Zonal tickets are valid for trains and buses. The private GKB rail line runs between Graz and Köflach and Graz and Wies-Eibiswald (via Deutschlandsberg); Austrian rail passes and zonal tickets are valid, but inquire before using European passes. Single tickets are valid for periods of one hour (one zone) up to five hours (22 zones). Zonal passes are available for 24 hours, one week, one month or one year. A 24 hour pass is often

cheaper than buying two single tickets, so inquire about the various options before purchasing.

Graz

☎ 0316 • pop 245,000 • 365m

The green of the parks, the red of the rooftops and the blue of the river combine to make Graz an attractive city in which to linger. It has a number of interesting sights and is a good base for a variety of excursions. The large student population (some 40,000 in three universities) helps to make Graz lively after dark.

Graz was considered a city as early as 1189, and in 1379 it became the seat of the Leopold line of the Habsburgs. Friedrich III, King of Germany, Emperor of Austria and Holy Roman Emperor, resided here and left his famous motto, AEIOU (*Austria Est*

Imperare Orbi Universo: Austria rules the world) inscribed in various places around town. In 1564, Graz became the administrative capital of Inner Austria, an area covering present-day Styria and Carinthia, plus the former possessions of Carniola, Gorizia and Istria. Once strongly fortified against Turkish attack, in 1784 Graz was one of the first European cities to dismantle its city walls.

Today, the second-largest city in Austria hosts prestigious fairs and festivals and has an important opera house and theatre. Graz offers a lot, but skiing is not part of the package. Strange, therefore, that the city should have sought to host the 2002 Winter Olympics. Its bid was unsuccessful.

Orientation

Graz is dominated by the Schlossberg, which rises over the medieval town centre. The River Mur cuts a north-south path west of the hill, dividing the old centre from the Hauptbahnhof (main train station). The Ostbahnhof (east train station) is south of the old town centre, close to the Messegelände

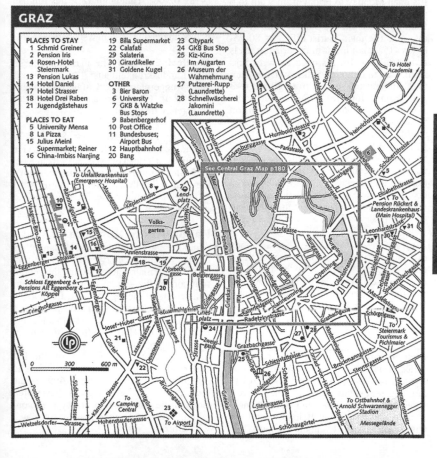

GRAZ

PLACES TO STAY		
1 Schmid Greiner	19 Billa Supermarket	23 Citypark
2 Pension Iris	22 Calafati	24 GKB Bus Stop
4 Rosen-Hotel Steiermark	29 Salateria	25 Kiz-Kino Im Augarten
13 Pension Lukas	30 Girardikeller	26 Museum der Wahrnehmung
14 Hotel Daniel	31 Goldene Kugel	27 Putzerei-Rupp (Laundrette)
17 Hotel Strasser	OTHER	28 Schnellwäscherei Jakomini (Laundrette)
18 Hotel Drei Raben	3 Bier Baron	
21 Jugendgästehaus	6 University	
	7 GKB & Watzke Bus Stops	
PLACES TO EAT	9 Babenbergerhof	
5 University Mensa	10 Post Office	
8 La Pizza	11 Bundesbuses; Airport Bus	
15 Julius Meinl Supermarket; Reiner	12 Hauptbahnhof	
16 China-Imbiss Nanjing	20 Bang	

(exhibition centre), where trade fairs are commonly held.

Tram Nos 3, 6 and 14 run from the Hauptbahnhof to Hauptplatz in the town centre. A number of streets radiate from this square, including Sporgasse, an important shopping street, and Herrengasse, the main pedestrian thoroughfare. South-east of Hauptplatz, Jakominiplatz is a major transport hub for local buses and trams.

Information

Tourist Offices There is an information office (☎ 80 75-21) in the Hauptbahnhof. It's open Monday to Friday from 9 am to 6 pm, and (in July and August) on Saturday from 9 am to 6 pm and Sunday from 10 am to 3 pm. The main tourist office (☎ 80 75-0, fax -15, email info@graztourismus.at) is at Herrengasse 16. It's open on weekdays from 9 am to 6 pm, on Saturday from 9 am to 3 pm, and on Sunday from 10 am to 3 pm. From 1 June to 31 September hours extend to 7 pm on weekdays and 6 pm on Saturday. Information about both the city and the province is available. Most of it is free, although there is a charge of AS10 for the *Old Town Walk* leaflet which has a clear map of the centre and sightseeing descriptions on the reverse. The provincial tourist board (see the Styria Orientation & Information section) sends information about Graz by post.

Money The Hauptbahnhof has a money exchange office and a Bankomat. Bankomats and banks are also to be found on Herrengasse. There's no longer an American Express (Amex) office but Bankhaus Krentschker, Hamerlinggasse 8, will exchange Amex travellers cheques without charging commission.

Post & Communications The main post office (Hauptpostamt Graz, A-8010) is at Neutorgasse 46, open on weekdays until 11 pm and weekends until 2 pm. There's another post office (Postamt A-8020) next to the Hauptbahnhof at Bahnhofgürtel 48, with many services available 24 hours.

The Jugendgästehaus (see Places to Stay) has Internet access (AS15 for 30 minutes) as do Café Zentral, Andreas Hofer Platz, which charges AS60 per hour (closed on Saturday after 1 pm and on Sunday), and Logo 1799 (email info@logo1799.or.at) at Karmeliterplatz, open on weekdays from 1.30 to 6 pm.

Travel Agency ÖKISTA (☎ 82 62 62-0) has an office at Raubergasse 20. It's open Monday to Friday from 9 am to 5.30 pm.

Bookshops The large English Bookshop (☎ 82 62 66), Tummelplatz 7, has English and French books. Buch und Presse in the Hauptbahnhof sells many English-language books, magazines and newspapers.

Medical Services The main hospital is the Landeskrankenhaus (☎ 385-0) at Auenbruggerplatz. The Unfallkrankenhaus (☎ 505-0), Göstingersrasse 24, provides emergency treatment.

Laundry Putzerei-Rupp (☎ 82 11 83), Jakoministrasse 34, houses self-service machines; it's open on weekdays from 8 am to 5 pm, Saturday 9 am to noon. Down the road, Schnellwäscherei Jakomini (☎ 81 10 20), Jakoministrasse 25, does service washes.

Hauptplatz to Hofgasse

Amid the clamour and bustle of Hauptplatz lies the Renaissance-style **Rathaus,** built in 1550. The female figures around the central fountain in the square represent the four main rivers of the region: Mur, Enns, Drau and Sann. At **Palais Saurau** on Sporgasse a figure of a Turk glares down from under the roof, while on Hofgasse the 15th century **Burg** now contains government offices. At the far end of the courtyard, on the left under the arch inscribed with AEIOU, is an ingenious double staircase (1499) – the steps diverge and converge as they spiral. Beyond the passage is a grassy area containing busts of famous people associated with Graz.

The **Domkirche** (cathedral) is a late-Gothic building dating from the 15th century, though it only became a cathedral in 1786. The interior combines Gothic and Baroque elements, with reticulated vaulting on the ceiling and many side altars. The exterior has a faded fresco showing life during the 1480 plagues.

The mannerist-Baroque **mausoleum** of Ferdinand II next door is a more impressive sight. Construction was started in 1614 by an Italian architect, Pietro de Pomis, who spent nearly 20 years on the project. After his death, Pietro Valnegro completed the structure. Inside, the exuberant stucco and frescoes were the work of Johann Bernhard Fischer von Erlach. Ferdinand, his wife and his son are interred in the crypt below, their tomb modestly set into the wall. In a clever arrangement, the dome of the crypt has a hole in the centre, allowing you to look up into the larger dome above. Pride of place in the crypt goes to the red marble sarcophagus of Ferdinand's parents, Charles II and Maria. However, only Maria lies within; Charles rests in Seckau Abbey (a former centre of the diocese of Styria) near Knittelfeld. The mausoleum is open daily from 11 am to noon and 2 to 3 pm (there's no lunch break in July and August). Admission costs AS10 (AS5 for children up to 15 years).

Heading back towards Hauptplatz, look out for figures emerging from an upper window in Glockenspielplatz to twirl to **Glockenspiel** music, every day at 11 am and 3 and 6 pm.

Landeszeughaus

The Landeszeughaus (provincial armoury) at Herrengasse 16 is a sight not to be missed. It houses an incredible array of gleaming armour and weapons, enough to equip about 30,000 soldiers. Most of it dates from the 17th century when the original armoury was built (in 1642). Its purpose was to provide a quick distribution point for equipping the local population when invasion was imminent. Some of the armour is beautifully engraved; other exhibits are crude and intimidating. The sheer weight of the metalware (such as the two-handed swords) suggests that battles were conducted in bizarre, staggering slow motion. The view from the 4th floor, of the Italian Renaissance courtyard of the Landhaus (Styrian Parliament building) next door and the Schlossberg beyond, is stunning.

The Landeszeughaus is open between 1 April and 31 October, Tuesday to Sunday from 9 am to 5 pm. Entry costs AS80 (students/seniors AS60), including a tour in English.

Churches

South-east of the Landeszeughaus is the **Stadtpfarrkirche** (parish church). It's worth peeking in at the stained glass: one small panel (left of the high altar, fourth from the bottom on the right) shows Hitler and Mussolini looking on as Christ is scourged.

Mariahilfkirche on Mariahilferplatz has a Baroque façade, created between 1742 and 1744 by Josef Hueber. Part of the church was built by de Pomis, who is buried inside.

Parks

Paths wind up the **Schlossberg** from all sides. The climb takes under 30 minutes and rewards walkers with excellent views. Along the way there are gardens and seating terraces. Alternatively, the **Schlossberg-bahn** (castle hill railway) runs from Sackstrasse up the Schlossberg every 15 minutes (public transport tickets are valid). At the top is an **open-air theatre**, a small **military museum** and a **bell tower** which dates from 1588 and which formed part of the now-demolished castle. To the south is the emblem of Graz, the **Uhrturm** (clock tower). Unusually, the larger hand on the clock face shows the hours; the minute hand was added much later. The townsfolk paid the French a ransom of 2987 florins and 11 farthings not to destroy the clock tower during the 1809 invasion.

East of the Schlossberg is the **Stadtpark**. With its large fountain and flower beds it's a relaxing place to sit or stroll.

STYRIA

Schlossberg Cave Railway

This is a good activity for those with kids. It's the longest grotto railway in Europe, winding for 2km around scenes from fairy tales. The entrance is on Schlossbergplatz; it's open daily from 10 am to 5 pm (6 pm in summer). Admission prices are on a sliding scale: AS35 for one adult or child, AS65 for two, AS85 for three, and so on. Next door is a new pedestrian tunnel through the hill, which has viewing windows into WWII air-raid caverns; admission is free.

Schloss Eggenberg

Schloss Eggenberg is at Eggenbergen Allee 90, 4km west of the centre (take tram No 1 to Schloss Eggenberg, backtrack a few metres and take the first street on the right). The Eggenberg dynasty made this its home in the 15th century; the Baroque palace was constructed by de Pomis around the original building. He was commissioned by Johann Ulrich (1568-1634), who was celebrating the power and prestige of being appointed governor of Inner Austria in 1625.

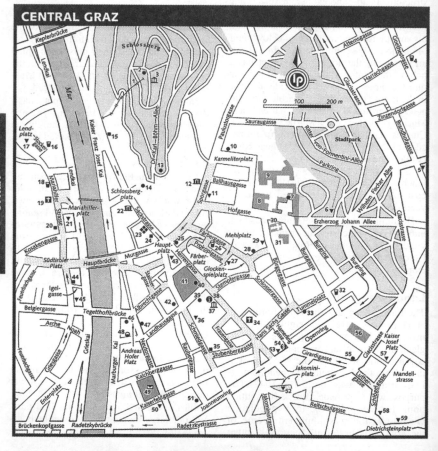

CENTRAL GRAZ

Astronomical themes and symbols dominate: the palace has 365 windows and 24 **Prunkräume** (state rooms). The Planet Hall is a riot of white stucco surrounding Baroque frescoes, painted by Hans Adam Weissenkircher. The frescoes portray the seven planets (all that were then discovered), the four elements and the 12 signs of the zodiac. Other rooms show mythological, classical and contemporary scenes. There's also a church, a Chinese room and games rooms. One room shows a portrait of Empress Maria Theresa painted as a slender figure even though by then she already weighed 100kg. The state rooms are open between 1 April and 31 October and can be visited by guided tour between 9 am and 5 pm, from Tuesday to Sunday. The tour is normally in German, though an English translation is possible (inquire when buying tickets).

The palace also houses two museums. The **Münzensammlung** (coin collection) displays coins and notes from the past 2500 years, plus other antiquities. The **Archäologie** collection covers early history and has as its prize exhibit the votive *Chariot of Strettweg* (7th century BC); this piece in bronze is dramatically lit in a dark room. The museums won't occupy visitors for more than about 30 minutes each, and are open from 1 February to 30 November, Tuesday to Sunday from 9 am to 5 pm.

The palace is set in extensive parklands where animals such as peacock and deer roam free and Roman stone reliefs can be seen. A café is open in summer. The grounds are open daily all year from 8 am to at least 5 pm (7 pm in summer). Combined admission to the park, state rooms and museums costs AS80 (concessionary and family tickets available). Entry to just the park and museums costs AS60; the park alone costs AS2.

Schloss Eggenberg, like the Landeszeughaus, forms part of the Landesmuseum Joanneum.

Other Attractions

The **Museum der Wahrnehmung** (Museum of Perception), Friedrichgasse 41, is an unusual if not over-large collection that explores sensory illusions. Admission costs AS40 (students/seniors AS30, families AS90) and it's open Wednesday to Monday from 2 to 6.30 pm.

CENTRAL GRAZ

PLACES TO STAY
15 Schlossberg Hotel
20 Hotel Mariahilf
24 Hotel Erzherzog Johann
35 Grazerhof
44 Grand Hotel Wiesler

PLACES TO EAT
5 Laufke
6 Promenade Café
11 Zur Goldenen Pastete
17 Food Market
21 Mohrenwirt
27 Gamlitzer Weinstube
29 Stainzerbauer
36 Landhaus Keller
43 Fast-Food Stands
45 Mangolds Vollwert Restaurant
50 Restaurant Gösser Bräu
52 Fast-Food Stands
53 Operncafé
57 Food Market

58 Restaurant Athen
59 Alt Wien

OTHER
1 Schlossbergbahn
2 Open-Air Theatre
3 Military Museum & Bell Tower
4 Café Harrach
7 Double Staircase
8 Schauspielhaus
9 Burg
10 Logo 1799
12 Palais Saurau
13 Uhrturm
14 Schlossberg Cave Railway
16 Neue Café Scherben
18 Brot & Spiele
19 Mariahilfkirche
22 Palais Attems; Styriarte & Steirischer Herbst Offices
23 Kastner & Öhler Department Store; Feinspitz

25 Kölz
26 MI Bar
28 Glockenspiel
30 Domkirche
31 Mausoleum
32 Kommod
33 English Bookshop
34 Stadtpfarrkirche
37 Landeszeughaus
38 Main Tourist Office
39 Landhaus Courtyard
40 Steirisches Heimatwerk
41 Rathaus
42 Casino
46 Hertz
47 Café Zentral
48 Bus Station
49 Main Post Office
51 ÖKISTA
54 Bankhaus Krentschker
55 Tageskasse
56 Opernhaus

STYRIA

At the southern end of the No 4 tram line is the **Arnold Schwarzenegger Stadion**, renamed in 1997 after the Styrian-born actor. Football (soccer) is played here, but the Stadion also houses the gym where Schwarzenegger worked out in his body-building days (admission is free). There's not much to see (some equipment, a few old photos) but plenty of tourists make the trip.

Activities

Bad Eggenberg, Janzgasse 21 (take tram No 1), is open daily from 8 am to 9.30 pm. A day pass for the swimming pool costs AS70 (AS45 for children and students) and the sauna costs AS140 (AS80 for children). A massage costs from AS220.

The main tourist office organises guided walks of the city (AS75), daily at 2.30 pm from April to October; Saturday only in winter.

Special Events

The Styriarte is a classical music festival held from late June to mid-July: contact the Styriarte Kartenbüro (☎ 82 50 00, fax 877 38 36), Sackstrasse 17, A-8010. Steirischer Herbst is an avant-garde festival held during October. Events include music, theatre, films, exhibitions and art installations, and are staged at a dozen different locations around town. Contact Steirischer Herbst Informationsbüro (☎ 82 30 07-0, fax 83 57 88, email stherbst@ping.at), Sackstrasse 17, or view their Web site at stherbst.at. Offices for both events are housed in Palais Attems.

The autumn trade fair, Grazer Herbstmesse International, takes place in the Messegelände (☎ 80 88-0), Messeplatz 1, for nine days starting in late September.

The Graz marathon takes place in late October.

Places to Stay – Budget

Except for the camp site and the Jugendgästehaus, Graz has few cheap places to stay, so try to book ahead. Even most private rooms (get the list from the tourist office) are pricey or a long way from the centre. Staff at the tourist office will book rooms (AS30 commission) but don't always get the lowest prices.

Camping Central (☎ 28 18 31, *Martinhofstrasse 3*) is open from 1 April to 31 October and a two person site costs AS254, including use of the swimming pool. The camp site is about 6km southwest of the city centre; take bus No 32 from Jakominiplatz.

The HI *Jugendgästehaus* (☎ 71 48 76, *fax -88, email jgh-graz@oejhv.or.at, Idlhofgasse 74*) has renovated rooms with private shower/WC; four-bed dorms cost AS220 per person, and singles/doubles cost AS300/500. Add AS20 first night's surcharge if you're only staying one or two nights. Reception is open from 7 am to 10 pm (closed 9 am to 5 pm at weekends and on holidays) and there's always daytime access. Laundry costs from AS40 to wash and dry. There are extensive lawns and parking, and self-service lunches cost AS65 (available to non-guests). The hostel has conference rooms and seminar deals. It's usually closed for Christmas and during January.

A short walk south of the Hauptbahnhof is *Hotel Strasser* (☎ 71 39 77, *fax 71 68 56, Eggenberger Gürtel 11*). It has functional but pleasant singles/doubles for AS440/660 with private shower, or AS340/560 without. There is a reasonably priced restaurant on the premises but no lift. Behind the Hauptbahnhof, *Pension Lukas* (☎ 58 25 90, *Waagner Biro Strasse 8*) offers similar rooms for AS350/550 with shower, or AS250/450 without; breakfast isn't included. The sleazy reputation of this place is no longer warranted.

Schmid Greiner (☎ 68 14 82, *Grabenstrasse 64*), north of Schlossberg, is a cosy and old-fashioned B&B pension, but the traffic outside can be noisy. Singles/doubles cost AS370/480 with hall shower but are cheaper in the low season.

Places to Stay – Mid-Range

Hotel Academia (☎ 32 33 30, *fax -3520, Untere Schönbrunngasse 7-11*) is a student residence used as a hotel from 1 July to 30 September. There are 170 single/double rooms with shower/WC and modern fittings costing AS480/760. *Rosen-Hotel Steiermark (☎ 38 15 03-0, fax -62, Liebiggasse 4)* has the same setup and it's closer to the university. Singles/doubles start at AS440/680.

Pensions generally provide the best three-star deals, though they tend to be farther from the town centre. An exception is *Pension Iris (☎ 32 20 81, fax -5, Bergmanngasse 10)*, where comfortable rooms with shower, toilet and TV cost about AS580/800. Double-glazing eliminates traffic noise.

Pension Alt Eggenberg (☎/fax 58 66 15, Baiernstrasse 3) offers singles/doubles with private shower/WC and satellite TV, good value at AS400/560. There's an inexpensive restaurant with a garden. It's west of the centre but easily reached by tram No 1 (the stop after Schloss Eggenberg). Nearby, at the terminal of tram No 1, is *Pension Köppel (☎/fax 58 55 47, Göstinger Strasse 25)*, where rooms have the same facilities but are more modern and cost AS470/740.

Pension Rückert (☎/fax 32 30 31, Rückertgasse 4) is on a quiet residential street east of the town centre. Rooms with shower/WC cost AS520/790; some singles with hall shower are available for AS420. Take tram No 1 to Tegetthoffplatz, walk 100m in the direction of the tram route then turn right.

At the centre of the old town is *Grazerhof (☎ 82 98 24, fax 81 96 33-40, Stubenberggasse 10)*. Smallish, innocuous rooms cost AS450/740, or from AS530/980 with private shower. The hotel adjoins two pedestrian streets, but the receptionist can tell you where to park.

Hotel Drei Raben (☎ 71 26 86, fax 71 59 59-6, Annenstrasse 43) is comfortable and convenient. Singles/doubles with bathroom and satellite TV start at about AS700/980. There are a few rooms using hall facilities costing AS410/700, and some triple rooms (AS1460).

Hotel Mariahilf (☎ 71 31 630, fax 71 76 52, Mariahilfer Strasse 9) has large rooms with shower/WC. Some are quite grand, but in others the furnishings are mixed and mismatched. Singles/doubles are overpriced in summer at AS940/1500, though in winter the rate drops to AS700/980.

Places to Stay – Top End

Schlossberg Hotel (☎ 80 70-0, fax -70, email schlossberg-hotel@steiermark-online .at, Kaiser Franz Josef Kai 30) is a charming four star hotel, small enough for guests to receive personal service. Singles/doubles start at AS1700/2300; rooms vary in size and style but all have character. There's a sauna and a fitness room (free for guests), a summer swimming pool and a rooftop terrace.

Hotel Erzherzog Johann (☎ 81 16 16, fax 81 15 15, Sackstrasse 3-5) is very central and housed in a 400-year-old building. Large, well-furnished singles/doubles start at AS1350/1990, with slightly lower prices in the low season (November to March except over New Year). The hotel is built around a pleasant, plant-strewn atrium (housing the quality 'winter garden' restaurant) and guests have free use of the sauna. Nearby parking costs AS160 per day.

Hotel Daniel (☎ 71 10 80, fax 71 10 85, email daniel@weitzer.com, Europaplatz 1), by the Hauptbahnhof, has good facilities for businesspeople, such as fax and computer services. Rooms cost from AS1190/1390.

The only five star hotel in town is the *Grand Hotel Wiesler (☎ 70 66-0, fax -76, email wiesler@sime.com, Grieskai 4)*. Its rooms start at AS2150/2800 and have excellent facilities, though they vary greatly in size. Guests have free use of the sauna; the solarium costs AS100.

Places to Eat

See also the bars listed in the Entertainment section for more eating options.

Self-Catering The main *food markets* are at Kaiser Josef Platz and Lendplatz and are open Monday to Saturday from 7 am to at least 12.30 am. There are also *fast-food stands* at Hauptplatz and Jakominiplatz.

Supermarkets include the large *Billa* at Annenstrasse 23 and a *Julius Meinl* below ground in the shopping centre opposite the Hauptbahnhof. *Laufke (Elisabethstrasse 6)*, also called Elisabethof, is a restaurant and expensive food store open each weekday to 11 pm.

Self-Service & Budget There are lots of excellent-value restaurants dotted around town. The university *Mensa*, downstairs at Schubertstrasse 2-4, serves main meals (including a vegetarian choice) costing from AS39 to AS60, with discounts for students. Food is served Monday to Friday from 11 am to 2 pm. The café on the ground floor is open Monday to Friday from 8 am to 3 pm, and has breakfasts for AS29. There are several other cheap places near the university which are popular with students: wander down Halbärthgasse and Harrachgasse.

The shopping centre opposite the Hauptbahnhof houses *Reiner*, open on weekdays from 8 am to 6.15 pm and on Saturday from 8 am to 4 pm. Self-service hot buffets cost less than AS65. There's a buffet-style restaurant called *Feinspitz* on the 2nd floor of the Kastner & Öhler department store on Sackstrasse. Tempting dishes start at AS60, and snacks and drinks are cheap.

As usual, weekday lunches in Chinese restaurants are a great deal: they start at a mere AS42 in *Calafati (Lissagasse 2)* near the Jugendgästehaus, or there's *China-Imbiss Nanjing (Annenstrasse 64)* east of the Hauptbahnhof.

La Pizza (☎ 71 03 22, Keplerstrasse 38) offers pizzas starting at AS60 and a free delivery service for orders over AS70; it's open daily from 11 am to 11 pm.

Mohrenwirt (Mariahilfer Strasse 16) is a small Gasthof with snacks and meals from AS20 to AS85. Ask the server about daily specials as they're not written down. Opening times are Saturday to Wednesday from 10 am to midnight.

A good place to try Austrian cooking (and about 70 different types of beer!) is *Goldene Kugel (Leonhardstrasse 32)*. It's open Sunday to Friday from 9 am to 1 am. Two-course lunches cost AS60 or AS70; evening dishes cost from AS75 to AS130. Close by is *Girardikeller (Leonhardstrasse 28)*, a cellar bar with free live music every Sunday except in summer. The food is very cheap – the weekday special is just AS50, and big pizzas with seven toppings cost AS65. It's open daily from 5 pm (6 pm at weekends) till 2 am.

Vegetarian delights are served at *Mangolds Vollwert Restaurant (Griesgasse 11)*, open weekdays from 11 am to 8 pm and Saturday from 11 am to 5 pm. Hot and cold buffets cost AS14 per 100g, daily dishes cost from AS43 to AS70, and there are various desserts. *Salateria (Leonhardstrasse 18)* is a similar place, with a weekday lunch menu for AS45. It's open from 10 am to 9 pm (closed holidays).

Alt Wien (Dietrichsteinplatz) is a simple restaurant with friendly staff. Austrian meals start at about AS60 and a salad buffet costs AS30/60 for a small/large plate. It's closed at weekends and on holidays.

Gamlitzer Weinstube (Mehlplatz 4) serves Styrian dishes for under AS140. Try the *Steirerpfandl* served in a pan (AS80): a tasty and filling combination of home-made pasta (*Spätzle*), cheese, minced meat and mushroom sauce. There are outside tables on the square; the restaurant is closed at weekends and on holidays.

Mid-Range & Top End The *Restaurant Gösser Bräu (Neutorgasse 48)* is a large place with a garden terrace and many different rooms. Dishes cost from AS65 to AS200 and there's a wide selection of local Gösser beers starting at AS31. It's open from 9 am to midnight daily (except most Saturdays).

Zur Goldenen Pastete (Sporgasse 28) is Graz's oldest inn. It serves affordable Styrian and vegetarian meals, and is closed on Sunday and holidays.

Restaurant Athen (☎ 81 61 11, Dietrichsteinplatz 1) is a Greek place where dishes start at about AS90; there's live music on Friday night, when it's usually necessary to book. It's open daily from 11 am (5 pm on Sunday and holidays) to midnight.

For atmosphere and quality, head to the 16th century *Landhaus Keller (☎ 83 02 76, Schmiedgasse 9)*. Flowers, coats of arms, medieval-style murals and soft background music contribute to the historical ambience. Dishes, including interesting Styrian specialities, start at AS125. In the summer, outside tables overlook the Landhaus courtyard. The restaurant opens Monday to Saturday from 11.30 am to midnight.

Equally atmospheric is *Stainzerbauer (☎ 82 11 06, Bürgergasse 4)*, with its wooden archways, numerous photographs and soft music. Styrian and Austrian specialities mostly cost between AS130 and AS225, though the weekday two course lunch is a bargain at AS80.

Grand Hotel Wiesler (see Places to Stay) has a gourmet restaurant, as do some of the other top hotels. *Pichlmaier (☎ 47 15 97, Petersbergen Strasse 9)* is a quality restaurant in the south-eastern suburb of St Peter. It serves Austrian and international dishes starting at AS200 and is open daily.

Cafés Graz has several traditional coffee houses, including *Operncafé (Opernring 22)* which is open daily from 7.30 am (Sunday 9 am) to midnight. There's free piano music from 7 pm on Wednesday. Another café is *Promenade* in the Stadtpark. It has decent food and outside seating and is open from 9 am to midnight daily.

Entertainment

Theatre & Opera Graz is an important cultural centre, hosting musical events throughout the year. A *Tageskasse (☎ 80 00, Kaiser Josef Platz 10)* sells tickets for the *Schauspielhaus* (theatre; ☎ *80 05*) and *Opernhaus* (opera; ☎ *80 08*), and dispenses information; seats cost from AS50 to AS500 (no commission charged). Students aged under 27 pay half-price. Opening hours are Monday to Friday, 8 am to 6.30 pm, Saturday till 1 pm. An hour before performances, students can buy leftover tickets for AS60 at the venue, and anybody can buy standing-room tickets for AS35 (theatre) or AS40 (opera). Both venues are closed in August. Look for free *Sommertheater* events in various venues around town.

Bars The *Grand Hotel Wiesler* (see Places to Stay) is famous for its jazz brunch on Sunday from 11 am to 2 pm (mid-October to late June). It attracts well known performers; AS315 admission includes the buffet. *Babenbergerhof (Babenbergerstrasse 39)* is a smallish bar with live jazz (free) on Monday and the first Tuesday in the month. Anna, the vivacious English-speaking hostess, treats her customers as friends. It's open from Monday to Friday and has cheap midday menus.

The area round the university has various places where you can mix with students, such as *Café Harrach* at Harrachgasse 26 (open from 9 am weekdays, 7 pm weekends). Just north of the university is *Bier Baron (Heinrichstrasse 56)*, a large, busy bar with rows of gleaming silver beer pumps, and a garden. Food is reasonably priced. The bar is open daily except Sunday from 11 am to 1 am (6 pm to midnight on Saturday and holidays).

Mehlplatz and Prokopigasse, in the centre of town, are full of relatively inexpensive, lively bars which offer snacks or meals until late. Like its Viennese parallel, this area has been dubbed the 'Bermuda Triangle'. The *MI Bar* (3rd floor) on Färberplatz gives a city panorama; it's open from 10 am, 4 pm on Sunday.

Kommod (Burggasse 15) is a bright and busy bar, often packed with students, where pizza and pasta cost from AS68; it's open daily from 5 pm to 2 am. *Neue Café Scherben (Stockergasse 2)*, off Lendplatz, is a more mellow bar, with paintings (for sale), plants and sofas; it's open daily from noon to 3 am. Its cellar bar is open in the evening for discos and live music (sometimes free).

Brot & Spiele (Mariahilfer Strasse 17) offers beer and cheap food from 4 pm; chess and pool tables are available. It's open from 10 am (Sunday and holidays from 1 pm) to 2 am daily.

Bang (Dreihackengasse 4) is a bar and disco with a mostly (but not exclusively) gay clientele. It's open on Friday and Saturday from 9 pm (AS40). There are also occasional cabaret shows (AS80).

Cinemas & Casino As in other cities, cinemas are cheaper on Monday (AS70). The *Royal English Cinema (☎ 826 133, Conrad von Hötzendorf Strasse 470)* screens English-language films. *Kiz-Kino Im Augarten (☎ 82 11 86, Friedrichgasse 24)* regularly shows films (mostly non-mainstream) in their original language (AS85; AS65 Monday to Wednesday). Graz *casino* is at Landhausgasse 10.

Shopping

Styria is known for painted pottery and printed linen. Other popular souvenirs include metal and china plates, steins, cow bells, dolls and statuettes. Quality handicrafts are available at Steirisches Heimatwerk at Herrengasse 10. Another souvenir shop in the town centre is Kölz, Hauptplatz 11. Opposite is Niedermeyer, Hauptplatz 7, the photography and electrical goods chain. The Kastner & Öhler department store is north of Hauptplatz. Citypark, Lazarettgürtel 55, is a shopping centre with 75 shops (take bus No 35 from Jakominiplatz).

A flea market is held at Karmeliterplatz on every third Saturday in the month from 6 am to 1 pm. Occasional handicrafts markets appear on Fäberplatz.

Getting There & Away

Air The airport (☎ 29 02-0) is 10km south of the town centre, just beyond the A2. Several flights a day go to/from Vienna, Munich, Frankfurt and Zürich. Innsbruck and Salzburg are serviced most days.

Bus Bundesbuses depart from outside the Hauptbahnhof and from the bus station at Andreas Hofer Platz, where there's a bus information office (open till 6 pm weekdays, 1 pm Saturday). Alternatively, call ☎ 0660-80 20 (charged at the local rate) for information. GKB buses (☎ 0316-59 87-0) run to Piber from Griesplatz or sometimes from Lendplatz. Watzke buses (☎ 0316-40 20 42) make the trip to the Austrian Open-Air Museum at Stübing, departing from Lendplatz.

Train Call ☎ 17 17 for train information. Direct IC trains to Vienna's Südbahnhof depart every two hours (AS310, two hours 40 minutes). Trains depart two-hourly to Salzburg (AS410, at least 4¼ hours), either direct or requiring a change at Bischofshofen. All trains running north or west go via Bruck an der Mur (AS100, 40 minutes), and it's sometimes necessary to change. Even if you want to go south-west to Klagenfurt you still have to go north to Bruck first; the total trip takes about 3½ hours. Trains to eastern Styria via Graz's Ostbahnhof originate at the Hauptbahnhof.

Two direct trains depart daily for Zagreb (AS264, 3½ hours). There are no direct services to Budapest. The quickest routing is north via Bruck (AS565, 5½ hours), though you could instead go east via Szentgotthárd (7½ hours).

Car & Motorcycle The A2/E59 from Vienna to Klagenfurt passes a few kilometres south of the city. Leading north from the A2, the A9 passes under the city and emerges to take a north-west course to the Salzkammergut, with the S35 branching off to Bruck an der Mur. To the south, the A9 heads to Maribor in Slovenia.

Car Rental City offices include: Avis (☎ 81 29 20), Schlögelgasse 10, and Hertz (☎ 82 50 07), Andreas Hofer Platz 1. See the Getting Around chapter for rates. Local operator Steinbauer Jeitler (☎ 71 50 83), Fabriksgasse 29, near Citypark shopping centre, may have lower prices.

Getting Around

To/From the Airport Bus No 631 runs daily from the Hauptbahnhof (the bay by Café Steirertreff). There are six a day in each direction (20 minutes). The first/last departures are at 5.10 am/6.15 pm from the Hauptbahnhof and at 5.55 am/7.20 pm from the airport. Buses stop en route at Griesplatz and the Hotel Weitzer.

Public Transport All of Graz is covered by one zone, zone 101. Single tickets (AS20) are valid for one hour, and you can switch between buses, trams and the Schlossbergbahn. Ten one-zone tickets cost AS150. A 24 hour pass costs AS40, a weekly pass AS92 and a monthly pass AS325 (valid from first use in each case). If you buy a city pass, it reduces regional travel fares by one zone.

Hourly and 24-hour tickets can be purchased from the driver; other passes can be purchased from Tabak shops, pavement ticket machines or the tourist office.

Other Transport You can park in areas marked as blue zones for a maximum of three hours between specified times (approximately shopping hours); buy tickets (*Parkschein*) at Tabak shops or the tourist office (AS8 per 30 minutes).

To call a taxi, dial ☎ 2801, 222 878 or 889. Taxis cost AS25 at taxi ranks or AS35 if you have to phone for one, plus AS12 per kilometre (AS13 per kilometre between 8 pm and 6 am).

You can rent bicycles from the Hauptbahnhof between 6 am and midnight daily.

Around Graz

The Graz tourist office has brochures in English giving plenty of ideas for trips near Graz; most are within a 40km radius of the city.

STYRIAN WINE ROUTES
Several tours of wine routes in the Graz region are available. The Graz tourist office has information on the routes – its *Weinführer* booklet includes maps. To explore these routes you really need your own transport. The train will take you to only one or two points on a certain route, for example it will get you to Gleisdorf, the starting point

of the Oststeirische Römerweinstrasse (East Styria Roman Wine Road), but then takes a very circuitous diversion before it rejoins the main route at Hartberg. To try to follow a route by bus would be slow and tedious, involving many changes.

One possibility is to hire a bicycle in Graz and take it on the train to one of the stations on a wine route. Deutschlandsberg is the main town on the Schilcher Weinstrasse (Schilcher Wine Road) and can be reached by hourly train from Graz (five zones from Graz, AS86; one hour). The train terminates at Wies-Eibiswald, which is also the end of this wine route. Ehrenhausen is the start of the Südsteirischen Weinstrasse (South Styria Wine Road) and can be reached by hourly trains from Graz (five zones, AS86; 45 minutes). Leibnitz, a station en route, is the start of the Sausaler Weinstrasse (Sausaler Wine Road).

DEUTSCHLANDSBERG
☎ 03462 • pop 7800 • 375m
This town is the centre of the production of Schilcher, a light, dry rosé. A good view of Deutschlandsberg can be had from **Burg Landsberg**, about 25 minutes walk from the town centre: head west from Hauptplatz and take the first right turn after crossing the railway tracks. The castle also contains a museum of early history. On the festival of Corpus Christi, church altars in town are specially decorated with flowers.

The tourist office (☎ 75 20), Hauptplatz 37, is open Monday to Saturday from 9 am to noon. After noon, you can often pick up brochures in the town hall next door.

Places to Stay & Eat
Deutschlandsberg offers a choice of guesthouses or private rooms, though most are out of the town centre. Convenient but relatively expensive is *Gasthof Kollar-Göbl* (☎ 26 42-0, fax -15, Hauptplatz 10), offering singles/doubles with shower/WC for about AS350 per person (reception closes at 3 pm on Sunday). Also on Hauptplatz is *Sorger Imbiss*, a meat shop with a self-service area for cheap hot food, and

China-Restaurant Peking, offering cheap weekday lunch menus.

Various Buschenschenken beckon on the outskirts of town; these are shown on the map in the holiday brochure available from the tourist office.

EHRENHAUSEN

☎ 03453 • pop 1200 • 258m

Ehrenhausen is smaller and more picturesque than Deutschlandsberg, and a better place to visit if you just want a fleeting glimpse of the wine region.

Orientation & Information

Marktplatz is the centre and the hub of the village. To walk there from the train station takes four minutes; turn left and cross the stream, then turn right. In the Rathaus at Marktplatz 2 is a rack holding tourist brochures, accessible during office hours (there's no tourist office). There's also a bank and Bankomat at Marktplatz. The post office is by the station.

Things to See & Do

Before embarking on the South Styria Wine Road there are a couple of things worth doing in town. The Eggenberg family was associated with Ehrenhausen, and purchased Schloss Ehrenhausen in 1543. A more interesting building, however, is the **mausoleum** of Ruprecht von Eggenberg (1546-1611), hero in battles against the Turks. It rests on a plateau above Marktplatz, and a path leads up just to the right of the Rathaus (less than 10 minutes walk). The white and yellow building has two large warriors gazing down from the terrace. The stucco inside is starkly white, with many embellishments clinging to the central dome and vines swirling around supporting pillars. There's a good view from the terrace down to Marktplatz.

Before climbing up, get the key from the manse (*Pfarrhof*) next to the **Pfarrkirche** on Marktplatz. Take the opportunity to explore the church itself: the altars inside are vivid Baroque, with lots of gold and painted statues. Don't leave Ehrenhausen without admiring the view from the western end of Marktplatz: the pastel colours of the houses in the foreground, topped by the church steeple and the mausoleum crowning the hill, form a fine picture.

Places to Stay & Eat

There are several private rooms available, or there's **Zur Goldenen Krone** (☎ 26 40, Marktplatz 24), offering singles/doubles with private shower/WC for AS350/600. The next stop north by train, Leibnitz, has a wider choice of places to stay; inquire at its tourist office (☎ 03452-767 11).

To find somewhere to eat you need look no farther than Marktplatz. It offers several choices, such as **Painer Gasthof & Fleischeri**, right by the church. It has tables inside and out, and serves local food. The three course lunch is AS65 and it's closed on Monday. Marktplatz also has a **Nah & Frisch** supermarket (through the Raiffeisen Bank arch; open on weekdays from 7.30 am to 6 pm and on Saturday from 7.30 am to 12.30 pm) and hosts a market on Friday afternoon.

AUSTRIAN OPEN-AIR MUSEUM

Seven provinces in Austria have open-air museums showing regional architecture. The Österreichischen Freilichtmuseum (Austrian Open-Air Museum) in Stübing is the best to visit as you get to sample the whole country in one go. The main complex is about 2km from end to end and is arranged in order as if the visitor is walking through Austria from east to west. First comes Burgenland, then Styria, Carinthia, the Danube Valley, Salzburg, Tirol, and finally Vorarlberg. Building No 20 is a west Styrian grocery, with old-fashioned goods on display and a few modern items for sale. No 38 is a Styrian schoolhouse with a classroom and an exhibition. Other highlights include the sgraffito decorations and unified structure of the farmhouse from Upper Austria (No 58), the crisscross construction of the barn (No 56), and the Salzburg *Rauchhaus,* or smoke house (No 77), so-called due to the absence of a chimney –

smoke was supposed to seep through chinks in the ceiling and dry grain in the loft.

Two to three hours is sufficient for a visit. Bring provisions for a picnic or visit the restaurant just outside the entrance. Smoking is not permitted in the complex as most buildings are timber.

The museum is open from 1 April to 31 October, daily except Monday, between 9 am and 5 pm. Entry costs AS75 (children AS30, students AS40). If you only want to see the exhibition hall near the entrance, admission costs AS20 (children/students AS10); it provides the background to this and other open-air museums in Austria and around Europe (text in German). At the entrance, buy the detailed booklet (in English) for AS25, giving a rundown on the 80-odd buildings in the complex.

A notice board by the ticket office announces when country-craft demonstrations take place. As these don't occur on a regular basis, it's worth telephoning (☎ 03124-53 700) before planning your visit. The buildings tend to look a bit similar after a while, unless there's something happening to liven things up. At the end of September Erlebnistag, a special fair with crafts, music and dancing, is held at the complex.

Getting There & Away

There are hourly trains from Graz to Stübing (two zones, AS38; 15 minutes). From the train station, walk left for 20 minutes, eventually passing over the rail tracks, then under them just before the entrance. A Watzke bus (☎ 0316-40 20 42) goes directly to the museum Monday to Saturday, departing from Lendplatz in Graz at 9 am and returning in the afternoon.

LURGROTTE

These caves, 20km north of Graz, are Austria's largest. They can be combined easily with the open-air museum on a day trip from Graz (do the caves first). The temperature in the caves is about 9°C.

There are two entrances to the Lurgrotte, and you can take a one hour tour from either entrance. The eastern one is at Semriach, from where daily tours (☎ 03127-83 19) are conducted between 10 am and 4 pm year-round (AS55). Infrequent buses to Semriach depart from Andreas Hofer Platz in Graz. If you also want to visit the open-air museum, it's easier to use the western entrance to the caves at Peggau. Tours (☎ 03127-25 80) are conducted daily from 9 am to 4 pm between 1 April and 31 October (AS60, or AS85 for a two-hour tour). Peggau is on the same train route as Stübing, and it's one zone farther from Graz (AS54). The caves are 15 minutes walk from the station.

PIBER & KÖFLACH
☎ 03144

Piber's claim to fame is the world-famous Lipizzaner stallion stud farm, 3km from the small town of Köflach.

Orientation & Information

Piber is about 40km west of Graz. Train travellers arrive first in Köflach, which has a tourist office (☎ 25 19-70, fax -79), Peter Rosegger Gasse 1, near Hauptplatz. Opening hours are Monday to Thursday from 8 am to noon and 1 to 4.30 pm, Friday from 7.30 am to 1 pm.

Bundesgestüt Piber

The Bundesgestüt Piber (Piber Stud Farm; ☎ 33 23) has been in operation since 1920 and now comes under the wing of the Ministry of Agriculture. The stud farm was moved here when the original location, Lipizza, became part of Slovenia after WWI. About 40 foals are born at the farm every year; of these only about five (just stallions) are of the right height and aptitude to be sent to the Spanische Reitschule (Spanish Riding School) in Vienna for training, which lasts at least five years. Even before training, each stallion is worth about AS200,000. Favoured veteran stallions return to the farm to service the mares – six different breeding lines are currently in operation. Foals are born dark and take between five and 12 years to achieve their distinctive white colouring.

The farm can be visited between Easter and 31 October. The guided tour takes about 70 minutes and costs AS120 (AS50 for students and children). Tours depart between 9 and 10.15 am and 2 and 3.15 pm but only if there are at least 20 people (which there invariably are). Visitors see a film (with English commentary on the English tour – phone ahead for details) and museum exhibits, then tour the stables to meet some of the equine residents.

To reach the stud farm from Köflach station, walk up Bahnhofstrasse, turn right along Hauptplatz (300m) and then left for a 3km walk along Piberstrasse (signposted). Buses along this road are infrequent.

Places to Stay & Eat

Staff at the Köflach tourist office will give details of pensions and private rooms. *Gasthof Bardel* (☎ *34 22, Fesselweg 1*) provides food and accommodation (singles/doubles costing AS350/600) right next to the stud farm.

Köflach's large *Pam Pam* supermarket is at Quergasse, off Bahnhofstrasse. *China-Restaurant Bei Le* on Bahnhofstrasse offers lunch menus costing between AS55 and AS65 (closed on Monday except holidays).

Getting There & Away

Köflach is the final stop for GKB private trains running approximately hourly from Graz (50 minutes). The fare is AS70 one way, or AS130 for a 24 hour pass. There are also GKB buses from Graz, leaving from Griesplatz or sometimes Lendplatz. For information call GKB (☎ 0316-59 87-0).

BÄRNBACH

☎ 03142 • pop 5160 • 432m

This small town is worth visiting primarily for the unique St Barbara Kirche, and can easily be combined with a trip to Piber. From the stud farm, return to Piberstrasse and then walk (buses are as rare as non-skiing Austrians) about 2km east (away from Köflach). You can't miss the church on the main road. Continue in the same direction for Hauptplatz and, across the

stream, the glass-making centre. A left turn at Hauptplatz will take you into Haupt-strasse and the road to the **Alt Kainach castle** (2km), which contains historical exhibits. Get tourist information from Bärnbach town hall (☎ 615 50-21, email stadtgemeinde@baernbach.at).

Things to See & Do

Although built after WWII, **St Barbara Kirche** needed renovating in the late 1980s. About 80% of the town population voted to commission the maverick Viennese artist Friedensreich Hundertwasser to undertake the redesign; work began in 1987 and was completed in 1988. It was a bold move: Hundertwasser is known for his unusual design concepts, particularly in discarding the straight line in building projects. The gamble paid off; the church is a visual treat inside and out, yet is still clearly a place of worship rather than a pseudo art gallery. Leave a donation and pick up the explanation card in English, which reveals the symbolic meaning behind the architectural design features.

The church is surrounded by 12 gates, each representing a different faith: Hinduism, Islam and so on, all connected by an uneven pathway. By the west façade is a powerful mosaic war memorial by Franz Weiss. The distinctive church steeple is topped by a gold onion dome. Features you wouldn't see in any other church include the bowed roof with green splodges along its flanks, the irregular windows, and the grass growing on the side porch roofs.

The interior also has striking and thoughtful touches: Hundertwasser's 'spiral of life' window (which reflects the afternoon sun onto the font); the modern art stations of the Cross by Rudolf Pointer; the glass altar and podium filled with 12 layers of different types of earth representing the 12 tribes of Israel; and the harmonious ceramics surrounding the image of Christ on the Cross in the chancel.

Bärnbach has been known for its glass-making for at least two centuries. The museum at the **Stölzle Glas Center** (☎ 629 50),

Glassblowing in Bärnbach

Glass is made from silica (usually sand), which is fused at high temperatures with borates or phosphates. Glass has been made for nearly 6000 years, though glassblowing with the aid of a pipe began only about 2000 years ago.

Glassblowers have plied their trade in the Bärnbach region for 300 years. In the old days they would establish camps in the forest, to make it easier to collect the 5000kg of wood that was required to produce 2kg of glass. The wood was needed to create potash, as well as to fire the ovens. Other materials required were quartz sand and lime.

The glass-making methods used in the Stölzle Glas Center are not substantially different to ones used all those years ago in the forest camps. The glass is melted in a large tank furnace which always contains about 8 tonnes of glass (over 1 tonne is used per day). The glass is kept molten at a temperature of 1200°C: the furnace is kept at this temperature 24 hours a day. If the furnace is ever shut off, it has to be done gradually, to avoid the risk of an explosion (to go from 1200°C to room temperature would require between five and seven days!).

The glassblower uses a 1.2m-long hollow iron pipe with a mouthpiece at one end. The end of the pipe is used to collect a small amount of molten glass, which the glassblower expands by blowing into the pipe. Several different glassblowers will work in turn on the same piece. It is necessary to periodically reheat the glass while it is being worked, using special ovens called muffels. Any handles or decorative pieces are added when the glass is hot, then it's placed in the cooling oven. It is cooled slowly (a process called annealing, which reduces brittleness) and each piece takes around four or five hours to pass through the 30m-long cooling oven.

The glass object is then ready to be cut, engraved, enamelled or painted to produce the finished product. A range of glassware can be admired and purchased in the factory shop.

Hochtregisterstrasse 1, is dedicated to glass and you can participate in a one hour tour of the factory. It's open from 1 April to 15 December, Monday to Friday from 9 am to 5 pm, Saturday from 9 am to 1 pm, and (May to October) Sunday and holidays from 9 am to 1 pm. Admission costs AS70 (AS130 for a family card). Guided tours are conducted in German (although you can phone ahead and request the English version) and commence at 9, 10 and 11 am and noon Monday to Thursday, and at 9, 10 and 11 am on Friday.

Places to Stay & Eat

There's an information board by the church, which lists accommodation and other facilities. Lodging is in small guesthouses such as *Gästehaus Lackner Hatzl* (☎ 625 85, *Hauptstrasse 62*), where rooms with shower/WC cost AS300 per person.

For self-caterers there's a *Billa* supermarket next to the town hall. Hauptstrasse has several places to eat: *Gasthaus Wolfgang Kuss* at No 4 has pizzas and Austrian food from AS70 (closed on Sunday and Monday); opposite is *Gasthaus Lind* (closed on Wednesday) which is similarly priced.

Getting There & Away

Bärnbach is on the Graz-Köflach train line, one stop (five minutes) before Köflach. The train station is 2km out of the town centre. To get to the train station from St Barbara Kirche, go to Hauptplatz and turn right down Dr Niederdorfer Strasse; continue until the rail tracks pass under the road, then take the next left. Regional buses stop in Bärnbach town centre.

Northern & Western Styria

MARIAZELL

☎ 03882 • pop 2000 • 868m

Mariazell is the most important pilgrimage site in Austria. It was founded in 1157 and a number of miracles have since been attributed to the Virgin of Mariazell, including Lewis I of Hungary's unlikely victory over the Turks in 1357. The town will be most crowded with pilgrims on 15 August (Assumption) and 8 September (Mary's 'name day').

Orientation

Mariazell is in the extreme north of Styria, close to Lower Austria and within the lower reaches of the eastern Alps. The train station (where you can rent bikes) is in St Sebastian, 1.5km north of Hauptplatz, the centre of Mariazell.

Information

Staff at the tourist office (☎ 23 66, fax 39 45, email tv-mzl@kom.at), Hauptplatz 13, will find rooms without charging. Ask about reductions given with the Gästekarte. Summer opening hours are Monday to Friday from 9 am to 12.30 pm and 2 to 5.30 pm, Saturday from 9 am to noon and 4 to 6 pm, and Sunday from 9 am to noon. Between 1 November and 30 April hours are Monday to Friday from 9 am to noon and 2 to 5 pm, and Saturday from 9 am to

noon. The post office (Postamt A-8630), Ludwig Leber Strasse, is just west of Hauptplatz.

Monday is the quietest day of the week, so many hotels and restaurants take their rest day then.

Basilika

This church on Hauptplatz is Mariazell's *raison d'être* and most visible feature. The original Romanesque church was converted to Gothic in the 14th century, then expanded and refitted as Baroque in the 17th century. The result from the outside is a strange clash of styles, with the original Gothic steeple bursting like a wayward skeletal limb from between two Baroque onion domes. The interior works better, with Gothic ribs on the ceiling combining well with Baroque frescoes and lavish stuccowork. Both Johann Bernhard Fischer von Erlach and his son Josef Emmanuel had a hand in the Baroque face-lift; the crucifixion group (1715) on the high altar is by Lorenzo Mattielli.

In the centre of the church is the **Gnadenkapelle** (Chapel of Miracles), a gold and silver edifice that houses the Romanesque statue of the Madonna. Within the church is the **Schatzkammer** (treasury) containing votive offerings spanning six centuries, mainly naive paintings. Entry to the Schatzkammer costs AS40 (students and children AS20); it's closed on Monday.

Activities

Skiers have the chance to throw themselves downhill from **Bürgeralpe** (1270m); a day pass costs AS270 (children AS165). There are a couple of restaurants at the top. In the summer, Bürgeralpe offers many different hiking trails, and a Freizeitpark with a museum showing different uses of wood. The adult cable car fare is AS70/100 up/return, or AS110/135 including entry to the Freizeitpark (open daily, May to October).

Gemeindealpe (1626m) is 5km northwest of Mariazell overlooking Mitterbach, but its chair lift is closed indefinitely.

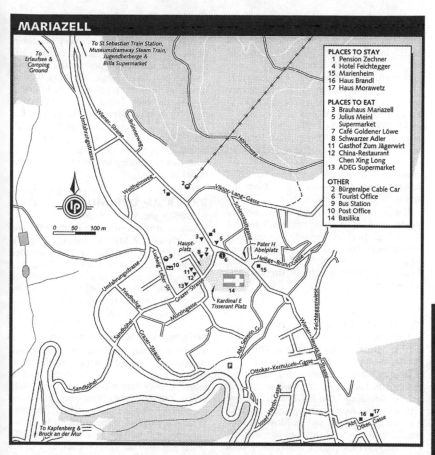

MARIAZELL

To St Sebastian Train Station,
Museumstramway Steam Train,
Jugendherberge &
Billa Supermarket

To
Erlaufsee &
Camping
Ground

Umfahrungsstrasse

Wiener-Strasse

Brunnweg

Weitheimweg

Ludwig-Leber-Str.

Umfahrungsstrasse

Friedhofsg.

Grazer-Strasse

Sandbühel

Grazer-Strasse

Sandbühel

Hauptplatz

Grazer Strasse

Mörtingasse

Kardinal E
Tisserant Platz

Kardinal E
Tisserant Platz

Pater H
Abelplatz

Heilige-Brunn-Gasse

Schiessstätteg.

Viktor-Lang-Gasse

Höhenweg

Wiener-Neustädter-Strasse

Feichteggerwiese

Abt-Severin-G.

Ottokar-Kernstock-Gasse

Josef-Haydn-Gasse

Abt-Otker-Gasse

To Kapfenberg &
Bruck an der Mur

0   50   100 m

PLACES TO STAY
1 Pension Zechner
4 Hotel Feichtegger
15 Marienheim
16 Haus Brandl
17 Haus Morawetz

PLACES TO EAT
3 Brauhaus Mariazell
5 Julius Meinl
  Supermarket
7 Café Goldener Löwe
8 Schwarzer Adler
11 Gasthof Zum Jägerwirt
12 China-Restaurant
  Chen Xing Long
13 ADEG Supermarket

OTHER
2 Bürgeralpe Cable Car
6 Tourist Office
9 Bus Station
10 Post Office
14 Basilika

STYRIA

From either peak you'll get a good view of **Erlaufsee**. This lake lies a few kilometres north-west of Mariazell and provides good opportunities for water sports such as windsurfing and scuba diving. Contact addresses of bodies running such sports are listed in the leaflet *Mariazellerland von A-Z*, which is available free from the tourist office. A slightly unusual way of getting to the lake is by the steam Museumstramway (AS80 return), which runs at weekends and on holidays between July and September.

Places to Stay

There is a *camp site* (☎ 21 16) at the south-eastern end of Erlaufsee, costing AS50 per adult, AS40 per tent and AS30 per car.

In July 1999, Mariazell's HI *Jugendherberge* (☎ 42 60, fax 2750, Erlaufseestrasse 49) will move into a brand new building by the Freizeitzentrum sports centre in St Sebastian. Telephone for details.

There are several options for rooms in private houses. *Haus Brandl* (☎ 28 66, Abt Otker Gasse 3) has rooms available in the summer only, costing AS195 per person, and *Haus Morawetz* (☎ *21 94, Abt Otker Gasse 7*) charges AS190 in summer and AS225 in winter. Both places are pleasant and are south-east of Hauptplatz.

Marienheim (☎/fax 25 45, Pater H Abelplatz 3) is run by nuns. Prices per person in this calm setting are AS300/330 in summer/winter with private shower/WC or AS250/280 without. Half/full-board is only an extra AS65/90 per day. *Pension Zechner* (☎/fax 25 81, Wiener Strasse 30) offers clean, fresh singles/doubles with shower/WC for AS280/560; some have TV. Rooms facing south-west (away from the street) have a fine view.

Plenty of elegant three and four-star hotels stand on or around Hauptplatz, and there's little to choose between them. *Hotel Feichtegger* (☎ 24 16, fax -80, Wiener Strasse 6) has loads of facilities, including a swimming pool; it charges from AS500 per person.

Places to Eat

There's an *ADEG* supermarket on Grazer Strasse and a *Julius Meinl* just north of the tourist office. There's also a *Billa* on Wiener Strasse near the train station.

Hauptplatz has many cafés and hotel restaurants, and it's easy to compare menus before deciding. *Café Goldener Löwe* serves various meals costing under AS100; it's closed after 7 pm and on Monday. Men should visit the WC upstairs to meet the Piss-Wand, a metal figure which will join in while you urinate. Next door, *Schwarzer Adler*, offers affordable set meals or more expensive à la carte dishes. Both places have an outside terrace.

Gasthof Zum Jägerwirt (Hauptplatz 2) looks deceptively small and cosy from the outside, but the left side has several adjoining rooms. Good, traditional dishes mostly cost over AS100. Next door, the *China-Restaurant Chen Xing Long* is worth trying for its weekday set lunches for AS60.

Brauhaus Mariazell (Wiener Strasse 5) brews its own beer and serves fairly expensive food; it's closed on Thursday.

Getting There & Away

A narrow-gauge train departs from St Pölten, 85km to the north, every two hours or so. It's a slow 2½ hour trip (AS130), though the scenery is good for the last hour. Unless you have a car, the only way to travel on without returning to St Pölten is to take the bus. There are several routes heading south, departing from the bus station (☎ 21 66) next to the post office. At least four Bundesbuses a day depart for Bruck an der Mur (AS100, 100 minutes) with two continuing to Graz (AS168, three hours in total).

BRUCK AN DER MUR
☎ 03862 • pop 15,000 • 491m

Bruck is at the confluence of the Mur and Mürz rivers (the Mürz is actually a significant waterway, but they probably decided 'Bruck an der Mur und der Mürz' was too much of a mouthful) and is at the junction of routes to all four points of the compass. If you're passing through, the town deserves a quick perusal.

Orientation & Information

The train station and a post office (Postamt A-8600) are at the eastern end of Bahnhofstrasse, and money can be exchanged at either; there's also a Bankomat here. Walk down Bahnhofstrasse and bear left at the roundabout for the town centre, Koloman Wallisch Platz. On the north side of the square you'll find the tourist office (☎ 890, email stadtmarketing@bruckmur.at) in the Rathaus. Updated computerised information is accessible daily. There's also another post office on Koloman Wallisch Platz.

Things to See & Do

Several paths wind up to the ruins of **Schloss Landskron;** the walk takes less than 10 minutes. Not much of the castle remains except a clock tower and a few cannons, and you don't quite gain enough height for an enhanced view, but at least it provides a pleasant setting for a picnic. One of the paths down again leads to Bauernmarkt, where there's a food and flower market beside the 15th century Gothic **Pfarrkirche** (parish church).

The remaining sights in Bruck are on Koloman Wallisch Platz. The **Rathaus** has an arcaded courtyard and houses a small museum. The **Kornmesserhaus** has an attractive arcaded frontage with fussy ornamentation that betrays both Gothic and Renaissance influences. This late 15th century building was erected at the behest of a rich merchant, Pankraz Kornmess, for whom it is named. There are other old historic houses lining the square, though the building at No 10 is more recent and boasts an Art Nouveau façade.

On the square itself is a fine Renaissance-style **wrought-iron well** created by Hans Prasser in 1626. Also here is the **Marien-säule**, a column dedicated to the Virgin Mary erected in 1710 after the town survived fire, plague and flooding.

Bruck is filled with street performers on the first Friday in August for the **Muren-schalk** free festival. North-west of Bruck are some Alpine lakes such as the tiny but

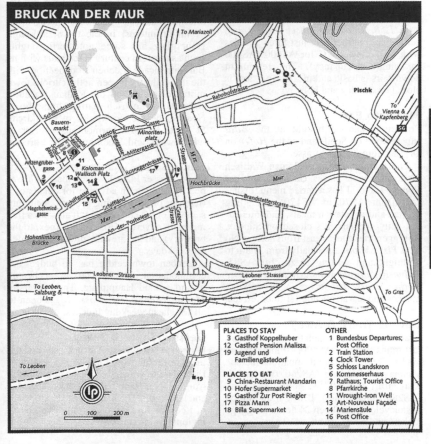

BRUCK AN DER MUR

PLACES TO STAY	OTHER
3 Gasthof Koppelhuber	1 Bundesbus Departures; Post Office
12 Gasthof Pension Malissa	2 Train Station
19 Jugend und Familiengästedorf	4 Clock Tower
	5 Schloss Landskron
PLACES TO EAT	6 Kornmesserhaus
9 China-Restaurant Mandarin	7 Rathaus; Tourist Office
10 Hofer Supermarket	8 Pfarrkirche
15 Gasthof Zur Post Riegler	11 Wrought-Iron Well
17 Pizza Mann	13 Art-Nouveau Façade
18 Billa Supermarket	14 Mariensäule
	16 Post Office

STYRIA

scenic **Grünersee**, about 25km from the town, near the source of the Laming River.

Places to Stay

There are only a few hotels in Bruck. The HI *Jugend und Familiengästedorf (☎ 584 58, fax -6, Stadtwaldstrasse 1)*, in the woods 10 minutes walk south of the centre is brand new. It has rooms starting at AS215 per person (AS265 for singles).

Gasthof Koppelhuber (☎ 516 38, Pischerstrasse 11) is beside the train station; take the stairs down to the left immediately after leaving the station. It offers simple, ageing but large rooms with hall shower for AS300/460. Add AS50 per person if you want breakfast. *Gasthof Pension Malissa (☎ 511 58, Koloman Wallisch Platz 9)* is a better deal but there are just three doubles with own shower/WC for AS600 (AS400 for single occupancy). The restaurant downstairs is basic and inexpensive, and is closed on Sunday and holidays.

Places to Eat

Provisions can be bought at the *Billa* supermarket on Schiffland or the *Hofer* on Dr Theodore Körner Strasse.

The southern end of Koloman Wallisch Platz has several places. *Gasthof Zur Post Riegler* at No 11 has a varied menu (dishes cost from AS70 to AS170), including Styrian and vegetarian meals, and interesting daily specials; it's closed on Sunday. Roseggerstrasse leads east from here; at No 32 is *Pizza Mann*, open daily from 11 am to midnight and serving pizzas for AS85. *China-Restaurant Mandarin (Dr Theodore Körner Strasse 16)* serves cheap weekday lunches and has an outside 1st floor terrace.

Getting There & Away

Bruck is the main rail hub for the region; all fast trains to Graz (AS100, 40 minutes) go via Bruck. Other major destinations include Vienna's Südbahnhof (AS240, two hours), Klagenfurt (AS260, 2½ hours) and Linz (AS280, three hours). Bruck train station has bicycle rental (open 24 hours), luggage lockers and a restaurant.

By road, the main autobahns intersect to the south-east of the town. If you're planning to cycle along the Mur, the tourist office can supply some useful maps.

LEOBEN

☎ 03842 • pop 35,000 • 540m

Leoben is a centre for metallurgical industries, yet still manages to garner accolades such as 'the most beautiful town in Styria' for its floral displays and parklands. Leoben achieved fame with the peace treaty signed here in 1797 by Napoleon and Emperor Franz II.

The tourist office (☎ 440 18, fax 482 18) is at Hauptplatz 12; it's closed on Friday afternoon and at weekends. There's little of major interest in the town, although Hauptplatz has some noteworthy sights such as the 17th century **Hacklhaus** with its Baroque façade. Leoben's connection with the iron industry is seen in the curious town motif (displayed on the Rathaus façade), showing an ostrich eating horseshoes. Nearby, the dreary exterior of **Pfarrkirche St Xaver** belies a harmonious interior of white walls and black-and-gold Baroque altars.

In the suburbs is the **Brauerei Göss** (☎ 20 90-0), Gösser Platz 1, which makes Gösser beer. Telephone in advance for details of a free tour of the brewing process, including samples of the end product. It also has a free museum, covering Göss Abbey (next to the brewery) and the brewing process; it's open on weekdays.

Leoben town centre has no budget accommodation, although you can eat cheaply in and around Hauptplatz. The university *Mensa (Franz Josef Strasse 18)* is open to all for cheap weekday lunches.

Getting There & Away

Leoben is 16km west of Bruck and is on the main rail route from there to Klagenfurt or Linz. The town centre is 10 minutes walk from Leoben Hauptbahnhof: cross the Mur and bear right. The brewery is 1½ km south of Leoben-Göss Bahnhof (only two-hourly regional trains stop).

EISENERZ

☎ 03848 • pop 9000 • 736m

Eisenerz is the main destination on the Steirische Eisenstrasse (Styrian Iron Road) extending north from Leoben. It's the largest ore mining centre in Central Europe, extracting 8200 tonnes per day.

Orientation & Information

The town is clustered at the foot of the remarkable Erzberg (Iron Mountain). The bus station is closest to the town centre, but even the train station is little more than five minutes walk to the north. The tourist office (☎ 37 00, fax 21 00) is at Freiheitsplatz 7, next to the Stadtmuseum. It's open Monday to Friday from 9 am to 1 pm (10 am to noon in winter) and 3 to 5 pm.

Things to See & Do

The town is attractively situated, allowing for some fine walks along the valley. Despite some grim terraced housing near the mine, Eisenerz has a charming old town centre, particularly around Bergmannsplatz, where some buildings sport sgraffito designs. There's also a fortified **Gothic church**; its walls were built in 1532 to protect against the Turks.

The **Stadtmuseum** covers folklore and mining and is open daily from May to October between 9 am and 5 pm, and on weekdays from November to April between 9 am and noon. Entry costs AS36 (students AS11).

The main reason to come to Eisenerz is the **Erzberg**. This peak has been completely denuded by opencast stope mining to such an extent that it resembles a step pyramid. The outcome is surprisingly beautiful, with its orange and purple shades contrasting with the lush greenery and grey crags of surrounding mountains.

The ironworks can be visited in two ways. A 90 minute 'Schaubergwerk' tour burrows into the mountain to the underground mines (abandoned in 1986). Tours are usually in German (English-language notes available). The 'Hauly Abenteuerfahrt' is a one hour tour of the surface works aboard a huge truck, with fine views along the way. Each tour costs AS150 (students AS70), or a combined ticket is AS270 (students AS130). Tours are conducted from 1 May to 31 October between 10 am and 3 pm (contact ☎ 32 00, fax -22, email erzberg@steirer-oberland.co.at). The departure point is a 10 minute walk from the centre, following the course of the river.

Places to Stay & Eat

Staff at the tourist office will help you find somewhere to stay. There are few private rooms, and the only one near the centre is *Karl Moser* (☎ 24 34, Flutergasse 11), where doubles (excluding breakfast) cost AS320 with shower/WC, AS260 without.

Near Bergmannsplatz is *Zur Post* (☎ 22 32, Lindmoserstrasse 10), where large singles/doubles with shower, WC and TV cost AS300/500. The restaurant serves good Styrian food for less than AS90. Close by, *Bräustüberl* (☎ 23 35, Flutergasse 5) has rooms with shower and WC for AS250/440; it also has a restaurant (closed on Monday).

There are a couple of supermarkets in town, as well as a few snack places, such as *Imbiss Moser* (Dr Karl Renner Strasse), that offers cheap hot food.

Getting There & Away

Every two hours, trains connect Eisenerz to Selzthal, a rail junction to the west (AS86, one hour; change at Hieflau). Bundesbuses run to Mariazell once a day (AS168, 2¼ hours). From Leoben, Bundesbus services run north to Eisenerz about every two hours (AS70, one hour), via Vordernberg Markt, which is as far as you can get by train, excluding the special Vordernberg-Eisenerz *Nostalgie* (nostalgic) train, which only runs in the summer.

ADMONT

☎ 03613 • pop 2900 • 641m

This small town at the entrance to the Gesäuse Valley is known for its **Benedictine abbey**. The tourist office (☎ 21 64, fax 36 48) is near the abbey church at Hauptplatz 4; it's closed at weekends and on Monday afternoon. The most important part of the abbey for visitors is the **Stiftsbibliothek** (abbey library), survivor of a fire in 1865 that severely damaged the rest of the abbey. It displays 150,000 volumes, and ceiling frescoes by Bartolomeo Altomonte. The best features are the statues (in wood, but painted to look like bronze) by Josef Stammel (1695-1765), especially the *Four Last Things* series. To understand the symbolism inherent in these works, buy the leaflet in English (it costs AS5, but staff at the tourist office will provide a free photocopy!). Admission to the Stiftsbibliothek costs AS60 and includes entry to a couple of other museums, one covering natural history, the other religious art and treasures. It's open daily from 1 April to 31 October, and in winter by appointment only (☎ 23 12). The abbey is 10 minutes walk from the station – turn left on leaving the station, then take the second right-hand turn.

There's a HI *Jugendherberge (☎ 24 32, fax 279 583)* about 1.5km south of the centre, sited in splendour in Schloss Röthelstein; it's closed from 1 November to 27 December. The castle is clearly visible above the trees: in the summer, walk up the steep trail cleared for the ski lift – the road route is much longer (3km, and no buses run). Accommodation in luxurious rooms with one to four beds costs AS300 per person; they have a private bathroom and some even have a TV. Phone ahead as it's often full with school groups (check-in from 7 am to 10 pm). There are several pensions near the abbey.

Getting There & Away
Admont is 15km east of Selzthal, on the route to Hieflau; trains run every two hours.

MURAU
☎ 03532 • pop 2600 • 830m

The Liechtenstein family was once dominant in the Murau region and built **Schloss Obermurau** in 1250. This was taken over by the Schwarzenberg family and converted to a Renaissance building in the 17th century.

There are short, infrequent tours of the interior in the summer.

Stadtpfarrkirche St Matthäus (St Matthew's Church) dates from the 13th century and is yet another Gothic church that was remodelled in Baroque style. Both elements work well together, as in the combination of the Gothic crucifixion group (1500) and the Baroque high altar (1655). The frescoes are from the 14th to 16th centuries. Enjoy the view of the church, castle and scenic centre from across the river, near the train station.

Murau Brauerei (☎ 326 60), Raffaltplatz 19-23, may let you join a tour of the brewery if you telephone in advance. The brewery museum opened in 1995; entry costs AS40 and it's closed on Friday afternoon and at weekends.

Skiing and walking are enjoyed on the nearby 2000m peaks, Kreischberg and Frauenalpe.

Places to Stay & Eat
If you decide to linger overnight, staff at the tourist office (☎/fax 27 20) by the train station will sort out a pension or private room. The HI *Jugendherberge (☎/fax 23 95, St Leonhard Platz 4)* has four and six-bed dorms with shower/WC costing AS160 per person in summer or AS215 in winter (add AS20 for stays of less than three nights). It's closed from 31 October to 26 December. The central *Gasthof Bärenwirt (☎ 20 79, Schwarzenbergstrasse 4)* has rooms costing AS200 per person, or AS320 with private shower/WC, and serves inexpensive regional food. The *Murau Brauerei* has a restaurant and beer cellar.

Getting There & Away
Murau is on highway 96 between Tamsweg and Judenburg. Heading west to Tamsweg, you can switch to highway 97 if you want to keep by the Mur River. Murau is also on a narrow-gauge private line connecting Unzmarkt and Tamsweg (Austrian rail passes valid, Inter-Rail and Eurail not valid; departures every two hours). More of a tourist excursion than a mode of transport is the steam train that

chugs to/from Tamsweg up to three times a week in the summer; return fare is AS180.

SCHLADMING

☎ 03687 • pop 4400 • 745m

Flanked by mountain ranges to the north and south, Schladming combines with neighbouring resorts **Rohrmoos** and **Haus** to create a large ski area; the skiing range is from 750m to 1894m. In summer, passes are available to ski the Dachstein Glacier (AS370 for one day). Another pass (the Top Tauern Skipass) links this ski area with neighbouring regions – see Radstadt in the Salzburg chapter.

The town tourist office (☎ 222 68, fax 241 38) is at Erzherzog Johann Strasse 213. Schladming has a HI *Jugendherberge* (*☎ 245 31, fax -88, Coburgstrasse 253*), closed from 1 November to 25 December.

Getting There & Away

Schladming is more easily reached from Salzburg province than from other places mentioned in this chapter. It is on the road and rail route that skirts the southern Salzkammergut.

Eastern Styria

This part of the province has no headline attractions, but it does have several castles surveying the undulating landscape.

STUBENBERG AM SEE

☎ 03176 • pop 2300 • 380m

Stubenberg is about midway between Gleisdorf and Hartberg, and either of these can provide a base for exploring the region.

This town is a centre for water sports and there's a good lookout point from the hill above the lake. The area between the lake and the nearby **Schloss Schielleiten** has a hot-air balloon festival in the second half of September. Dozens of colourful balloons rising in front of the yellow façade of the Schloss create a dramatic scene.

A few kilometres south, **Schloss Herberstein** (☎ 882 50) adjoins a deep gorge. It has an Italianate arcaded courtyard and furnished rooms that can be toured from March to October, daily between 10 am and 5 pm; entry costs AS125. Walking down from the car park, you pass an animal park, home to 120 different species.

Places to Stay & Eat

Stubenberg itself has a range of inexpensive places to stay, including private houses. For information on accommodation, contact the tourist office (☎ 88 82), on the 1st floor of the Gemeindeamt building. There is a *camp site (☎ 83 90)* by the lake. Eating options in the resort include *Pizzeria Erla (☎ 88 89, Buchberg 70)*, by the lake, which also has rooms.

Getting There & Away

Occasional Bundesbuses via Stubenberg run to/from Hartberg and Gleisdorf; dial ☎ 0660-80 20 for details (call charged at local rate). No train goes close to Stubenberg; the only rail track takes slow local trains that run from Graz to Hartberg, travelling a circuitous route via Gleisdorf and Fürstenfeld. By road, highway 54 connects Gleisdorf and Hartberg, from which a signposted turn-off to the north leads to Stubenberg. One or two buses run daily to Schloss Herberstein from Gleisdorf, continuing on to Stubenberg.

BAD BLUMAU

☎ 03383

Fans of the architectural style of Friedensreich Hundertwasser won't want to miss this unusual place. It's a whole health resort designed by him and featuring his characteristic trademarks – uneven floors, grass on the roof, colourful ceramics and golden spires; it opened in May 1997. If you can afford to stay, contact the *Rogner-Bad Blumau Hotel (☎ 5100-0, fax -808, email spa.blumau@rogner.com)*. Doubles cost AS1600/2200 in low/high season, including use of swimming pools and sauna but not the various health treatments on offer. The hotel organises guided tours of the resort for non-guests.

Getting There & Away

Bad Blumau is a short detour south of the A2/E59, the highway connecting Graz and Vienna. Blumau (the main village, about 300m from the resort) is on the rail line between Hartberg and Fürstenfeld.

RIEGERSBURG
☎ 03153

Riegersburg is 10km south-west of Fürstenfeld. The main attraction here is **Schloss Riegersburg**, an impressive 13th century castle which offers fine views of the Grazbach Valley. Formerly a crucial bastion against invading Hungarians and Turks, it now has a couple of museums among its numerous rooms; one features witchcraft, the other expounds the history of the owners, the Liechtenstein family. A war memorial is a reminder of fierce fighting in 1945, when Germans occupying the castle were attacked by Russian troops. The Schloss (☎ 821 31) can be visited from Easter to 31 October, daily from 10 am to 5 pm. Entry costs AS85 (students AS50) for one museum or AS120 (AS80) for both. For more information, contact the town tourist office (☎ 86 70).

The Riegersburg HI *Jugendherberge* (☎ *82 17, Im Cillitor*) is part of the castle walls; it's open from 1 May to 31 October.

Getting There & Away

Infrequent buses run from Graz (AS100, 90 minutes); you have to change at Gleisdorf, except on Sunday. The nearest train station is Feldbach, a 15 minute bus journey.

Carinthia

Carinthia (Kärnten) is known primarily for its many lakes: there are 1270 within the province, of which about 200 have bathing facilities. The most famous of these is Wörther See (Lake Wörth); it's waters are warmed by thermal springs. Many lakes provide ideal opportunities for angling; tourist offices have information on permits (these can be expensive) and regulations about official fishing seasons and the size of fish you can keep. The attraction of water sports means that summer is the main season in Carinthia (it proclaims itself Austria's sunniest province), though it also offers winter sports.

Carinthia shares an area of outstanding natural beauty, the Hohe Tauern National Park, with neighbouring Salzburg province and Tirol. This mountainous area is covered in the Hohe Tauern National Park Region chapter.

Orientation & Information

Carinthia is the fifth largest Austrian province, with an area of 9533 sq km and a population of 548,000, 3% of whom speak Slovene. The terrain ranges from gentle hills to precipitous Alpine peaks. The main river is the Drau.

The administrative capital is Klagenfurt, but the provincial tourist board is in nearby Velden: Kärntner Tourismus (☎ 04274-52 100, fax -50, email info@carinthia.com), Casinoplatz 1, A-9220 Velden. See the Velden section for directions to the office. You can book rooms and obtain information via the 24 hour Carinthia 'hotline' (☎ 0463-30 00), based in Klagenfurt.

The Kärnten Card, which is available from early May to early October from tourist offices and hotels, gives free access to 90 attractions – museums, cable cars, swimming pools and much else, as well as free use of public transport. It's valid for three weeks and costs AS365 (AS150 for children aged under 14).

Highlights

- Take a summertime stroll around Klagenfurt's Europapark

- Bathe in warm Wörther See, heated by thermal springs

- Explore historic Friesach surrounded by its moat and hillside castles

- Visit Burg Hochosterwitz, with its impressive girdle of gate towers

- Enjoy a range of excursions from Villach, particularly to Burgruine Landskron

There's also the Kultur Card Kärnten (AS250), which gives discounts of between 10 and 20% on arts and cultural events. It's valid for one year from purchase so it's only really of interest to visitors staying for a relatively long time and residents.

Getting Around

As in other provinces, Carinthia is divided into regional zones for public transport, with the option of buying single tickets or passes valid for 24 hours, seven days, 30 days or one year. For information, call the Verkehrsverbund Kärnten hotline (☎ 0463-500 830) between 7 am and noon, Monday to Friday.

CARINTHIA

CARINTHIA (KÄRNTEN)

Klagenfurt

☎ 0463 • pop 87,000 • 446m

Klagenfurt is an enjoyable city with a pleasant climate. The town centre itself is worthy of exploration, but the big draw for tourists is Europapark, in particular the world-in-miniature Minimundus. Wörther See, which extends west from Klagenfurt, is another well known attraction.

After twice being destroyed by fire, Klagenfurt became the capital of Carinthia in 1518, courtesy of Maximilian I. The symmetrical town plan was conceived by Domenico de Lalio, but he was only one of several architects who contributed to the Italianate flavour of the centre. The old city walls were razed in 1809 following the occupation of the town by French forces.

Orientation

Klagenfurt lies 30km from Slovenia and 60km from Italy. The town centre is enclosed by a square of ring roads, with Neuer Platz (New Square) at its heart. North of Neuer Platz is Alter Platz (Old Square), which is surrounded by narrow streets and arcaded courtyards. One block west of Neuer Platz is Heiligen Geist Platz, the hub for local buses.

The Hauptbahnhof (main train station) is just over 1km south of Neuer Platz. Wörther See is about 4km west of the city centre, with Europapark on its eastern shore.

Information

Tourist Offices The main tourist office (☎ 53 72 23, fax 53 72 95, email klagenfurt-info@w-see.or.at) is in the Rathaus on Neuer Platz. Summer opening hours are Monday to Friday from 8 am to 8 pm, and weekends and holidays from 10 am to 5 pm; from 15 October to 30 April, hours are Monday to Friday from 8 am to 5 pm. Staff will find rooms (no commission) and bike rental is available (AS50 for three hours or AS90 for the day).

A smaller tourist office by the entrance to Minimundus in Europapark is open daily from May to early October between 9 am and 8 pm.

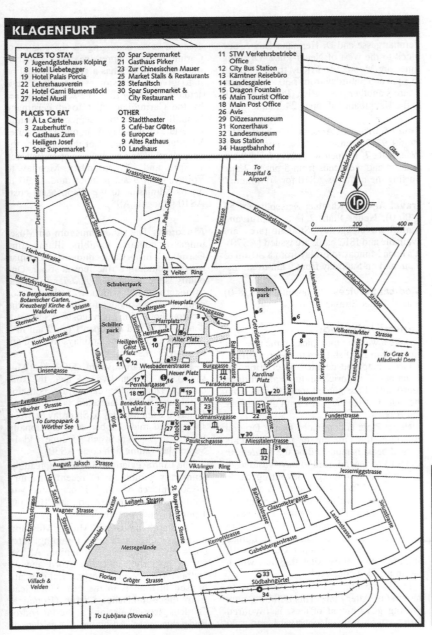

KLAGENFURT

PLACES TO STAY
7 Jugendgästehaus Kolping
8 Hotel Liebetegger
19 Hotel Palais Porcia
22 Lehrerhausverein
24 Hotel Garni Blumenstöckl
27 Hotel Musil

PLACES TO EAT
1 À La Carte
3 Zauberhutt'n
4 Gasthaus Zum
  Heiligen Josef
17 Spar Supermarket

20 Spar Supermarket
21 Gasthaus Pirker
23 Zur Chinesischen Mauer
25 Market Stalls & Restaurants
28 Stefanitsch
30 Spar Supermarket &
  City Restaurant

OTHER
2 Stadttheater
5 Café-bar G@tes
6 Europcar
9 Altes Rathaus
10 Landhaus

11 STW Verkehrsbetriebe
  Office
12 City Bus Station
13 Kärntner Reisebüro
14 Landesgalerie
15 Dragon Fountain
16 Main Tourist Office
18 Main Post Office
26 Avis
29 Diözesanmuseum
31 Konzerthaus
32 Landesmuseum
33 Bus Station
34 Hauptbahnhof

CARINTHIA

Post & Communications The main post office (Postamt 9010) is on the corner of Pernhartgasse and Dr Hermann Gasse, one block to the west of Neuer Platz. Opening times are Monday to Friday from 7.30 am to 8 pm and Saturday from 7.30 am to 1 pm. There's another post office (Postamt 9020) at the Hauptbahnhof, open 24 hours.

Email & Internet Access Café-bar G@tes (☎ 50 97 77, email gates@happynet.at), Waagplatz 7, is open weekdays from 9 am to 2 am and weekends from 5 pm to 2 am. Surfing the net costs AS10 for 10 minutes.

Travel Agency Kärntner Reisebüro (☎ 56 4 00-0), Neuer Platz 2 is a helpful and central travel agency. Student fares are available and ISIC cards are issued (AS70). It's open Monday to Friday from 8.30 am to 6 pm and on Saturday from 9 am to noon.

Medical Services The hospital (☎ 538-0) is at St Veiter Strasse 47.

Central Attractions

To take a walking tour, pick up the relevant brochure in English from the tourist office. It has a map and detailed descriptions of monuments, historic buildings and hidden courtyards. Free guided tours depart from the tourist office daily at 10 am during July and August.

Neuer Platz is dominated by the Dragon Fountain, the emblem of the city. This winged beast is modelled on the *Lindwurm* (dragon) of legend, said to have resided in a swamp here long ago, devouring cattle and virgins. Markets and festivals are held in the square, which also has a statue of Empress Maria Theresa dating from 1873.

Alter Platz is the oldest part of the city and contains a number of historic buildings. On the corner with Wiener Gasse you'll find the 17th century Altes Rathaus, which has an arcaded courtyard.

The 16th century **Landhaus** stands just to the west of Alter Platz. This building, now housing government offices, is favoured with a two storeyed courtyard and two steeples. The interior walls of its Wappensaal (Hall of Arms) are painted with 655 coats of arms belonging to the estates of Carinthia. More impressive than the walls is the ceiling, which has a gallery painted on it to give the illusion it is vaulted; it is actually perfectly flat. The scene, rendered by the Carinthian artist Josef Ferdinand Fromiller (1693-1760), depicts the Carinthian estate owners paying homage to Charles VI. Stand in the centre of the room for the best effect. The Landhaus is open between 1 April and 31 September, Monday to Friday, from 9 am to noon and 12.30 to 5 pm. Admission to the Wappensaal costs AS10 (students AS5).

Museums The **Landesmuseum** on Museumgasse contains exhibits illuminating Carinthia's history and culture since Roman times, including a fine mosaic floor. One oddity is the *Lindwurmschädel*, a fossilised rhinoceros head which was the not-so-comely artist's model for the head of the Dragon Fountain. Entry costs AS30 (students AS15) and it's open from 9 am to 4 pm daily (Sunday and holidays from 10 am to 1 pm).

The **Diözesanmuseum** (Diocesan Museum), on Lidmanskygasse near the 16th century Domkirche (cathedral), contains religious art. The museum is open from 10 am to 2 pm Monday to Saturday between 1 June and mid-October, and additionally from 3 to 5 pm between 15 June and 14 September (admission costs AS30).

The **Landesgalerie**, Burggasse 8, features temporary exhibitions of recent art (entry AS30, children AS15). It's open Monday to Saturday from 9 am to 6 pm, and 10 am to 1 pm on Sunday and holidays.

The **Bergbaumuseum** (Mining Museum) covers, would you believe it, mining; entry costs AS50 (students and seniors AS25). It's open daily between 1 April and 31 October from 9 am to 6 pm. Exhibits are housed in tunnels in the hill which lead from the **Botanischer Garten** (Botanical Gardens; free admission) at the far end of Radetzkystrasse. Adjoining the gardens is the **Kreuzbergl Kirche**, with mosaic stations of the cross on the approaching path, and walking trails up the hill behind.

Europapark Vicinity

Europapark and Wörther See are centres for summer activities, generally available from May to September, although balmy weather can extend the season. Bus Nos 10, 11, 12, 20, 21 and 22 from Heiligen Geist Platz run to Minimundus, though usually only Nos 10, 11 and 12 continue the short distance to Strandbad.

Minimundus This is the most touristy offering in the park, but it's quite fun, especially for children. Detailed 1:25 scale models of about 160 famous international buildings are displayed. The models are numbered, not labelled (you can pick up a catalogue for AS30) but some buildings are instantly recognisable: the miniature of St Peter's Basilica in Rome is one of the most impressive. The Eiffel Tower, the Statue of Liberty and the Taj Mahal are also featured, along with many Austrian buildings. A café and restaurant (normal-sized) are on site.

Minimundus is open daily from 9 am to 5 pm (late April and early October), 9 am to 6 pm (May, June and September) and 9 am to 7 pm (July and August; it's open till 9 pm on Wednesday and Saturday during these months). Admission costs AS90 for adults and AS30 for children.

Reptilienzoo This reptile zoo offers a chance to shudder at a variety of snakes, spiders and similar creatures. Brief but informative signs in English provide information on the various species: spiders hear, taste and smell through their legs, and the blue poison arrow frog from Suriname, despite being under 4cm long, can produce enough poison to kill 10 humans or 20,000 mice. Outside are squat crocodiles, giant turtles and model dinosaurs. It's open daily year-round from 8 am to 5 pm (6 pm in summer) and entry costs AS75 (students AS65, children AS35).

Strandbad This private beach on the lake has cabins (AS30 per day), wooden piers, shady grassy areas, a nude sunbathing terrace (for men on Tuesday, Thursday and

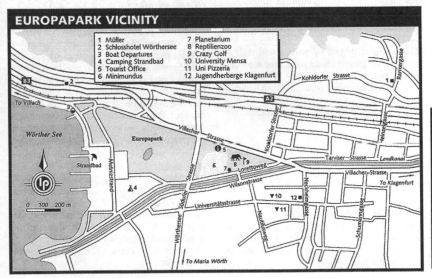

EUROPAPARK VICINITY

1 Müller
2 Schlosshotel Wörthersee
3 Boat Departures
4 Camping Strandbad
5 Tourist Office
6 Minimundus
7 Planetarium
8 Reptilienzoo
9 Crazy Golf
10 University Mensa
11 Uni Pizzeria
12 Jugendherberge Klagenfurt

Wörther See
Europapark
Strandbad
To Villach
To Maria Wörth
Kohldorfer Strasse
Villacher Strasse
Tarviser Strasse
Lendkanal
To Klagenfurt
Lorettoweg
Wilsonstrasse
Universitätsstrasse
Ranivergasse
Heinzelgasse
Neckheimgasse
Schumanngasse
Nautilusweg
Südufer Strasse
Metnitzstrand
Wörthersee Strasse

0   100   200 m

Saturday; for women on other days) and a restaurant. It's open daily in the summer from 8 am to around 8 pm. A day card costs AS35 (AS15 for children) and a family card AS50 (one adult) or AS80 (two adults). After 3 pm entry costs AS20 for adults and AS15 for children.

Adjoining the beach complex is a place where you can hire rowing boats (AS24), pedal boats (AS42) and motorboats (AS66) for 30 minutes.

Other Attractions Europapark is a fine place for a stroll, with winding pathways, fountains, statues and colourful flowerbeds. There's a skateboarding course and tennis courts nearby. Next to the Reptilienzoo is a **planetarium** where a 45 minute show with German commentary costs AS75 (students/seniors AS65, children AS45). There's a crazy golf course opposite (AS30 per person per round), table tennis (AS25 per hour), pool/billiards (AS10 per game) and you can rent bicycles for the same prices as at the tourist office.

The departure point for cruises on the lake is only a few hundred metres north of Strandbad. See the Wörther See section in this chapter for information on timetables and lakeside resorts.

Castles
Klagenfurt is ringed by castles and stately homes. The tourist office has a free map detailing routes, which is ideal if you have your own transport. These are close enough to be visited on a cycling tour (see the Getting Around section for more details).

Special Events
There are several free festivals, including the Klagenfurter Stadtfest, a two day festival in early July. Contact the tourist office for details of all festivals.

Places to Stay – Budget
Staying in Klagenfurt entitles visitors to a *Gästekarte* (guest card), giving various discounts and available from hotels, hostels and camp sites.

Camping Strandbad (☎ 21 1 69) is in a good location by the lake in Europapark. There is a shop with a buffet on site and campers have free use of the Strandbad swimming complex. The camp site is open from 1 May to 30 September and costs AS50 per adult (AS25 for children up to age 14), plus AS100 for a large site (including electricity, parking and hot water) or AS20 for a small site (under 20 sq metres). In the high season, from 20 June to 20 August, the price per person rises to AS80 for adults and AS40 for children. A resort tax of AS12 must be added.

The HI *Jugendherberge Klagenfurt* (☎ 23 00 19, fax -13, email oejhv-kaern ten@oejhv.or.at, Neckheimgasse 6), near Europapark, has modern facilities and four-bed dorms with private shower/WC costing AS190 per person. Single/double occupancy of a dorm costs AS290/480. Reception is closed between 9 am and 5 pm, though you can leave your bags during the day. Front door keys are available. To get there from the centre, take a Strandbad bus (Nos 10, 11 and 12), but check with the driver before embarking as some take a different route.

The HI *Jugendgästehaus Kolping* (☎ 569 65, fax -20, Enzenbergstrasse 26) is only 800m east of Neuer Platz, but it's only open from 10 July to 10 September. Rooms with shower cost AS200 for a single or AS160 per person for doubles/triples; add AS20 for a single night stay. Open for the same period is *Mladinski Dom* (☎ 356 51, fax -11, Mikshalle 4), run by the Slovenian hostel association. It's 1km east of Völkermarkter Ring and has single/double/triple rooms costing between AS210 and AS280 per person.

There are about a dozen homes that offer private rooms for between AS180 and AS320 per person, but these are mostly in the suburbs. An exception is *Lehrerhausverein (Bäckergasse 17)*, with seven beds (using hall shower) in rooms of varying size costing AS280 per person; reserve one week ahead. Apply to Rauter Anita (☎ 51 38 40) at Adlergasse 11, on the next street to the east.

Hotel Liebetegger (☎ *569 35, fax -6, Völkermarkter Strasse 8)* is the only central budget hotel. Rooms with modern fittings cost AS400/800 with shower/WC and TV or AS250/400 without; breakfast costs AS50.

The other budget places are a bit out of the way. *Müller* (☎/*fax 212 54, Rankengasse 21)* is not too badly placed between the centre and Europapark. Rooms are fairly plain, starting at AS260 per person, and some have a private shower. The restaurant is good value and a haunt for chess players.

Places to Stay – Mid-Range & Top End

If you have your own transport, consider staying at *Waldwirt* (☎ *426 42, fax 466 80, Josefiwaldweg 2)*, on the Kreuzbergl hill north-west of the city. It's a small place with a swimming pool; singles/doubles start at AS420/760.

To stay in style overlooking the lake, go to *Schlosshotel Wörthersee* (☎ *211 58, fax -8, Villacher Strasse 338)*. Rooms are well presented, some with balcony, and all with cable TV, bathroom or shower and WC; it also has a stretch of private beach. Singles/doubles start at AS490/690. There's parking, but no lift.

Hotel Garni Blumenstöckl (☎ *577 93, fax -5, 10 Oktober Strasse 11)* is in a 400-year-old building with rooms around a flora-filled courtyard. This small family-run place has rooms with bath/WC and cable TV starting at AS580/980.

On the opposite side of the junction is *Hotel Musil* (☎ *51 16 60, fax -4, 10 Oktober Strasse 14)*. This historical building also has an interesting structure, with rooms grouped around an attractive oval atrium. Rooms have antique furniture and modern amenities, and are kitted out in a variety of styles ranging from rustic to Maria Theresa Baroque. All rooms are doubles, starting at AS1490 (AS1290 for single occupancy).

The central *Hotel Palais Porcia* (☎ *51 15 90, fax -30, Neuer Platz 13)* has a sumptuous lounge on the 3rd floor, with portraits, period furniture and ornate mirrors. Most rooms match this opulence and cost from AS950/1350 to AS2400/4800.

Places to Eat

Eating cheaply in the town centre isn't too hard. Several snack stands dot the area, or you can stock up at one of the *Spar* supermarkets on Adlergasse or Dr Hermann Gasse. On Bahnhofstrasse there's another *Spar* supermarket – this one has a self-service *City* restaurant, where daily set menus cost AS59.

A fruit and vegetable *market* occupies Benediktinerplatz from Monday to Saturday, bolstered by a flower market on Thursday and Saturday morning. There are several tiny restaurants in the market arcade, where meals only cost about AS50.

Stefanitsch on Lidmanskygasse is a food shop serving weekday lunch specials for about AS60 (open shop hours with early closing at 1 pm on Wednesday). On the same street, at No 19, is *Zur Chinesischen Mauer*, a Chinese restaurant with weekday lunch menus costing from AS63 to AS99 (open daily).

West of town and convenient for the Jugendherberge and Europapark is the university *Mensa* (*Universitätsstrasse 90)* which is open to all. Cheap meals are available year-round, Monday to Friday from 11 am to 2.30 pm. The university building opposite houses a café, open daily from 8 am to midnight. Close by at Universitätsstrasse 33 is *Uni Pizzeria*, with pavement tables and tasty food costing from AS70 to AS225 (open daily from 11 am to midnight).

Gasthaus Zum Heiligen Josef (*Osterwitzgasse 7)* serves local cuisine, including vegetarian choices, starting at AS85 (closed on Monday). Across the road is *Zauberhutt'n*, offering good Italian food starting AS60 served in a rustic environment; it's closed Saturday lunchtime and on Sunday. Both places have outside tables.

Gasthaus Pirker (*Adlergasse 16)* is another good place for Austrian food, costing from AS70 to AS190. It has a comfortable interior, recently refurbished, and a bar area. Opening hours are Monday to Friday from 8 am to midnight.

For more expensive dining, try hotel restaurants, such as the one in the *Hotel Musil* (see Places to Stay). This hotel has its own bakery: incredibly elaborate cakes are sold in its shop and café. Fancy guzzling a Lindwurm-shaped confection? You have the opportunity here.

The restaurant in the *Schlosshotel Wörthersee* (see Places to Stay) is highly rated for regional cuisine. In summer it's open daily, lunch and evening; in winter, it's closed on Monday and until 5 pm.

One of the top restaurants in town is the aptly named *À La Carte* (☎ *51 66 51, Khevenhüller Strasse 3*), a small, formal, expensive but popular place – book ahead. Austrian and international main courses cost AS160 or more; cover charge is AS50 (closed on Sunday and Monday).

Entertainment

I once overheard a disgruntled young traveller describe Klagenfurt as 'the city of the dead'. It's not that bad, though it must be admitted that the city centre can be surprisingly quiet. Try the area around Pfarrplatz and Herrengasse, where there are a couple of decent bars. For later, louder clubbing, head east along Völkermarkter Strasse to the industrial zone, where there are several discos and clubs.

You can see plays, operettas and operas at the *Stadttheater* (☎ *540 64, Theaterplatz 4*) ; it's closed mid-June to mid-September. The ticket office is open Tuesday to Saturday from 9 am to noon and 4 to 6 pm; standing-room tickets are sometimes available. The *Konzerthaus* (*Miesstaler Strasse 8*) puts on other musical events. There's a yearly or monthly booklet with a timetable of events available from the tourist office.

Getting There & Away

Air The airport (☎ 415 00-0) is 3km north of the city centre; there are five flights a day to Vienna (with Tyrolean Airways; ☎ 07144-44 44-83) and two a day each to Zürich (Crossair; ☎ 17 89) and Frankfurt (Tyrolean). The only other options are chartered flights.

Bus Bundesbuses depart from outside the Hauptbahnhof; call ☎ 543 40 for route details. See the Wörther See Getting Around section for information on buses to resorts at the lake.

Train Trains to Graz depart every one to two hours (AS330, three hours); these go via Bruck an der Mur (AS260), 170km to the north-east. IC trains run to Vienna every two hours; the journey takes 3½ hours. Trains to western Austria, Italy, Slovenia and Germany go via Villach (AS68; takes 30 to 40 minutes, with two to four trains per hour). Heading to Ljubljana, you can avoid the trip to Villach by taking the local line from Klagenfurt to Rosenbach (AS68, 30 minutes), and continuing from there. However, these non-express trains are less frequent, so saving time depends on getting a good connection. Call ☎ 1717 for train information between 7 am and 6.30 pm daily.

Car & Motorcycle Since the opening of a bypass, the A2/E66 between Villach and Graz skirts the north of Klagenfurt.

Car rental offices include:

Avis
  (☎ 559 38) Villacher Strasse 1A
Europcar
  (☎ 51 45 38) Völkermarkter Ring 9
Hertz
  (☎ 561 47) St Ruprechterstrasse 12

Getting Around

To get to the airport, take bus No 42 from the Hauptbahnhof via the town centre, or bus No 45 from Heiligen Geist Platz.

City buses cost AS22 for one journey (including changes) and AS50 for a 24 hour pass. These are the prices when bought from the driver; they're AS20 and AS40, respectively, when purchased in advance from the STW Verkehrsbetriebe office on Heiligen Geist Platz (open weekdays from 6.30 am to 2.30 pm). Bus services are sparse in the evening; free timetables are available from the tourist office or STW office. Bus Nos 40, 41 and 42 run from the Hauptbahnhof to the town centre.

As well as renting bikes, the tourist office provides a *Radwandern* cycle map, listing sights and distances. Tours (the longest being 34km) are arranged by themes. You can rent bikes from the Hauptbahnhof for the standard rate and the counter is open daily from 6.30 am (7 am on Sunday) to 10.30 pm. For taxis, call ☎ 311 11 or ☎ 27 11. The 'Nacht Taxi' (☎ 537 262) scheme allows half-price travel by taxi from 10 pm to 5 am; you must buy vouchers in advance from the Rathaus.

Central Carinthia

WÖRTHER SEE
Wörther See is one of the warmer lakes in the region owing to thermal springs: the average water temperature between June and September is 21°C. Summers in this part of Carinthia are very hot in any case, so it's an ideal location for frolicking amid the lapping waves, or for the serious pursuit of water sports. The lake stretches from west to east between Velden and Klagenfurt and the long, thin shoreline provides unfolding vistas on a boat trip.

The northern shore has the best transport access and is the busiest section. On this side, the first main resort west of Klagenfurt is **Krumpendorf**. This place has plenty of parkland and facilities for tennis, golf and water sports. The tourist office, the Kurverwaltung (☎ 04229-23 13), is in the Rathaus at Hauptstrasse 145.

The next resort to the west is **Pörtschach**, which has a distinctive tree-lined peninsula with a curving bay on either side. Along the lake shore is a pleasant promenade lined with flowers. The resort has a golf course and the usual water sports. Contact the tourist office (☎ 04272-23 54), Hauptstrasse 153, for details.

On the southern shore lies **Maria Wörth**, a small resort dominated by two churches. The largest combines Gothic, Baroque and Romanesque elements; the smaller 12th century Winterkirche features Romanesque frescoes of the apostles. On the hill southwest of Maria Wörth is **Pyramidenkogel**, a

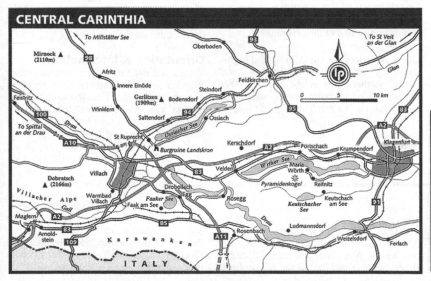

CENTRAL CARINTHIA

rather ugly tower that nevertheless provides fine views of Wörther See and the surrounding mountain ranges. It reaches 905m, 435m higher than the lake. It's open between April and October and entry costs AS60 (children AS25). Further details of these attractions are available from the tourist office (☎ 04273-2240, fax 3703, email maria-woerth-info@w-see.or.at).

For accommodation details, contact the tourist offices in the individual resorts.

Getting Around

Bus & Train Bundesbuses travel along both shores of the lake, stopping at all the main resorts. Bus 5179 runs between Villach and Klagenfurt four to seven times a day each way, taking 45 minutes to cover the 23km of the Velden-Klagenfurt leg, travelling along the northern shore. Bus 5310 runs along the southern side of the lake between Klagenfurt and Velden via Maria Wörth, but there are only a few departures each day and none on Sunday. For bus information, call ☎ 0463-500 830 on weekdays from 7 am to noon.

The railway line between Klagenfurt and Villach runs along the northern shore of the lake. Regional trains stop at Krumpendorf, Pörtschach and Velden; express trains stop at only one or two of those stations.

Car & Motorcycle The A2/E66 and highway 83, which runs closer to the shore, are on the northern side of the lake. On the southern side, the route is classified as a main road, but it's much smaller.

Bicycle A circuit of the lake is about 50km, well within the limits of most casual cyclists, especially with an overnight stop somewhere. The *Rent a Radl* leaflet, available from the Klagenfurt tourist office, lists 20 places around the lake that rent bikes between about May and September; such bikes can be returned to any of these outlets. Rates are AS30/50 for one/three hours, AS90 for 24 hours and AS300/500 for one/two weeks. Ask about student/child rates. Bikes can also be hired at the Klagenfurt,

Krumpendorf, Pörtschach and Velden train stations but there's a AS45 surcharge if you don't return it to the same station.

Boat STW (☎ 0463-211 55, fax -15), St Veiter Strasse 31, Klagenfurt, runs steamers on the lake from early May to early October. Boats call at both sides, stopping at Klagenfurt, Krumpendorf, Sekirn, Reifnitz, Maria Wörth, Pörtschach, Dellach, Weisses Rössl, Auen and Velden, and return by the same route, departing from Klagenfurt at least every two hours. The longest trip (Klagenfurt-Velden) takes 1¾ hours and costs AS115 one way or AS170 return. A stopoff is allowed en route. Alternatively, the special *Rundfahrtkarte* (round-trip) ticket, also costing AS170 (AS150 if purchased before boarding) allows unlimited stops en route. The same ticket for a family costs AS380 (AS330 in advance). A four week pass costs AS400 for adults (photo required); child fares are about half-price. STW also runs evening cruises with music and dancing.

VELDEN

☎ 04274 • pop 8000 • 450m

This resort town exudes an aura of affluence and is one of the most popular holiday destinations on the lake.

Orientation & Information

Velden is ranged round the western end of Wörther See. The train station is about 10 minutes walk from Karawankenplatz, the central hub of the resort: turn right on leaving the station, then left down the side street where the main road forks.

The tourist office, the Kurverwaltung (☎ 21 03-0, fax -50, email office@velden .co.at), Seecorso 2, is just to the south of Karawankenplatz. Winter opening hours are Monday to Friday from 9 am to 5 pm; hours in July and August are Monday to Friday from 8 am to 8 pm, Saturday from 9 am to 6 pm and Sunday from 9 am to 5 pm. For the rest of the summer opening hours are shorter than this. Staff at the office can help find rooms but won't make bookings.

The provincial tourist office (☎ 52 100), Casinoplatz 1, is open on weekdays from 8 am to 5 pm (4 pm on Friday). It is in the cream-coloured house by the church – the absence of signs makes it seem as if it's hiding from tourists, though staff are helpful when you locate it.

Things to See & Do

Velden hasn't much in the way of sights, but you could admire the Baroque doorway of the 16th century former palace, now a hotel, on Seecorso. The **casino** is at Europaplatz on Am Corso and is open daily from 3 pm.

Apart from strolling around enjoying the relaxed atmosphere, the main attractions are water activities. Several **beaches** charge an entrance fee (between AS45 and AS90 per day), and rowing boats (AS40 per hour) and motorboats (AS160) are available for hire. There is also sailing, windsurfing, water-skiing and scuba diving.

Land-based activities include tennis and golf. All contact addresses and prices are available from the tourist office.

The hills north of Velden provide good views of the Karawanken mountain range to the south.

Four kilometres south of Velden is the Rosegg **Wildpark** (animal park; ☎ 523 57), open daily between April and November. Entry costs AS80/40 for adults/children. Infrequent buses run to Rosegg from Velden, but only on schooldays.

Places to Stay & Eat

In Velden you can choose from many hotels, pensions, private rooms or holiday apartments, though most are closed in winter. It's best to elicit the help of staff at the tourist offices. Prices are higher in the summer peak season, and these prices (per person) are quoted below.

Some of the central but still reasonably cheap pensions include: *Gästehaus Hutter* (☎ 24 40, Schubertweg 1), open year-round, where rooms with balcony cost AS240; *Haus Perdacher* (☎ 28 57, Sternberg-strasse 3), which has a garden and rooms with shower/WC for AS260; *Haus Berginz*

(☎ 24 38, fax -4, Rosentaler Strasse 19), which has a swimming pool and rooms with shower/WC and balcony starting at AS335; and *Seehaus Ogris* (☎ 20 79, fax -42, Seecorso 34), where rooms with shower/WC and satellite TV start at AS450.

Hubertushof (☎ 26 76, Europaplatz 1) is a four star hotel, with rooms starting at AS950 per person; facilities include an indoor swimming pool, sauna and fitness room. Its restaurant serves quality regional cuisine (main courses starting at AS170).

For self-caterers, supermarkets include an *ADEG* by Karawankenplatz and a *Julius Meinl* at Europaplatz. Walk along Seecorso to find various places to buy inexpensive fast food, such as *Wurstsalon* (open summer only). The chic *Pavillon*, Seecorso 8, offers Italian and Austrian food starting at AS78 (open from noon to 1 am). *China-Restaurant Xiangianghof* (Am Corso 2A) serves weekday lunch menus with starter costing upwards of AS59.

Getting There & Away

Trains to/from Villach (AS34, 10 to 15 minutes) and Klagenfurt (AS52, 15 to 20 minutes) run every 30 to 60 minutes.

VILLACH
☎ 04242 • pop 55,000 • 500m

Villach is an important transport hub for routes into Italy and Slovenia and the influence of both can be discerned in the town's ambience and inhabitants. Villach has several sights and serves as a base for exploring nearby lakes and other attractions. See the Around Villach section for details.

Orientation & Information

The old town centre is south of the Drau River. North of the river are the Hauptbahnhof, the bus station and a post office (open daily from 7 am to 10 pm), all close together on Bahnhofplatz. From the well-equipped Hauptbahnhof (containing a train information office, shops, restaurants and snack bars), walk south down Bahnhofstrasse and bear left down Nikolaigasse for the tourist office (☎ 244 44-0, fax -17, email

CARINTHIA

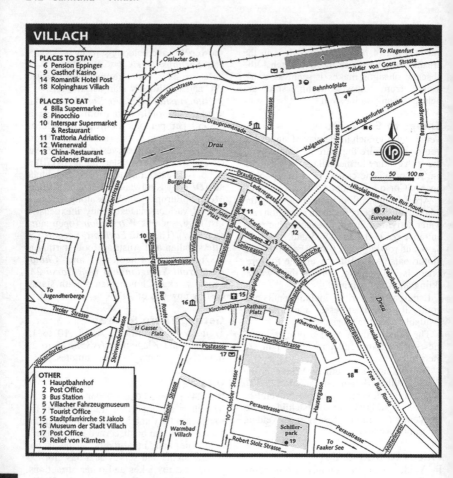

VILLACH

PLACES TO STAY
6 Pension Eppinger
9 Gasthof Kasino
14 Romantik Hotel Post
18 Kolpinghaus Villach

PLACES TO EAT
4 Billa Supermarket
8 Pinocchio
10 Interspar Supermarket
   & Restaurant
11 Trattoria Adriatico
12 Wienerwald
13 China-Restaurant
   Goldenes Paradies

OTHER
1 Hauptbahnhof
2 Post Office
3 Bus Station
5 Villacher Fahrzeugmuseum
7 Tourist Office
15 Stadtpfarrkirche St Jakob
16 Museum der Stadt Villach
17 Post Office
19 Relief von Kärnten

villach.information@telecom.at), Europaplatz 2; it's a few hundred metres. The office is open Monday to Friday from 8 am to 12.30 pm and 1.30 to 6 pm, and Saturday from 9 am to noon.

The post office on Postgasse (Postamt 9501) is open Monday to Friday from 7 am to 5.30 pm.

Things to See & Do

The small yellow city bus that completes a circuit of the centre every 20 minutes is free. The tourist office provides a map with English text guiding visitors through a walk of the old town; alas, there's nothing spectacular to see. The pedestrian-only hub of the town is the long, slender Hauptplatz, at the southern end of which stands **Stadtpfarrkirche St Jakob** (parish church of St Jakob). This Gothic church has a tower (open in the summer; entry AS20), a rococo altar, carved gravestones and an unusual pulpit.

Perhaps the best attraction here is the **Relief von Kärnten**, housed in Schillerpark,

Peraustrasse, south of the old town. This huge relief map of Carinthia covers 182 sq metres and depicts the province at a scale of 1:10,000 (1:5000 vertically, to exaggerate the mountains). It can help you plan your trip (or track your progress) through the region, and there are some interesting photos on the walls. The building is open from 2 May to 31 October, daily except Sunday and holidays, from 10 am to 4.30 pm (entry AS20, children AS10). Open for the same hours is the **Museum der Stadt Villach**, Widmanngasse 38. It covers local history, archaeology and medieval art (AS30, students AS20); combination tickets covering both attractions are available.

The **Villacher Fahrzeugmuseum**, Draupromenade 12, displays motorcycles and cars, mostly from the 1950s and 60s. Many are crammed together without any apparent regard for their condition or curiosity value. The bicycles with tiny motors are quite fun. Entry costs AS60, and it's open daily from 10 am to noon and 2 to 4 pm (9 am to 5 pm on Sundays and holidays, and 10 am to 5 pm from mid-July to mid-September).

Special Events

On the first Saturday in August the pedestrian centre is taken over by a folklore festival, the Kirchtag, which is held from noon to midnight. Entry is AS60. Some events begin during the preceding week.

Places to Stay

The HI *Jugendherberge* (☎ 563 68, fax -20, Dinzlweg 34) is about 1km west of the pedestrian centre. From H Gasser Platz, head west along Tiroler Strasse over the railway tracks and then bear right on St Martiner Strasse. Dinzlweg is the first on the left. The hostel has four-bed dorms with private shower/WC for AS170 per person, and dinner costs AS80. Don't abuse their hospitality in the serve-yourself breakfast. Doors are open during the day (though reception is closed from 10 am to 5 pm), and getting a key means you can avoid the 10 pm curfew. You can also rent bikes (AS30 per hour or AS120 per day).

Pension Eppinger (☎ 24 3 89, Klagenfurter Strasse 6) is set back from the street, through a green gate, and has courtyard parking. Rooms are perfectly adequate: singles/doubles with shower cost AS280/380; doubles/triples with shower/WC cost AS420/520. Breakfast isn't available.

Kolpinghaus Villach (☎ 270 71-0, fax -4, Hausergasse 5), by the car park, is also convenient. Singles/doubles with shower cost AS310/410, and there are 94 beds.

Gasthof Kasino (☎ 244 49, fax -4, Kaiser Josef Platz 4) is two blocks west of Hauptplatz. Renovated singles/doubles are fairly large and cost AS400/700 with shower and WC (some with TV). It has a garage (free for guests) and an inexpensive restaurant (closed on Sunday).

Romantik Hotel Post (☎ 261 01-0, fax -420, email romantik-hotel@magnet.at, Hauptplatz 26) is in a historic building with a garden and a sauna (free for guests). Rooms with bathroom or shower, WC and satellite TV vary in style and price, starting at AS750/1200, or AS450/950 for small rooms. It's also possible to stay in Warmbad Villach (see the Around Villach section) – there are actually more hotels and pensions there than in Villach itself. Staff at the Warmbad Villach tourist office (☎ 04242-372 44) find rooms commission-free.

Places to Eat

There's a *Billa* supermarket opposite the train station, and various snack places close by. Near the pedestrian area is *Interspar*, a shopping and supermarket centre on Ringmauergasse. It has a self-service restaurant, open Monday to Friday from 8.30 am to 7.30 pm and on Saturday from 8 am to 5 pm. Meals are cheap anyway (costing from AS56 to AS85) but look out for half-price deals after 6 pm. The salad buffet is AS11 per 100g.

At the northern end of Hauptplatz there's a *Wienerwald* with a takeaway section. On Hauptplatz itself there's *China-Restaurant Goldenes Paradies*, above the Julius Meinl supermarket, where weekday lunch menus cost from AS55 to AS65. You can also seek out the cafés in the pedestrian centre that give a flavour of Slovenia or, particularly, Italy; many have outside tables.

Pinocchio (Lederergasse 15) serves excellent and enormous pizzas starting at AS70; it's open daily. *Trattoria Adriatico (☎ 263 74, Bambergergasse)* is a quality Italian place with good seafood specialities. Prices are reasonable – pasta dishes start at AS70 and other meals cost upwards of AS130 (plus AS20 cover charge). It's closed at weekends.

The *Romantik Restaurant Postillon* of the Romantik Hotel Post (see Places to Stay) has an ambience that tries to live up to its name. It's open daily and provides acclaimed regional specialities costing upwards of AS100; the three course set menu costs AS140.

Getting There & Away

Villach is on three Austrian IC express rail routes, serving Salzburg (AS270, 2½ hours), Lienz (AS180, 70 minutes) and Klagenfurt (AS68, 30 minutes). It is also the junction at which two international EC routes diverge and head south. Direct services go to many destinations, for example Venice (AS184, 3½ hours), Ljubljana (AS116, 1¾ hours) and Zagreb (AS214, four hours). Rail journeys to Italy are subject to an unpopular (and hopefully temporary) Italian *Aufpreis* (surcharge).

Villach is equally well served by roads. The autobahns cross in a confusion of slip roads 4km east of the centre. Various bus routes radiate from Villach; call ☎ 2020-1510 for Bundesbus information.

AROUND VILLACH

Three kilometres south of the town centre is **Warmbad Villach**, a complex of thermal pools (33°C) and rejuvenating radioactive mineral waters, reputed to hinder the ageing process rather than cause unpleasant mutations. Nearly 40 million litres of water gush daily from six springs.

Kinetotherapy, mud baths, massages, saunas and other treatments are on offer in plush hotels and at Kurzentrum Heilbad Thermalbad Warmbad (☎ 370 00), which is open all year. If you just want to enjoy the waters, a day pass for its indoor thermal pool (with water slide, whirlpools and so on) costs AS120. Erlebnistherme Warmbad (☎ 378 89) is open all year, and entry to its adventure pool (with water slide etc; indoor and outdoor facilities) costs AS105, or AS80 after 4 pm. Zillerbad Warmbad (☎ 30 01 373) is open from May to October in good weather, and its open-air pool costs AS50 (AS45 for half a day). City bus No 1 goes to Warmbad (AS22).

East of Villach many lakes, big and small, provide plenty of swimming and boating opportunities. The largest are **Faaker See**, close to the Karawanken range, and **Ossiacher See**, a long, narrow lake only 4km north-east of Villach. Boats on Ossiacher See complete a crisscross tour of the lake in 2½ hours (AS125), with departures from Steindorf and, in high season, St Andrä. They're every 75 minutes or so in the high season (from early May to early October). Boats also navigate the Drau River between Villach Kongresshaus and Wernberg Bad (AS100) up to four times a day between 30 April and 8 October. Both of these services are operated by Ossiacher See und Drauschiffahrt (☎ 04242-580 71, email ods-schiffahrt@erlebnis.net). Full tours cost AS125 and AS110, respectively; a combined ticket for both tours is AS180.

A little north of Ossiacher See, off the road to Radenthein, is **Elli Riehl's Puppenwelt** (Puppet World; ☎ 04248-23 95), Winklern 14, Einöde. There are about 600 cute little dolls, which mainly appeal to small children; it's open from Easter to 15 October (AS50, children AS25).

Between Villach and Ossiacher See is **Burgruine Landskron**. The castle, partially in ruins, is famous for its 40 minute *Adler-Flugschau* (bird of prey show; ☎ 04242-428 88), in which captive predators are released to soar and swoop above the crowds. Shows are conducted at 11 am and 3 pm daily between May and September (also at 6 pm in July and August). A more recent attraction is the Affenberg (monkey mountain;

☎ 04242-430 319), open from 9.30 am to 5.30 pm, Friday to Sunday between Easter and 31 October, and daily from 1 May to 30 September. Entry to each attraction costs AS60 for adults or AS30 for children. There's a great view of the castle from the nearby village of St Andrä, with the Karawanken peaks as a backdrop.

The backdrop to the north of Ossiacher See is Gerlitzen (1909m), one of the main areas for winter **skiing**; a day pass costs AS330. Another nearby ski area is Dobratsch (2166m; day pass AS275), in the Villacher Alpen about 12km west of Villach. In summer this area is ideal for walking and mountain cycling, and at 1500m there's an **Alpine garden** (AS20) containing flora from the southern Alps. It's open daily between mid-June and 31 August from 9 am to 6 pm. To reach the garden, follow the Villacher Alpenstrasse from the town. This is a toll road (AS160 for cars, AS70 for motorcycles, bicycles free), though from about November to March it's free. It's closed to caravans.

Places to Stay & Eat

There are several *camp sites* by both Ossiacher See and Faaker See, as well as hotels, pensions, private rooms and holiday apartments. The tourist office in St Ruprecht (☎ 04242-420 00, fax 427 77), near Ossiacher See, covers the whole region, and staff will find rooms without charging. You can also refer to the region-wide accommodation brochure obtainable from the Villach tourist office. There are tourist offices for individual lake resorts.

Standard Austrian inns abound. More expensive options for regional cuisine include: *Das Kleine Restaurant* in the *Warmbaderhof Hotel* (☎ 04242-300 10-80, *Kadischenallee 24, Warmbad Villach)*, and *Karnerhof* (☎ 04254-21 88, *Karnerhofweg 10)* in the village of Egg on Faaker See (closed Monday).

Getting There & Around

From Villach Hauptbahnhof hourly trains run to Warmbad Villach (AS19) and along the northern shore of Ossiacher See; trains to Faaker See are less frequent. Bundesbuses run to both lakes from Villach bus station, but distances are so short that it's easy and more pleasant to explore the region by bicycle. You can hire bikes at Villach, Faak am See, Bodensdorf and Steindorf train stations, and from many other places.

Eastern Carinthia

The best sights in eastern Carinthia are north of Klagenfurt, on or close to highway 83 and the rail route between Klagenfurt and Bruck an der Mur. There are mountain ranges on either side: the Seetaler Alpen and Saualpe to the east and the Gurktaler Alpen to the west.

FRIESACH

☎ 04268 • pop 7000 • 636m
Friesach has a peaceful, unhurried air that belies the bristling fortifications on every hill top. It is Carinthia's oldest town, once important for its key location on the Vienna-Venice trade route. Friesach became part of the diocese of Salzburg in 860. Ensuing centuries saw invasions by the Bohemians, Hungarians, Turks and French, until the town came under the wing of the Habsburgs in 1803.

Orientation & Information

Friesach lies in the Metnitz Valley. At the centre of town, the picturesque Hauptplatz is a few minutes walk from the train station along Bahnhofstrasse: turn left on leaving the station and follow the road as it branches right. In summer, the tourist office (☎ 43 00, fax 42 80), Hauptplatz 1, opens Monday to Friday from 9 am to noon and 2 to 6 pm, and on Saturday from 9 am to noon. For the rest of the year, it's open from 10 am to noon on Monday, Wednesday and Friday.

Things to See & Do

Friesach is unique in Austria in retaining a filled moat around its ancient city walls. Flower borders seduce strollers who meander along the bank. North of the moat is a **Dominican monastery**; its 13th century Gothic church is open to the public, and is noted for its wooden crucifix and a sandstone statue of the Virgin.

Linger in Hauptplatz, an enchanting square with a Renaissance fountain. Just to the north is the **Stadtpfarrkirche**, which has a fine 12th century font and a distinctive tiled roof. To see the interior of the slender 14th century **Heiligblutkirche** (Church of the Holy Blood), visible on the hill to the south-west of Hauptplatz, you need to ask for the key from the *Pfarrhof* (manse) at the Stadtpfarrkirche.

Ranged along the hills rising above Hauptplatz to the west stand four ancient fortifications, all providing excellent views of the town and valley. The northernmost is the

Burg Geyersberg; the farthest south is the Virgilienberg Ruins. The middle two are the most easily visited from the town. A path winds up by the Heiligblutkirche to the **Rotturm**, a 13th century tower of which little remains. A better view is from **Peters-kirche**, accessible by paths ascending from in front of the Stadtpfarrkirche. To see the Gothic interior of Peterskirche, ask for the key at the house next door.

Behind Peterskirche, **Petersberg** houses the town museum, open daily between 10 am and 5 pm from May to October (entry AS40, students and seniors AS20, children AS10). The Petersberg castle is also the site for open-air theatre (anything from Shake-speare to Brecht) in summer. Obtain details and tickets (prices ranging from AS120 to AS200) from the tourist office.

Maypole Madness

Anybody travelling in Austria during May is certain to see many maypoles, as nearly every village and town raises one. The maypole (*Maibaum*) is traditionally erected on 1 May, often at night.

The 'pole' is actually a sturdy tree trunk, 30 or even 40m long, usually topped off by a small Christmas tree from which hang circles of pine branches. The maypole is dedicated to someone, either a local celebrity, the village girls, innkeepers or, in these more egalitarian times, simply 'everybody'. The raising of the maypole is quite a performance, and is well worth stopping to watch.

It can take 25 men three hours to raise the pole from horizontal to vertical, using a combination of hurdle-like supports, elongated pitchforks and brute strength. They force it upwards inch by exhausting inch, each upward movement accompanied by cheers of encouragement from other villagers. An alternative to pitchforks is a series of long, supporting poles, each attached to the maypole by a noose. Each noose is gradually manoeuvred down towards the base of the maypole while the other poles/nooses take the strain. Once vertical, the maypole rests in a small pit, and is fixed in place by hammering large wood splints around the base. The night I witnessed the raising of a maypole the local villagers indulged in an all-night party, which comprised music from a rather amateurish local brass band, accompanied by synchronised clapping from the onlookers, and much guzzling of frothy beer and fried sausages.

'It's a tradition that the party goes on all night,' a villager told me. 'We have to make sure nobody steals the maypole.' As if anyone could! But as an excuse for an all-night party, it's not a bad one.

At the end of May, often the last Sunday in the month, the maypole is pulled down and chopped up – another good excuse for a party.

Friesach has two medieval festivals: the Altstadtfest in the first weekend of June, and the Ritterfest in mid-July. The townsfolk don ancient costumes, and stage duels and other events. Friesach's historic past will be featured in a summer-long exhibition in 2001; the tourist office will provide details, and you can call 0463-549 54 or visit www.carinthia.com/landesausstellung.

Places to Stay

Zum Goldenen Anker (☎ 23 13, Bahnhofstrasse 3) is by Hauptplatz and offers variable but good value rooms with cable TV. Singles/doubles cost AS240/480, or AS330/580 with private shower. Reception is in the attached restaurant; phone ahead at weekends, when the restaurant is closed. Simple meals in this small Gasthof cost from AS65 to AS110.

Weisser Wolf (☎ 22 63, Hauptplatz 8) has comfortable rooms with shower and TV costing AS380/660; some also have WC. Meals in the restaurant start at AS90; it's closed on Monday.

The only four star hotel in Friesach is *Metnitztalerhof (☎ 25 10-0, fax -54, email metnitztalerhof@burgenstadt.at, Hauptplatz 11)*. Singles/doubles with shower, WC and TV start at AS540/880; some have a big balcony with good views. There's also a reasonably priced restaurant with outside tables overlooking the square.

Places to Eat

Explore the places round Hauptplatz, such as the hotels mentioned in Places to Stay. *Restaurant Kupferdachl (Langegasse 2)*, off the south-western corner of Hauptplatz, serves regional food starting at AS65 and offers pizzas after 5 pm (closed Tuesday).

For self-caterers, supermarkets include a *Spar* on Hauptplatz and an *ADEG* near the train station on Bahnhofstrasse.

Getting There & Away

Friesach is on the railway line between Vienna's Südbahnhof (3¾ hours) and Villach (70 minutes), with hourly express trains running in both directions. Bruck an der Mur (AS200, 110 minutes) and Klagenfurt are on this route. Slower trains also run to Klagenfurt, 55 minutes away, every hour (AS100 one way or AS120 for a day pass). Bundesbuses run to Friesach from Klagenfurt via St Veit approximately hourly. You can hire bicycles at the train station.

GURK

This small town, some 18km west of the Friesach-Klagenfurt road, is notable for its **Dom**. It was built between 1140 and 1200 and is one of the finest examples of Romanesque architecture in Austria. The relatively plain exterior of the cathedral is dominated by two huge onion domes capping square-sided twin towers. The interior has Gothic reticulated vaulting on the ceiling, and most of the church fittings are Baroque or rococo. The early Baroque high altar is particularly impressive: it's laden with 72 statues and 82 angels' heads.

The frescoes in the Episcopal Chapel, dating from around 1200, are made all the more affecting by their primitive colours. The chapel can be viewed by guided tour only, at 1 pm daily from April to October. The Dom is open daily, all year.

Those with children might be interested in visiting the nearby **Zwergenpark** (Dwarfs Park) populated by garden gnomes. It has a mini-railway and is open from May to October (AS60, children AS40). For information call ☎ 04266-85 20.

Getting There & Away

Gurk cannot be reached by rail, and Bundesbus No 5371 goes there from Klagenfurt (via St Veit an der Glan) only three times a day (twice on Sunday). Private transport makes a visit much easier: the town is on highway 93.

ST VEIT AN DER GLAN

☎ 04212 • pop 13,000 • 476m

St Veit was historically important as the seat of the dukes of Carinthia from 1170 until 1518, when the dukes skipped down the road to Klagenfurt and the town diminished in status.

Orientation & Information

St Veit is near the junction of primary road routes to Villach (highway 94) and Klagenfurt (highway 83). To get to the pedestrian-only town centre from the Hauptbahnhof (where you can usually pick up a free map), walk left down Bahnhofstrasse for 600m and then go one block right.

The tourist office (☎ 55 55-31, fax -80) is in the Rathaus at Hauptplatz 1, in the heart of the pedestrian area. It's open on weekdays and on Saturday in summer.

Things to See & Do

The town centre can keep visitors occupied for a couple of hours. Places of interest line the long **Hauptplatz**, with a fountain at either end and a central column erected in 1715 as a memorial to plague victims. The north-eastern fountain, the Schüsselbrunnen, is surmounted by a bronze statue, created in 1566. This figure is the town mascot: its hand is raised as if in greeting, yet at the same time a jet of water spits forth from its mouth. The south-western fountain bears a statue of local medieval poet, Walther von der Vogelweide.

The most impressive façade on Hauptplatz belongs to the **Rathaus**. Its Baroque stuccowork was applied in 1754 and features a double-headed eagle on the pediment. St Veit (the saint, not the town) stands between the eagle's wings. Walk through the Gothic vaulted passage to admire the arcaded courtyard, bedecked with sgraffito designs.

Close to the town hall is the **Verkehrsmuseum** (Transport Museum) at Hauptplatz 29. It does a reasonable job of making the development of transport in the region seem interesting, and displays old travel documents, motorcycles, model trains and mannequins wearing uniforms; there are no English labels. The WWII display includes photos of bomb-damaged Villach and Klagenfurt train stations; appropriately, the guard dummy in this section sports a ludicrous Hitler moustache! It's open daily from 1 May to 15 October and entry costs AS35 (students AS20). There's also a city museum (in the former ducal castle on Burggasse, one block north of Hauptplatz) and a Romanesque Stadtpfarrkirche, adjoining Hauptplatz.

The colourful, mosque-like Hotel St Veit (see Places to Stay) was built in 1998 and has astrological symbols by Ernst Fuchs.

Places to Stay

There is a range of inexpensive places to stay in St Veit, including private rooms. The *camp site* (☎ 22 90) is 1.5km east of the centre, off Völkermarkter Strasse.

Gasthof Steirerhof (☎ 24 42, Klagenfurter Strasse 38), five minutes walk south of the centre, offers adequate rooms with hall showers costing AS260 per person. *Gasthof Sonnhof* (☎ 24 47, Völkermarkter Strasse 37), on the way to the camp site, has good singles/doubles with shower/WC and balcony costing AS280/500, and a good-value restaurant (closed Monday). From the station, leave by the eastern exit, take the path leading south and bear right when it joins the road.

Weisses Lamm (☎ 23 62, fax -62, Unterer Platz 4-5) offers four star comfort starting at about AS460 per person. The visually striking *Hotel St Veit* (☎ 46 60-0, fax 660, Friesacher Strasse 1) charges AS900/1200.

Places to Eat

Opposite the Hauptbahnhof is a *Billa* supermarket. Nearby, at Bahnhofstrasse 32 (opposite the *Spar* supermarket), is *Pizza Max*, a cheap takeaway and eat-in restaurant; it's closed Saturday lunchtime and Monday. The *Interspar* supermarket on Völkermarkter Strasse has a self-service restaurant where hot meals cost from AS45 to AS80. The *TOBI* supermarket, on Ossiacher Strasse by the post office, also has a very cheap restaurant, where three-course set lunches cost AS59 and AS69.

There are lots of comfortable places to eat in the compact pedestrian area, many with outside tables. Just west of Hauptplatz is *Gasthof Traube* (Oktober Platz 2), which has a garden and inexpensive regional food (closes Monday at 2 pm). Nearby is *Pukelsheim (☎ 24 73, Erlgasse 11)*, serving pricey, upmarket Austrian and regional meals (closed Monday).

Getting There & Away

St Veit is 33km south of Friesach and 20km north of Klagenfurt. Hourly express trains on the Vienna-Villach route stop at St Veit; the journey to Villach takes 45 minutes. Fares are AS68 to Friesach (30 minutes) and AS36 to Klagenfurt (20 minutes).

Bundesbuses run to Klagenfurt, Maria Saal and Friesach about every hour.

BURG HOCHOSTERWITZ

This fortress drapes itself around the slopes of a hill and is a stunning sight, especially when viewed from the north-west. The visual impact is due mainly to the 14 gate towers and their connecting walls that circle the hill to the summit. These were built between 1570 and 1586 by Georg Khevenhüller, the then owner, to protect against Turkish invasion. It certainly looks impregnable, and the information booklet (in English; AS30) outlines the different challenges presented to attackers by each gate – they're something of a medieval forerunner to the multiple levels in modern computer adventure games!

The castle itself was first mentioned in documents in 860. A small museum features family portraits and arms and armour (one suit would fit a 2m-tall giant). Entry costs AS70 (students AS35) and it's open daily between Palm Sunday and 31 October, from 9 am to 5 pm (from 8 am to 6 pm between May and September). There's a cheap restaurant in the grounds.

Getting There & Away

Regional trains on the St Veit-Friesach route stop at Launsdorf Hochosterwitz station, 3km north-east of the car park and the first gate, where a lift will take you directly to the castle for AS40. Infrequent buses from either Klagenfurt or St Veit will get you 1km closer (to the Brückl crossroads). If you don't have time to visit, you can at least absorb the sight of the castle to the east of the train.

MAGDALENSBERG

Four kilometres south of Burg Hochosterwitz, this 1058m peak provides an excellent 360 degrees panorama from its summit. There's also a Roman archaeological open-air museum here (open 1 May to 31 October, AS40) and a Gothic chapel. The road up approaches from the south. Buses from Klagenfurt arrive once a day on schooldays (at 2.35 pm), and depart five minutes later. This means taking the bus is not viable, unless you're prepared to walk down the hill to one of the nearby villages to pick up another bus or a train.

MARIA SAAL
☎ 04223 • pop 3200
On a fortified hill stands the pilgrimage church of Maria Saal. Its twin spires are visible from afar.

Orientation & Information

This small town is 10km north of Klagenfurt. The road from the train station splits in two and encloses the church hill. Behind the church is Hauptplatz, with a bank and several restaurants. The tourist office (☎ 22 14, fax -22), Am Platz 7, is in the centre of Hauptplatz.

Things to See & Do

The church was built in the early 15th century from volcanic stone. Originally Gothic, it later received Romanesque and Baroque modifications. The exterior south wall is embedded with relief panels and ancient gravestones: look for the Keutschach family tombstone in red marble, and the Roman mail wagon carved into one of the stones used in the building of the church. There are unusual outbuildings within the walled enclosure. The interior of the church is nicely proportioned when looking down the nave. Overhead, the ceiling is fan-vaulted and there are frescoes of people growing out of bulbous flowers (that's not as hallucinatory as it sounds – it

CARINTHIA

represents the genealogy of Christ). The image of the Virgin on the high altar dates from 1425; on either side of the main altar are Gothic winged altars. There's an explanatory pamphlet, in English, available in the church.

About 500m north of the church is the **Kärntner Freilichtmuseum** (Carinthian Open-Air Museum; ☎ 31 66). It contains over 30 typical or historical Carinthian rural dwellings and features demonstrations of country crafts. It is open daily except Monday from 10 am to 6 pm, between about 1 May and mid-October (weather permitting). Entry costs AS60 for adults, AS130 for families and AS30 for students.

Getting There & Away

There are no official left-luggage facilities in the small train station, but the ticket clerk may look after your bags if you ask nicely. Maria Saal is on the same Vienna-Klagenfurt rail route as Friesach and St Veit, but only the slower hourly regional trains stop here. Fares are AS36 to St Veit and AS19 to Klagenfurt; both journeys take about 10 minutes. Buses run to both places from below the church.

Western Carinthia

Excluding the Hohe Tauern National Park (see the following chapter), the main points of interest in western Carinthia are close to the primary road route north from Villach, the A10/E55 which ultimately leads to Salzburg. It has a toll section between Rennweg and a point north of the Tauern Tunnel (AS140, AS100 for motorcycles); to avoid the toll, take highway 99.

The rail route from Villach takes a more westerly course after Spittal an der Drau, before also turning north. It is shadowed by highway 106 (later 105), the road to Bad Gastein. However, driving this way necessitates using the railway car-shuttle service (*Autoschleuse Tauernbahn*) through the tunnel from Mallnitz-Obervellach in Carinthia to Böckstein in Salzburg. The fare for cars is AS200 one way (AS120 if purchased in advance from Austrian motoring clubs, some banks and garages) or AS320 return (valid for two months). The price for motorcycles is AS100/160. For information on services through this tunnel, telephone ☎ 04784-600 390 in Mallnitz-Obervellach or ☎ 06434-26 63 39 in Böckstein. Departures are every 30/60 minutes (summer/winter), except at night.

GMÜND

☎ 04732 • pop 2700 • 749m

Gmünd's ancient city walls, still partially intact, are a reminder of its former strategic importance – it was owned by a succession of powerful rulers, not least the Archbishops of Salzburg. Gmünd was founded in the 11th century.

The walled centre is attractive, with small streets leading off Hauptplatz and running beneath a succession of arches. The most impressive old building is the 13th century **Alte Burg** on the hill. Although it's partially in ruins, cultural events are still held inside.

Also a mere stone's throw from Hauptplatz is the privately owned **Porsche Museum**. A Porsche factory was sited in Gmünd from 1944 to 1950, and the first car to bear that famous name (a 356) was handmade here. One of these models is on display (only 52 were built), together with about 15 other models and a couple of the wooden frames used in their construction. There's a film (in German) on Dr Porsche's life and work. The museum is open all year, daily from 9 am to 6 pm (10 am to 4 pm from mid-October to mid-May). It's rather pricey for a small museum (AS70).

Places to Stay & Eat

Gmünd has inexpensive private rooms as well as pensions, hotels and holiday apartments. Staff at the tourist office (☎ 22 22), in the Rathaus on Hauptplatz, can outline accommodation options. There are a couple of places on Hauptplatz, and these have affordable restaurants. There's also a restaurant in the Alte Burg; meals start at AS85, and it's open daily.

The tourist office also has information about Trebesing, a village with several hotels, 4km down the road: dubbed 'Europe's first Babydorf', it's an interesting place to stay if you have young kids, as it has extensive facilities for children.

Getting There & Away
Gmünd is not on a rail route, though buses do go there from Spittal an der Drau (30 minutes; no buses on Sunday), including bus No 5132, which continues north to Salzburg province.

SPITTAL AN DER DRAU
☎ 04762 • pop 16,200 • 556m
Spittal is an important economic and administrative centre in upper Carinthia. Its name comes from a 12th century hospital and refuge that once succoured travellers on this site.

Orientation & Information
The tourist office (☎ 34 20, fax 32 37) is at Burgplatz 1, at the side of the main tourist attraction, Schloss Porcia. Opening hours are Monday to Friday from 9 am to 6 pm (8 pm in July and August) and Saturday from 9 am to noon. From the train station, walk down Bahnhofstrasse and cut across Stadtpark, a 10 minute walk.

The post office (Postamt 9800) near the train station opens daily from 7 am to 9 pm.

Things to See & Do
Schloss Porcia is an excellent Renaissance edifice, built between 1533 and 1597. The Italianate arcaded courtyard is particularly eye-catching. The upper floors contain the Museum für Volkskultur (entry AS45, students AS20), a regional museum which gives an effective evocation of life in the locality, covering art, artefacts, rustic crafts and culture. Of interest are the primitive wooden skis and the crudely carved school desks. Many signs are in English. From 15 May to 31 October it's open daily from 9 am to 6 pm; at other times opening hours are Monday to Thursday from 1 to 4 pm. Cultural events are also held in the Schloss.

Spittal's nearest mountain, offering inspiring views, is the Goldeck (2142m), to the south-west. In summer, the peak can be reached by cable car (AS145 one way, AS195 return) or by the Goldeckstrasse toll road (cars AS160, motorbikes AS80; reductions with Gästekarte). The road stops 260m short of the summit. In winter, the peak is the domain of skiers: day passes cost AS320 (reductions for children, young people aged under 18 and seniors). The cable car doesn't run from mid-April to mid-June or from mid-September to mid-December.

Special Events
On a weekend in late June every odd-numbered year (1999, 2001 etc) the historical legend of Katharina von Salamanca (said to haunt Schloss Porcia in retribution for the violent death of her son) is re-enacted in the Salamanca Festival, held in the town centre. Admission is free.

Places to Stay
Staff at the tourist office will track down accommodation free of charge. *Draufluss Camping* (☎ 24 66) is about 3.5km from the town centre on the southern bank of the Drau River; it's open April to October. The most central HI *Jugendherberge* (☎ 32 52, fax -4, Zur Seilbahn 2) is near the base of the Goldeck cable car. From the train station, turn right and cross under the rail tracks. The hostel has basic cooking facilities and a good-value restaurant, but may close in off-season (phone ahead); check-in opens at 5 pm. Dorm beds cost AS90 and breakfast is AS30. Non-HI members pay AS10 extra but don't get a guest stamp. Single occupancy may be possible for a AS50 surcharge. Another HI *Jugendherberge* (☎ 27 01) at the Goldeck mid-station (1650m) is accessible only by cable car; dorm beds are AS180.

There are few convenient pensions, so you may have to resort to private rooms such as the central *Gästehaus Edlinger* (☎ 29 48, Mozartstrasse 9); doubles with shower/WC cost AS560. *Gasthof Brück-enwirt* (☎ 27 72, An der Wirtschaftsbrücke

SPITTAL AN DER DRAU

PLACES TO STAY
1 Gästehaus Edlinger
3 Hotel Salzburg
8 Pension Hübner
11 Gasthof Weiss
13 Gasthof Brückenwirt
19 Jugendherberge

PLACES TO EAT
4 Spar Supermarket & Restaurant; Gerngross Department Store
5 Rathaus Café
9 Café-Restaurant Formosa
10 Café-Restaurant Zellot
12 Wirtshaus Zum Spittl
20 Tennis Halle Restaurant

OTHER
2 Post Office
6 Schloss Portia & Museum Für Volkskultur
7 Tourist Office
14 Swimming Pool
15 Post Office
16 Bundesbus Departures
17 Train Station
18 Goldeck Cable Car

2) is a few minutes walk east of the town centre, by the Lieser River. It's a chalet-style inn with balconies, a garden and friendly staff. Singles/doubles (all with a sink) are AS280/560 with private shower/WC, or AS230/460 without. Just over the Lieser is *Gasthof Weiss* (☎ 23 41, *Edlingerstrasse 1A*), charging AS300/490 for rooms with shower/WC, but it only ever has vacancies at weekends.

Near Schloss Porcia is *Pension Hübner* (☎ 21 12, *fax 352 59, email huebner@*

carinthia.com, Schillerstrasse 20), run by the owners of the shop of the same name. All rooms have a private shower and satellite TV, and most have attached WC. Singles cost from AS330 to AS420, doubles from AS550 to AS740, depending on the room, season and length of stay. This pleasing place is usually open from 1 May to 30 September but phone ahead for winter stays. There are also apartments with kitchens (minimum stay five days), and bicycles are free for guests to use.

Opposite Stadtpark, *Hotel Salzburg* (☎ *31 65, fax -65, Tiroler Strasse 22)* has good rooms with period furniture, shower/WC and satellite TV costing AS420/700.

Places to Eat

On Neuer Platz there's a Gerngross store, with a *Spar* supermarket and self-service restaurant (open normal shop hours).

The *Tennis Halle Restaurant*, by the Jugendherberge, serves surprisingly good (and inexpensive) food; the *Forelle* (trout) for AS125 is excellent. *Rathaus Café (Ebnergasse 5)* has a 1st floor terrace, a pub ambience and meals costing less than AS125. It's open Monday to Saturday from 7 am to midnight or later.

Wirtshaus Zum Spittl (Edlinger Strasse 1) has a welcoming interior and a garden, and serves Austrian food and pizzas costing from AS68 to AS150 (closed Wednesday). *Café-Restaurant Formosa (Hauptplatz)* is one of several cheap Chinese restaurants.

Cuisine served in the stylish *Café-Restaurant Zellot (☎ 21 13, Am Torbogen)* changes according to monthly festivals; prices are mid-range. The walls provide exhibition space for up-and-coming local artists. It's closed on Sunday and (except in July and August) Monday.

Getting There & Away

Spittal-Millstättersee railway station is at an important rail junction: two-hourly IC services run north to Bad Gastein (AS100, 52km) and west to Lienz (AS116, 67km, one hour). Villach (AS68, 30 minutes) is 37km to the south-east. The route north via Mallnitz-Obervellach yields some excellent views as the railway track clings high to the side of the valley (sit on the left).

Bundesbuses leave from outside the train station, including about 12 a day to Gmünd. Call ☎ 39 16 for information.

MILLSTATT

☎ 04766 • pop 3300 • 588m

Millstatt lies 10km east of Spittal an der Drau on the northern shore of Millstätter See. The lake is attractively situated, bordered by tree-lined hills on its southern side and a sprinkling of small resorts on its northern shore.

Orientation & Information

Millstatt is roughly in the middle of the 12km-long northern shore of Millstätter See. The Millstatt tourist office, the Kurverwaltung (☎ 20 22-0, fax 34 79), is housed in the Rathaus, in the town centre at Marktplatz 8. The comprehensive *Informationen-Veranstaltungen* booklet covers the whole lake and provides information on festivals and events, sports facilities and prices, transport timetables and much else. Across the square at No 14 is the Millstätter See tourist office (☎ 37 00, fax -8, email info@millstatt-see.co.at), with touch-screen computer information outside.

Things to See & Do

The resort is dominated by a **Benedictine abbey**, founded in 1070. The abbey's Romanesque church has a distinctive inner doorway, complete with grotesque faces peering from the columns. The heavy Gothic ceiling vaulting vies for attention with the gold statues and Baroque altars. The fresco of the Last Judgement (1513-16), to the right of the high altar, is by Urban Görtschacher. In the arcaded courtyard stands an old linden tree; there's an even more ancient tree (about 1000 years old) outside. The **Stiftsmuseum** (abbey museum) deals with the history of the town and the geology of the region; it's open daily between mid-May and 30 September, from 9 am to noon and 2 to 6 pm (entry AS30, children AS20).

The lake is up to 141m deep and teems with possibilities for **water sports** such as sailing, scuba diving, swimming, waterskiing, windsurfing, and fishing. Several types of boat are available for hire. Simply strolling along the Seepromenade, lined with statues and flowers, is pleasant. **Boat cruises** (☎ 20 75) operate from 1 May to mid-October; a full circuit of the lake costs AS125 and takes two hours (child/family fares available).

East of Millstatt is **Bad Kleinkirchheim**, a spa resort and winter skiing centre (AS340 for a day pass). Its tourist office (☎ 04240-82 12) can provide details.

Places to Stay & Eat

The summer season is from Easter to mid-October, with the highest prices (those quoted here) applicable from June to September. Many quiet, mid-priced B&Bs line Alexanderhofstrasse and Tangernerweg, to the west of the resort centre. Millstatt has some winter tourism, but most hotels, pensions and private rooms close at this time. The winter hibernators don't open until late May, including the places mentioned below – check availability with the tourist office outside summertime.

Cheap and central is *Gasthof Zum Brunnen* (☎ 20 80, *Marktplatz 30*), where basic singles/doubles cost AS240/420, or AS290/520 for the few rooms with shower/WC; add AS40 for a single night stay. Nearby, *Haus Aigner-Haberl* (☎ 21 11, *Mirnockstrasse 39*) only has doubles with hall shower which cost AS380. There's a café downstairs.

Haus Josef Pleikner (☎ 20 36, *Seemühlgasse 57*) has rooms costing from AS295 to AS350 per person, most with private shower/WC. It has parking facilities and private lake access. It's above and part of

Pizzeria Peppino (closed on Sunday, open in winter), serving pizzas starting at AS62, plus schnitzels and spaghetti. Seemühlgasse is between Kaiser Franz Josef Strasse and the boat station. Several restaurants overlook the lake, but they're more expensive.

For self-caterers there's an *ADEG* supermarket not far from the lakeside at Kaiser Franz Josef Strasse, near Schwarzstrasse. It is open on weekdays from 8 am to 12.30 pm and 2 to 6.30 pm, and on Saturday from 7.30 am to 12.30 pm.

Hotel See-Villa (☎ 21 02, fax 22 21, *Seestrasse 68*) has a good restaurant where main dishes, including fish specialities, start at AS140. Menu prices are reduced by 20% if you stay here: rooms start at AS590 per person, and have bath or shower, WC, telephone and balcony.

For pub entertainment, try *Full House* (*Kaiser Franz Josef Strasse*), near Seemühlgasse. This small American bar has live music.

Getting There & Away

Regular Bundesbuses to Millstatt depart from outside Spittal train station (AS32, 20 minutes), with some continuing to Bad Kleinkirchheim (a further 40 minutes). The road from Spittal stays close to the lake shore. Hourly buses run to Villach (100 minutes) via Radenthein.

Klagenfurt's Wappensaal (Hall of Arms) features 655 coats of arms of the estates of Carinthia.

MARK HONAN

Riverside walks and cycle rides by the Drau are popular among visitors to charming Villach.

AUSTRIAN NATIONAL TOURIST OFFICE/MARKOWITSCH

The dramatic Hohe Tauern National Park provides a perfect habitat for the chamois and the marmot

Some come to look at Grossglockner, Austria's highest peak, while others actually make the ascent.

Hohe Tauern National Park Region

Austria's highest peak and its tallest water-fall, the longest glacier in the eastern Alps, snow-capped crags, lush valleys, soaring bearded vultures, skipping ibexes, burrowing marmots – all this and more awaits the visitor to the Hohe Tauern National Park (Nationalpark Hohe Tauern), accessible by roads twisting past some of the finest views in the country.

Orientation

In 1971 the provinces of Carinthia, Salzburg and Tirol agreed to the creation of a national park; regions were added in stages until it became Europe's largest national park, comprising 1787 sq km. Salzburg has contributed 805 sq km, Tirol 610 sq km, and Carinthia 372 sq km. The most famous route in Austria, the Grossglockner Road, starts in Salzburg and ends in Carinthia. Its highest point is the mighty Grossglockner (3797m), which straddles the border between East Tirol and Carinthia. On the western side of the park stands the second-highest peak in the region, Grossvenediger (3674m), the high point of the border between East Tirol and Salzburg.

The boundaries of the park are extremely irregular, but it can be split into three sections for convenience: west of the Felber Tauern Road (containing Grossvenediger), the vicinity of Grossglockner, and the eastern portion between Mallnitz and Bad Gastein. Zell am See, Bad Gastein and Lienz border the park and are covered in this chapter.

Information

The Hohe Tauern National Park is open all year and there's no admission charge; however, most of the roads to and through the park have toll sections, and some are impassable or closed in winter (see the Getting Around section later in this

Highlights

- Marvel at the stunning vistas on the Grossglockner Road
- View the mighty Grossglockner and the Pasterze Glacier from Franz Josefs Höhe
- Walk alongside the spectacular 380m-high Krimml Falls
- Enjoy the active life – skiing, walking and windsurfing around Zell am See
- Soak in the 19th century aura of Bad Gastein, a favourite with cure-seekers since the Middle Ages

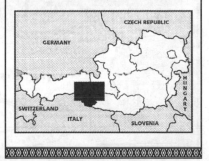

chapter). This is a protected nature area but not a wilderness area: 60,000 people live within its borders in 29 communities.

All tourist offices in places bordering the park have information on Hohe Tauern, including the offices in Zell am See, Krimml, Bad Gastein and Lienz; they should also be able to provide free maps of the park. The *Experience in Nature* map (in English) shows information offices and overnight accommodation spots. It also highlights many tour suggestions, with descriptions on the reverse side.

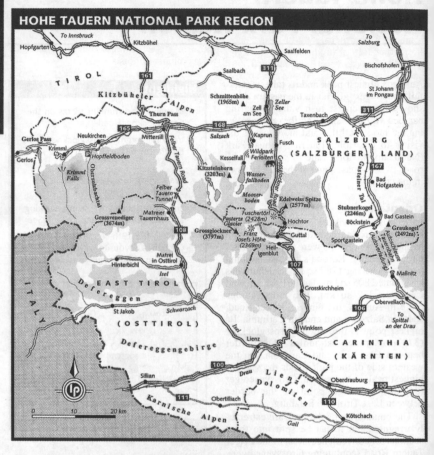

HOHE TAUERN NATIONAL PARK REGION

The office which has jurisdiction over the whole park is known as the Nationalparkrat (☎ 04875-51 12, fax -21, email nprht@netway.at), Rauterplatz 1, A-9971 Matrei in Osttirol. The town is on the southern side of the Felber Tauern Road. In addition, there is a Nationalparkverwaltung office run by each province and covering its own portion of the park. The one for Tirol (☎ 04875-51 61, fax -20, email npht.tirol@netway.at) shares the same address as the Nationalparkrat. The one for Salzburg (☎ 06565-65 58, fax -18, email nationalpark@salzburg.or.at), A-5741 Neukirchen am Grossvenediger 306, is at Neukirchen in the north-west of the national park region, near Krimml. The Carinthia office (☎ 04825-61 61, fax -16, email hohetauern@nationalpark-kaernten.or.at) is at Döllach 14, A-9843 Grosskirchheim. You could also investigate the national park's Web site: www.npht.sbg.ac.at/npht. Information on accommodation options is available from these offices.

Things to See & Do

Walking while enjoying the unspoiled environment is the main activity in the park. Freytag & Berndt produces nine 1:50,000 walking maps covering the national park and surrounding areas. As this is a conservation area, there are several things *not* to do, such as straying from the marked trails, littering, lighting fires or disturbing the flora and fauna.

The park has more than 300 mountains above 3000m, and 246 glaciers. There are also numerous rivers, lakes, waterfalls and ravines. For information on the Grossglockner Road, see that section in this chapter.

Another popular excursion is to **Grossvenediger**, a peak permanently coated with ice and snow and flanked by glaciers. The closest you can get by road is the Matreier Tauernhaus Hotel (1512m) at the southern entrance to the Felber Tauern Tunnel. You can park here and within an hour's walk gain fine views of the mountain. A more athletic option is to park at the Hopffeldboden parking area, south of Neukirchen, and walk south along the Obersulzbachtal (Obersulzbach Valley). It is a 10 hour walk to Grossvenediger, with a mountain refuge about halfway. Another possibility is to approach from the south; there's a car park at Hinterbichl, at the end of the road running west from Matrei. It's a similar distance to Grossvenediger, again with a mountain refuge along the way.

Skiing areas are just beyond the borders of the park, at places such as Zell am See and Bad Gastein.

Places to Stay & Eat

Camping is not permitted within the park, though there is a summer *camp site* at Matrei (☎ 04875-51 11), and two others on the road leading west from there (one is open year-round).

For short excursions to the park, it's easy to base yourself somewhere like Zell am See or Lienz. Within the park, some small-scale guesthouses provide food and accommodation, but they are widely scattered. If you plan to undertake major walking expeditions you should schedule your overnight stops in advance. Contact the regional or local tourist offices for accommodation lists.

On the food front, regional specialities include *Erdapfelnidei* (potato noodles), *Fleischkrapfen* (meat-filled dumplings) and *Kasnocken* (cheese dumplings).

Getting Around

The authorities are determined to limit the flow of traffic through the park. It is possible that private vehicles will one day be banned altogether. This is certainly envisaged for the Grossglockner Road, where visitors would have to rely on buses or shuttle taxis, but this won't happen anytime soon. See the Grossglockner Road section for information on travelling this route in the meantime. Getting around by Bundesbus is made more attractive by special passes; such deals change periodically, so make inquiries upon arrival. In 1998, for example, a one week pass was available, covering the Grossglockner south region; it cost AS270. Buying zonal day or week passes for provincial transport should work out significantly cheaper than buying single tickets.

The Felber Tauern Road (Felbertauernstrasse) is open year-round. There is a 5.5km-long tunnel at the East Tirol-Salzburg border: the toll is AS140 for cars (AS130 in winter) and AS110 for motorcycles. Bundesbuses operate along this road (such as those on the Lienz-Kitzbühel route).

ZELL AM SEE
☎ 06542 • pop 9700 • 758m

Zell am See is ideally situated. It enjoys a picturesque location between its namesake lake, the Zeller See, and the ridged slopes of the Schmittenhöhe mountain. It's also a convenient base for excursions, including trips along the Grossglockner Road.

Zell am See has teamed up with **Kaprun** to create the Europa Sports Region. Sports brochures, available from the tourist office

HOHE TAUERN NATIONAL PARK

ZELL AM SEE

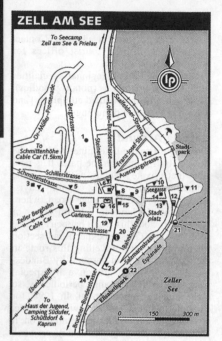

ZELL AM SEE

PLACES TO STAY
2   Hotel Salzburgerhof
3   Haus Haffner
7   Haus Raßer
8   Zum Hirschen
9   Sporthotel Lebzelter
14 Buchner
15 Gasthof Steinerwirt
18 Hubertus

PLACES TO EAT
4   Va bene
5   Ampere
6   China-Restaurant Fünf Planeten
10 Wienerwald
11 Grand Hotel
13 Moby Dick Fischrestaurant
19 Spar Supermarket
23 Pizza Mann
24 Restaurant Kupferkessel

OTHER
1   Freizeitzentrum
12 B17
16 Post Office
17 Bundesbus Station
20 Tourist Office
21 Boat Departures
22 Train Station

in either place, will usually cover the whole region. Kaprun is pretty and lively, and it has good access to ski slopes, but isn't so convenient for water sports.

Orientation

Zell am See lies on the western bank of the Zeller See. Almost adjacent to the main resort is Schüttdorf, barely clinging to the south side of the lake; it is generally cheaper for accommodation.

Information

The tourist office, or Kurverwaltung (☎ 770-0, fax 720 32, email zell@gold.at), is at Bruckner Bundesstrasse 1, a few minutes walk from the train station. It is open Monday to Friday from 8 am to noon and 2 to 6 pm, and on Saturday from 9 am to noon. In the high season, hours lengthen and include Saturday afternoon and Sunday

morning. There's an accommodation board in the foyer with a free telephone (accessible daily from 8 am to midnight).

The post office (Postamt 5700) is on Postplatz; it's, open Monday to Friday from 7.30 am to 6.30 pm and on Saturday between 7.30 and 11 am (10 am in winter).

If you want to stay in Kaprun, contact its tourist office (☎ 06547-86 43-0, fax 81 92-0, email kaprun@gold.at) for advice on accommodation. You should ask to be given the *Gästekarte* (guest card) wherever you stay.

Skiing

This region has a long history of skiing. In 1927 the first cable car in Salzburg province (the fifth in Austria) was opened on Schmittenhöhe, and the first glacial ski run was opened on Kitzsteinhorn in 1965. The Europa Sports Region operates 60 cable cars and lifts, giving access to over 130km of runs for people of all abilities. Ski passes for the region cost AS795 for a two day minimum (cheaper in the low season; reductions for senior citizens, young people and children). Ski buses are free for ski pass holders. Ski rental prices are about AS190 per day.

The **Schmittenhöhe cable car** reaches 1965m. Other cable cars from Zell am See ascend to the ridge on either side of this point. These operate from mid-December to mid-April. There are several black (difficult) runs that twist between the tree-lined flanks of the mountain. For weather conditions, call ☎ 736 94, or check the live TV pictures shown in the tourist office and cable car stations.

Kaprun is the closest resort to **Kitzsteinhorn** (3203m), offering year-round glacier skiing. Start early in the day during the high season to avoid long queues. Ascent options include the Gletscherbahn underground railway or the cable car that soars over the glacier and up to 3029m (less than 200m from the summit). A day pass for Kitzsteinhorn or Schmittenhöhe costs AS420, with reductions in the low season and for non-skiers. First-timers can try a cheap taste of winter skiing on the Maiskogel lift, costing AS135 after 2 pm. The short Lechnerberg lift costs just AS20 for one ride. For information on weather conditions on the Kaprun slopes, call ☎ 06547-84 44.

Other Activities

Staff at the tourist office can provide maps and information on cycling and walking. From Schmittenhöhe you can gaze at 30 peaks over 3000m. The **Pinzgauer Spaziergang walk** from here takes less than seven hours and exploits to the full the magnificent views; the path is marked, and a map is available from the tourist office. There is very little change in altitude along the way. You descend via the Schattbergbahn cable car to Saalbach (which is another excellent skiing area), and take the Bundesbus back from there to Zell am See (the last departure is at 6.30 pm). From June to mid-October there are guided walks from Schmittenhöhe

Alpine Reservoirs

South of Kaprun is a series of reservoirs in a picturesque setting of Alpine peaks. There are walking paths and restaurants in the vicinity. The southernmost of the accessible reservoirs, the Mooserboden (2036m), stores 89.9 million cubic metres of water; two-thirds of this quantity is meltwater from the Pasterze Glacier in the Hohe Tauern National Park, which is transported through a 12km tunnel from another reservoir farther south. Mooserboden has two dams at its northern end and an electricity plant. Water spills down to the Wasserfallboden reservoir (1672m), and is then pumped up again to create yet more electricity. The smooth arches of the dams provide a striking contrast to the rugged irregularity of the mountain peaks. Near Kaprun is the Klamm reservoir and the main stage power plant.

The Mooserboden reservoir is a viable day trip from Zell am See in summer. Bundesbuses run year-round beyond the Klamm reservoir and as far as the Kesselfall Alpenhaus, which is the limit of car travel. Transport from here runs from mid-May to mid-October and costs AS195 (seniors AS159) return: a shuttle bus goes to the Lärchwand funicular, which ascends 431m and connects with another shuttle bus to Mooserboden, where there's a restaurant, an information centre and a museum with free admission.

to other places. These are free with the lift ticket (AS180 up, AS125 down, or AS230 return; reductions with the Gästekarte).

Golf and tennis are among the other sports offered in the region. In the centre of town on Steinergasse is the Freizeitzentrum (☎ 785-0), with an adventure swimming pool, saunas, steam room and massage, as well as tenpin bowling and an ice stadium. It is open daily from 10 am to 10 pm.

From early May to early October, boats depart from Zell am See Esplanade and complete a 40 minute circuit of the lake (AS80, children AS40). Boats also shuttle passengers across the lake, occasionally stopping at Seecamp Zell am See (AS22 one way, AS38 return). Rowing boats, pedal boats and motor boats can be hired from various places between April and October. Anglers need a fishing permit. Of the other resorts around the lake, Thumersbach has a water-skiing school and Prielau has a windsurfing and sailing school.

Another option for water lovers is rafting on the Salzach River. Rafting Center Taxenbach (☎ 06543-6352), 20km east of Kaprun, charges AS490 for a two hour trip. Bundesbus No 3441 goes there, and trains run to Taxenbach-Rauris from Zell am See. Alternatively, local agents such as Adventure Service (☎ 735 25) will sell you a complete package from Zell am See.

Special Events

Zell am See celebrates a full calendar of seasonal events, including two lake festivals. The first, in mid-July, features sporting events, and the second, in early August, has music and costume parades.

Places to Stay – Budget

Seecamp Zell am See (☎ 721 15, *Thumersbacher Strasse 34, Prielau*) is near the northern shoreline (head clockwise from the town) and open year-round. It charges AS87 per person and upwards of AS50 per site. *Camping Südufer* (☎ 562 28, *Seeuferstrasse 196*), south of the lake, is cheaper at AS60 per adult.

The HI *Haus der Jugend* (☎ 571 85, fax -4, *Seespitzstrasse 13, Schüttdorf*), is a 15 minute walk around the lake. Exit the train station on the lake side (Zum See) and take the footpath along the shore (it's moderately lit). Turn left at the end. Beds in two or four-bed rooms with attached shower/WC and lockers cost AS180 for one night or AS155 per night for longer stays. Those over 15 years pay an overnight tax of AS10.50 in summer or AS11.50 in winter.

The food is good and you should pre-order dinners (AS65). Getting a key circumvents the curfew and day closure; check-in is from 4 pm. It's closed during November.

Nearby Kaprun also has a HI *Jugendherberge* (☎ 06547-85 07, fax -3, *Nikolaus Gassner Strasse 448*); closed in September.

Private rooms are another cheap option in Zell am See. *Haus Haffner* (☎ 723 96, *Schmittenstrasse 29*) is just west of the Zeller Bergbahn cable car and has 12 rooms. Single/double rooms with hall shower cost AS220/400, or AS280/510 with shower/WC. *Haus Rasser* (☎ 726 58, fax 720 53, *Loferer Bundesstrasse 1*), above a shop on the main street, has 13 beds and charges AS320/600 for singles/doubles with shower/WC. Book in advance.

Buchner (☎/fax 726 36, *Seegasse 12*) is in the centre on a pedestrian street, though there's parking around the back. Rooms are average-sized with wood furnishings, and some have a balcony. Prices are AS300 per person (AS320 in winter) or AS350 with private shower/WC.

Places to Stay – Mid-Range & Top End

The price difference between the low and high seasons (the latter is quoted here) is more marked in this category. Some prices drop in summer.

Hubertus (☎ 724 27, fax -27, *Gartenstrasse 4*), by the Zeller Bergbahn cable car, is a chalet-style place with parking. Rooms with private facilities cost AS470/740.

The central *Gasthof Steinerwirt* (☎ 725 02, fax -47, *Dreifaltigkeitsgasse*) has rooms with shower/WC and TV costing from AS300 to AS480 per person. It's by the pedestrian zone but has parking. Nearby, *Sporthotel Lebzelter* (☎ 776-0, fax 724 11, *Dreifaltigkeitsgasse 7*) has better rooms and more facilities, including a sauna and cellar bar. Prices start at AS680/1270.

Zum Hirschen (☎ 774, fax 471 66, *Dreifaltigkeitsgasse 1*) has facilities including a sauna, steam bath and solarium, and is in an ideal central location. Prices start at AS1010/1820 for singles/doubles.

Hotel Salzburgerhof (☎ *765-0, fax -66, email 5sterne@salzburgerhof.at, Auerspergstrasse 11*) is also central. It's a big chalet with a rustic-style interior, complemented by the traditional dress worn by staff. All modern comforts are provided in this five star place. The indoor swimming pool, sauna and fitness room are free for guests, and there's ample parking. Prices start at AS1350/2500.

Krone (☎ *574 21, fax -7, email krone@ aon.at, Kitzsteinhornstrasse 16*) is south of the lake in Schüttdorf, and has a sauna, steam bath, fitness room and a small swimming pool. Rooms with private shower/WC in this chalet-style place cost AS700/1400.

Places to Eat

For self-caterers, there are several central supermarkets, including a *Spar* (*Bruckner Bundesstrasse 4*).

Pizza Mann (*Bruckner Bundesstrasse 9*) serves a range of pizzas costing AS85, or there's *Va bene* (*Schmittenstrasse 27*), offering Italian food starting at AS68; it's closed on Tuesday.

There's a branch of the chicken fast-food chain *Wienerwald* at Seegasse 5. Fish meals are cheap and cheerful at *Moby Dick Fischrestaurant* (*Kreuzgasse 16*), which is open shop hours.

China-Restaurant Fünf Planeten (*Loferer Bundesstrasse 3*) has the usual cheap midday menus. For inexpensive Austrian fare, you could try the restaurant at *Gasthof Steinerwirt* (see Places to Stay).

Restaurant Kupferkessel (*Bruckner Bundesstrasse 18*), near the train station, is a former petrol station and retains the old forecourt. It has seating areas ranged around a central bar and a youthful ambience (but not exclusively so). The menu is varied and reasonably priced (dishes starting at AS70), including pizza, pasta, fish and steaks, as well as vegetarian and Austrian food, and there's a salad bar. Opening hours are 11 am (5 pm Sunday) to 2 am (1 am Sunday).

Ampere (☎ *723 63, Schmittenstrasse 12*) has a bar on the ground floor and a classy restaurant upstairs. It has regular festivals during which different types of cuisine are served; main courses are usually over AS165, except for some cheaper vegetarian options. Lunches are not served. It is closed on Sunday and for two weeks in early May and again in late November.

The Zirbenstube (pine room) of *Zum Hirschen* (see Places to Stay) is similarly priced and serves quality Austrian fare in a wood-panelled interior. It closes in the low season. The gourmet restaurant in the *Hotel Salzburgerhof* (see Places to Stay) serves main courses at around the AS250 mark. The restaurant in the *Grand Hotel* (☎ *788, Esplanade 4*) is another culinary temple.

Entertainment

Zell am See has a reasonable choice of bars and discos. *Ampere* (see Places to Eat) is popular with the après-ski crowd.

B17 is a WWII theme bar on Salzmannstrasse; it's open 5 pm to 2 am nightly.

Getting There & Away

Zell am See is on the IC rail route with hourly trains connecting Salzburg province and Tirol. Destinations include Salzburg (AS140, 1½ hours), Kitzbühel (AS100, 45 minutes) and Innsbruck (AS240, two hours). It is also at the head of the narrowgauge railway line to Krimml Falls (see the Krimml Falls Getting There & Away section). You can hire bikes at the train station.

Bundesbuses leave from outside the train station and/or from the bus station, behind the post office. They run to various destinations including Kaprun (AS30, 17 minutes), Krimml Falls (approximately hourly) and Salzburg (about four a day). See the Grossglockner Road Getting There & Away section for details of buses to Lienz via Franz Josefs Höhe.

Zell am See is on highway 311 running north to Lofer, where it joins the 312 connecting St Johann in Tirol with Salzburg (passing through Germany). It's also just a few kilometres north of the east-west highway linking St Johann im Pongau with Tirol (via the Gerlos Pass).

KRIMML FALLS

About 55km west of Zell am See, these triple-level falls are an inspiring sight and attract hordes of visitors in summer. In winter, the slopes above the village of Krimml become a ski area, and the falls just one more static lump of ice.

Orientation & Information

The Krimmler Wasserfälle (Krimml Falls) are on the north-western edge of the national park, within the protected area.

Krimml Ort (village), at an elevation of 1076m, is about 500m north of the path to the falls, on a side turning from highway 165, which goes towards the falls. There are parking spaces (about AS45 per day) near the path to the falls, which branches to the right just before the toll booths for the Gerlos Pass road (see the Gerlos Pass section later in this chapter).

The tourist office (☎ 06564-72 39, fax 75 50) is in the village centre next to the white church. Opening hours are Monday to Friday from 8 am to noon and 2.30 to 5.30 pm, and Saturday from 8 to 10 am. In the low season, hours are much reduced. The post office is next door. There's another information office on the way up to the falls.

Viewing the Falls

The Krimml Falls path (Wasserfallweg) is 4km long. The combined height of the falls is 380m, over three main sections connected by a fast-flowing, twisting river and rapids. This lessens the immediate impact, but also means you can ascend for 1½ hours or more and enjoy ever-unfolding vistas. The highest free fall of water is 65m, in the lower falls. The middle section is mostly dissipated into a series of mini-falls, the highest being 30m, and the upper section has a free fall of 60m. The trail is steep in certain sections, but many elderly people manage the incline.

The ticket and information offices are a few minutes walk along the path. Entry costs AS15 (AS5 for children) between May and October; there's no charge during the rest of the year as the offices are not staffed. A short distance past the offices is the first viewpoint of the lower falls, where a curtain of spray beats down onto a plinth of rock. Every few hundred metres further small paths deviate from the main trail and offer alternative viewpoints of the falls; each gives a worthwhile perspective. The excellent view back towards Krimml can often be seen through the treetops.

After about an hour's walk you'll reach the Gasthof Schönagel (1300m), where you can take refreshments and buy souvenirs. This point is just above the middle level of the falls. After another five to 10 minutes the terrain opens out and you can see the final, upper section of the falls. A steep, further 20 minutes walk will bring you to the top of that level (known as the Bergerblick viewpoint) for a truly memorable view over the lip of the falls and back down to the valley.

If you stop off at all or most of the viewpoints on the way up, it'll take about two hours to reach Bergerblick – more if you stop for food. A fast, straight descent can take as little as 40 minutes. If you're unable or unwilling to walk up to the falls, a national park taxi can take you to the upper levels; ask the tourist office to make a reservation. Private cars are not allowed on this route.

Places to Stay & Eat

Unless you want to continue walking past the third level of the falls and along the Krimmler Ache (Krimml River), Krimml is easily visited as a day trip from Zell am See. There are places to stay either in the village or on the way up to the falls; staff at the Krimml Ort tourist office can advise on accommodation options.

Near the church in Krimml is an *ADEG* supermarket, useful for creating a picnic. There are snack stands and restaurants (with reasonable prices) on the walk to the falls, and *Gasthof Schönagel* above the middle section of the falls.

Getting There & Away

Krimml can be reached from either the west or the east. The only rail route is the narrow-gauge Pinzgauer Lokalbahn from Zell am See (AS100, 1½ hours). It calls at many places (including Schüttdorf, near the Zell am See Haus der Jugend) on its pleasant trip through small villages and cow pastures (AS100, 90 minutes). Departures are approximately hourly with the last train back to Zell am See at 5.37 pm. In summer, Bundesbuses run from Krimml train station to the falls, but only as far as Krimml Ort at other times; the bus fare is covered by your train ticket. Alternatively, you can do the whole trip by Bundesbus from Zell am See in 1½ hours (AS100; last return bus at 6.05 pm). Krimml Ort is only a few hundred metres short of the path to the falls. The Krimml Falls path starts near the beginning of the Tauernradweg (cycle path) to Salzburg (175km) and Passau (325km).

GERLOS PASS

This pass (1507m) is north-west of Krimml and is a scenic route to the Zillertal (Ziller Valley). Just to the south-west of Krimml there are fine views of the whole of the Krimml Falls; farther on, peaks and Alpine lakes abound. There is a toll on this route: AS90 for cars or AS50 for motorcycles.

Bundesbuses make the trip from Krimml to the Zillertal in summer (AS194 return; last bus to Zell am Ziller at 4.20 pm). By car, you can avoid using the toll road; take the old route, signposted 'Alte Gerlosstrasse'. This 11km stretch of road branches off from highway 165 at Wald im Pingau, a few kilometres east of Krimml (on the road to Zell am See) and joins the new Gerlos road just west of the toll section.

GROSSGLOCKNER ROAD

The Grossglockner Hochalpenstrasse (High Alpine Road) was built between 1930 and 1935, following the course of an important trading route between Italy and Germany since the Middle Ages. The present road takes visitors on a magical 50km journey between 800 and 2500m above sea level,

The sure-footed chamois has hooves especially adapted to its life on the mountainside.

traversing a range of geographical features and climatic conditions. You'll find a dozen restaurants along the route, some of which offer accommodation.

Even before reaching the national park, the trip south from Zell am See is picturesque. Cows graze in green fields and white peaks appear over the steep sides of the valley. **Wildpark Ferleiten**, south of Fusch, is home to more than 200 Alpine animals including chamois, marmots, wolves and bears. Admission costs AS55 (children AS35) and it's open daily from May to November).

Once through the toll gate near the Wildpark, the road rises steeply. At 2260m there's an Alpine **Natur Schau** (nature show), a small museum of flora, fauna and ecology (free admission). A little farther on and up is **Fuschertörl** (2428m), where there's a restaurant, *Dr Franz Rehrl Haus*, and excellent views on both sides of the ridge. From here a 2km side road (no coaches allowed) goes up to **Edelweiss Spitze** (2577m), where there's an even better panorama.

Continuing south, the road descends, then rises again. At Knappenstube (2450m) there are traces of medieval gold mining.

The peak of activity was in 1557 when 900kg of gold was found here; much of it went to swell the already bulky coffers of the archbishopric of Salzburg. Hochtor (2503m) is the highest point on the road, after which there is a steady descent to Guttal (1950m). Here the road splits: to the left is Heiligenblut and the route to Lienz, to the right is the Gletscherstrasse (Glacier Road). This 9km road ascends to **Franz Josefs Höhe** (2369m), the viewing area for Grossglockner.

Taking the Gletscherstrasse, the initial views south to the Heiligenblut valley are fantastic, yet you soon concentrate on the approaching massif of Grossglockner itself (sit on the left for the best views). At Franz Josefs Höhe there are places to park, eat, sleep and buy souvenirs. The Grossglockner looms from across a vast tongue of ice, the Pasterze Glacier. The cracks and ridges in this 10km-long mass of ice create a marvellous pattern of light and dark. Steps lead down to the edge of the glacier, or, for ease, you can take the Gletscherbahn (AS60 one way, AS98 return; departures every 10 minutes). There are several walks that start from Franz Josefs Höhe. The most popular is the Gamsgrubenweg, winding above the glacier and leading to a waterfall; allow up to 1½ hours return.

Getting There & Away

The Grossglockner Road (highway 107) is open to traffic from May to November, daily between 5 am and 10 pm. There's a toll section between Wildpark Ferleiten and a point just north of Heiligenblut (AS350 for cars, AS230 for motorbikes). An eight day pass (consecutive days) is AS410/310. You can walk or cycle along the road free of charge; the hills are steep (up to 12% gradient), but hardy mountain cyclists manage the trip. For recorded information on road conditions, call ☎ 04824-26 06.

Franz Josefs Höhe is accessible from north and south by Bundesbus. Toll charges of AS40 are included in the ticket price. From Zell am See (AS145/229 single/return) the buses run between mid-June and early October, taking two hours and 10 minutes. Depending on the season, up to three morning buses depart Zell am See with the same number returning in the afternoon; you could have up to five hours at the site in the high season (early July to early September) without staying overnight.

Buses from Lienz to Franz Josefs Höhe (1¾ hours) only run between late June and late September, with additional buses from mid-July to mid-September. It's possible to spend up to six hours at the site on a same-day trip. The return trip is covered under Carinthia's zonal transport tickets; a 24 hour pass costs AS158.

In the high season, you can get from Zell am See to Lienz (or vice versa) and still have plenty of time at Franz Josefs Höhe. Outside the high season this same-day trip is only possible travelling north (Lienz to Zell am See).

HEILIGENBLUT

☎ 04824 • pop 1250 • 1300m

Heiligenblut is both a summer and winter resort, close to the boundaries of the national park.

Orientation & Information

This beautifully situated village is 39km north of Lienz. The tourist office (☎ 20 01-21, fax -43, email heiligenblut-glockner@netway.at) is on the main street, close to the 'Hotel Post' bus stop. It's open Monday to Friday from 8.30 am to noon and 2.30 to 6 pm and, in the high season, on Saturday from 9 am to noon and 4 to 6 pm. Close by, in the Gästehaus Schober, is a national park information office (☎ 27 00), open daily from 30 June to 30 September. There are some museum exhibits, and from 4 to 6 pm on weekdays in the same office there's someone from the Bergführerinformationsbüro (mountain guides office) available to give advice on climbing and walking.

Things to See & Do

Heiligenblut's **church** was built between 1430 and 1483; its slender pale steeple is clearly visible from far away on the

Gletscherstrasse. The church's ceiling and altar are both late-Gothic in style, and it contains many statues of saints. The high altar is winged, with intricate figures carved in relief. The tabernacle is purported to contain a tiny phial of Christ's blood, hence the name of the village (*Heiligenblut* means holy blood).

Most of the **skiing** above the resort is done from the Schareck (2604m) and Gjaidtroghöhe (2969m) peaks. A one day lift pass costs AS330, or AS260 if purchased after noon. Mountaineering is another popular local pursuit.

Places to Stay & Eat

Glocknercamping (☎ 20 48) is open summer and winter. There's a HI *Jugendherberge* (☎/fax 22 59, Hof 36) near the church and below the *ADEG* supermarket. It is closed from 1 October to 26 December and costs AS170 for a dorm bed (reception is closed from 11 am to 5 pm).

Staff at the tourist office can provide information about hotels, pensions, private rooms, apartments and farmhouses. At the budget end, prices start at about AS200 per person in winter, AS180 in summer.

Restaurants are not too expensive. *Café Dorfstüberl* near the tourist office serves pizza and Austrian food from about AS85.

Getting There & Away

In addition to the Bundesbuses to Franz Josefs Höhe, buses run year-round to/from Lienz (AS72 one way, AS120 return; 70 minutes). They go approximately hourly, though there are fewer at weekends, especially on Sunday.

BAD GASTEIN

☎ 06434 • pop 5600 • 1100m

Bad Gastein is the chief resort in the scenic north-south Gasteiner Tal (Gastein Valley). Bad Gastein's fame rests on its radon-rich hot springs, which have attracted cure-seekers since the Middle Ages. It used to be called Badgastein until, in 1997, the local authorities decided that two names were better than one.

Orientation & Information

Bad Gastein clings to the valley slopes; this means there are lots of hills and plenty of scenic vantage points. Tumbling through the centre in a series of waterfalls is the valley river, the Gasteiner Ache.

The train station is on the west side of town. The town centre, Kongressplatz, is down the hill to the east: make your way down near the Hotel Salzburger Hof. You can save some legwork by going to the car park at the top of Haus Austria and taking the lift down.

To reach the tourist office (☎ 25 31-0, fax -37, email fvv.badgastein@aon.at), Kaiser Franz Josef Strasse 27, go left from the train station exit and walk down the hill. It is open Monday to Friday from 8 am to 6 pm and on Saturday from 10 am to 1 pm. In high season, hours include Saturday afternoon and Sunday, depending on demand. Staff will find accommodation free of charge, and a Gästekarte is available. Computer information in the foyer is accessible 24 hours.

The post office (Postamt 5640) is next to the train station, and is open Monday to Friday from 8 am to 7 pm and on Saturday from 8 to 10 am.

Things to See

Bad Gastein became popular in the 19th century and many of the building façades reflect the grandeur of that era. It's worth taking a stroll around town to soak up the ambience. From the eastern bank by the Wasserfallbrücke (waterfall bridge), a path runs south up the hill. At the upper bridge, take Kötschachtaler Strasse and follow it eastwards up to the Hotel Schillerhof: from here you have one of the best views of the town and the valley. Work your way down via paths and roads to the small church with the dark tiled roof. This is **Nikolauskirche**, built in the 14th and 15th centuries round a central pillar. It is Gothic in style and charmingly simple inside, with an uneven flagstone floor and faded, childlike murals.

The **Gasteiner Museum** is on the 2nd floor of Haus Austria in the town centre and is open daily from 10.30 am to noon and 3.30 to 6 pm (entry AS30). It displays minerals, paintings, crafts, and photos of historic events and famous visitors (including a shot of the infamous Goebbels taken in 1938). There are also models and costumes from the **Perchten Festival** when participants wear tall, incredibly elaborate hats. This occurs every four years on 6 January (the next is in 2002). You can see more festival paraphernalia on the 3rd floor of Haus Austria (free admission).

Health Treatments

The tourist office will provide copious information in English on the beneficial effects of Bad Gastein treatments. The radon-enriched water is the product of 3000 years of geological forces. Back then it was merely rain water; now, apparently, it has the ability to revitalise and repair human cells, alleviate rheumatism, improve male potency, reduce female menopausal problems, and much else. The radon is absorbed through the skin and retained in the body for nearly three hours. No doubt patients emerge from treatments not only feeling fully refreshed, but also able to explain Einstein's theory of relativity while simultaneously leaping tall buildings with a single bound.

The waters of the hot springs are piped to all major hotels and pensions, which offer their own health treatments. **Felsenbad** (☎ 22 23), opposite the train station, has an indoor swimming pool (dug into sheer rock) and several steaming outdoor pools. Admission costs AS143 (children AS75), including saunas and lockers. It is open daily from 9 or 9.30 am to 8 pm or 9.30 pm, depending on season. Curative massages in its **Thermalkurhaus** (☎ 27 11-0) cost AS210 (partial) or AS260 (full massage). The Gastein water can also be drunk to beneficial effect here.

Activities

Winter is the main season thanks to the extensive **skiing**. The whole valley is covered by the Gastein Super Skischein, giving access to 59 lifts (ranging from 800 to 2800m) and over 250km of ski runs, most at intermediate level. The pass will cost you AS410/2250 for one day/one week, with reductions for seniors, children and in the low season (bus and train transfers included). Bad Gastein's main peaks are the Stubnerkogel (2246m) and the Graukogel (2492m). A one day ski pass covering only Bad Gastein and Bad Hofgastein (see the Around Bad Gastein section in this chapter) costs AS400. Cross-country skiing is also possible here.

In summer, both peaks are excellent for **walking**. The two sections of the Stubnerkogelbahn cable car (near the train station) cost AS145 up, AS60 down, or AS170 return. Fares for the Graukogelbahn (near Hotel Schillerhof) are the same prices.

Places to Stay – Budget

Phone ahead in the off-season as many places close during that time. *Camping Erlengrund* (☎ 27 90) is 2km north of Bad Gastein in Kötschachdorf, accessible by Bundesbus. It's open year-round.

The HI *Jugendherberge* (☎ 20 80, fax 506 88, Ederplatz 2) is about 1km south of the train station. It's open all day (10 pm curfew) year-round. Dorm beds cost AS150 in summer and AS190 in winter, plus sheets (AS20) and tax (AS17); doubles cost a little more. It even has a sauna.

There are many private rooms which you can find by walking around (for example, there's a clutch behind the Eurospar supermarket) – the tourist office leaflet lists some. *Haus Erika* (☎ 22 16, Stubnerkogelstrasse 40), near the Stubnerkogelbahn, has 12 rooms with private shower/WC costing from AS200 to AS300 per person. The owner is friendly (but speaks minimal English) and the walls are decked with interesting pictures.

Pension Laura (☎ 27 04, fax 52 10, Bismarckstrasse 20) is a small place near Nikolauskirche, open year-round. It has cheerful rooms with private shower/WC and TV, and there's a sauna and radon baths on the premises. It represents good value –

BAD GASTEIN

PLACES TO STAY
1 Pension Laura
4 Hotel Mozart
6 Hotel Schillerhof
15 Hotel Salzburger Hof
22 Bergfriede
24 Haus Erika
26 Jugendherberge

PLACES TO EAT
7 Brasserie
9 Café Weissmayr
10 Le Café de Gastein
12 Pizzeria Pub
13 Prälatur Restaurant
16 Bayer Imbiss
23 Eurospar Supermarket
25 Bayr Stüberl

OTHER
2 Nikolauskirche
3 Tourist Office
5 Graukogelbahn
8 Casino
11 Kur und Kongresshaus
14 Gasteiner Museum;
    Haus Austria
17 Train Station; Bahnhof Restaurant
18 Stubnerkogelbahn
19 Post Office
20 Felsenbad
21 Thermalkurhaus

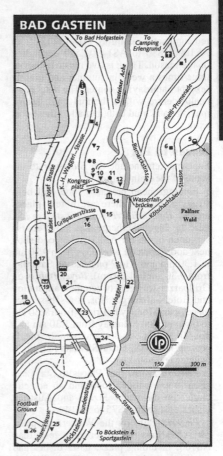

high season prices are AS290/490/690 for singles/doubles/triples.

Bergfriede (☎ *20 11, K H Waggerl Strasse 23*) is a pension with its own restaurant. It has double rooms for AS400 with hall shower or AS560 with private shower (either a room cubicle or en suite bathroom). The furnishings are almost museum pieces: rustic and old-fashioned, with painted designs. The writer Karl Heinrich Waggerl was born in this house in 1897.

Places to Stay – Mid-Range & Top End

Hotel Mozart (☎ *26 86-0, fax -62, Kaiser Franz Josef Strasse 25*) offers pleasant singles/doubles with high ceilings, shower/ WC and cable TV for AS600/1100, and there's a radon bath on site (AS130).

Hotel Schillerhof (☎ *25 81, fax -61, Kötschachtaler Strasse 5*) has fine views and use of the outdoor swimming pool (summer only), sauna and fitness room is included in the price; other health and beauty treatments cost extra. Fresh, clean rooms vary in size and facilities; some have a balcony. Prices are AS1050/1900 in winter and just AS520/840 in summer.

Hotel Salzburger Hof (☎ *20 37, fax 38 67, Grillparzerstrasse 1*) is convenient for the train station. Rooms are standard for four star class, though the singles are a little too compact for comfort. Prices range from AS1090/1880 to AS1490/2580 depending on the season. There is live music in the bar three times a week in summer and nightly (except Saturday) in winter. The hotel has a health centre with a thermal pool, sauna, massage and mud bath, but all of these cost extra.

Places to Eat

Supermarkets include the *Eurospar* to the south of the train station.

Finding cheap prepared food will be a struggle, though there are a few places around. *Bayr Stüberl (Schareckstrasse 15)*, near the Jugendherberge, has a two course set lunch menu for AS85 and a food shop next door (open on weekdays from 9.30 am to 1.30 pm and 3 to 7 pm, and on Saturday from 9.30 am to 1.30 pm). *Bayer Imbiss* on Grillparzerstrasse, between the train station and Hotel Salzburger Hof, is a self-service place open Monday to Friday from 7.30 am to 6 pm and on Saturday from 1.30 am to 1 pm. It serves snacks and simple meals costing from AS35 to AS85 and has a deli counter and salad bar.

Pension Laura (see Places to Stay) has good, unpretentious food and an eclectic clutter on the walls. Pizzas and Austrian dishes cost from AS75 to AS149.

Pizzeria Pub, by the Wasserfallbrücke, offers various meals costing less than AS100, including pizza, pasta dishes and schnitzels, and beer costs AS36 for 0.5L. It is open daily from 11 am to 1.30 am.

Le Café de Gastein on Kongressplatz has a comfortable ambience and sofa seating. It serves meals costing from AS75 to AS150, including several vegetarian choices, and it's open daily from 7.30 am to 11 pm. At *Café Weissmayr*, nearby on Kaiser Franz Josef Strasse, dishes cost between AS85 and AS185. There's also a three course menu for AS128. It's open daily from 9 am to midnight.

Hotel Mozart (see Places to Stay) has a restaurant with a range of meals and prices.

The smaller meals start at AS70, though most of the main dishes cost between AS105 and AS200.

The *Bahnhof Restaurant* is a high-quality, comfortable and popular place, despite its relatively humble location in the train station. Dishes mostly cost over AS100 although the three course set menu (AS130), available lunch and dinner, is affordable and filling. The kitchen is open daily from 11 am to 2 pm and 5 to 9 pm.

The *Prälatur Restaurant* in the five star Arcotel Elisabethpark (☎ 25 51-0, *Kaiser Franz Josef Strasse 5*) has an excellent reputation with high prices to match. Another gourmet choice is *Brasserie (☎ 51 0 15, Kaiser Franz Josef Strasse 16)*. The food (dishes costing between AS150 and AS270) combines Austrian and French styles. The restaurant is open in the evening from Monday to Saturday and is usually closed over the summer.

Getting There & Away

Express trains trundle through Bad Gastein every two hours, connecting the resort to points both north and south, such as Spittal-Millstättersee (AS100, 50 minutes), Salzburg (AS140, 1¾ hours), and Innsbruck (AS310, three hours). There are good views to the right of the train when travelling north from Bad Gastein to Bad Hofgastein. Travelling south, also sit on the right, as the view is good after the second tunnel.

To take your car south, you need to use the railway car shuttle service (Autoverladung) through the tunnel that starts at Böckstein (AS200 one way). See the Western Carinthia section in the Carinthia chapter for more details.

Bicycles can be hired at the train station.

AROUND BAD GASTEIN

Three kilometres south of Bad Gastein, at the head of the Gasteiner Tal, is **Böckstein** (1131m), a village with a museum and a Baroque church. It also has a medieval gold mine which has been converted into a health treatment centre, the Gasteiner Heilstollen (☎ 37 53-0). Patients are delivered by a small tunnel train 2.5km into the mountain, where they take their cure (AS650 per trip). A full cure takes at least 10 trips over three weeks (book well in advance), and the centre is open from mid-January to late October.

Leading west from Böckstein is a toll road (AS50, but included in the Gastein Super Skischein) to **Sportgastein** (1588m), a recently created centre for skiing and other sports. Seven kilometres north of Bad Gastein is **Bad Hofgastein** (858m), another spa centre, with good winter sports facilities. Bad Gastein, Bad Hofgastein and Böckstein are all linked by both bus and rail; Sportgastein can be reached by infrequent buses.

There are two access roads to the national park (with parking spaces at the terminus): the road to Sportgastein is one; the other turns east just south of Bad Gastein and follows the Kötschachtal.

East Tirol

East Tirol (Osttirol) covers 2020 sq km and has a population of 42,000. It is a region circled by mighty Alpine ranges, including the Lienzer Dolomiten (Lienzer Dolomites) and the Karnische Alpen (Carnic Alps) to the south. This factor, together with the loss of South Tirol to Italy after WWI, has made East Tirol somewhat isolated from the rest of Tirol. The opening of the Felber Tauern Tunnel in 1967 improved access to fellow Tiroleans, but the region retains strong social and economic links with its eastern neighbour, Carinthia. The Hohe Tauern National Park accounts for over 25% of East Tirol's territory.

East Tirol is shown in the provincial map in the Tirol chapter. See the Tirol chapter introduction for information on VVT transport tickets, which are valid for travel between Tirol and East Tirol.

Skiing resorts in East Tirol include St Jakob, Sillian and Obertilliach. Obertilliach is on highway 111, on the south side of the Lienzer Dolomites. Sillian is near the Italian border, on the main highway 100

heading west from Lienz. St Jakob lies farther north, on a much more precipitous and spectacular route into Italy, which crosses a high mountain pass (2052m) in the Defereggengebirge.

LIENZ

☎ 04852 • pop 13,000 • 686m

The administrative capital of East Tirol, Lienz combines winter sports and summer walking with a relaxed, small-town ambience. The jagged Dolomites crowd the southern skyline. Lienz has been inhabited since Roman times, and was granted a town charter in 1252.

Orientation

The Italian influence is evident in Lienz (it's only 40km from the border): restaurants usually offer Italian menu translations ahead of English, and various shopkeepers proclaim their facility in that language.

The town centre is within a 'v' formed by the junction of the rivers Isel and Drau. The pivotal Hauptplatz is directly in front of the train station; three other squares lead from it. Hauptplatz has lots of parking – it's a Kurzparkzone with a 90 minute limit during indicated hours.

Information

Tourist Offices The local tourist office (☎ 652 65, fax -2, email lienz@netway.at) is just off Hauptplatz, at Europaplatz 1. It's open Monday to Friday from 8 am to 6 pm, and on Saturday from 9 am to noon. In the high seasons (June to September and mid-December to Easter) it's also open on weekdays till 7 pm, on Saturday from 5 to 7 pm and on Sunday morning. Staff will find accommodation (even private rooms) free of charge; if the office is shut, there's an accommodation board outside with a free telephone. Wherever you stay, ask your host for the Gästekarte, and get it stamped at the tourist office.

The regional tourist office, the Osttirol Werbung (☎ 653 33, fax -2, email osttirol@netway.at), is on the 2nd floor of Albin

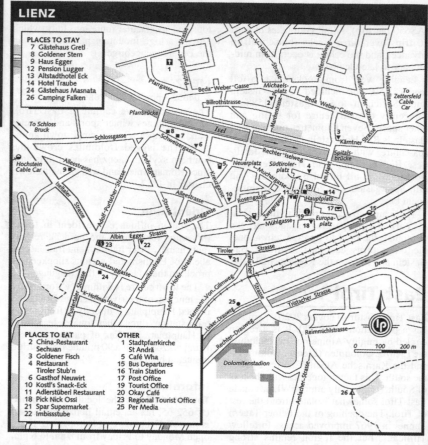

LIENZ

PLACES TO STAY
7 Gästehaus Gretl
8 Goldener Stern
9 Haus Egger
12 Pension Lugger
13 Altstadthotel Eck
14 Hotel Traube
24 Gästehaus Masnata
26 Camping Falken

PLACES TO EAT
2 China-Restaurant Sechuan
3 Goldener Fisch
4 Restaurant Tiroler Stub'n
6 Gasthof Neuwirt
10 Kostl's Snack-Eck
11 Adlerstüberl Restaurant
18 Pick Nick Ossi
21 Spar Supermarket
22 Imbissstube

OTHER
1 Stadtpfarrkirche St Andrä
5 Café Wha
15 Bus Departures
16 Train Station
17 Post Office
19 Tourist Office
20 Okay Café
23 Regional Tourist Office
25 Per Media

Egger Strasse 17. It's closed at the weekend and on Friday afternoon.

Post & Communications The post office (Postamt 9900) is on Hauptplatz, virtually opposite the train station. Its opening hours are Monday to Friday from 7.30 am to 7 pm and Saturday from 8 to 11 am; currency exchange is available.

There's not yet an Internet café in Lienz, but you can surf and send emails by prior arrangement at Per Media (☎ 653 56, email office@permedia.co.at), Amlacher Strasse 12/205, in the Osttiroler Wirtschaftspark (open office hours).

Schloss Bruck

This well-preserved 13th century castle overlooks the town from the west. It is the former seat of the counts of Görtz and houses the **Heimatmuseum** which exhibits local crafts and items connected with folklore. It includes a Romanesque chapel (from the 15th century) sporting colourful frescoes. The museum also displays 19th and 20th century art by East Tirolean artists. A whole gallery is devoted to Albin Egger-Lienz (1868-1926), who dwelt on themes of toil, conflict and death. Expunge his morose vision with the view from the castle tower. The museum is open between Palm Sunday and 1 November, Tuesday to Sunday from 10 am to 5 pm, except between mid-June and mid-September when it is open daily from 10 am to 6 pm. Admission costs AS50 (students AS25).

Stadtpfarrkirche St Andrä
Stadtpfarrkirche St Andrä (St Andrew's Church) is north of the Isel River. This impressive Gothic building is noted for its murals (some dating from the 14th century), organ loft (1616) with winged organ and two 16th century tombstones, sculpted in red Salzburg marble. There's also a 'Schöne Madonna' (1430), displaying the classic 'S' stance of this style. Albin Egger-Lienz is buried in the memorial chapel in the graveyard. There's a good view of the Dolomites from the church area – visit in the early evening when the peaks catch the sun.

Activities
South of the Drau River is the Dolomitenstadion, a sports complex comprising a stadium, swimming pool and tennis courts.

Downhill **skiing** takes place on the **Zettersfeld**, where runs are mostly medium to easy. The Zettersfeld cable car station is north of the Isel (a free bus runs from the train station in the summer and winter high seasons). The top section of the cable car is complemented by five ski lifts at elevations of between 1660 and 2278m. **Hochstein** (2057m) is another skiing area, with its cable car station west of the centre. One-day ski passes covering all local lifts cost AS320 and the ski lifts run from 1 December to Easter, depending on snow. There are also several cross-country trails in the valley. Dolomitenlauf is a famous cross-country skiing championship that takes place on the third Sunday in January. Downhill ski rental starts at AS210 per day

(including boots) and cross-country equipment costs around AS120.

In the summer, good **walking** trails await in the mountains or along the valley to surrounding villages. Ask for the tourist office's *Hiking Tips* brochure. The cable cars come back into service for the summer season: the ride to Hochstein, which operates from late May to mid-September, costs AS100 return for both sections of the chair lift; the Zettersfeld cable car (running from mid-June to late September) costs AS100 return, or AS140 including the chair lift. A seven day pass for all Zettersfeld and Hochstein lifts costs AS300; children pay half-price.

Cycling paths for city and mountain bikes radiate from Lienz.

Special Events
On the second weekend in August Lienz hosts its annual Stadtfest, when it costs AS60 to enter the town centre to view and partake in the celebrations. Summer also sees a series of events representing Tirolean culture, as well as free concerts on Hauptplatz and in other squares (at 8 pm on Wednesday and Sunday).

Places to Stay – Budget
Camping Falken (☎ 640 22, *Eichholz 7*) is south of the Drau, and is closed from November to mid-December. Prices are about AS80 per person, AS55 for a tent and AS35 for a car.

Lienz offers plenty of private rooms and a single night's stay is often possible. Prices start at around AS130 per person, though the cheapest choices are a little way out of town. ***Haus Egger*** (☎ 720 72, *Alleestrasse 33*) is quiet, fairly central and excellent value at AS170 per person (up to 10 beds are available). You eat breakfast with the family and will be plied with food until you beg for mercy.

Gästehaus Gretl (☎ 621 06, fax -4, *Schweizergasse 32*) has big singles/doubles with private shower and WC costing AS280/520, and there's courtyard parking. Ring the bell of the ceramics shop if nobody's about (it's run by the same family). Along the road, **Goldener Stern** (*☎/fax 621 92, Schweizergasse 40*) offers white rooms in the old-fashioned *Gasthof* (inn) or in the more modern garden annexe. Single/double rooms cost AS360/780 with shower/WC and TV, or AS290/540 without (there's a seasonal AS20 charge to use the hall shower). Both here and Gretl are closed from Easter to late May; Gretl is also shut over the winter.

Pension Lugger (*☎ 621 04, Andrä Kranz Gasse 7*) is plain but adequate, and right in the town centre. Doubles cost AS500 with private shower, but without breakfast. There's just one single for AS250 using the shared bathroom.

Gästehaus Masnata (*☎ 655 36, Drahtzuggasse 4*) offers a couple of spacious modern doubles with private WC/shower or bath, costing AS520. There are also three excellent apartments with kitchens, sleeping two or three, costing AS530 in winter or AS480 in summer. The minimum stay in an apartment is a week.

Places to Stay – Mid-Range & Top End

Altstadthotel Eck (*☎ 647 85, fax -3, Hauptplatz 20*) has an ideal location, nicely decorated corridors, a restaurant and a historical ambience. Large rooms with high ceilings, shower/WC, satellite TV, sofa and comfortable chairs start at AS370/740.

Hotel Traube (*☎ 644 44, fax 641 84, Hauptplatz 14*) is an atmospheric, stylish hotel with a rooftop indoor swimming pool. Its large rooms have all the usual amenities and prices start at AS650 per person in winter and AS990 per person in the summer high season. They may also have special package deals.

Places to Eat

Supermarkets include an **ADEG** on Hauptplatz and a **Spar** on Tiroler Strasse.

Imbissstube (*Albin Egger Strasse 5*) specialises in tasty rotisserie chicken, sprinkled with delicious spices; in fact that's usually all it does. The smell of the chickens siz-

zling on the spit outside is enough to make vegetarians join Meat Eaters Anonymous. This simple place is open daily from 10.30 am to 9 pm. A half-chicken (*Hendl*) with a bread roll costs just AS32.

China-Restaurant Sechuan (*Beda Weber Gasse 13*), north of the Isel, is open daily and has a choice of 15 weekday lunch menus costing AS55. **Kostl's Snack-Eck** (*Kreuzgasse 4*) is a bakery and snack bar with tables inside and out. Cheap snacks, pizzas and schnitzels cost less than AS60, and it's open Monday to Saturday from 8 am to 8 pm.

Pick Nick Ossi (*Europaplatz 2*) is a new place near the town centre. The ground floor is a restaurant serving a range of cheap food (pizzas, grills, and snacks), and there's a games room downstairs. It's open Monday to Saturday from 11 am to 2 am.

The **Adlerstüberl Restaurant** (*Andrä Kranz Gasse 5*) is a good place to try Tirolean specialities; most cost over AS100, though lunch and evening daily specials are somewhat cheaper. It's open daily from 8 am to midnight. **Restaurant Tiroler Stub'n** (*Südtiroler Platz 2*) offers tasty regional dishes starting at AS80, including the filling *Tirolerstub'n Platte* (costing AS440 for two). There are lots of outside tables, which overlook the square, and food is served daily till 11 pm.

Gasthof Neuwirt (*Schweizergasse 22*) has local, Austrian and other grilled dishes costing from AS95 to AS200, and a daily vegetarian menu. There are many different rooms; on the walls of the *Fischerstube* (Fisherman's Room) is a rogue's gallery of stuffed fish that didn't quite make it onto the dinner plate. The fish that do, though, are very appetising: the *Forelle Neuwirt* (trout) swims under a sea of mushrooms and tomatoes, and costs AS145. Another Gasthof with a good restaurant is **Goldener Fisch** (*Kärntner Strasse 9*).

One of the best restaurants in town is in the **Hotel Traube** (see Places to Stay). Most meat and fish dishes cost over AS175, or there's a three course set menu for about AS200 (open daily).

Entertainment

The *Okay Café* in the Creativ Center off Zwergergasse is a dark and smoky bar where beer costs about AS35 for 0.5L. In the back room, there are concerts ranging from rock to avant-garde every week (entry AS150 to AS250). It is open Monday to Saturday from 8 pm to 3 am.

Café Wha (Schweizergasse 3) is a bar frequented by a varied mix of young locals, attracted by the music, beer (AS31 for 0.5L) and pool tables. It's open from 6 pm to 2 am daily except Monday.

Getting There & Away

Bus The bus departure point is in front of the train station. The ticket and information office (☎ 649 44 or 670 67) is only open Monday to Friday from 7.45 to 8.15 am and 5 to 6.20 pm. There are bus connections to the East Tirol ski resorts of St Jakob, Sillian and Obertilliach, as well as northwards to the Hohe Tauern National Park (see the Grossglockner Road section for more details). Buses to Kufstein and Kitzbühel are quicker and more direct than the train. Buses run to Kitzbühel (110 minutes) three times a day from Monday to Saturday.

Train Most train services to the rest of Austria go east via Spittal-Millstättersee, where you usually have to change trains. Trains to Salzburg take about three hours (AS310). This is also one route to Innsbruck, changing at Schwarzach-St Veit. However, a quicker and easier route to Innsbruck is to go west via Sillian and Italy. Austrian rail passes are valid for the whole trip only on 'corridor' trains (*not* the one at 1.53 pm) – see the Innsbruck Getting There & Away section in the Tirol chapter for more details. Lienz train station has bike rental and currency exchange facilities.

Car & Motorcycle To head south, you must first divert west or east along highway 100, as the Dolomites act as impassable sentries. For details of road routes to the north, see the Getting Around section at the beginning of this chapter.

Tirol

The province of Tirol (sometimes spelled Tyrol) is the engine that drives Austrian tourism: in 1997 it had over seven million visitors, nearly twice as many as its nearest rival, Salzburg province. The reason they all come is the Alps. This is classic Austrian scenery, with quaint wooden chalets amid the foothills of precipitous peaks.

Numerous highly developed resorts offer myriad sporting opportunities, particularly skiing. In summer, walking takes over, but winter remains the busiest season. The more sedentary visitor can simply enjoy the magnificent views and fresh Alpine air.

The Tiroleans are a proud lot, as evident in the traditional saying: 'Bisch a Tiroler, bisch a Mensch' – 'If you're Tirolean, you're a (real) person'. The implied putdown of non-Tiroleans isn't really directed at foreigners, it's more a dig at their fellow Austrians, particularly the Viennese. They could easily adapt the saying: if you're in Tirol, you're somewhere.

For information on East Tirol see the Hohe Tauern National Park Region chapter.

History

Despite the difficult Alpine terrain, Tirol has experienced influxes of tribes and travellers since the Iron Age. In 1991, the 5500-year-old body of a man was discovered preserved in ice in the Ötztal Alps (see the boxed text 'Entombed in Ice' later in this chapter). The Brenner Pass (1374m) allowed the region to develop as a north-south trade route.

Emperor Maximilian's fondness for Innsbruck increased the region's status. Under his rule (1490-1519) the town became an administrative capital and an artistic and cultural centre. The duchy of Tirol was ruled from Vienna after the death of Archduke Sigmund Franz in 1665.

In 1703 the Bavarians attempted to capture the whole of Tirol, having contested control of parts of the north of the

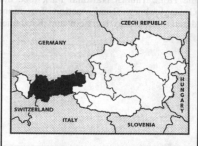

Highlights

- Enjoy mountain vistas and year-round sports throughout the province
- Admire the Goldenes Dachl (Golden Roof) in Innsbruck against the spectacular backdrop of the Nordkette Mountains
- Stroll through the gardens and museum collections of Schloss Ambras in Innsbruck
- Visit the larger-than-life bronze statues in Innsbruck's Hofkirche
- Guzzle Gauderbier during the rural Gauderfest in Zell am Ziller
- Indulge in skiing and après-ski activities in chic Kitzbühel

province for many centuries. In alliance with the French (during the War of the Spanish Succession), they reached as far as the Brenner Pass before being beaten back.

Another Franco-Bavarian alliance during the Napoleonic Wars saw Tirol incorporated into Bavaria. In 1809 Andreas Hofer led a successful fight for independence, only to have Vienna return Tirol to Bavaria under a treaty later that year. Hofer continued the struggle, and was shot by firing squad on Napoleon's orders on 20 February 1810.

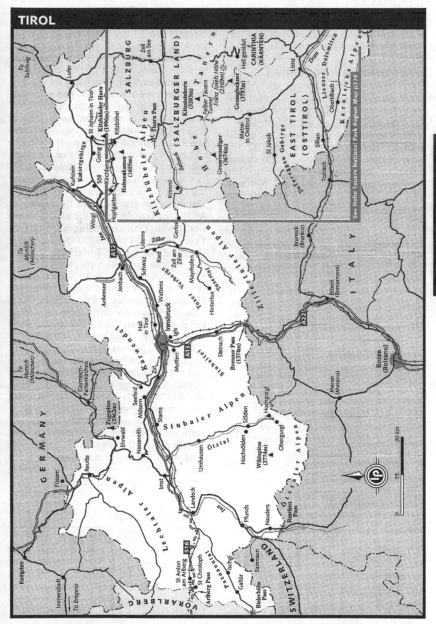

A further blow was dealt by the Treaty of St Germain (1919): prosperous South Tirol was ceded to Italy and East Tirol was isolated from the rest of the province.

Orientation & Information

River valleys wind through the Alpine ranges that crowd the skyline. The most important is the Inn Valley, which provides the main east-west passage through Tirol.

Tirol is an ideal playground for skiers, walkers, mountaineers and anglers, and tourist offices release plenty of glossy material to promote these pursuits. The provincial tourist board, Tirol Werbung (☎ 0512-72 72, fax -7, email tirol.info@tis.co.at), is at Maria Theresien Strasse 55, A-6010 Innsbruck. It's open Monday to Friday from 8 am to 6 pm. Useful free guides in English distributed by the office include the *Walking Guide Tirol*, detailing walking itineraries, mountain huts and mountaineering schools; *Cycling Guide Tirol*, outlining cycling routes and bike-friendly guesthouses; *Winter Guide Tirol*, listing sporting options; and *Cultural Guide Tirol*, containing museum information.

Tirolean Cuisine

Specialities include *Tiroler Gerstlsuppe*, a barley soup; *Gebackene Schinkenfleckerl*, soufflé with square noodles and ham; *Schlutzkrapfen*, ravioli filled with spinach and cheese; *Tiroler Rindersaftbraten*, sliced braised beef with parmesan; *Tiroler Saftgulasch*, a goulash with diced bacon that is often served with polenta; and *Tiroler Kirchtagskrapfen*, fritters filled with dried pears, prunes and poppy seed.

Getting Around

Regional transport comes under the wing of the Verkehrsverbund Tirol (VVT). Its head office (☎ 0512-36 59 20) is at Bodem Gasse 9, Innsbruck. The system is rather complicated, with different types of ticket available for each journey. A brochure (in German only) explains the options. Prices cover journeys on city buses, trams, Bundesbuses and also ÖBB (Austrian Federal Railway) trains. VVT fares for journeys within Tirol are often lower than the 'normal' ÖBB train fare for long trips but more expensive for shorter ones, so ticketing clerks need to check the rate under both systems. Fares quoted in this chapter are either ÖBB or VVT, depending on which is the lowest. Also, make sure you're getting the best ticket for your purposes: VVT zonal day passes are often much cheaper than single tickets. If you're staying in Innsbruck, it's generally worth paying extra to add city travel onto your regional tickets, instead of buying a day pass separately.

Streckenkarten tickets are 'ordinary' VVT tickets, priced according to distance. The minimum price is AS18 for a single or AS33 for a city day pass; the maximum for any trip in Tirol (including to/from East Tirol) is AS154 or AS280. Additionally, Tirol is divided into 12 overlapping transport regions, each with its own system of passes *(Netzkarten)* for unlimited travel. However, Innsbruck is a special case, even though it apparently falls within three regions. A pass for any region (excluding travel within Innsbruck city) costs AS155 per day or AS275 for a week, or it's AS325/AS600 per day/week for all 12 regions. To add travel in Innsbruck to one of the three regional cards that cover the vicinity there's a small extra charge (AS5 for one-way trips, or AS11 for a day pass). Travel in small towns is usually covered under the regional passes, but if you *only* want to travel in a particular town get a city pass instead, costing AS33 for a day or AS72 for a week.

Monthly and yearly tickets are also available, and there are reductions for children, senior citizens and families.

Innsbruck

☎ 0512 • pop 120,000 • 575m

Innsbruck dates from 1180, when the small market settlement on the north bank of the Inn expanded to the south bank. This was made possible by a bridge that had been built a few years previously and which gave the settlement its name, Ynsprugg.

In 1420 Innsbruck became the ducal seat of the Tirolean line of the Habsburgs. Emperor Maximilian I built many of the monuments that survive today; Archduke Ferdinand II and Empress Maria Theresa also played a part in shaping the city. More recently, the capital of Tirol has become an important winter sports centre, staging the Winter Olympics in 1964 and 1976.

The diverse attractions of the city, coupled with beautiful scenery and top-class skiing, make Innsbruck a destination that offers something for everybody.

Orientation

Innsbruck is in the valley of the Inn River, scenically squeezed between the northern chain of the Alps (the Karwendel) and the Tuxer Vorberge (Tuxer mountains) to the south. Extensive mountain transport facilities radiate from the city and provide ample walking and skiing opportunities, particularly to the south and west. The town centre is very compact, with the Hauptbahnhof (main train station) just a 10 minute walk from the pedestrian-only old town centre (Altstadt). The main street in the Altstadt, Herzog Friedrich Strasse, connects with Maria Theresien Strasse. It's a major thoroughfare but is closed to private transport.

Innsbruck's exhibition centre is on Ingenieur Etzel Strasse, about 1km north of the Hauptbahnhof.

Information

Tourist Offices The main tourist office (☎ 53 56, fax -43), Burggraben 3, is on the ground floor. It sells ski passes and public transport tickets and staff will book hotel rooms (AS40 commission). It's open Monday to Saturday from 8 am to 7 pm and Sunday and holidays from 9 am to 6 pm.

There's a smaller branch in the Hauptbahnhof (☎ 58 37 66), open daily from 9 am to 9 pm (10 pm June to September). Further offices are at the city approach of the main highways: on the A12 autobahn to the east and west, and on the Brenner Pass road in the south. They are open daily from 10 am to 8.30 between June and September and

Monday to Saturday from noon to 7 pm between October and May. Another office is on Kranebitter Allee to the west, open mid-June to 30 September daily from noon to 7 pm (10 am to 9 pm in July and August).

Although all of these tourist offices are privately run, they provide plenty of free literature in English, including a brochure containing details of summer and winter sightseeing opportunities and activities, plus practical information. Simple city maps are free, and there's a more detailed map costing AS10; however, this map is available free at some hotels and at the city-run tourist board (☎ 598 50, fax 7, email info@innsbruck.tvb.co.at), above the main tourist office. It closes at 6 pm on weekdays, noon on Saturday.

'Club Innsbruck' is a guest card, obtainable free from your accommodation, which gives various discounts. It also entitles you to join free guided mountain walks, run from June to September; contact the tourist office for details.

The Innsbruck Card gives one free admission to all of the main sights in and around Innsbruck, as well as travel on cable cars and free use of public transport for the duration. It's available from the main tourist office and costs AS230/300/370 for 24/48/72 hours.

In the Hauptbahnhof, staff at the *Jugendwarteraum* (youth waiting room) can give useful tips on sights, entertainment and HI accommodation. It is closed from mid-July to mid-September; hours are otherwise Monday to Friday from 11.30 am to 6.30 pm and Saturday from 10 am to 7 pm.

Money The Hauptbahnhof has exchange facilities (compare rates and commission between the ticket counters and the exchange office) and a Bankomat. The tourist office also exchanges money.

Post & Communications The main post office is at Maximilianstrasse 2 (Hauptpostamt A-6010). Normal hours are 7 am to 11 pm daily, though there is also a 24 hour counter around the side. Another post office

TIROL

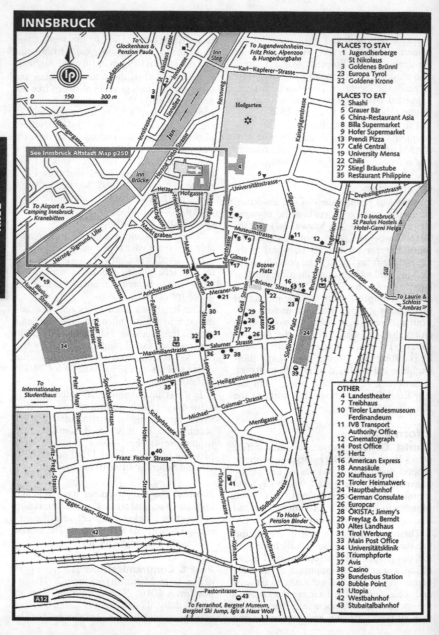

INNSBRUCK

PLACES TO STAY
1 Jugendherberge
  St Nikolaus
3 Goldenes Brünnl
23 Europa Tyrol
32 Goldene Krone

PLACES TO EAT
2 Shashi
5 Grauer Bär
6 China-Restaurant Asia
8 Billa Supermarket
9 Hofer Supermarket
13 Prendi Pizza
17 Café Central
19 University Mensa
22 Chilis
27 Stiegl Bräustube
35 Restaurant Philippine

OTHER
4 Landestheater
7 Treibhaus
10 Tiroler Landesmuseum
   Ferdinandeum
11 IVB Transport
   Authority Office
12 Cinematograph
14 Post Office
15 Hertz
16 American Express
18 Annasäule
20 Kaufhaus Tyrol
21 Tiroler Heimatwerk
24 Hauptbahnhof
25 German Consulate
26 Europcar
28 ÖKISTA; Jimmy's
29 Freytag & Berndt
30 Altes Landhaus
31 Tirol Werbung
33 Main Post Office
34 Universitätsklinik
36 Triumphpforte
37 Avis
38 Casino
39 Bundesbus Station
40 Bubble Point
41 Utopia
42 Westbahnhof
43 Stubaitalbahnhof

See Innsbruck Altstadt Map p250

To Glockenhaus &
Pension Paula

To Jugendwohnheim
Fritz Prior, Alpenzoo
& Hungerburgbahn

To Airport &
Camping Innsbruck
Kranebitten

To Internationales
Studentenhaus

To Innsbruck,
St Paulus Hostels &
Hotel-Garni Helga

To Laurin &
Schloss
Ambras

To Hotel-
Pension Binder

To Ferrarihof, Bergisel Museum,
Bergisel Ski Jump, Igls & Haus Wolf

is at Brunecker Strasse 1-3, just to the north of the Hauptbahnhof. It is open Monday to Saturday from 6.30 am to 9 pm.

Free Internet access is provided in the bar at Utopia (see under Entertainment). In Jugendherberge St Nikolaus (see Hostels under Places to Stay – Budget) it costs AS10 for 10 minutes. In the tourist office there are free computer terminals hooked into the Tirol Internet pages.

Bookshops Freytag & Berndt (☎ 57 24 30), Wilhelm Greil Strasse 15, sells many maps plus some travel books and novels in English. It is open Monday to Friday from 8.30 am to 1 pm and 2 to 6 pm, and on Saturday from 9 am to noon. You can get English-language newspapers from Buch und Presse in the Hauptbahnhof.

Travel Agencies American Express (☎ 58 24 91-0), Brixnerstrasse 3, with full travel and financial services, is open Monday to Friday from 9 am to 5.30 pm and on Saturday from 9 am to noon. ÖKISTA (☎ 58 89 97), Wilhelm Greil Strasse 17, is open Monday to Friday from 9 am to 5.30 pm.

Medical Services The Universitätsklinik (University Clinic; ☎ 504-0), part of the Landeskrankenhaus, is at Anichstrasse 35.

Laundry Bubble Point, Andreas Hofer Strasse 37, is self-service and costs AS45 per wash (including powder), plus a minimum AS10 to dry. Opening hours are Monday to Friday from 7 am to 10 pm, and Saturday and Sunday from 7 am to 8 pm.

Walking Tour

Start by absorbing the Baroque façades along Herzog Friedrich Strasse; most of these buildings were built in the 15th and 16th centuries. They make a fine picture, with the impressive Nordkette mountains soaring above them to the north. The fussy rococo ornamentation of the Helblinghaus, the last building on the left as you walk north, was created in the 18th century.

For an overview of the city, climb the 14th century **Stadtturm** (city tower), also on Herzog Friedrich Strasse. It's open daily between 1 March and 31 October from 10 am to 5 pm, except in July and August it's open till 6 pm. Entry costs AS22 (students and children AS11).

The **Goldenes Dachl** (Golden Roof), across the square, comprises 2657 gilded copper tiles which shimmer atop a Gothic oriel window (built in 1500). Emperor Maximilian used to observe street performers from the 2nd floor balcony, which has a series of scenes depicted in relief (including, in the centre, the emperor himself with his two wives). The balustrade on the 1st floor bears eight coats of arms. Inside the building is a new, rather small museum devoted to Maximilian, the **Maximilianeum**; admission costs AS60 (students AS30). A combined ticket costing AS79 also covers the Stadtturm and Hofkirche.

Behind the Goldenes Dachl is **Dom St Jakob** (St James' Cathedral). Its interior is over-the-top Baroque. Much of the sumptuous art and stuccowork were completed by the Asam brothers from Munich, though the Madonna above the high altar is by the German painter Lukas Cranach the Elder.

Returning to Herzog Friedrich Strasse, continue south along the equally imposing Maria Theresien Strasse. The tall, slender **Annasäule** (St Anne's Column) was erected in 1706 to mark the repulsing of a Bavarian attack in 1703. A statue of the Virgin Mary stands at the top; St Anne is depicted at the base. Next, to the left, is a fine Baroque façade belonging to the **Altes Landhaus**, built in 1728 and now the seat of the provincial government. Another 200m south is the 1765 **Triumphpforte** (Triumphal Arch) which commemorates the marriage of the then emperor-to-be, Leopold II.

Hofburg

The Hofburg (Imperial Palace) on Rennweg dates from 1397, but has been rebuilt and extended several times since then. A major influence was Maria Theresa, who imposed her favourite Baroque and rococo styles;

TIROL

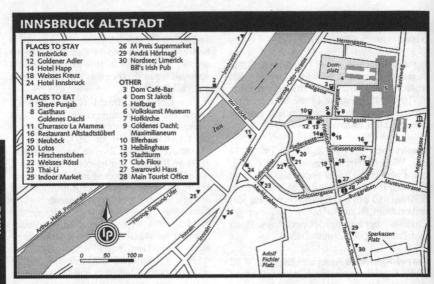

INNSBRUCK ALTSTADT

PLACES TO STAY
2 Innbrücke
12 Goldener Adler
14 Hotel Happ
18 Weisses Kreuz
24 Hotel Innsbruck

PLACES TO EAT
1 Shere Punjab
8 Gasthaus
    Goldenes Dachl
11 Churrasco La Mamma
16 Restaurant Altstadtstüberl
19 Neuböck
20 Lotos
21 Hirschenstuben
22 Weisses Rössl
23 Thai-Li
25 Indoor Market

26 M Preis Supermarket
29 Andrä Hörtnagl
30 Nordsee; Limerick
    Bill's Irish Pub

OTHER
3 Dom Café-Bar
4 Dom St Jakob
5 Hofburg
6 Volkskunst Museum
7 Hofkirche
9 Goldenes Dachl;
    Maximilianeum
10 Elferhaus
13 Helblinghaus
15 Stadtturm
17 Club Filou
27 Swarovski Haus
28 Main Tourist Office

0   50   100 m

the Hofburg pales into insignificance, however, when compared with her other home, Schloss Schönbrunn (see the Vienna chapter). The grand rooms are decorated with numerous paintings of Maria Theresa and her family; the faces of her 16 children look strangely identical (particularly in the white room) – maybe the artist was intent on avoiding royal wrath arising from sibling rivalry in the beauty stakes. The impressive **Riesensaal** (Giant's Hall) is a 31m-long state room with ceiling frescoes and much marble, gold and porcelain embellishment.

The Hofburg is open daily from 9 am to 5 pm. Entry costs AS55 (students/seniors AS35), and a booklet in English costs AS25. Tours are available, but they're usually conducted in German only. Renovations will cause some re-organisation of rooms until about 2000.

Hofkirche

The Hofkirche (Imperial Church) opposite the Hofburg, on Burggraben, contains the massive but empty sarcophagus of Maximilian I, decorated with scenes from his life.

Most of the reliefs were created by Flemish sculptor Alexander Colin (1527-1612), who also produced the kneeling bronze figure of the emperor (1584). The tomb is considered the finest surviving example of German Renaissance sculpture, though the overall display is only a partial realisation of the initial plans. The Renaissance metal grille was designed in 1573 by Georg Schmiedhammer from Prague. Maximilian is actually buried in Wiener Neustadt.

The twin rows of 28 sombre, giant bronze figures which flank the sarcophagus are memorable, if strangely unsettling. Habsburgs and other dignitaries are depicted. The bronze has been polished to a sheen in certain places by the hands that have touched it; a certain private part of Emperor Rudolf is very shiny indeed! King Arthur (König Artur), the legendary English king, was designed by Albrecht Dürer, as were the images of Theoderic of the Ostrogoths and Count Albrecht IV.

Tirolean hero Andreas Hofer (1767-1810) is also entombed in the church. The steps by the entrance lead to the **Silberne**

Kapelle (Silver Chapel), wherein stands an image of the Virgin with embossed silver. The tombs of Archduke Ferdinand II and his wife, a commoner, are also inside.

The Hofkirche is open daily from 9 am to 5 pm (5.30 pm in July and August) and entry costs AS20 (students AS14), except on Sunday afternoon and holidays when it's free. Combined tickets (AS50; students AS39) are available which include the adjoining Volkskunst Museum (Folk Art Museum). This collection includes utensils and musical instruments, though most space is devoted to a series of rooms from Tirolean dwellings. It's open Monday to Saturday from 9 am to 5 pm, Sunday and holidays from 9 am to noon. Entry to the museum alone costs AS40 (students AS25).

Tiroler Landesmuseum Ferdinandeum

This museum, at Museumstrasse 15, houses a good collection of art and artefacts, including Gothic statues and altarpieces and a collection of Dutch and Flemish masters. The original reliefs from the Goldenes Dachl are to be found here, and there's a 1:20,000 scale relief map of Tirol in the basement. It's open daily from 10 am to 5 pm (Thursday also from 7 to 9 pm) between May and September; from October to April it's open Tuesday to Saturday from 10 am to noon and 2 to 5 pm and on Sunday and holidays from 10 am to 1 pm. Entry costs AS50 (students AS30).

Schloss Ambras

South-east of the town centre, this fine Renaissance castle can easily occupy visitors for several hours. Archduke Ferdinand II acquired the castle in 1564, the year he became ruler of Tirol, and greatly extended the original building, shifting the emphasis from fortress to palace. He was responsible for creating the impressive Renaissance Spanische Saal (Spanish Hall), a long room with a wooden inlaid ceiling and frescoes of Tirolean nobles gazing from the walls. The grisaille (grey relief) around the courtyard of the upper castle is also noteworthy.

Archduke Ferdinand was the instigator of the Ambras Collection. There are three main elements to the collection. The Rüstkammer (Armour Collection) mostly comprises 15th century pieces, as well as Ferdinand's wedding armour, which inexplicably lacks a lapel for the carnation. The Kunst und Wunderkammer (Art and Wonders Collection) is more interesting. There are some beautiful objects on display here, alongside many oddities.

The Nuremberg Plate (1528) seems innocuous at first glance, but closer inspection reveals several perpetrators doing something unmentionable to a victim's posterior. The Portraitgalerie contains room upon room of portraits of Habsburgs and other nobles. Portrait No 158 (Room 10) shows a whiskered Charles VIII masquerading as a peasant, wearing a hat masquerading as an armchair. Maria Anna of Spain (No 126, Room 22) wins the prize for the most ludicrous hairstyle. When portraits of Habsburgs begin to pall, you can unwind by strolling in the extensive castle gardens.

Opening hours between 1 April and 31 October are 10 am to 5 pm daily except Tuesday; admission costs AS60 (students, seniors and children AS30). Between 1 December and 31 March you can only visit the interior on a guided tour conducted in German (AS25 plus the admission fee). The tours start at 2 pm daily except Tuesday.

To get there take tram No 6 or bus K; tram No 3 will also take you reasonably close. Another option is to take the special shuttle bus from the Altes Landhaus (AS30 return), which departs on the hour between 10 am and 5 pm in summer and at 1.45 pm only in winter.

Bergisel

On the southern outskirts of Innsbruck, Bergisel was the site of the famous battle in 1809 at which Andreas Hofer defeated the Bavarians. The Bergisel Museum contains memorials to Tirolean freedom fighters from this and other battles (open March to October; AS25, or AS15 for students).

Alpenzoo

The zoo is north of the Inn River on Weiherburggasse, about 1.5km from the town centre. It features a comprehensive collection of Alpine animals, including amorous bears and combative ibexes. It is open daily from 9 am to 6 pm (5 pm from late September to late March). Admission costs AS70 (students and children AS30). To get there, walk up the hill from the northern end of Rennweg or take the Hungerburgbahn (the funicular to Hungerburg), which is free if you buy your zoo ticket at the bottom.

Next to the Hungerburgbahn lower station is a circular building; within is the **Rundgemälde**, a 1000 sq metre panorama painting of the Battle of Bergisel. It's open from 9 am to 5 pm daily between 1 April and 30 October; admission costs AS28.

Skiing

There are five main ski areas around Innsbruck, and most have been used in Olympic competitions. All are connected by ski buses which are free to anyone with the 'Club Innsbruck' card. The closest ski region to the city is the Hungerburg area, to the north. The others are to the south or the west: Igls, Mutters, Tulfes and Axamer Lizum. Skiing is varied, with most runs geared to intermediates. At Bergisel there's a ski jump which, rather disconcertingly, overlooks a graveyard. A one day ski pass costs from AS265 to AS365 depending on the area, though the Glungezer lifts cost only AS250 on weekdays.

You can ski year-round on the Stubai Glacier, which is a popular excursion from Innsbruck (see the Around Innsbruck section). The glacier and the five Innsbruck regions are included in the Glacier Ski Pass which starts at AS1260 for three days. The Super Ski Pass additionally covers the Arlberg and Kitzbühel areas; it costs AS1780 for four days skiing within six days. The regional passes are sold by the tourist office; buy passes for the individual areas at the ski lifts. Rental of skis, boots and poles starts at AS180 per day for downhill and AS90 for cross-country.

Walking

Above the Hungerburgbahn soars the two-section Nordkette cable car. This reaches the Hafelekar belvedere at 2334m. This area is ideal for walking and offers spectacular views. Special services run to Seegrube (1905m, the mid-station on Nordkette) till 11.30 pm on Friday evening so that the lights of Innsbruck can be enjoyed from above; call ☎ 29 33 44 for information.

Language Courses

The university conducts intensive German-language courses during July and August. For further details of courses you should contact the Innsbrucker Hochschulkurse Deutsch (☎/fax 58 72 33, email ihd-univ-innsbruck@uibk.ac.at; during summer, ☎ 507-4418), Universität Innsbruck, Innrain 52, A-6020 Innsbruck. A three week course (60 hours) costs AS5500 and a six week course (120 hours) costs AS10,800. German-language courses are also available at ISICO (☎ 57 21 60; fax 57 72 63), Colingasse 3, A-6020 Innsbruck, from April to June and September to November.

Organised Tours

Sightseeing bus tours of the city depart daily at noon (and also at 2 pm from June to September) from outside the Hauptbahnhof. They last two hours and cost AS160 (children AS70, or free if under six years). Tourist offices and specified travel agents make tour bookings.

Special Events

The best known annual event is the series of early music concerts (Festwochen der Alten Musik) conducted over most of July and August. This is dominated by Baroque operas and prices range from AS260 to AS800, with a 20% reduction for people aged under 27. The venues include Schloss Ambras, the Landestheater and the Hofkirche. The main tourist office sells tickets and runs a Festwochen Hotline (☎ 561 561).

From 26 November to 22 December, there's a Christmas market in the Altstadt.

Places to Stay – Budget

Camping A few kilometres west of the town centre, *Camping Innsbruck Kranebitten (☎/fax 28 41 80, Kranebitter Allee 214)* is open from April to October. Prices are AS75 per person, AS40 for a tent and AS40 for a car. There is a restaurant on site.

Private Rooms The tourist office has lists of private rooms in Innsbruck and Igls costing from AS180 to AS280 per person. Igls is a few kilometres south of town; get there by tram No 6 or bus J. Further afield is the friendly *Haus Wolf (☎ 54 86 73, Dorfstrasse 48, Mutters)*. Rooms with one to three beds cost AS190 per person, including a big breakfast. It's surrounded by wonderful scenery and guests say that the effort of getting there is well worthwhile. Take the Stubaitalbahn (Stubai Valley railway) from Südtiroler Platz in front of the Hauptbahnhof (AS25, 30 minutes; stop: Birchfeld), which departs every 50 minutes till 10.30 pm.

Hostels A convenient hostel for the centre is *Jugendherberge St Nikolaus (☎ 28 65 15, fax -14, email yhnikolaus@tirol.com, Innstrasse 95)*. This is also reception for the *Glockenhaus* pension, up the hill at Weiherburggasse 3, which has more secluded singles/doubles with private shower/WC for AS345/470 (breakfast is served in the hostel). The hostel is HI-affiliated but it seems more like an independent backpacker place. There's a cellar bar, which can be noisy, and Internet access. Dorm beds cost AS160 for the first night and AS145 for additional nights, including sheets. Doubles without shower cost AS390. Shower tokens are AS10 and check-in is from 5 to 10 pm, though you can usually leave bags during the day. Get a key for late nights out. The attached restaurant is open to non-residents; it serves inexpensive Austrian food and is a good place for socialising. The hostel also offers excursion packages. You can walk here from the Hauptbahnhof (about 2km), or take the half-hourly bus K from outside the station.

Two HI hostels on Reichenauerstrasse are served by bus No O from Museumstrasse. Dorm beds at *Innsbruck (☎ 34 61 79, fax -12, email yhibk@tirol.com)*, at No 147, cost upwards of AS146 for the first night, AS116 thereafter (AS7 reduction for those aged under 18). Curfew is at 11 pm and the building is closed from 10 am to 5 pm. It has a kitchen, double rooms (AS500) and very slow washing machines (AS45). *St Paulus (☎ 34 42 91, fax 39 83 19)*, at No 72, offers beds in large dorms for AS120. Breakfast costs AS30 and there's a kitchen and a bar. Curfew is approximately 11.30 pm and the doors are locked from 11 am to 5 pm. The hostel is only open from mid-June to early September.

Another hostel to try in the summer is *Jugendwohnheim Fritz Prior (☎ 58 58 14, fax -4, Rennweg 17B)* where beds cost AS120, breakfast is AS45 and sheets are AS20; check-in opens at 5pm (open during July and August).

Student Rooms As in Vienna, student accommodation is pressed into service as tourist hotels in the summer, from July to August or September.

Internationales Studenthaus (☎ 501, fax -15, Rechengasse 7) is the most convenient. It's right by the university to the west of town and has 567 beds. Singles/doubles with private shower and WC cost AS425/750, or AS325/570 with hall shower. Reception is open 24 hours.

Hotels & Pensions *Goldenes Brünnl (☎ 28 35 19, St Nikolaus Gasse 1)* is on the other side of the river from the Altstadt. It's basic, good value and often full (phone ahead); singles/doubles with hall showers cost AS280/480. Reception is in the restaurant, and is open till midnight; it's closed on Tuesday in the low season.

Innbrücke (☎ 28 19 34, Innstrasse 1) is convenient for the Altstadt. Rooms are fairly simple but large, and cost AS400/700 with shower/WC or AS320/500 without.

Ferrarihof (☎ 58 09 68, fax 57 10 62, Brennerstrasse 8) is south of town, just off

TIROL

the main road. Single/double rooms with either private or hall shower cost AS290/480. Reception is in the bar downstairs, open from 8 am to midnight. There is plenty of parking space.

Laurin (☎ *34 11 04, Gumppstrasse 19)* is behind the station, near to a stop for tram No 3. Singles/doubles cost AS330/500, or AS420/600 with private shower, and there's a lift and parking spaces.

Up the hill towards the zoo is *Pension Paula* (☎/fax *29 22 62, Weiherburggasse 15)*. Prices are AS420/660 with private shower/WC or AS320/540 without. There's no convenient public transport but parking is no problem. It's popular, so book ahead.

Places to Stay – Mid-Range & Top End

Hotel-Pension Binder (☎ *334 36, fax -99, email info@hotelbinder.at, Dr Glatz Strasse 20)* is behind the Hauptbahnhof, close to the route of tram No 3. This amenable place has rooms with cable TV and telephone. Single/double rooms cost AS580/900 with private shower and WC or AS490/660 with shared facilities.

Hotel-Garni Helga (☎ *26 11 37, fax -6, Brandlweg 3)* is a slightly better deal. Rooms with shower/WC, TV and telephone cost AS550/720 and the hotel has a sauna and an indoor swimming pool. It's 3km north-east of town, just across Grenobler Brücke and off highway 171, the road to Salzburg. Bus O runs close by.

Goldene Krone (☎ *58 61 60, fax 58 01 89-6, email r.pischl@tirol.com, Maria Theresien Strasse 46)* is near the Triumphpforte, and is convenient for both the Altstadt and the Hauptbahnhof. Smallish but well equipped singles/doubles start at AS840/1200 in this three star place.

Also in the three star category, the best place in the Altstadt is *Weisses Kreuz* (☎ *594 79, fax -90, email hotel.weiss .kreuz@eunet.at, Herzog Friedrich Strasse 31)* where rooms cost AS450/840 or AS770/1140 with private shower/WC. The 'superior' doubles for AS1300 are worth the extra cost. This 500-year-old inn played

host to a 13-year old Mozart and all of the rooms are spacious, neat and comfortable. Prices drop slightly in winter. If it's full, try *Hotel Happ* (☎ *58 29 80, fax -11)* across the street at No 14 which is almost as atmospheric; rooms with shower/WC and TV cost AS700/1200. Reception closes at noon on Wednesday in the low season.

The four star *Goldener Adler* (☎ *57 11 11, fax 58 44 09, Herzog Friedrich Strasse 6)* has welcomed many famous people through its portals in the past 600 years – see the plaque by the entrance. The public areas have an abundance of character, rather more, in fact, than the modern, comfortable but somewhat sanitised rooms. Prices start at AS1080/1600.

Hotel Innsbruck (☎ *598 68, fax 57 22 80, Innrain 3)* is near the river in the Altstadt. Good on-site facilities include a sauna (AS80), swimming pool (free) and garage parking (AS150). Singles/doubles cost from AS1000/1400.

The only five star place in town is the *Europa Tyrol* (☎ *59 31, fax 58 78 00, email hotel@europatyrol.com, Südtiroler Platz 2)*, opposite the Hauptbahnhof. The rooms (starting at AS1350/1950) and lobby are as grand as you would expect, and it has a top-class restaurant.

Places to Eat

Some of the bars listed in the Entertainment section also serve food.

Self-Catering There is a large indoor food and flower *market* by the river in Markthalle, Herzog Sigmund Ufer, open normal shop hours. Opposite, on Innrain, is a large *M Preis* supermarket, open Monday to Friday from 7.30 am to 6.30 pm and on Saturday from 7.30 am to 5 pm. A *Billa* and a *Hofer* are close together on Museumstrasse.

Self-Service & Budget Restaurants Like other cities, Innsbruck has various snack stands providing cheap filling fodder such as sausages, chips and burgers. Some of these only come out at night to reel in the going-home-half-drunk trade.

Andrä Hörtnagl, adjoining Burggraben and Maria Theresien Strasse, has a supermarket and cheap restaurant. *Neuböck (Herzog Friedrich Strasse 30)* is a meat shop serving sit-down meals for under AS100 (open daily till 6 or 6.30 pm). Equally cheap is *Nordsee (Maria Theresien Strasse 11)*, serving fast fish meals; it's open on weekdays till 7 pm and on Saturday till 3 or 5 pm.

The university *Mensa (Herzog Sigmund Ufer 15)*, on the 1st floor, serves good lunches between 11 am and 1.30 pm from Monday to Friday and sometimes on Saturday (not in summer). There's a choice of self-service or a slightly more expensive section with table service. Either way you can eat well for between AS45 and AS80. It's closed over Christmas/New Year.

China-Restaurant Asia (Angerzellgasse 10) offers excellent three-course weekday lunch specials – you get a lot of food for AS69. It is open daily from 11.30 am to 2.30 pm and 6 pm to midnight. Another Chinese restaurant is *Lotos (Seilergasse 5)* in the Altstadt. It has an all-you-can-eat buffet at lunchtime on weekdays for AS85.

Nearby, *Thai-Li (Marktgraben 3)* serves tasty Thai food stating at AS125, plus three-course lunch menus for AS85 and AS95 from Monday to Saturday.

Prendi Pizza (Viaduktbögen 5) offers a selection of over 30 pizzas costing from just AS50 to AS90 (open 11 am to midnight daily). For more expensive Italian food, and outside tables by the river, there's *Churrasco La Mamma (Innrain 2)*; open daily from 9 am to midnight.

Shashi (Innstrasse 81) is a small place with a jovial English-speaking host. Big pizzas start at AS60 and Indian meals costing about AS95 include rice, papadams and bread. Also good for Indian food is *Shere Punjab (Innstrasse 19)* where curry with rice starts at AS85. Both places are open daily.

Restaurant Philippine (☎ 58 91 57, Müllerstrasse 9) is a specialist vegetarian restaurant, decked out in light colours. It has a wide selection of main dishes costing from AS85 to AS170, and a fine salad buffet at AS48/88 for a small/big plate. It is open Monday to Saturday from 10 am to midnight (the kitchen closes at 10 pm). English-language menus are available.

The *Café Central (Gilmstrasse 5)* is a Viennese-style coffee house, which offers English newspapers, Austrian dishes for between AS75 and AS125, and piano music on Sunday from 8 to 10 pm. It's open daily from 7.30 am to 11 pm.

Mid-Range & Top End Restaurants For colourful décor and Mexican food starting at AS100, try *Chilis* on Adamgasse. It's open daily from 8 am to midnight.

Stiegl Bräustube (Wilhelm Greil Strasse 25) almost has a beer hall atmosphere, though it's a bit too restrained to qualify. Stiegl beer is AS35 for 0.5L and dishes from the extensive menu cost from AS80 to AS270. It's closed on Sunday and holidays.

Offering creative yet affordable cuisine in a comfortable, arcaded room is *Grauer Bär (Universitätsstrasse 5)*. Most main courses cost over AS135; it's open daily.

Most places in the Altstadt are a bit expensive, and generally serve a combination of Tirolean, Austrian and international food. *Gasthaus Goldenes Dachl (Hofgasse 1)* provides a civilised environment for tasting Tirolean specialities such as *Bauerngröstl*, a pork, bacon, potato and egg concoction served with salad (AS120). It is open daily from 7.30 am to midnight.

Weisses Rössl (☎ 58 30 57, Kiebachgasse 8) is good for regional food costing from AS80 to AS200, including set menus. It's closed on Sunday and holidays. Opposite is *Hirschenstuben (☎ 58 29 79, Kiebachgasse 5)*, which has vaulted rooms and a menu that encompasses both local and Italian dishes (AS90 to AS245). It is closed on Monday lunchtime, Sunday and holidays, and from mid-June to late July. Both of these places get busy in the high season, so book ahead.

For upmarket eating, *Restaurant Altstadtstüberl (☎ 58 23 47, Riesengasse 13)* is one of the best places to try Tirolean food, often with an Italian influence. Main dishes vary with the availability of ingredients, and cost in the region of AS120 to AS240. It's closed on Sunday and holidays.

Goldener Adler (see Places to Stay – Mid-Range & Top End) has three restaurants, all with main courses costing from AS135 to AS265. The one on the 1st floor is the most elegant, but the cellar-style Goethe Stube (open evenings only, and not in low season) on the ground floor has the added attraction of a zither player from 7 pm. All three restaurants are open daily.

Entertainment
Ask at the tourist office about 'Tirolean evenings' (AS220 for brass bands, folk dancing, yodelling and one drink). Innsbruck has its own symphony orchestra; it and other ensembles perform regularly in various venues. Schloss Ambras hosts a series of classical music concerts in summer. Between mid-May and late September medieval brass music is performed from the Goldenes Dachl balcony every Sunday at 11.30 am.

The *Landestheater* (☎ 520 74, *Rennweg 2*) stages year-round performances ranging from opera and ballet to drama and comedy. Get information and tickets (commission charged) from the tourist office.

Cinemas around town are cheaper on Monday when all seats cost AS70. *Cinematograph* (☎ 57 85 00, *Museumstrasse 31*) shows independent films in their original language; tickets are always AS70.

Utopia (☎ 58 85 87, *Tschamlerstrasse 3*) has a venue for theatre, art, parties and live music in the cellar on around five nights each week; entry costs from AS40 to AS200 (AS20 reduction for students). There's also a café-bar (with free Internet access) open Monday to Saturday from 6 pm to midnight. Some fixtures from its former incarnation as a factory are still in place, creating a distinctive environment.

Treibhaus (☎ 58 68 74, *Angerzellgasse 8*) has live music most nights (in a circus-style tent in summer). Entry costs from AS100 to AS250, though free jazz enlivens

Sunday lunchtimes. There's also a play area for kids, and pizzas and other meals are served. It's open daily till 1 am.

Elferhaus (☎ 58 28 75, *Herzog Friedrich Strasse 11*) is a popular student hang-out. It's a long, narrow bar and restaurant with live music on the 11th of the month (free entry). Food costs from AS78 to AS140 and there is a huge selection of beer from Austria and elsewhere (starting at AS36 for 0.5L). This place gets very busy and stuffy; it's open daily from 10 am to 2 am.

A more affluent clientele frequents the *Club Filou* (*Stiftgasse 12*), in the Altstadt. This chic bar and restaurant is open daily from 6 pm to 4 am. The downstairs bar opens at 10 pm and has a dance floor, but doesn't get lively till midnight; the drinks are expensive in this section (AS38 for a glass of wine, AS48 for a small beer).

Dom Café-Bar (*Pfarrgasse 3*) is a busy, dimly-lit drinking establishment in the Altstadt, with good pasta and other dishes starting at AS90. It is open daily from 5 pm to 1 or 2 am.

The Austrian craze for Irish bars has reached Innsbruck in the form of *Limerick Bill's Irish Pub* (*Maria Theresien Strasse 9*); Guinness is AS56 a pint (0.58L) and there's occasional live Irish music. It's open daily from 3.30 pm to 1 am. *Jimmy's* (*Wilhelm Greil Strasse 17*) is popular with snowboarders.

You'll find a clutch of late-night bars and clubs nestled in the railway arches along Ingenieur Etzel Strasse. This district is called the Viaduktbögen; the busiest area is from 500 to 1200m north of the train station.

Innsbruck has a *casino* at Landhausplatz, open daily from 3 pm.

Shopping
Tirolean crafts include embroidered fabrics, wrought iron and glassware. There are many souvenir shops in the cobbled streets of the Altstadt offering loden hats, wood carvings, grotesque masks and other Tirolean products. The Tiroler Heimatwerk shop is at Meraner Strasse 2. Swarovski Haus, Herzog Friedrich Strasse 39, sells

Springtime blooms on Herzog Friedrich Strasse, Innsbruck.

Time to relax, Innsbruck.

Typical Tirolean village scene.

Traditional Innsbruck houses line the banks of the Inn River.

Bird's-eye view from Innsbruck city tower.

Giant bronze figures in Innsbruck's Hofkirche.

Innsbruck nestles in the Inn River valley between the Alps and the Tuxer mountains, Tirol.

Baroque Martinsturm, the emblem of Bregenz.

'Three Towers', Montafon Valley, Vorarlberg.

crystalware. Kaufhaus Tyrol, Maria Theresien Strasse 33, is a large department store. A flea market appears on the pedestrian part of Burggraben on Saturday morning.

Getting There & Away

Air The small airport (☎ 225 25) is at Fürstenweg 180. Tyrolean Airways (☎ 22 22-0) is the main carrier and flies daily to Vienna and Zürich, and on most days to Amsterdam and Frankfurt.

Bus The Bundesbus station is by the Hauptbahnhof. The ticket office is near the Jugendwarteraum in the smaller of the Hauptbahnhof's two halls.

Train The Hauptbahnhof is the most convenient Innsbruck station, though some local trains also stop at the Westbahnhof (which is actually to the south) and at Hötting (to the west).

Fast trains depart every two hours for Bregenz and Salzburg. From Innsbruck to the Arlberg, most of the best views are on the right-hand side of the train. Regular express trains head north to Munich (via Kufstein) and south to Verona. Kitzbühel can be reached hourly (AS134; direct service every second hour).

Four daily trains (three on Sunday) go to Lienz, passing through Italy. The 1.53 pm train is an international train; it costs AS206; if you're travelling on an Austrian rail pass you must pay AS74 extra for the Italian section. The other trains are Austrian 'corridor' trains, and you can disembark in Italy; these only cost AS154 (a VVT fare), and Austrian rail passes are valid for the whole trip.

For train information, call ☎ 1717 between 7 am and 9 pm.

Car & Motorcycle The A12 and the parallel highway 171 are the main roads heading west and east. Highway 177, to the west of Innsbruck, heads north to Germany and Munich. The A13 is a toll road (AS110) running south through the Brenner Pass to Italy. En route you cross the Europabrücke

(Europe Bridge); this is 777m long and passes over the Sill River at a height of 190m, making it Europe's highest bridge. Toll-free highway 182 follows the same route, passing under the bridge.

Car Rental Offices include:

Avis
  (☎ 57 17 54) Salurner Strasse 15
ARAC-Eurodollar
  (☎ 34 31 61) Amraserstrasse 84
Budget
  (☎ 58 84 68) Leopoldstrasse 54
Europcar
  (☎ 58 20 60) Salurner Strasse 8
Hertz
  (☎ 58 09 01) Südtiroler Platz 1

Getting Around

To/From the Airport The airport is 4km to the west of the town centre. It's served by bus F, which leaves every 15 or 20 minutes from Maria Theresien Strasse (AS21). Taxis charge about AS120 for the same trip.

Public Transport Tickets on buses and trams cost AS21 (from the driver; valid upon issue), or AS60 for a block of four when bought in advance. Tickets bought in advance must be stamped in the machines at the outset of the journey. Advance purchase passes cost AS33 for one day, AS45 for 24 hours and AS115 for one week (Monday to Sunday). They're not valid for the Hungerburgbahn. The fine for riding without a ticket is AS450. Advance tickets can be bought at Tabak shops, the tourist office and the IVB transport authority office (☎ 53 07-103) at Museumstrasse 23. The IVB office is open weekdays from 7.30 am to 6 pm and can also issue VVT tickets (see the North-Eastern Tirol Getting Around section).

Parking on unmarked streets is not restricted. Most streets near the centre have a blue line; you can park on these for a maximum of 1½ or three hours during set times (approximately shop hours). The charge is AS5/10/20 for 30/60/90 minutes; get tickets from the pavement dispensers. Parking garages (such as the one under the Altstadt) cost about AS200 per day.

Taxis cost AS52 (AS57 after 10 pm and on Sunday), plus about AS19 per kilometre. Numbers for radio taxis are ☎ 20 20 70 and 53 11.

Bicycle Rental The office in the Hauptbahnhof is open daily from 7 am to 6.30 pm (6 pm on Saturday).

Around Innsbruck

If you're using Innsbruck as a base to visit the area, remember that VVT tickets allow you to add an Innsbruck pass to the cost of the ticket (see the Getting Around section at the beginning of this chapter).

IGLS

Igls is just a few kilometres south of Innsbruck, at the terminus of tram No 6 (Innsbruck city tickets are valid). This charming and picturesque resort achieved world recognition as a site for the 1976 Winter Olympics, for which a toboggan and bobsleigh run was built. Igls is covered by the Innsbruck ski pass. Staff at its tourist office (☎ 0512-37 71 01), Hilberstrasse 15, can help you find accommodation.

HALL IN TIROL

☎ 05223 • pop 13,000 • 574m

Hall lies 9km east of Innsbruck. It enjoyed past importance for its salt mines and now seeks a new role as a tourist destination. Staff at the tourist office (☎ 562 69), Wallpachgasse 5, will do their best to convince you that this is a worthy endeavour; the office is open on weekdays and Saturday morning. Hall has an attractive old town centre, and it's certainly viable to pay a visit on the way to or from Innsbruck.

If you do stop off, explore the area round Oberer Stadtplatz, the centre of the town. The 15th century **Rathaus** is distinctive and has a courtyard with crenated edges and mosaic crests. Ascend the stairs and turn left to view an impressive wood-panelled room. Across the square, the **Pfarrkirche** (parish church; 13th century) has an off-

centre chancel and is predominantly Gothic in style. Less than 200m to the east is the **Damenstift**, a convent founded in 1557 and graced by a Baroque tower.

A little south of the town centre is **Burg Hasegg**, site of the tower that has become an emblem of the town. This castle had a 300 year career as a mint for silver coins (*Thalers*, the root of the modern word 'dollar'). It is now a municipal museum that elucidates the town's history. Entry to the museum and castle costs AS60, including a tour (possible in English). It's open daily in summer; check with the tourist office about visiting at other times.

Getting There & Away

Highway 171 goes almost through the town centre, unlike the A12/E45 which is over the Inn River to the south. The train station is about 1km south-west of the centre; it is on the main Innsbruck-Wörgl train line, but only regional trains stop there. Innsbruck (AS38 return) can also be reached by bus; buses skirt the town centre and also stop near the train station.

WATTENS

This small town is 20 minutes east from Innsbruck by Bundesbus or train. The main reason to visit is for the **Swarovski Kristallwelten** (Crystal Worlds), a well-presented series of light-and-sound displays featuring the famous Swarovski crystals. Entry costs AS75 (free for children up to age 12, and with the Innsbruck Card) and it's open daily from 9 am to 6 pm. Spending over AS100 in the shop entitles you to a AS25 discount off the entry fee. It's at Kristallweltenstrasse 1, a 20 minute walk south-east of Wattens train station.

SCHWAZ

☎ 05242 • pop 11,000 • 535m

Schwaz, 18km east of Hall, is another former mining town, except that silver and copper was the bounty sought (much of it finding its way to the Hall mint). During its heyday in the 15th and 16th centuries it was the second most populous town in Tirol after Innsbruck. Houses built during these prosperous years survive in and around the central Stadtplatz.

For information on the town, contact the tourist office (☎ 632 40) at Franz Josef Strasse 23.

Things to See & Do

The large **Pfarrkirche**, dating from the 15th century, bears 15,000 copper tiles on its roof. Although the church has a Gothic structure, it has a Baroque interior. A similar combination can be seen in the **Franziskanerkirche**, which has 15th century wall paintings in the cloisters depicting Christ's Passion.

About 1.5km east of the town is **Schau Silberbergwerk**, a former silver mine which you can visit on a tour following a mini-train ride into the mountain (AS150; children AS75); allow two hours. It's open daily, but closed most of January. Between the mine and the town centre is the **Haus der Völker**, Husslstrasse, with temporary ethnological displays (open daily, AS70).

Getting There & Away

Schwaz is on the same transport routes as Hall. Similarly, only regional trains stop; the trip to/from Innsbruck takes 25 minutes and costs AS104 return.

STUBAI GLACIER

Year-round skiing is possible on this glacier – a popular excursion from Innsbruck – and the pistes are varied enough to cater for most skiers. The summer skiing area is at an elevation of between 2900 and 3300m. Walkers are attracted to the network of footpaths lower down in the valley. The Stubaital (Stubai Valley) branches off from the Brenner Pass route a little south of the Europabrücke and runs south-west. The glacier itself is about 40km from Innsbruck.

Getting There & Away

The journey there takes 80 minutes by hourly 'STB' bus from Innsbruck Bundes-bus station; buy one-way tickets from the driver (AS84) and return tickets in advance

(AS152); the last bus back is usually at 5.30 pm. Stubai Glacier ski passes cost AS420 for one day or AS280 for the afternoon. Many places in Innsbruck offer complete packages to the glacier, which compare favourably with going it alone. The tourist office package in summer costs AS599, including transport, passes and equipment rental. In winter, the STB bus is free with 'Club Innsbruck', and the price for the tourist office package reduces to AS540.

SEEFELD

☎ 05212 • pop 2800 • 1180m

This prosperous, attractively situated resort hosted the Olympic Nordic skiing competitions in 1964 and 1976. Seefeld is popular year-round, but especially in winter.

Orientation & Information

Seefeld lies between Innsbruck and the German border on the Seefelder Sattel (Seefeld Saddle), a glacier-formed channel through the Northern Limestone Alps.

The train station (which rents bikes) is just 200m east of the main square, Dorfplatz. The tourist office (☎ 23 13, fax 33 55, email info@seefeld.tirol.at), Kloster Strasse 43, is on the northern side of Dorfplatz, open Monday to Friday from 8.30 am to 12.15 pm and 3 to 6 pm, and on Saturday from 8.30 am to 12.15 pm. In the high season, hours are Monday to Saturday from 8.30 am to 6.30 pm, Sunday from 10 am to 12.30 pm and (from December to March) 4 to 6 pm.

The post office (Postamt 6100) is also on Kloster Strasse.

Things to See & Do

Pfarrkirche St Oswald dates from the 15th century. Above the Gothic doorway is a decorative tympanum, depicting the 14th century martyrdom of St Oswald and the miracle of the host (an event which caused the church to become a pilgrimage site; see the boxed text later in this section). Other features include the winged Gothic altar, the wooden font and the fine ceiling vaulting in the chancel. Ascend the inside stairs to view

Glacier Watching

With fears of global warming growing, glaciers are increasingly under scrutiny. Of the world's supply of fresh water, 80% is stored in ice and snow, and 97% of this is in Antarctica and Greenland. Glaciers are also important in the rest of the world. Without glacier meltwater, many areas at the foot of high mountain ranges would be desert or steppes. Most Austrian glaciers are in Tirol and Vorarlberg. The Pasterze Glacier in the Hohe Tauern National Park is the largest in the eastern Alps.

There's much more to glaciers than lumps of ice. They begin as snow which, over the course of years, is compressed to firn (sometimes called névé). A depth of about 10m of fresh snow reduces to a depth of 1m of firn, which eventually evolves into ice. Surprisingly, ice takes longer to form in 'cold' glaciers (those below 0°C) than in 'temperate' glaciers. Glaciers are filled with air bubbles, created during the transformation of snow to ice, and the gas content of these bubbles may be modified by water flows in a temperate glacier.

The ice at the bottom of glaciers (in the ablation zone) may be centuries old, making it possible to measure past environmental pollution. The eruption of Krakatoa volcano in Indonesia in 1883 can be measured in glacial ice, and there are traces of the 1977 Sahara dust storms in Alpine glaciers. The peak of nuclear testing and fallout, 1963, is a benchmark year in dating glacial ice.

Glaciers are always moving; whether retreating (shrinking) or advancing (growing), the ice always moves down the valley. You might think the movement so slow as to be insignificant. Not so. The pylon feet of glacier ski lifts are set in the ice and may have to be repositioned several times each year, as is the case on the Kitzsteinhorn Glacier in Salzburg province. Over summer, huge crevasses open in the ice and must be filled before skiing starts in winter. Even filled, they can still be hazardous – never leave the marked trails when skiing on glaciers. Ice avalanches from glaciers are another significant hazard.

Cross Section of a Glacier

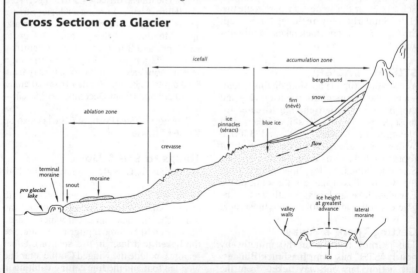

the **Blutskapelle** (Chapel of the Holy Blood), housing paintings by Michael Huber and some 18th century stuccowork.

Seefeld receives plenty of affluent, fur-clad tourists, who take leisurely strolls round the streets and footpaths, or opt for a horse-drawn carriage. The walk south to the **Wildsee** (lake) is pleasant, or climb the small hill behind the church for good views of the resort, the lake and surrounding peaks. For longer walks, inquire at the tourist office for information about its summer excursions (AS150).

Downhill **skiing** is mainly geared towards intermediates and beginners. The local ski pass costs AS330 (children AS205) for one day. The two main areas are Gschwandtkopf (1500m) and Rosshütte (1800m), the latter being reached by a funicular and thereafter connecting to higher lifts and slopes on the Karwendel range. The resort's speciality is cross-country skiing, with 200km of trails (*Loipe*) across the valley. They go all the way to **Mösern**, 5km distant, where there are excellent views of the Inn River and peaks beyond.

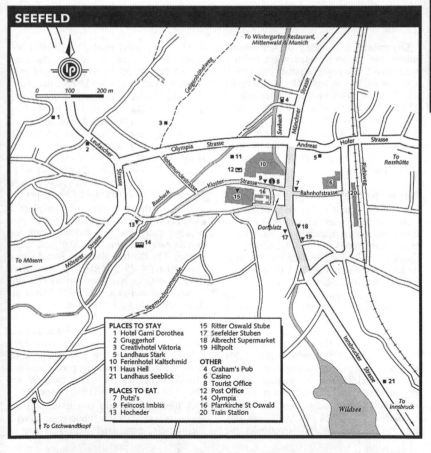

SEEFELD

PLACES TO STAY
1 Hotel Garni Dorothea
2 Gruggerhof
3 Creativhotel Viktoria
5 Landhaus Stark
10 Ferienhotel Kaltschmid
11 Haus Hell
21 Landhaus Seeblick

PLACES TO EAT
7 Putzi's
9 Feincost Imbiss
13 Hocheder

15 Ritter Oswald Stube
17 Seefelder Stuben
18 Albrecht Supermarket
19 Hiltpolt

OTHER
4 Graham's Pub
6 Casino
8 Tourist Office
12 Post Office
14 Olympia
16 Pfarrkirche St Oswald
20 Train Station

TIROL

The Miracle of the Host

These days, miracles are thin on the ground, but back in the Middle Ages miracles such as that commemorated on the tympanum of Pfarrkirche St Oswald in Seefeld could make the reputation of a town or village.

During the Easter communion of 1384, a local bigwig named Oswald Milser (no relation to the church's patron saint) decided he was too important to settle for an ordinary communion wafer; instead, he demanded a large clerical one. The timid priest obeyed, whereupon the floor of the church softened beneath Oswald's feet and began to swallow him up. The priest retrieved the wafer from the greedy citizen and the ground firmed up again, saving Oswald. He subsequently repented, and died penniless two years later. The wafer, once examined, was discovered to have been miraculously marked with blood, presumed to be that of Christ; hence the apartment in the church which held the miraculous wafer is called the Blutskapelle (Chapel of the Holy Blood).

TIROL

Olympia is a complex of saunas and indoor and outdoor heated pools (with a water slide). The pools are open daily from 9.30 am to 10 pm and entry costs AS88 (children AS44) with the Gästekarte or AS160 (AS120) including the saunas (open from 1 pm). Massages are also available.

Seefeld has a **casino** near the train station, for those tourists who feel weighed down by their bulging pockets; it's open from 3 pm daily.

Places to Stay

Staff at the tourist office will search for accommodation free of charge, and will answer telephone enquiries on this matter daily except Sunday from 8.30 am to 8 pm. Check with the office on what's left open in the low season (not much!). A Gästekarte is available for overnighters.

The cheapest option is a room in one of the many private houses though, as in hotels and pensions, prices will be higher in winter. In fact, more upmarket places have four price levels through the year; the highest (quoted here) may be nearly double the low season prices, and stays of less than three days might incur a surcharge. Many top-end hotels offer discounts on green fees for the golf course.

Landhaus Seeblick (☎ 23 89, fax -50, *Innsbrucker Strasse 165)* overlooks the

Wildsee and most rooms have wood balconies and a view of the lake. Recently renovated, all rooms are equipped with shower/WC and cost AS330 per person.

About 200m north-east of the tourist office is *Landhaus Stark* (☎ 21 04, *Andreas Hofer Strasse 144)* which has an annexe above the bank. Rooms cost AS240 per person or AS400 with private shower/WC. *Haus Hell* (☎ 24 27, fax -51, *Olympiastrasse 290)* is only a small place, but has an indoor swimming pool; rooms have shower/ WC and TV and start at AS520 per person.

Half a kilometre west of Dorfplatz is *Gruggerhof* (☎ 32 54, *Leutascher Strasse 64)*, where rooms with balcony, sink and hall shower cost from AS220 to AS250 per person. On the hill above is *Hotel Garni Dorothea* (☎ 25 27, fax -73, *Kirchwald 391)*. This three star place has a swimming pool, sauna and other facilities. Prices are from AS580 to AS740 per person in rooms with shower/WC and TV.

The four star *Ferienhotel Kaltschmid* (☎ 21 91, fax -116, *Olympia Strasse 101)*, behind the tourist office, also has good facilities, such as a swimming pool, sauna and fitness room. Rooms vary greatly in size and price (AS990 to AS1950 per person).

A hint that Seefeld is a haven for big spenders is the fact that it boasts seven five-star hotels, compared with just one in

Innsbruck. *Creativhotel Viktoria (☎ 44 41, fax 44 43, Geigenbühelweg 589)* is small and cosy with just 14 suites, each reflecting a different epoch. Prices start at AS1950 per person.

Places to Eat

Feincost Imbiss on Dorfplatz is a shop that sells cheap, hot food to eat in or take away. Wiener schnitzel and salad costs AS73 and a half-chicken and chips is AS69. Opening hours are Monday to Saturday from 8.30 am to 1 pm and 3 to 6 pm, and Sunday from 10 am to noon. Also cheap for simple food (schnitzels, pizza, burgers and so on) is the nearby *Putzi's*, which has both a takeaway section and a sit-down café.

Dorfplatz has plenty of other places to eat, mostly in the mid-price category. Leading south from Dorfplatz is Innsbrucker Strasse, where there's an *Albrecht* supermarket. Opposite is *Seefelder Stuben*, offering Austrian and Italian food from about AS80 to AS220, served between 11 am and 11 pm. Farther along on the same side of the road are a couple of pizzerias.

The *Bahnhof Restaurant* in the train station is a bit rough-and-ready, attracting male drinkers and card players, but it also serves big platefuls of tasty food. Try the *Tiroler Gröstel* (AS89), a heaped fry-up of meat, potatoes and onion, served with a bowl of salad. It's open daily till 9 pm.

The hotels *Hiltpolt (Innsbrucker Strasse 18)* and *Hocheder (Kloster Strasse 121)* have good, central, mid-range restaurants. For expensive gourmet food, there's the *Wintergarten* in Hotel Tümmlerhof *(☎ 25 71, Münchner Strasse 215)* or the more central *Ritter Oswald Stube* in the Hotel Klosterbräu *(☎ 26 21, Kloster Strasse 30)*.

For après-ski drinking, try the New Zealander-owned *Graham's Pub* behind the Hotel Eden on Münchner Strasse. It shows sports on satellite TV and has live music once a week.

Getting There & Away

Seefeld is 25km north-west of Innsbruck, just off highway 117, which is the route into Germany. The road follows the floor of the Inn Valley till it rises sharply (1:7 gradient) near Zirl. The train track starts climbing the north side of the valley much sooner after departing Innsbruck, providing spectacular views across the whole valley (sit on the left). Trains run hourly and take 40 minutes (AS52 one way, AS98 return). Fares to Germany from Seefeld are AS46 to Mittenwald and AS84 to Garmisch-Partenkirchen.

EHRWALD

Ehrwald's crowning glory is the **Zugspitze** (2962m), which marks the border between Austria and Germany, and looms mightily over the village. A modern, fast cable car (AS385 return) sails to the top, where there's a restaurant and a magnificent panorama. All of the main Tirolean mountain ranges can be seen, as well as the Bavarian Alps and Mt Säntis in Switzerland. North of the Zugspitze is Garmisch-Partenkirchen, Germany's most popular ski resort, which also offers access to the mountain summit.

Ehrwald is linked with other resorts in Austria (including Seefeld) and Germany (including Garmisch-Partenkirchen) under the Happy Ski Pass (AS910, children AS650; minimum three days).

For information on accommodation and activities, you can contact the tourist office (☎ 05673-23 95) in the town centre. Staff book rooms free of charge, or there's an accommodation board with free telephone.

Getting There & Away

To reach Ehrwald from Seefeld by train you have to pass through Germany, but Austrian rail passes are valid for the whole trip (AS97). In the other direction, trains come from Reutte but, other than from Ehrwald, Reutte itself can be reached by rail only from Germany.

Drivers can follow either rail route, or approach from the south via the Fern Pass (1216m); it's open all year and has a maximum gradient of 1:8. Bundesbuses go to/from Reutte (AS53) and Imst (AS67, via Nassereith and the Fern Pass).

North-Eastern Tirol

This part of the province is dominated by two east-west mountain chains, the Kitzbüheler Alpen and the Zillertaler Alpen. A road and rail route between Innsbruck and Salzburg diverts into Germany near Kufstein; an alternative route that dips south between the Kitzbüheler Alpen is slower but more scenic.

THE ZILLERTAL

The Zillertal (Ziller Valley) is well developed for summer and winter sports. It is one of the most densely populated valleys in the region and attracts plenty of tourists. The Zillertal runs south between the Tuxer Alpen and the Kitzbüheler Alpen. Guarding the entrance to the valley is Jenbach (population 6000), which stands on the north bank of the Inn River. The narrow Ziller River meanders along the length of the broad valley. Small resorts provide all amenities, but attractive cow pastures, chalets and church spires are offset by unsightly lumber yards and electricity pylons. The farthest resort from Jenbach, at the head of the valley, is Mayrhofen.

All of the resorts have a tourist office, and there's an office for the whole valley (☎ 05288-871 87, fax -1, email zillertal-werbung@netway.at). The magazine *Zillertaler Gästezeitung* (partially in English) covers the valley in great detail. It has lists of sights and events and provides a lot of practical information.

There are five camp sites within the valley. Uderns, about one-third of the way south into the valley, has a HI *Jugendherberge* (☎ 05288-620 10, fax 628 66, Finsingerhof, Finsing 73) open all year. Accommodation prices at most places are usually slightly higher in the winter. Most beds are in chalet-style properties, whether pensions, private rooms, holiday apartments or farmhouses. Ask staff at the tourist office for help in finding somewhere (they usually won't charge), as there are dozens of options in each resort. Wherever you stay, inquire about the resort's Gästekarte.

Activities

The main **skiing** resort is Mayrhofen (see the Mayrhofen section later in this chapter), but there is downhill and cross-country skiing elsewhere. The Zillertaler Super-skipass covers all 151 lifts in the valley; it starts at AS1240 (children AS740) for the minimum four days, or AS1440 (AS860) including the glacier ski lifts. Ski buses connect resorts.

Walking is strongly emphasised in summer. A famous network of trails is the Zillertaler Höhestrasse in the Tuxer Alpen. Trails lead from the resorts of Ried, Kaltenbach, Aschau, Zell and Ramsau. Mountain huts at elevations of around 1800m provide overnight accommodation. Between early June and early October a six day Z-Ticket is available, covering the whole valley and valid for one use per day of cable cars, trains, buses and swimming pools; it costs AS480 per adult and child or family tickets are available.

Other sporting possibilities include rafting on the Ziller River, tennis, paragliding and cycling. The Ziller and its tributaries are also good for fishing, but permits are only valid for certain stretches.

Special Events

From late September to early October the cow herds are brought down from the high pastures, an event known as the Huamfahrerfest. The cows wear elaborate headdresses for the occasion, and the clanging of cow bells accompanies the efforts of amateur musicians. In Zell am Ziller they come down on the first Sunday in October, an event called Almabetrieb. In Mayrhofen the descent occurs on the first and second Saturdays in October, when the sprawling *Krämermarkt* takes over the village centre. Its wares include food, curios, crafts and cow bells.

Getting There & Away

All trains along the Inn Valley (including IC and EC trains) stop at Jenbach. Destinations include Innsbruck (30 minutes), Kufstein (30 minutes) and Kitzbühel (one hour).

Getting Around

The Zillertal is serviced by a private railway line, the Zillertalbahn. For information on this service, call ☎ 05244-606-0, based in Jenbach, the departure point for trains and buses up the valley and elsewhere. A steam train (*Dampfzug*) runs twice a day in summer: it takes 80 minutes to reach the last stop, Mayrhofen. If you just want to get from A to B, take the normal train (*Triebwagen*) as it costs about half the price. Departures from Jenbach are 22 minutes past the hour between 7.22 am and 6.22 pm. Austrian and European rail passes are not valid, but the regional VVT ticket, costing AS155/275 for one day/week is.

Buses also run down the valley every hour or so; the last from Jenbach at 9.05 pm and the last from Mayrhofen at 7.10 pm.

ZELL AM ZILLER

☎ 05282 • pop 2000 • 580m

A former gold mining centre and now the main market town in the valley, Zell am Ziller (also known as Zell im Zillertal) retains its sense of fun, especially during the Gauderfest (see Special Events later in this section).

Orientation & Information

The tourist office (☎ 22 81, fax -80, email tourist.info.zell@netway.at) is at Dorfplatz 3A, near the train tracks: from the Zell am Ziller train station, turn right along Bahnhofstrasse and right again at the end, a five minute walk. The office is open Monday to Friday from 8.30 am to 12.30 pm and 2.30 to 6.30 pm; in the high season it also opens on Saturday.

At the other end of Dorfplatz is the post office, with bus stops at the rear.

Things to See & Do

Off Dorfplatz is the **Pfarrkirche**, built in 1782 to an unusual circular design, with side altars all the way around and interior wall scenes in pastel colours by Franz-Anton Zeiller (1716-93). Outside, most of the graves feature similar but distinctive black metal crosses with tracery surrounds.

Pizza-Air is not some fancy new delivery service for Italian food; it offers piloted **paragliding** trips of three to 25 minutes duration (AS700 to AS1500). It is based in Pizza-Café Reiter (☎ 228 90, or mobile 0664-200 42 29), Zellbergeben 4, on the western side of the Ziller River.

One round of the Paragliding World Cup is held in Zell in late May. The tourist office will provide copious information on all activities and organise free guided walks in summer. Ask about the **Abenteuer Goldbergbau**, a two hour year-round tour of a nearby goldmine (AS130). Zell has a new Freizeitpark with adventure swimming pools, tennis courts and much else.

Special Events

Wafting around hot air currents (with or without the aid of a paraglider) is not recommended after a bellyful of Gauderbier, an incredibly strong beer (reputedly over 10% alcohol) brewed specially for the Gauderfest. This festival takes place on the first weekend in May (admission around AS80 per day), and participants show off long-established rural skills: playing music, dancing and drinking heavily. The lavish main procession (participants wear historic costumes) and wrestling (separate bouts for humans and rams) take place on Sunday.

Places to Stay & Eat

Camping Hofer (☎ 22 48, Gerlosstrasse 33) is east of the train tracks. Charges in winter/summer are AS67/62 per person, and AS85/65 for a site.

Rooms in chalet-style homes are found everywhere in and around Zell. Near the camp site is *Gasthof Waldheim* (☎/fax 23 22, Hainzenberg 2), offering rooms with shower/WC for AS280 per person; they have Tirolean music in the restaurant once a week. *Früstückspension Kerschdorfer* (☎/fax 25 11, Unterdorf 18) is 250m from Dorfplatz; head for the river and turn right. It has pleasant singles/doubles with private shower/WC for AS290/520, some with a balcony. There's a TV room, and a 1st floor terrace overlooking tennis courts and trees.

If you have more money to spend, look to the hotels on or near Dorfplatz, such as *Hotel Bräu* (☎ *23 13, fax -17*) where well equipped rooms cost AS720/1320, and there's off-street parking and a sauna (free for guests). Its restaurant has wood pan-elling, old stoves and a mid-price menu including Austrian and international dishes.

For self-caterers, there's a *Billa* super-market on Bahnhofstrasse. Large pizzas at *Pizza-Café Reiter* (see Things to See & Do earlier in this section) mostly cost between AS95 and AS115. It's a good après-ski place too.

Perhaps the best place for a cheap feed is *SB Restaurant* (*Unterdorf 11*), a self-service place on Dorfplatz, open daily from 11 am to 9 pm. It serves snacks, soups and salads plus simple meals costing from AS50 to AS85. It's an annexe to the *Zeller Stube*, a Gasthaus serving large portions for between AS80 and AS250.

Getting There & Away
The Triebwagen train to Mayrhofen (13 minutes) costs AS22 and the train to Jenbach (44 minutes) is AS51. There are special reduced fares on the Gauderfest weekend. Zell am Ziller is the start of the Gerlos Pass route to the Krimml Falls; most Bundesbuses start from Mayrhofen (see the Mayrhofen Getting There & Away section).

MAYRHOFEN
☎ 05285 • pop 3600 • 630m
A picturesque chalet village, Mayrhofen guards the approach to four Alpine valleys.

Orientation & Information
Am Marktplatz leads from the train station to Durster Strasse. The tourist office (☎ 67 60, fax -33, email mayrhofen@zillertal .tirol.at) is in Europahaus, a conference centre on Durster Strasse. It's open Monday to Friday from 8 am to 6 pm and in the high season on Saturday from 9 am to 1 pm and 3 to 6 pm and on Sunday from 9 am to noon. Pick up the comprehensive brochure *Mayrhofen from A-Z*; it's free and written in

English. Outside Europahaus is an elec-tronic 24 hour accommodation board.

Things to See & Do
Mayrhofen offers legion **skiing** and **walking** opportunities. It is also the home of the Zillertal mountaineering school (☎ 628 29) at Hauptstrasse 458. Inquire at the tourist office about guided walks (free with the Gästekarte). Return cable car fares on Ahorn and Penken are AS145 in summer; the peaks and valleys all around provide fine vistas.

Mayrhofen's local ski pass, valid for ski lifts on Ahorn, Penken and Horberg (28 in total), costs AS350 for one day. The resort also provides easy access to year-round skiing on the Huntertux Glacier, reaching an altitude of 3250m. In winter, a day pass costs AS420 and free ski buses go there (a 20km, 45 minute trip). In summer, a day pass costs AS350 but there are fewer lifts and Bundesbuses are the only transport (hourly, AS85 return).

Erlebnisbad is a swimming pool complex (☎ 625 59) at Waldbadstrasse, with indoor and outdoor pools, an aquaslide, whirlpools and saunas. There are two white-water rafting schools (details at the tourist office).

Keep an eye out for events staged in the Europahaus, such as Tirolean evenings.

Places to Stay
Campingplatz Kröll (☎ *625 80*), in the north of the village at Laubichl, is open all year. Camping costs AS55 per adult, plus AS25 each for a car and tent. Its Gästehaus has singles/doubles costing AS190/340 or AS280/520 with private shower/WC.

Duftner Rosa (☎ *637 08, Maidlergasse 547*) has the cheapest private rooms in the village centre. Simple rooms without shower are only AS160 per person.

Landhaus Alpenrose (☎ *622 19, fax 630 29, Wiesl 463*) is near the ski lift. All rooms bar one have a balcony and there are parking places. Rooms cost AS240 with a bathroom or AS220 with a shower cubicle.

The *Gästehaus Hornegger* (☎ *627 10, Brandberg Strasse 359*) is surrounded by fields but is still central. Rooms with shower/WC cost AS290/580, including a good breakfast.

Hotel-Garni Central (☎ *623 17, fax -33, Hauptstrasse 449*) offers modern, comfortable rooms with shower/WC, telephone, TV and balcony for AS400/760. Apartments can work out cheaper and have kitchens.

Places to Eat

Supermarkets include a *Billa* and a *Spar*, both on Brandberg Strasse.

China-Restaurant Singapore (*Scheulingstrasse 371*) is open daily from 11.30 am to 2.30 pm and 5.30 to 11.30 pm. It offers a range of set lunches including starter costing upwards of AS70 (there are menus in English).

Just off Am Marktplatz on Schwendaustrasse is *Zum Kaiserbründl*, open daily from 9 am to 1 am. Pizzas and Austrian dishes cost between AS70 and AS210, and there's a patio in the garden and a cheap takeaway counter. *Café Edelweiss* (*Brandberg Strasse 352*) serves a similar range and standard of food from AS80 to AS250.

Gourmets in search of Tirolean and international dishes might try the rather presumptuously named *Die Gute Stube* in the plush Hotel Elisabeth (☎ *67 67, Einfahrt Mitte 432*). It's open daily and main dishes are between AS230 and AS360. The hotel also houses *Mamma Mia*, serving cheap Italian food; it's open from 11 am to 12.30 am daily. You can choose any sort of pasta to go with your sauce, starting at AS75. As in other ski resorts, the restaurants may close during quiet periods between season, so phone ahead to check.

Entertainment

Mo's Eiscafe (*Hauptstrasse 417*) is an American-style bar with affordable food; there's free live music at 9 pm from Tuesday to Saturday (open daily). *Scotland Yard* (*Scheulingstrasse 372*) is a British-style pub, opening at 7 pm nightly.

Getting There & Away

By Triebwagen train, it's AS60 each way to Jenbach (55 minutes). Bundesbuses to Krimml Falls via Zell am Ziller and the Gerlos Pass depart up to five times a day in summer. Including the toll, the fare is AS132 (90 minutes; bikes can be carried) or AS194 return. See the Krimml Falls section in the Hohe Tauern National Park Region chapter for more details.

ACHENSEE

Achensee (Lake Achen) is the largest lake in Tirol, about 9km long and 1km wide. But size isn't everything – its beautiful situation amid forested mountain peaks is what brings in the tourists during summer. The Achenseebahn, a private cogwheel steam train, makes the trip from Jenbach (AS160 one way, AS230 return; only Bundes-Netzkarte and Österreich Puzzle rail passes valid). There are up to six departures a day between early May and late October. Boat tours of the lake cost AS130 and take nearly two hours, and the departure from Seespitz is co-ordinated with the arrival of the train from Jenbach. Several resorts around the lake offer water and winter sports.

KITZBÜHEL

☎ 05356 • pop 8200 • 762m

Kitzbühel was founded way back in the 9th century BC. It developed as a copper and mining centre, and is now a fashionable and prosperous winter resort. It's a place where you're assailed by plenty of glitz and glamour – not least in the tourist brochures.

Orientation & Information

Bahnhof Kitzbühel, the main train station (where you can hire bikes), is 1km north of the hub of the resort, Vorderstadt. The tourist office (☎ 621 55-0, fax 623 07, email office@tourist-kitzbuehel), Hinterstadt 18, is in the pedestrian-only part of the town centre. It's open Monday to Friday from 8.30 am to noon and 2.30 to 6 pm, and on Saturday from 8.30 am to noon. In the winter high season, it's open from 8.30 am to 6.30 pm on weekdays and between 8.30 am and noon and 4 and 6 pm at weekends. There's lots of information in English; the pocket-sized *Kitzbühel Portrait*, produced summer and winter, will tell you everything you need to know about activities and events. Staff will find accommodation free of charge, or you can make use of the electronic accommodation board and free telephone outside. The Gästekarte offers various discounts to overnighters.

Opposite the tourist office is a travel agency, Eurotours (☎ 713 04); it's open daily in the high season and changes money.

The post office (Postamt 6370) is on Josef Pirchl Strasse.

Things to See & Do

Picturesque gabled houses dominate the pedestrian centre – get that camera clicking! Kitzbühel has a couple of interesting churches just north of Vorderstadt. **Pfarr-kirche St Andreas** was built in the 15th century; Gothic features such as the nave remain despite the subsequent Baroque face-lift. Some of the interior frescoes are by local artist Simon-Benedikt Faistenberger (1695-1759) who added to the work of his grandfather, creator of the high altar. Faistenberger also had a hand in the adjoining **Liebfrauenkirche**, which has a sturdy square tower. Both churches are north of Kirchplatz, near the town centre.

Another cultural diversion is provided by a visit to the **Heimatmuseum**, Hinterstadt 34, including sections on local history and winter sports (entry AS30, students AS5). It's open Monday to Saturday from 9.30 am to 12.30 pm.

The tackier side of glamour can be seen in the Miss Austria beauty pageant, held over two days in early March. Late July sees tennis stars compete in the Austrian Open, which is held at the tennis stadium just off Jochberger Strasse.

Skiing

Kitzbühel runs are suitable for all ability levels. The ski area extends from 800 to 2000m and offers 160km of pistes accessed by 60 ski lifts. The Hahnenkamm (1655m), south-west of the town, was the first downhill piste to be opened in Austria in 1928.

There's a huge network of runs and lifts on the ridge up and behind. The Hahnenkamm professional downhill ski race takes place in January and is a spectacular event.

Across the valley to the north-east is Kitzbüheler Horn (1996m), which has mostly intermediate runs. This is also a favoured mountain for snowboarders. The ski region includes the peaks around the nearby resort of Kirchberg (see that section later in this chapter), and extends as far as Thurn Pass in the south, the gateway to Salzburg province and the Felber Tauern Tunnel.

A one day general ski pass costs AS420 in the high season (approximately Christmas, New Year and from February to mid-March) and AS390 at other times. Use of ski buses is included. The two day pass (AS800) includes free entry to the swimming pool. Before 21 December and after mid-March some pensions offer guests 50% 'Skihit' reductions on ski passes – inquire in advance if they're part of the scheme. A day's equipment rental is about AS180 for downhill gear or AS105 for cross-country skiing equipment.

The Kitzbüheler Alpen ski pass includes the whole region (260 lifts, 680km of runs) and costs AS1980 for six days.

Walking

Dozens of summer walking trails surround the town and provide a good opportunity to take in the scenery. The tourist office organises free guided walks for Gästekarte holders and supplies free walking maps. Get a head start to the heights with the three day cable car pass costing AS390 (AS490 including Bundesbus trips). Individual ascent tickets cost AS170 (AS150 with Gästekarte; children half-price) on either Hahnenkamm or Kitzbüheler Horn, and the descent is free with the ascent ticket. Of the two peaks, vista vultures generally consider the view to be superior from Kitzbüheler Horn: the jagged Kaisergebirge range dominates to the north, and beyond the Kitzbüheler Alps the Grossglockner and Grossvenediger are visible in the south.

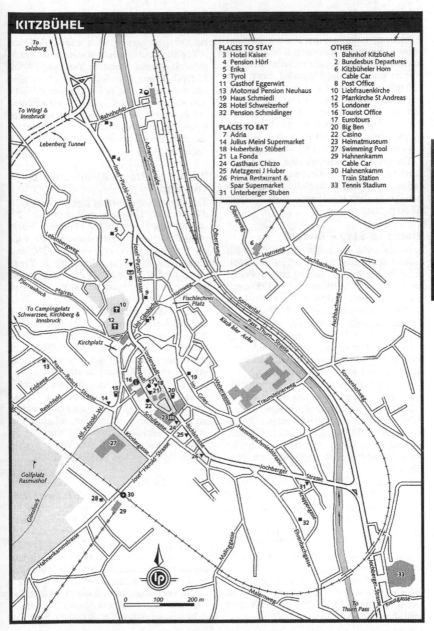

KITZBÜHEL

To Salzburg

To Wörgl & Innsbruck

Lebenberg Tunnel

To Campingplatz Schwarzsee, Kirchberg & Innsbruck

Kirchplatz

Golfplatz Rasmushof

Bahnhofstr

Josef-Pirchl-Strasse

Lebenbergweg

Pfarrau

Pfarraubach

Franz-Reisch-Strasse

Feldweg

Reischfeld

Alfr.-Petrold-Weg

Achenpromenade

Untr.Glättstoasse

Vorderstadt

Hinterstadt

Klostergasse

Josef-'Herold'-Strasse

Ölbergweg

Hornweg

Fischlechner Platz

Sonnental

Kitzbichler Ache

Pass-Thurn-Strasse

Im Gries

Weberbasse

Bichlstrasse

Schulgasse

Hammerschmiedstrasse

Jochberger Strasse

Kapsergasse

Ehrenbachgasse

Traunsteinerweg

Sonnenhofweg

Aschbachweg

Hornweg

Aschbachweg

Hahnenkammstrasse

Glanzbach

Malerweg

Malingasse

Jochberger-Strasse

Kreuzgasse

To Thurn Pass

PLACES TO STAY
- 3 Hotel Kaiser
- 4 Pension Hörl
- 5 Erika
- 9 Tyrol
- 11 Gasthof Eggerwirt
- 13 Motorrad Pension Neuhaus
- 19 Haus Schmiedl
- 28 Hotel Schweizerhof
- 32 Pension Schmidinger

PLACES TO EAT
- 7 Adria
- 14 Julius Meinl Supermarket
- 18 Huberbräu Stüberl
- 21 La Fonda
- 24 Gasthaus Chizzo
- 25 Metzgerei J Huber
- 26 Prima Restaurant & Spar Supermarket
- 31 Unterberger Stuben

OTHER
- 1 Bahnhof Kitzbühel
- 2 Bundesbus Departures
- 6 Kitzbüheler Horn Cable Car
- 8 Post Office
- 10 Liebfrauenkirche
- 12 Pfarrkirche St Andreas
- 15 Londoner
- 16 Tourist Office
- 17 Eurotours
- 20 Big Ben
- 22 Casino
- 23 Heimatmuseum
- 27 Swimming Pool
- 29 Hahnenkamm Cable Car
- 30 Hahnenkamm Train Station
- 33 Tennis Stadium

TIROL

0   100   200 m

There is an **Alpine flower garden** (free admission) on the slopes of the Kitzbüheler Horn, open in the summer. You can drive up as far as the Alpenhaus: the toll of AS30 per car and AS20 per person includes a reduction on prices in the restaurant there. The 120 different types of flower bloom at different times: most are in the spring (June), and summer (mid-July to mid-August), though some tardy species wait till autumn (September). Hahnenkamm has a free museum, open summer and winter.

The scenic **Schwarzsee** lake, about 3km north-west of the town centre, is a fine location for summer swimming. There are two beach complexes, each costing about AS40 per day.

Places to Stay – Budget

A single night surcharge (AS20 to AS40) usually applies on top of published rates, but try to negotiate in the low season. Prices are higher at Christmas and in February, July and August, peaking in the winter high season – top prices are quoted here.

Campingplatz Schwarzsee (☎ 628 06, *Reither Strasse 24*) is on the shores of the Schwarzee. It is open year-round and costs a hefty AS99 per person plus AS110 for a site. Local trains stop at Schwarzsee.

Many private homes have rooms available. They offer up to 10 beds apiece; AS200 per person is usual, though farther-flung farmhouses will be cheaper. *Haus Schmiedl* (☎ 627 48, *Im Gries 15*) is basic, but only one block east of Vorderstadt; singles/doubles with hall shower cost AS210/400.

Despite its three stars, *Hotel Kaiser* (☎/fax 647 08, *Bahnhofstrasse 2*) courts youth groups and backpackers, charging from AS180 to AS320 per person in four-bed rooms with bunks and shower/WC. Singles/doubles start at AS420/480. It's closed from mid-April to mid-May; phone ahead for availability.

Pension Hörl (☎/fax 631 44, *Josef Pirchl Strasse 60*) offers simple but pleasant rooms starting at AS270/500 or AS300/560 with shower.

Pension Schmidinger (☎ 631 34, *Ehrenbachgasse 13*) has good-value rooms for AS290 per person with shower/WC or AS240 without. Student discounts are available. *Motorrad Pension Neuhaus* (☎/fax 622 00, *Franz Reisch Strasse 23*) is also central; singles/doubles cost about AS380/760 with shower/WC, AS340/680 without. Prices drop in the low season and for longer stays and motorcyclists get a discount in summer. Both pensions are usually open in the off season.

Places to Stay – Mid-Range & Top End

The atmospheric *Gasthof Eggerwirt* (☎ 624 37, fax -22, *Untere Gänsbachgasse 12*), down the steps from the churches, has a painted façade. Single/double rooms with private shower/WC cost AS740/1360 and parking is available. Close by is *Tyrol* (☎ 624 68-0, fax 629 74-21, *Josef Pirchl Strasse 14*) where similar rooms cost from AS630/1260.

Hotel Schweizerhof (☎ 627 35-0, fax -57, *Hahnenkammstrasse 4*) is near the Hahnenkamm cable car station. Well-equipped rooms start at AS1550/2400, but ask about reasonably priced packages that include sports or beauty treatments.

Erika (☎ 648 85, fax -13, email hoteler ika@netway.at, *Josef Pirchl Strasse 21*) has excellent facilities such as an indoor swimming pool, sauna, steam bath, solarium and massage service. Rooms in this period building have private shower/WC and cable TV; half board starts at AS1500/2500.

Places to Eat

For self-caterers there is a *Julius Meinl* supermarket behind the tourist office on Franz Reisch Strasse and a *Spar* supermarket on Bichlstrasse.

Metzgerei J Huber (*Bichlstrasse 12*) is a shop with a sit-down section serving some inexpensive snacks and hot food. Along the road is *Prima*, a branch of the self-service chain, open daily from 9 am to 9 pm in the high season. In the low season it closes at 6.30 pm weekdays, at 3 pm on Saturday and all day Sunday. Prices are low (two-course set menus cost AS68 and AS78), even if the food is uninspiring. Look for reduced prices an hour before closing. There's a 1st floor sun terrace.

Huberbräu Stüberl (*Vorderstadt 18*) has more atmosphere. It serves good Austrian cooking at very reasonable prices, including excellent three-course menus, which cost between AS85 and AS115, and it's open daily. After the kitchens close at around 10 pm, it remains popular with drinkers till about midnight; beer costs AS32 for 0.5L.

Adria (*Josef Pirchl Strasse*) is near the post office and is open in the off season; it's less crowded than places in the centre. Italian dishes start at AS72 and it is open daily from 10 am to midnight.

La Fonda (*Hinterstadt 13*) is a surprisingly cheap Tex-Mex place with a bar, a pool table and a good atmosphere. Most meals cost less than AS80 and it's open from 5 pm (closed Tuesday).

Gasthaus Chizzo (*Josef Herold Strasse 2*) is a good place to try Austrian food, which costs from AS95 to AS245. Meals are served in a large room with lots of wood decor, and there's an adjoining bar.

Gasthof Eggerwirt (see Places to Stay – Mid-Range & Top End) offers quality local cuisine costing from AS100 to AS260 in frescoed rooms. The daily three course menu is around AS160.

Book ahead in the high season for *Unterberger Stuben* (☎ 661 27-0, Wehrgasse 2), a rustic but elegant restaurant; it's closed Wednesday lunchtime, on Tuesday and in the low season. It has an extensive menu, with dishes starting at AS100 up to a gourmet extravaganza costing AS820. Try some of the *Kohlroulade auf Trüffelkartoffel* (cabbage stuffed with veal, served with truffles and mashed potato) for AS185.

Entertainment

Kitzbühel has many discos and pubs – there are several on Hinterstadt. You can meet other English-speakers at *Big Ben* on Vorderstadt or at the *Londoner* on Franz Reisch Strasse, a bar usually crammed with young drinkers.

If you've more money than you need (unlikely in Kitzbühel), you can always lighten your pockets in the **casino**, Hinterstadt 24 (open nightly from 7 pm).

Getting There & Away

There are approximately hourly train departures from Bahnhof Kitzbühel to Innsbruck (AS144, 1¼ hours) and Salzburg (AS240, 2½ hours). Regional trains between Wörgl and Zell am See stop at Kitzbühel Hahnenkamm train station, which is closer to the town centre than Bahnhof Kitzbühel.

Getting to Lienz by train is awkward: two changes are required and it takes more than four hours. The bus is direct and takes only two hours leaving from outside Bahnhof Kitzbühel daily at 5 pm (AS154; buy the ticket from the driver). There's an additional weekend departure at 10.40 am. The bus to Kufstein costs AS84 (AS137 return) and takes one hour, though there are only one or two departures a day.

Heading south to Lienz, you pass through some marvellous scenery. Highway 108 (the Felber Tauern Tunnel) and highway 107 (the Grossglockner Road, which is closed in winter) both have toll sections; for details, see the Hohe Tauern National Park Region chapter.

KIRCHBERG
☎ 05357

This resort provides access to the same ski slopes as Kitzbühel and is a slightly cheaper base than its famous neighbour – as one skier described it, people wear Swatches not Rolexes.

The tourist office (☎ 23 09, fax 37 32, email kirchberg.tvb@netway.at) at Hauptstrasse 8 has an accommodation board outside with a free telephone.

Many travellers looking for work in the ski season base themselves here. A good place to start out is *Haus Austria* (*mobile* ☎ 0664-261 02 18, Lendstrasse 26-28). It provides beds in shared rooms with shower/

WC costing just AS110 per person for job seekers who arrive in autumn. Add AS30 for breakfast and AS60 for dinner. During the rest of the year singles/doubles cost AS260/300. You can inquire about the rooms at Haus Austria at the next-door *La Bamba* (*☎/fax 45 43*) as the two places work closely together. La Bamba is a bar with a pool table and also serves Mexican food (open from 4 or 5 pm).

Although smaller than Kitzbühel, Kirchberg can be lively at night. English-speakers generally crowd into the *London Pub* on Schlossergasse.

Getting There & Away
Ski buses make the 6km trip from Kitzbühel every 10 or 15 minutes during the day. Bundesbuses run during the summer. Train departures to Kitzbühel (AS19, 10 minutes) are hourly till 10.05 pm.

ST JOHANN IN TIROL
☎ 05352 • pop 6500 • 660m
Ten kilometres north of Kitzbühel, St Johann is a typical Tirolean chalet resort. Skiing here is suitable for all abilities, but especially intermediates; a day ski pass for the area costs AS330 (children AS175). The Baroque Pfarrkirche (1723-32) contains paintings and stuccowork by Simon-Benedikt Faistenberger.

Places to Stay & Eat
Accommodation is available to suit a range of budgets. To find somewhere to stay, go to the tourist office (☎ 63 33 50, fax 652 00), Poststrasse 2, which has an accommodation board with a free telephone outside.

The Huberbräu brewery has been soothing parched throats in St Johann since 1727. The best place to imbibe is the *Huberbräu Bräustuberl (Brauweg 2)*, above the brewery itself. The square-sided tower is 500m from the train station, and is clearly visible. Light or dark beer costs AS30 for 0.5L, and there are inexpensive Austrian favourites on the menu. It's open daily from 10.30 am to 10 pm. There's a good view over the town from tables inside or out.

Getting There & Away
St Johann is on the IC rail route between Zell am See and Innsbruck, and is the stop before Kitzbühel when travelling west. It is also at an important road junction, where the north-south highway 161 intersects with the east-west highway 312. Bundesbuses between St Johann and Kitzbühel (AS19) are frequent.

WÖRGL
☎ 05332 • pop 8500 • 511m
This town has nothing of interest to tourists but it is an important transport junction. At Wörgl the two-hourly 'corridor' train to Salzburg (via Germany) splits off from the hourly express route that stays in Austria. Road routes also split, with the A12 taking the more northerly route through Germany. Highway 311 stays with the other train line, but drivers have a third option of a route to Salzburg, highway 312 via St Johann and Lofer, which also passes through a section of Germany.

Contact the tourist office (☎ 760 07), Bahnhofstrasse 4A, if you anticipate having to spend the night in Wörgl.

KUFSTEIN
☎ 05372 • pop 15,000 • 503m
Tourists are drawn to Kufstein, near the German border, by its lakes and medieval castle.

Orientation & Information
Kufstein is the northernmost Austrian town in the Inn Valley. The train station is on the west bank of the Inn River, a three minute stroll from the core of the town, Stadtplatz, on the east bank.

This is where you'll find the tourist office (☎ 622 07, fax 614 55, email kufstein@ netway.at), Unterer Stadtplatz 8. Opening hours are Monday to Friday from 8.30 am to 12.30 pm and 2 to 5 pm; in summer it's open till 6 pm on weekdays and on Saturday from 9 am to noon. Staff will reserve accommodation without charging commission. If you decide to stay overnight, ask for the Gästekarte, which has different benefits in summer and winter. Many shops accept payment in Deutschmarks.

The post office (Postamt 6332) is on Oberer Stadtplatz and is open Monday to Friday from 7 am to 7 pm and on Saturday from 8 to 11 am.

Things to See & Do

Control of the town has been hotly contested by Tirol and Bavaria through the ages. The first recorded reference to the fortress, **Festung Kufstein**, was in 1205 when it was owned by Bavaria. Kufstein swapped hands twice before Maximilian I took the town for Tirol in 1504. The bulky Kaiserturm (Emperor's Tower) was added to the fortress in 1522. In 1703 the town was razed by fire during a siege by the Bavarians. The siege failed, but the Bavarians belatedly won the prize in 1809 during the Napoleonic Wars, only to have it returned to Austria five years later as a result of the Congress of Vienna.

Festung Kufstein dominates the town from its hill overlooking Stadtplatz. It's open daily from Easter to 26 October, and entry is a pricey AS100. Inside is a wide-ranging but not over-large **Heimatmuseum** that includes temporary exhibitions. Displays are imaginatively presented and incorporate creative lighting and excerpts of suitable music.

Elsewhere in the fortress you can view the **Heldenorgel** (Heroes Organ), below the Kaiserturm. This massive instrument has 4307 pipes, 46 organ stops and a 100m gap between the keyboard and the tip of the pipes; the resultant delay in the sounding of the notes makes playing it a tricky business. Keep an ear out for recitals at noon and (in summer) 6 pm – the music can easily be heard from Stadtplatz and elsewhere, though there's also a special listening auditorium on Stadtplatz by the church (AS10).

There is a lift to the fortress (AS30 return, closed in winter), but the 15 minute walk up is not demanding. After 5 pm and in the winter you can roam the castle grounds without paying, and enjoy the fine views of the valley below.

The **lakes** around Kufstein are an ideal destination for cyclists; you can rent bikes in the train station. Bundesbuses visit some of the lakes – get a timetable from the tourist office. The smaller, closer lakes are in the wooded area west of the Inn River, where there's a network of walking trails. Hechtsee, 3km to the north-west, and Stimmersee, 2.5km to the south-west, are both attractively situated, and both have swimming areas with entrance fees. Hechtsee is flanked by two other lakes, Egelsee and Längsee. Larger lakes such as the Walchsee, Hintersteinersee and the Thiersee are farther afield, to the east. A free city bus goes to Hechtsee twice a day in summer.

Places to Stay

There is a *camp site (☎ 622 29-55, Salurner Strasse 36)* by the river, 1km south of Stadtplatz. It charges AS53 per adult, AS32 per tent and AS38 per car.

For a budget place, ask at the tourist office for help in finding a private room in town or in a farmhouse. Prices range from around AS160 to AS250 per person.

Hotel Gisela (☎ 645 20, Bahnhofplatz 4) is an oldish building opposite the train station. According to local reports it's not very well run, but it is cheap and convenient, and probably OK for a short stay. Doubles with shower/WC cost AS580 and singles with hall shower are AS280.

West of the station (take the footpath over the tracks) and next to the church is *Kirchewirt – Toni Stüberl (☎ 625 12, fax 614 30, Zellerstrasse 17)*, with parking and balconies. Smallish rooms with shower/WC cost AS320/560.

A few blocks south-east of the fortress are a couple of places on Mitterndorfer Strasse. *Pension Striede (☎ 623 16, fax -33)* at No 20 costs AS295 per person, and is attached to an orthopaedic centre. Hospital-like rooms have a private shower/WC and a balcony or access to the large garden. *Fremdenheim Maier (☎ 622 60)* at No 13 costs AS320 per person, also with private shower/WC. It has a bar and restaurant (closed Saturday afternoon and Sunday).

To stay in the centre of town, go to *Hotel Gasthof Goldener Löwe* (☎ *621 81-0, fax -8, email stadthotels@netwing.at, Oberer Stadtplatz 14*). This attractive place has a restaurant and nearby garage parking. Single/double rooms starting at AS530/900 are equipped with shower/WC, TV and telephone.

Places to Eat

Less than 200m north of Oberer Stadtplatz, along Reischsstrasse, is the Inntal Center, with shops and a large supermarket. On the 1st floor *(not* the ground floor café with the same name) is a *Prima* self-service restaurant with a terrace. It has the usual wide choice offered by this chain plus daily set menus with soup or dessert costing AS68 and AS78. It's open normal shopping hours.

For more ambience, the area to explore is Unterer Stadtplatz. A pleasant pedestrian area, it has several restaurants with outside tables, and the prices aren't too bad. There's even a *Spar* supermarket at No 27 for picnics: it's open Monday to Friday from 8 am to 7.30 pm and on Saturday from 7.30 am to 1 pm.

Café Restaurant Auracher (Unterer Stadtplatz 11) serves Austrian dishes starting at about AS69, including daily specials and the option of reduced-price 'seniors' meals. Around the corner is a pizza restaurant where pizzas cost from AS60 to AS100; it's open from 11 am to 2 pm and 5 to 11 pm. Across the street is *Café Hell*, open daily till 6 pm. It provides a range of cakes and ice creams and similar meals to Auracher (it's under the same ownership). The best thing about this place is the outside terrace overlooking the river.

Getting There & Away

The trip to Kitzbühel (AS84, change at Wörgl) usually takes under an hour. The easiest road route is also via Wörgl.

Kufstein is on the main Innsbruck-Salzburg 'corridor' train route; trains to Salzburg (AS270, 1¼ hours) only run every two hours, but those to Innsbruck (AS127, 50 minutes) are hourly, as some trains

funnel down from Germany – Munich is on a direct line, a little over an hour away.

One or more Bundesbuses run to Lienz each day; they take 3¼ hours and call at Kitzbühel 75 minutes after departure. Buses leave from outside the train station.

KAISERGEBIRGE

Running east of Kufstein is the Kaisergebirge range, a rugged landscape soaring to 2300m and extending as far as St Johann in Tirol. It exercises walkers, mountaineers and skiers alike. The Kaisergebirge is actually two ranges, split by the east-west Kaisertal (Kaiserbach Valley). The northern range is the Zahmer Kaiser (Tame Emperor) and the southern is the Wilder Kaiser (Wild Emperor) – no medals for guessing which has the smoother slopes. The cable chair up Wilder Kaiser from Kufstein costs AS100 (AS130 return).

SÖLL

☎ 05353 • pop 3000 • 720m

Söll is a well known ski resort 10km south of Kufstein. It had a reputation for attracting boozy, boisterous visitors who were at least as interested in après-ski as *actuel-ski*. Recently, however, the resort has attempted to move more upmarket and regain its traditional Tirolean charm, with some success.

The highest skiing area overlooking the resort is Hohe Salve at 1827m. A one day ski pass for Söll lifts costs AS350. Söll has combined with neighbouring resorts Itter, Hopfgarten, Kelchsau, Westendorf and Brixen to form the huge Skiwelt area (88 lifts, 250km of pistes), for which a one day pass costs AS370, including free ski buses (for example, from Kufstein).

Staff at the tourist office (☎ 52 16, fax 61 80) in the centre of the village will provide you with further information and can help with finding accommodation.

Getting There & Away

Söll is on highway 312 between Wörgl and St Johann in Tirol. It is not on a train line, but Bundesbuses run from Wörgl every couple of hours (fewer on Sunday).

Western Tirol

The Inn River slices through mountain ranges from east to west until it reaches Landeck, at which point it twists south and goes into (or more accurately, flows out of) Switzerland. The Arlberg ski region traverses the provincial border between Tirol and Vorarlberg, and is covered in the Vorarlberg chapter.

STAMS
☎ 05263

Stams is a small town visited primarily for its **Cistercian abbey**, founded in 1273 by Elizabeth of Bavaria, mother of Conradin, the last of the Hohenstaufens. The exterior is dominated by two sturdy Baroque towers, added in the 17th century. The most impressive feature of the church interior is the high altar (1613): the intertwining branches of this version of the 'tree of life' support 84 saintly figures surrounding an image of the Virgin. Near the entrance is the **Rose Grille**, an exquisite iron screen made in 1716. Guided tours are possible (☎ 55 73).

The town's small tourist office (☎ 67 48) is only open on Monday, Tuesday, Thursday and Friday from 8.30 to 11.30 am.

Getting There & Away

Stams is in the upper Inn Valley, on the rail route between Innsbruck and Landeck, but only regional trains stop there. From Innsbruck train fares are AS68 one way, AS136 return. Both the A12/E60 and highway 171 pass near the abbey.

THE ÖTZTAL

The Ötztal (Ötz Valley) is the most densely populated of the three river valleys that run north from the **Ötztaler Alpen** (Ötztal Alps) until they drain into the Inn River. The Ötztaler Alpen guard the border to Italy and are home to numerous glaciers that shimmer between soaring peaks. The highest summit in the region is Wildspitze (3774m). Mountaineers, walkers and skiers can find plenty to occupy themselves. Contact the various tourist offices about accommodation; prices are 30 to 50% lower in summer.

The Ötztal is dotted with villages in picturesque locations along the banks of the Ötztaler Ache. From Umhausen it is possible to walk to the **Stuibenfall** waterfall in about 40 minutes: take the path by the tourist office (☎ 05255-52 09, fax -5, email umhausen@netway.at).

One of the most popular resorts for skiers is **Sölden** (1377m), which has a mountain annexe, Hochsölden (2090m). Some of the pistes are long and demanding and include glacier skiing; a one day ski pass costs AS400. The Giggijoch cable car climbs up to a special snowboarding area above Hochsölden. The Gaislachkogel cable car rises to 3058m and provides sweeping views of the whole Ötztaler Alpen. The tourist office (☎ 05254-22 12-0, fax 31 31, email oetztalarena@netway.at) can give details on local amenities, such as the mountaineering school and the ski schools. It's in the centre of Sölden, near the Giggijoch cable car.

Three kilometres south of Sölden is **Zwieselstein**, where the Venter Ache (Venter stream) branches to the south-west. Paths lead up to Wildspitze from the end of this valley.

Farther south is **Obergurgl** (1930m), another well known skiing resort, and the highest parish in Austria. Pistes are mostly suitable for beginners and intermediates and continue right to the edge of the village. Hohe Mut (2659m) is a justly famous lookout, accessible by chair lift. Obergurgl is actually at the head of the valley, but the road doubles back on itself and rises to **Hochgurgl** (2150m). Here the pistes are a little steeper and the views equally impressive. One tourist office (☎ 05256-466, fax 353, email tvbgurgl@netway.at) and one ski pass (AS420 per day) cover both resorts.

Just beyond Hochgurgl, where the road makes a sharp right-hand turn, is another viewing point, the **Windegg Belvedere** (2080m). The road continues into Italy where it joins the course of the Timmelsbach River.

TIROL

TIROL

Entombed in Ice

In September 1991 German hikers in the Ötztal Alps came across the body of a man preserved within the Similaun Glacier. Police and forensic scientists were summoned to the scene. They carelessly hacked the body out of the ice, not yet aware of the importance of the find. The body had been found some 90m within Italy, but was appropriated by the Austrians and taken to Innsbruck University to be studied.

Although a Swiss woman quickly identified the body as that of her father, who had disappeared on the glacier in the 1970s, experts initially decided it was about 500 years old: the ice man, nicknamed 'Ötzi' or 'Frozen Fritz', was thought to have been a soldier serving under Archduke Ferdinand. Carbon dating, however, revealed he was nearly 5500 years old, placing him in the late Stone Age.

Ötzi became big news. More so because the state of preservation was remarkable: even the pores of the skin were visible. In addition, Ötzi had been found with 70 artefacts, including a copper axe, bow and arrows, charcoal and clothing. Over the next six years he was thoroughly examined and analysed. Physiologically he was found to be no different to modern humans. His face was reconstructed, right down to his dark hair and blue eyes. X-rays showed he had suffered from arthritis and frostbite, and his ribs had been broken. He had died between late August and late September.

Despite these discoveries, the experts could not agree on what had brought Ötzi up 3000m into the Alps. Perhaps he had sheltered in a cave from a wintry squall, but had frozen to death. Or maybe he'd been a shaman, communing with spirits in the cave. A hunter, taking flight? A shepherd, returning with his herd to Italy from the summer pastures in Austria? And what had he been doing with a copper axe, when he predated the Bronze Age? Conflicting theories raged back and forth. The tussle over jurisdiction of the body was another issue. Innsbruck University reluctantly and permanently relinquished Ötzi to the Italians in 1998, when he became the centrepiece of a new museum in Bolzano.

Not everybody was worried about such controversies. Several Austrian and Italian women contacted the university shortly after the discovery and requested that they be impregnated with Ötzi's frozen sperm. The scientists could not oblige: although well-preserved in many respects, Ötzi no longer had a penis. 'We don't know if it's shrunk or has been eaten by an animal', one scientist explained. Alas, Ötzi would not become the oldest father in the world.

Getting There & Away

No trains enter the valley. Stop off at Ötztal Bahnhof on the Innsbruck-Landeck IC route and pick up a Bundesbus from there. In the summer and winter high seasons buses depart approximately hourly (only every two hours in the low season) and go as far as Obergurgl (AS94, 90 minutes). From approximately mid-July to mid-September two morning buses continue as far as Timmelsjoch, on the Italian border.

If you have your own transport you should be able to get at least as far as Hochgurgl all year, but the road beyond into Italy (via the Timmelsjoch Pass) is generally blocked by snow in winter. It's also a toll road; the one-way cost is AS85/65 for cars/motorcycles.

REUTTE

☎ 05672 • pop 5300 • 854m

Reutte is the administrative capital of the Ausserfern district. You might pass through the town if you're going to Füssen in Germany (home of King Ludwig's castles) or Ehrwald, but there's no compelling reason to linger. The tourist office (☎ 623 36, fax 654 22), Untermarkt 34, will try to convince you otherwise, especially by promoting nearby skiing and walking.

The town has a HI *Jugendherberge* (☎ 723 09, *Prof Dengel Strasse 20*), open from mid-June to late August.

Getting There & Away

Train routes to and from Reutte run via Germany. Bundesbuses (☎ 625 58) provide connections to many parts of Tirol, as well as to Füssen in Germany (AS32, or AS62 for a day return; 40 minutes).

Highway 314, running north-south, runs a couple of kilometres to the east of Reutte.

IMST

☎ 05412 • pop 7500 • 830m

Imst is beautifully situated and has a couple of interesting buildings in the old centre.

It's mainly known for its **Shrovetide festival**, the Schemenlaufen (ghost dance), which takes place every four years, the next being in 2000. The centrepiece of this occasion is a colourful procession of 'ghosts', which the less credulous spectator will realise are actually locals wearing elaborate costumes and masks.

The tourist office (☎ 69 10-0, fax -8) at Johannesplatz 4 can tell you about rafting on the River Inn.

Getting There & Away

Imst is linked with other parts of Austria by Bundesbus (☎ 662 66 for information), which is also how you can get to Imst from the nearest train station, Imst-Pitztal (AS18). Buses depart approximately every 40 minutes and it takes eight minutes to complete the 3km trip. The town is slightly to the north of the main east-west roads (the A12 and highway 171).

TIROL

Fantasy Castles

Some of Germany's prime attractions are a short trip by car or bus from Reutte, including the fantastic castles of Ludwig II (1845-86), last king of Bavaria and cousin of the Empress Elisabeth. Ludwig was found drowned in suspicious circumstances in Lake Starnberg. Perhaps it was as well that he died without heirs, for he was at least a couple of slices of Brot short of a Bavarian breakfast. The so-called 'mad monarch' had three obsessions in life: Richard Wagner, swans and building castles. The first two are clearly seen in the decorations of the third.

Ludwig's most famous creation is Neuschwanstein, a mishmash of architectural styles that inspired Walt Disney's Fantasyland castle. It is beautifully situated on a pine-clad hill, with a backdrop of shimmering peaks and a deep blue lake. Images of swans are everywhere, including in light fittings, door handles and basin taps. A large painted image on the walls of Ludwig's study indicates that his musings were generally less than erudite: it shows Ludwig being intimately attended by near-naked nymphs. The setting for the scene is a grotto, which is exactly what Ludwig had built in the next room.

A little way down the hill is Hohenschwangau. This was not built by Ludwig but is where he lived as a child. Structurally it is not as eccentric as its neighbour, but it is still well worth a visit. The castles are situated a few kilometres from Füssen and are accessible by guided tour (in English). Füssen is about 15km north of Reutte.

Farther east is Ludwig's Schloss Linderhof. This is visited mainly for its grounds, particularly the ludicrous Wagner-inspired golden conch boat. To get there from Reutte, take the minor road that skirts the northern shore of the Plansee.

LANDECK
☎ 05442 • pop 7500 • 816m

Landeck is an important transport junction, guarding the routes to Vorarlberg, Switzerland and Italy. The town has been standing sentinel for centuries, as demonstrated by its hillside fortifications.

Orientation & Information

Landeck is split into several spread-out communities. The town centre proper is east of the right-angle bend of the Inn River, where that river converges with the Sanna. The train station is 1.5km to the east: walk left on leaving the station and stay on the same side of the river (even though the main built-up area seems to be on the other side). City buses also make the trip (AS18 one way, AS33 return).

The main street in the centre is Malserstrasse, where you'll find the tourist office (☎ 623 44, fax 678 30, email tvbland eck@netway.at), open Monday to Friday from 8.30 am to noon and 2 to 6 pm and on Saturday from 8.30 am to noon. Ask about its free guided tours run from May to September. You can change money here, as well as in the post office (Postamt 6500) across the street.

Things to See & Do

The Stadtpfarrkirche, behind the tourist office, was built in 1493 and displays Gothic features such as network vaulting and a winged altar (16th century). On the hill above stands Schloss Landeck. Originally built in the 13th century, a fire destroyed it 500 years later and the subsequent rebuilding was not true to the original form. It now contains a museum of local history (open from late May to 26 October, AS25). There's a fine view of the valley from the castle tower.

Like everywhere in Tirol, Landeck attracts the odd skier or two. Free ski buses go to nearby Zams, where the Venet cable car rises to Krahberg (2208m). The ski area is not huge, but it has runs for all abilities; a one day ski pass costs AS295. In the summer, Landeck's main season, the same area is ideal for walking; the cable car costs AS130 one way or AS155 return.

Landeck also offers river rafting and kayaking: contact Sport Camp Tirol (see Places to Stay).

Places to Stay

Check the board outside the tourist office. The town has a Gästekarte.

Sport Camp Tirol (☎ 646 36, fax 640 37, Mühlkanal 1), off Flirstrasse on the north bank of the Sanna River, is open year-round. Prices are AS60 per person, AS40 for a car, and AS40 or more for a tent. It also has a couple of bungalows costing AS175 per person.

The best option for a cheap bed is to search for a room in a private house. The most likely hunting area is west of the Inn and south of the train line; there's a path leading uphill near the rail tracks (the road is less direct). Here you'll find *Landhaus Zangerl* (☎ 626 76, Herzog Friedrich Strasse 14), where rooms with balcony and private shower/WC cost just AS180 per person. On the same road is *Pension Paula* (☎ 633 71), offering singles/doubles for AS310/520.

Tourotel Post (☎ 69 11, fax -71, Malserstrasse 19) is attached to and run by the Wienerwald restaurant. It provides comfortable, renovated rooms with shower/WC, TV and telephone for AS690/980. There's a solarium and sauna on the premises.

Places to Eat

There are various places to eat near the post office along Malserstrasse. This street also has two supermarkets, a *Hofer* and a *Spar*.

Prima (Malserstrasse 36), a self-service place, has a varied menu. Two-course daily specials cost AS68 or AS78, and there's a salad buffet and pastries. It is open Monday to Friday from 7.30 am to 6 pm and on Saturday from 7.30 am to 5 pm.

Wienerwald (Malserstrasse 19) offers the usual chicken-oriented meals costing from AS80 to AS120; it's open daily between 7 am and midnight. *Gasthof Vorhofer* (Maisengasse 10), behind the tourist office, is a typical Austrian inn serving food starting at AS85 and staging periodic culinary festivals. It's closed Monday.

For more expensive, quality cuisine, try the restaurant in the four star *Hotel Schrofenstein* (☎ *623 95, Malserstrasse 31*).

Getting There & Away

Landeck is on the east-west IC express train route, 50 minutes from Innsbruck (AS127) and one hour and 50 minutes from Bregenz (AS200). Bundesbuses head in all directions, departing from outside the train station and/or from the bus station in the town (near where the railway track crosses the Inn; ☎ 644 22-30 for information). Several bus routes run south down the Inn Valley as far as Pfunds (AS67). Less frequent services continue into Switzerland and the Unterengadin (Engadine Valley; bus No 4220). Various buses run to Nauders, where you can transfer to an Italian bus to Merano in Italy (four or five a day; total trip at least 3¾ hours).

The A12/E60 into Vorarlberg passes by Landeck, burrowing into a tunnel as it approaches the town. Highway 315, the Inn Valley road, passes through the centre of town and stays on the east side of the river.

THE INN VALLEY

The Inn Valley (Inntal) extends for 230km within Tirol. Its initial stretch, south of Landeck, is the only section not shadowed by railway tracks. There's little of major interest in this region, though **Pfunds** is picturesque. Many homes here are similar in design to those found in the Engadine, a region in Graubünden, Switzerland, farther up the Inn Valley.

South of Pfunds, you have the choice of continuing along the Inn and into Switzerland or turning left to Nauders, and thereafter into South Tirol (Italy) by way of the

Reschen Pass (1508m; open year-round). Either road offers a corniche section with fine views.

Places to Stay

Pfunds has a HI *youth hostel* (☎ *05474-52 44, fax -4, Haus Dangl, No 347*) which is open all year. Beds cost AS200. The small tourist office (☎ 05474-52 29) near the bus stop can give you directions.

Getting There & Away

Regular buses run from Landeck through the valley and into Switzerland and Italy. See under Getting There & Away in the earlier Landeck section.

THE PAZNAUNTAL

The Paznauntal (Paznaun Valley) runs parallel to the Inn Valley, but farther to the west. It's divided from its more famous neighbour by the Samnaun mountain chain. The main settlement in the valley is **Ischgl** (population 1100; altitude 1400m). This attractive resort is considered to be one of Austria's best ski areas, despite (or because of) its relative isolation. It shares its skiing pass (AS440 for one day; reductions for seniors and children) with Samnaun, a duty-free area in Switzerland. The tourist office (☎ 05444-52 66, fax 56 36) in the centre of Ischgl can tell you more.

Getting There & Away

Only a secondary road (188) runs along the valley, crossing into Vorarlberg at Bielerhöhe where there are good views. This pass (2036m) is closed in winter and to caravans at all times. There's a toll of AS150 for cars and AS140 for motorcycles. The road rejoins the main highway near Bludenz. Regular Bundesbuses travel along the valley as far as Galtür (10km beyond Ischgl); they originate in Landeck.

TIROL

Vorarlberg

The small state of Vorarlberg extends from the plains of Bodensee (Lake Constance) in the north to the Silvretta group of Alpine peaks in the south. It offers many outdoor activities as well as access to Liechtenstein, Switzerland and Germany. The provincial capital, Bregenz, hosts a spectacular annual music festival.

The local people speak an Alemannic dialect of German which is closer to Schwyzertütsch (Swiss-German) than to standard German. This is a lingering legacy of Germanic Alemanni tribes who raided southwards and had settled in eastern Switzerland and Vorarlberg by the 6th century. In the early 15th century, Vorarlberg suffered great damage during the Appenzell War with the Swiss Confederation. Relations with its neighbour improved later: in 1918 the state became independent of Tirol and sought union with Switzerland, a move blocked by the Allied powers in the postwar reorganisation of Europe.

Orientation

At 2600 sq km, Vorarlberg is the smallest Austrian province after Vienna, and is home to 331,000 people. The Arlberg skiing region is split between Vorarlberg and Tirol, and is covered in this chapter.

Information

The provincial tourist board is Vorarlberg Tourismus (☎ 05574-425 25-0, fax -5, email info@vbtour.co.at), Postfach 302, A-6901 Bregenz. Prospective visitors with children should contact the office in advance for details of the many activities for kids available throughout the province during July and August. Also ask for the A3 size map of Vorarlberg, with sightseeing information (in English) on the reverse side.

Getting Around

There are six overlapping transport regions in Vorarlberg, covering the north-west

Highlights

- Enjoy the watery attractions of Bodensee

- Stroll around the quaint old town centre of Bregenz

- Experience a musical production on a floating stage during the Bregenz Festival

- Ski during the day and party at night in St Anton, one of Austria's top winter resorts

(Rheintal), west (Oberland), south (Bludenz), south-west (Walgau), east (Arlberg) and north-east (Bregenzerwald). Kleinwalsertal in the east is not covered by these regions. A travel pass for a single region costs AS90 (families AS120) for one day or AS190 for one week. A travel pass for all the regions costs AS150 (families AS180) per day or AS280 for a week. Children, seniors and disabled people pay half-price. Passes are available for city transport only in Bregenz, Dornbirn, Feldkirch, Bludenz, Lech and Götzis; day passes cost AS25 (families AS35) and one-week passes are AS70.

For further transport information, contact the provincial Verbundbüro (☎ 05572-336 60), Zollgasse 10, Dornbirn.

VORARLBERG

BREGENZ
☎ 05574 • pop 27,100 • 352m

Bregenz is a compact provincial capital. It was the seat of the counts of Bregenz after the 8th century and was part of Bavaria during the Napoleonic Wars.

Bregenz's most compelling attraction is Bodensee, which provides the setting for the annual music festival that places the town firmly on the cultural map of Austria.

Orientation
Bregenz is on the eastern shore of Bodensee. The town centre is about 10 minutes walk east of the train station. Local buses also make the trip (AS13, or AS25 for a day card); bus No 1 continues to the Pfänder cable car.

The newer part of town is near the boat landing stage; the older part, known as the Oberstadt, is inland.

Information
The tourist office (☎ 433 91-0, fax -10, email tourismus@bregenz.vol.at), Bahnhofstrasse 14, is open Monday to Friday from 9 am to noon and 1 to 5 pm, and on Saturday from 9 am to noon. During the Bregenz Festival, hours are Monday to Saturday from 9 am to 7 pm and Sunday from 4 to 7 pm. It provides good city maps, and listings of accommodation, consulates and activities. It also sells permits (AS80 per day) for fishing from the lake shore. The provincial tourist office (see the Information section at the beginning of the chapter), Römerstrasse 7/I, is open Monday to Friday from 9 am to 5 pm.

The post office (Postamt 6900) is on Seestrasse and is open Monday to Saturday from 7 am until 7 pm, Sunday and holidays from 9 am until noon.

Things to See & Do
The **Oberstadt** certainly merits a stroll; a good walking route is described in the tourist office leaflet 'Bregenz at a Glance'. Quaint homes with shutters and frescoes line cobbled streets; some houses are built into the old city walls.

The centrepiece and town emblem is the bulbous, Baroque **Martinsturm** (St Martin's Tower), built in 1599. It's topped by the largest onion dome in Central Europe. On the ground floor there's a church with 14th century frescoes, and on the upper floors is a small military museum, with the benefit of good views. It's open over Easter and from May to September, Tuesday to Sunday, from 9 am to 6 pm.

The half timbered **Altes Rathaus** (old town hall) was designed by the Baroque architect Michael Kuen and built in 1662. Farther south, off Thalbachgasse, **Stadtpfarrkirche St Gallus** (parish church) has a plain exterior, but the Baroque and rococo interior is surprisingly light and delicate.

Near the shore of Bodensee, the **Vorarlberg Landesmuseum**, Kornmarktplatz 1, outlines the region's history and culture, and has a collection of works by Swiss-born

VORARLBERG

BREGENZ

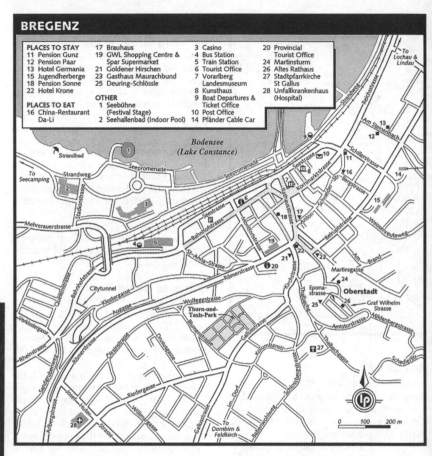

PLACES TO STAY	17 Brauhaus	3 Casino	20 Provincial
11 Pension Gunz	19 GWL Shopping Centre &	4 Bus Station	Tourist Office
12 Pension Paar	Spar Supermarket	5 Train Station	24 Martinsturm
13 Hotel Germania	21 Goldener Hirschen	6 Tourist Office	26 Altes Rathaus
15 Jugendherberge	23 Gasthaus Maurachbund	7 Vorarlberg	27 Stadtpfarrkirche
18 Pension Sonne	25 Deuring-Schlössle	Landesmuseum	St Gallus
22 Hotel Krone		8 Kunsthaus	28 Unfallkrankenhaus
	OTHER	9 Boat Departures &	(Hospital)
PLACES TO EAT	1 Seebühne	Ticket Office	
16 China-Restaurant	(Festival Stage)	10 Post Office	
Da-Li	2 Seehallenbad (Indoor Pool)	14 Pfänder Cable Car	

artist Angelika Kauffmann (1741-1807). It is open Tuesday to Sunday from 9 am to noon and 2 to 5 pm; entry costs AS20 (students AS10). A little way along Seestrasse is the **Kunsthaus**, a new art museum, open Tuesday to Sunday from 10 am to 6 pm (9 pm on Thursday; closed on Monday). Admission costs AS50 (students AS30). The **casino**, behind the train station, is open daily from 3 pm.

The peak of the **Pfänder** (1064m) offers an impressive view of the lake and beyond;

to the east, the Allgäuer Alpen range can be seen. A cable car operates year-round (except during maintenance) daily from 9 am to 6 pm (7 pm in summer). Fares are AS88 up, AS63 down and AS125 return. Walk south through the woods from the top station to find a viewing table. At the top there is also a *Greifvogelflugschau* (bird of prey show) from early May to late September, daily at 11 am and 2.30 pm (AS44, children AS23), and an animal park (free entry).

Bodensee Excursions

Bodensee (Lake Constance) is a major summer holiday resort for Austrian, German and Swiss tourists. As well as many water sports, there are interesting sights around the lake which can easily be visited by boat tour from Bregenz. There are plenty of youth hostels and cosy guest-houses if you want to stay overnight.

Considered in anticlockwise order (the direction the boats travel), the closest place to Bregenz is **Lindau** in Germany. Of interest in this island village are a Bavarian lion monument and an old Rathaus (town hall) with murals. **Friedrichshafen** is where Graf Zeppelin built his overgrown cigar-shaped balloons, an achievement commemorated in the town's Zeppelin museum. Picturesque **Meersburg** has many half-timbered houses built in the classical German style, and two castles overlooking the vineyard-patterned hills. **Überlingen** has the Cathedral of St Nicholas, with a four storey altar (dating from the 17th century) and a dozen side altars. **Konstanz** (Constance), the largest town on the lake and linked to Meersburg by car ferry, has a Gothic cathedral and a lively student population. The flower island of **Mainau** is close by.

Switzerland has fewer points of interest around the lake. The Swiss annexe of Konstanz, **Kreuzlingen**, contains nothing of great sightseeing importance. **Arbon** has a historical museum in a 16th century castle, and some half-timbered houses. **Rorschach** has a craft museum in its historic Kornhaus. A short train ride south from Rorschach is **St Gallen**, with an excellent late-Baroque cathedral and adjoining rococo library, plus many buildings with oriel windows in the old town centre.

The international **Bodensee Festival** takes place from early May to early June. Most events (concerts, cabaret, theatre etc) are on the German side of the lake, particularly around Friedrichshafen. The Bregenz tourist office has a comprehensive timetable of Bodensee boats, trains and buses.

There is an open-air bathing complex just to the north-west of the train station. The **Strandbad** (AS34, students AS28) is open from around mid-May to 1 September. It has lakeside access, a couple of pools and a self-service restaurant. Entry to the **Seehallenbad** (indoor pool) costs AS43 (students AS32; open in winter, closed on Monday).

Special **boat excursions** out of Bregenz are operated in the summer by Österreichischen Bundesbahnen (ÖBB; Austrian Federal Railways). Schedules are available from the boat station, train station or tourist office.

Sailing and **diving** are on offer at Lochau, 5km north of town.

Special Events

The Bregenz Festival takes place from late July to late August. Operas, orchestral works and theatrical productions, featuring international performers, are performed on the **Seebühne**, a vast, open-air floating stage at edge of the lake, behind the train station. Contact the Kartenbüro (☎ 407-6, fax -400), Postfach 311, A-6901 Bregenz, about nine months before the festival, for information and tickets, which cost anything from AS150 to AS1800.

Places to Stay

Seecamping (☎ 718 95, Bodangasse 7) is a lakeside camping ground 3km west of the train station. A site costs AS60 each per person, tent and car, plus AS17 tax. It's open from mid-May to mid-September. Cheaper camp sites can be found slightly inland.

The HI *Jugendherberge* (☎ 428 67, fax -4, Belruptstrasse 16A) is open from 1 April to 30 September. Yes, it comprises those two long sheds that look like army barracks. A bed costs AS126, plus AS32 or AS16 for sheets if required. It's closed from 9 am to 5 pm: reception (from 5 to 8 pm) is in the farthest hut, below which is a small room (door to left of the stairs) where you can leave your bags or wait during the day. Avoid the 10 pm curfew by getting a key.

Rooms in private houses cost around AS200 per person and are invariably good value; some are scenically situated on the lower slopes of the Pfänder. These, and holiday apartments, appear on the tourist office accommodation list. Stays of under three days may not be possible, or will incur a surcharge. Staff at the tourist office will book rooms for AS30 commission, which is an especially useful service during the festival. Expect prices during the festival to be higher than those quoted here.

Pension Gunz (☎ *436 57, Anton Schneider Strasse 38*) has simple singles/doubles with private shower for AS360/680. Reception is in the café downstairs; it's closed on Tuesday, so you may not be able to check in without phoning in advance.

Pension Sonne (☎*/fax 425 72, Kaiserstrasse 8*) is convenient, family-run and open year-round. A room costs AS440/800 with shower/WC and AS350/640 without.

Pension Paar (☎ *423 05, Am Steinenbach 10*) is a small two star place near the boat landing stage. Singles/doubles using hall showers cost AS360/640; it's open from May to October.

Hotel Krone (☎ *421 17, fax 459 43, Leutbühl 3*) is ideally central, though not famous for its friendliness. Doubles start at AS500 (AS720 with private shower/WC), and are huge and well-kept.

Hotel Germania (☎ *427 66-0, fax -4, email germania@bregenz.at, Am Steinenbach 9*) is a four star place that particularly tries to attract cyclists. It has a bike workshop, sells accessories and organises bike tours (rental available). It also has garage parking, a fitness room and a sauna, all free for guests. Healthy meals are offered in the quality restaurant (closed Sunday evening).

Singles/doubles with bathroom, TV and telephone start at AS790/1190.

Places to Eat

Some of the places mentioned under Places to Stay are worth trying for food.

In the *GWL shopping centre*, on Römerstrasse, there's a *Spar* supermarket with a self-service café-restaurant. Meals cost from AS55 to AS110, and there's a salad buffet for AS10 per 100g. It's open Monday to Friday from 9 am to 6 pm and on Saturday from 9 am to 4 pm. The pricier restaurant on the 1st floor has serving staff and access to a terrace.

Open daily, *China-Restaurant Da-Li* (*Anton Schneider Strasse 34*) has lunch menus on weekdays from AS65 including soup or spring roll.

Brauhaus (*Anton Schneider Strasse 1*) offers a beery atmosphere in its *Bräustubel*, or a calmer environment in its restaurant. Both have the same menu, offering Austrian and vegetarian dishes from AS75 to AS210. It's open daily from 9 am to 1 am.

Goldener Hirschen (*Kirchstrasse 8*) has good Austrian food costing from AS70 to AS155, served in a traditional room with heraldic crests, antlers and lots of wood. It's closed on Tuesday. *Gasthaus Maurachbund* (*Maurachgasse 11*) is also a good place for Austrian food, albeit more expensive (from AS115 to AS275; closed on Thursday).

The best restaurant in Bregenz is *Deuring-Schlössle* (☎ *478 00, Ehregutaplatz 4*). This elegant building in the old town is the refined setting for gourmet dishes from around AS220, including fish from the lake. You can opt to have a different, specially selected glass of wine with each course of a multi-course menu. The kitchen is open from noon to 2 pm and 6.30 to 9.30 pm (closed on Monday). Accommodation is also available.

Getting There & Away

For Rheintalflug flights (see Air in the Getting Around chapter of this book) go to the office at Bahnhofstrasse 10 (☎ 488 00).

Bundesbuses to destinations in Vorarlberg (including Dornbirn; 30 minutes) leave from outside the train station. Trains to Munich (AS397) go via Lindau; trains for Konstanz (AS168) go via the Swiss shore of the lake. There are also regular departures to St Gallen and Zürich. Trains to Innsbruck take less than three hours and depart every one to two hours. Trains to Bludenz (AS82), calling at Feldkirch en route (AS58), are more frequent; for return trips to both places buy a day pass instead. The train station has a bike rental counter (open daily from 6 am to 9.40 pm), a train information office and an ATM Bankomat.

Boat services operate from late May to late October, with a reduced schedule from early March. For information on this so-called *Weissen Flotte* (white fleet), call ☎ 428 68. From Bregenz to Konstanz by boat (AS143; via Lindau) takes about 3½ hours and there are up to six departures per day. Rail pass holders no longer get a discount on Bodensee ferries (except with the Bundes-Netzkarte, and with Eurail on a couple of Switzerland-Germany ferries).

A Bodensee pass (AS336 for 15 days) entitles the holder to half-price tickets on boats, trains and buses. Alternatively, buy transferable day passes (AS252 per set of three) valid for free travel on boats. Inquire also about the Bodensee family card, which allows free travel for children.

BREGENZERWALD

This is the area around Bregenz; it has a regional tourist office (☎ 05559-555-0, email bregenzerwald@bregenzerwald.at) in Egg. It is less wooded than the name implies (*Wald* means forest), being a combination of tree-lined hills, small villages and open pastures. Skiing (both downhill and cross-country) and walking are popular. The most dramatic natural feature is the **Rappenlochschlucht** (Rappenloch Gorge), through which the raging Dornbirner Ache flows.

The best source of information on exploring the gorge is the tourist office (☎ 05572-221 88, email dt@dornbirntourismus.vol.at) in the Rathaus in nearby

Dornbirn. Dornbirn itself is the largest town in Vorarlberg, with a population of 40,000, but has no major tourist sights.

Getting There & Away
Frequent IC trains stop at Dornbirn on their way to/from Bregenz, eight minutes away. Otherwise, private transport, Bundesbus, bike or foot is the way to explore the region. The Bundesbus from Dornbirn to Ebnit (at least four a day in summer, two in winter) will take you close to the Rappenlochschlucht.

FELDKIRCH
☎ 05522 • pop 29,000 • 450m
Feldkirch has a long history: its town charter was granted in 1218, and 'Feldkirichun' appeared in records as early as 842. It's also the gateway to Liechtenstein, a parcel-sized principality to the west famous for its postage stamps and wines.

Orientation & Information
The town centre is a few minutes walk south of the train station (turn left upon exiting). The tourist office (☎ 734 67, fax 798 67, email fktour@fkwerb.vol.at), Herrengasse 12, is in the centre; Herrengasse leads off from Domplatz (Cathedral Square). Opening hours are Monday to Friday from 9 am to 6 pm (closed for lunch in winter), and Saturday from 9 am to noon. Staff here can reserve rooms free of charge.

The post office (Postamt 6800) is opposite the train station.

Things to See & Do
The town retains an aura of its medieval past, with old patrician houses lining the squares in the centre, and a couple of towers surviving from the ancient fortifications. Both Neustadt and Marktplatz have arcaded walkways. The cathedral, known as **Domkirche St Nikolaus** (or St Nicholas' Church), has late-Gothic features and fine stained glass. The painting to the right of the altar is by local boy Wolf Huber (1480-1539), a leading member of the Danube school.

The 12th century **Schloss Schattenburg** dominates the town, and can be reached by stairs or road. This castle was the seat of the counts of Montfort until 1390. Extensive views can be enjoyed from the keep, and the museum (AS25, students AS10; closed on Monday and during November) has displays of religious art and historical artefacts. The castle is also the setting for folklore evenings (details available from the tourist office).

There's a **Wildpark** (animal park), in which 200 species roam, about 1km to the north-west of the town centre. Entry is free.

At **Laterns** there are ski slopes, with lifts up to 1785m. From Feldkirch it's about 30 minutes by car, but over an hour by Bundesbus (change at Rankweil). A one day ski pass costs A315 (family cards available).

Special Events

Since 1993 Feldkirch has hosted the **Schubertiade** summer music festival, formerly held at Hohenems. This annual event is a justly famous celebration of Schubert's work, and has been joined by similar events in Schwarzenberg (east of Dornbirn), and in Lindau and Achberg (both in Germany). It occurs in late June; bookings are accepted shortly after the preceding year's event has finished, and it's sometimes necessary to book this far ahead. Contact Schubertiade GmbH (☎ 05576-720 91, fax 754 50), Postfach 100, A-6845 Hohenems.

Other festivals include a **wine festival** on the second weekend in July and a **jugglers' festival** on the first weekend in August. In winter there's a Christmas market.

Places to Stay

The HI *Jugendherberge* (☎ 731 81, fax 793 99, Reichsstrasse 111) is 1.5km north of the train station (bus No 2 trundles past) in a historic building that formerly served as an infirmary. It has been completely modernised inside and has good facilities. A bed in a dorm (eight beds or more) costs AS134, and rooms (with at least two beds) are AS184 per person. Dinners cost AS77. There's a AS25 heating surcharge in winter,

and a price reduction of AS20 if you have your own sheets/sleeping bag. Curfew is at 10 pm, or you can get a key for AS14. Reception is open during the day, except on Sunday when it's closed from 10 am to 5 pm. The hostel is closed for two weeks in early December.

Private rooms are an economical alternative, but you'll find hotels and pensions surprisingly expensive – Switzerland may be nearby but that's no excuse to charge Swiss prices.

The best deals are away from the town centre: *Gasthof Engel* (☎ 720 56, Liechtensteiner Strasse 106) is less than 2km south-west of the centre in Tisis. It has singles/doubles for AS340/540 using hall shower, and a restaurant (closed Monday), garden and parking.

Gasthof Löwen (☎ 728 68, fax 378 57, Egelseestrasse 20) is 1km west of the centre, beyond the railway line. Rooms start at AS380/680 with shower and AS330/500 without. Its restaurant is closed on Monday.

Stadthotel Clunia (☎ 702 54, fax -4, Reichsstrasse 177) is a small place close to the train station, behind the post office. Small singles/doubles cost AS500/900 with private shower/WC and TV, or AS450/800 without.

Hotel Central Löwen (☎ 720 70-0, fax -5, Neustadt 17) has good-sized modern rooms with TV and en suite bathroom. Prices are AS660/1040 for singles/doubles, including use of the sauna and steam bath.

If you want to camp, *Waldcamping* (☎ 743 80) offers a quiet location for summer and winter camping in Gisirigen; take bus No 2 from the train station to the last stop (3.5km).

Places to Eat

There's a *Spar* supermarket (Neustadt 19) in the town centre. A larger supermarket and general store (selling everything from washing machines to bicycles) is *Interspar* (St Leonhards Platz), open weekdays from 9 am to 7.30 pm and on Saturday from 8 am to 5 pm. It has a cheap café with meals for under AS80.

China-Restaurant Asien (Schmiedgasse 4), open daily, has special weekday lunches from AS66. For Austrian food try *Johanniterhof (Marktgasse 1)*, with outside tables on the square and meals starting at AS82. *Gasthof Lingg*, overlooking Marktplatz from Kreuzgasse, is a bit more upmarket; it's closed on Monday.

Another place for good food but without excessive prices is the restaurant inside *Schloss Schattenburg* (closed on Monday and during November).

Getting There & Away

Two buses per hour (one at weekends) depart for Liechtenstein from in front of the train station, calling at Katzentrum (behind the tourist office) en route. To reach Liechtenstein's capital, Vaduz (AS32; 40 minutes away), it's sometimes necessary to change buses in Schaans. Liechtenstein has a customs union with Switzerland, so you will pass through Swiss customs before entering Liechtenstein. Trains to Buchs, on the Swiss border, pass through Schaans, but only a few stop there. Buchs has connections to major destinations in Switzerland, including Zürich and Chur. Bundesbuses to destinations in Vorarlberg also depart from outside the train station.

Feldkirch is on the main road and rail route between Bregenz (AS58) and Tirol.

BLUDENZ

☎ 05552 • pop 14,500 • 588m

Bludenz is a pleasant, unassuming town, standing at the meeting point of five valleys: Klostertal, Montafon, Brandnertal, Grosswalsertal and Walgau.

Granted its town charter in 1274, Bludenz was the seat of the Habsburg governors from 1418 to 1806. The arrival of the railways in the late 19th century allowed the town, a former silver mining centre, to become an important commercial base. At the same time there was an influx of settlers from the Val Sugana, in northern Italy, resulting in today's Italianate ambience. Textiles, chocolate and beer are Bludenz's main industries.

Orientation & Information

The town centre is on the northern bank of the Ill River. The tourist office (☎ 621 70, fax 675 97, email bludenz@bludenz.vol.at), Werdenbergerstrasse 42, is five minutes walk from the train station: walk up Bahnhofstrasse and turn left at the post office (Postamt 6700), on the corner of Bahnhofstrasse and Werdenbergerstrasse. The tourist office is open Monday to Friday from 8 am to noon and 2 to 5.30 pm, and (in July and August only) on Saturday from 9 am to noon. Post office hours are Monday to Friday from 7 am to 8 pm (cash counters till 5 pm), and Saturday from 8 am to noon. You can change money at the tourist office as well as the post office. East of the tourist office is a small pedestrian-only area.

Things to See & Do

One of Bludenz's most enjoyable features can't even be seen. Almost anywhere you wander in the centre, the rich, enticing aroma of chocolate will fill your nostrils. The **Suchard chocolate factory** is right opposite the train station; there are no conducted tours but there is a shop where you can buy the produce at decent prices. It's open Monday to Friday from 9 to 11.30 am and 1.30 to 4.30 pm (4 pm on Friday). Chocolate also plays an important part in the children's **Milka chocolate festival** in mid-July when 1000kg of the stuff is up for grabs in prizes.

For other attractions, join one of the free city tours organised by the tourist office; they depart from the tourist office at 10 am on Monday between June and September. The most distinctive architectural feature in town is the parish church, **St Laurentiuskirche** (Church of St Lawrence). It was built in 1514 and has an unusual octagonal, onion-domed spire. Several covered staircases lead up to the church; one has a war memorial within. There's also a **Stadtmuseum** (city museum) at Kirchgasse 9, open from June to early September (closed Sunday and holidays).

Bludenz is a good base for exploring the surrounding valleys. There are 15 **skiing**

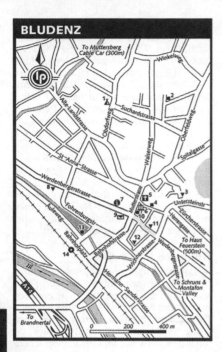

BLUDENZ

1	Camping Seeberger
2	Landhaus Muther
3	Schlosshotel
4	Haus Manahl
5	St Laurentiuskirche
6	Stadtmuseum
7	Tourist Office
8	Braugaststätte Fohrenburg
9	Post Office
10	Herzog Friedrich
11	SB Restaurant & Spar Supermarket
12	Gasthaus Hirschen
13	Suchard Chocolate Factory Shop
14	Train Station

areas within a 40km radius. Ski bus transport to/from Bludenz is sometimes included in the price of ski passes (for example with the AS360 one day pass for Sonnenkopf). Ski passes are obtained from the relevant resort; if you don't yet have your pass but are wearing ski clothes, you may not have to pay for the bus. A private train takes skiers to Schruns (AS28, 20 minutes; rail passes valid), a resort to the south-east. Walking and cycling are other popular activities. A cable car (☎ 668 38) goes up to Muttersberg at 1384m (AS100 return; reductions for seniors). Catch the No 1 bus to the cable car station or walk 1km north of the town centre.

Places to Stay

Ask for the *Gästekarte* if you stay overnight in town. *Camping Seeberger* (☎ 625 12, *Obdorfweg 9*) is open all year. It costs

AS228 for a two person site, and is about 600m north-west of the centre.

Staff at the tourist office will reserve accommodation without charging any commission. Private rooms are the best value for budget travellers, even though a surcharge of AS30 to AS50 per day usually applies for stays under three days. *Haus Manahl* (☎ 676 55, Herrengasse 11) is in the heart of town. The house is actually a few steps up from Herrengasse, with the No 11 on the garden fence. It has four doubles (hall showers) for AS460; single occupancy costs AS300.

Rooms in the suburbs give you more for your money but are less convenient. *Haus Feuerstein* (☎ 320 32, Schillerstrasse 22), 1km east of the pedestrian-only area, costs AS250/420 for singles/doubles. *Landhaus Muther* (☎ 657 04, Alemannstrasse 4) is a similar distance north. It's a pleasant place to stay and costs AS350/600 for rooms with private shower/WC.

The ideally central *Herzog Friedrich* (☎ 627 03-0, fax -81, Mutterstrasse 6) has a restaurant and sports three stars. The exterior is fairly stark but the rooms (AS490/880, with shower/WC, TV and telephone) betray a gentler touch.

Places to Eat

In the pedestrian-only area in the town centre is the Kronenhaus department store at Werdenbergerstrasse 34. Inside is a *Spar*

VORARLBERG

supermarket, open Monday to Friday from 8.30 am to 6 pm, and Saturday from 8 am to 1 pm (4 pm on Langersamstag). Upstairs is the *SB* self-service restaurant, with meals from AS66, a salad buffet, and alcoholic beverages.

Gasthaus Hirschen (Sturnengasse 19) has a restaurant serving Austrian food in comfortable, rustic surroundings. Meals cost from AS85 to AS230, including a cheap lunch menu with soup. It has a tree-lined beer garden across the street.

Braugaststätte Fohrenburg (Werden-bergerstrasse 53) is a large place with several sections, including garden seating. It has Austrian food for AS90 to AS210, but the main attraction is the many varieties of local Fohrenburger beer (from AS34 per 0.5L). That's hardly surprising as the brewery is across the road. Opening hours are Monday to Saturday from 9 am to midnight, and Sunday from 9 am to 11 pm.

Schlosshotel (☎ 630 16, Schlossplatz 5) is the town's only four star hotel and has one of the best restaurants in town.

Getting There & Away
Bludenz is on the east-west IC rail route, two hours from Innsbruck (AS210) and 45 minutes from Bregenz (AS82).

The east-west A14 road passes just south of the Ill River and the town centre. The Silvretta Road, leading to Silvretta Stausee (reservoir) and the Bielerhöhe Pass (2036m) into Tirol, heads south-east from Bludenz along the Montafon Valley. There's a toll for cars of AS150 to cross the pass (AS140 for motorbikes).

Bundesbuses run down all five valleys around Bludenz. Call ☎ 627 46 for details of prices and timetables.

BRANDNERTAL
☎ 05559
The Brandnertal (Brand Valley) runs south-west of Bludenz. Thirteen kilometres from Bludenz is the resort of **Brand** (elevation 1037m). It offers accommodation and winter sports (AS335 for a day skiing pass; reductions for young people and seniors).

There have been good reports about the ski school. Contact the tourist office (☎ 555-0, fax -20) for more information.

The climbing road from Brand provides good views and ultimately leads to **Lün-ersee** (sounds like a mad name for a lake). To reach the lake, at 1907m, you have to make a 400m ascent by cable car (mid-May to mid-October only). Lünersee has been dammed to produce hydroelectric power. Overlooking the lake is the Schesaplana peak (2965m), straddling the Swiss border, which can be climbed from the lake in about three hours.

Getting There & Away
There is a Bundesbus every one to two hours from Bludenz as far as Brand Inner-tal, a 40 minute journey. The further 20 minute bus trip (7km) to the Lünerseebahn cable car station is run only in the summer, as the road (1:8 gradient) is often blocked by snow in winter.

KLEINWALSERTAL
This oddity of a place is more German than Germany. It's in the east of Vorarlberg, most of it is surrounded by German territory. Furthermore, access from the south is precluded by the towering Allgäuer Alpen, meaning the only way in or out is through Germany.

The area is treated as de facto German territory when it comes to customs and border controls: you'll see it marked on maps as a *Zollanschlussgebiet* (customs connection area) or *Zollausschlussgebiet* (customs exclusion area), depending upon the orientation of the cartographer. This special status has existed since 1891, though it's no longer significant now there's an open border between Austria and Germany (under the Schengen Agreement; see the Visas & Documents section in the Facts for the Visitor chapter). Inevitably, the cultural and economic links of the place are with Germany rather than Austria. Here the Deutschmark is a more shopkeeper-friendly currency than the Schilling and, yes, they even speak German.

VORARLBERG

The region was settled by migrants from the Swiss canton of Valais (Wallis) in about 1300. The isolation of the area meant traditional culture, crafts and costume held sway until well into the 20th century. Nowadays, however, the population mainly ministers to the needs of affluent skiers.

Orientation & Information

The Kleinwalsertal occupies about 100 sq km, and has three main resorts: Riezlern (1100m), Hirschegg (1124m) and Mittelberg (1218m). Together they provide plenty of variety for downhill skiers (30 lifts linked by one ski pass) and cross-country skiers (over 40km of trails). Although the valley is scenically rewarding, it's probably not worth the effort of getting here unless you're a ski enthusiast. Nevertheless, each resort has a tourist office which will try to convince you otherwise; the largest is in Hirschegg (☎ 05517-51 14-0, email kwt_tourismus@verkehrsamt.vol.at).

Hotels and restaurants are expensive; the only cheap accommodation is in the mountains above the resorts.

Getting There & Away

Kleinwalsertal is on highway 201, running north from Mittelberg to Oberstdorf and Sonthofen in Germany. A right turn at Sonthofen (highway 199) leads to Reutte, in Tirol. A few kilometres farther north on the 201 is Immenstadt, where highway 308 will allow you to re-enter Vorarlberg from the north. The nearest rail line terminates at Oberstdorf, close to the Austrian border, from where there are infrequent buses to Kleinwalsertal. Another option is the Bundesbus from Reutte.

Arlberg Region

The Arlberg region, shared by Vorarlberg and Tirol, comprises several linked resorts and is considered to have some of the best skiing in Austria. St Anton is the largest and least elitist of these fashionable chalet resorts but, even there, budget travellers can kiss their savings goodbye.

The winter season is long, with snow reliable till about mid-April. Summer is less busy (and cheaper), though still popular with walkers. Even so, some of the restaurants, bars and discos that swing during the ski season are closed. Most others will close between seasons, and open for summer from late June to October. Many guesthouses and some hotels do likewise.

Skiing

A single ski pass covers the whole region. It is valid for 85 ski lifts, giving access to 260km of prepared pistes and 180km of high Alpine deep-snow runs. Passes cost AS470 for one day, AS1300 for three and AS2300 for seven. Skiers staying in Lech, Zürs, Stuben, St Anton and St Christoph get a reduction of nearly 10% on passes of six days or more, and low-season passes are also about 10% cheaper. The low seasons run from late November to pre-Christmas, early to late January, and from late March (after mid-April, the end-of season discount reaches 50%). Various other tickets are available, such as a cheaper beginner's ticket or a points-system ticket. Children get reductions on all tickets, and just AS100 buys a season ticket for kids aged under six. Seniors only receive reductions on some types of ticket.

Downhill equipment rental in the resorts starts at AS190 for skis and poles, and AS90 for boots.

Getting There & Away

The largest resort in the region is St Anton. For information about getting there see the St Anton Getting There & Away section. St Anton and St Christoph are close to the eastern entrance of the Arlberg Tunnel, the toll road connecting Vorarlberg and Tirol. The tunnel toll is AS130 for cars and minibuses. You can avoid the toll by taking the B197, but no vehicles with trailers are allowed on this winding road.

Getting Around

Bundesbuses run between St Anton and Lech, stopping at St Christoph and Zürs en route. They are hourly (till about 6 pm) in winter, reducing to four a day in summer; the full trip costs AS46, or AS90 return. Taking a minibus taxi, which can be shared between up to eight people, is another option: the trip from St Anton to Lech costs AS550. Some routes (for example from Zürs to Alpe Rauz, a ski area near St Christoph) are included with the ski pass.

ST ANTON AM ARLBERG
☎ 05446 • pop 2300 • 1304m

This is the largest resort, enjoying an easy-going atmosphere and vigorous nightlife. Actually lying across the border, in Tirol, St Anton has been characterised by its large population of Australasian 'ski bums' who work through the ski season, though their presence may gradually diminish now that jobseekers from the EU have an advantage in finding work.

St Anton's main problem is its popularity: try to avoid the weekend crowds. The resort is to host the World Alpine Skiing Championships in February 2001. This will probably mean that new facilities will be built before then. There are already plans to shift the rail track so that it runs beside the Rosanna River in the centre of the resort.

Orientation
St Anton is strung out along the northern bank of the Rosanna River. The train station is near the centre (a pedestrian-only zone) and most of the ski lifts. Farther east and on the northern side of the railway tracks is the area called Nasserein. Farther east still is St Jakob, with its own train station (only two local trains a day stop there) but no convenient ski lifts, except for a new run ending at Nasserein.

Information
The tourist office (☎ 226 90, fax 2532, email st.anton@netway.at) is in the Arlberg Haus, less than five minutes walk from the train station and set back from the road. It's open daily in the high season and from Monday to Friday between seasons, with hours adjusting to demand. Outside is an accommodation board, hotel lists and free telephone, so you can sort out somewhere to stay at any time.

The post office (Postamt 6580) is near the Rosanna River, off the northern end of the pedestrian zone. Sport Jennewein, a sports shop by the rail tracks, offers Internet access for AS5.

In the Ferienpark to the west of the town is St Anton's **museum**, devoted to skiing and local culture; entry is AS20.

Activities
St Anton went down in skiing history as the place where Hannes Schneider pioneered the Arlberg method in the early 20th century. The resort offers some of the best **skiing** in Austria for experts, with many difficult runs, both on and off-piste. In fact, St Anton is one of the best resorts in Austria for off-piste skiing on powder snow. Cable cars go all the way up to Valluga (2811m), from where experts can go off-piste all the way to Lech (with a ski guide only). Galzig (2185m) is along the way to Valluga. There are nursery slopes on Gampen (1846m) and Kapall (2333m), but generally the skiing is not suited to beginners.

Snowboarders favour Galzig or Rendl. The Rendl area is on the southern side of the Rosanna River, where lifts go as high as Gampberg (2407m). There's also a 4km-long **toboggan** run, starting from Gampen, swinging by the Rodelhütte restaurant and ending near the Alte St Anton restaurant. Toboggan rental at sports shops costs about AS60 per day.

Six kilometres to the west of St Anton is **St Christoph** (1800m), a much smaller place with only about six hotels, all expensive. It has lifts going to the Galzig area.

In the summer, **walking** takes over from skiing. A Wanderpass valid for all lifts costs AS390 for one week or AS750 for the summer season. A version of the one week pass costing AS510 includes admission to the swimming pool and other attractions.

Other activities include indoor swimming, sauna, massage, ice skating, tennis and squash.

VORARLBERG

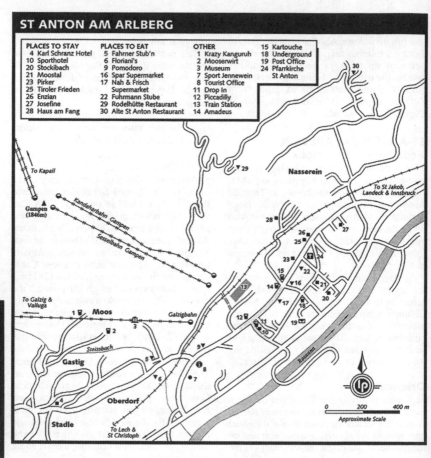

ST ANTON AM ARLBERG

PLACES TO STAY
4 Karl Schranz Hotel
10 Sporthotel
20 Stockibach
21 Moostal
23 Pirker
25 Tiroler Frieden
26 Enzian
27 Josefine
28 Haus am Fang

PLACES TO EAT
5 Fahrner Stub'n
6 Floriani's
9 Pomodoro
16 Spar Supermarket
17 Nah & Frisch
　　Supermarket
22 Fuhrmann Stube
29 Rodelhütte Restaurant
30 Alte St Anton Restaurant

OTHER
1 Krazy Kanguruh
2 Mooserwirt
3 Museum
7 Sport Jennewein
8 Tourist Office
11 Drop In
12 Piccadilly
13 Train Station
14 Amadeus

15 Kartouche
18 Underground
19 Post Office
24 Pfarrkirche
　　St Anton

Places to Stay

There are nearly 200 B&Bs in and around St Anton, and a similar number of holiday apartments. Accommodation prices are significantly higher in winter. The prices quoted here are the *per person* prices for the winter season. Many places have six different prices levels through the year – two in summer and four in winter. Summer prices can be as low as half the price of those in winter. Short stays usually incur a surcharge.

There's not a lot to choose between the simpler B&Bs in terms of value for money, but watch for those that charge extra to use a shower (the places listed below don't). To make a choice based on location you'll need the tourist office brochure showing prices and map positions – this is especially important as St Anton has no street names! (Houses are merely numbered instead.) Booking ahead will save a lot of frustration at peak times. Otherwise, check the board outside the tourist office for vacancies.

Places to Stay – Budget

Generally, the farther from the town centre, the cheaper it gets. St Jakob's main street has *Franz Schuler* (☎ *3108, No 33*) and *Josef Sailer* (☎ *2814, No 120*). Both cost around AS250 with hall shower; Sailer has some rooms with private shower. The Nasserein area is also slightly cheaper.

Not far from the pedestrian area, beyond Pfarrkirche St Anton in the main street, is *Enzian* (☎/fax *2403, No 177*), which has rooms with private shower/WC and TV for AS400. Next door is the pleasant *Tiroler Frieden* (☎ *2247, No 149*). It's full of groups for most of the winter, but gives low summer prices (AS140 per person on a shared-room basis) to those looking for work in November. *Josefine* (☎ *2651, No 334*), a little farther north-east, off the main street and opposite the Goldenes Kreuz guesthouse, is a friendly place, open in the winter only. It has just a few singles/doubles with hall shower for about AS300.

Stockibach (☎/fax *2072, No 484*) has rooms with shower for about AS430; it's down the turn-off by the church. The place is open in the off season, but is full with Swedish groups in February and March.

Places to Stay – Mid-Range & Top End

The following pensions have clean modern rooms with shower/WC and cable TV, and on-site saunas. *Pirker* (☎ *2310, fax -22, No 241*) is north of the pedestrian zone on the main street and has rooms for AS550; there's a restaurant next door. *Moostal* (☎/fax *2831, No 487*) is nearby, off the main street; rooms cost from AS560. *Haus am Fang* (☎ *3543; fax -4, No 508*), north of the main street, has a genial hostess and rooms from AS500 to AS600. All of these places have apartments available, but Haus am Fang and Pirker have no single rooms.

Sporthotel (☎ *3111, fax -70, No 52*) is a four star hotel in the pedestrian zone, with an indoor swimming pool, a sauna and lots of other facilities included in the price (AS1700). *Karl Schranz Hotel* (☎ *297 70, fax 2555-5, No 372*), up on the hill across the train tracks, is a better value four star hotel, though it lacks the swimming pool and is just under 1km from the town centre. This Tirolean-style place is owned by the eponymous skier; singles/doubles with half-board cost AS1300/2300 (credit cards not accepted). Reception closes at 10 pm.

Places to Eat

Some of the bars mentioned in the Entertainment section also serve food. Restaurants and bars are described in the *St Anton Revue*, a detailed free magazine in English available from the tourist office.

Self-caterers have a choice of supermarkets. There's a *Nah & Frisch* in the pedestrian zone, open daily till 6.30 pm (2 to 6 pm on Sunday). The nearby *Spar* supermarket is open daily from 7 am to 9 pm (10 am to 8 pm on Sunday and holidays), though hours reduce off-season. A deli counter inside serves hot takeaway lunches from Monday to Saturday (from AS55 to AS75); meals must be pre-ordered by 10 am, and collected between 11 am and noon. The other way to save money on food is to use the few takeaway stands in town, such as the one in front of the tourist office.

Restaurants have few or no dishes below AS100. English speakers favour *Pomodoro*, near the tourist office, where pizzas start at AS87. It's open from about 5 pm, depending on the season, and closed in summer. *Floriani's*, across the train tracks, has pizzas at similar prices, as well as Austrian food. It's open from about 4 pm and closed on Monday.

The train station has two linked restaurants, *Tiroler Wirtshaus Stub'n* and the quainter *Pasta Restaurant* (open evenings only, access from the platform). They share the same menu, which includes lots of vegetarian pasta dishes (from AS95), and the option of cheaper, smaller portions. *Fuhrmann Stube*, north of the pedestrian zone, is a family-friendly place with good value Austrian food. It's open daily.

Fahrner Stub'n (☎ *2353*), opposite Floriani's, is open from 3 or 5 pm (but usually closed in summer). This small, comfortable place serves good Austrian and Tirolean food for around AS100 to AS220.

Most of the top hotels in the resort have quality restaurants, which are also open for the summer season. *Jagerstube*, in the Karl Schranz Hotel (see Places to Stay), is open to non-guests and serves good local fare; it's open till 9pm. *Brunnenhof (☎ 2293)*, in St Jakob, has the reputation of being one of the best restaurants in Arlberg; main courses are around AS230 to AS320; it's closed from May to November.

Entertainment

Lively après-ski bars on the lower slopes include *Krazy Kanguruh* (which does good burgers too) and *Mooserwirt*. Each has a disco, and small beers cost around AS40. In the centre of the village is *Piccadilly*, with live music; it has a AS50 cover charge. *Underground* is another good venue (cover charge around AS50; free in the low season). It has two parts, each with live music: a bar/disco downstairs and a ground floor bistro with decent food (open from 4 pm to 3 am). *Kartouche*, by the Hotel Schwarzer Adler, has English football via satellite, and a DJ (free entry). Other dance venues include *Drop In* (small cover charge), open from around 9 pm to 3 am.

These places are usually closed throughout summer. An exception is *Amadeus*, a comparatively cheap bar (beer costs AS42 for half a litre) with pool tables, darts and taped rock music (open from around 9 pm to 2 am).

Getting There & Away

St Anton is on the rail route between Bregenz (AS88) and Innsbruck (AS131), less than 1½ hours from either place. For train information call ☎ 05446-2402 385. Bundesbuses depart from stands opposite the tourist office.

Getting Around

Free local buses go to outlying parts of the resort (such as St Jakob). They only run till about 6.30 pm, though in winter there's also an hourly night bus (AS30).

WESTERN ARLBERG
☎ 05583

The following resorts are all within Vorarlberg. The northernmost is Lech (1450m). This upmarket resort is a favourite with royalty, film stars, and anybody who likes to pretend to be such from behind dark glasses. Ski runs are mainly medium and easy, with some advanced off-piste possibilities. A cable car goes up Rüflikopf (2362m), but most of the lifts and runs are on the opposite side of the valley, on the Krigerhorn (2178m) and Zuger Hochlicht (2377m). The Lech ski school (☎ 23 55-0) can arrange helicopter skiing (from AS3200 for four people). Lech's tourist office (☎ 2161-0, email lech-info@lech.at) is in the centre of the resort, on the main road. It's open daily in the high season.

Six kilometres to the south lies Zürs (1716m), a smaller resort but with its own tourist office (☎ 22 45, email zuersinfo@zuers.at) on the main street. A cable car ascends to Trittkopf (2423m); across the valley the Zürsersee cable car climbs to 2206m, where there's a lake and a further lift to whisk you to 2450m.

One kilometre south of Zürs is the Flexen Pass (1773m), after which the road splits: the western fork leads to Stuben (1407m), the eastern to Tirol and St Christoph.

Places to Stay

The cheapest options are in private rooms or holiday apartments, but it's wise to book in advance. If you just arrive on spec, seek the help of the local tourist office; the Lech and Zürs offices each have an accommodation board and free telephone that are always accessible.

Despite its upmarket profile, Lech has a HI *Jugendherberge (☎ 24 19, fax -4)*, 2km to the north-east of the main resort in the village of Stubenbach. It's closed in May, June, and from mid-September to mid-December. It costs from AS280 per person (AS160 in summer); check-in is from 4 pm.

A bargain place near the centre of Lech, on the road towards Stubenbach, is *Pension Brunelle (☎ 29 76)*, charging from AS330 per person in winter and AS190 in summer. It has hall showers and there's a small sun terrace. *Haus Guido* (☎ 29 61) has rooms from AS440 (AS220 in summer) per person: it's north of the Lech River, just west of the centre.

Places to Eat

Eating cheaply in Lech is all but impossible, unless you stock up at one of the two *supermarkets* (open daily in season) in the centre. *Hager Metzgerei*, east of the post office, serves affordable hot and cold meats, including grilled chicken, but it's closed from 12.30 to 3 pm and after 6.30 pm. Farther along the same road is *Charly Pizza* (open daily), where most pizzas cost AS100 or more.

In the centre of Lech, by the Rüflikopf lift, is *Haus Ambrosius*. This place offers several choices costing less than AS100, including a salad buffet. If you have adequate funds there are plenty of quaint places in Lech where you can eat very well.

In Zürs, the *Sporthotel Zürser See* (☎ 227 10) occasionally lays on live music to entertain its alfresco diners.

Getting There & Away

The Flexen Pass is open all year, but has been known to be blocked in winter. Lech can also be approached from the north, via the turning at Warth (1494m). Infrequent Bundesbuses travel this route in summer, terminating at Reutte.

Salzburg Province

Salzburg province (Salzburger Land) has something to appeal to everyone. The city of Salzburg draws visitors from near and far; it's a tourist magnet second only to Vienna. To the east of the city is a sublime landscape of mountains and lakes, the Salzkammergut (covered in the following chapter). To the south are found mightier mountain ranges, towering above ski villages, cascading waterfalls and spa resorts. Salzburg province also has the lion's share of the Hohe Tauern National Park, covered in that chapter earlier in this book.

History

Salzburg, the provincial capital, was the chief town in the region as far back as Roman times. In about 696 St Rupert established a bishopric there, which was subsequently elevated to an archbishopric with authority over the dioceses of Bavaria.

The archbishops increasingly became involved in temporal matters and in the 13th century were granted the titles of Princes of the Holy Roman Empire. Their powers extended to an area up to twice the size of present-day Salzburg province and included parts of Bavaria and Italy.

Economic strength was built on mining: there were some gold mines (now within Tirol and Carinthia) but salt, the so-called 'white gold', had been more important since Celtic times. This is acknowledged in various place names (salt being *Hall* in Celtic and *Salz* in German). See the Salzkammergut chapter for more on salt mining.

Wolf Dietrich von Raitenau (1587-1612) was one of Salzburg's most influential archbishops and instigated the Baroque reconstruction of the city. However, an unsuccessful dispute with powerful Bavaria over the salt trade led to his imprisonment, during which he died.

Paris Lodron (1619-53) managed to keep the principality out of the Thirty Years' War. Salzburg was also neutral during the

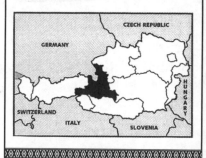

War of the Austrian Succession a century later, but about this time its power and prosperity began to diminish. During the Napoleonic Wars Salzburg was controlled by France and Bavaria, before becoming part of Austria in 1816.

Orientation

Salzburg province is roughly triangular and totals 7154 sq km. It's home to 482,000 people, and borders Germany and Italy.

The Salzach River rises in the south-west of the province, flows east, turns north at St Johann im Pongau, and marks the border with Germany north of Salzburg city.

Information

The provincial tourist board is Salzburger Land Tourismus GmbH (☎ 0662-66 88, fax -66, email info@szgtour.co.at), Alpenstrasse 96, A-5300 Hallwang bei Salzburg, Postfach 1. This office primarily deals with marketing and postal or telephone inquiries; Salzburg has an office for personal callers (see the Salzburg Information section).

Tourist offices sell the Salzburger Sommer Joker, a card which gives free entry to 100 attractions in Salzburger Land. It's available from 10 May to 26 October and costs AS495 for 16 days. It includes a 24 hour Salzburg Card (see the Salzburg Information section).

Salzburg

☎ 0662 • pop 144,000 • 425m

Salzburg stands in a breathtaking setting and contains magnificent architectural treasures. The Baroque spires of the old town, with the Festung Hohensalzburg (fortress)

SALZBURG PROVINCE (SALZBURGER LAND)

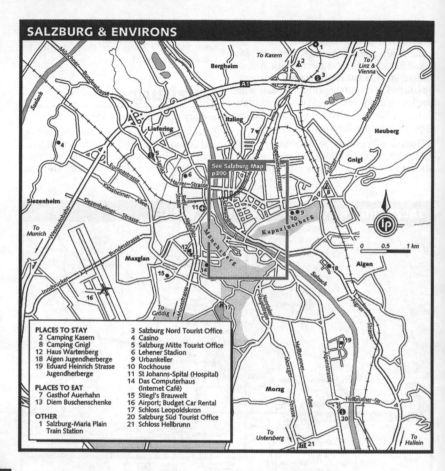

SALZBURG & ENVIRONS

PLACES TO STAY
2 Camping Kasern
5 Camping Gnigl
12 Haus Wartenberg
18 Aigen Jugendherberge
19 Eduard Heinrich Strasse
    Jugendherberge

PLACES TO EAT
7 Gasthof Auerhahn
13 Diem Buschenschenke

OTHER
1 Salzburg-Maria Plain
   Train Station
3 Salzburg Nord Tourist Office
4 Casino
5 Salzburg Mitte Tourist Office
6 Lehener Stadion
9 Urbankeller
10 Rockhouse
11 St Johanns-Spital (Hospital)
14 Das Computerhaus
    (Internet Café)
15 Stiegl's Brauwelt
16 Airport; Budget Car Rental
17 Schloss Leopoldskron
20 Salzburg Süd Tourist Office
21 Schloss Hellbrunn

rising behind, are an unforgettable sight. The old town is a UNESCO World Cultural Heritage site.

The city's descent into poverty in the 18th century was a blessing in disguise: it ensured that the historic buildings which are now attracting high-spending tourists were repaired rather than replaced. Another fortuitous factor in Salzburg's tourist pre-eminence was the birth of Wolfgang Amadeus Mozart (1756). The city that gave the composer scant encouragement during his lifetime now can't get enough of him (or the influx of well-heeled music lovers).

The influence of Mozart is everywhere. There is Mozartplatz with its Mozart statue, the Mozarteum music academy, Mozart's birthplace and Mozart's residence. His music dominates alike grand festivals and the more humble outpourings of street musicians. Chocolate confections and liqueurs are even named after him. Devotees of a rather different musical genre are also drawn to the city in surprising numbers: in

1964 the city and nearby hills were alive to filming of *The Sound of Music*.

Salzburg also offers plenty for budget travellers. It costs nothing to walk around and take it all in. Entering churches, courtyards and gardens places no demands on shallow pockets.

Orientation

The city centre is split by the Salzach River. The compact old part of town, mostly pedestrian-only, is on the left bank (known as *linkes Salzachufer*), with the Festung Hohensalzburg dominant on the Mönchsberg. Most attractions are on this side of the river. The new town, the centre of business, is on the right bank (*rechtes Salzachufer*), along with most of the cheaper hotels. You may also hear people talk of the old town as being on the south or west bank.

Mirabellplatz, on the right bank, is a hub for both local buses and city and country tours. A little farther north is the Hauptbahnhof and the Bundesbus station.

Information

Tourist Offices The main office (☎ 889 87-330) is at Mozartplatz 5, in the old town. It's open from 9 am to 7 pm daily between April and October (8 pm in July and August); between November and March, it's open from 9 am to 6 pm Monday to Saturday. In the same office is a ticket service (☎ 84 03 15) for events around town (commission charged).

The Salzburger Land Tourismus office (☎ 84 32 64) is in the same building; go through the door then right. It's open weekdays from 9 am to 5.30 pm, Saturday from 9.30 am to 3.30 pm and (July and August only) Sunday from 10 am to 3.30 pm.

Other information offices are at arrival points to the city:

Airport
(☎ 85 20 91), Innsbrucker Bundesstrasse 95, west of the city; open daily from 9 am (or earlier) to 9.30 pm
Hauptbahnhof
(☎ 889 87-340), platform 2A; open daily from

9 am to 8 pm (from 8.30 am to 9 pm between 1 May and 31 October)
Salzburg Mitte
(☎ 889 87-350), Münchner Bundesstrasse 1, in the north-west; open from 9 am to 7 pm daily between April and October (till 8 pm in July and August), and from 10.30 am to 5 pm Monday to Saturday between November and March
Salzburg Nord
(☎ 66 32 20), Autobahnstation Kasern, on the A1 from the north-east; open from around 9.30 am to 7 pm daily between June and September (flexible hours)
Salzburg Süd
(☎ 889 87-360), at Park & Ride Parkplatz, Alpensiedlung Süd, Alpenstrasse, in the south; open the same hours as Mitte

Staff at all of the branch tourist offices will book rooms in hotels and pensions, but not in private houses; commission is AS30. They also sell a town map, *Stadtplan*, for AS10, though you could just as easily make do with the free *Hotelplan*. The free *Salzburg Sights* leaflet details opening hours and entry fees for important sights.

Salzburg Information (☎ 889 87-0, fax -32, email tourist@salzburginfo.or.at), at Auerspergstrasse 7, is the head office. It deals with marketing and congress inquiries and isn't really set up for personal calls from tourists but it will send out tourist brochures (☎ 889 87-430, fax -435). Advance hotel reservations placed through this office (☎ 889 87-314, fax -32) are free. Opening hours are Monday to Thursday 8 am to 4 pm and Friday from 8 am to 1 pm.

Tourist offices and hotels sell the Salzburg Card. This provides free entry to 24 museums and sights, reduced entry to a further 10 attractions (such as the Marionetten Theater and the Untersberg cable car) and free public transport for the duration. The price is AS200/270/360 for 24/48/72 hours, and it could certainly save you money if you're busy enough. Salzburg Plus is a pre-paid card that has the Salzburg Card benefits but also covers meals, accommodation and shows. The price depends on what you include; inquire at tourist offices.

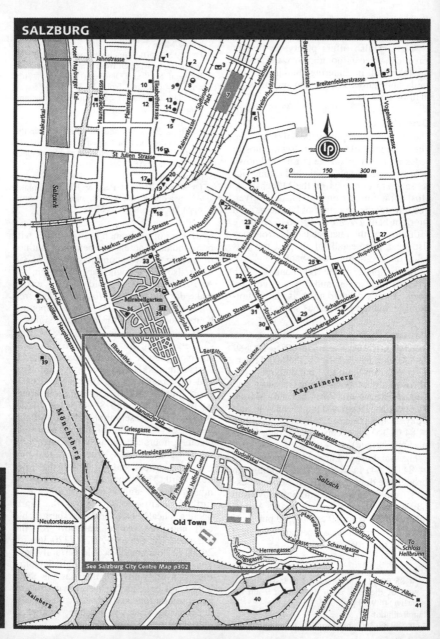

SALZBURG

See Salzburg City Centre Map p302

SALZBURG

PLACES TO STAY					
5	Elizabeth Pension	2	Eurospar Supermarket &	13	Hertz
6	Sandwirt		Restaurant	14	Avis
10	Pension Adlerhof	15	Billa Supermarket	16	Shell 24 Hour Garage
11	Haunspergstrasse	18	K+K StieglBräu	17	Motzko
	Jugendherberge		Restaurant	20	Motzko Reise
12	Hotel Hohenstauffen	19	Imbiss Wurst	21	Europcar
22	Lasserhof	24	Reform Haus Gfrerer	26	Salzburger
23	International Youth Hotel	25	Restaurant		Weissbierbrauerei
27	Pension Bergland		Wegscheidstuben	31	Norge Exquisit
29	Hotel Restaurant Hofwirt	28	Billa Supermarket	32	ÖKISTA
30	Wolf Dietrich			33	Kongresshaus
39	Schloss Mönchstein	**OTHER**		34	Albus Bus to Gaisberg
41	Jugendgästehaus	3	Post Office	35	Schloss Mirabell
		4	Eurodollar	36	Dwarf's Garden
PLACES TO EAT		7	Hauptbahnhof	37	HOSI
1	Bayerischer Hof	8	Bundesbus Station	38	Augustiner Bräustübl
		9	Laundrettes	40	Festung Hohensalzburg

Money Normal banking hours are Monday to Friday from 8.30 am to 12.30 pm and from 2 to 4.30 pm, though some branches and exchange offices are open longer, particularly in the summer. Currency exchange in the Hauptbahnhof is available daily from 7 am to 9 pm between June and October, and from 7.30 am to 8.30 pm between November and May. At the airport you can exchange money at the exchange booth daily from 8 am to 4 pm, and at the information office from 4 to 9.30 pm. Bankomats are all over the place. Some places will accept payment in Deutschmarks, but make sure the conversion rate is competitive.

American Express (☎ 80 80) is next to the tourist office at Mozartplatz 5. Amex travellers cheques are exchanged free of charge. It is open Monday to Friday from 9 am to 5.30 pm and on Saturday till noon. After hours (till 8 pm), Hotel Weisse Taube, Kaigasse 9, exchanges Amex cheques at the same rate (no commission).

Post & Communications The post office at the Hauptbahnhof (Bahnhofspostamt 5020), Südtiroler Platz 17, is open daily from 6 am to 11 pm, including for money exchange. In the town centre, the main post office (Hauptpostamt 5010), Residenzplatz 9, is open Monday to Friday from 7 am to 7 pm (money exchange till 5 pm), and Saturday from 8 to 10 am.

The Internetcafe (☎ 84 43 77, email computerhau@dascom.or.at) in Das Computerhaus, Rainbergstrasse 30A, has 30 computers and charges AS25 for 15 minutes. There's coffee but no café atmosphere; it's open daily from 9 am to midnight.

Travel Agencies ÖKISTA (☎ 88 32 52), at Wolf Dietrich Strasse 31, is open Monday to Friday from 9 am to 5.30 pm and on Saturday till noon. Young Austria (☎ 62 57 58-0), at Alpenstrasse 108A, is open from 9 am to 5 pm Monday to Friday and till noon on Saturday.

Bookshops Motzko (☎ 88 33 11), Elisabethstrasse 1, stocks English-language books. Across the road, on Rainerstrasse, is its travel branch, Motzko Reise. By platform 2A in the Hauptbahnhof is a Buch und Presse shop, with international newspapers and magazines.

Medical Services & Emergency The Landeskrankenhaus (hospital), St Johanns-Spital (☎ 44 820), is at Müllner Hauptstrasse 48, just north of the Mönchsberg;

☎ 141 for an ambulance. The police headquarters (☎ 63 83-0) are at Alpenstrasse 90.

Gay & Lesbian Travellers The Homosexuelle Initiative, HOSI (☎ 43 59 27), has a branch at Müllner Hauptstrasse 11. It runs a bar at this address on Tuesday, Wednesday, Friday and Saturday evenings.

Laundry Norge Exquisit (☎ 87 63 81), Paris Lodron Strasse 16, offers self-service machines (AS57 to wash, AS25 to dry and AS28 for soap), service washes (AS185) and dry-cleaning. It's open weekdays from 7.30 am to 6 pm, Saturday from 7.30 am to noon. There are also laundrettes opposite the Bundesbus station.

Walking Tour

Take time to wander around the many plazas, courtyards, fountains and churches in the Baroque old town. Start by absorbing the bustle of Domplatz and the adjoining Kapitelplatz and Residenzplatz. The hubbub from the market competes with the clip-clop of horses' hooves and the rhythms of classical and folk street musicians. Portrait painters add to the scene. Residenzplatz also has a Glockenspiel that chimes at 7 and 11 am and 6 pm.

The vast **Dom** (cathedral) on Domplatz has three bronze doors symbolising – from left to right as you face them – faith, hope and charity. Constructed between 1614 and 1657, this was the first building north of the Alps to exhibit the Italian Baroque style. Inside, admire the dark-edged stucco, the dome and the Romanesque font where Mozart was baptised. A museum, the Dommuseum, contains ecclesiastical treasures and oddities; it's open daily from early May to mid-October (entry AS40, students AS10).

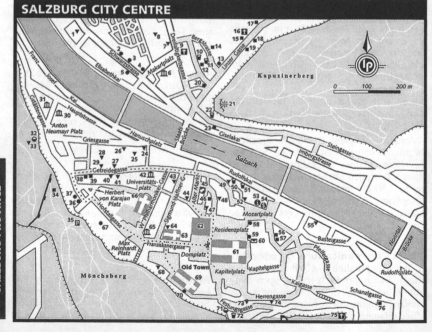

SALZBURG CITY CENTRE

From here, turn left at the first courtyard off Franziskanergasse for **Stiftskirche St Peter**, dating from 847. This abbey church is remarkable for its Baroque ostentation. It's as if a dozen churches have been plundered to fit this one out: the walls are crammed with emotive paintings, swirling stucco and 15 side altars. There's also a fine organ with a clock and statues. The graveyard contains catacombs (*Katakomben*) which you can visit, open daily from 10.30 am to 3.30 pm (entry AS12, students AS8).

Returning to Franziskanergasse is the **Franziskanerkirche** (Franciscan Church), revealing Romanesque, Gothic and Baroque elements spanning the 13th to 18th centuries. The best feature is the Baroque high altar, presumed to be by Johann Bernhard Fischer von Erlach, complementing the carved Madonna by Michael Pacher.

The western end of Franziskanergasse opens into Max Reinhardt Platz, where you'll see the back of Fischer von Erlach's **Kollegienkirche** (Collegiate Church) on Universitätsplatz. This church is considered an outstanding example of Baroque, more for its overall structure than for the décor. The interior is bare and almost austere compared with the fussy ornamentation of Stiftskirche St Peter. The few embellishments don't overly impress: the cherubs and clouds above the altar are a bit ridiculous and the gold figures below lack subtlety.

Walk left on leaving the church to reach Herbert von Karajan Platz and the **Pferdeschwemme** (horse trough), a rather elaborate drinking spot for the archbishops' mounts. Created in 1700, this is a horse-lovers' delight, with rearing, equine pin-ups surrounding Michael Bernhard Mandl's 'horse tamer' statue. (There are also impressive horsey fountains in Residenzplatz and Kapitelplatz.) From the horse trough, turn right around the corner and join the

SALZBURG CITY CENTRE

PLACES TO STAY		43	Hotel Elefant	23	Filmkulturzentrum
12	Schwarzes Rössl	44	Café Tomaselli	30	Carolino Augusteum
14	Trumer Stube	47	Café Konditorei Fürst		Museum
15	Institut St Sebastian	48	An Bing Chinese	31	Haus der Natur
17	Amadeus		Restaurant	32	Mönchsberg Lift
18	Junger Fuchs	49	Zum Mohren	35	Altstadt Garage
19	Goldene Krone	52	K+K Restaurant am	36	Festspiele Ticket Office
20	Hotel Gablerbräu		Waagplatz	37	Pferdeschwemme
34	Naturfreundehaus	55	University Mensa	42	Mozarts Geburtshaus
38	Blaue Gans	64	Toscana Café (Mensa)	45	British (UK) Consulate
39	Goldener Hirsch	68	St Peter's Stiftskeller	50	Tom's Bierklinik
46	Zur Goldenen Ente	73	Weisses Kreuz	51	Zur Frommen Hell
56	Hotel Wolf	74	St Paul's Stub'n	53	City & Provincial
57	Hotel Weisse Taube				Tourist Offices
76	Hinterbrühl	**OTHER**		54	American Express
		2	Mozarteum	58	Glockenspiel
PLACES TO EAT		3	Marionetten Theater	59	Salzburger Heimatwerk
1	Vegy Vollwertimbiss	4	Landestheater	60	Main Post Office
7	Café Gelateria San Marco	5	Salzburger	61	Dom (Cathedral)
8	Mozarteum Mensa		Landesreisebüro	62	Residenz Gallery
24	Zum Eulenspiegel	6	Mozart-Wohnhaus	63	Franziskanerkirche
25	Wilder Mann	9	Dreifaltigkeitskirche	65	Rupertinium
26	Julius Meinl Supermarket	10	Zum Fidelen Affen	66	Kollegienkirche
27	McDonald's	11	Schnaitl Musik Pub	67	Festspielhaus
28	Sternbräu	13	Inlingua	69	Stiftskirche St Peter
29	Eduscho	16	Sebastianskirche; Mausoleum	70	Catacombs
33	Café Winkler		of Wolf Dietrich	71	Festungsbahn
40	Nordsee	21	Kapuzinerberg Viewpoint	72	Stieglkeller
41	Fabrizi Espresso	22	Shrimps Bar	75	Stift Nonnberg

SALZBURG PROVINCE

bustling crowds along **Getreidegasse**, where many shops have distinctive wrought-iron signs. Some interesting passageways and courtyards lead from this street. Turning right down Alter Markt will bring you back to Residenzplatz.

Festung Hohensalzburg

In many ways the fortress is the high point of a visit to Salzburg. It takes about 15 minutes to walk up the hill from the old town, or you can use the Festungsbahn funicular (AS24 up, AS34 return) from Festungsgasse 4. The fortress was extended by the archbishops over many centuries. By far the greatest influence on its present structure was Leonhard von Keutschach, Archbishop of Salzburg from 1495 to 1519. His symbol was the turnip, and this peculiar motif appears 58 times around the castle, usually as a wall relief. Entry costs AS35, but it's worth paying another AS35 for the multilingual guided tour which allows entry to parts of the castle not otherwise seen.

The 40 minute tour covers grisly torture chambers, the lookout tower and impressive state rooms (featuring a fine tiled stove, Gothic carvings and Leonhard's state-of-the-art en suite toilet). At the end, you're left to roam around the two small museums covering history, arms, WWII photos and more tools of the torture trade. Allow about 20 minutes for each museum.

If you don't join the tour you can still enjoy the sweeping views, explore the courtyards, see a slide show (regular showings in English) and visit the terrace café. The outlook over the city is simply stupendous. The view to the south is of Alpine peaks, including the Untersberg (1853m); in the foreground, the isolated house in the middle of the big field once belonged to the archbishop's groundskeeper, though tour guides will tell you it was the home of the shunned official executioner.

The castle is open daily: between November and March from 9 am to 5 pm; in April, May, June and October from 9 am to 6 pm; and between July and September from 8 am to 7 pm. However, the museums

shut earlier, and if you take a late tour they may be closed by the time you finish; it's possible to see the museums before joining the tour.

Below the castle on its eastern side is **Stift Nonnberg**, the oldest convent in German-speaking lands, founded by St Rupert around 700. Its church is late-Gothic and you can often hear the choir singing in the afternoon.

Museums & Galleries

The outstanding **Haus der Natur** (Museum of Natural History) is at Museumplatz 5. You could spend hours wandering round its many diverse and well-presented exhibits. In addition to the usual flora, fauna and mineral displays, it has exhibits on physics and astronomy (unfortunately, all signs are in German) plus bizarre oddities such as a stomach-churning display of deformed animals on the 4th floor. There are also many tropical fish and an excellent reptile house with lizards, snakes and alligators. It even has an inexpensive terrace café with lunch menus. The museum is open daily from 9 am to 5 pm and entry costs AS55 (students AS30).

Overlooking Residenzplatz, the **Residenz** was built between 1596 and 1619. This less than modest home allows you to see the Baroque luxury which the archbishops endured while they sweated over sermons about humility and charity. Johann Michael Rottmayr created some of the frescoes, which are well complemented by rich stuccowork and furnishings. It can be visited by guided tour only, daily in July and August, and from Monday to Friday during the rest of the year; entry costs AS50 (with students/seniors AS40). Entry to the **Residenz Gallery** costs the same, or get a combined ticket for AS80 (concessions AS70). European art from the 16th to 19th centuries is on display and includes good Dutch and Flemish works. It's open daily from 10 am to 5 pm (closed Wednesday from October to March).

In the **Rupertinium**, Wiener Philharmoniker Gasse 9, 20th century art comprises its

Musical Mozartistry

Born in 1756, Wolfgang Amadeus Mozart was only 35 when he died in 1791, yet he composed some 626 pieces: 24 operas, 49 symphonies, over 40 concertos, 26 string quartets, seven string quintets and numerous sonatas for piano and violin. Praise for his music came from many quarters – Haydn believed him to be the 'greatest composer' and Schubert effused that the 'magic of Mozart's music lights the darkness of our lives'.

Mozart was born in Salzburg (one of seven children – only two survived) and started his career at a young age. His musician father, Leopold, taught him to play the harpsichord at age three. Two years later, Leopold gave his son a small violin, but without musical instruction. A few days afterwards, young Mozart asked a quartet if he could join in. The musicians laughingly agreed, but were amazed when the prodigy played his part perfectly. One went as far as to call it witchcraft. Mozart senior was quick to exploit his son's astounding talent. Along with Wolfgang's sister 'Nannerl' (four years older and also exceptionally gifted), they toured Europe, giving recitals and receiving plaudits wherever they went. Wolfgang spent one-third of his short life on the road.

At the age of six, Wolfgang performed for Empress Maria Theresa at Schönbrunn. By the time he was eight he had toured London, Paris, Rome, Geneva, Frankfurt and the Hague. Four of his sonatas were published before he turned nine, and he could write down complex pieces after just one hearing. In 1770, though only 14 years old, Mozart was appointed director of the archbishop of Salzburg's orchestra but departed for Paris in 1777 after an argument with his employer. In 1781 he settled in Vienna. Here Mozart had his most productive years, his music encompassing light-hearted and joyous themes, dramatic emotions and melancholic gloom.

Although always musically prolific, Mozart was a compulsive gambler and lost large sums of money at billiards, ninepins and cards. He was also something of a ladies' man – at age 24 he proclaimed, 'If I had married everyone I jested with, I would have well over 200 wives'. On 4 August 1782 in Stephansdom he married Constanze Weber, the younger sister of a former girlfriend.

Mozart was dispatched to the earth on a rainy December day after a meagerly attended and frugal funeral. His body was wrapped in a sack and doused with lime (in accordance with an imperial decree to prevent epidemics) before being buried in a ditch in St Marxer Friedhof (Cemetery of St Mark) in Vienna.

The film *Amadeus* (1985) by Milos Forman and Peter Shaffer, portrayed Mozart as infuriating, enthusiastic, volatile, emotionally immature and effortlessly gifted, an interpretation perhaps not far removed from the truth (though Mozart once announced that nobody had worked harder than himself at studying musical composition).

not particularly stunning permanent collection, but most space is devoted to temporary exhibitions. The building dates from the 17th century. Entry costs AS40 (students/seniors AS20). It's open daily in summer and Tuesday to Sunday the rest of the year, always with late opening (to 9 pm) on Wednesday.

The **Carolino Augusteum Museum**, at Museumplatz 1, has an interesting collection covering local history with recourse to paintings by local artists, Roman mosaics, Gothic statues and utensils. There are some illuminating room interiors evoking historical periods and styles but no signs in English. Admission costs AS40 (seniors AS30, students AS15) and it is usually closed on Monday, with late opening (to 8 pm) on Tuesday.

There are two Mozart museums; they're popular, pricey, and cover similar ground. Both contain musical instruments, sheet music and other memorabilia of the great man. **Mozarts Geburtshaus** (birthplace), Getreidegasse 9, is where he lived for the first 17 years of his life. Displays include the mini-violin that Wolfgang played as a toddler. Entry costs AS70 (students/seniors AS55).

The **Mozart-Wohnhaus** (Mozart's Residence), Makartplatz 8, has more to offer if you only want to visit one Mozart museum. This is where he lived for seven years from 1773 and the building has been restored to its original structure (it was damaged in WWII). Commentary and musical excerpts are delivered via hand-held devices activated by infrared signals and there's a slide show that concentrates on Mozart's early years and extensive travels. (The later Vienna-based years are all but ignored. I wonder why?) Entry costs AS65 (concessions AS50) or AS110 (AS85) in combination with the Geburtshaus. Downstairs is the **Mozart Ton- und Filmmuseum**, an archive of celluloid homages to the maestro. It's open on Monday, Wednesday and Friday from 9 am to 1 pm, and on Tuesday and Thursday from 1 to 5 pm; entry is free.

Less aesthetic tastes are catered for in **Stiegl's Brauwelt**, Bräuhausstrasse 9, a brewery tour and exhibition; two beers are included in the entry price (AS96). It's closed on Monday and Tuesday. You can also tour the **Mozartkugeln factory** (☎ 891 10), Hauptstrasse 14-16, where Mozart confectionery is made. However, it's south of town in Grödig, and there's no convenient public transport (bus No 55 to Grödig leaves you 15 minutes walk away).

Schloss Mirabell

This palace in Mirabellgarten was built by the worldly prince-archbishop Wolf Dietrich for his mistress, Salome Alt, in 1606. Salome bore the archbishop at least 10 children (sources disagree on the exact number – poor Wolf was presumably too distracted by spiritual matters to keep count himself). Johann Lukas von Hildebrandt gave the building a more Baroque appearance in 1727. Its attractive gardens featured in *The Sound of Music*, and this is a great place to relax. A most harmonious and oft photographed view is obtained from the northern end. Concerts and other extravaganzas are held in the palace. Take a look inside at the marble staircase, adorned with Baroque sculptures by George Raphael Donner.

From the palace, cross Makartplatz and have a look at the interior of the **Dreifaltig-keitskirche** (Holy Trinity Church). It was created by Johann Bernhard Fischer von Erlach at the end of the 17th century; the dome fresco by Rottmayr depicts a congested celestial scene.

Mausoleum of Wolf Dietrich

This restored mausoleum, in the graveyard of the 16th century Sebastianskirche (St Sebastian Church) on Linzer Gasse, has some interesting epitaphs. In a wonderful piece of arrogance, the archbishop commanded the faithful to 'piously commemorate the founder of this chapel' (that is, himself) and 'his close relations', or expect 'God Almighty to be an avenging judge'. Mozart's father and widow are buried in the graveyard.

Walks

The old town is squeezed between the Kapuzinerberg and Mönchsberg hills, both of which have a good network of footpaths. There is a viewpoint at the western end of the Kapuzinerberg, with ramparts built during the Thirty Years' War: climb up in 10 minutes from the stairs near the southern end of Linzer Gasse. On Mönchsberg, consider walking from Festung Hohensalzburg down to the Augustiner Bräustübl (see the later Entertainment section).

Language Courses

German language courses are offered at:

Amadeus Fereinschule
(☎ 88 24 70, fax 88 00 96, email amadeus@via.at) Dreifaltigkeitsgasse 9
IFK Deutschkurse
(☎/fax 84 96 11, email office@ifk-ca.ac.at) Prof Mag Linecker
Inlingua
(☎ 87 11 01, fax -85, email inlinguasbg@fc.alpin.or.at) Linzer Gasse 17-19

Prices and courses are comparable to those mentioned in the Language Courses section in the Vienna chapter. Inlingua gives a discount to Salzburg Card holders.

Organised Tours

One-hour walking tours of the old city (AS80) leave at 12.15 pm daily (except Sunday during winter) from the main tourist office. Coach tours of the city and environs usually have free hotel pick-up. Some also leave from Mirabellplatz, including the renowned Sound of Music Tour.

The Oscar-winning film was a flop in Austria but this tour is by far the most popular with English-speaking visitors. Tours last from three to four hours and cost around AS350. They take in major city sights featured in the movie and include a visit to the Salzkammergut. If you go in a group with the right mix of tongue-in-cheek enthusiasm, as I did, it can be brilliant fun. I have fond memories of elderly 'youths' skipping in the summer house, chanting 'I am 16 going on 17', and manic Julie Andrews impersonators flouncing in the fields, screeching 'the hills are alive' in voices to wake the dead. On the other hand, people who have gone with a serious group have reported it was quite dull. A lot depends on the approach of the guide; make sure they don't deviate from the itinerary unless you want them to.

Other organised tours explore Bavaria, Salzbergwerk (salt mines), the city and the Salzkammergut. Tours are conducted by various agencies, the most prominent of which are Salzburg Panorama Tours (☎ 87 40 29) and Salzburg Sightseeing Tours (☎ 88 16 16); both are on Mirabellplatz. The Sound of Music Tour arranged through the Jugendgästehaus (see Hostels – Left Bank in the Places to Stay section) is about the cheapest.

Special Events

The Salzburger Festspiele (Salzburg International Festival) takes place from late July to the end of August and includes music ranging from Mozart (of course!) to contemporary. This is the high point in Salzburg's cultural calendar, and a time when the city takes on a new vitality; just beware of the crowds. Several events take place each day in different locations with as many as 175 orchestral, operatic and theatrical events staged. Prices vary from AS50 to AS4200; the cheapest prices are for standing-room tickets, which can usually be pre-booked. Most sell out months in advance. Write for information as early as October to: Kartenbüro der Salzburger Festspiele, Postfach 140, A-5010 Salzburg. People under 26 years old are eligible for reduced price deals. Try checking closer to the event for cancellations – inquire at the ticket office (☎ 84 45 01, fax 84 66 82, email info@salzbfest.co.at), Herbert von Karajan Platz 11. Its opening hours during the festival are 9.30 am to 5 pm daily.

Other important music festivals are at Easter (Osterfestspiele for one week) and the Whit Sunday weekend (Pfingstkonzerte). Mozart Week is in late January.

The Sound of Dollars

The 1965 Hollywood musical *The Sound of Music* immortalised the story of the von Trapp family. The movie adaptation of their lives paints a vivid picture of a devoted family whose high morals guide them towards a better life but the events that lay ahead of the real von Trapp family followed a rather less harmonious course.

After climbing every mountain to escape Nazi-occupied Austria, the von Trapp family finally arrived in a tiny mountain village in Italy. Having left their home and fortune behind the family suddenly had to work for a living and so turned to singing. The Trapp Family Singers were an immediate success and began touring Europe and eventually America. The now famous family emigrated to America and in 1939 bought a farmhouse in the hills of Stowe, Vermont, and founded the Trapp Family Music Camp and Lodge.

In 1947 Captain von Trapp died, but the family continued performing until 1957, when the von Trapp children were free to lay down their lederhosen and concentrate on their own families and careers. Most of the children remained working together at the lodge, while Maria worked as a missionary in New Guinea with Father Wasner, the family priest who had fled Austria with them.

In 1980 the lodge burnt down, but the wealthy von Trapps were able to rebuild it as a 93 room hotel and cross-country ski centre with an additional 100 time-share apartments.

Maria von Trapp died in 1987 aged 82. Her death ignited a family feud which continues today and has split the once devoted von Trapp family in two. The dispute is over the value of stock held by the shareholders in The Trapp Family Lodge Incorporation. The holdings include the Trapp Family Music Camp Lodge, 2200 acres of land in Stowe and some of the royalties to the film.

The bitter dispute caused the family members to oust Maria's youngest son, Johannes, from his position as president of the corporation. He won back control but caused further tension by reorganising the company. Unhappy family members cashed in their shares in the corporation and were paid around US$2.5 million. The dissenting family members believed they were owed more and took the dispute to the highest court in Vermont. The court ordered The Trapp Family Lodge Inc to pay them US$3 million.

Despite the continuing family feud, the Trapp Family Lodge remains a major attraction. With 150,000 visitors a year, the hills of Vermont are alive, no longer to the sound of music, more likely to the rustle of money.

Wendy Bashford

Places to Stay – Budget

Accommodation is at a premium during the Salzburger Festspiele, so book ahead (you may pay even higher prices than the summer prices quoted here). In more expensive places, prices are usually lower in winter. The tourist office's *Hotelplan* lists accommodation options.

Camping Just north of the A1 Nord exit, *Camping Kasern* (*☎/fax 45 05 76, Carl Zuckmayer Strasse 4)* costs AS60 per adult and AS35 each for a car and tent; it's open from 1 April to 31 October. *Camping Gnigl* (*☎ 64 30 60, Parscher Strasse 4)*, east of Kapuzinerberg, costs marginally less and is open from mid-May to mid-September.

Hostels – Right Bank If you're travelling to party, head for the *International Youth Hotel* or Yo-Ho (*☎ 87 96 49, fax 87 88 10, Paracelsusstrasse 9)*. There's a bar with loud music and cheap beer (AS25 for 0.5L), and no school groups. Guests get some discounts on local sights. The staff are almost exclusively young, native English-speakers. Not surprisingly, it is very popular; phone reservations are accepted no earlier than one day before. Beds per person cost AS130 (eight bed dorm), AS150 (four bed dorm, own key) and AS180 (double room, own key). It's open all day, with check-in anytime, and there's a 1 am curfew. Showers cost AS10, lockers AS10 and sheets (if required) AS20. Breakfast costs from AS30 to AS55, dinner from AS60 to AS75. The hotel also organises outings and shows *The Sound of Music* daily.

The HI *Jugendherberge* (☎ 87 50 30, fax 88 34 77, Haunspergstrasse 27) west of the Hauptbahnhof is only open in July and August, and costs AS166 per person in four-bed dorms. Reception and check-in is from 7 am to 2 pm and 5 pm to midnight.

Institut St Sebastian (☎ 87 13 86, fax -85, Linzer Gasse 41) is attached to Sebastianskirche, literally and administratively, and has a student atmosphere. There's a roof terrace and kitchens, and dorm beds for AS180 plus AS30 for sheets. Singles/doubles cost AS380/660 with shower/WC or AS330/620 without. Prices are about 10% lower in winter and you can check in during the day. The church bells are loud in some rooms.

A further HI *Jugendherberge* (☎ 62 32 48, fax -4, Aigner Strasse 34), south of the Kapuzinerberg in Aigen, is slightly inconveniently located, though you can walk to the old town in 20 minutes (or take bus No 49). It's open year-round and a dorm bed costs AS160. Check in from 5 pm.

Hostels – Left Bank The *Naturfreundehaus* (☎ 84 17 29, Mönchsberg 19), also called Gasthaus Bürgerwehr, is clearly visible high on the hill between the fortress and Café Winkler. Take the stairway up from near Max Reinhardt Platz, or the Mönchsberg lift (AS16 up, AS27 return) from A Neumayr Platz. It offers dorm beds for AS120 (showers AS10) and marvellous views. It's open all day but has a 1 am curfew. The restaurant provides breakfast starting at AS30 and hot meals from AS65 to AS110. The restaurant is open year-round but rooms are only available from mid-May to 1 September; and it's sometimes too cold to open the dorms so phone ahead and check. It's closed on Friday.

The HI *Jugendgästehaus* (☎ 84 26 70-0, fax 84 11 01, Josef Preis Allee 18) is large, modern and busy, and probably the most comfortable hostel. Eight-bed dorms cost AS160, four-bed rooms are AS210 and two-bed rooms are AS260; prices are per person and reduce by AS10 after the first night. Telephone reservations are accepted, or you should turn up at 11 am to be sure of a bed – reception is only open in small shifts during the rest of the day. It has good showers, free lockers, a bar, a small kitchen, and bike rental for AS95 per day. Daily Sound of Music tours are the cheapest in town at AS300 for anybody who shows up by 8.45 am or 1.30 pm. The film is also shown daily.

South of town is a year-round HI *Jugendherberge* (☎ 62 59 76, fax 62 79 80, Eduard Heinrich Strasse 2); beds cost AS160 in six-bed dorms. Bus Nos 51 or 95 will get you within 400m (stop: Polizeidirektion). Check in from 5 pm.

Private Rooms Salzburg's private rooms aren't quite the bargain they are elsewhere in Austria: they cost a minimum of AS250 per person anywhere near the city centre. Ask for the tourist office's list of private rooms and apartments.

If you're prepared to travel, Kasern, just north of the city limits, offers better value and a choice of several places. They're all within 10 minutes walk of the local train station, Salzburg-Maria Plain (AS19 from the Hauptbahnhof) – some places will even pick you up from there if you call ahead. The terminus of bus No 15 would also get you within walking distance. From the train station, walk up the hill along Bergstrasse to find a couple of private rooms, including *Seigmann* (☎ 45 00 01) at No 66. At the crossroads, turn left to find places on Panoramaweg. *Christine* (☎ *45 67 73, Panoramaweg 3)* has two to four-bed rooms for AS180 per person; solo travellers will have to share. Next door at No 5 is *Lindner* (☎ *45 66 81)*, with similar prices. Both places work together (the hostesses are sisters) and each provides a good breakfast.

Hotels & Pensions *Sandwirt* (☎/*fax 87 43 51, Lastenstrasse 6A)* is behind the Hauptbahnhof and back from the street (behind the post office building). Singles/doubles/triples with hall shower cost AS300/460/600; doubles/triples with private shower are AS520/660 and four-bed rooms are AS800. The rooms are clean, and reasonably large and quiet. There's courtyard parking.

Rooms in the *Elizabeth Pension* (☎/*fax 87 16 64, Vogelweiderstrasse 52)* are generally smaller but they have been recently renovated and the hosts are friendly. It's close to the Breitenfelderstrasse stop of bus No 15, which heads for the town centre every 15 minutes. Singles/doubles cost AS300/460 with hall shower or AS350/540 with private shower cubicle. Singles are not available in July or August.

Schwarzes Rössl (☎ *87 44 26, fax -7, Priesterhausgasse 6)* is a student residence that welcomes tourists between July and September. Singles/doubles using a hall shower cost AS400/660.

Junger Fuchs (☎ *87 54 96, Linzer Gasse 54)* has singles/doubles/triples for AS260/380/480 without breakfast. The rooms are simple but fair-sized, and better than the cramped corridors would suggest. The good location for the price makes it one of Salzburg's better budget deals. Room rates are the same year-round.

Places to Stay – Mid-Range

Right Bank Near the Hauptbahnhof is *Pension Adlerhof* (☎ *87 52 36, fax 87 36 636, Elisabethstrasse 25)*. Some rooms are modern with pine fittings, others have old-style painted furniture, and there's a Baroque breakfast room. Singles/doubles with private shower/WC cost AS550/750;

two doubles costing AS650 use hall facilities. Parking is limited.

Goldene Krone (☎ *87 23 00, Linzer Gasse 48)* offers singles/doubles with private shower/WC for AS570/970; some of the rooms have church-like groined ceilings which add a bit of character. *Amadeus* (☎ *87 14 01, fax -7)*, across the road at No 43-45 offers a similar standard for about AS700/1150, but with cable TV. It has a dazzling blue and white breakfast room.

Cheaper, but about 1km to the east, is the *Pension Bergland* (☎ *87 23 18, fax -8, email pkuhn@sol.at, Rupertgasse 15)* which charges AS530/820 for rooms with private shower/WC and cable TV; some cheaper rooms don't have full private facilities. The owner painted the many pictures that hang in this friendly, family-run place. Bikes are available for hire at AS75 per day.

Close to the old town is *Trumer Stube* (☎ *84 47 76, fax 87 43 26, email hotel .trumer-stube@eunet.at, Bergstrasse 6)*. Also family-run, it provides clean and pleasant doubles with shower/WC and cable TV for AS980; single occupancy (AS725) is not possible in summer.

Hotel Restaurant Hofwirt (☎ *87 21 72-0, fax 88 14 84-99, Schallmooser Hauptstrasse 1)* has three-star singles/doubles costing AS780/1400 and there's free private parking.

Left Bank *Haus Wartenberg* (☎ *84 84 00, fax -5, Riedenburger Strasse 2)* offers renovated rooms in a building dating back 400 years. Singles/doubles with shower/WC cost AS650/980 and there are a few older rooms (with hall shower) for AS400/750. It's within walking distance from the old town, and many bus routes run along nearby Neutorstrasse.

The following places are in the old town: the convenience means you pay significantly more. Parking can be limited, though many places have an arrangement for reduced prices at parking garages.

Hinterbrühl (☎ *84 67 98, Schanzlgasse 12)* is fairly basic and one of the cheapest places in the old town. Singles/doubles with hall shower cost AS420/520; breakfast is AS50. Reception is in the restaurant downstairs, open daily from 8 am to midnight.

Blaue Gans (☎ 84 13 17, fax -9, *Getreidegasse 43*) underwent substantial renovations in 1998. Modern rooms with private facilities cost AS850/1250.

Hotel Wolf (☎ 84 34 53-0, fax 84 24 23-4, *Kaigasse 9*) charges from AS780/1040. Appealing rooms are kitted out in modern or rustic style and have shower/WC and cable TV.

Zur Goldenen Ente (☎ 84 56 22, fax -9, *Goldgasse 10*) is a 700-year-old house which retains some original features. Rooms are variable but all have private bath/shower and TV. Prices are around AS710/1150 and reception is open daily.

Places to Stay – Top End

All places mentioned here provide rooms with private bath or shower, WC, TV and telephone.

Lasserhof (☎ 87 33 88, fax -6, *Lasserstrasse 47*) offers singles/doubles starting at AS930/1540, some with balcony. Some rooms have a strange mix of modern and rustic fittings. There's free parking on the street, and bicycles are available free of charge to guests.

Wolf Dietrich (☎ 87 12 75, fax 88 23 20, email *office@salzburg-hotel.at*, *Wolf Dietrich Strasse 7*) has excellent facilities including an indoor pool, sauna, solarium, bar and restaurant. Rooms cost from AS1090/1760; the décor emulates homely elegance, with some success. Garage parking costs AS110.

Nearer the old town, *Hotel Gablerbräu* (☎ 889 65, fax -55, *Linzer Gasse 9*) offers reasonable-sized rooms for AS1200/1900 and a lobby area on each floor.

Hotel Hohenstauffen (☎ 87 21 93, fax -51, *Elisabethstrasse 19*) is convenient for the Hauptbahnhof and parking is no problem. The stylish rooms are all different – some even have a four-poster bed. Singles/doubles cost AS990/1690 in high season, AS790/1290 at other times.

Goldener Hirsch (☎ 84 84-0, fax 84 33 49, email *goldhirsch@salzburg.co.at*, *Getreidegasse 37*) is a classy five star hotel. There are 70 rooms in three houses; they vary in size and colour scheme but all are in rustic style. Rooms cost from AS2200/3400, excluding breakfast. The valet parking service costs AS250 per day.

Schloss Mönchstein (☎ 84 85 55-0, fax 84 85 59, email *moenchstein@salzburginfo.or.at*, *Mönchsberg Park 26*) is as palatial as the name suggests. Its pastoral, isolated setting favours those with their own transport, and it has a tiny chapel that's popular for weddings. Prices start at AS2200/2900 per person.

Places to Eat

Salzburg need not be expensive for food. Quick, hot snacks or meals can be had at various deli shops and outdoor food stands, including in the old town. While sightseeing, nip into *Eduscho* at Getreidegasse 34 (and elsewhere): a small, strong cup of coffee costs only AS8; you'll have to stand.

To experience the best of Salzburg's coffee-house culture, go to Alter Markt. *Café Tomaselli* is the city's most famous café; *Café Konditorei Fürst* is opposite and also worth a visit. Both have lots of cakes and outside tables, though only Tomaselli has English-language newspapers.

You can also eat at some of the places mentioned in the Entertainment section.

Self-Catering On Universitätsplatz and Kapitelplatz there are market stalls and food stands. Also in the old town, there's a small *Julius Meinl* supermarket on Griesgasse. On the right bank, there are several supermarkets on Schallmooser Hauptstrasse, including a *Billa*. *Eurospar* is opposite the Hauptbahnhof. The *Shell* garage on St Julien Strasse has a shop open 24 hours, with snacks, provisions and alcohol. A fruit and vegetable market occupies some of Mirabellplatz on Thursday morning.

Self-Service Restaurants The best budget deals are in the university Mensas.

Menus for students (show ISIC card) start from as low as AS38; non-students AS45 to AS65. Lunch is from 11.30 am to 2 pm, but don't go too late as the better choices run out. They're closed at weekends.

The *Mozarteum Mensa* is between the Aicher Passage and Mirabellgarten. On the left bank are the university Mensas. The most convenient is called the *Toscana Café*, in the courtyard at Sigmund Haffner Gasse 11. It's open weekdays from 9 am to at least 4 pm (3 pm Friday). The *Mensa* at Rudolfs-kai 42 has the same menus and opening times, except it's closed in summer.

The Hauptbahnhof houses *Eurosnack*, a burger and schnitzel place open daily from 10 am to 9 pm. *Eurospar*, nearby in Südtiroler Platz, has a self-service restaurant. Meals cost around AS60, reducing to half price after 6 pm (closes 7 pm weekdays, 5 pm Saturday). *Imbiss Wurst* (Rainerstrasse 24) serves half a chicken for AS32; it closes at 6 pm weekdays, noon on Saturday. There's a *McDonald's* at Getreidegasse 26 and a *Nordsee*, the fast fish chain, opposite at Getreidegasse 27.

Budget Restaurants – Right Bank *Café Gelateria San Marco (Dreifaltigkeitsgasse 13)* is a small place, good for cheap pizza/pasta from AS50 to AS75. It's open Monday to Saturday from 9 am to 10 pm.

Restaurant Wegscheidstuben (Lasserstrasse 1) has a three course menu for AS118, available lunchtime and evening. It's an archetypal Austrian place, frequented by locals, and is open Tuesday to Saturday from 8 am to midnight and Sunday lunchtime.

One of the few vegetarian places in town is *Vegy Vollwertimbiss (Schwarzstrasse 21)*. This shop and restaurant offers a salad buffet starting at AS35 and a lunch menu for AS87, including soup. It is open Monday to Friday from 10.30 am to 6 pm.

Reform Haus Gfrerer (Lasserstrasse 18) sells health food and natural products; it's open normal shop hours and has a dining area. It has lunch specials for just AS45 and a small/large salad buffet for AS29/55.

Budget Restaurants – Left Bank Salzburg has its share of Chinese restaurants. Some, like *An Bing (Goldgasse 13)*, have inexpensive weekday lunch menus.

Weisses Kreuz (☎ 84 56 41, Bierjodlgasse 6) offers Austrian food costing over AS100, but a better choice is its menu of Balkan specialities. *Djuvec* (rice, succulent pork and paprika) for just AS72 is excellent, or try the Balkan Plate (a selection of five dishes) for AS122. It's closed on Tuesday except in July and August.

It's almost as if they're trying to keep *St Paul's Stub'n (Herrengasse 16)* a secret. It's the yellow house, completely anonymous but for the 1st floor terrace tables and a tiny sign. Pasta and tasty pizzas (from AS72 to AS94) are served upstairs until late. Sitting together on long tables makes it easy to meet the students who drink there. It's open daily from 6 pm to 12.30 am.

Fabrizi Espresso (Getreidegasse 21) is a café in a small, pretty courtyard. This calm retreat serves hot meals (about AS90) as well as cakes and snacks. It's open daily until 7 pm (6 pm at weekends and holidays).

Hotel Elefant (Sigmund Haffner Gasse 4) has several dining areas, with the same menu. Meals, including vegetarian dishes, start at AS85. It's closed on Tuesday.

A cheap place, especially for its location in the old town, is *Wilder Mann (Getreidegasse 20)*; Austrian fare starts at AS60. It's closed on Sunday.

Diem Buschenschenke (Neutorstrasse 34) is a wine tavern of the type normally found in wine-growing regions. Compile a meal from the hot and cold buffets; it's open daily from 4 pm to midnight.

Worth visiting for the view, though the food's good value too, is the *Naturfreundehaus* restaurant, up on Mönchsberg (see under Hostels – Left Bank in the Places to Stay – Budget section).

Mid-Range Restaurants – Right Bank *Bayerischer Hof (☎ 469 70-0, Kaiserschützenstrasse 1)*, near the Hauptbahnhof, is surprisingly cheap considering it's part of a four star hotel. There are various choices below AS100, including the all-you-can-eat midday buffet. It's closed at weekends.

Further north is *Gasthof Auerhahn* (*Bahnhofstrasse 15*); it's reasonably priced (dishes AS80 to AS220) and has a good reputation locally. It's closed on Sunday evening and Monday, except in August.

K+K StieglBräu Restaurant (*Rainerstrasse 14*) has several large rooms, cheap weekday lunches, three choices of beer and a garden. The food is Austrian, costing from AS95 to AS195, and there's a salad bar. It's open daily from 11 am to midnight.

Mid-Range Restaurants – Left Bank *Sternbräu*, in a courtyard between Getreidegasse 36 and Griesgasse 23, is a bit touristy but it has a nice garden and many dining rooms. It serves good Austrian food, including fish specials, costing from AS85 to AS215; it's open daily from 9 am to midnight. The adjoining courtyard contains the self-service *Pavillon* (open Easter to September) and *La Stella*, serving Italian food.

St Peter's Stiftskeller, in a courtyard by Stiftskirche St Peter, is also rather touristy, but the outside tables are a fine place to relax on a sunny summer's day, to the accompaniment of live accordion music. There are also many evocative dining rooms; main dishes cost from AS98 to AS255 and it's open daily.

The atmospheric, rustic restaurant in *Zur Goldenen Ente* (see the Places to Stay – Mid-Range section) offers tempting meat dishes, including duck and boar. Meals start at around AS100 and the restaurant is closed at weekends.

Zum Mohren (☎ 84 23 87, Judengasse 9) is a cellar restaurant with some eye-catching decorative features. Most main dishes cost over AS170, though a few vegetarian or salad-based meals are only about AS100. It's closed on Sunday.

West of Mönchsberg is *Restaurant Wartenberg* in Haus Wartenberg (see the Places to Stay – Mid-Range section). It has an informal atmosphere and simple décor. The frills are reserved for the Austrian fare, which has a good reputation. There are

some cheaper choices, but most main dishes cost over AS150; it's closed on Sunday and holidays.

Top-End Restaurants *K+K Restaurant am Waagplatz* (☎ 84 21 56, Waagplatz 2) has something for most people: outside tables, medieval parties in the cellar (for groups), and cheapish food in the casual ground floor *Stüberl*. Upstairs, the restaurant is more formal and restrained. Quality Austrian fare is around AS130 to AS260 and there's a selection of wines and spirits.

Zum Eulenspiegel (☎ 84 31 80, Hagenauerplatz 2), by Mozarts Geburtshaus, has several floors. It has pleasant surroundings and good food costing from AS150 to AS270 (though the cartoon menus betray downmarket leanings). It's shut on Sunday.

Café Winkler (☎ 84 77 38, Mönchsberg 32) has the advantage of combining good views with appetising food but doesn't quite have the high-class ambience you would expect for the price. Meals start at AS265 à la carte or at AS120 from the simpler all-day menu, and the cover charge is at least AS25. It's closed on Monday.

The restaurant in the *Goldener Hirsch* (see the previous Places to Stay – Top End) offers gourmet food for about AS350. The hotel also houses *s'Herzl*, a less formal rustic restaurant with similar dishes and the same kitchen as its gourmet sibling, but much cheaper (dishes from AS130).

At the top of the range is the *Paris Lodron* restaurant in Schloss Mönchstein (see the previous Places to Stay – Top End). Enjoy lavishly prepared food in an opulent setting, all shining silverware and soft classical music. Dishes top AS300 and are presented with pride and panache. Reserve in advance.

Entertainment
Music & Theatre The *Marionetten Theater* (☎ 87 24 06-0, Schwarzstrasse 24) has been delighting visitors for 80 years. These ingenious puppets sing and dance to recordings of famous operas and ballets from May to September, and at Christmas,

Easter and during Mozart Week in January. Tickets are pricey at AS250 to AS480. Less frivolous musical events are staged at the next door *Mozarteum* (☎ *87 31 54*). Special Mozart concerts are performed at various locations round town, sometimes in historical costumes.

The *Landestheater* (☎ *87 15 12, Schwarzstrasse 22*) sometimes has musicals and ballets as well as plays. The *Festspielhaus* (☎ *84 45 01, Hofstallgasse 1*) is the main venue for operas and operettas and is built into the sheer sides of the Mönchsberg.

Szene (☎ *84 34 48, Anton Neumayr Platz 2*) stages avant-garde productions in summer, encompassing dance, theatre and music. The *Kongresshaus* (☎ *889 87, Auerspergstrasse 7*) has occasional cultural and artistic presentations.

Urbankeller (☎ *87 08 94, Schallmooser Hauptstrasse 50*) incorporates a Jazzclub, which hosts live jazz most Fridays. Close by, the *Rockhouse* (☎ *88 49 14, Schallmooser Hauptstrasse 46*) is Salzburg's main venue for rock and pop bands; admission starts at AS70.

Bars & Clubs *Augustiner Bräustübl* (*Augustinergasse 4-6*) proves that monks can make beer as well as anybody: the quaffing clerics have been running this huge beer hall for years. It's atmospheric and Germanic, even though it's mostly filled with tourists. Beer is dispensed from the self-service counter, either in 1L (AS56) or 0.5L (AS28) mugs. Meat, bread and salad ingredients (pricey) are available from the shops in the foyer. Eat inside or in the large, shady beer garden. It's open daily from 3 pm (2.30 pm on holidays and at weekends) to 11 pm.

Stieglkeller (☎ *84 26 81, Festungsgasse 10*) is another beer hall. It's even more touristy, as indicated by the live Sound of Music show (AS360) in the summer, but there is a good garden overlooking the town. Food in the restaurant costs between AS90 and AS180, and there's cheaper self-service beer upstairs (AS31 for 0.5L). Opening hours are 10 am to 10 pm daily, though it's closed from October to April.

Salzburger Weissbierbrauerei, on the corner of Rupertgasse and Virgilgasse, is a small brewery creating its own very palatable dark and cloudy brew. It is being remodelled in 1999, but currently has two sections: Bräugasthof Rupertihof has hot food, and beer for AS30/39 (0.3/0.5L). It's open nightly from Monday to Saturday and perhaps also for weekday lunches. Across the shady courtyard is the Bräustüberl self-service section where the draught beer is a few Schillings cheaper and there are pretzels and cuts of cold meat.

Zum Fidelen Affen (*Priesterhausgasse 8*) is a popular student-style place where everybody sits at long tables. There's decent Austrian food for around AS95 and it's open from 5 pm to midnight (closed on Sunday).

The *Schnaitl Musik Pub* (*Bergstrasse 5*) has pool, videos and a local clientele. Most Fridays (not in summer) there's live rock or indie music; cover charge, when applicable, is up to AS100. It's open daily from 7.30 pm to 2 am (6.30 pm to 1 am in winter).

The liveliest area for bars, clubs and discos is the area near the Radisson Hotel on Rudolfskai. Claustrophobes beware – these places get packed. *Tom's Bierklinik*, in a passage at Rudolfskai 22, allows the indecisive to dither over a choice of 100 types of beer (from AS42 for 0.5L); it's open daily from 8 pm to 4 am. In the next passage along, *Zur Frommen Hell* is an American theme bar (open Monday to Saturday from 8 pm to 2 am). Between the two passages is the *Vis-à-Vis* bar, which is less loud, less frantic and more sophisticated than the other places nearby, and is open daily from 7 pm to about 5 am.

The vicinity of the Mönchsberg lift has some late-night bars. There are also a couple on Steingasse, including the *Shrimps Bar* at No 5, where the food is worth a taste.

Other Entertainment The *Filmkulturzentrum* (☎ *87 31 00, Giselakai 11*) has Hollywood and non-mainstream films in the original language (AS90). Salzburg's *casino* is open from 3 pm in Schloss Klessheim in the north-west.

SV Salzburg is one of Austria's leading football (soccer) teams, and plays at the Lehener Stadion, Schumacherstrasse. The team attracts a lot of juvenile support and crowd trouble is almost unknown; tickets cost from AS200. Bus Nos 1, 2 and 27 go there from the Hauptbahnhof.

Shopping

Not many people leave without sampling some Mozart confectionery. Chocolate coated combinations of nougat and marzipan cost around AS5 per piece (cheaper in supermarkets) and are available individually or in souvenir packs. These are sold throughout Austria but it's only in Salzburg that you'll find whole window displays devoted to Mozart merchandise, the chocolate joining forces with liqueurs, mugs and much else.

Getreidegasse is the main street for shopping and souvenirs. Elsewhere in the old town, souvenir shops are La Point, Alter Markt 1, and round the corner at Kopfberger, Judengasse 14. Salzburger Heimatwerk (☎ 84 41 19), Residenzplatz 9, has glassware, CDs, books, china and fabrics relating to the province.

Getting There & Away

Air The airport (☎ 85 80-251) has regular scheduled flights to Amsterdam, Berlin, Brussels, Frankfurt, London, Paris, Zürich and elsewhere, including main Austrian cities. British Airways (☎ 84 21 08) has an office at Griesgasse 29. Lauda Air (☎ 84 85 45-0) is at Rainbergstrasse 3A. For Austrian Airlines or Swissair, call ☎ 85 44 11.

Bus Bundesbuses depart from outside the Hauptbahnhof on Südtiroler Platz where timetables are displayed. There's a Bahnbus information office at the Hauptbahnhof, next to Eurosnack; for Postbus information, call ☎ 167.

There are at least four departures a day to Kitzbühel (2¼ hours), changing at Lofer. Buses to Lienz only run between July and September (change at Franz Josefs Höhe). Numerous buses leave for the Salzkammergut between 6.30 am and 8 pm – destinations include Bad Ischl (AS100), Mondsee (AS60), St Gilgen (AS60) and St Wolfgang (AS90).

Train Salzburg is well served by IC and EC services. For train information call ☎ 1717, available daily from 7 am to 8.30 pm. Tickets (no commission) and train information are also available from Salzburger Landesreisebüro (☎ 88 28 22-11), Schwarzstrasse 11.

Fast trains leave hourly for Vienna's Westbahnhof (AS410, takes three hours and 20 minutes), travelling via Linz (AS200, one hour and 20 minutes). The express service to Klagenfurt (AS330, three hours) runs via Villach.

The quickest way to Innsbruck is by the 'corridor' train through Germany; trains depart at least every two hours (AS350, two hours) and stop at Kufstein. There are trains to Munich every 30 to 60 minutes (AS274, but ask about special weekend deals; takes about two hours), some of which continue to Karlsruhe via Stuttgart.

Car & Motorcycle Three autobahns converge on Salzburg and form a loop round the city: the A1 from Linz, Vienna and the east, the A8/E52 from Munich and the west, and the A10/E55 from Villach and the south. The quickest way to Tirol is to take the road to Bad Reichenhall in Germany and continue to Lofer (highway 312) and St Johann in Tirol.

Car Rental Offices include:

Avis
  (☎ 87 72 78) Ferdinand Porsche Strasse 7
Budget
  (☎ 87 50 38) Innsbrucker Bundesstrasse 95, by the airport
Eurodollar
  (☎ 87 16 16) Vogelweiderstrasse 69
Europcar
  (☎ 87 42 74) Gabelsbergerstrasse 3
Hertz
  (☎ 87 66 74) Ferdinand Porsche Strasse 7

Hitching Getting a lift to Munich is notoriously difficult. Consider taking the bus or train across the border before you waste too much time on the autobahn slip road.

Getting Around

To/From the Airport Salzburg airport is less than 4km west of the city centre at Innsbrucker Bundesstrasse 95. Bus No 77 stops outside and terminates at the Hauptbahnhof. This bus runs from around 7 am to 10 pm and doesn't go via the old town (though it intersects with bus No 29, which will take you there). A taxi to the airport from the centre costs about AS120.

Bus Bus drivers sell single bus tickets for AS20. Other tickets must be bought from Tabak shops or tourist offices: day passes (valid for a calendar day) are AS40; single tickets (AS15 each) and 24-hour passes (AS32 each) are both sold in units of five. Prices are 50% less for children aged six to 15 years; those under six years travel free.

The transport information office (☎ 62 05 51-553) is at Griesgasse 21. Bus routes are shown on city and hotel maps: bus Nos 1, 2, 6 and 51 start from the Hauptbahnhof and skirt the pedestrian-only old town.

Bus Taxi 'Bus taxis' operate nightly from 11.30 pm to 1.30 am for a cost of AS35. Hanuschplatz is the departure point for suburban routes on the left bank, and Theatergasse for routes to the right bank.

Taxi Taxis cost AS33 (AS43 from 10 pm to 6 am) plus AS11 or AS12 per kilometre inside the city or AS20 or AS22 per kilometre outside the city. To book a radio taxi (AS10 surcharge), call ☎ 81 11 or ☎ 17 15.

Car & Motorcycle Driving in the city centre is hardly worth the effort. Parking places are limited and much of the old town is only accessible by foot. The largest car park near the centre is the Altstadt Garage under the Mönchsberg. Attended car parks cost around AS25 per hour. Rates are lower on streets with automatic ticket machines

(blue zones): a three hour maximum applies (AS42, or AS7 for 30 minutes) on weekdays from 9 am to 7 pm and on Saturday from 9 am to noon.

Bicycle The bike rental office in the Hauptbahnhof is open 24 hours and charges standard rates. The bikes for rent in Residenzplatz in summer are much more expensive (AS60 for one hour, AS190 for a day). They also organise biking tours; call ☎ 88 48 39.

Fiacre Rates for a fiacre for up to four people are AS380/740 for 25/50 minutes. They line up on Residenzplatz.

Around Salzburg

Hellbrunn, Gaisberg and Untersberg are best visited as an excursion from Salzburg. Hallein and Werfen can also be visited as a day trip or explored in a more leisurely fashion en route to sights farther south. Between Hallein and Werfen, another excursion is to the Gollinger Wasserfall (Golling Falls).

HELLBRUNN

Four kilometres south of the centre of Salzburg's old town is the popular **Schloss Hellbrunn**, built in the 17th century by bishop Marcus Sitticus, Wolf Dietrich's nephew. In the grounds is a Wasserspiele section containing many ingenious trick fountains and water-powered figures. They were installed by the bishop and are activated by the tour guides, who all seem to share the bishop's infantile sense of humour. Expect to get wet!

Tickets for the Wasserspiele cost AS70 (students AS35). It's open daily from April to October, with the last tour at 4.30 pm or later (up to 10 pm in July and August). You can also tour the Baroque Schloss (AS30; same opening times as the Wasserspiele) and visit the small **Volkskundemuseum** (Folklore Museum) on the hill, open from 9 am to 5 pm; entry costs AS20, but it's included in the Wasserspiele ticket price.

There is no charge to stroll round the attractive gardens; these are open year-round till dusk. **Tiergarten Hellbrunn** is also in the grounds; entry costs AS70, students AS50. This zoo is naturalistic and open-plan: the more docile animals are barely confined. It is open daily and last entry ranges from 4 pm in winter to 7 pm in summer, though in summer there are also night visits on Friday and Saturday (last entry 9 pm) under an artificial moon.

Getting There & Away
Bus No 55 stops directly outside the Schloss every half-hour (AS20, city passes valid). Pick it up from Salzburg's Hauptbahnhof or Rudolfskai in the old town. The last bus back to the city is at 10.30 pm.

GAISBERG
The Gaisberg (1287m) is east of Salzburg old town, at the edge of the city limits. A lookout point provides an excellent panorama of the town and the Salzkammergut. Unless you have your own transport, the only way up is to take the Albus Bus (☎ 42 40 00) from the northern end of the Aicher Passage on Mirabellplatz (AS30 each way, 30 minutes). Check schedules as they are very infrequent. From November to March the bus only goes as far as Zistelalpe, about 1.5km short of the summit.

UNTERSBERG
This is the peak to the south of the town, reaching to a height of 1853m. The panorama of Tirolean and Salzburg Alpine ranges is more spectacular than from Gaisberg. The summit is accessible by cable car (AS125 up, AS105 down, or AS205 return) which runs year-round except for about two weeks in April and six weeks from 1 November. Get to the valley station by city bus No 55 to St Leonhardt.

HALLEIN
☎ 06245 • pop 20,000 • 461m
The main reason to visit Hallein is the Salzbergwerk (salt mine) at Bad Dürrnberg, on the hill above the town. The town was

once settled by Celts, who provided its name.

Orientation & Information
The train station is east of the Salzach River: walk ahead, bear left and then turn right to cross the river for the town centre (five minutes). En route you pass near the tourist office (☎ 853 94, fax 851 85-13), Mauttorpromenade, on the narrow island adjoining the Stadtbrücke. It is open Monday to Friday from 9 am to 4.30 pm. In summer it's open from 9 am (10 am Saturday, 4 pm Sunday) to 9 pm.

The post office (Postamt 5400) is opposite the train station.

Things to See & Do
The sale of salt from the **Bad Dürrnberg mine** filled Salzburg's coffers with much revenue during its ecclesiastical principality days. It is believed inhabitants were mining salt as long as 4500 years ago, but production has now been replaced by guided tours (AS180, students AS160); see under Information in the Salzkammergut chapter for more details of Salzbergwerk tours. At this mine there's the bonus of a brief raft trip on the salt lake. The mine (☎ 852 85-15) is open daily from 9 am to 5 pm (11 am to 3 pm from 1 November to 31 March). Overalls are supplied for the tour.

If you don't have a car, the easiest way to reach Bad Dürrnberg is to take the cable car, a 10 minute walk from the train station. The return fare is AS110, or AS250 (students AS220) including entry to the mines. A cheaper option is the 5km, 11 minute bus ride (AS19) from outside the station, but departures are infrequent at weekends. You could also walk to the mine, but it's a steep 40 minute climb: from the tourist office, walk up to the church with the bare concrete tower, turn left along Ferchl Strasse, and follow the sign pointing to the right after the yellow Volksschule building.

Hallein has some elegant 17th and 18th century houses in Salzach style, and the **Keltenmuseum** (Celtic Museum) at Pflegerplatz 5. The museum displays interesting

Celtic artefacts and details the history of salt extraction in the region (English notes available). It's open from around April to October, and entry costs AS50 (students/seniors AS30).

Special Events

The Halleiner Stadtfestwoche is 10 days of diverse events in late June, including live music (from classical to world music), street theatre, clowns and processions. Some of these events are free.

Places to Stay & Eat

Hallein has a HI *Jugendherberge* (☎ 803 97, fax -3, Schloss Wispach, Wiespach-strasse 7), open from 1 April to 30 September. It's 1.4km north of both the station (route signposted) and the town centre, but at least staying there allows you to pay just AS10 to swim in the Freibad next door (AS50 normally). This former stately home has beds in large dorms for AS160 (AS170 for a single night). There's a shower/WC on every floor and good breakfasts. Reception is closed from around noon to 5 pm.

Anna Rieger (☎ 752 54, Gamperstrasse 28), near the cable car station, provides the only central private rooms; there are two doubles (hall shower) for AS390.

In the town centre, *Pension Miki* (☎ 802 29, Ederstrasse 2) has singles/doubles for AS350/600 with shower/WC or AS310/540 without. Reception is in the café, which closes at 9 pm and on Sunday. Close by is *China-Restaurant Sun-Ly* (Ederstrasse 6), serving reasonable weekday lunches starting at AS60.

The bargain in the pedestrian zone is *Café Europa* (Thunstrasse 12), a rather smoky Gasthof offering schnitzel and chips for just AS48, two-course menus for AS55 and other cheap Austrian fare. It has a self-service annexe called *Schnitzel Max*, where prices are a few Schillings lower. It's open daily from 10 am to 10 pm.

Head west to the edge of the pedestrian zone and turn left to reach *Gästehaus Unterholzerbräu* (☎ 812 03, Oberhofgasse

4), also known as Gasthaus Röck. It serves Austrian food, fish and grills costing from AS75 to AS190, and has a couple of double rooms with hall shower for AS460. It's closed on Tuesday.

For self-caterers, there's a *Billa* supermarket situated near the tourist office on Mauttorpromenade.

Getting There & Away

Hallein is 30 minutes or less from Salzburg by bus or train (both AS40; departures every 30 to 60 minutes). Hallein train station rents bikes.

BERCHTESGADEN

Although this town is in Germany, it is easy to visit from Salzburg. It achieved fame (or perhaps notoriety) for the **Eagle's Nest**, a retreat built by Adolf Hitler on the Kehlstein summit. The **Salzbergwerk** (☎ 08652-600 20) north of town proves the Germans are also able to turn salt into money – proceeds from Berchtesgaden have long contributed to Bavaria's power and wealth. Popular tours follow a similar schedule to those in Hallein and the Salzkammergut, except they're cheaper here: DM19.50 (around AS135) for adults, DM9.50 for children.

Five kilometres south of Berchtesgaden is **Königssee**, an attractive lake providing boat tours and a scenic setting for walks. This area is a national park, and some people consider that it offers the best walking in Germany.

If you plan to stay overnight in or around Berchtesgaden, contact the town tourist office (☎ 08652-9670), opposite the train station in Königsseer Strasse, for advice about accommodation options.

Getting There & Away

Berchtesgaden is 30km south of Salzburg on highway 160. Direct buses run from the city, or it's less than an hour by rail (take a Munich train and change at Freilassing). Some of the tour operators in Salzburg offer a half-day tour of Berchtesgaden, the Eagle's Nest and Königssee.

WERFEN

☎ 06468 • pop 3000 • 525m

Picturesque Werfen provides access to a top attraction, the Eisriesenwelt ice caves.

Orientation & Information

The town stands on the northern side of the Salzach River, five minutes walk from the train station: cross the river and head towards the castle. The tourist office (☎ 5388, fax 7562, email info@werfen.at) is at Markt 35, in the centre of the town. It is open Monday to Friday from 9 am to 5 pm, except from mid-July to mid-August when it's open on weekdays till 7 pm and on Saturday from 5 to 7 pm. Staff will book accommodation for no commission.

Eisriesenwelt Höhle

These caves in the mountains are the largest accessible ice caves in the world. They contain 30,000 sq metres of ice and about 42km of passages have been explored. During a 75 minute tour you visit several immense caverns, containing some beautiful and elaborate ice shapes. Unfortunately, the powerful illumination provided by a series of magnesium flares is all too brief. The caves were first entered in 1879 but it was Alexander von Mörk who pioneered the most extensive exploration, and his ashes lie in the 'cathedral' cave.

Take warm clothes because it can get cold inside, and you need to be fairly fit (older people may find the stairs a bit difficult because of the altitude). The caves are open from 1 May to early October. The tour (in German) visits about one-fiftieth of the caves and costs AS90.

Getting to the caves is a bit of an effort, though the trip offers fantastic views. A minibus service (AS70 return) operates from the station along the steep (up to 23 degrees) 6km road to the car park, which is as far as cars can go. A 15 minute walk brings you to the cable car (AS110 return); from the top station it is a steep 15 minute walk to the caves. Allow at least four hours for the return trip from the train station, or three hours from the car park (peak-season

queues may add an hour). The whole route can be walked, but it's a hard four hour ascent, rising 1100m above the village.

You can also explore the Dachstein ice caves near Obertraun; see the Salzkammergut chapter for details.

Burg Hohenwerfen

Burg Hohenwerfen stands on the hill above the village, in an extremely photogenic location. Originally built in 1077 for an archbishop of Salzburg, the present building dates from the 16th century. The entry fee includes an exhibition (displays change periodically) and a guided tour of the interior (in English if there's sufficient demand – otherwise get the English notes); this covers the chapel, dungeons, arsenal and belfry. The best part is a dramatic falconry show in the grounds. The walk up from the village takes 20 minutes. It can be visited daily from April to October and entry costs AS100 (students AS90).

Both the fortress and the caves can be fitted into a day trip from Salzburg if you start early; visit the caves first, and be at the fortress by 3 pm for the falconry show.

Places to Stay & Eat

Private rooms start at about AS160 per person. There are four places on Hirschenhöhstrasse, behind Gasthof Lebzelter.

Guesthouses in town include *Kärntnerhof* (☎ 5214, fax 7175, Markt 31), providing biggish singles/doubles with shower/WC for AS305/580. About half of the rooms have a balcony and there's a large dining area (including a terrace at the back) serving affordable Austrian food. *Goldener Hirsch* (☎ 5342, Hauptstrasse 28) is cheaper at AS280/540, and there's a garden, but the rooms have a shower cubicle instead of a proper bathroom.

A range of restaurants await on the main street. There are also supermarkets for self-caterers. *Bella Grotta Pizzeria (Markt 39)* offers pizzas starting at AS65; there are outside tables and it's open daily. If you have the money, go to *Zur Stiege* (☎ 5256, fax -4, Markt 10); its restaurant has a very good reputation, with meals from AS190. Rooms with shower/WC and TV start at AS340 per person.

Gasthof Lebzelter Obauer (☎ 5212, fax -12, Markt 46) also has rooms (from AS550 per person) which have all the comforts expected of a four star place, but it's really known for its restaurant, which is acclaimed as one of the finest in the whole of Austria. Main courses cost from AS200 to AS400. You have to make reservations in advance, especially as rest days vary.

Getting There & Away

Werfen can be reached from Salzburg by highway 10. Trains from Salzburg (AS80) run approximately once an hour and the journey takes 50 minutes.

Southern Salzburg Province

The principal attractions in the south are covered in the Hohe Tauern National Park Region chapter. The following places are worth a look if you're passing through the south-east of the province. Tamsweg and Mauterndorf are both within the Lungau region; staff at the Lungau tourist office (☎ 06477-8988, fax -20, email info@ lungau.co.at) can tell you about ski passes and accommodation.

TAMSWEG

☎ 06474 • pop 5000 • 1024m

Tamsweg is the main town in the Lungau region. If you're passing through you may want to stop off to look at St Leonhard-kirche, a 15th century Gothic church on a hill outside the town. It has some impressive stained glass windows, particularly the so-called Goldfenster (gold window) to the right of the chancel. After the discovery of a statuette of St Leonard, an event depicted in the Goldfenster, the church became a well known pilgrimage site.

In the centre of town, the attractive Marktplatz is lined with rustic-style inns as well as the 16th century Rathaus, a rather grander, turreted edifice.

Tamsweg is known for its Samsonumzug (Samson Procession) which takes place on two days in late July and on a couple of other special (variable) dates in summer. The biblical character and other famous figures are depicted in giant size and paraded through the streets.

Getting There & Away

Tamsweg is at the terminus of a private rail line that branches off from the Vienna-Klagenfurt main line at Unzmarkt. See the Murau section in the Styria chapter for details. A two-hourly Bundesbus runs to and from Salzburg (2½ hours), usually via Mauterndorf and Radstadt.

The town is a 10km detour from highway 99, which connects Radstadt and Spittal an der Drau.

MAUTERNDORF

☎ 06472 • pop 1600 • 1122m

Mauterndorf's tourist office (☎ 7279, fax 7657) is called the Fremdenverkehrsverband. Both a summer and winter resort, Mauterndorf has the added attraction of a castle. This was built by the archbishops of Salzburg in the 13th century on the site of a Roman fort. In 1339 the castle chapel (with Gothic frescoes) was added and in 1452 a winged altar was installed. The castle houses a regional museum, and is the venue for various cultural events. It is believed that in the Middle Ages the main road passed directly through the castle courtyard. This facilitated the collecting of tolls from road users, but presumably also entailed a defence risk. The locals were lucky not to encounter a Trojan horse trundling along the road.

Moosham, 6km south of Mauterndorf, has a castle formerly owned by the archbishops of Salzburg.

Getting There & Away

Mauterndorf is on highway 99. Bundesbuses go along this route, but Mauterndorf is not on a railway line.

n a hill behind Salzburg, Festung Hohensalzburg dominates the Baroque spires of the old town.

alzburg's traditional old-town shops ...   ... and traditional-style transport.

MARK HONAN

Pacher's altar in St Wolfgang's pilgrimage church was constructed in Italy and carried over the Alps.

MARK HONAN

Wolfgangsee – water-sports paradise.

MARK HONAN

Painted skulls in Hallstatt's bone house.

AUSTRIAN NATIONAL TOURIST OFFICE/TRUMLER

The view from Traunkirchen village on Traunsee

RADSTADT

☎ 06452 • pop 4000 • 856m

Radstadt retains much of its medieval fortification but most visitors flock to participate in winter skiing.

Orientation & Information

The town centre is uphill from the train station: a town plan in the station foyer shows the best paths. The tourist office (☎ 7472, fax 6702, email radstadt-info@ magnet.at) is in the centre at Stadtplatz 17, open Monday to Friday from 8 am to noon and 2 to 6 pm, and (except in off-season) on Saturday from 9 am to noon. In the winter additional hours are Saturday 4 to 6 pm and Sunday from 9 to 11 am. Staff at the tourist office will book rooms for no commission, including cheap private rooms (no minimum stay). Next door is an accommodation board with a free telephone, accessible daily from 7 am to midnight.

Things to See & Do

The walled centre of town, with three round turrets, is an impressive sight. One tower, the **Kapuzinerturm**, houses a museum dealing with local history and culture (entry AS20, open 1 June to 30 September). There is another museum in **Schloss Lerchen** (entry AS35, closed April, May and mid-November to Christmas). The **Stadtpfarr-kirche** (parish church) combines Gothic and Romanesque elements and has an interesting graveyard.

Radstadt and neighbouring skiing areas combine to form the huge **Sportwelt Amadé** skiing district; 120 lifts give access to 320km of pistes, mostly suitable for intermediates and beginners. A high-season lift pass costs AS380 for one day. If this doesn't give you enough choice, you can opt instead for the Top Tauern Skipass, valid for 270 lifts (700km of runs) in Salzburg province and Styria; it costs AS2030 for six days or AS2160 for seven days.

The same mountains attract walkers in summer. Overlooking Radstadt to the north is the **Rossbrand** (1770m). If you wear rose-tinted spectacles as you make the ascent, you might believe the tourist office's claim that this is the most famous viewpoint in the eastern Alps.

Places to Stay & Eat

Radstadt has a few hotels, guesthouses and pensions, but by far the most beds are provided by numerous private homes, farmhouses and holiday apartments.

There are cheaper places, but if you just want something central and decent, try *Gasthof Torwirt (☎ 5541, fax 5139, Hoheneggstrasse 12)*, which has single/double rooms for AS410/720, or *Hotel Post (☎ 4306, fax -90, Stadtplatz 8)*, which has rooms from AS610/1020. Both offer rooms with shower/WC and cable TV, though Hotel Post has more on-site facilities, including a restaurant.

Gasthof Löcker (Schernbergstrasse 13) has rooms with shower/WC and TV for AS410/720. Its restaurant offers Austrian food from AS70 to AS150 and is closed on Tuesday. *China-Restaurant Mauer*, next door at No 15, has weekday lunch menus for less than AS70, including soup or spring roll; it's open daily.

3P, near the Stadtpfarrkirche on Karl Berg Gasse, is a pub with pool tables and also serves some food.

Close to the tourist office, on Hoheneggstrasse, are two *Spar* supermarkets.

Getting There & Away

Radstadt is on the route of two-hourly IC trains running between Innsbruck and Graz – both are about three hours away. Kitzbühel, Zell am See and Bruck an der Mur are also along this route.

From Radstadt, highway 99 runs into Carinthia. This climbs to the Radstädter Tauern Pass at 1739m and is not recommended for caravans. Just to the west is a busier north-south route, the A10/E55, which avoids the high parts by going through a 6km tunnel.

The Salzkammergut

This 'earthly paradise', as described by Franz Josef I, is a popular holiday region to the east of Salzburg. The lure of the many lakes means summer is the main season, but winter has its attractions too. It's an area where you can simply relax and take in the scenery, or get involved in the numerous sports and activities on offer. In summer, walking and water sports are favoured; in winter, some walking paths stay open but downhill and cross-country skiing are more popular. Some pensions and private rooms close for the winter.

A winter ski pass is available from ski lift stations for the Salzkammergut-Tennengau region, which includes 80 cable cars and ski lifts serving 145km of ski runs. It costs AS1390 (children AS890) for five days, AS1590 (AS990) for six days, AS1770 (AS1120) for seven days and AS2520 (AS1590) for 10 days. It is also valid for a number of free ski buses. Look for low-season offers in January and after mid-March, when you might get six or seven days for the price of five. One-day passes are offered for specific resorts.

If you plan to fish, be sure to check with the local tourist office about permits, permitted seasons and other regulations – these vary from lake to lake and can be quite specific. At Wolfgangsee, for example, fishing is allowed from the bank or a boat, but not between 10 pm and 6 am, and live bait is allowed but not multiple fishing equipment.

Orientation

In this region of mountains and lakes, most taller mountains are in the south and most larger lakes in the north. The Salzkammergut is split between three provinces. Upper Austria takes the lion's share including the largest lake, Attersee, its two neighbours, Mondsee and Traunsee, and the ever popular Hallstätter See in the south. Bad Ischl, also in Upper Austria, is the geographical and administrative centre of the

Highlights

- Savour the varied attractions of Hallstatt, from stunning views to decorated human skulls
- Explore the wondrous Dachstein ice caves at Obertraun
- Discover the antique ceramics and lakeside castles of Gmunden
- Admire Pacher's magnificent altar in the pilgrimage church of St Wolfgang
- Take in the captivating panorama of lakes and mountains from the Schafberg

Salzkammergut. East of Hallstätter See is a small region within Styria, comprising Bad Aussee and its lakes. Salzburg province has most of Wolfgangsee, and some less important lakes to the west and north-west.

Information

In addition to the local tourist offices – there is one in almost every resort – the provincial tourist offices can be helpful, though they usually only hold resort brochures for their own region within the Salzkammergut. See the Salzburg, Upper Austria and Styria chapters for addresses and opening times of these offices. The provincial tourist office in Salzburg city has some useful information, including bus and train schedules and a list of camping grounds. The Upper Austria provincial tourist office in Linz also has a good supply of brochures. In Styria, information is held in the main Graz tourist office (for personal callers) and the provincial office (for information by post), also in Graz.

The Salzkammergut has its own tourist board, known as the Ferienregion Salzkammergut (☎ 06132-269 09-0, fax -14, email salzkammergut@upperaustria.or.at), Wirer-

strasse 10, Postfach 130, A-4820 Bad Ischl. It mostly has general information, however, and isn't geared to receive personal callers, so for the specifics you'd be better off contacting other offices.

The Salzkammergut is dotted with hostels and affordable hotels, but the best deals are probably rooms in private homes or farmhouses – despite the prevalence of single-night surcharges (about AS30). Tourist offices can supply lists of private rooms, as well as details of Alpine huts at higher elevations. Most resorts have a

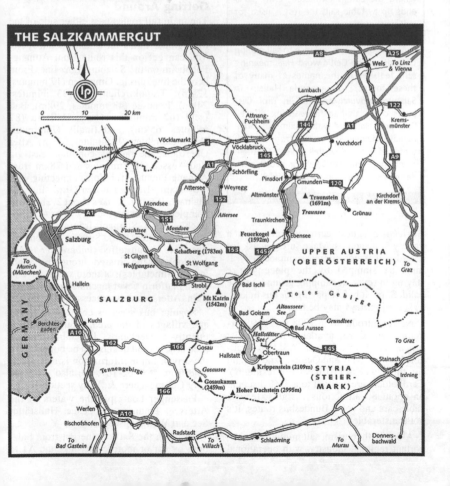

THE SALZKAMMERGUT

Salt Mines

As its name suggests, the Salzkammergut was important for the mining of salt, the 'white gold' that gave the region its prosperity. Mines at Hallstatt, Bad Ischl and Altaussee are still in production. Salt mining is a lengthy process: it takes 10 to 15 years for the brine in each new section to reach a height and saturation level at which it is economical to pump it out. Brine from these mines goes to Ebensee where the salt is extracted. Only 10% ends up as table salt; the rest is used for industrial purposes.

Several other towns in Austria owe their existence or past importance to salt mining or trading. The Celtic word *Hall*, meaning salt, features in the names of many of these towns, for example Hallein in Salzburg province and Hall in Tirol. Disputes over salt had far-reaching effects: Salzburg's 'salt war' with Maximilian, Duke of Bavaria, over the profits from the salt trade led to the downfall of Wolf Dietrich, archbishop-prince of Salzburg. Worth pondering as you season your schnitzel!

Gästekarte (guest card) which offers a variety of discounts. Make sure you ask for a card if it is not offered spontaneously. It must be stamped by the place you're staying in (even at camping grounds) to be valid. Show it before paying for bus tickets, as some journeys may be free.

Newly introduced in 1998 was the Salzkammergut Card, available from tourist offices and hotels. It costs AS65, is available between May and October, and is valid for three weeks (10 days for residents). Cardholders are entitled to a 25% discount on about 80 attractions – sights, ferries, cable cars and some Bundesbus routes. It's not transferable.

Along with tourism, salt mining is an important regional industry, with operational

mines at Hallstatt, Bad Ischl and Altausee. All three mines offer tours, each slightly different but adhering to a similar formula: visitors don mining overalls, take a mini-train ride to the mine and slide down wooden tunnels. Beyond this, the content of the tours is pretty thin and they're rather expensive. If you can only afford one guided tour in the mountains, I'd recommend the ice caves at Obertraun instead. Details of all of these tours are provided in the relevant sections for each of these towns.

Getting Around

The main rail routes pass either side of the Salzkammergut, but the area can be crossed by regional trains on a north-south route. You can get on this route from Attnang-Puchheim on the Salzburg-Linz line. From here the line runs to: Gmunden (17 minutes, 12km); Traunkirchen Ort (33 minutes, 24km); Ebensee (43 minutes, 29km); Bad Ischl (62 minutes, 46km); Hallstatt (87 minutes, 65km); and finally Obertraun-Dachsteinhöhlen (91 minutes, 67km). After Obertraun, the railway continues east via Bad Aussee (104 minutes and 78km from Attnang-Puchheim) before connecting with the main Bischofshofen-Graz line at Stainach-Irdning. It takes about 2½ hours to complete the 108km journey from Attnang-Puchheim to Stainach-Irdning (and the trains are often late). Smaller stations on this route are unstaffed (*unbesetzter Bahnhof*; look for the crossed-through rectangle icon on timetables); at these you'll have to use a platform ticket machine or pay on the train. Attersee is also accessible by rail.

Regular bus services connect all towns and villages in the area, though less frequently at weekends. Timetables can be seen at stops and tickets can be bought from the driver. Some information is also available from ☎ 0662-167; see also the Salzburg Getting There & Away section.

Passenger boats ply the waters of the Attersee, Traunsee, Mondsee, Hallstätter See and Wolfgangsee.

To reach the Salzkammergut from Salzburg by car or motorcycle, take the A1 to reach the north of the region, or highway 158 to Bad Ischl. Travelling north-south, the main road is the highway 145 (the Salzkammergut Bundesstrasse) which follows the rail line for most of its length.

Bad Ischl

☎ 06132 • pop 13,000 • 468m

This spa town's reputation snowballed after Princess Sophie took a treatment here to cure her infertility in 1828. Within two years she had given birth to Franz Josef I; two other sons followed. Rather in the manner of a salmon returning to its place of birth, Franz Josef made an annual pilgrimage to Bad Ischl, making it his summer home and hauling much of the European aristocracy in his wake. However, deviating from salmon behaviour, Franz Josef returned to his spiritual home to make not love but war – usually on deer, but ultimately on the whole world.

Orientation & Information

Bad Ischl town centre is compactly contained within a bend of the Traun River.

The tourist office or *Kurdirektion* (☎ 277 57-0, fax -77, email office@kd-badischl .or.at) is west of the train station at Bahnhofstrasse 6. It is open Monday to Friday from 8 am to 6 pm, Saturday 9 am to 4 pm and Sunday from 9 to 11.30 am. The Gästekarte (also called a Kurkarte) gives reductions on many admission prices, though this is offset by the nightly *Kurtaxe* (from AS12 to AS19).

The post office (Postamt 4820) is further west on Bahnhofstrasse, it's open until 7 pm weekdays and until 11 am Saturday (8 pm and noon in summer). There are moneychanging facilities at the post office and train station. You can also hire bikes daily between 7 am (11 am on Sunday) and 6 pm at the train station.

Things to See & Do

Stroll around town, admiring the plentiful Biedermeier-style buildings; if you walk along the Esplanade you'll reach the **Stadt-**

museum (city museum), which deals with local history and culture (entry AS50; closed in November and on Monday except in July and August). Across the river is the **Lehárvilla** (entry AS55), former home of the operetta composer Franz Lehár. For longer walks, see the tourist office's suggestions on the reverse of the city map. Also ask about the free guided city walks in summer.

Franz Josef's summer residence was the **Kaiservilla**. He stayed in this villa for 60 years, from 1854 to 1914, and it was here that he signed the declaration of war on Serbia that started WWI. The emperor had the habit of getting up for his daily bath as early as 3.30 am – not a typical regimen for someone on holiday. The villa was his hunting lodge (though rather grand for that purpose) and contains an obscene number of hunting trophies; most of his victims are now no more than antlers on the wall, but the 2000th (!) chamois he shot is presented in its stuffed entirety.

The villa can be visited only by guided tour, which is given in German, but there are written English translations. The tour takes 40 minutes, costs AS100 and includes entry to the Kaiserpark grounds (which

Franz Josef, a regular at Bad Ischl, became emperor when just 18 years old.

THE SALZKAMMERGUT

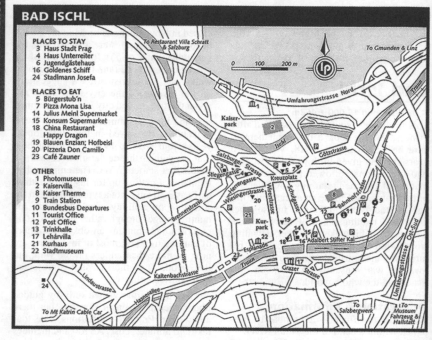

BAD ISCHL

PLACES TO STAY
3 Haus Stadt Prag
4 Haus Unterreiter
6 Jugendgästehaus
16 Goldenes Schiff
24 Stadlmann Josefa

PLACES TO EAT
5 Bürgerstub'n
7 Pizza Mona Lisa
14 Julius Meinl Supermarket
15 Konsum Supermarket
18 China Restaurant
   Happy Dragon
19 Blauen Enzian; Hofbeisl
20 Pizzeria Don Camillo
23 Café Zauner

OTHER
1 Photomuseum
2 Kaiservilla
8 Kaiser Therme
9 Train Station
10 Bundesbus Departures
11 Tourist Office
12 Post Office
13 Trinkhalle
17 Lehárvilla
21 Kurhaus
22 Stadtmuseum

costs AS35 on its own). The Kaiservilla is open 1 May to mid-October daily, from 9 to 11.45 am and 1 to 4.45 pm; from Easter to 30 April it's open weekends only.

The small **Photomuseum**, nearby in the park in the Marmorschlössl building, has some interesting old photographs and cameras (entry AS15; students AS10). It's open from 1 April to 31 October daily, from 9.30 am to 5 pm.

Bad Ischl's local peak is **Mt Katrin** (1542m) which provides views and walking trails. In summer, the cable car costs AS160 return. In winter, the mountain offers downhill skiing (AS230 for a day pass). The area also has some cross-country skiing trails.

There's a **Salzbergwerk** (salt mine; ☎ 239 48-31) to the south of town in Perneck: walk there in 40 minutes or take the infrequent bus service. Tours cost AS135 and there are several conducted daily from 1

May to late September. Also to the south, in Sulzbach, is the **Museum Fahrzeug** (transport museum), open daily from 1 April to 31 October (entry AS70). It's about 4km south of the town centre and the Bad Goisern Bundesbus runs there.

The tourist office has information on health treatments such as those in the Kaiser Therme (☎ 233 24-0), at Bahnhofstrasse 1. To get a taste of the waters, visit the **Trinkhalle** (drinking hall) on Auböckplatz (open in the summer) or the Kaiser Therme.

Special Events

Free *Kurkonzerte* (spa concerts) are performed once or twice a day (except Tuesday) during summer; ask the tourist office for venues and times. An operetta festival takes place in July and August; for details and reservations contact Büro der Operettengemeinde Bad Ischl (☎ 238 39,

fax 233 84), Wiesingerstrasse 7, A-4820.
The Ischler Stadtfest in late August features
two days of diverse music.

Places to Stay

Staff at the tourist office will help find
rooms free of charge, or you can use the 24
hour accommodation board in the foyer.

The HI *Jugendgästehaus* (☎ 265 77, fax
-75, Am Rechensteg 5) is in the town centre
behind Kreuzplatz. Dorms (with up to five
beds per room) cost AS140 per person,
singles/doubles are AS190/340 plus tax)
and dinner is AS55. Check-in is from 5 to 7
pm and the hostel is closed for a couple of
weeks at Christmas.

Haus Unterreiter (☎ 244 71, Stiegengasse 1) has four singles and two doubles
for around AS160 per person, with hall
shower; there are TVs in most rooms. Go
through the arch and climb the stairs at the
back of the small Nah & Frisch supermarket. Many other homes offer private
rooms, but none are so central. The staff do
not speak English.

B&B pensions offer reasonable value.
Stadlmann Josefa (☎ 231 04, Mastalier-
gasse 21) has basic rooms from AS190 per
person, some with private shower, but it's
west of the centre. More convenient is
Haus Stadt Prag (☎/fax 236 16, Eglmoos-
gasse 9), providing large singles/doubles
with shower/WC for AS370/680.

Goldenes Schiff (☎ 242 41, fax -58,
email gruber@goldenes-schiff.co.at, Adalbert Stifter Kai 3) overlooks the river and
offers four star comfort from AS580/880 in
the low season and AS680/1080 in the high
season (river views cost extra). The hotel
has a solarium, a good restaurant and
parking places – and they're proud of their
horsehair mattresses.

Places to Eat

For self-caterers, a *Julius Meinl* supermarket is on Pfarrgasse, but the *Konsum* on
Auböckplatz is cheaper.

The *China Restaurant Happy Dragon*,
on Adalbert Stifter Kai by the Schröpfer-
platz bridge, overlooks the river and has

outside tables. Lunch menus are AS64 (not
Sunday or holidays) and other dishes, including Indian meals, from about AS90. It's
open daily and the food is above average.

Pizzeria Don Camillo (Wiesingerstrasse
5) has decent pizza and spaghetti from
AS55 and salads from AS35 to AS75. It's
open daily and has outside tables overlooking the Kurpark. Smaller and even cheaper
(pizzas from AS50 to AS65) is *Pizza Mona
Lisa* (Kreuzplatz 12), which also does take-
aways; it's closed Monday.

For Austrian food, try *Bürgerstub'n*
(Kreuzplatz 7), back from the street in a
courtyard; it's closed Sunday. It has white
walls, lots of plants, and meals priced from
AS95 to AS195. The salad buffet costs
AS40 or AS60.

Blauen Enzian (Wirerstrasse 2) is also
back from the main street. This informal
place offers a varied menu (from AS80 to
AS170 per dish) covering pasta, regional
and national food and salads; it's closed
Sunday. Next door is *Hofbeisl*, an atmospheric place for a drink.

Sample imperial elegance on the Esplanade at *Café Zauner*, open from 1 May
to 30 September. Gourmets may want to
head 2km north-west out of town to *Restaurant Villa Schratt* (☎ 276 47, Steinbruch
43), where dishes start at AS200; it's closed
Tuesday and Wednesday.

Getting There & Away

Bundesbuses leave from outside the train
station. There are hourly buses to Salzburg
(AS100, 85 minutes) between 5.05 am and
8.10 pm, via St Gilgen. To St Wolfgang
(AS40), you often have to change at Strobl
(the bus will be waiting and the same ticket
is valid). Buses run to Hallstatt every
couple of hours (AS50, 50 minutes), with
some continuing to Obertraun.

Trains depart hourly (see Getting Around
earlier in the chapter). It costs AS36 to Hallstatt but, unlike the bus, you must add the
cost of the boat from Halstatt station (see
the Hallstatt Getting There & Away section
later in this chapter). The fare to Gmunden

is AS68 (45 minutes); the train to Salzburg via Attnang-Puchheim costs AS190.

Most major roads in the Salzkammergut go to or near Bad Ischl; highway 158 from Salzburg and the north-south highway 145 intersect just north of the town centre.

Southern Salzkammergut

The Dachstein mountain range provides a 3000m backdrop to the lakes in the south. Transport routes go round rather than over these jagged peaks.

HALLSTÄTTER SEE

This lake, at 508m, is the big draw in the south. Hallstatt is the most famous resort and gets hordes of day-trippers. Just 5km round the lake lies Obertraun, the closest resort to the Dachstein ice caves. Either place would make a suitable base from which to explore the locality. The Hallstatt-Dachstein region became a UNESCO World Cultural Heritage site in 1997.

From around June to August (weather depending), three boats a day depart from Hallstatt on a circular excursion round the lake costing AS80, a 75 minute trip; disembarkation is possible.

HALLSTATT

☎ 06134

Hallstatt has a history stretching back 4500 years. The Hallstatt Period (800 to 400 BC) refers to the early Iron Age in Europe and was named after the settlers who worked the salt mine; near the mine entrance, 2000 flat graves were discovered dating from 1000 to 500 BC. In 50 AD, the Romans were also attracted by the rich salt deposits. Nowadays the village is prized mainly for its picturesque location.

Orientation & Information

Seestrasse is the main street; some other streets are mere pedestrian paths. Turn left from the ferry to reach the tourist office (☎ 8208, fax 8352) at Seestrasse 169. It is

open Monday to Friday from 9 am to 5 pm and weekends from 10 am to 2 pm; from 1 September to 30 June it is closed at weekends and between noon and 1pm. The office sells an invaluable information brochure for AS10, which includes accommodation options (the regional office should provide this brochure for free). It also sells an English-language walking guide (AS70). For those staying in the village, Gästekarte benefits include reduced admission to the Dachstein ice caves.

The post office (Postamt 4830) is around the corner from the tourist office, and changes money.

Things to See & Do

Hallstatt is set in idyllic, picture-postcard scenery, wedged between the mountains and the lake. The tour buses that roll in stay only a few hours and then the village returns to a calmer state. Join everyone else strolling down the quaint streets, snapping up souvenirs and photographs in equal measure.

The Catholic **Pfarrkirche** (parish church) was built in the 15th century and has Gothic frescoes and two winged altars: the better one, dating from 1510, shows saints Barbara and Katharina, with Mary in the middle. You shouldn't miss the macabre **Beinhaus** (bone house; entry AS10) by the church; it contains rows of neatly stacked skulls, upon which have been painted flowery designs and the names of their former owners. These human remains have been exhumed from the too-small graveyard since 1600.

The village has two small **museums**, one devoted to local early history (the Prähistorisches Museum) and the other to local crafts and fauna (the Heimatmuseum). They're worth a look, although exhibit signs are only in German. Combined entry costs AS50 (reductions for students and Gästekarte holders), though the history museum closes from November to March. Some Celtic and Roman excavations can be seen (free) in Janu, a shop opposite the tourist office.

Above the village on the Salzberg (salt mountain) is the **Salzbergwerk** (salt mine). Tours (usually in German, plus a short English film) dwell on the fate of a 3000-year-old miner, found preserved in the salt in 1735. It's open 1 May to 26 October, daily from 9.30 am. The last tour is at 4.30 pm from late May to mid-September; at other times it's at 3 pm. Entry costs AS135 (AS120 with the Gästekarte). A funicular costing AS95 return (AS80 if you have a Gästekarte) will take you to **Rudolfsturm** (Rudolf's Tower – there's an excellent view from the public terrace), 15 minutes walk from the mine. Alternatively, either of two scenic walking trails will get you from Hallstatt to the tower in 45 minutes.

Gasthof Hallberg is the base for Hallstatt's **scuba diving** school, and the **ski** school is at the Gasthof Zauner; see the following Places to Stay & Eat.

Hallstatt has an unusual **Corpus Christi procession**: the shoreline is so crowded that some participants take to the water in boats.

Places to Stay & Eat

Some private rooms in the village are only available in summer; others require a minimum three night stay. Prices are around AS200 per person. It's best to elicit the help of the tourist office, which will willingly ring round for you without charge. There's an accommodation board with free phone in Lahn (the southern part of the village). Lahn has the cheapest private rooms.

A camp site at *Campingplatz Höll* (☎ 8329, Lahnstrasse 7) costs AS55 per person, AS40 per tent and AS30 per car. It's open from 15 April to 15 October.

The HI *Jugendherberge* (☎ 8212, Salzbergstrasse 50) is open from around 1 May to 30 September, depending on the weather. Beds cost AS100, with breakfast and sheets another AS25 each. Some dorms have lots of beds and are cramped; it's often full with groups. Check-in is only from 5 to 6 pm.

TVN Naturfreunde Herberge (☎/fax 8318, Kirchenweg 36) is just below the road tunnel, by the waterfall. It has dorm beds for AS110, plus AS40 each for sheets and breakfast (if required). As in the Jugendherberge, some rooms are OK, others are cramped. It's run by the *Zur Mühle Gasthaus*, which shares the building. Zur Mühle has the best food prices in the village, with pizza and pasta from AS68 and Austrian food from AS75. It's closed on Wednesday and from 2 to 4 pm, when there's also no TVN check-in.

Go to *Bräu Gasthof* (☎ 8221, fax -4 Seestrasse 120) if you want typical Austrian food in an old-fashioned atmosphere (or to sit outside by the lake). Meals cost from AS60 to AS145. It's open daily, but only from 1 May to 26 October. Doubles with private WC and shower are available all year for AS800, or AS880 with balcony.

Kongress Stuberl by the tourist office is another good place to eat (from AS85). *Amigos (Seestrasse 156)* has reasonably priced Tex-Mex meals. For self caterers there's a *Konsum* supermarket in Lahn.

Gasthof Hallberg (☎/fax 8395, Seestrasse 113) has pizzas and Austrian food for AS95 to AS160. It also has a few rooms for AS530 per person with private WC and shower. *Gasthof Zauner* (☎ 8246, fax -8, Marktplatz 51) is run by the same family. It has good rooms with shower/WC, TV and telephone, some with balcony and view of the lake. Singles/doubles are AS645/1190 (AS855/1610 for half-board). The restaurant is known for its good food (especially fish) and wines. Dishes cost above AS100, and the restaurant is closed from 2 November to Christmas.

Getting There & Away

There are around six buses a day to/from Obertraun and Bad Ischl, but none after 4.50 pm. Get off the Bundesbus at the Parkterrasse stop for the centre and the tourist office, or at Lahn (at the southern end of the road tunnel) for the Jugendherberge hostel.

Hallstatt train station is across the lake. The boat service from there to the village (AS23) coincides with train arrivals (at least 10 a day from Bad Ischl; total trip 45 minutes). Car access into the village is restricted: from early May to late October, electronic gates are activated. Staying overnight gives free parking and a pass to open the gates.

OBERTRAUN
☎ 06131

This spread-out village appears to be totally enclosed within a crater of mountains; it's a trick of perspective, but a pleasing one.

Orientation & Information

Obertraun is on the northern bank of the Traun River, at the start of the narrow and steep-sided valley leading east to Bad Aussee. The tourist office (☎ 351, fax 342-22, email tourismus@obertraun.or.at) is in the Gemeindeamt, open Monday to Friday from 8 am to noon and 2 to 5 pm. In the high season it's open till 6 pm and on Saturday from 9 am to noon. The Dachstein ice caves are south of the river, a pleasant 20 minute walk through the woods (take path No 7; signposted).

The resort Gästekarte entitles you to a variety of useful discounts.

Dachstein Caves

The best of these caves are the **Rieseneis-höhle** (Giant Ice Caves); ask at the ticket office about tours in English. The caves are millions of years old and extend for nearly 80km in places. The ice itself is no more than 500 years old but is increasing in thickness every year – the 'ice mountain' is 8m high, twice as high as when the caves were first explored in 1910. There are some unusual and beautiful formations, such as the 'ice chapel'.

The **Mammuthöhle** (Mammoth Caves) are basically more of the same except without the ice formations. They are worth seeing, if only for the atmospheric slide show projected within a far cavern, accompanied by swelling music mingling with the sound of ceaselessly dripping water. The tour is in German only.

Both sets of caves are 10 minutes walk from the first stage of the Dachstein cable car (station Schönbergalm) at 1350m; near the station is the ticket office for the caves.

Dachstein or Werfen?

Unless you're a caving buff, you'll probably want to see either the caves at Dachstein or those at Werfen (south of Salzburg) but not both. The costs involved are about the same, so how to choose between them?

Werfen, in Salzburg province, is undeniably the more impressive in terms of sheer scale. Dachstein is said to have more beautiful ice formations, but this is probably only because they are better lit and the tour allows more time to study them. Dachstein is also less physically strenuous and has the advantage of tours in English. In either case, the view across the valley from the entrance is excellent.

Political purists may get excited about another difference: the Dachstein caves are managed by the local authority, whereas Werfen is a private enterprise.

The cable car operates every 20 minutes; a return ticket costs AS168. The caves are open from 1 May to mid-October. Entry costs AS90 for each cave or AS130 for a combined ticket. Each tour takes nearly an hour; be at the ticket office at the latest by 3 pm in summer and 2 pm in autumn to have time to do both tours.

The **Koppenbrüllerhöhle** are part of the same Dachstein cave system, and are down the valley towards Bad Aussee. This water-filled cave can be visited on a guided tour, which costs AS90, between 1 May and 30 September.

Other Attractions

The Dachstein cable car has three stages, the highest being **Krippenstein** at 2109m; various viewpoints and walking trails await, which provide excellent vistas of the Dachstein range to the south and Hallstätter See to the north. In winter this is also a ski region (AS290 for a one day pass). Uniquely, you can indulge in nude cross-country skiing up here (inquire at the tourist office).

Obertraun has a grassy **beach** area (free entry) with changing huts, a small waterslide, a children's play area and boat rental.

Places to Stay & Eat

Look for the many private rooms (from AS160) and holiday apartments in the village. *Campingplatz Hinterer* (☎ 265) is by the lake, south of the river.

The HI *Jugendherberge* (☎ 360, fax -4, Winkl 26) is 15 minutes walk from the train station: cross the river and take the first street on the left. It costs AS182 (A162 if aged under 19); add AS20 for a single night's stay. Those aged under 19 save AS5 on the price of lunch (AS70) and dinner (AS75). You can only check in between 5 and 8 pm but a storage room (unlocked) is available for leaving bags during the day. Get a key to avoid the 10 pm curfew.

Rooms at *Gasthof Höllwirt* (☎ 394, fax -4, Hauptstrasse 29) cost from AS300 to AS420 per person with private shower. The good restaurant, where meals mostly cost over AS100 (closed Wednesday till 6 pm).

Obertrauner Hof (☎ 456-0, fax -78, Hauptstrasse 90) has a range of room prices depending upon the length of stay and season. Expect to pay around AS400 per person for a big room with shower and toilet. The restaurant is also good, with meals starting at about AS80. It's closed on Tuesday except in July and August.

Near the beach and boat landing point is a *skittles alley (Kegelbahn)* with pizzas for AS60 to AS90; it's open from 3 pm (10 am at weekends) until midnight, but closed on Monday except in summer. By the tourist office is a *Konsum* supermarket, which is open Monday to Friday from 7.30 am to noon and 3 to 6 pm and Saturday from 7 am to noon.

Getting There & Away

Buses between Hallstatt and Obertraun are patchy, with only five or fewer running per day, but it's possible to hitch, or the walk takes 50 minutes. Four or five boats per day

go between Obertraun and Hallstatt in summer (AS40, 25 minutes).

You can rent bicycles from Obertraun-Dachsteinhöhlen, the train station for the village. Obertraun-Koppenbrüllerhöhle is the station for the water cave, and trains only stop here in summer when the caves are open.

BAD AUSSEE
☎ 03622 • pop 5100 • 650m

Bad Aussee is the chief Styrian town in the Salzkammergut. It provides access to two lakes, as well as being a health resort. Everywhere in town there's the sound of rushing water, emanating from the swiftly flowing Traun.

Orientation & Information

The train station is 2km south of the town, which has Kurhausplatz at its centre. The tourist office (☎ 523 23, fax 523 24) is in the town centre, at the corner of the Kurpark – the park is the geographical point (*geografischer Mittelpunkt*) on which the whole country would pivot. The office is open Monday to Friday from 8 am to noon and 2 to 6 pm, Saturday 10 am to noon. In July and August hours are weekdays from 8 am to 7 pm, Saturday from 9 am to 12.30 pm, Sunday 10 am to 12.30 pm. Across the street is the post office (Postamt 8990), with a bus information counter.

Things to See & Do

Bad Aussee has a couple of Gothic churches, and the **Kammerhof Museum** (entry AS40), covering local history and salt production, housed in the 17th century Kammerhof on Chlumeckyplatz (AS40). A sauna, swimming pool and various health treatments are available at the nearby **Kurzentrum** (☎ 532 03-0).

Four kilometres north of the town is **Altausseer See**, a small lake with the village of Altaussee on its western side. From the village there is access to the **Altaussee Salzbergwerk**, where art treasures were secreted during WWII. Several tours (AS130) are conducted daily between 10 am and

4 pm from 1 May to 31 October and at 2 pm on Thursday during the rest of the year. Call ☎ 713 32-51 for information. A scenic road, the Panoramastrasse, climbs most of the way up Loser (1838m), the main peak overlooking the lake. The toll for the return trip is AS40 for cars plus AS67 per person, and AS50 for motorbikes. You'll need snow chains if you wish to travel the road during the winter.

Grundlsee, 5km north-east of Bad Aussee, is a longer, thinner lake, with a good viewpoint at its western end as well as walking trails and water sports (including a sailing school). Extending from the eastern tip of the lake are two smaller lakes, **Toplitzsee** (where the Nazis tested weapons and dumped counterfeit currency) and **Kammersee**. Boats tour all three lakes from May to October (AS130 for the full tour). Call ☎ 8613 for information.

Special Events

Ascension Day, usually in late May/early June, sees the start of the four day Narzissenfest with processions, music, and

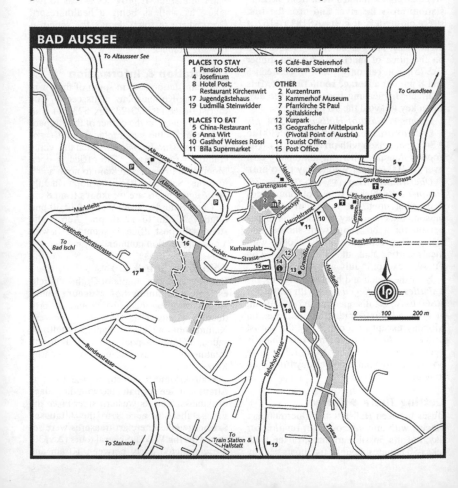

BAD AUSSEE

PLACES TO STAY
1 Pension Stocker
4 Josefinum
8 Hotel Post;
   Restaurant Kirchenwirt
17 Jugendgästehaus
19 Ludmilla Steinwidder

PLACES TO EAT
5 China-Restaurant
6 Anna Wirt
10 Gasthof Weisses Rössl
11 Billa Supermarket

16 Café-Bar Steirerhof
18 Konsum Supermarket

OTHER
2 Kurzentrum
3 Kammerhof Museum
7 Pfarrkirche St Paul
9 Spitalskirche
12 Kurpark
13 Geografischer Mittelpunkt
   (Pivotal Point of Austria)
14 Tourist Office
15 Post Office

To Altausseer See

To Grundlsee

Altausseer-Strasse

Altausseer Traun

Marktleite

Jugendherbergesstrasse

To Bad Ischl

Gärtengasse

Chlumeckypl

Hauptstrasse

Grundlseer-Strasse

Kirchengasse

Grundlseer

Tauscherinweg

Mühlleite

Ischler-Strasse

Kurhausplatz

Stainzerhausplatz

Bahnhofstrasse

To Stainach

To Train Station & Hallstatt

0   100   200 m

animals made of flowers. Entry costs from AS100 to AS150 per day.

Places to Stay

Staff at the tourist office will help to find accommodation free of charge and there is an information touch-screen outside. Many homes around Altausseer See and Grundlsee offer cheap private rooms; these and pensions are listed in the Bad Aussee brochure available from the tourist office.

The HI *Jugendgästehaus* (☎ 522 38, fax -88, Jugendherbergsstrasse 148) is a modern off-white building on the town's hill. Beds cost from AS180 in rooms with one to four beds, with shower. Reception is open all day in July and August, otherwise it's closed from 1 to 5 pm; daytime check-in is usually possible during reception times. It's 15 minutes walk by road, but there are shorter (unlit) footpaths.

Ludmilla Steinwidder (☎ 551 24, Bahnhofstrasse 293), 600m towards the train station from town, has private rooms for about AS180 per person.

Josefinum (☎ 521 24, Gartengasse 13) is the bargain in the centre. It has 13 singles (AS227 with shower/WC, AS207 without) and three doubles (AS397 or AS417 with shower/WC); add AS20 for a single night stay. It's run by nuns so be on your best behaviour (no smoking inside bedrooms). Telephone ahead for evening arrival.

Pension Stocker (☎ 524 84, Altausseer Strasse 245), 500m north-west of Kurhausplatz, has been extensively renovated. Pristine rooms with shower/WC and TV are around AS300 per person. It has a large garden overlooking tennis courts, and off-street parking.

The *Hotel Post* (☎ 535 55, fax 536 66, Kirchengasse 162) has rooms with shower/WC, cable TV and kitchenette. Prices are AS480 per person, AS580 including breakfast.

At the eastern end of Grundlsee, in Gössl, are two *camp sites*: call ☎ 8181 or 8689. A HI *Jugendherberge* (☎ 8629, fax -4) is situated nearby in Wienern, and is open from 1 May to 31 October.

Places to Eat

Restaurant Kirchenwirt in the Hotel Post (see Places to Stay) has a wide choice of Austrian food, with dishes costing between AS85 and AS185. A similar place is *Gasthof Weisses Rössl (Hauptstrasse 156),* which is closed on Wednesday evening and Thursday.

Anna Wirt (Kirchengasse 28) is a Heuriger with good hot and cold buffets – look out for the smoked trout. It's open from 5 pm weekdays and from 10 am Saturday (closed Sunday). Across the river is *China-Restaurant*.

Café-Bar Steirerhof (Ischler Strasse 81) is a bar open from 8 pm; its house pizza (AS85) has lots of toppings.

There's a *Konsum* supermarket on Bahnhofstrasse, south of the tourist office, and a *Billa* on Hauptstrasse.

Getting There & Away

Bad Aussee is on the rail route from Bad Ischl to Stainach-Irdning, with trains running hourly in both directions.

Regular bus services run from the train station to both lakes, calling at Bad Aussee en route; the fare to either lake or to Bad Aussee is AS20.

GOSAUSEE
☎ 06136

This small lake is flanked by some impressively precipitous peaks, such as the Gosaukamm (2459m). The view is good from the lake and there's also a cable car (AS130, AS90 in the low season) that goes up to Zwieselalm (1587m) from mid-May to mid-October. Before reaching the lake on highway 166, you pass through the village of **Gosau**, where there's a tourist office (☎ 8295, fax 8255).

Getting There & Away

Gosau is at the junction to the only road to the lake and can be reached by highway 166 from Hallstätter See. Bundesbus services run to the lake from Bad Ischl (AS70), via Steeg on Hallstätter See, approximately every one to two hours.

THE SALZKAMMERGUT

Northern Salzkammergut

The main lakes of interest are Traunsee – with the three resorts of Gmunden, Traunkirchen and Ebensee – and Wolfgangsee, which is home to the resorts of St Wolfgang and St Gilgen, and which also provides access to the Schafberg peak (1783m).

TRAUNSEE

The eastern flank of this lake (the deepest in Austria at 192m) is dominated by rocky crags, particularly Traunstein (1691m). The resorts are strung along the western shore and are connected by rail. Infrequent Bundesbuses run between the resorts sometimes continuing to Bad Ischl. Boats operated by Traunsee Schiffahrt (☎ 07612-652 15) tour the shoreline, from Gmunden to Ebensee, between 1 May and 26 October; frequencies peak in July and August. The full one-way trip costs AS80 (children AS50). For several journeys, investigate the Punktekarte: AS250 worth of travel for AS210. The famous paddle steamer *Gisela,* once boarded by Franz Josef, takes to the waves in July and August on Saturday and holidays (a AS15 surcharge applies).

GMUNDEN

☎ 07612 • pop 14,000 • 440m

Gmunden is known for its castles and ceramics. It was established in 909 and received a town charter in 1278. Gmunden was a former administration centre for both the Habsburgs and the salt trade.

Orientation & Information

The town centre is on the western bank of the Traun River and has the Rathausplatz at its heart. Just to the west is the tourist office (☎ 643 05, fax 714 10, email info .gmunden@upperaustria.or.at), Am Graben 2, open Monday to Friday from 8 am to 6 pm, Saturday (and Sunday in July and August) from 10 am to 6 pm. Hours from mid-September to mid-May are Monday to

Thursday from 8 am to noon and 2 to 6 pm, Friday till 5 pm. Staff at the office will find rooms free of charge. The post office (Postamt 4810) is 200m up the hill on Bahnhofstrasse.

Things to See & Do

Start explorations in the Rathausplatz, which contains the Rathaus, complete with a ceramic glockenspiel that chimes tunes at 10 am, noon, 2, 4 and 7 pm. More ceramics can be seen in the **Kammerhof** just to the east, open Tuesday to Saturday from 10 am to noon and 2 to 5 pm, and Sunday and holidays from 10 am to noon (AS20, children free). It covers antique Gmunden ceramics and local history and has an art gallery on the top floor.

North of the Rathausplatz is the **Pfarrkirche** (parish church), a Gothic building later remodelled as Baroque and noted for an altar (dating from 1678) by Thomas Schwanthaler.

Off Bahnhofstrasse, midway between the Hauptbahnhof and the centre, is a **ceramics factory** (☎ 786), Keramikstrasse 24, which has free guided tours for groups from Monday to Thursday (telephone ahead to join a tour). More porcelain and other valuable artefacts can be seen in the elegant environment of **Schloss Weyer**, Freygasse 27, east of the Traun. Entry is AS60 and it's open May to September, Tuesday to Friday from 10 am to noon and 2 to 6.30 pm.

Walks along the Esplanade are enjoyable. Head south for 1.5km to reach **Toscana Park**, a protected nature area on a peninsula, which contains a castle (**Landschloss Ort**; now a forestry school). Connected by a causeway is another castle, **Seeschloss Ort**; this 17th century edifice, jutting into the lake, is clearly visible from the Esplanade and forms a fine picture. The castle has achieved recent fame through being portrayed as a hotel in a German sitcom, *Schlosshotel Orth* – fans of the series often ask to stay here, though there are no bedrooms! It's being renovated: there's a new restaurant, an attractive arcaded courtyard and a small chapel (free entry).

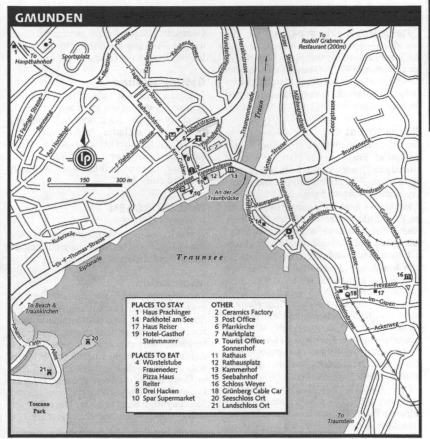

GMUNDEN

PLACES TO STAY	OTHER
1 Haus Prachinger	2 Ceramics Factory
14 Parkhotel am See	3 Post Office
17 Haus Reiser	6 Pfarrkirche
19 Hotel-Gasthof	7 Marktplatz
Steinmaurer	9 Tourist Office;
	Sonnenhof
PLACES TO EAT	11 Rathaus
4 Würstelstube	12 Rathausplatz
Fraueneder;	13 Kammerhof
Pizza Haus	15 Seebahnhof
5 Reiter	16 Schloss Weyer
8 Drei Hacken	18 Grünberg Cable Car
10 Spar Supermarket	20 Seeschloss Ort
	21 Landschloss Ort

The town has schools for sailing, water-skiing and windsurfing and a **beach** (AS60 per day) just south of Toscana Park.

Gmunden provides access to the **Grünberg** lookout (984m). A cable car (AS123 return) ascends from the east side of the lake, or it's easy to walk up.

Places to Stay

Private rooms are the best deal for budget travellers. *Haus Prachinger*, (☎ 755 35, *Kaltenbrunerstrasse 36*), on the tram route from the Hauptbahnhof, has two doubles for AS340; it costs AS25 to use the hall shower. *Haus Reiser* (☎/fax 724 25, *Freygasse 20*) is near Schloss Weyer and has a TV room, garden, five doubles, one single and one triple; prices are about AS260 per person, with private shower/WC.

Hotel-Gasthof Steinmaurer (☎ 704 88, fax -31, *Traunsteinstrasse 23*) is by the Grünberg cable car and across the road from a public beach. Attractive singles/doubles have shower/WC, telephone and balcony and cost AS650/1050. The restaurant has outside seating.

Parkhotel am See (☎ 642 30, fax -66, *Schiffslände 17)* is near the eastern bank of the Traun. It's a four star place with rooms for around AS890/1380 but it's closed from late September to late May. Hotel facilities include a solarium, garage, restaurant and lakeside garden.

Places to Eat

For self-caterers, there's a large *Spar* supermarket at Franz Josef Platz; it's open Monday to Thursday from 8 am to 6.30 pm, Friday from 7.30 am to 7.30 pm and Saturday from 7.30 am to 5 pm.

For snacks there are a couple of stands on the Esplanade, or there's *Reiter (Rinnholz Platz 6)*, a meat store with cheap hot and cold meals and a couple of tables; it closes at 1 pm and on Sunday.

Würstelstube Fraueneder (Tagwerker Strasse 1) is a small, simple place with Austrian food for under AS70 (open daily from 9 am to 10 pm). Next door is *Pizza Haus*, a takeaway place with a small eat-in area (closed till 5 pm on weekends). Chinese restaurants include *Sonnenhof (Teatergasse 4)*, in a courtyard behind the tourist office. It is open daily; weekday lunches cost from AS65 to AS80.

Drei Hacken (Am Graben 10), open daily, has a garden, a basic bar area and palatable food. The menu is standard Austrian fare, including specials with soup, from AS80 to AS160.

Rudolf Grabners Restaurant (☎ 641 69, Scharnsteiner Strasse 15) is deceptively plain-looking from the outside, but it's gourmet quality; reserve ahead (closed Thursday). It also has rooms (AS390/640).

Getting There & Away

Three rail lines converge on Gmunden. Two loop down from Lambach on the Linz-Salzburg route and terminate at Gmunden Seebahnhof, the closest station to the town centre. However, Lambach is bypassed by express trains, one of these lines is for goods trains only and the other is a slow private line which requires a change at Vorchdorf-Eggenberg. This means that Gmunden Hauptbahnhof, on the Salzkammergut Attnang-Puchheim to Stainach-Irdning line, is the easiest to get to.

Getting Around

The Hauptbahnhof (which rents bikes) is 2km north-west of the town centre: tram G regularly departs from outside it to Franz Josef Platz, including after every train arrival. Single tickets cost AS16, but a *Tagesnetzkarte* (day card; AS22) is also valid for the two local bus lines. A family day card costs AS33.

TRAUNKIRCHEN
☎ 07617 • pop 1500

Traunkirchen is an attractive hamlet on a spit of land about halfway along the western shore of the Traunsee.

Information

The small but helpful tourist office in the town centre, the Tourismusbüro (☎ 2234, fax 3340, email info.traunkirchen@upper austria.or.at), is part of the Gemeindeamt building. Staff can provide room listings, sights information in English and a useful walking map with English text. From June to October the office is open Monday to Friday from 8 am to noon and 2 to 4 pm and Saturday from 8 am to noon. The rest of the year it's open weekday mornings only.

Things to See & Do

The main point of interest in the village is the wooden **Fischerkanzel** (Fisherman's Pulpit) in the parish church. It was carved in 1753 and depicts the miracle of the fishes, with the apostles standing in a tub-shaped boat and hauling in fish-laden nets. The composition, colours (mostly silver and gold) and detail (even down to wriggling, bug-eyed fish) create a vivid impression. The church has some fine Baroque altars and portraits of the apostles (Judas is notable by his absence). The church was built by the Jesuits before their suppression in 1773.

The spire on the hill belongs to the **Johannesbergkapelle**, a chapel built in the 14th century or earlier. On the southern side of the hill (the opposite side to the parish church) is a war memorial.

Festival **processions** take place on 5 January and Corpus Christi.

Places to Stay & Eat

Ask the staff at the tourist office to help you find accommodation (they don't charge commission). *Strand-Camping* (☎ *2281*) is by the lake at Viechtau, north of the resort; it's open from 1 May to 30 September. Costs are AS50 per adult, plus AS40 per tent and AS15 for a car.

Seepension Zimmermann (☎ *2371, fax 2360*) is central and right by the lake. It has a grassy terrace and beach area and doubles cost about AS550. On the main street, 60m from the tourist office, is *Goldener Hirsch* (☎/fax *2260*), an inn offering rooms with shower and WC for AS330/600; many have a balcony. The restaurant has good Austrian food, including fish specialities, for about AS65 to AS125. Both places are closed in winter.

Next to the tourist office is a *Konsum* supermarket, open Monday to Friday from 7.30 am to noon and 3 to 6 pm and Saturday from 7 am to noon.

Getting There & Away

Traunkirchen Ort is on the north-south train line, 12km from Gmunden (AS36) and 5km from Ebensee (AS19). It's a four minute walk to the centre from this unstaffed train station; take the path that passes under the tracks. The main Traunkirchen station is one stop north (AS19 from Gmunden) but it's farther from the resort.

EBENSEE

☎ 06133 • pop 8700 • 425m

This town is on the southern shore of the Traunsee.

Orientation & Information

Most of Ebensee is on the eastern bank of the Traun, though the town centre is on the western bank. This is where you'll find the tourist office (☎ 8016, fax 4655, email info.ebensee@upperaustria.or.at), in the Rathaus at Hauptstrasse 34 by the Landungsplatz train station. Opening hours are Monday to Friday from 8 am to noon and 2 to 5 pm, extending to 6 pm in July and August, including Saturday.

Things to See & Do

There is little to see in the town itself. Take the cable car that climbs up to **Feuerkogel** (1592m), where there are walking trails leading across a flattish plateau. Within an hour's walk is Alberfeldkogel (1708m) with an excellent view over the two Langbath lakes. The cable car leaves hourly and costs AS152 up, AS128 down, or AS197 return. Feuerkogel also provides access to winter **skiing** (AS280 for a day pass; easy to medium slopes).

The tourist office will give you details of the many **water sports** on offer, which include fishing, scuba diving, windsurfing and sailing.

Places to Stay & Eat

Ask for the local Gästekarte if you stay in the resort. Around a dozen homes offer private rooms for about AS150 per person; these are listed in the tourist office's accommodation brochure.

The HI *Jugendherberge* (☎ *6698, fax -85, Rindbachstrasse 15*) is 15 minutes walk anticlockwise round the lake and is open from April to October. A bed in a renovated dorm with shower/WC costs AS130/150 for people under/over 19 years. Add AS20 for a single-night stay.

Gasthof Himmel (☎ *5463, Berggasse 27*) is closed Thursday and *Gasthof Kofler* (☎ *5342, Berggasse 1*) is closed Tuesday and Wednesday; each charges around AS250 per person and has an inexpensive restaurant. Berggasse is near the tourist office: head south-west on Hauptstrasse, then take the first street on the right, the first left, and the first right again. On Hauptstrasse itself you'll find the inexpensive *Pizzeria Flamingo*.

Gasthof Auerhahn (☎/*fax 5320, Bahnhofstrasse 55)*, by Ebensee train station, has good Austrian food from AS75 (closed Wednesday). It also has simple rooms (AS280/480) with kitchenette.

Midway between the two train stations, on Bahnhofstrasse, are two supermarkets, a *Billa* and a *Konsum*. *China-Restaurant Jasmin* is also nearby. It is open daily and has cheap lunchtime menus all during the week.

Getting There & Away

The train station for the centre and the boat landing stage is Ebensee-Landungsplatz. The larger Ebensee station is less than 15 minutes walk to the south. The town is 17km north of Bad Ischl (AS36) and the same distance south of Gmunden.

GRÜNAU

If you want to get off the beaten track, consider going to Grünau, east of Traunsee, where there's a new hostel, the *Tree House Backpacker Hotel* (☎ 07616-84 99, fax 85 99, email treehousehostel@hotmail.com, Grünau 525)*, also known as Schindlbach. Rooms with one to four beds and shower/WC cost from AS165 to AS200 per person. There's a sauna, tennis courts, Internet access and two bars and a skiing area is close by. Two-hourly trains run to Grünau from Wels (one hour).

ATTERSEE

The largest lake in the Salzkammergut is flanked mostly by hills, with mountains in the south. Resorts cling to the shoreline, offering the usual water leisure activities. The main resort is **Attersee**, which has a museum and a couple of churches. Its tourist office (☎/fax 07666-7719) is at Nussdorferstrasse 15; staff will help you to find accommodation.

There are two boat circuits of the lake during the summer including a 75 minute tour (AS75) from Attersee town which explores the north and a 2½ hour tour (AS130) commencing from **Weyregg** and heading south.

Weyregg has a HI *Jugendherberge* (☎ 07664-2780, fax -4, Weyregg 3)*, open from 1 May to 30 October.

Getting There & Away

Two lakeside towns, Attersee and Schörfling, are connected to the rail network, each by a line branching from the main Linz-Salzburg route (though only regional trains stop): for Kammer-Schörfling change at Vöcklabruck and for Attersee town change at Vöcklamarkt. An hourly bus runs from Kammer to Weyregg, but services stop late afternoon.

WOLFGANGSEE

This lake is easily accessible from Salzburg and plays host to hordes of summer and weekend visitors escaping the city. In addition to the two main resorts, St Wolfgang and St Gilgen, it has **Strobl** on the eastern shore (population 2750), a pleasant but unremarkable place. It's at the start of a scenic toll road (AS30 per car and per person) to Postalm (1400m). Wherever you stay, ask about the local Gästekarte.

A ferry service operates from Strobl to St Gilgen, stopping at various points en route. Services are from 1 May to 26 October, but more frequent during the high season from late June to early September. The journey from St Wolfgang to St Gilgen (AS52) takes 40 minutes and boats sail approximately hourly from 8.45 am to 5.15 pm (7.55 pm in the high season). In the other direction, the first departure from St Gilgen is at 9.20 am. Holders of Austrian and European rail passes get a 20% fare reduction.

A historic path, the pilgrim's way, connects St Gilgen and St Wolfgang via the western shore. It's a half-day walk.

Schafberg

Wolfgangsee is dominated by the 1783m Schafberg mountain on its northern shore. At the summit you'll find a hotel, a restaurant and phenomenal views over mountains and lakes (especially Mondsee, Attersee and, of course, Wolfgangsee). If you don't fancy the three to four hour walk from St

Wolfgang, ascend by the cogwheel railway which runs from 1 May to 26 October. Departures are approximately hourly between 9 am and 5 pm but the trip is so popular that you probably won't be able to get on the next train to leave: queue early, purchase a ticket for a specified train and then go for a wander along the lake or around St Wolfgang until your train departs.

It takes 40 minutes to reach the top station, which is only a few metres short of the hotel and viewing point. The fare is AS140 up or AS250 return; holders of Austrian and European rail passes get a 15% fare reduction.

ST WOLFGANG
☎ 06138 • pop 2800 • 549m

St Wolfgang was founded in 976 by the Bishop of Regensburg, Germany (who was later canonised) and has achieved renown as a place of pilgrimage.

Orientation & Information
The main streets are Pilgerstrasse and Michael Pacher Strasse, which join at the pilgrimage church. The tourist office (☎ 2239, fax -81, email info@stwolfgang .gv.at), Pilgerstrasse 28, is in the centre, between the church and the post office. It's open Monday to Friday from 8 am to noon and 2 to 5 pm, Saturday from 8 am to noon. In July and August, weekday opening hours are 8 am to 6 pm.

Things to See & Do
The major sight is the **pilgrimage church**, built in the 14th and 15th centuries. This incredible church is virtually a gallery of religious art, with several altars (Gothic to Baroque), a showy pulpit, a fine organ and many statues and paintings. The best piece is the winged high altar built by Michael Pacher between 1471 and 1481, which has astonishing detail on the carved figures and Gothic designs. The church wardens were once so protective that the wings were kept closed except for important festivals. Now they are always open, except for eight weeks before Easter.

The Baroque double altar by Thomas Schwanthaler is also worth a look. It was commissioned in 1675, reputedly to replace Pacher's effort which was considered old-fashioned and thus slated for destruction. According to an apocryphal story, it was Schwanthaler himself who persuaded the then abbot to retain Pacher's high altar. The church is open daily from 7.30 am to dusk.

Beside the church is a bronze **fountain** from 1515. A lengthy inscription includes rather condescending advice to poor pilgrims: if they can't afford wine, they should 'make merry' with the fountain's waters.

A tourist office booklet (free) details the many **water sports** on offer. A few minutes walk anticlockwise round the lake is the start of the Schafberg railway.

Places to Stay
Camping Appesbach (☎ 2206, Au 99) is on the lakeside, 1km from St Wolfgang in the

Pacher's Religious Art

Michael Pacher was the dominant figure in Austrian religious art in the 15th century. He was born in Bruneck (Southern Tirol, now in Italy) in 1435 and died in Salzburg in 1498. His work was rooted in traditional Bruneck art but he also absorbed Dutch and, in particular, northern Italian influences. Pacher was a master of perspective and colouring and gave an impression of fluidity and movement to his statue groups. This is seen in his altar in the pilgrimage church in St Wolfgang. In creating this altar, as in several others, Pacher was aided by his brother Friedrich.

Pacher's style was much imitated, for example in the impressive altar in Kefermarkt, Upper Austria. His paintings and carvings are found in many museums, such as the Landesmuseum Ferdinandeum in Innsbruck (where Friedrich Pacher's work is also featured) and the Orangery of the Unteres Belvedere in Vienna.

direction of Strobl. Open from Easter to 1 October, a site costs AS75 per person and from AS70 for a tent and car.

St Wolfgang has some good *private rooms* (from AS170 per person), either in village homes or in farmhouses on the surrounding hills. Lists are available from the staff at the tourist office who will phone places on your behalf.

Gästehaus Raudaschl (☎ 2329, fax -6, Pilgerstrasse 4), opposite the tourist office, has single/double rooms for AS320/560 with shower; doubles with use of hall showers cost AS400.

Sporthotel Wolfgangerhof (☎ 223 470, fax 250 99, Pilgerstrasse 132) is a three star chalet hotel with a restaurant, swimming pool, sauna and solarium. It's a bargain considering the facilities available: rustic-style singles/doubles with shower/WC, TV and balcony cost AS450/800.

St Wolfgang's most famous hotel is *Im Weissen Rössl (☎ 23 06-0, fax -41, email hpeter@weissesroessl.co.at, Im Stöckl 74)* which, as the White Horse Inn, was the setting for Ralph Benatzky's operetta of the same name. Rustic or modern-style rooms have all amenities and start from AS850/1600. Service is good and the restaurant is highly regarded.

Places to Eat

Buy picnic materials at the *Konsum* supermarket 100m from the Schafberg cogwheel railway ticket office, towards the village centre. There are smaller supermarkets in the centre.

The main street has plenty of eating options ranging from cheap snack joints to quaint touristy restaurants. The centre is compact enough to explore before making a choice. *Pizzeria Mirabella (Pilgerstrasse 152)* has 1st floor tables overlooking the street; pizzas (from AS75) are served from 11.30 am to 3 pm and 6.30 to 9.30 pm.

Sporthotel Wolfgangerhof (see Places to Stay) has a good restaurant with a 1st floor terrace. Austrian meals, including goulash, schnitzels and fish, start at AS78. Try the home-made Apfelstrudel (AS34). It's open

daily till 10 pm (9 pm in winter) and there are also children's menus.

Getting There & Away

The only road to St Wolfgang approaches from the east from Strobl. The Bundesbus service from St Wolfgang to St Gilgen (AS40) and Salzburg (AS90) goes via Strobl, where you usually have to change buses. For the centre of the resort, alight immediately after the St Wolfgang road tunnel. Wolfgangsee ferries stop at the village centre (stop: Markt) and at the Schafberg railway.

ST GILGEN
☎ 06227 • pop 3000 • 550m

St Gilgen is only 29km from Salzburg, and this ease of access has boosted its popularity. Apart from the very scenic setting, there's not too much to see in the town.

Information

The local tourist office (☎ 2348, fax 726 79, email stgilgen@ping.at) is in the Rathaus at Mozartplatz 1. It's open daily in July and August, weekdays and Saturday morning for the rest of summer and only Monday to Friday for the rest of the year.

Things to See & Do

Near the Rathaus is the house where Mozart's mother was born, which now contains a few memorials to the musician. The Muzikinstument-Museum der Völker, Sonnenburggasse 1, has two rooms filled with obscure musical instruments from around the world, plus (summer only) a 25 minute film show on Mozart. Opening times are: 1 June to 15 October, Tuesday to Sunday from 9 to 11 am and 3 to 7 pm; 7 January to 31 May, Monday to Thursday from 2 to 5 pm, Sunday from 3 to 6 pm. Entry is AS45.

Like all lakeside resorts, St Gilgen offers water sports such as windsurfing, water-skiing and sailing. The Strandbad, just to the north of the boat station, is a beach charging AS30 (AS50 for the indoor pool). A little farther, beyond the yacht club, is a small, free beach with a grassy area.

The mountain rising over the resort is **Zwölferhorn** (1520m); a cable car (AS120, or AS180 return) will whisk you to the top where there are good views and walks. Skiers ascend in winter.

Places to Stay & Eat

St Gilgen has a very good HI youth hostel, *Jugendgästehaus Schafbergblick (☎ 2365, fax -75, Mondseestrasse 7)*. It's almost like a hotel in its facilities and attitude, though it does receive the usual school groups. Prices are from AS120 to AS264 per person, in anything from singles to 10-bed dorms, with or without WC and lake view but always with shower, including a fine buffet breakfast. It's closed for five weeks around Christmas. Check-in is from noon to 1 pm or 5 to 7 pm, and you get a key for night-time access. Staying here also gives free entry to the swimming pool.

Staff at the tourist office will help you to find somewhere to stay, or there's an accommodation board, accessible 24 hours every day, opposite the bus station. The cheaper places (private rooms etc) are mostly away from the centre, though *Kendlerhof (☎ 7254, fax 7156, Streicherplatz 6)* is just off the pivotal Mozartplatz and has good breakfasts and solicitous hosts. Singles/doubles cost around AS300/540, or AS360/640 with shower (depending on the season and length of stay). It's open from 1 May to 31 October.

Gasthof Rosam (☎ 2591, Frontfestgasse 2), two minutes from the St Gilgen boat station, charges AS350/540 for rooms with shower and WC. The small restaurant area serves large portions of good Austrian food for AS80 to AS150 until 9 pm. The Gasthof is open from Easter to 31 October.

Pizzeria Bianco (Ischler Strasse 18), by the lake, has pizza and pasta for around AS75, and a salad buffet in summer, when it's open daily (Friday to Sunday in winter). Weekday lunch menus from AS69 are available from *China-Restaurant Hong Kong (Schwarzenbrunner Strasse)*, just off Mozartplatz. *Gasthof Zur Post (☎ 2239, fax 2698, Mozartplatz 8)* is recommended for

slightly pricier regional food (about AS85 to AS190; closed Monday during the off-season) in a rustic-style chalet with a pictorial scene painted on the façade. Rooms with shower/WC and cable TV cost AS450 per person; there's no lift.

Getting There & Away

St Gilgen is 50 minutes from Salzburg by Bundesbus (AS60), with hourly departures until early evening; some buses continue on to Stobl and Bad Ischl. The bus station is near the base station of the cable car. Highway 154 provides a scenic route north to Mondsee. For details of the ferry service to/from St Wolfgang, see the Wolfgangsee section earlier in this chapter.

MONDSEE
☎ 06232 • pop 3000 • 493m

This lake is noted for its warm water; coupled with its closeness to Salzburg (30km away), this factor makes it a popular lake for swimming and other water sports. The village of Mondsee is on the northern tip of the crescent-shaped lake. The tourist office (☎ 2270, fax 4470, email mondsee land.tourismus@upperaustria.or.at) is at Dr Franz Müller Strasse 3, between the church and the lake. It's open daily in summer, weekdays only for the rest of the year.

Segelschule Mondsee (☎ 3548-200, fax -232), Robert Baum Promenade 3, is the largest **sailing school** in Austria. It offers sailing and windsurfing courses, plus boat/board rental costing from AS130/100 per hour.

The main cultural interest in the village is the 15th century **parish church**. The Baroque façade was added in 1740. This large church achieved brief fame when featured in the wedding scenes of *The Sound of Music* movie, but it's worth visiting in any case for its many altars and statues.

Next door, in part of the former abbey, is a **museum** devoted to local history and crafts, including archaeological finds from the Mondsee Culture of the late Stone Age and early Bronze Age. It's open daily between 1 May and mid-October, weekends and holidays only to the end of October. Entry is AS30 (students AS15).

Places to Stay & Eat

For lists of hotels and restaurants, ask at the tourist office. Mondsee has a HI *Jugendgästehaus* (☎ 2418, fax -75, Krankenhausstrasse 9), where prices start at AS150 per person; it's closed from mid-December to mid-January. *Gasthof Grüner Baum* (☎ 2314, Herzog Odilo Strasse 39) has large doubles with shower/WC for AS600. There's no check-in when the restaurant is closed, from 2 to 5 pm and on Tuesday.

Imbissstube (M Guggenbichler Strasse 5) is behind the post office; it has a stand-up buffet section and is closed on Sunday.

It serves sausage snacks and Austrian meals costing AS25 to AS130. For self-caterers there's a *Spar* supermarket close by on Rainerstrasse. On Marktplatz are several pricier places with good atmosphere and food. Try *Gasthof Blaue Traube* (☎ 2237, fax -7) at No 1, which also has singles/doubles from AS490/780.

Getting There & Away

Plenty of Bundesbus routes run to/from Mondsee, including an hourly service from Salzburg (AS60) that takes 40 to 55 minutes. Services to St Gilgen are very infrequent, though ask in the tourist office about the travel agent's shuttle bus that runs in summer (AS70; bikes carried free).

Upper Austria

Upper Austria (Oberösterreich) occupies almost 12,000 sq km and is home to more than 1.3 million people. The province's most important holiday area contains the lakes and mountains of the south-west (see the Salzkammergut chapter). Elsewhere, Upper Austria offers abbeys, quaint and attractive towns in the north and east and a not-so-attractive reminder of Nazi occupation, the Mauthausen concentration camp. Adolf Hitler was born in the province, in Braunau am Inn. His favourite city was Linz, for which he had great (unrealised) plans, including making it the architectural jewel of the Danube. Here he wanted to retire, had he not been forced to retire sooner than planned in a Berlin bunker.

Orientation & Information
Upper Austria is mostly flat, with the Danube running west to east. The river is an important trade artery but this section is less scenic than that in Lower Austria.

The provincial capital is Linz, also the location of the provincial tourist board, Oberösterreich Touristik (☎ 0732-77 30 24, fax 77 30 25, email info@touristik.at), Kapuzinerstrasse 3, A-4021 Linz.

Getting Around
Regional transport in Upper Austria is linked under Oberösterreichischer Verkehrsverbund tickets. Prices depend on the number of zones you travel in, and you can buy single tickets as well as daily, weekly, monthly or yearly passes. If you have a city pass for Linz, Wels or Steyr, you get a one zone discount for regional travel. For information, call ☎ 0660-5047.

Linz

☎ 0732 • pop 203,000 • 266m

Linz is an industrial town and a busy Danube port; important industries are iron, steel and chemicals. The southern suburbs

UPPER AUSTRIA

show a depressing skyline of belching smokestacks but past these you'll find a surprisingly charming and picturesque old town centre.

In Roman times Linz was a fortified camp called Lentia which soon achieved importance for its position on trade routes. Linz was granted the status of regional capital in 1490 by Friedrich III, who was then a resident of the town.

Orientation
Linz lies on both sides of the Danube, with the old town and most attractions on the south bank. Hauptplatz, a spacious square, is the hub; it is mostly car free and abuts Landstrasse, a shopping street with a pedestrian-only section. The Hauptbahnhof

UPPER AUSTRIA

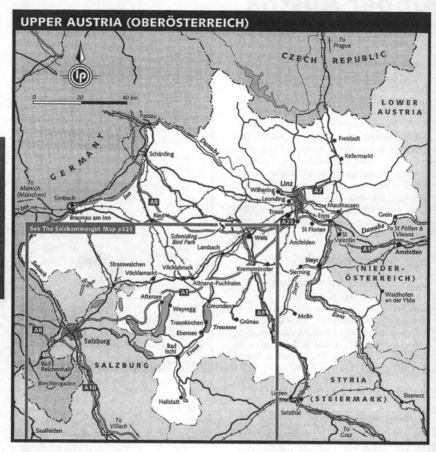

UPPER AUSTRIA (OBERÖSTERREICH)

(main train station) is about 1km to the south and has good facilities (and probably the most expensive lavatories in the country – AS6.50 a go!).

Information

Tourist Offices The tourist office (☎ 7070-1777, fax 77 28 73, email info .linz@upperaustria.or.at), Hauptplatz 1, is open Monday to Friday from 8 am to 7 pm, Saturday from 7 am to 7 pm, and Sunday and holidays from 10 am to 7 pm. From 1 November to 30 April it closes an hour earlier. Staff will search out accommodation free of charge.

The Sparda Bank in the Hauptbahnhof has a free telephone line to the tourist office. It's open Monday to Friday from 8 am to 6 pm, Saturday from 8 am to 2 pm and there's a computer touch screen outside with tourist information.

Personal callers are welcome at the provincial tourist office (see the Orientation & Information section at the start of this chapter), which is open Monday to Friday from 9 am to noon and 1 to 5 pm.

The tourist office and hotels sell the Linz City Card (AS299) providing a meal/drinks voucher worth AS150, a free city tour and free admission to some attractions, including the Ars Electronica Center. The Junior version for children under 14 years old costs AS99.

Post & Communications The main post office (Postamt 4020), opposite and to the west of the Hauptbahnhof, is open for postal services from 7 am to 8 pm on weekdays and from 7.30 am to 8 pm on Saturday; telephones can be used daily from 6 am to midnight. There's another post office (Postamt 4010) on Domgasse.

Travel Agencies American Express (☎ 66 90 13), Bürgerstrasse 14, is open Monday to Friday, 9 am to 5.30 pm and on Saturday, 9 am to noon. It has full financial and travel agency services and charges no commission for cashing Amex travellers cheques.

ÖKISTA (☎ 77 58 93) is at Herrenstrasse 7; it's open Monday to Friday from 9 am to 5.30 pm.

Medical Services The Krankenhaus (hospital; ☎ 78 06-0) is 1km east of the town centre at Krankenhausstrasse 9. Emergency treatment is available at the Unfallkrankenhaus (☎ 69 20-0), Blumauerplatz 1.

South Bank

Follow the walking tour of the town centre outlined in the pamphlet available from the tourist office (in English).

The large Hauptplatz is surrounded by Baroque buildings, including the **Altes Rathaus**, which retains some earlier Renaissance elements. A focal point of the square is the **Dreifaltigkeitssäule** (trinity column) sculpted in Salzburg marble in 1723. This 20m-high Baroque pillar commemorates deliverance from war, fire and plague. A flea market occupies Hauptplatz on Saturday from 7 am to 2 pm (in winter it's at a spot in front of the Neues Rathaus).

Just west of Hauptplatz is the **Landhaus** on Klosterstrasse, the seat of the provincial government. It was constructed between 1564 and 1571. Wander into the arcaded courtyard to see the **Planet Fountain** (1582), which predated the arrival of the great German astronomer Johann Kepler who taught for 14 years in a college once sited here.

Up the hill to the west of Hauptplatz is **Schloss Linz**. This castle has been periodically rebuilt since 799 and provides a good view of the many church spires in the centre. Friedrich III once resided here. It also houses the **Schlossmuseum**, or Landesmuseum, open Tuesday to Friday from 9 am to 5 pm, weekends and holidays from 10 am to 4 pm (admission AS50; temporary exhibitions cost extra). Displays cover art, artefacts and weapons, starting with the Bronze Age, passing through Roman times and winding up in the 19th century.

The neo-Gothic **Neuer Dom** (New Cathedral), built in 1855, features exceptional stained glass, including a window depicting the history of the town. At 131m high, its spire is the second-highest in Austria after Stephansdom in Vienna. The **Alter Dom** (Old Cathedral) is where Anton Bruckner had a 12 year stint as church organist. The style is 17th century Baroque, with the usual stucco and marble décor.

Other churches described in the tourist office's walking tour include the **Minoritenkirche** (Minority Church) featuring paintings on the side altars by Johann Schmidt of Krems, and the **Stadtpfarrkirche** (parish church), with a tomb containing the heart of Friedrich III.

Linz has its share of greenery. **Danube Park** trails alongside the river and boasts unusual metal sculptures. The **Botanischer Garten** (botanical garden) flaunts a plethora of cacti and orchids (entry AS10; kids free).

North Bank

Clearly visible from the old town is the **Pöstlingberg** (537m) on the north bank, providing fine views. At the summit is a

UPPER AUSTRIA

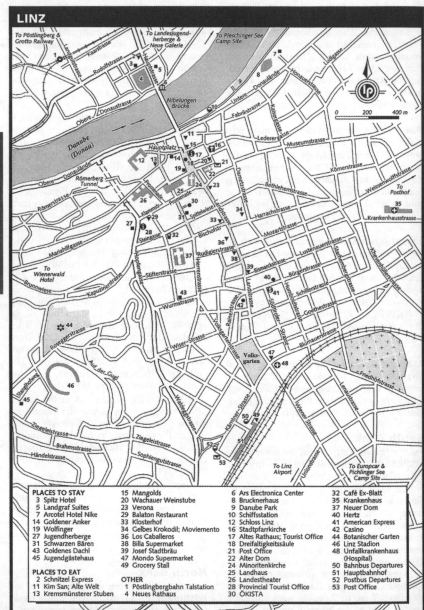

LINZ

To Pöstlingberg &
Grotto Railway

To Landesjugend-
herberge &
Neue Galerie

To Pleschinger See
Camp Site

Langgasse

Kaarstrasse

Rudolfstrasse

Hauptstrasse

Nibelungen
Brücke

Untere Donaulände

Obere Donaustrasse

Honauerstrasse

Ludlgasse

Fabrikstrasse

Lederergasse

Museumstrasse

Kaiserstrasse

Danube
(Donau)

Obere Donaulände

Römerberg
Tunnel

Hauptplatz

Körnerstrasse

Weissenwolffstrasse

To
Posthof

Krankenhausstrasse

Promenade

Klammstr.

Spittelwiese

Landstrasse

Bethlehemstrasse

Harrachstrasse

Mozartstrasse

Lustenauerstrasse

Starhembergstrasse

Dametzstrasse

Bischofstr.

Rudigierstrasse

Herrenstrasse

Mariahilfgasse

To
Wienerwald
Hotel

Brunnwiese

Kapuzinerstrasse

Stifterstrasse

Hopfengasse

Wurmstrasse

Bismarckstrasse

Bürgerstrasse

Schillerstrasse

Goethestrasse

Blumauerstrasse

Landstrasse

Humboldtstrasse

Südtiroler Strasse

Khevenhüllerstrasse

Rosegger-strasse

Auf der Gugl

Stadhofweg

Ziegeleistrasse

Brahmsstrasse

Händelstrasse

Sophiengutstrasse

Ziegeleistrasse

Wiser-Strasse

Waldeggstrasse

Volksgartenstrasse

Rainerstrasse

Volks-
garten

Kärntner Strasse

Wiener Strasse

Unionstrasse

Friedhofstrasse

Lenaustrasse

To
Europcar &
Pichlinger See
Camp Site

To Linz
Airport

0   200   400 m

PLACES TO STAY
3 Spitz Hotel
5 Landgraf Suites
7 Arcotel Hotel Nike
14 Goldener Anker
19 Wolfinger
27 Jugendherberge
31 Schwarzen Bären
43 Goldenes Dachl
45 Jugendgästehaus

PLACES TO EAT
2 Schnitzel Express
11 Kim San; Alte Welt
13 Kremsmünsterer Stuben

15 Mangolds
20 Wachauer Weinstube
23 Verona
29 Balaton Restaurant
33 Klosterhof
34 Gelbes Krokodil; Moviemento
36 Los Caballeros
38 Billa Supermarket
39 Josef Stadtbräu
47 Mondo Supermarket
49 Grocery Stall

OTHER
1 Pöstlingbergbahn Talstation
4 Neues Rathaus

6 Ars Electronica Center
8 Brucknerhaus
9 Danube Park
10 Schiffsstation
12 Schloss Linz
16 Stadtpfarrkirche
17 Altes Rathaus; Tourist Office
18 Dreifaltigkeitssäule
21 Post Office
22 Alter Dom
24 Minoritenkirche
25 Landhaus
26 Landestheater
28 Provincial Tourist Office
30 ÖKISTA

32 Café Ex-Blatt
35 Krankenhaus
37 Neuer Dom
40 Hertz
41 American Express
42 Casino
44 Botanischer Garten
46 Linz Stadion
48 Unfallkrankenhaus
   (Hospital)
50 Bahnbus Departures
51 Hauptbahnhof
52 Postbus Departures
53 Post Office

twin-spired Baroque church dating from the 18th century. The walk up is gentle, or you can take the Pöstlingbergbahn that runs every 20 minutes till 8 pm. It costs AS40 return (or AS48 including a ride on tram No 3 from the town centre to the lower station (Pöstlingbergbahn Talstation) – get this ticket from the tourist office). At the top is a **grotto railway** (AS50; children AS25) that meanders past scenes from fairy stories. It runs from the Saturday before Palm Sunday to 2 November.

At the northern side of the Nibelungen Brücke (bridge) is the new **Ars Electronica Center** exhibiting interactive computer wizardry and giving free internet access. There are lots of computer simulations, with numerous staff on hand to explain what's going on. An impressive exhibit is the Cave of Virtual Reality, which allows you to take a 3D trip though space and time (explore the universe, visit a Renaissance city). There's also a virtual reality flying machine that will whisk you over Linz (expect to queue). Displays require high maintenance, so some exhibits will probably be out of action during your visit. It's open Wednesday to Sunday from 11 am to 7 pm and entry costs AS80 (students/seniors AS40).

The **Neue Galerie** at Blütenstrasse 15 exhibits German and Austrian art from the 19th and 20th centuries, with the likes of Klimt and Schiele well represented. Entry costs upwards of AS60 (students/seniors AS30), depending on exhibitions. It's open daily from 10 am to 6 pm (10 pm on Thursday), except from June to September when it's closed from 1 pm on Saturday and all day Sunday.

Special Events

The famous **Brucknerfest** is held during September, for which tickets are from AS220 to AS1100, or from AS40 to AS50 for standing room. Concerts are held primarily at the city's premier music venue, Brucknerhaus (☎ 77 52 30, fax 7612-201), Untere Donaulände 7, A-4010. The Brucknerfest kicks off with the Klangwolke 'cloud of sound' weekend in Danube Park,

when there's free music and lasers sear the night sky.

The Linz city festival in late May brings free rock, jazz and folk to the streets around Urfahrmarkt on the north bank. The Ars Electronica (technology exhibition with avant-garde music) takes place in early September and in late July there's a street artists' festival.

Places to Stay – Budget

Camping *Pichlinger See* (☎ 30 53 14) is about 16km south-east of town at Wiener Bundesstrasse 937; infrequent Bundesbuses run there from the Hauptbahnhof. It's open from March to November and has a restaurant. *Pleschinger See* (☎ 24 78 70) is in a protected area (no motor vehicles) on the north bank by the Danube cycle track, about 5km north-east of the Nibelungen Brücke. It's open from May to September and a site costs AS45 per adult and AS45 per tent.

Hostels There are three HI hostels in Linz, all offering rooms with private shower/WC. The *Jugendgästehaus* (☎ 66 44 34, fax 60 21 64, Stanglhofweg 3), near Linz Stadion, has singles/doubles for AS318/436 and four-bed dorms for AS158 per person. Morning check-in is possible on weekdays, otherwise it's from 6 pm.

The *Landesjugendherberge* (☎ 73 70 78, fax -15, Blütenstrasse 19-23), in a tower block on the north bank, has two to five-bed rooms costing AS10 per person (AS105 for those aged under 19), plus AS25 in winter. It's intended for groups but individuals can stay. Take the lift within the multistorey car park. Meals are cheap: breakfast costs AS20, lunch is AS35 and dinner is AS25. You can check in when reception is open: weekdays from 7 am to 10 pm, weekends from 7 am to 10 am and 5 to 10 pm. Reception may close as early as 6 pm in winter, so phone ahead.

The *Jugendherberge* (☎ 78 27 20, fax 78 17 894, Kapuzinerstrasse 14) is small, central and more personal. Beds cost AS160/130 for people over/under 19 years, and breakfast is AS30. There's a washing

UPPER AUSTRIA

machine, common room and no curfew. Check-in is from 5 to 8 pm, and the hostel is usually closed from November to 1 March. Phone to check.

Hotels & Pensions There aren't many budget places in town. The cheapest hotel is *Goldenes Dachl* (☎ 7 58 97, *Hafnerstrasse 27*), one block south of the Neuer Dom. Singles/doubles with hall shower cost AS260/460, without breakfast.

Wienerwald (☎ 77 78 81, fax 78 46 73, *Freinbergstrasse 18*) is next to the western terminus of bus No 26 (last one leaves town at 7.46 pm!), 1.5km from the town centre. It has a restaurant serving the usual chicken dishes. The rooms are reasonably large and decent value at AS330/530 with a private shower in the hall or AS290/490 with no access to a shower. Credit cards are accepted and there's ample parking.

Places to Stay – Mid-Range & Top End

Goldener Anker (☎/fax 77 10 88, *Hofgasse 5*), off Hauptplatz, has singles/doubles for AS305/590, or AS450/670 with private shower/WC. It's attractively priced considering its central location, on a street with cafés and bars. Optional breakfast costs AS75 per person and the restaurant is closed at weekends.

Schwarzen Bären (☎ 77 24 77, fax -47, *Herrenstrasse 9-11*) provides comfortable if unremarkable accommodation in a convenient location. Prices start at AS480/720, or AS680/880 with private shower/WC and satellite TV. Garage parking costs AS50 per night.

Wolfinger (☎ 77 32 91, fax -55, *Hauptplatz 19*) is a stylish place in the pedestrian zone. The historical ambience is accentuated by archways, stuccowork and period furniture. Rooms with shower/WC and TV start at about AS820/1200, with the best rates at weekends.

Arcotel Hotel Nike (☎ 76 26-0, fax -2, *Untere Donaulände 9*), next to the Brucknerhaus, has an office block appearance and charges AS1500/2000 for rooms with good views. Facilities include an indoor swimming pool. More affordable is the Best Western *Spitz Hotel* (☎ 73 64 41-0, fax 73 08 41, *Fiedlerstrasse 6*), where rooms cost AS950/1550. Longer staying guests are normally accommodated at the *Landgraf Suites*, nearby at Hauptstrasse 12, where rooms contain a kitchenette.

Places to Eat

Linz is the home of a tempting almond pastry and raspberry cake, the *Linzer Torte*.

Self-caterers can find supermarkets including a *Mondo* at Blumauerplatz and a *Billa* on Landstrasse. There are plenty of cheap *Würstel* (sausage) *stands* lining the Volksgarten on Landstrasse. The Hauptbahnhof contains snack stands and a sit-down restaurant. A grocery stall outside is open daily from 10 am to around 8 pm.

Mangolds (Hauptplatz 3) is a self-service vegetarian restaurant open from 11 am to 8 pm (closes at 5 pm on Saturday and all day Sunday and holidays). There are cheap set menus, and the buffet costs AS14 per 100g. Another place with lots of veggie choices is *Gelbes Krokodil (Dametzstrasse 30)*; it's not open at weekend lunchtimes.

Schnitzel Express is a self-service place on Hauptstrasse, just north of Nibelungen Brücke. Schnitzels start at only AS45 and it's open daily from 10 am to 10 pm.

Josef Stadtbräu (Landstrasse 49) has a big beer garden. All-you-can-eat weekday brunches cost AS79 and other meals are under AS100; beer is brewed here too. There's live music from 5 pm on Sunday (not in summer).

Verona, in a courtyard off Taubenmarkt, is an Italian restaurant serving big pizzas starting at AS59. There are many Chinese restaurants scattered around town, including *Kim San*, in a courtyard off Hauptplatz. Set menus are available at lunchtime and in the evening.

Los Caballeros (Landstrasse 32) is a Mexican restaurant offering a special deal at weekday lunchtimes: AS78 buys you an all-you-can-eat meal. It's open daily from 11 am to 2 pm. *Balaton Restaurant*

(*Klammstrasse 7*) serves inexpensive Hungarian cuisine in a comfortable environment; it's closed Monday. For simple, cheap Austrian food in a quiet wine tavern, try *Wachauer Weinstube (Pfarrgasse 20)*; it's closed at weekends and on holidays.

Klosterhof (Landstrasse 30) is a large and popular eatery in a 17th century building. Each dining room has a different ambience and there's a huge beer garden. It's open daily from 9 am to midnight and meals start at about AS85.

The expensive choice for gourmets is *Kremsmünsterer Stuben (☎ 78 21 11, Altstadt 10)*. Typical Austrian dishes (from AS195) have been adapted to suit more refined tastes. This place is closed Monday lunchtime and all day Sunday.

Entertainment

Café Ex-Blatt, on the corner of Steingasse and Waltherstrasse, caters for students, as do many bars in the centre. It has candles on tables, walls crammed with pictures, pizza for AS84 and beer costs AS36 for 0.5L. It's open daily till 1 or 2 am. *Alte Welt (☎ 77 00 53, Hauptplatz 4)*, has music and cultural events most nights, as well as reasonable food; it's closed on Sunday.

The *Posthof (☎ 77 05 48, Posthofstrasse 43)* is a centre for contemporary music, dance and theatre, particularly avant-garde events. Programmes at the *Landestheater (☎ 76 11-100, Promenade 39)* are generally more traditional. *Moviemento (Dametzstrasse 30)* shows original-language, non-mainstream films (AS85).

There is a *casino* in the Hotel Schillerpark, Rainerstrasse 2-4; it's open daily from 3 pm. *Linz Stadion (☎ 573 11, Roseggerstrasse 41)* stages sports events and major pop concerts.

Getting There & Away

Air Linz airport mostly handles national and charter flights. For information call the airport direct on ☎ 07721-600-0. Austrian Airlines and Swissair (☎ 1789) are at Schubertstrasse 1; from Landstrasse, walk east down Bismarckstrasse for three blocks.

Bus Bundesbuses depart from stands near the Hauptbahnhof: Bahnbuses from the stands to the north, and Postbuses from beyond the small park to the west. Allow sufficient time to locate your departure point. There's a bus information counter at each location, or call ☎ 16 71 or 60 70 80.

Train Linz is on the main rail route between Vienna and Salzburg, with express trains hourly in both directions. Slower trains also service this and other routes. At least two trains depart daily for Prague (AS302 each way, AS522 for a weekend return). They are direct in summer; change at Summerau at other times. For train information call ☎ 17 17.

Car & Motorcycle The city has good road connections. The east-west A1/E60 passes the south of the city; the A7 branches north from there and skirts the old city centre.

Boat The Schiffsstation is at Untere Donaulände 1, on the south bank just east of Nibelungen Brücke. Wurm + Köck boats (☎ 78 36 07) run westwards from early April to 31 October, but the full trip as far as Passau (AS242 one way, AS284 return) only operates from 1 May to 25 October, running daily. The trip takes seven hours Linz-Passau and five hours Passau-Linz.

Ardagger (☎ 07479-64 64-0) runs boats from Linz to Krems; see the Danube Valley section in the Lower Austria chapter for details.

Getting Around

Linz airport is 12km south-west of the town. A taxi would cost up to AS300. Hourly trains from Linz Hauptbahnhof run to the nearest train station, Hörsching (AS17; direction: Salzburg), which is 30 minutes walk from the airport. Alternatively, there should be a free airport bus running from Linz; inquire in the train information office in the Hauptbahnhof.

Public transport includes trams (such as the No 3 between the Hauptbahnhof and Hauptplatz) and buses, but by early evening some services stop or become infrequent. Get single tickets (AS18; correct change required) from pavement dispensers, which also supply day passes (AS36) and weekly passes (AS120, valid Monday to Sunday), as do Tabak shops. Drivers don't sell tickets – buy and validate tickets before boarding.

Linz has offices for all the major car hire firms including Avis (☎ 66 28 81), Europaplatz 7; Europcar (☎ 60 00 91), Wiener Strasse 91; and Hertz (☎ 78 48 41), Bürgerstrasse 19. There's free car parking at Urfahrmarkt.

You can hire bikes at the Hauptbahnhof daily from 6 am to 9.30 pm.

Around Linz

The following places can be visited on day trips from Linz, but to fully experience the character of these towns, you should plan to stay overnight. If you enjoy rococo interiors, consider also visiting the **Cistercian abbey** at Wilhering, 9km west of Linz, on the south bank of the Danube. The abbey church is breathtaking for its extremely elaborate but delicate ornamentation.

MAUTHAUSEN
☎ 07238 • pop 4500

Nowadays Mauthausen is a pleasant small town on the north bank of the Danube east of Linz, but its status as a quarrying centre prompted the Nazis to site a *Konzentrationslager* (concentration camp) here. Prisoners toiled in the granite quarry and all too often perished on the so-called *Todesstiege* (Stairway of Death) leading from the quarry to the camp. Some 200,000 prisoners died or were executed in the camp between 1938 and 1945. The museum tells the story of this and other camps (such as those at Ebensee and Melk) using German text, charts, artefacts and many harrowing photos. Visitors can see the inmates' living quarters (each designed for 200, but housing up to 500) and gas chambers. In the camp and on the approach to the quarry there are numerous poignant memorials to the deceased.

The camp is open between 1 February and mid-December, from 8 am to 4 pm (6 pm April to September), and charges an entry fee of AS25 (students and seniors AS10). Some people might feel that charging to see such horrors is inappropriate; in other countries, camps such as Auschwitz and Dachau have free entry.

On the way through Mauthausen, pause for awhile in the centre. On the side of the house at Heindlkai 31, by the main road, there's a scene in relief showing a sadistic dentist at work. Round the corner, facing the Danube, is Chalet Wedl, with a colourful façade and some distinctive features, such as the giant spider's web on the metal gate. West along Heindlkai are places to stay and eat, as well as the tourist office (☎ 2243), which is open daily till 7 pm from 1 May to 31 September. In winter, information is available next door at Gasthof Zur Traube (☎ 2023-0).

Getting There & Away

Mauthausen train station is about 1.5km east of the town centre and can be reached from Linz in about 30 to 50 minutes (AS68), depending upon connections in St Valentin. You can rent a bike from the station, which eases the 5km journey to the camp (signposted KZ Mauthausen). If you want to walk, you can do it in 40 minutes: walk through the town (12 minutes) and then take the signposted *Fussweg* (footpath) to the right after the Freizeitzentrum (bikes can take this route too).

The bus from Linz takes 55 minutes and gets you about 3km closer to the camp than the train. Another option is to take the Donauschiffahrt Ardagger boat from the Schiffsstation in Linz (AS70 each way) on Sunday, Tuesday, or Thursday, returning the next day.

ST FLORIAN
☎ 07224 • pop 5600 • 300m

This town has one of the best abbeys in Upper Austria, if not the whole country, and is easily accessible from Linz. St Florian was a Roman who converted to

Christianity and was drowned in the Enns River (in 304) for his pains. In many Austrian churches he is represented wearing Roman military uniform and dousing flames with a bucket of water.

Orientation & Information

St Florian is a market town 15km south-east of Linz. The centre of town is Marktplatz, where there's a small tourist office (☎/fax 56 90) at No 3, open Monday to Friday from 9 am to 1 pm (closed December and January). The post office (Postamt 4490) is also here.

Augustiner Chorherrenstift

The Baroque spires of this Augustinian abbey are visible from anywhere in town. The abbey dates from at least 819 and has been occupied by the Augustinians since 1071. The Baroque appearance was created between 1688 and 1751 by Carlo Carlone and Jakob Prandtauer. The main entrance, framed by statues, is especially impressive, particularly when bathed in the afternoon sunlight.

The interior is accessible by a guided tour (one hour) which takes in lavish apartments, resplendent with rich stucco and emotive frescoes. They include 16 emperor's rooms (once occupied by visiting popes and royalty) and a library housing 125,000 volumes. The Marble Hall is dedicated to Prince Eugene of Savoy, a Frenchman who led the Habsburg army to victory over the Turks in many battles. Prince Eugene's Room contains an amusing bed featuring carved Turks.

The high point of the interior is the **Altdorfer Gallery**, displaying 14 paintings by Albrecht Altdorfer (1480-1538) of the Danube school. There are eight scenes of Christ and four of St Sebastian – all vivid and dramatic with an innovative use of light and dark. Altdorfer cleverly tapped into contemporary issues to depict his biblical scenes (for example, one of Christ's tormentors is clearly a Turk).

The **Stiftskirche** (abbey church) is almost overpowering in its extensive use of stucco and frescoes. The altar is made from 700 tonnes of Salzburg marble, and the huge organ (1774) was the largest in Europe at the time it was built. Anton Bruckner was a choir boy in St Florian and was church organist from 1850 to 1855; he is buried in the crypt below his beloved organ. Also in the crypt are the remains of 6000 people, their bones and skulls stacked in neat rows.

Abbey tours cost AS60 (students AS55) and run daily from Easter to 31 October at 10 and 11 am and 2, 3 and 4 pm. They're usually in German (notes in English), though phone (☎ 89 02-10) to see if you can join an English tour. The Stiftskirche can be visited without joining a tour.

Attached to the abbey is the **Historisches Feuerwehrzeughaus** (Fire Brigade Museum), open from 1 May to 31 October, daily except Monday from 9 am to noon and 2 to 4 pm. It displays historic fire engines, hoses, buckets and other fire-fighting paraphernalia (admission AS25, students AS15).

Schloss Hohenbrunn

Less than 2km west of town is Schloss Hohenbrunn, built between 1722 and 1732 in Baroque style; the architect was Jakob Prandtauer. This stately home houses a fairly interesting museum of hunting and fishing (Jagd und Fischereimuseum). Blood sports are celebrated in art, ornaments, implements, weapons and even the castle stuccowork. It is open between 1 April and 31 October from 10 am to noon and 1 to 5 pm. It's closed Monday except public holidays. Admission costs AS30 (students AS25).

Places to Stay & Eat

St Florian has about seven small-scale places to stay. *Zum Goldenen Pflug* (☎ 42 26, Speiserberg 3), near the abbey gates, has singles/doubles with shower/WC starting at AS300/500.

Gasthof Erzherzog Franz Ferdinand (☎ 42 45-0, fax -9, Marktplatz 13) is the largest (71 beds) and fanciest (three star) place. Rooms with shower/WC, TV and radio cost upwards of AS460/820.

For self-caterers there's a *Spar* supermarket by the Lagerhaus bus stop. *Gasthaus Goldener Löwe (Speiserberg 9)*, by the abbey gates, serves Austrian dishes costing from AS85 to AS120. It has a courtyard and garden and is closed Wednesday.

Down the hill at Linzer Strasse 11 is *Zum Grünen Baum*. Ageing rooms with shower/WC cost AS320/480. Its restaurant has two-course lunch menus (AS62 and AS82) and an evening 'Heurigen Buffet'; it's closed Sunday evening. On the corner with Speiserberg, is *Gasthof Zur Traube*, offering Austrian food and lunches for about AS70 (closed Friday lunchtime and Thursday).

Getting There & Away

St Florian is not accessible by train. Buses depart from the Postbus stop at Linz Hauptbahnhof and take 25 minutes to reach St Florian (AS24). Several buses do the trip (frequent departures), but allow time to locate the right bus, as they don't all have St Florian marked on the front. Buses to Sierning and Molln call at Hohenbrunn after St Florian (AS24 from Linz).

STEYR

☎ 07252 • pop 43,000 • 310m

Like Linz, Steyr has an attractive town centre despite its heavy industries; it was also the first town in Europe to have electric street lighting (1884). The iron industry has been the backbone of its prosperity since the Middle Ages. Steyr made armaments in WWI and WWII and, in 1944, was bombed for its trouble. During the Allied occupation it was a frontier town between the US and Soviet zones.

Orientation & Information

The picturesque town centre is contained within the converging branches of the Enns and Steyr rivers. The Hauptbahnhof, on the eastern bank of the Enns, is about eight minutes walk from the pivotal Stadtplatz. The tourist office (☎ 532 29-0, fax -15, email steyr-info@ris.at) is in the Rathaus, at

Stadtplatz 27; it's open Monday to Friday from 8.30 am to 6 pm, and Saturday from 9 am to noon. At Christmas time, Saturday hours extend to 4 pm and it's open Sunday from 10 am to 3 pm. (Steyr is busy then because nearby Christkindl has a post office issuing special Christmas postmarks.)

To the west of the Hauptbahnhof is the main post office (Hauptpostamt 4400), open Monday to Friday, 7.30 am to 7 pm and Saturday, 8 am to 11 pm. Cash can be exchanged during these hours, but not travellers cheques. Another post office is at Grünmarkt 1, adjoining Stadtplatz, where there are several Bankomat machines.

Things to See & Do

Steyr's main points of interest are clustered on or around Stadtplatz. A 17th century fountain is at the centre of the long, narrow square. One of the most noteworthy buildings is the 18th century **Rathaus**, with a church-like belfry and a rococo façade. Opposite, at No 32, is the 13th century **Bummerlhaus**, a symbol of the town with its Gothic appearance and steep gable.

Other buildings round the square have distinctive arcades and courtyards – some house modern businesses: wander into the

Steyr was home to Franz Schubert, the inspiration behind 'Schubertiade' musical evenings.

The Augustinian abbey at St Florian, Upper Austria, decorated between 1688 and 1751, is renowned both for its outstanding Baroque exterior and for the rich stucco and emotive frescoes of its interior.

JON DAVISON

The inner courtyard of Benedictine Stift Melk.

MARK HONAN

The renowned vine-growing area of Dürnstein.

MARK HONAN

Picturesque Dürnstein, with the ruins of Kuenringerburg perched on a hill above the village.

bank at No 9 and the clothes shop at No 14. You can admire the fine façade of **No 12**, with its angels and crests, and see where Franz Schubert lived at No 16.

Two highly visible buildings at the northern end of the Stadtplatz area are **Schloss Lamberg**, which was restored in Baroque style in 1727 after a fire damaged the town centre, and **Michaelerkirche** (1635), just across the Steyr River where it meets the Enns, which has a large gable fresco.

At the southern end of Stadtplatz is **Marienkirche** (St Mary's Church), a mix of Gothic and Baroque styles, with an extremely ornate high altar and pulpit. The alcoves for the side altars are rich in stucco; the one to the left of the entrance contains a statue of St Florian.

A little way up the hill to the west is the **Stadtpfarrkirche**, a Gothic creation from the 15th century. It shares some features with Stephansdom in Vienna, just as it shared the same architect, Hans Puchsbaum, but it's a much cruder work. Down the steps to the south is the **Heimatmuseum**, in the 17th century granary Innerberger Stadel, Grün-

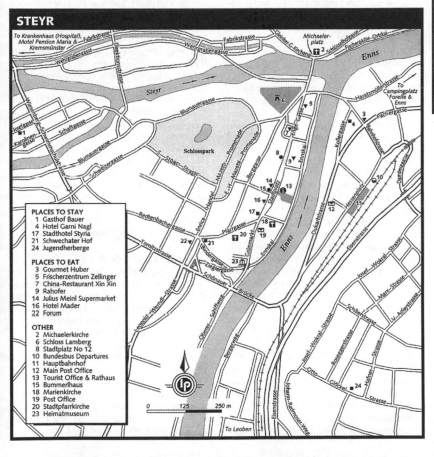

STEYR

To Krankenhaus (Hospital),
Motel Pension Maria &
Kremsmünster

PLACES TO STAY
1 Gasthof Bauer
4 Hotel Garni Nagl
17 Stadthotel Styria
21 Schwechater Hof
24 Jugendherberge

PLACES TO EAT
3 Gourmet Huber
5 Frischerzentrum Zellinger
7 China-Restaurant Xin Xin
9 Rahofer
14 Julius Meinl Supermarket
16 Hotel Mader
22 Forum

OTHER
2 Michaelerkirche
6 Schloss Lamberg
8 Stadtplatz No 12
10 Bundesbus Departures
11 Hauptbahnhof
12 Main Post Office
13 Tourist Office & Rathaus
15 Bummerlhaus
18 Marienkirche
19 Post Office
20 Stadtpfarrkirche
23 Heimatmuseum

0   125   250 m

To Leoben

UPPER AUSTRIA

markt 26. It has displays of history, culture and folklore, including mechanical puppets. Entry is free and it's open from 10 am to 4 pm except on Monday and (from November to March) Tuesday.

Places to Stay

Campingplatz Forelle (☎ 780 08, *Kermatmüllerstrasse 1A, Münichholz*) is about 2km north of town on the eastern bank of the Enns (take bus No 1 from the centre). It is open from May to September.

The HI *Jugendherberge* (☎/fax 455 80, *Hafner Strasse 14*) is behind and to the south of the Hauptbahnhof: pass under the tracks via Damberggasse, take the second street on the right after the overpass bridge and then bear right on Viktor Adlerstrasse. It's closed for Christmas and New Year and dorm beds cost just AS76 (AS69 for those aged under 19); reception is open from 3 pm on weekdays and 5 pm on weekends.

Other than these options, budget travellers will have a problem in Steyr. The few cheap choices (including private rooms) are inconveniently far from the centre. *Hotel Garni Nagl* (☎ 529 76, *Kollergasse 1*), off Bahnhofstrasse, is an exception. It charges AS300/500/720 for singles/doubles/triples with private shower cubicle.

Motel Pension Maria (☎ 710 62, fax -66, *Reindlgutstrasse 25*), 2km west of the town centre, is a short walk beyond the Krankenhaus (where bus No 2 stops). Singles/ doubles/triples with private shower/WC and cable TV cost AS270/540/690. It's closed on Friday and Saturday so phone ahead to book on these days. *Gasthof Bauer* (☎ 544 41, *Josefgasse 7*) is on an island in the Steyr River, accessible from the town centre. This small place has rooms with shower/WC starting at AS330/660 (closed Tuesday).

Schwechater Hof (☎ 530 67, fax 477 054, *Leopold Werndl Strasse 1*), behind the Stadtpfarrkirche, has a rustic restaurant; singles/doubles with shower/WC, cable TV and telephone cost AS580/850.

Stadthotel Styria (☎ 515 51, fax -51, *Stadtplatz 40*) is the next category up, with

rooms starting at AS790/1040 plus a sauna and solarium (free for guests).

Places to Eat

The *Julius Meinl* supermarket (*Stadtplatz 30*) is open daily except Sunday from 7.30 am to 6.30 pm (5 pm Saturday). There are snack stands on Stadtplatz, which also hosts an open-air market on Thursday and Saturday mornings. The *Forum* department store (*Leopold Werndl Strasse 2*) houses a *Spar* supermarket as well as a cheap self-service restaurant.

Frischerzentrum Zellinger (*Enge Gasse 13*) is a grocery shop with a self-service café at the rear. Meals cost just AS49 to AS69 and it's open Monday to Friday from 7.30 am to 6 pm and Saturday from 7 am to noon. The misleadingly titled *Gourmet Huber* (*Bahnhofstrasse 3*) is a similar, smaller, simpler place. *China-Restaurant Xin Xin* (*Enge Gasse 20*) offers lunch menus with soup (starting at AS55) from Monday to Saturday.

Schwechater Hof (see the previous Places to Stay) has an inexpensive rustic restaurant with a garden. *Hotel Mader* (☎ 533 58, *Stadtplatz 36*) provides reliable Austrian cuisine; most dishes cost over AS100. It has several different sections, including a garden; it's closed Sunday. Across the square, *Rahofer* (*Stadtplatz 9*) serves good Italian food and also has a courtyard (closed Sunday and Monday).

Getting There & Away

Trains from Linz (40 minutes, AS84) are direct every two hours, or require a change at St Valentin. Trains continue south into Styria. Steyr Hauptbahnhof has a restaurant, a bike rental service, a left-luggage counter and a travel information office.

Bundesbuses and city buses leave from outside the Hauptbahnhof to the north, where there's a bus information booth open Monday to Friday, 8 am to 3 pm. Two buses a day go to St Florian. Buses run to Linz (70 minutes) approximately hourly. Steyr is on highway 115, the road branching from the A1/E60 and running south to Leoben.

WELS

☎ 07242 • pop 62,000 • 317m

Wels is an agricultural hub with a historic and appealing centre. Most of the country-side comes to town for the agricultural fair and Volksfest carnival, which together take over Wels in early September.

The tourist office (☎ 434 95, fax 479 04, email office@tourism-wels.at) is at Stadt-platz 55.

Things to See & Do

The focal point of the town is the long **Stadtplatz**, lined with historic buildings and eye-catching façades. Branching off are several attractive courtyards (for example, at Stadtplatz 34). Audio guides (AS20) or written tour notes (free) for the centre are available from the tourist office. At the western end of Stadtplatz, in the former leather workers' district, is a tower, the **Led-ererturm** (1618), and at the eastern end is the Stadtpfarrkirche, with a fine Roman-esque porch and Gothic stained glass. Op-posite the church, Stadtplatz 24 bears paintwork from 1570 and was occupied by Salome Alt, the mistress of Salzburg's prince-archbishop Wolf Dietrich.

Behind Stadtplatz 14 is the stately **Kul-turzentrum Burg** where Maximilian I breathed his last in 1519. It now houses a museum: among the exhibits are two room interiors (rustic and Biedermeier), and some ingenious small puppets activated from un-derneath. North of the tourist office, at Pollheimer Strasse 17, is the **Stadtmuseum**, containing Roman finds including the *Venus of Wels*, a small, beautiful bronze statue. Both museums are free and are closed on Monday and in the afternoon at weekends and on holidays.

Places to Stay & Eat

Staff at the tourist office can help you find somewhere to stay. The HI *Jugendher-berge (☎ 235 75-7, fax -6, Dragonerstrasse 22)* is just five minutes walk north-west of Stadtplatz and is open all year (you can check in from 5 pm onwards); dorm beds cost AS111.

The town has many cheap places to eat, including two self-service restaurants: *SB Am Eck* at Bahnhofstrasse 13, and *Reiter* at Stadtplatz 63 (both are open during normal shop hours). Stadtplatz has other restaurants for a range of tastes and budgets, and there's a *Spar* supermarket just beyond the Leder-erturm. There are a surprising number of Chinese restaurants in the town centre. *Pfeffermühle (☎ 455 97, Gärtnerstrasse 7)*, on the northern side of the train station (not the side with the bus station), is another. It has a garden, weekday lunch menus starting at AS65, off-street parking and sizeable singles/doubles with private shower cubicle for AS350/640.

Getting There & Away

The train station (where you can hire bikes) is 1.25km north of Stadtplatz. The bus station is in front of the train station. The town is on the express rail route between Linz and Salzburg, just 16 minutes south-west of Linz (AS52, several per hour). There's also a line running to Passau on the German border.

Bundesbuses run to numerous destina-tions including Ebensee, Gmunden, Bad Ischl, Lambach and Linz.

LAMBACH

☎ 07245

The small town of Lambach is 10km south-west of Wels. Its **Benediktinerstift** (Benedictine abbey) was founded in 1056, though much of the present edifice dates from the 17th century when the church was rebuilt in Baroque style. The abbey has a theatre (the only one of its kind in Austria) but more striking are the Romanesque frescoes from the 11th century. They are extremely well preserved and betray the influence of the styles of south-eastern Europe, unusual in Austria. They can only be accessed by guided tour (☎ 283 55 for information).

Getting There & Away

Lambach is on the Linz-Salzburg rail route but, unlike Wels, IC and EC trains don't stop here. Local trains to/from Wels (AS36) take 11 minutes.

SCHMIDING BIRD PARK

This is Austria's largest bird park (*Vogelpark*) home to 350 species. It also has an interesting ethnological museum. Combined entry costs AS120 (children AS40) and it's open from 9 am to 5 pm daily between mid-March and mid-November.

The park is about 7km north-west of Wels, accessible by bus No 2438 from there (infrequent at weekends). Alternatively, Haiding train station on the Wels-Passau route is about 2km north of the park.

KREMSMÜNSTER

☎ 07583

There is another **Benedictine abbey** at Kremsmünster, overlooking the Krems Valley. Although it was established in 777, it too owes much to Baroque remodelling in the early 18th century. Stuccowork and frescoes are much in evidence in the church, library and **Kaisersaal** (Emperor's Hall). The most acclaimed piece in the treasury is the *Tassilo Chalice*, made of gilded copper and donated to the monks by the Duke of Bavaria in about 780. These sights can be visited daily on a regular one hour guided tour (several daily, less frequent in winter). The **Sternwarte** (observatory tower) houses a wide-ranging museum collection. This can be visited on a separate guided tour taking 90 minutes, from 1 May to 31 October only. Each tour costs AS55 (students AS30, children AS25). Also of interest are the five fish ponds from the late 17th century, sporting statues and arcades (AS10 entry).

About 1.5km east of Kremsmünster is a **musikinstrumenten museum** in Schloss Kremsegg (open daily; AS70). Staff at the Kremsmünster tourist office (☎ 72 12), Rathausplatz 1, will tell you more.

Getting There & Away

Kremsmünster is on the IC rail route between Linz and Graz via Selzthal (direct trains every two hours). Kremsmünster Markt station is 25 minutes from Linz (AS68). Buses from Wels (30 minutes) run regularly on weekdays, less so at weekends.

FREISTADT

☎ 07942 • pop 6700 • 560m

This medieval fortified town is one of the main sights in the Mühlviertel region. Freistadt was important for its position on the salt route to Bohemia.

Orientation & Information

The compact town centre is within the old city walls. Right in the centre is Hauptplatz, with a small tourist office, the Mühlviertler Kernland (☎ 757 00, fax 757 01, email info.stflorian@netway.at) at No 14. It is open Monday to Friday from 9 am to noon and 1 to 5 pm, and also Saturday from May to September. Staff will reserve accommodation free of charge, including bookings for private rooms.

Immediately to the west of the city wall is the main north-south route, highway 125; knnown as Linzer Strasse in the south of the town, Promenade where it abuts the old centre and Prager Strasse in the north. There's a post office (Postamt 4240) at Promenade 11.

Things to See & Do

The city walls, with several gates and turrets, are mostly intact and surrounded by a grassy fringe. **Hauptplatz** has some interesting buildings with ornate façades. On the southern side of the square is the 14th century parish church, which is Gothic with a Baroque tower. Waaggasse, just west of Hauptplatz, is lined with striking architecture, including some with sgraffito designs.

Just beyond the north-eastern corner of Hauptplatz is a **Schloss** (1390), with a square tower topped by a tapering red-tiled roof. Inside is the **Heimathaus**, a regional museum (admission AS10, students and seniors free) open for tours from Tuesday to Friday and at weekends from May to October. It contains the usual historical and cultural displays as well as a collection of

Beer For All

Freistadt's brewery makes several varieties of Freistädter Bier, and has been in operation since 1777. The relationship between the town and its brewery is unlike that of any of the other 65-odd breweries in Austria: this is a *Braucommune*, owned jointly by the 149 households located within the town walls. A share in the brewery is conferred by owning one of these houses – people who sell lose their stake to the purchaser, so don't expect to find too many of these homes on the market! Realistically, the brewery cannot be taken over by any competitor, as the business would have to buy the whole town in order to take control.

In the old days, the owners of the brewery would get their share of the profits in liquid form, which would be distributed in *Eimer Bier* containers holding 56L. Each owner might get up to 130 containers! Nowadays, for better or worse, owners instead get a cash payment of equivalent value.

All of the guesthouses and inns in the town serve the local brew, and each outlet is entitled to send its regulars on a free tour of the brewery once a year (usually on a Tuesday). The tour guide will tell you that the brewery makes an average of 120,000L of beer a week, and that the bottling plant can handle up to 14,000 bottles per hour. The tour concludes with a free sampling of the produce. You might be lucky enough to be able to go along if you get friendly with an inn owner at the right time of year. Alternatively, telephone the brewery office (☎ 757 77) during office hours to ask if you can join a tour.

600 works of engraved and painted glass (*verre églomisé*).

The town's brewery, at Promenade 7, has a small gallery displaying brewing-related art (free entry; closed Monday).

Places to Stay

There is a *camping ground* (☎ 725 70) just outside the old centre, to the west of the Feldaist River by the Tenniscenter.

The non-HI *Jugendherberge* (☎ 743 65, *Schlosshof 3)* is in front of the Schloss, open June to September. Reception is open from 5 to 8 pm, but phone ahead as the owner's not always around. Private rooms (about AS170 per person) can be found on the tourist office's hotel list.

Früstückspension Hubertus (☎ 723 54, *Höllplatz 3)*, in the south-western corner of the old centre, has singles/doubles with shower/WC for AS230/400 plus a café and parking places. Nearby *Pension Pirklbauer* (☎ 724 40, fax -5, *Höllgasse 2-4)* has similar rooms for AS230/480, with satellite TV and a bit more style; it also has a garden.

Hotel Zum Goldenen Adler (☎ 721 12, fax -44, *Salzgasse 1)*, in the historic centre, has the best facilities in town, including a small outdoor pool and terrace, sauna and solarium. Rooms have shower/WC, telephone and cable TV and cost AS515/830.

Places to Eat

Two large supermarkets, *Hofer* and *Spar*, are opposite each other on Linzer Strasse. In the old town there's a *Julius Meinl* (*Eisengasse 13)*. Nearly next door is *Haider Imbiss*, serving snacks and small meals costing from AS23 to AS69. It is open Monday to Friday from 7.30 am to 6 pm and Saturday from 7 am to 12.30 pm. *Ratscherrnstube (Hauptplatz 1)* caters for locals, with Austrian dishes costing from AS50 to AS100; it's closed Monday.

For tasty regional specialities, try the elegant restaurant in the *Hotel Zum Goldenen Adler* (see the previous Places to Stay), or there's the atmospheric *Hotel-Gasthof Deim (Böhmergasse 8-10)* with some Gothic and rustic features, and food starting at AS90. Both are open daily.

Getting There & Away

Freistadt is on a direct rail route from Linz (AS100, 70 minutes); departures are two-hourly. This line wriggles its way north to Prague. Czech rail fares are lower than those in Austria, so you can save money by buying (in Czech currency) onward tickets once you've crossed the border.

Freistadt train station is 3km south-west of the centre: to avoid the walk and not rely on very infrequent buses, hire a bike from the station.

Highway 125, the main route from Linz, passes adjacent to the walled centre and continues towards Prague.

KEFERMARKT

☎ 07947

There's one particular reason to visit Kefermarkt: the **Church of St Wolfgang**, also known as the Pfarrkirche. Although it's not as famous as the pilgrimage church in the village of St Wolfgang in Salzkammergut, its Gothic altar (the Flügelaltar) is of comparable beauty and similar design. The identity of the 15th century sculptor is not known. The altarpiece of limewood is 13.5m high, with latticework fronds rising towards the ceiling. At the centre are three expressive figures, carved with great skill (left to right as you face them): St Peter, St Wolfgang and St Christopher. The wings of the altar bear religious scenes in low relief. The rest of the decorations in the church are Baroque. It closes at 6 pm.

Places to Stay & Eat

If you want to stay, there are a couple of adjacent places at Oberer Markt, down the hill from the church. *Horner (☎ 62 20)* offers singles/doubles with shower for AS320/500. No arrivals are accepted on Tuesday when the restaurant is shut. *Zehethofer (☎ 62 77)* charges AS260/520 for rooms using hall shower but is cheaper for Austrian fare (AS60 to AS120).

Getting There & Away

Kefermarkt is 10km south of Freistadt and the church is about 1km north of the train station. The fare from Freistadt is AS19. If you hire a bike at Freistadt station you can return it at Kefermarkt station (or vice versa), though this will cost an extra AS45.

BRAUNAU AM INN

☎ 07722 • pop 17,000 • 352m

Isolated from the rest of the province, Braunau has achieved unwanted attention as the birthplace of Hitler. It would prefer to be described as *die gotische Stadt* (the Gothic city).

Orientation & Information

Braunau is within spitting distance of Germany: the central Stadtplatz connects to a bridge over the Inn River and thence to the German town of Simbach.

Stadtplatz is about 1km from the train station: turn right outside the station, veer left under the road bridge and continue along Linzer Strasse. Stadtplatz is straight on, but following the 'i' sign to the right will bring you to an unstaffed information centre with leaflets, an accommodation board with access to a free telephone, and free backpack-sized lockers (usually full).

The tourist office (☎ 626 44, fax 843 95), in the Volksbank at Stadtplatz 9, is open Monday to Friday from 9 am to noon and (between 1 May and 30 September) from 2.30 to 5.30 pm.

Things to See & Do

Braunau's sights could occupy you for a couple of hours – follow the walking tour of

UPPER AUSTRIA

the centre prescribed by the tourist office (notes in English). **Stadtplatz** is a long square lined with elegant homes in pastel shades, with a 13th century gate tower at the southern end. The spire of the parish church, **Stadtpfarrkirche St Stephan**, is one of the tallest in Austria – to find out how tall, you'll have to measure it yourself: the tourist office claims that it's 100m; guidebooks variously describe it as 99m, 96m or 95m. Close by is the former church, St Martin's, containing a war memorial.

The walking tour omits **Hitler's Geburtshaus** (birth house) at Salzburger Vorstadt 15, just south of Stadtplatz. Hitler was born here in 1889 with the unprepossessing moniker of Adolf Schicklgruber. His family remained here for a further two years before moving to Linz. In 1938, when Hitler stormed through Braunau at the head of his troops and tanks, he did not stop at his old house.

The town tries to play down its Hitler connection. The *Führer* is ignored in most tourist literature. No plaque marks his birthplace. In 1989 a belated, oblique acknowledgment came with the placing of a lump of stone from Mauthausen on the pavement outside the house. Even this fails to mention Hitler: its inscription reads *Für Frieden Freiheit und Demokratie nie wieder Faschismus millionen Tote Mahnen.* (For peace, freedom and democracy. Never again fascism. Millions of dead admonish.)

Places to Stay

There's camping at the *Freizeitzentrum* (☎ *873 57*) in the south of town, off Salzburger Strasse. It's open from 1 April to 30 September and a site costs AS55 per person and AS50 per tent.

The HI *Jugendherberge* (☎ *816 38, Osternbergerstrasse 57, Osternberg*) is a 2km bus ride south of Stadtplatz (take a bus labelled 'Ostenberg'). Check-in is from 4 to 7 pm (telephone for later arrivals) and it closes over Christmas and Easter. Beds cost AS140 and optional breakfast is AS25.

Ideally situated at Stadtplatz 23 is *Hotel Gann* (☎ *632 06*). Singles/doubles with

shower cost AS280/510, or AS350/560 with shower/WC and TV. Rooms costing AS230/400 have no access to a shower. Equally convenient is the nearby *Gasthaus Puchmayr* (☎ *632 73, Johann Fischer Gasse 6*), above a Chinese restaurant. It's a smaller place, charging AS300/500 for rooms with private shower/WC.

Next to the train station, *Gasthof Gfrörer* (☎ *633 20, fax -33, email wgb.com@aon.at, Bahnhofstrasse 50*) has rooms with shower/WC and telephone for AS310/510.

Places to Eat

For self-caterers there's a *Billa* supermarket at Am Berg, behind Hitler's Geburtshaus, and a *Julius Meinl* on Stadtplatz.

Stadtplatz has a range of places to eat. *Reiter,* at No 15, is a grocery shop serving hot meals costing from AS38 to AS85. It's open Monday to Friday from 9 am to 6 pm (1 pm on Wednesday) and Saturday from 9 am to noon. *Bogner,* at No 47, has outside tables and serves Austrian food starting at AS68 (closed Sunday lunchtime). It calls itself 'Austria's smallest brewery' and has several home-brewed beers to try. *Chinatown,* at No 26 (access via a side road), has a choice at midday (except Sunday) of Chinese menus starting at AS56 or an all-you-can-eat buffet for AS79. *Pizzeria Portofino (Salzburger Vorstadt 13)* offers a large range of pizzas starting at AS60.

Gasthaus zum Schiff (*Stadtplatz 3*), offers good regional dishes costing from AS70 to AS170. It's closed on Monday and Tuesday from October to April.

Getting There & Away

Braunau is the terminus of the regional train service from Steindorf bei Strasswalchen (AS68; 45 minutes). Steindorf is on the Linz-Salzburg IC rail route. Braunau also has rail connections to Wels. To take a train from Braunau to Simbach in Germany costs AS19; trains go from there to Munich. Cars to Munich can take highway 12 (the E552).

Braunau receives plenty of touring cyclists (and you can hire bikes at the train station): the town is on the Inntal Radweg, following the Inn River through Germany and down to Innsbruck, and in the other direction reaching the German border town of Passau (where further cycling routes follow the Danube). Another bike track follows the Salzach River to Salzburg.

Lower Austria

Lower Austria (Niederösterreich) is rather overshadowed by Vienna, which it surrounds. Although the city is a separate province, all things, it seems, revolve round the national capital. Literature from the provincial tourist office takes pride in the fact that Lower Austria is 'The Province on Vienna's Doorstep'.

Efforts to forge a separate identity were not helped by Vienna's former status as Lower Austria's provincial capital, while also the federal capital and having its own provincial government. In 1986 St Pölten became the capital of Lower Austria and the task of exploiting the province's accessibility from Vienna, while at the same time trying not to be overwhelmed by the city, began in earnest.

It's not a futile endeavour. Lower Austria has plenty to offer in its own right: the Danube (Donau) Valley is justly praised for its wines, castles and abbeys, the Wienerwald attracts walkers and spa seekers, and Semmering is a famous holiday region in the south.

Orientation

Lower Austria is the country's largest province, covering 17,174 sq km, and has the largest population (1.5 million) of any region except Vienna. Geographically, it is dominated by the Danube Valley, which is also the focus of tourism. The land is relatively flat and fertile (it has the highest percentage of land under cultivation in Austria) though mountains reach 2000m high in the south.

Information

St Pölten has gradually absorbed the administrative functions of the province, but the tourist information office is still in Vienna; contact Niederösterreich Touristik-Information (☎ 01-513 80 22, fax -30, email noe.tourist-info@ping.at), 01, Walfischgasse 6. Direct all written enquiries to this

address. The city tourist office in St Pölten holds only localised information on the province.

St Pölten

☎ 02742 • pop 50,000 • 267m

Nearly 2000 years ago St Pölten was known as Aelium Cetium, but the town all but disappeared with the departure of the Romans. The arrival of the Augustinians in the 8th century saw it regain importance, and the country's newest provincial capital has the oldest municipal charter, granted in 1159. It also has a smattering of Baroque buildings:

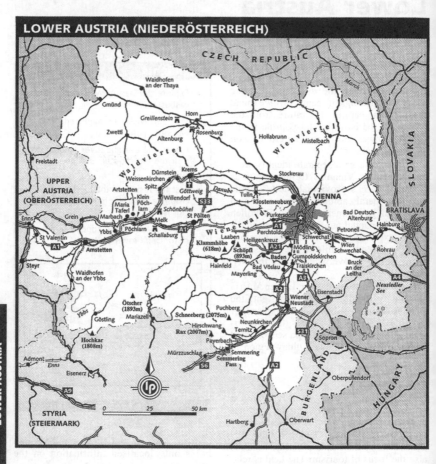

LOWER AUSTRIA (NIEDERÖSTERREICH)

Baroque master Jakob Prandtauer was once a resident.

Orientation & Information

The town centre is a compact, mostly pedestrian-only area to the west of the Traisen River. The tourist office (☎ 353 354, fax 333-2819, email st.poelton.gov .ti@telecom.at), inside the Rathaus on Rathausplatz, is 500m walk from the Hauptbahnhof (main train station). Opening hours are Monday to Friday from 8 am to 6 pm. From Easter to late October it's also open on Saturday from 9.30 am to 5.30 pm and on Sunday from 10 am to 5 pm. Ask for the *St Pölten City Guide* (in German, but with useful listings) and the city map (*Stadtplan*). Next door is a travel agency; outside is an accommodation map and free telephone to hotels and guesthouses.

The Hauptbahnhof (which has money-exchange counters open daily and a Bankomat) has a similar accommodation search facility outside.

The post office (Postamt 3100) is near the Hauptbahnhof. Its opening hours are Monday to Friday from 7 am to 8 pm, Saturday from 7 am to 1 pm.

Things to See & Do

Follow the walking tour of the town centre outlined in English in the tourist office's *Sankt Pölten barock* leaflet, or hire the office's taped walking tour for AS20. The architecture is not exclusively Baroque – Kremser Gasse 41 has an Art Nouveau

façade by Josef Olbrich, the creator of the Secession building in Vienna.

Rathausplatz is the hub of the town and has at its centre a **Dreifaltigkeitssäule** (Trinity Column), constructed in 1782. Several eye-catching buildings line the square, including the rococo **Franziskanerkirche** (Franciscan Church), completed in 1770. This has side altar paintings by Kremser Schmidt.

Close to Rathausplatz are several places of interest, including the **Institut der Englischen Fräulein** at Linzer Strasse 11, a

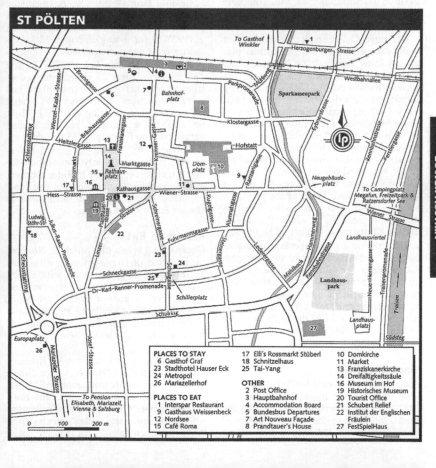

ST PÖLTEN

LOWER AUSTRIA

PLACES TO STAY	17 Elli's Rossmarkt Stüberl	10 Domkirche
6 Gasthof Graf	18 Schnitzelhaus	11 Market
23 Stadthotel Hauser Eck	25 Tai-Yang	13 Franziskanerkirche
24 Metropol		14 Dreifaltigkeitssäule
26 Mariazellerhof	OTHER	16 Museum im Hof
	2 Post Office	19 Historisches Museum
PLACES TO EAT	3 Hauptbahnhof	20 Tourist Office
1 Interspar Restaurant	4 Accommodation Board	21 Schubert Relief
9 Gasthaus Weissenbeck	5 Bundesbus Departures	22 Institut der Englischen
12 Nordsee	7 Art Nouveau Façade	Fräulein
15 Café Roma	8 Prandtauer's House	27 FestSpielHaus

convent founded in 1706, which has a classic Baroque façade, and several frescoes by Paul Troger in the chapel. The tiny **Museum im Hof**, Hess Strasse 4, dwells on recent history, particularly from a worker's viewpoint. Admission is free and it is open from 9 am to noon on Wednesday, Friday and Saturday.

Across the road is the **Historisches Museum**, Prandtauerstrasse 2, which covers history from Roman times to the mid-19th century. Entry is AS20 (students AS10) and the museum is open Tuesday to Sunday from 9 am to 5 pm. The house at Rathausgasse 2 has a Baroque façade, complete with a relief of Schubert (the composer was a frequent visitor).

Herrenplatz has a small morning **market** (daily except Sunday) which expands into the adjoining Domplatz on Thursday and Saturday. Domplatz was the heart of the ancient Roman town. The 13th century **Domkirche** (cathedral) has a 77m tower and much Baroque ornamentation, which was added in the early 18th century. The interior, with lashings of fake marble and gold, was designed by Jakob Prandtauer. Note the painted figure that seems about to fall on you if you stand before the altar, and the hole in the organ that captures the stained glass image behind. Many of the paintings here are by Daniel Gran, who lived at Wiener Strasse 8 for a while. Prandtauer lived at Klostergasse 1, north of Domplatz.

The Freizeitpark is a sports and leisure complex to the north-east of the town, by Ratzersdorfer See (Ratzerdorf Lake). Cultural (and administrative) activities are mostly centred in the new Landhausviertel, by the Traisen River between the two bridges. Here you'll find the **FestSpielHaus** (theatre), exhibition centre, shops, offices and much else.

Places to Stay

Budget options are very limited, especially since the HI youth hostel closed through lack of funds. There are a few private rooms, but none in the centre. *Camping-platz Megafun* (☎ 251 510) is 3km to the north-east of the centre in the Freizeitpark, and is open year-round. Prices here are AS50 per person and AS30 for a tent.

Mariazellerhof (☎ 769 95, fax -8), on Europaplatz, has single double rooms with shower/WC, cable TV and telephone from AS390/600. Many rooms have kitchen facilities. *Pension Elisabeth* (☎ 727 14, fax -8, Mariazeller Strasse 164), 1.5km south of Mariazellerhof, is owned by the same family. It's marginally cheaper but there are no kitchens. For either place phone ahead, as reception is closed on some days from 10 am to 4 pm.

Gasthof Graf (☎ 52 7 57, Bahnhofplatz 7) has rather seedy rooms with or without private shower and WC, and charges from AS390/620 for a single/double. Make inquiries in its cheap restaurant.

Stadthotel Hauser Eck (☎ 733 36, fax 783 86, Schulgasse 2) is near the pedestrian zone. This Art Nouveau place has comfortable rooms with shower/WC, cable TV and telephone starting at AS460/780. It has a lift and a restaurant, and can arrange garage parking for only AS25 a night.

Metropol (☎ 707 00-0, fax -133, Schiller-platz 1) is the town's only central four star hotel. It charges AS1050/1660 for modern, standardised singles/doubles, but you don't get that much more for your money than in Hauser Eck's better rooms.

Places to Eat

Cheap eating is less of a problem. North of the train line, on Herzogenburger Strasse, is an *Interspar* shopping centre with a self-service restaurant (1st floor; menus from AS56) and a supermarket. Fast food, schnitzel-style, is available at *Eurosnack* in the Hauptbahnhof and *Schnitzelhaus* at Schiessstattring 27, both of which are open daily.

Within the pedestrian area of Kremser Gasse is a branch of *Nordsee*, with eat-in or takeaway fish meals from about AS65; it's open normal shopping hours. *Tai-Yang* (*Schneckgasse 12*) is a Chinese restaurant offering weekday set lunches, which start at AS55; it's open daily.

Café Roma (Rathausplatz 5) mainly serves ice cream and drinks, but often has one lunch dish (such as spaghetti bolognese) for a give-away price – as low as AS12! It's open daily.

Austrian food starts at around AS60 at *Gasthaus Weissenbeck (Ranzonigasse 3)*. It's open from 9 am to midnight, except on Wednesday, when it closes at 2 pm. *Elli's Rossmarkt Stüberl (Rossmarkt 5)* has Austrian food from AS65, including several vegetarian options; it closes at 2 pm on Saturday and all day Sunday.

About 1km north of the Hauptbahnhof is *Gasthof Winkler (☎ 364 944, Mühlweg 64)*, a more elegant place with good regional and seasonal dishes costing from AS80 to AS250; it closes on Sunday at 2 pm and all day Monday. On Sunday lunchtime there's an extensive buffet for AS150.

Getting There & Away

St Pölten is 60km west of Vienna, on the hourly express train route running from Vienna's Westbahnhof (AS102; 35 minutes) to Linz (AS180) and Salzburg (AS336). From St Pölten, trains run north to Krems (AS54) and south to Mariazell.

St Pölten has equally good road connections: the east-west A1/E60 passes a few kilometres south of the city and the S33 branches north from there, bypassing St Pölten to the east, and continuing to Krems. The east-west highway 1 passes through the city centre, from which highway 20 branches south to Mariazell.

Bundesbuses and taxis depart from outside the Hauptbahnhof. Bundesbuses to Klosterneuburg via Tulln run from Monday to Friday; 85 minutes. There are also buses to Melk (Monday to Friday, 35 minutes) and Krems (40 minutes).

The Danube Valley

The historical importance of the Danube Valley as a corridor between east and west ensured that control of this area was hotly contested. Consequently there are hundreds of fortresses in Lower and Upper Austria,

including many monasteries and abbeys with defences to match conventional castles. The Wachau section of the Danube, between Krems and Melk, is the most scenic, with wine-producing villages, forested slopes, vineyards and imposing fortresses at nearly every bend.

The *Gästekarte* for the Wachau and Nibelungengau region offers a host of benefits for anyone staying in the region (approximately between Ybbs and Krems). If you stay in one resort you can get the benefits for *all* resorts, such as free entry to Melk's open-air swimming pool in the summer. Cards are provided with your accommodation and are funded by the nightly resort tax of around AS10 per adult, which is usually included in the price of your room. The Wachau-Nibelungengau regional office (☎ 02732-856 20, fax 874 71, email 106131 .3451@compuserve.com) is on the 1st floor at Undstrasse 6, A-3504 Krems, and is open on weekdays from 9 am to 4.30 pm.

This section covers the main Danube Valley attractions in order from west to east.

Getting Around

A popular way of exploring the Wachau region is by boat. DDSG Blue Danube (☎ 01-588 80, fax -440, email ddsg.blue .danube@telecom.at) operates steamers between Melk and Krems from early April to late October, with three departures daily (one a day in April and October). The full trip takes 100 minutes going downstream and an hour longer going upstream (that is, Krems to Melk). The one way fare is AS190, AS260 return. The trip as far as Spitz, halfway between Melk and Krems, costs AS100 (AS140 return) from either town. Boats also stop at Dürnstein. A commentary en route (in English) highlights points of interest. The stretch from Krems to Vienna is less interesting; DDSG runs boats along this stretch in Summer, one in each direction on Sunday only. National and European rail passes entitle the holder to a discount of 20% off DDSG's Wachau fares. Bicycles can be taken on the boats free of charge.

Brandner (☎ 07433-25 90-0, email schiffahrt@brandner.at) runs two daily boats between Krems and Melk, 1 May to 26 October, with stops at Dürnstein and Spitz. Fares are similar to those of DDSG, but bicycles are charged at AS20. Ardagger (☎ 07479-64 64-0) travels from Linz (in Upper Austria) to Krems, including a stop at Weissenkirchen, on Sunday, Tuesday and Thursday (7¾ hours), returning from Krems to Linz on Monday, Wednesday and Friday (10¼ hours). The service runs from late April to late October; the fare is AS470 each way, and bikes are carried for AS30.

The route by road is also scenic and cycling is extremely popular in summer. There is a bicycle track along the south bank from Vienna to Krems, and along both sides of the river from Krems to Linz. East of Vienna, a bicycle track runs north of the river to Hainburg. Most tourist offices in the region can provide useful cycling information. If you're driving, Highway 3 links Vienna and Linz and stays close to the north bank of the Danube for much of the way.

The rail track that runs along the north bank of the Danube takes slow local trains (2nd class only). It makes 31 stops on the 120km, three hour trip between Krems and St Valentin, including at Dürnstein, Weissenkirchen, Spitz, Emmersdorf, Klein Pöchlarn, Grein and Mauthausen. But only one train a day completes the full route (four in summer): most trains only run between Krems and Emmersdorf and between Grein and St Valentin. Some of the small stations are unstaffed; you must buy a ticket from ticket machines or on the train.

WEST OF MELK

Grein, in Upper Austria, is a small town on the north bank of the river, with a castle (mostly 15th century) which has a fine arcaded courtyard. On the premises is a museum devoted to navigation and shipping on the Danube. It's open from 1 May to 31 October and it's closed on Monday; entry costs AS30.

About 15km south of Grein is **Amstetten**, the main town in the vicinity (population

22,000). It has little of tourist interest, though it is on both the A1 and the main rail route (express trains stop here) between Linz and Vienna. The Ybbs River, a tributary of the Danube, runs south of the town.

Continuing south another 25km, you reach **Waidhofen an der Ybbs**, a stunningly attractive riverside town, with historic gabled houses, arcaded courtyards and dramatic onion domes. Get there by train from Amstetten in 30 minutes, en route to Eisenerz (see the Styria chapter).

Travelling eastward along the Danube from Grein, you soon pass into Lower Austria and a rocky, wooded section of the river. After Ybbs, the next boat stop is at Marbach. Three kilometres along a road that wriggles northwards from here is the pilgrimage church of **Maria Taferl**. This Baroque creation with two onion domes was the work of Jakob Prandtauer, who also worked on the abbey at Melk.

About 5km north-east of Maria Taferl, taking minor roads, is **Artstetten**, notable for a castle that has been much modified in the last 700 years. It was formerly owned and occupied by Archduke Franz Ferdinand, to whom a museum (☎ 07413-83 02) is devoted. The assassination of the archduke and his wife sparked WWI. The tomb of the unlucky pair is in the church. The museum is open daily from 9 am to 5 pm between 1 April and 2 November; entry costs AS70 (students AS55, children AS40). Artstetten is 3km north of Klein Pöchlarn, which is across the river from its larger cousin, Pöchlarn. There's no bridge, but these places are linked by ferry. Danube steamers stop at the Pöchlarn side.

MELK

☎ 02752 • pop 6500 • 228m

Lying in the lee of its imposing monastery-fortress, Melk is an essential stop on the Danube trail.

Historically, the site of Melk was of great importance to both the Romans and the Babenbergs. In 1089 the Babenberg margrave Leopold II donated the castle to Benedictine monks, who converted it into a fortified abbey. Fire destroyed the original edifice, which was completely rebuilt between 1702 and 1738 according to plans by Jakob Prandtauer and his follower, Josef Munggenast. Extensive restorations were completed in 1995.

Orientation & Information

The train station is 300m from the town centre. Walk 50m down Bahnhofstrasse to reach the post office (Postamt 3390), open till 6 pm (5 pm for money exchange) on weekdays and 10 am only on Saturday. Turn right for the Jugndherberge or carry straight on, taking Bahngasse for the central Rathausplatz.

Turn right at Rathausplatz for the tourist office (☎ 523 07-32, fax -37) on Babenbergerstrasse 1. It's closed from November to March (unless staff happen to be there); otherwise it's open on weekdays from 9 am to noon and 2 to 6 pm, on Saturday from 10 am to 2 pm, and on Sunday (except in April and October) from 10 am to 2 pm. In July and August, Monday to Saturday hours stretch to 9 am to 7 pm. Staff at the office will make room reservations.

Bicycles can be rented at the train station.

Stift Melk

This Benedictine abbey dominates the town from its commanding hill site, and provides an excellent view from the terrace. Monks have resided here for over 900 years. Visitors are permitted to roam the abbey buildings unaccompanied, but regular guided tours highlight interesting details and are well worth the small extra charge.

The huge **monastery church** is enclosed by the buildings, but still dominates the complex with its twin spires and high octagonal dome. The inside is Baroque gone mad, with endless prancing angels and gold twirls, but is still extremely impressive. The theatrical high altar scene, depicting St Peter and St Paul (the two patron saints of the church), is by Peter Widerin. Johann Michael Rottmayr did most of the ceiling paintings, including those in the dome.

Other high points are the library and the

mirror room: both have painted tiers on the ceiling (by Paul Troger) to give the illusion of greater height. The ceilings are slightly curved to aid the effect. Imperial rooms, where various dignitaries stayed (including Napoleon), contain museum exhibits.

The monastery is open from the Saturday before Palm Sunday to All Saints' Day (1 November), from 9 am to 5 pm, except between May and September when it closes at 6 pm. Entry costs AS55, or AS30 for students aged under 27 years, and the guided tour is AS15 extra. During winter it can be visited by guided tour only (☎ 523 12). Even in summer, phone ahead (☎ 523 12-232) to ensure you get on an English-language tour. If you also want to visit Schloss Schallaburg (see later section), get a combined ticket.

Old Town Centre

Other interesting buildings around town date mostly from the 16th and 17th centuries. Try the walking tour outlined in the tourist office map, particularly along the pedestrian-only Hauptstrasse and Sterngasse. Don't miss the excellent façade of the Altes Posthaus at Linzer Strasse 3-5.

Special Events

The Melker Sommerspiele in July and August features open-air theatre. Whitsuntide Baroque concerts are held in Stift Melk during May.

Places to Stay & Eat

Camping Melk, signposted as Fährhaus Jensch, is 1km out of town, to the west of the canal where it joins the Danube. The camp site is open from around April to October. Charges, excluding resort tax, are AS35 per adult, AS35 per tent and AS25 for a car. The reception is in the restaurant *Melker Fährhaus* (☎ 532 91, *Kolomaniau 3*), open Wednesday to Sunday (daily in summer) from 8 am to midnight. When it is closed, just camp and pay later. The restaurant has good lunchtime menus including soup from about AS75. Self-caterers can stock up at the *Spar* supermarket, in the town centre at Rathausplatz 9. It's open on weekdays from 7 am to 6 pm, and on Saturday from 7 am to noon.

The HI *Jugendherberge* (☎ *526 81, fax 542 57, Abt Karl Strasse 42)*, 10 minutes walk from the station, has good showers and four-bed dorms, as well as sports and games facilities and parking spaces. A bed costs AS150 (AS126 for those aged under 19), plus a AS25 surcharge for the first night only. The reception is closed from 10 am to 5 pm, but during the day you can reserve a bed and leave your bags in the *Fahrradraum* (bicycle room) to the left of the entrance. The hostel is closed from 1 November to mid-March.

The tourist office accommodation leaflet lists private rooms, which are reasonable value, even though most are away from the centre of town.

Gasthof Goldener Stern (☎ *522 14, fax -4, Sterngasse 17)* offers good prices for the centre: singles/doubles with hall shower are around AS300/520 and rooms are quite large. The restaurant (closed on Tuesday in winter) serves a variety of Austrian dishes starting at AS80.

Gasthof Weisses Lamm (☎ *540 85, Linzer Strasse 7)* has four doubles with private shower/WC for AS550, and one single for AS350. On the premises is *Pizzeria Venezia* (open daily), offering many tasty pizzas starting at AS60, cheap weekday lunches, and some Greek dishes.

The *Gasthof zum Goldenen Hirschen* (☎ *522 57, Rathausplatz 13)* is a 16th century house; pleasant, compact singles/ doubles with private shower and (usually) WC cost AS381/622. Its *Rathauskeller* restaurant (open daily) has daily fixed-price menus with soup for about AS90, and other dishes from AS75.

Hotel Goldener Ochs (☎ *523 67, fax -6, Linzer Strasse 18)* is an old house, but has large rooms with modern furnishings, private shower/WC and cable TV. Prices are AS620/920, reducing in the low season. The place has a comfortable restaurant (closed on Tuesday and Sunday in winter), garden, sauna (free for guests) and solari-

um. Nearby at No 7 is *China Restaurant Krone*, with cheap midday menus.

Melk's gourmet restaurant is in a hotel, *Stadt Melk* (☎ *525 47, Hauptplatz 1)*, where main dishes cost from AS245 to AS295; it's open daily. The proprietor maintains an extensive wine cellar – the wine menu is as thick as a book. Stylish rooms in this three star place cost AS750/980.

Getting There & Away

Boats leave from the canal by Pionierstrasse, 400m to the north of the abbey. Direct trains to Melk depart from Vienna's Westbahnhof (AS142) and take an hour. Some trains involve changing at St Pölten but that will only add about 10 minutes to the trip.

SCHLOSS SCHALLABURG

This splendid Renaissance castle-cumpalace, 5km south of Melk, is a rewarding excursion. The architectural centrepiece is a two storey arcaded Renaissance courtyard with magnificent terracotta arches. The rich red-brown carvings set against whitewashed walls cry out to be photographed. There are some 400 terracotta images, completed between 1572 and 1573. The largest figures support the upper storey arches – note the court jester sniggering in the corner. Below these are pictorial scenes and a series of mythological figures and masks. A recorded commentary, which costs AS10, explains the significance of some of the images. Every year the castle hosts a prestigious exhibition.

The castle is open from late April to late October, and entry to the complex and exhibition costs AS80 for adults, AS50 for seniors and AS30 for students. A reduced combination ticket which includes Melk's monastery costs AS115. There's an excellent mid-range restaurant in the castle.

Getting There & Away

There's only one Bundesbus a day from Melk to Schallaburg (AS30), departing in the morning. Hiring a bike from Melk train station gives more flexibility.

MELK TO DÜRNSTEIN

In addition to the many vineyards, look for peaches and apricots that are grown on this 30km-long passage of the Danube. Even the steepest hills are terraced and cultivated.

Shortly after departing Melk you pass the 12th century **Schloss Schönbühel**, standing high on a rock on the south bank, which officially marks the beginning of the Wachau region. There's also a Servite monastery (the Servites were a mendicant order of friars) dating from the 17th century. Immediately afterwards, on the same side, are the ruins of **Burg Aggstein**, a 12th century castle complex built by the Kuenringer family. These so-called 'robber barons' are said to have imprisoned their enemies on a ledge of rock (the Rosengärtlein), where the hapless captives faced starvation, unless they opted for a quicker demise by throwing themselves into the abyss below.

On the opposite bank **Willendorf** soon appears, where a 25,000-year-old sandstone statuette of Venus was discovered (see the boxed text 'The Venus of Willendorf'); another statuette, made from a mammoth tusk, was also found here.

A farther 5km brings **Spitz** into view, a peaceful village with attractive houses. The parish church at Kirchenplatz is unusual for its chancel, which is out of line with the main body of the church. Another noteworthy feature is the 15th century statues of the 12 apostles lining the organ loft; most wear an enigmatic expression, as if being tempted by an unseen spirit to overindulge in the communion wine. It's a Gothic church with crisscross ceiling vaulting, yet has Baroque altars. The fountain in front and the vine-covered hills rising behind make a pretty picture. One hill, the Tausendeimerberg, is so-named for its reputed ability to yield a thousand buckets of wine per season. The tourist office (☎ 02713-23 63) in the village centre can give information about accommodation.

The Venus of Willendorf

Unbeknown to the inhabitants of Willendorf, for approximately 26,000 years the area was home to one of the most famous prehistoric sculptures of the human form. Discovered by archaeologist Josef Szombathy in 1908, it has since become an icon of the original 'Earth Mother'. There is much debate about what clues the 5cm-tall sandstone figure can reveal about life in 24,000 BC. Some believe the sculpture shows the esteemed role of women in prehistoric society and that mankind worshipped a female deity or Earth Mother.

Others reject Venus' status as goddess, arguing that the attention to detail, from her plaited hair to her dimpled arms, suggests that the artist used a living model, although a lack of face and feet would seem to refute this. If, however, the figure was modelled on that of a real woman, her generous body reveals clues about that woman's status. In a hunter-gatherer society, such a body would equate with an unusually sedate lifestyle, implying again the probability of her special status within the society.

The tiny figurine may have served as a good luck charm, carried on hunting missions to ensure a fruitful catch. The red ochre staining could represent blood spilt while foraging, or menstrual blood, indicating that Venus was a symbol used to promote fertility.

Whatever the Venus of Willendorf signified in prehistoric times, today her great age and voluptuous form make her a symbol of fertility, procreativity and nurturing, as well as a modern-day commodity in reproduction art. A replica is now on show in the Naturhistorisches Museum (Natural History Museum) in Vienna, the original being too precious to be displayed.

Lisa Ball

Six kilometres farther along the north bank is **Weissenkirchen**. Its centrepiece is a fortified parish church on a hill. This Gothic church was built in the 15th century and has a Baroque altar. The garden terrace, if open, provides good views of the Danube. Below the church is the charming Teisenhoferhof arcaded courtyard, with a covered gallery and lashings of flowers and dried corn. The Wachau Museum is here containing work by artists of the Danube school. The museum is open from 1 April to 31 October (closed on Monday) and entry costs AS20 (students AS10). The tourist office (☎ 02715-26 00) is in the village centre.

After Weissenkirchen the river sweeps to the right and yields a fine perspective of Dürnstein.

Getting There & Away

DDSG, Brandner and Ardagger boats stop at Spitz, and Ardagger vessels also call at Weissenkirchen. The Wachau railway runs along the north bank, connecting all of the villages on that side. Krems to Spitz costs AS36; you can hire bikes at Spitz train station. Drivers wishing to stay close to the river can choose a road on either bank.

DÜRNSTEIN

☎ 02711 • pop 1000 • 209m

One of the prime destinations in the Wachau, Dürnstein achieved notoriety in the 12th century when King Richard I (the Lionheart) of England was imprisoned here.

Orientation & Information

From the train station, walk ahead and then right for the village walls (about five minutes). En route you pass the tourist office (☎ 200), in a little hut in the corner of the eastern car park. It's open in the afternoon only from April to October. You can get information from the Rathaus (☎ 219, fax 442) on Hauptstrasse, the main street, all year during office hours (weekdays from 9 am to noon and 1.30 to 4 pm). The boat landing stage is below the dominating feature of the village centre, the blue and white parish church.

Things to See & Do

High on the hill, commanding a marvellous view of the curve of the Danube, stand the ruins of **Kuenringerburg**, the castle where Richard was incarcerated from 1192 to 1193. His crime was to have insulted Leopold V; his misfortune was to be recognised despite his disguise when journeying through Austria on his way home from the Holy Lands; his liberty was achieved only upon the payment of a huge ransom of 35,000kg of silver (which partly funded the building of Wiener Neustadt). It was here that the singing minstrel Blondel attempted to rescue his sovereign. The walk up from the village takes about 15 to 20 minutes.

In the village, Hauptstrasse is a cobbled street with picturesque 16th century houses, wrought-iron signs and floral displays. Views are also good where the road descends at the western end of the village.

The meticulously restored **Chorherrenstift** (abbey church) is all that remains of the former Augustinian monastery. Founded in 1410, it received its Baroque facelift in the 18th century (overseen by Josef Munggenast, among others). The exterior has plenty of saints and angels adopting pious poses on and around the pristine blue and white steeple; the interior effectively combines white stucco and dark wood balconies. Kremser Schmidt did many of the ceiling and altar paintings. Entry costs AS25 and includes access to the porch overlooking the Danube and a photo exhibition detailing the renovations. It's open daily from 9 am to 6 pm, 1 April to 31 October.

East of the centre is **Kuenringerbad**, a swimming and sports complex.

Places to Stay & Eat

Pension Altes Rathaus (☎/fax 252, Hauptstrasse 26) is reached through an attractive courtyard. It has singles with hall shower for AS280 and doubles with private shower/ WC for AS630. *Pension Böhmer* (☎ 239, Hauptstrasse 22) has smaller rooms with shower/WC for AS350/550. Private rooms are cheaper: *Maria Wagner* (☎ 232, Hauptstrasse 41) has doubles starting at AS360.

Gasthof Sänger Blondel (☎ 253, fax -7, *Klosterplatz*) has rooms from AS660/920 with shower/WC and TV. Its restaurant (closed on Sunday evening and Monday) has a shady courtyard and food starting from AS90. For food, also try the cheaper and plainer **Goldener Strauss** *(Hauptstrasse 18)*, which has a small garden; it's closed on Tuesday.

Gartenhotel Weinhof (☎ 206, fax -88, *Dürnstein 122)* is about 1km west of the centre, with a range of rooms in either the main building or the annexe. It's only open in summer; expect to pay about AS680/960. Guests enjoy numerous facilities including a sauna, outdoor swimming pool, garden and restaurant.

Alter Klosterkeller is a *Buschenschank* (wine tavern) on Anzuggasse, just outside the village walls (on the eastern side) and overlooking the vineyards. Wine costs AS20 a *Viertel* (0.25L), and a variety of cold snacks and meals, priced from AS25 to AS90, is served. It's open from 3 pm (2 pm on weekends), closed on Tuesday. For other wine taverns, get the calendar of opening times from the tourist office.

Restaurant Loibnerhof (☎ 02732-828 90, *Unterloiben 7)*, 1.5km east of Dürnstein, is highly regarded and reasonably priced; it's closed on Monday and Tuesday.

Getting There & Away
Krems and Weissenkirchen are about 20 minutes away by boat (AS95). By train, the fare is AS19 to either; trains run hourly.

KREMS
☎ 02732 • pop 23,000 • 202m
Krems lies on the north bank of the Danube, surrounded by terraced vineyards. It was first mentioned in documents in 995, and has been a centre of the wine trade for most of its history.

Orientation & Information
Krems comprises three linked parts: Krems to the east, the smaller settlement of Stein (formerly a separate town) to the west, and the connecting suburb of Und. Hence the local witticism: *Krems Und Stein sind drei Städte* (Krems and Stein are three towns).

The centre of Krems stretches along a pedestrian-only street, Obere and Untere Landstrasse. The tourist office (☎ 826 76, fax 700 11) is between Krems and Stein at Undstrasse 6, in the Kloster Und building. It's part of the Austropa travel agency, and sells packages to Austrian attractions. It's open on weekdays from 9 am to 7 pm and weekends from 10 am to noon and 1 to 7 pm. Between 1 November and 30 April hours are weekdays only from 9 am to 6 pm. Room reservations are made free of charge, and there's a free phone and accommodation board outside.

The main post office (Postamt 3500) is at Brandströmstrasse 4-6. The boat station is on Donaustrasse, approximately 2km west of the train station.

Things to See & Do
There are several Renaissance and Baroque houses lining Untere and Obere Landstrasse in Krems, and Steiner Landstrasse in Stein; a peaceful stroll along these cobbled streets is rewarding. Quaint courtyards hide behind some of the old façades, and the odd remnant of the city walls remains. The distinctive **Steinertor** on Obere Landstrasse dates from the 15th century and is the town emblem. Near the **Linzertor,** in Stein, is the house occupied from 1756 by the artist Martin Johann Schmidt, often known as Kremser Schmidt.

Krems has several churches with interiors worth investigating. **Pfarrkirche St Veit**, on the hill at Pfarrplatz, is fitted out in Baroque style, though it had earlier Gothic and Romanesque incarnations. The ceiling frescoes are by Kremser Schmidt. The 15th century **Piaristenkirche** (Piarist Church) on Frauenbergplatz, behind Pfarrkirche St Veit, has Gothic vaulting, huge windows and Baroque altars.

The **Kulturverwaltung Museum** is a former Dominican monastery (the Dominikanerkirche), an atmospheric building which houses two museums: the Historisches Museum displaying religious and

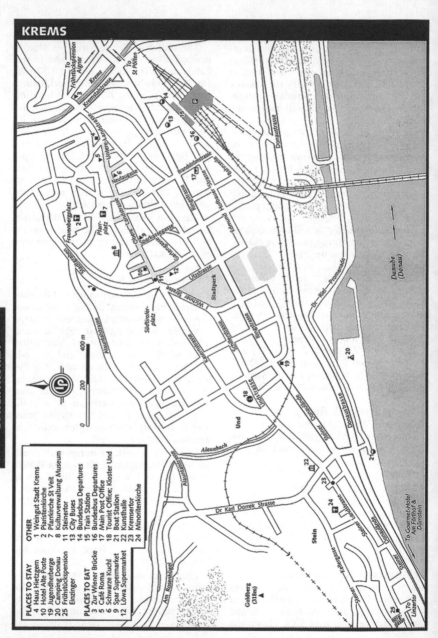

KREMS

LOWER AUSTRIA

modern art (with plenty of paintings by Kremser Schmidt), and the Weinstadtmuseum giving an exposition of wine-making. It's open from 1 to 6 pm Wednesday to Sunday, and 9 am to 6 pm on Tuesday (closed on Monday) between March and November; entry costs AS40.

Close to the Kremsertor is an arts centre, the **Kunsthalle** (☎ 826 69, fax -16, email office@krems.kunsthalle.at). Temporary displays organised by the centre are sometimes held in the **Minoritenkirche** in Stein.

The street plan from the tourist office (AS10) details other points of interest. Wine buffs can enjoy wine tasting daily except during winter (AS140) in the Kloster Und, home of a wine college. Weingut Stadt Krems, Stadtgraben 11, allows free tastings prior to possible purchase.

Special Events

In August every year Krems hosts its Niederösterreichische Landesmesse, a folklore festival, expanding to international scope every second year (next in 2000). The annual Donau festival of the arts, with some events held in Krems, runs from mid-June to early July.

Places to Stay

Camping Donau (☎ 844 55, *Wiedengasse 7),* east of the boat station, is open from Easter to mid-October and a site costs AS50 per person, from AS30 for a tent and AS40 for a car.

The HI *Jugendherberge* (☎ 834 52, *Ringstrasse 77)* has excellent facilities for cyclists, such as a garage and an on-site repair service. A bed in a four/six-bed dorm is S150/160, plus a AS20 surcharge for stays of one or two nights. It's closed from 9 am to 5 pm, check-in is from 5 to 8 pm. It's open from 1 April to 30 October.

In other places, a surcharge of AS10 to AS30 for a single-night stay is common. As ever, private rooms are a good deal, and details of these are in the tourist office's accommodation brochure. *Haus Hietzgern* (☎ 761 84, *Untere Landstrasse 53)* is ideally central and has an Art Nouveau façade. There are two doubles and two triples with shower/WC, available from 1 June to 31 August for AS295 per person.

Frühstückspension Aigner (☎ 845 58, *Weinzierl 53)* is a *Weinbau* (wine producer) and there's a *Heuriger* (wine tavern) next door. Singles/doubles with private shower/WC and TV cost AS410/640. Bundesbuses go along this road, though it's less than 20 minutes walk from the train station.

In Stein, *Frühstückspension Einzinger* (☎ 823 16, *fax -6, Steiner Landstrasser 82)* offers elegant, old-style rooms round an attractive courtyard; singles/doubles with shower/WC and TV cost AS350/680.

Hotel Alte Poste (☎ 822 76, *fax 843 96, Obere Landstrasse 32)* is a 500-year-old house. It has good singles/doubles for AS310/600, or AS480/720 with private shower, and an enchanting courtyard.

Gourmet-Hotel Am Förthof (☎ 833 45, *fax -40, Förthofer Donaulände 8),* 500m west of Stein, is a small hotel with an outdoor swimming pool. Rooms (all with bath or shower, WC and TV) cost from AS700/1000 to AS900/1500, depending on the size and season.

Places to Eat

Supermarkets include a *Spar* on Obere Landstrasse and a *Löwa* in the shopping centre by the Steinertor.

Near where Untere and Obere Landstrasse join there are several snack and takeaway bars. *Café Roma* on Untere Landstrasse is an ice cream and drinks place, but often has one lunch dish (such as spaghetti bolognese) for a give-away price of AS20 or less. It's open daily. Further west at No 8 is *Schwarze Kuchl*, with food for around AS65 to AS95. It's open weekdays, 8 am to 7 pm, and Saturday from 8 am to 1 pm.

The restaurant *Zur Wiener Brücke* (☎ 821 43, *Wiener Strasse 2),* also called Gasthof Klinglhuber, has terrace seating overlooking the Krems River. Tasty Austrian food costs from AS120 to AS220, though are some cheaper, light meals are served; it's open daily from 7 am to at least 10 pm.

Hotel Alte Poste (see Places to Stay) has a pleasant restaurant and tables in a courtyard. Dishes start from AS90 and local wine from AS30 per Viertel. It's closed Tuesday evening and Wednesday.

As its name implies, the *Gourmet-Hotel Am Förthof* (see Places to Stay) is also a good place to eat, particularly for regional specialities. Meals are priced from AS90 to AS300; it's open daily (kitchen till 10 pm).

Don't omit a visit to a Heuriger; most are out of the centre and provide an authentic experience in eating and drinking. They're only open for two or three-week bursts during the year: get the timetable from the tourist office.

Getting There & Away

Four daily Bundesbuses (two or three at weekends) depart for Melk from outside the train station. The fare is AS70 and it takes 65 minutes. Buses also go between Krems and Stein. There are trains every hour to Franz Josefs Bahnhof in Vienna; they cost AS119 and take about an hour.

Bikes can be rented at the train station, Camping Donau and some hotels. Cyclists are very welcome in Krems; some hotels have bike garages and repair facilities.

AROUND KREMS
Stift Göttweig

This abbey was founded in 1083 and given to the Benedictine order 11 years later. Six kilometres south of Krems, the abbey's position on a hill makes its towers and onion domes clearly visible from afar (and you can view to afar from the garden terrace or the restaurant in the abbey grounds). What remains today is mostly the Baroque work begun in 1719 following a devastating fire. The plans for rebuilding were never fully realised, resulting in an asymmetric but impressive complex. The abbey church has ceiling frescoes (dating from 1739) by Paul Troger; Kremser Schmidt also contributed to the church and to the imperial apartments, which are part of the abbey. It's open daily from late March to November; entry costs AS60, or AS70 with a guided tour.

Getting There & Away A few buses leave from outside Krems train station, but the only one on Sunday is at 1 pm, returning at 3.57 pm. Going via train (the St Pölten line) is another possibility.

WALDVIERTEL

North and west of Krems is the Waldviertel, a less visited forested region, which is ideal for off-the-beaten-track walking and outdoor sports. You'll also find affordable accommodation, a typical ambience of rural Austria, and a smattering of historical buildings. English is not so widely spoken in these parts. For more on local attractions, including Stift Zwettl, contact the Tourismusregion Waldviertel (☎ 02822-541 09-0, fax -36, email tourismus@wvnet.at), Hamerlingstrasse 2, A-3910 Zwettl.

An important site in the region is the Benedictine **Stift Altenburg**, founded in 1144. In the ensuing centuries it was all but destroyed by plundering hordes, until extensive Baroque rebuilding began in 1650. The abbey library (with ceiling frescoes by Paul Troger) and the crypt (featuring frescoes by Troger's pupils) are among the most impressive examples of their kind in Austria. The abbey church was created by Josef Munggenast between 1730 and 1733. The church contains some of Troger's best frescoes (in the central dome, and above the high and side altars). The gilded organ dates from 1773. Guided tours are conducted daily except Monday from Easter to 1 November (AS80, students AS40; 90 minutes). For information call ☎ 02982-3451. You can visit the church without taking one of these tours.

A few kilometres south of Altenburg is **Schloss Rosenburg**, a multi-turreted edifice built between the 14th and 17th centuries. It's open from Easter to 15 November and has daily tours and occasional falcon shows (☎ 02982-2911). A similar distance west of Altenburg is **Schloss Greillenstein**, which was built in the late 16th century but had an entrance tower added in 1700. There are tours of the interior from 1 April to 31 October daily (AS65).

Getting There & Away

Rosenburg is on a rail line that runs north from Krems (55 minutes). For the other destinations you'll have to rely on Bundesbuses if you don't have your own transport; call ☎ 02732-825 36-390 in Krems for bus information.

Zwettl is on a rail line but it's a very circuitous route from Krems, involving two changes, whereas the Bundesbus is direct (50 minutes).

TULLN

☎ 02272 • pop 12,300 • 180m

Formerly a Roman camp called Comagena, and named as a town settlement in 791, Tulln calls itself the 'Birthplace of Austria' and was in effect the nation's first capital.

Orientation & Information

Tulln is 29km west of Vienna, on the south bank of the Danube River. The centre of town is the pedestrian-only Hauptplatz. The tourist office (☎ 658 36, fax 658 38) is one block north at Minoritenplatz 2. It's open on weekdays from 9 am to noon and 2 to 6 pm, and weekends from 1 to 6 pm; from 1 October to 30 April, hours are weekdays only from 9 am to noon. Staff reserve rooms without charging commission.

Tulln train station (with bike rental facilities) is 15 minutes walk south-east of Hauptplatz; from the station, turn right into Bahnweg, right at Brückenstrasse, and left onto Wiener Strasse. Tulln Stadt is an S-Bahn station (for suburban trains from Vienna), just five minutes walk south of Hauptplatz along Bahnhofstrasse.

Things to See & Do

Next to the tourist office, in the Minoritenkloster, is a complex of museums, the **Tullner Museen**. Collections cover the city's history, both ancient and modern (including geology and Roman finds); one section deals with fire-fighting. Entry to all parts costs AS30 (AS20 for seniors and students) and it's open Wednesday to Friday from 3 to 6 pm, on Saturday from 2 to 6 pm, and on Sunday from 10 am to 6 pm.

On the riverside is the **Egon Schiele Museum**, open Tuesday to Sunday from 9 am to noon and 2 to 6 pm (5 pm in winter). Entry costs AS30 (AS20 for seniors and students). The exhibition vividly presents the life story of the Tulln-born artist – ask for the extensive English notes. Schiele is famous for his provocative nudes and he was briefly imprisoned in 1912 following the seizure of 125 erotic drawings (some were of pubescent girls, and Schiele was also in trouble for allowing children to see his explicit works). Appropriately, the premises are a former jail and contain a mock-up of his cell, though Schiele was actually jailed in Neulengbach. There are 100 of his works on display (plus copies), mostly sketches and early paintings.

Churches of interest include the newly restored **Minoritenkirche** (18th century) and **Pfarrkirche St Stephan** (12th century Romanesque, with alterations in Gothic and Baroque style). Behind the latter is a 13th century polygonal funerary chapel, with frescoes depicting some not very evil-looking devils. The crypt below is filled with exhumed bones (no public access).

The town offers a variety of sports near the Yachthafen (yacht harbour), to the east of the centre. The adjoining swimming pool complex costs AS40 per day (students AS30); it's closed on Monday. The tourist office has plenty of information for cyclists.

Places to Stay & Eat

Donaupark Camping (☎ 652 00, fax 652 01), east of the centre near the river, is open from mid-May to early October. A site (including parking) costs AS50, plus AS70.50 per adult.

Beside the river and 500m west of the Egon Schiele Museum is *Alpenvereins Herberge* (☎ 626 92), with dorm beds for AS163 or a mattress on the floor for AS133. It's open from 1 May to 31 October.

Some families offer private rooms for about AS250 per person; find them on the tourist office list. A similar price is charged at *Gasthof Zum Grünen Baum* (☎ 625 05, Wiener Strasse 43) in Langenlebarn, 4km towards Vienna. It has five rooms with private shower, a restaurant and parking.

Hotel-Restaurant zur Rossmühle (☎ 624 11-0, fax -33, Hauptplatz 13) has an imperial aura and a veritable jungle of plants in the lobby, complete with tweeting birds. The high-ceilinged singles/doubles have shower/WC and TV, and cost from AS590/880. The restaurant (open daily) is good quality, with interesting presentations of national dishes for AS130 to AS220.

China Restaurant Asia (Brudergasse 5), off Hauptplatz, has good weekday lunch menus from AS58, with plenty of food; it's open daily. For good Austrian cooking, go to *Albrechtsstuben (Albrechtsgasse 24)* where three-course lunch menus start at AS60, and other meals cost from AS70 to AS180. This place has a garden and is frequented by locals; it's closed on Sunday evening and on Monday.

For self-caterers there's a *Löwa* supermarket on Hauptplatz.

Getting There & Away

Tulln is reached by train or S-Bahn (line 40) from Vienna's Franz Josefs Bahnhof (AS51). The train is quicker (25 minutes), but only stops at the main Tulln station, while the S40 stops at Tulln Stadt. Heading west, trains go to Krems (AS68) or St Pölten (AS78). The road to/from Vienna is highway 14, via Klosterneuburg.

KLOSTERNEUBURG
☎ 02243

Overlooking the river at Klosterneuburg is a large Augustinian abbey, **Stift Klosterneuburg**, founded in 1114. The abbey buildings are mostly Baroque and can be visited daily on a 45 minute guided tour in German (AS50; students AS15). The abbey church is also Baroque, despite its neo-Gothic spires. An annexe to the church contains St Leopold's Chapel. This houses the **Verdun Altar**, which is covered with 51 enamelled panels showing biblical scenes. It was constructed in 1181 by Nicholas of Verdun and is an unsurpassed example of medieval enamelwork.

At Klosterneuburg is the *Donaupark Camping* site *(☎ 858 77)* by the Danube. It's open all year round. A HI *Jugendherberge (☎ 835 01, Hüttersteig 8)*, in the Maria Gugging district, is accessible by bus from the train station; it's open from 1 May to mid-September.

Getting There & Away

Klosterneuburg is on the S-Bahn route from Vienna to Tulln (AS17 from Franz Josefs Bahnhof): Klosterneuburg-Kierling is the station closest to the abbey. Alternatively, walk there from Kahlenberg (at the end of bus No 38A from Vienna).

PETRONELL
☎ 02163 • pop 1250 • 190m

The village of Petronell lies close to the Danube, 38km east of Vienna. In Roman times it was the site of Carnuntum, a regional capital believed to have had 50,000 inhabitants. Ruins of that town extend as far as Bad Deutsch-Altenburg, 4km to the east.

Orientation & Information

Petronell train station is 1km south of the main street, Hauptstrasse. Get tourist information from the Archaeological Park (☎ 337 70, fax 337 75, email info@carnuntum.co.at).

Bad Deutsch-Altenburg's tourist office (☎ 02165-624 59) is at Badgasse 17.

Things to See & Do

The relics of Carnuntum's former glories are not particularly stunning, but they do make a reasonably diverting day. They include a grass-covered amphitheatre that formerly seated 15,000 and an archaeological park on the site of the old civilian town. This park includes ruins of the public baths, a reconstructed temple, and tours and activities for children. It is open daily from late March to 31 October; entry costs AS35. The **Heidentor** (Heathen Gate) was once the south-west entrance to the city and now stands as an isolated anachronism amid fields of corn.

Bad Deutsch-Altenburg has a museum devoted to the Carnuntum era, at Badgasse 40-46. It is open Tuesday to Sunday from 10 am to 5 pm; entry costs AS60. Bad Deutsch-Altenburg is also a health spa, with iodine sulphur springs (28°C).

Tiny **Rohrau**, 6km south of Petronell, is the birthplace of Josef Haydn. Signs will point you to the house where the event took place: it's now a museum (☎ 02164-22 68) devoted to the composer. Entry costs AS20 and it's closed on Monday. The 16th century Schloss Harrach in Rohrau has an art gallery (☎ 02164-2253). It's open from Easter to 1 November (closed on Monday).

Places to Stay & Eat
Gasthof Zum Heidentor (☎ 2201, Hauptstrasse 129) has singles/doubles with shower/WC and TV for AS300/500. The restaurant (closed on Monday) offers a lunch menu with soup for AS60 (Tuesday to Saturday only), and has a beer garden and children's play area. There's a *Denk* supermarket nearby on Hauptstrasse.

Hotel Marc Aurel (☎ 2285, Hauptstrasse 173) is a three star place charging AS500/720 for rooms with shower/WC and TV. The restaurant (open daily) has Austrian dishes for under AS100.

Bad Deutsch-Altenburg has a wider choice of places to stay. At the cheaper end, try *Pension Mittermayer (☎ 02165-62 8 74, Badgasse 20)* with simple, pleasant rooms for AS260/480 using hall shower. *Pension Riedmüller (☎ 02165-62 4 73 0, Badgasse 28)* charges AS300 per person (with private shower/WC) and has a café. *Stephanstub'n (Badgasse 34)* has affordable Austrian food and night-time dancing; it's open daily.

Getting There & Away
From Vienna, an hourly train (S7) departs Wien Nord station at 33 minutes past the hour, calling at Wien Mitte station three minutes later. The fare is AS68, or AS51 if you already have a Vienna city travel pass. Bad Deutsch-Altenburg station is an extra zone from Vienna, so the fare is AS85 (AS68 with pass). Bundesbuses to Rohrau

and the Neusiedler See area in Burgenland are infrequent.

The cycle path from Vienna goes along the north bank of the Danube, crosses to the south at Bad Deutsch-Altenburg, and continues into Slovakia.

Wienerwald

The Wienerwald (Vienna Woods) is a place to get off the beaten track and enjoy nature. **Walking** is popular, with numerous trails meandering through the trees. **Schöpfl** (893m) is the highest point, and has a panoramic lookout (with an Alpine hut open year-round). The signposted walk to Schöpfl lookout takes about two hours, starting from the car park off the Hainfeld-Laaben road, near the Klammhöhe Pass. Walking and cycling trails are shown on the *Wienerwald Wander und Radkarte*, available free from regional tourist offices.

Attractive settlements speckle the Wienerwald, such as the wine-growing centres of Perchtoldsdorf, Mödling and Gumpoldskirchen. Inquire at the respective tourist offices about accommodation. The tourist board for the Wienerwald (☎ 02231-621 76, fax 655 10) is at Hauptplatz 11, A-3200 Purkersdorf, just west of Vienna.

Mödling (population 20,300) was once favoured by the artistic elite escaping from Vienna: Beethoven's itchy feet took him to Hauptstrasse 79 from 1818 to 1820, and Schönberg stayed at Bernhardgasse 6 from 1918 to 1925. Mödling tourist office (☎ 02236-267 27, fax 416 32) is at Elisabethstrasse 2, behind the Rathaus.

Mayerling has little to show now, but the bloody event that occurred there (see the boxed text 'Mystery at Mayerling' on the next page) still draws people to the site. The Carmelite convent can be visited on a daily guided tour (AS20). Six kilometres to the north-east is **Heiligenkreuz**, where Maria's grave can be seen. The chapter house of the 12th century Cistercian abbey here is the final resting place of most of the Babenberg dynasty, which ruled Austria until 1246. The church and the cloister both combine

Mystery at Mayerling

It's the stuff of lurid pulp fiction: the heir to the throne found dead in a hunting lodge with his teenage mistress. It became fact in Mayerling on 30 January 1889, yet for years the details of the case were shrouded in secrecy and denial. Even now a definitive picture has yet to be established – the 100th anniversary of the tragedy saw a flurry of books on the subject, and Empress Zita claimed publicly that the heir had actually been murdered.

The heir was Archduke Rudolf, 30-year-old son of Emperor Franz Josef, husband of Stephanie of Coburg, and something of a libertine who was fond of drinking and womanising. Rudolf's marriage was little more than a public façade by the time he met the 17-year-old Baroness Maria Vetsera in the autumn of 1888. The attraction was immediate, but it wasn't until 13 January of the following year that the affair was consummated, an event commemorated by an inscribed cigarette case, a gift from Maria to Rudolf.

On 28 January Rudolf secretly took Maria with him on a shooting trip to his hunting lodge in Mayerling. His other guests arrived a day later; Maria's presence, however, remained unknown to them. On the night of the 29th, the valet, Loschek, heard the couple talking until the early hours, and at about 5.30 am a fully dressed Rudolf appeared and instructed him to get a horse and carriage ready. As he was doing his master's bidding, two gun shots resounded through the still air. He raced back to discover Rudolf lifeless on his bed, with a revolver by his side. Maria was on her bed, also fully clothed, also dead. Just two days earlier Rudolf had discussed a suicide pact with a former mistress. Apparently he hadn't been joking.

Almost immediately the cover-up began. Count Hoyos, a guest at the lodge, told Maria's mother that it was Maria who killed both herself and the archduke with the aid of poison. The official line was proffered by Empress Elisabeth, who claimed Rudolf died of heart failure. There was no hint of suicide or a mistress. The newspapers swallowed the heart failure story, though a few speculated about a hunting accident. It was only much later that Rudolf's suicide letter to his wife was published in her memoirs, in which he talked of going calmly to his death.

Throughout the lies and misinformation, the real victim remains Maria. How much of a willing party she was to the suicide will never be known. What has become clear is that Maria, after her death, represented not a tragically curtailed young life but an embarrassing scandal that had to be discreetly disposed of. Her body was left untouched for 38 hours, after which it was loaded into a carriage in such a manner as to imply that it was a living person being aided rather than a corpse beyond help. Her subsequent burial was a rude, secretive affair, during which she was consigned to the ground in an unmarked grave (her body was later moved to Heiligenkreuz). Today the hunting lodge is no more – a Carmelite nunnery stands in its place.

Romanesque and Gothic styles. The abbey museum contains 150 clay models by Giovanni Giuliani (1663-1744), a Venetian sculptor who also created the Trinity column in the courtyard. Tours of the abbey buildings are conducted hourly every day and cost AS40 (students AS25). Maria's grave can be seen without joining the tour.

Heiligenkreuz's tourist office (☎ 02258-8720) is near the abbey.

Between Mödling and Heiligenkreuz, boat tours can be taken on Europe's largest underground lake, **Seegrotte Hinterbrühl** (☎/fax 02236-263 64). This former mine flooded with 20 million litres of water in 1912 and consequently shut down. It reopened to tourists as a display mine in 1932. The site was used by the German Army to build aircraft during WWII. The tours (in English) last 45 minutes and cost AS50 (children AS25). Hinterbrühl is open daily, April to October from 8.30 am to noon and 1 to 5 pm, and November to March from 9 am to noon and 1 to 3.30 pm.

Getting There & Away

To explore this region, it's best if you have your own transport. Trains skirt either side of the woods and the bus service is patchy. Bundesbus Nos 1140 and 1142 run regularly between Baden and St Pölten, usually stopping at Heiligenkreuz and sometimes also at Mayerling. Mödling is a stop on the S-Bahn and regional train routes between Vienna's Südbahnhof and Baden, and frequent buses go between Mödling and Hinterbrühl.

The main road through the area is the A21 that loops down from Vienna, passes by Heiligenkreuz, then curves north to join the A1 just east of Altlengbach.

BADEN

☎ 02252 • pop 23,500 • 230m

On the eastern edge of the Wienerwald, the spa town of Baden has a long history. The Romans were prone to wallow in its medicinal springs. Beethoven came here many times in hope of a cure for his deafness. The town flourished in the early 19th century when it was adopted by the Habsburgs as their favourite summer retreat. Baden mostly closes down in winter.

Orientation & Information

The centre of town is the pedestrian-only Hauptplatz; the train station is 500m southeast. A couple of minutes walk west of Hauptplatz is the tourist office (☎ 44531-59, fax 807 33) at Brusattiplatz 3, open Monday to Saturday from 9 am to 6 pm, and on Sunday and holidays from 9 am to noon. From November to Easter, hours are weekdays only from 9 am to 5 pm.

The VIP Card (free if you stay three nights or more) gives very useful benefits, such as discounts on entry prices and free walking tours.

Things to See & Do

Baden exudes health and 19th century affluence, an impression endorsed by the many Biedermeier-style houses. The **Dreifaltigkeitssäule** on Hauptplatz dates from 1714.

The town attracts plenty of promenading Viennese at the weekends. All and sundry make for the **Kurpark**, a magnificent setting for a stroll. Rows of white benches are neatly positioned under manicured trees in front of the bandstand, where free spa concerts (*Kurkonzerte*) are performed every day except Monday from May to September at 4.30 pm. Elaborate flower beds complement monuments to famous artists (Mozart, Beethoven, Strauss, Grillparzer etc). The **Undine Brunnen** (fountain) is a fine amalgam of human and fish images. The **casino** has gaming tables (open from 3 pm; dress code) and slot machines (from 1 pm; no dress code). ID is required for entry.

The **Emperor Franz Josef Museum**, Hochstrasse 51, north of the centre, displays local folklore. Entry costs AS30 and the museum is closed on Monday and in winter. The **Rollett Museum**, Weikersdorfer Platz 1, south-west of the centre, covers aspects of the town's history (like the bomb damage in WWII). The most unusual exhibit is the collection of skulls, busts and death masks amassed by the founder of phrenology, Josef Gall (1752-1828). This apparently cranky science, which held that criminal characteristics could be inferred from the shape of the skull, links disturbingly with modern claims of the discovery of a 'criminal gene'. The museum is closed on Monday; entry costs AS20. Beethoven's former house at Rathausgasse 10 is now a museum, but there's not much to see. Entry costs AS20 and the museum has limited opening hours. There's also a doll and toy museum (entry AS20; closed on Monday) at Erzherzog Rainer Ring 23.

Baden's reputation as a health spa rests on its 14 **hot springs**, with a daily flow of

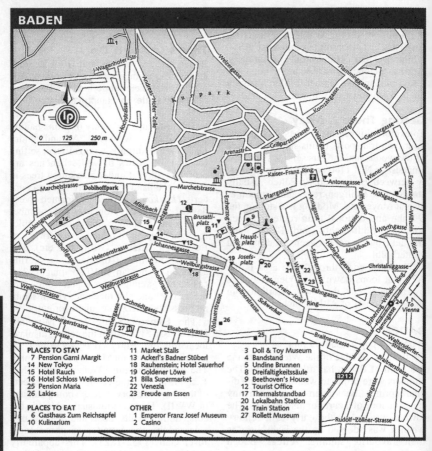

BADEN

PLACES TO STAY
7 Pension Garni Margit
14 New Tokyo
15 Hotel Rauch
16 Hotel Schloss Weikersdorf
25 Pension Maria
26 Lakies

PLACES TO EAT
6 Gasthaus Zum Reichsapfel
10 Kulinarium

11 Market Stalls
13 Ackerl's Badner Stüberl
18 Rauhenstein; Hotel Sauerhof
19 Goldener Löwe
21 Billa Supermarket
22 Venezia
23 Freude am Essen

OTHER
1 Emperor Franz Josef Museum
2 Casino

3 Doll & Toy Museum
4 Bandstand
5 Undine Brunnen
8 Dreifaltigkeitssäule
9 Beethoven's House
12 Tourist Office
17 Thermalstrandbad
20 Lokalbahn Station
24 Train Station
27 Rollett Museum

6.5 million litres. The waters emerge at a temperature of 36°C and are enriched with sulphur, chlorine and sulphates. The town has various indoor and outdoor pool complexes, for medicinal or frivolous purposes. In the latter category is the Thermalstrandbad, at Helenenstrasse 19-21, with sulphur and normal pools, plus imported sand. Entry costs from AS64 per day; the pool is open from 1 May to 30 September. The Kurmittelhaus, which houses the tourist office on Brusattiplatz, is also a spa centre.

Special Events

In June, a rose festival is held in the Rosarium gardens in the Doblhoffpark and an operetta festival begins. May to September is the season for trotting races (*Trabenen*; entry around AS30), held at the track 1.5km to the east of the town centre.

Places to Stay

Unfortunately, the few private rooms are the only option for those on a tight budget; get a list from the tourist office. *Lakies*

(☎ 229 38, Vöslauerstrasse 11), 250m south of Josefsplatz, has singles with shower for AS180, and one double. The *New Tokyo* Japanese restaurant *(☎ 243 03, Johannesgasse 1)* has large, if fairly bare, doubles with shower for AS600.

Pension Garni Margit (☎ 897 18, Mühlgasse 15-17) is 500m east of Hauptplatz. It has a homey ambience and a garden, but the singles/doubles for AS340/600 have no access to a shower. Pay AS400/650 or more for private facilities. The three star *Pension Maria (☎ 430 33, fax -32, Elisabethstrasse 11)* has rooms with shower/WC for AS430/650. There's an outdoor swimming pool and off-street parking.

Hotel Rauch (☎ 445 61, Pelzgasse 3) is next to the Doblhoffpark, in a typical Baden building with high ceilings. Rooms (with WC and mini-baths) cost up to AS480/800, depending on the size and season.

Hotel Schloss Weikersdorf (☎ 483 01-0, fax -150, Schlossgasse 9-11), also adjoining the park, has a genuine castle ambience and fixtures, which is usually reflected in room furnishings. Singles/doubles with shower/WC and cable TV start at AS825/1350, though there are cheaper rooms in the annexe, which houses the sauna and indoor swimming pool (both free for guests).

Places to Eat

There's a *Billa* supermarket at Wassergasse 14. On the same street, by Bahngasse, is *Freude am Essen*, a self-service place offering sausage snacks and simple Austrian meals for under AS90. It's open on weekdays (not Wednesday) from 9 am to 6.30 pm, and on Saturday from 9 am to 3 pm. *Kulinarium* has similar prices and opening times, but it's not self-service. It's by Brusattiplatz, where there are market stalls selling food and flowers.

Several Chinese restaurants provide inexpensive fare: *Goldener Löwe (Braitnerstrasse 1)*, for example, has a variety of lunch menus (Monday to Saturday) for about AS59, and outside tables overlook the Schwechat River. *Venezia (Wassergasse 29)* is an Italian restaurant with bigger-than-the-plate pizzas costing from AS42 to AS105. Both are open daily.

Ackerl's Badner Stüberl (Gutenbrunnerstrasse 19) is a typically Austrian place with mid-price food; it's closed on Tuesday. The plush Hotel Sauerhof houses *Rauhenstein (☎ 412 51-6, Weilburgstrasse 11-13)*, a gourmet restaurant serving international dishes costing upwards of AS200 (open evenings only, from 6 to 11.30 pm), and a café-restaurant open daily from 7 am to 7 am, with meals starting at AS130 and a Sunday lunchtime buffet (AS370).

Baden is not known for its nightlife, but to combine wine and dining, ask the tourist office for the opening schedule of the various Heurigen. *Gasthaus Zum Reichsapfel (Spiegelgasse 2)* is like a small beer hall, with several varieties of ale on tap. It also serves inexpensive meals and snacks, including various vegetarian choices.

Getting There & Away

IC trains don't stop at Baden, but regional and S-Bahn services do: two to four trains an hour run to Wiener Neustadt (AS34) and Vienna's Südbahnhof (AS51, or AS34 with a Vienna city pass; 20 to 25 minutes). For the same price from Vienna, you could instead take the Lokalbahn tram that goes from Kärntner Ring (opposite Hotel Bristol) to Josefsplatz in Baden (every 15 minutes; the journey takes an hour). Austrian and European rail passes are, apparently, valid for half-price travel on this service, though none of the staff seem sure of the rules.

The north-south road routes, highway 17 and the A2, pass a few kilometres to the east of the town.

Southern Lower Austria

This region includes the edge of the Alps, the highest and best known peak being Schneeberg at 2075m. In the south-east are several mountains approaching 2000m, such as Hochkar and Ötscher (both have chair lifts).

WIENER NEUSTADT

☎ 02622 • pop 40,000 • 265m

First known simply as Neustadt (new city) or Nova Civitas, this city was built by the Babenbergs in 1194. It became a Habsburg residence in the 15th century, during the reign of Friedrich III. His son, Maximilian I, was born in the town. Wiener Neustadt was severely damaged in WWII and only 18 homes were unscathed. Historic buildings that were damaged have been restored.

Orientation & Information

The centre of town is the large Hauptplatz, where you'll find the tourist office (☎ 235 31-468, fax -390) at No 3, in the Rathaus complex. It is open Monday to Friday from 8 am to noon and 1 to 5 pm, and on Saturday from 8 am to noon. Unfortunately, the tourist office doesn't have a great deal of information in English, but it does at least have a free booklet, called *Cultural Promenade*, which describes the central sights and gives their locations on a map. Most of the streets leading off Hauptplatz are for pedestrians only.

The train station is less than 1km to the south-west. It has bike rental, a travel agency and a Bankomat. Next door is the main post office (Postamt 2700), open Monday to Friday from 7 am to 7 pm, Saturday from 7 am to 4 pm, and Sunday and holidays from 7 to 10 am.

Things to See & Do

Spacious **Hauptplatz** is lined with elegant buildings, not least the three parts of the Rathaus (first mentioned in 1401), featuring an arcade and colourful crests. An outdoor market fills the square daily except Sunday, though the busiest days are Wednesday and Saturday. East of Hauptplatz is **Neukloster**, a 14th century Gothic church with striking Baroque fittings.

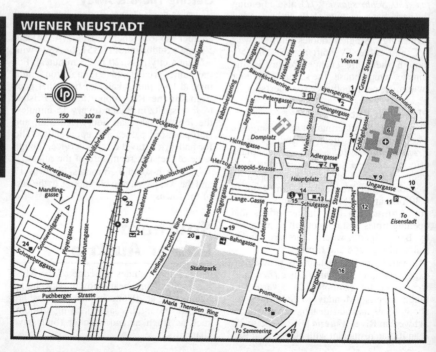

WIENER NEUSTADT

The Romanesque **Dom** (cathedral; erected in 1279 but subsequently much rebuilt) has a rather bare and grey exterior, and two severe-looking square towers. The interior has an unbalanced look, caused by the chancel being out of line with the nave, and the asymmetric arch that connects the two. Fifteenth century wooden apostles peer down from pillars, and there's a Baroque high altar and pulpit.

The imposing **castle** on Burgplatz houses a military academy, founded by Empress Maria Theresa in 1752, and later commanded by the young Rommel, before he became a 'foxy' Nazi general. The castle with its four towers dates from the 13th century, though it had to be completely rebuilt after WWII. Within the complex is **St Georgs Kapelle**, with a fine late-Gothic interior. Maximilian I, who was born in the castle, is buried under the altar. On the outside wall is the Wappenwand (Heraldic Wall) comprising 15th century carvings of 107 coats of arms. This wall was all that survived the bombing during WWII (the stained glass had already been removed to the Altaussee salt mines in the Salzkammergut). The statue below the window is Friedrich III, whose AEIOU motto also appears on the wall. The military guard will show you round (ring the bell if the door's shut).

At the eastern end of the Stadtpark is a **Wasserturm** (water tower), built between 1909 and 1910. Its shape intentionally apes the gilded goblet (*Becher*) donated to the townsfolk by King Matthias Corvinus of Hungary after he took the town in 1487. A copy of this chalice can be seen in the **Stadtmuseum** at the intersection of Wiener Strasse and Petersgasse (the original is housed in the Rathaus). Admission costs AS30 and the museum is open daily except Monday and Saturday, from 10 am.

Wiener Neustadt is a convenient base for those wishing to undertake an excursion to Schneeberg (see the Schneeberg section later in this chapter).

Places to Stay

The HI *Jugendherberge* (☎ 296 95, *Promenade 1)* is the white house in the Stadtpark, near the water tower. It has four-bed dorms including modern bathroom facilities at AS135.50, and single/double rooms for AS185.50 – prices are per person. Breakfast is not included in the price; you can pay an extra AS35 or there is a kitchen. Get a key for late entry. Check-in is from 5 to 8 pm on the 1st floor, but phone ahead as it's run by a family, and they may not always be around; the place is often full anyway.

Wiener Neustadt has just five hotels and pensions, and no real budget choice. The cheapest place is the recently re-modelled *Gasthof Friedam* (☎ 230 81, *Schneeberggasse 16)*, less than 10 minutes walk west of the train station. Singles/doubles (twin beds) with shower/WC and cable TV cost AS420/560, and the restaurant (closed on Wednesday) has a cheap lunch menu.

Hotel Zentral (☎ 237 93, *fax -5, Hauptplatz 27)* is very central. Rooms have shower/WC, satellite TV and telephone, and cost from AS620/995.

Hotel Corvinus (☎ 241 34, fax 241 39, Bahngasse) is a four star place. Comfortable rooms with modern furniture and facilities are AS940/1440. There's a sauna, steam bath and whirlpool (free for guests), off-street parking and a plush restaurant.

Places to Eat

There are *Billa* supermarkets on Bahngasse and Hauptplatz. Hauptplatz also has several *Würstel* stands. Near the tourist office is *Weisses Rössl*, with Austrian food from AS80. It's open till 7.30 pm, and is closed Saturday afternoon and on Sunday.

Schnitzelhaus, the fast-food Schnitzel chain, is on Grazer Strasse; it's open daily from 10 am to 10 pm. *Pizza Mann*, 150m north on Grazer Strasse, is good value for eat-in or take-away pizzas.

To the north is Eyerspergring. On this street is *Sport Café*, with snooker and pool tables (open daily from 2 pm to midnight), and *Stargl-Wirt*, a specialist schnitzel place. The schnitzels cost around AS130; it closes at 2 pm at weekends.

Ungargasse, running east from Hauptplatz, has two good places to eat. *Stüberl Zum Ungartor*, at No 21, has tasty Austrian food for AS75 to AS180. It has a comfortable ambience, despite the chalked menu board outside; it's closed on Monday. *China-Restaurant Hong Kong*, at No 27, has weekday lunch menus from AS52, including a starter. It's open daily.

Getting There & Away

The 35 minute train journey from Vienna's Südbahnhof to Wiener Neustadt costs AS85 (two to four departures per hour). There are trains almost hourly to the Hungarian shopping town of Sopron (AS51, 45 minutes), and Austrian rail passes are valid for the whole trip. Bundesbuses depart from the northern end of Wiener Neustadt train station. You can get to Eisenstadt from here.

The city has excellent road links: options from Vienna include the A2 or highway 17.

SEMMERING

☎ 02664 • pop 1100 • 1000m

This spread-out mountain resort, which became a favourite with moneyed tourists at the turn of the century, is famed for its clean air. Semmering also has skiing facilities.

Orientation & Information

Semmering sits on a south-facing slope above the Semmering Pass. There's no real centre to the resort: it's mostly ranged along Hochstrasse which forms an arc above the train station. Parking is not a problem.

Outside the train station (which has a restaurant and left luggage facilities, but no bike rental) there's a map. Go left and follow the paths to 'Passhöhe'. In 20 minutes you reach the Kurverwaltung tourist office (☎ 2539-5, fax -6). It's by the bank where Hochstrasse branches from highway 306, and is open Monday to Friday from 8 am to noon and 1 to 5 pm. The Tourismusregion Süd-alpin regional tourist office (☎ 2539-1, fax 2335) is on the 1st floor, and is open on Monday, 8 am to 2 pm, and Tuesday to Friday, 8 am to 4 pm.

Things to See & Do

Outdoor activities are the resort's main draw, including **walking**: the tourist office can sell you the *Wanderkarte* map (text in German) or give you brochures outlining scenic walks. Overlooking Semmering to the south is the **Hirschenkogel** (1340m), on which a new cable car is being built. It attracts walkers or skiers (AS305 for a day pass), depending on the season, and there's a restaurant at the top. A day pass for all three local ski regions costs AS335.

The resort has a golf course (☎ 2471), mini-golf, tennis courts, two ski schools (☎ 2471, ☎ 8538) and a swimming pool and sauna complex in the four star Hotel Panhaus (☎ 8181).

An excursion can be made to the north along the scenic **Höllental** (Hell's Valley), a deep, narrow gorge created by the Schwarza River. Along the route from Semmering (by winding, local roads) you pass the Raxblick viewpoint. A little farther on is Hirschwang, where in 1926 Austria's first cable car was built. You can ascend to 1540m (AS188 return) for a 360° panorama. Hirschwang is where you join the Höllental.

Places to Stay & Eat

Most places close during the off season (from Easter until sometime in May, and in November). Semmering has few options for budget travellers, other than a couple of private rooms. Unless stated otherwise, all of the places below are on Hochstrasse, near the two tourist offices. The higher end of Hochstrasse is where the more expensive hotels reside. Also on this street is a *Billa* supermarket, open Monday to Friday from 7.30 or 8 am to 7 or 7.30 pm, and Saturday from 7.30 am to 5 pm.

Haus Mayer (☎ 2251, fax 2252, No 257) has good-value rooms with shower and balcony costing from AS240 to AS300 per person, but only takes nonsmokers.

Haus Tonn (☎ 2264, No 108) charges AS220/460 for singles/doubles using hall shower. It also has doubles with private shower for AS560.

Pension Löffler (☎ 2304, fax -8, No 174) has good, largish rooms for AS400/700, with shower, WC and satellite TV. Its restaurant has good food for between AS70 and AS160, and outside tables. There's a three course lunch menu for AS130 and a two course deal for senior citizens (AS90).

Hotel-Restaurant Berghof (☎ 2320, fax -4, No 271) is round the corner from the tourist offices. It has pleasant singles/doubles with shower/WC and TV for AS390/780; doubles also have a balcony. Austrian food costs from AS80 to AS170.

The family-managed *Hotel-Restaurant Belvedere* (☎ 2270, fax 226 742, No 60) has excellent facilities for a three star place: use of the swimming pool, sauna and solarium are all included in the price, and there's a large garden and patio area. Rooms have shower/WC, TV and balcony, and cost from AS420 per person in summer or AS520 in winter. The restaurant (open daily) has regional dishes (AS80 to AS250) including fish and seasonal specialities.

Getting There & Away

From Semmering, the rail route to the north-east passes through some impressive scenery of precipitous cliffs and forested hills (make sure you sit on the right). The route, incorporating many bridges and tunnels, was Europe's first Alpine railway and was completed in 1854 by Karl Ritter von Ghega. The most scenic section is the 30 minute stretch between Semmering and Payerbach (AS52). There's a direct service from Semmering to Vienna's Südbahnhof (AS155). Travelling south-west to Graz (AS156), you must first take a regional train to Mürzzuschlag.

By road (highway 306), the Semmering Pass (985m) marks the border between Lower Austria and Styria. Excursions along the Höllental are easiest if you have your own transport. Bundesbuses do run to Hirschwang and Raxblick, but departures are infrequent.

SCHNEEBERG

The popular ascent up Schneeberg by cog-wheel steam train is a full day excursion, providing excellent views and good walks. The top station, Hochschneeberg, is at 1795m. Nearby is a hotel and restaurant, and a viewing terrace by a small chapel dedicated to the Empress Elisabeth (wife of Franz Josef). From the station, a path leads to Klosterwappen and Fischerhütte; these are each about a 70 minute walk from the station, and 20 minutes from each other.

The path to both is initially the same. After 30 minutes it splits: the steeper left-hand path goes to **Klosterwappen** (2075m), identifiable by the radar and cross on the ridge. This fork provides the best view of the Raxalpe range and the upper reaches of the Höllental, with the ribbon-like road winding its way on the far side of the valley. A path goes down into the valley, while a flattish walk along the ridge will bring you to the *Fischerhütte* restaurant (food served till 7 pm). Up the hill behind the restaurant is the Kaiserstein viewpoint (2061m), with a beehive-shaped monument to Emperor Franz I. The most impressive part of the view from here is the Breite Ries, a bowl-shaped area of erosion with stark grey and red cliffs.

Getting There & Away

There are trains from Wiener Neustadt to Puchberg am Schneeberg (50 minutes), where you board the Schneeberg cogwheel. A special leaflet (in English) giving times of the Schneeberg train is available at many train stations. Trains operate from late April to early November, and the full ascent from Puchberg to Hochschneeberg takes about 85 minutes (AS160 up, AS130 down, AS270 return). Austrian rail passes are valid. Trains depart frequently according to

demand (which is usually high). There are guaranteed ascents at 8.30 and 11.55 am, with descents at 2.05 and 4 pm, and further guaranteed trains running in summer, particularly in August.

Puchberg itself has places to stay and eat. For more information about the trains, or special all-in tickets (including overnight accommodation and/or meals), you should get in touch with the Puchberg train station on ☎ 02636-22 25 0.

To walk from Puchberg up to Hochschneeberg takes three hours or more. Klosterwappen is on the long-distance path, the Nordalpenweg, running from Bodensee (in Vorarlberg) to the Wienerwald.

Language

This German language guide contains pronunciation guidelines and basic vocabulary to help you get around Austria. For background information on Austria's language milieu see the Language section at the end of the Facts about Austria chapter.

It may be a surprise to know that German is, in fact, a close relative of English; English, German and Dutch are all known as West Germanic languages. The High German that is used today comes from a regional Saxon dialect. The fact that many German words survive in the English vocabulary today makes things a lot easier for native English speakers. While that's good news, the bad news is that, unlike English, German has retained clear formal distinctions in gender and case.

The polite form of address in German involves using the third person plural with verb forms, eg *Haben Sie ...?*, as against *Hast du ...?* (Do you have ...?). In this guide the polite form is used unless otherwise indicated. If in doubt it's alwayss best to use the polite form. Note that in German all nouns are written with a capital letter.

If you want a more comprehensive guide to the language get hold of Lonely Planet's *German phrasebook*. In it you'll find everything you need to know about German grammar along with a vast array of useful phrases divided into chapters such as Meeting People, Going Out, Social Issues, Shopping and Activities; there's also a special section on varieties of German (such as that spoken in Austria).

Pronunciation

Unlike English or French, German has no real silent letters: you pronounce the **k** at the start of the word *Knie* (knee), the **p** at the start of *Psychologie* (psychology), and the **e** at the end of *ich habe* (I have).

Vowels As in English, German vowels can be pronounced long, as the 'o' in 'pope', or short, as in 'pop'. As a rule, vowels are long before one consonant and short before two consonants: the **o** is long in the word *Dom*, 'cathedral', but short in the word *doch*, 'after all'.

a	short, as the 'u' in 'cut' or long, as in 'father'
au	as the 'ow' in 'vow'
ä	short, as in 'cat' or long, as in 'care'
äu	as the 'oy' in 'boy'
e	short, as in 'bet' or long, as in 'obey'
ei	as the 'ai' in 'aisle'
eu	as the 'oy' in 'boy'
i	short, as in 'it' or long, as the 'ee' in 'see'
ie	as the 'ee' in 'see'
o	short, as in 'not' or long, as in 'note'
ö	as the 'er' in 'fern'
u	as in 'pull'
ü	similar to the 'u' in 'pull' but with lips stretched back

Consonants Most German consonants sound similar to their English counterparts. One important difference is that **b**, **d** and **g** sound like 'p', 't' and 'k', respectively when word-final.

b	as in 'be'; as 'p' when word-final
ch	as in Scottish *loch*
d	as in 'do'; as 't' when word-final
g	as in 'go'; as 'k' when word-final (except after **i**, when it's as 'ch' in Scottish *loch*)
j	as the 'y' in 'yet'
qu	as 'k' plus 'v'
r	can be trilled or guttural, depending on the region
s	as in 'sun'; as the 'z' in 'zoo' when followed by a vowel
sch	as the 'sh' in 'ship'
sp, st	as 'shp' and 'sht' when word-initial

tion	the 't' is pronounced as the 'ts' in 'its'
v	as the 'f' in 'fan'
w	as the 'v' in 'van'
z	as the 'ts' in 'its'

Basics

Good day.	*Grüss Gott.* (pol)
Hello.	*Servus/Grüss Dich/ Griassdi.* (inf)
Goodbye.	*Auf Wiedersehen. Pfiati/Ciao* (inf)
Yes/No.	*Ja/Nein.*
Please.	*Bitte.*
Thank you.	*Danke.*
That's fine/ You're welcome.	*Bitte sehr.*
Sorry. (excuse me, forgive me)	*Entschuldigung.*
Do you speak English?	*Sprechen Sie Englisch?*
How much is it?	*Wieviel kostet es?*
What's your name?	*Wie heissen Sie?*
My name is ...	*Ich heisse ...*

Getting Around

What time does the ... leave?	*Wann fährt ... ab?*
What time does the ... arrive?	*Wann kommt ... an?*
boat	*das Boot*
bus (city)	*der Bus*
bus (intercity)	*der (überland) Bus*
plane	*das Flugzeug*
tram	*die Strassenbahn*
train	*der Zug*

What time is the next boat?	*Wann fährt das nächste Boot?*
I'd like to hire a car/bicycle.	*Ich möchte ein Auto/ Fahrrad mieten.*

I'd like a ...	*Ich möchte eine ...*
one-way ticket	*Einzelkarte*
return ticket	*Rückfahrkarte*

1st class	*erste Klasse*
2nd class	*zweite Klasse*
left luggage lockers	*Schliessfächer*
timetable	*Fahrplan*

Where is the bus stop?	*Wo ist die Bushaltestelle?*
Where is the tram stop?	*Wo ist die Strassen- bahnhaltestelle?*
Where is the train station?	*Wo ist der Bahnhof (Bf)?*
Where is the ferry terminal?	*Wo ist der Fährhafen?*
Can you show me (on the map)?	*Können Sie mir (auf der Karte) zeigen?*
I'm looking for ...	*Ich suche ...*

Go straight ahead.	*Gehen Sie geradeaus.*
Turn left.	*Biegen Sie links ab.*
Turn right.	*Biegen Sie rechts ab.*
near	*nahe*
far	*weit*

Around Town

a bank	*eine Bank*
the city centre	*die Innenstadt*
doctor	*der Arzt*
the ... embassy	*die ... Botschaft*
my hotel	*mein Hotel*
hospital	*das Krankenhaus*
library	*die Bibliothek*
the market	*den Markt*
the newsagency	*der Zeitungshändler*
the pharmacy	*die Apotheke*
the police	*die Polizei*
the post office	*das Postamt*
a public toilet	*eine öffentliche Toilette*
the telephone centre	*die Telefonzentrale*
the tourist office	*das Fremden- verkersbüro*

Signs

EINGANG	Entrance
AUSGANG	Exit
VOLL/BESETZT	Full/No Vacancies
AUSKUNFT	Information
OFFEN	Open
GESCHLOSSEN	Closed
POLIZEIWACHE	Police Station
ZIMMER FREI	Rooms Available
TOILETTEN (WC)	Toilets
HERREN	Men
DAMEN	Women

bridge	Brücke
castle	Schloss/Burg
cathedral	Dom
church	Kirche
island	Insel
lake	See
main square	Hauptplatz
monastery/convent	Kloster
mosque	Moschee
mountain	Berg
old city	Altstadt
ruins	Ruinen
square	Platz
tower	Turm

| What time does it open/close? | Um wieviel Uhr macht es auf/zu? |

Accommodation

Where is a cheap hotel?	Wo ist ein billiges Hotel?
What is the address?	Was ist die Adresse?
Could you write the address, please?	Könnten Sie bitte die Adresse aufschreiben?

hotel	Hotel
guesthouse	Pension, Gästehaus
youth hostel	Jugendherberge
camping ground	Campingplatz

| Do you have any rooms available? | Haben Sie noch freie Zimmer? |

I'd like ...	Ich möchte ...
a single room	ein Einzelzimmer
a double room	ein Doppelzimmer
a room with a bath	ein Zimmer mit Bad
to share a dorm	einen Schlafsaal teilen
a bed	ein Bett

| for one/two nights | eine Nacht/zwei Nächte |

| How much is it per night/person? | Wieviel kostet es pro Nacht/Person? |
| Is breakfast included? | Ist Frühstück inbegriffen? |

| Where is the bath/shower? | Wo ist das Bad/die Dusche? |

Food

grocery	Lebensmittelgeschäft
delicatessen	Delikatessengeschäft
restaurant	Restaurant/Gaststätte
breakfast	Frühstück
lunch	Mittagessen
dinner	Abendessen

I'd like the set lunch, please.	Ich hätte gern das Tagesmenü, bitte.
Is service included in the bill?	Ist die Bedienung inbegriffen?
I'm a vegetarian.	Ich bin Vegetarier (m) Vegetarierin. (f)

Time & Days

What time is it?	Wie spät ist es?
today	heute
tomorrow	morgen
yesterday	gestern
in the morning	morgens
in the afternoon	nachmittags

Monday	Montag
Tuesday	Dienstag
Wednesday	Mittwoch
Thursday	Donnerstag
Friday	Freitag
Saturday	Samstag, Sonnabend
Sunday	Sonntag

Health

antiseptic	Antiseptikum
aspirin	Aspirin
condoms	Kondome
constipation	Verstopfung
contraceptive	Verhütungsmittel
diarrhoea	Durchfall
medicine	Medizin
nausea	Übelkeit
sunblock cream	Sunblockcreme
tampons	Tampons

I'm allergic ...	Ich bin gegen ... allergisch.
to antibiotics	Antibiotika
to penicillin	Penizillin

Emergencies

Help!	*Hilfe!*
Call a doctor!	*Holen Sie einen Arzt!*
Call the police!	*Rufen Sie die Polizei!*
I'm lost.	*Ich habe mich verirrt.*

I'm ...	*Ich bin ...*
diabetic	*Diabetikerin* (f)
	Diabetiker (m)
epileptic	*Epileptikerin* (f)
	Epileptiker (m)
asthmatic	*Asthmatikerin* (f)
	Asthmatiker (m)

Numbers

0	*null*	11	*elf*
1	*eins*	12	*zwölf*
2	*zwei*	13	*dreizehn*
3	*drei*	14	*vierzehn*
4	*vier*	15	*fünfzehn*
5	*fünf*	16	*sechzehn*
6	*sechs*	17	*siebzehn*
7	*sieben*	18	*achtzehn*
8	*acht*	19	*neunzehn*
9	*neun*	20	*zwanzig*
10	*zehn*	21	*einundzwanzig*

22	*zweiundzwanzig*
23	*dreiundzwanzig*
24	*vierundzwanzig*
25	*fünfundzwanzig*
30	*dreissig*
40	*vierzig*
50	*fünfzig*
60	*sechzig*
70	*siebzig*
80	*achtzig*
90	*neunzig*
100	*hundert*
1000	*tausend*

one million	*eine Million*

Austrian Words

Though the grammar is the same as standard German, there are also many words and expressions that are used only by Austrians. Some words will be used throughout the country, others are only in use in particular regions, though they will probably be generally understood. Most would not automatically be understood by non-Austrian German speakers. On the other hand, the 'normal' German equivalent would be understood by Austrians.

Most of the greetings and farewells that we've included in the list of useful phrases are common only to Austria. *Servus* is an informal greeting, and can also be used when taking your leave. The word has been adopted as a motto by the Austrian national tourist office. *Grüss dich* or *Griassdi* (literally 'greet you') is also a familiar, informal greeting. It's especially used by people who don't want to bring God into the conversation (as in *Grüss Gott* – 'Greet God'). For 'goodbye', *Auf Wiederschauen* is the standard phrase (in Germany also); *Pfiati* or *Ciao* is less formal.

It's quite possible you may want to tell people that you've been drinking. If you're tipsy you can say *Ich bin beschwipst* or *Ich habe einen Schwips*. If you're definitely the worse for wear, the Viennese dialect expression is *I'hob an dulliö*. If you're very drunk, you could say *Ich bin zu*, though everyone will probably have figured that out by then.

Some useful Austrian words are: *Blunzen* (black pudding); *Erdäpfel* (potato); *Faschiertes* (minced meat); *Gerstl* (money); *Karfiol* (cauliflower); *Maroni* (roasted chestnut); *Maut* (toll charge); *Müch* (milk); *Obers* (cream); *Paradeiser* (tomatoes); *Scherzl* (crust of bread); and *Stamperl* (glass for Schnapps). See the Food section in the Facts for the Visitor chapter for more useful food-related words. To request the bill in a restaurant, simply say 'Zahlen, bitte'.

Words that are more specifically Viennese include:

Beisl	small tavern for food and drink
Bim	tram
Haberer	friend
Stiftl	glass (for wine)
Verdrahn	to sell

Glossary

Abfahrt – departure (trains)
Achterl – glass holding 0.125L
Ankunft – arrival (trains)
ANTO – Austrian National Tourist Office
ATM – see *Bankomat*
Ausgang – exit
Autobahn – motorway
Autoreisezug – motorail train

Bad – bath (spa resort)
Bahnhof – train station
Bahnsteig – train station platform
Bankomat – automated teller machine (ATM), cashpoint
Bauernhof – farmhouse
Beisl – small tavern or restaurant
Berg – hill or mountain
Besetzt – occupied, full
Bezirk – (town or city) district
Biedermeier period – 19th century art movement in Germany and Austria; applies particularly to a decorative style of furniture from this period
Bierkeller – beer cellar
Brauerei – brewery
Bundesbus – state bus, run by the railway (Bahnhbus) or the post office (Postbus)
Bundesländer/Länder – federal provinces
Bundesrat – Federal Council (upper house – government)
Burg – castle/fortress
Buschenschank/Buschenschenken – wine tavern(s)

Dirndl – traditional skirt
Dorf – village
D train – medium-fast train

EC – EuroCity, express train
EEA – European Economic Area, comprising European Union states plus Iceland, Liechtenstein and Norway
Einbahnstrasse – one-way street
Eingang, Eintritt – entry
Elektroboot – motor boat

EN – EuroNight, international and domestic night train
E train – fast train
EU – European Union

Fahrplan – timetable
Feiertag – public holiday
Ferienwohnungen self-catering holiday apartments
Festung – castle/fortress
Flohmarkt – flea market
Flughafen – airport
Flugpost – air mail
Föhn – hot, dry wind which sweeps down from the mountains, mainly in early spring and autumn
FPÖ – Freedom Party (politics)
Freizeitzentrum – sports and leisure centre
Friedhof – cemetery

Gästekarte – guest card
Gasthof – inn
Gemeindeamt – office of the local authority
Gemütlichkeit – 'cosiness'; a quality much valued by Austrians
Gendarmerie – police
Glockenspiel – carillon
Glockenturm – clock tower
Gondelbahn – gondola

Hafen – harbour, port
Haltestelle – Bus or tram stop
Hauptbahnhof – main train station
Hauptpost – main post office
Heuriger/Heurigen – wine tavern(s)

IC – InterCity, express train
Imbiss – snack bar

Kaffeehaus/Café Konditorei – coffee house
Kärnten – Carinthia (Austrian province)
Konsulat – consulate
Krügerl – glass holding 0.5L

Kurzparkzone – short-term parking zone

Land/Länder – province(s)
Landesmuseum – provincial museum
Landtag – provincial assembly (government)
Langersamstag – 'long' Saturday, the first Saturday of the month; shops open up to 5 pm instead of 1 pm (less common since shopping hours were liberalised)
Langlauf – cross-country skiing
Luftseilbahn – cable car

Maut – toll (or indicating a toll booth)
Mehrwertsteuer (MWST) – value-added tax
Mensa – university restaurant
Mitfahrzentrale – hitching organisation

Nationalrat – National Council (lower house – government)
Not(ruf) – emergency (call)

ÖAMTC – national motoring organisation
ÖAV – Austrian Alpine Club
ÖBB – Austrian federal railway
ÖKISTA – student travel agency
ÖVP – Austrian People's Party (politics)

Parkschein – parking voucher
Pfarrkirche/Stadtpfarrkirche – parish church
Pfiff – glass containing 0.25L
Platz – town or village square
Polizei – police
Postamt – post office
Postlagernde Briefe – poste restante

Radler – mixture of beer and lemonade
Rathaus – town hall
Ruderboot – rowing boat
Ruhetag – 'rest day', on which a restaurant is closed

S-Bahn – suburban train system
SC – SuperCity, express train
Schlepplift – ski lift

Schrammelmusik – popular Viennese music for violins, guitar and accordion
Secession movement – early 20th century movement in Vienna seeking to establish a more functional style in architecture; led by Otto Wagner (1841-1918)
Selbstbedienung (SB) – self-service (restaurants, laundries etc)
Sesselbahn – chair lift
SPÖ – Social Democrats (politics)
Stadtmuseum – city museum
Standseilbahn – funicular
Steiermark – Styria (Austrian province)
Stift – abbey
Strandbad – designated bathing area on a lake or river, usually with an entry fee
Studentenheime – student rooms

Tabak – tobacconist
Tagestellar/Tagesmenu – the set meal or menu of the day in a restaurant
Tal – valley
Telefon-Wertkarte – phonecard
Tierpark – zoo
Tor – gate
Tretboot – paddleboat (pedalo)

U-Bahn – urban underground rail system
Urlaub – holiday

Vienna Circle – group of philosophers centred on Vienna University in the 1920s and 1930s
Vienna Group (Wiener Gruppe) – art/literary movement formed in the 1950s, whose members incorporated surrealism and dadaism in sound compositions, textual montages and actionist happenings
Viertel – 0.25L (drinks); also a geographical district

Wäscherei – laundry
Wien – Vienna
Würstel Stand – sausage stand

Zimmer frei/Privat Zimmer – private rooms (accommodation)

LONELY PLANET

Phrasebooks

L onely Planet phrasebooks are packed with essential words and phrases to help travellers communicate with the locals. With colour tabs for quick reference, an extensive vocabulary, and use of script, these handy pocket-sized language guides cover day-to-day travel situations.

- handy pocket-sized books
- easy to understand Pronunciation chapter
- clear & comprehensive Grammar chapter
- romanisation alongside script to allow ease of pronunciation
- script throughout so users can point to phrases for every situations
- full of cultural information and tips for the traveller

'...vital for a real DIY spirit and attitude in language learning'
– *Backpacker*

'the phrasebooks have good cultural backgrounders and offer solid advice for challenging situations in remote locations'
– *San Francisco Examiner*

Arabic (Egyptian) • Arabic (Moroccan) • Australia *(Australian English, Aboriginal and Torres Strait languages)* • Baltic States *(Estonian, Latvian, Lithuanian)* • Bengali • Brazilian • Burmese • Cantonese • Central Asia • Central Europe *(Czech, French, German, Hungarian, Italian, Slovak)* • Eastern Europe *(Bulgarian, Czech, Hungarian, Polish, Romanian, Slovak)* • Egyptian Arabic • Ethiopian (Amharic) • Fijian • French • German • Greek • Hill Tribes • Hindi/Urdu • Indonesian • Italian • Japanese • Korean • Lao • Malay • Mandarin • Mediterranean Europe *(Albanian, Croatian, Greek, Italian, Macedonian, Maltese, Serbian, Slovene)* • Mongolian • Nepali • Papua New Guinea • Pilipino (Tagalog) • Quechua • Russian • Scandinavian Europe *(Danish, Finnish, Icelandic, Norwegian, Swedish)* • South-East Asia *(Burmese, Indonesian, Khmer, Lao, Malay, Tagalog Pilipino, Thai, Vietnamese)* • Spanish (Castilian) *(also includes Catalan, Galician and Basque)* • Spanish (Latin American) • Sri Lanka • Swahili • Thai • Tibetan • Turkish • Ukrainian • USA *(US English, Vernacular Talk, Native American languages, Hawaiian)* • Vietnamese • Western Europe *(Basque, Catalan, Dutch, French, German, Greek, Irish)*

Lonely Planet Journeys

J OURNEYS is a unique collection of travel writing – published by the company that understands travel better than anyone else. It is a series for anyone who has ever experienced – or dreamed of – the magical moment when they encountered a strange culture or saw a place for the first time. They are tales to read while you're planning a trip, while you're on the road or while you're in an armchair, in front of a fire.

These outstanding titles explore our planet through the eyes of a diverse group of international writers. JOURNEYS books catch the spirit of a place, illuminate a culture, recount a crazy adventure, or introduce a fascinating way of life. They always entertain, and always enrich the experience of travel.

MALI BLUES
Traveling to an African Beat
Lieve Joris (translated by Sam Garrett)

Drought, rebel uprisings, ethnic conflict: these are the predominant images of West Africa. But as Lieve Joris travels in Senegal, Mauritania and Mali, she meets survivors, fascinating individuals charting new ways of living between tradition and modernity. With her remarkable gift for drawing out people's stories, Joris brilliantly captures the rhythms of a world that refuses to give in.

THE GATES OF DAMASCUS
Lieve Joris (translated by Sam Garrett)

This best-selling book is a beautifully drawn portrait of day-to-day life in modern Syria. Through her intimate contact with local people, Lieve Joris draws us into the fascinating world that lies behind the gates of Damascus. Hala's husband is a political prisoner, jailed for his opposition to the Assad regime; through the author's friendship with Hala we see how Syrian politics impacts on the lives of ordinary people.

THE OLIVE GROVE
Travels in Greece
Katherine Kizilos

Katherine Kizilos travels to fabled islands, troubled border zones and her family's village deep in the mountains. She vividly evokes breathtaking landscapes, generous people and passionate politics, capturing the complexities of a country she loves.

'beautifully captures the real tensions of Greece' – *Sunday Times*

KINGDOM OF THE FILM STARS
Journey into Jordan
Annie Caulfield

Kingdom of the Film Stars is a travel book and a love story. With honesty and humour, Annie Caulfield writes of travelling in Jordan and falling in love with a Bedouin with film-star looks.

She offers fascinating insights into the country – from the tent life of traditional women to the hustle of downtown Amman – and unpicks tight-woven Western myths about the Arab world.

LONELY PLANET

Lonely Planet Travel Atlases

Lonely Planet has long been famous for the number and quality of its guidebook maps. Now we've gone one step further and produced a handy companion series: Lonely Planet travel atlases – maps of a country produced in book form.

Unlike other maps, which look good but lead travellers astray, our travel atlases have been researched on the road by Lonely Planet's experienced team of writers. All details are carefully checked to ensure the atlas corresponds with the equivalent Lonely Planet guidebook.

- full-colour throughout
- maps researched and checked by Lonely Planet authors
- place names correspond with Lonely Planet guidebooks
- no confusing spelling differences
- legend and travelling information in English, French, German, Japanese and Spanish
- size: 230 x 160 mm

Available now: Chile & Easter Island • Egypt • India & Bangladesh • Israel & the Palestinian Territories • Jordan, Syria & Lebanon • Kenya • Laos • Portugal • South Africa, Lesotho & Swaziland • Thailand • Turkey • Vietnam • Zimbabwe, Botswana & Namibia

---

Lonely Planet TV Series & Videos

Lonely Planet travel guides have been brought to life on television screens around the world. Like our guides, the programmes are based on the joy of independent travel, and look honestly at some of the most exciting, picturesque and frustrating places in the world. Each show is presented by one of three travellers from Australia, England or the USA and combines an innovative mixture of video, Super-8 film, atmospheric soundscapes and original music.

Videos of each episode – containing additional footage not shown on television – are available from good book and video shops, but the availability of individual videos varies with regional screening schedules.

Video destinations include: Alaska • American Rockies • Australia – The South-East • Baja California & the Copper Canyon • Brazil • Central Asia • Chile & Easter Island • Corsica, Sicily & Sardinia – The Mediterranean Islands • East Africa (Tanzania & Zanzibar) • Ecuador & the Galapagos Islands • Greenland & Iceland • Indonesia • Israel & the Sinai Desert • Jamaica • Japan • La Ruta Maya • Morocco • New York • North India • Pacific Islands (Fiji, Solomon Islands & Vanuatu) • South India • South West China • Turkey • Vietnam • West Africa • Zimbabwe, Botswana & Namibia

The Lonely Planet TV series is produced by: Pilot Productions
The Old Studio
18 Middle Row
London W10 5AT UK

LONELY PLANET

Guides by Region

Lonely Planet is known worldwide for publishing practical, reliable and no-nonsense travel information in our guides and on our web site. The Lonely Planet list covers just about every accessible part of the world. Currently there are nine series: travel guides, shoestring guides, walking guides, city guides, phrasebooks, audio packs, travel atlases, diving and snorkelling guides and travel literature.

AFRICA Africa – the South • Africa on a shoestring • Arabic (Egyptian) phrasebook • Arabic (Moroccan) phrasebook • Cairo • Cape Town • Central Africa • East Africa • Egypt • Egypt travel atlas • Ethiopian (Amharic) phrasebook • The Gambia & Senegal • Kenya • Kenya travel atlas • Malawi, Mozambique & Zambia • Morocco • North Africa • South Africa, Lesotho & Swaziland • South Africa, Lesotho & Swaziland travel atlas • Swahili phrasebook • Trekking in East Africa • Tunisia • West Africa • Zimbabwe, Botswana & Namibia • Zimbabwe, Botswana & Namibia travel atlas
Travel Literature: The Rainbird: A Central African Journey • Songs to an African Sunset: A Zimbabwean Story • Mali Blues: Traveling to an African Beat

AUSTRALIA & THE PACIFIC Australia • Australian phrasebook • Bushwalking in Australia • Bushwalking in Papua New Guinea • Fiji • Fijian phrasebook • Islands of Australia's Great Barrier Reef • Melbourne • Micronesia • New Caledonia • New South Wales & the ACT • New Zealand • Northern Territory • Outback Australia • Papua New Guinea • Papua New Guinea (Pidgin) phrasebook • Queensland • Rarotonga & the Cook Islands • Samoa • Solomon Islands • South Australia • Sydney • Tahiti & French Polynesia • Tasmania • Tonga • Tramping in New Zealand • Vanuatu • Victoria • Western Australia
Travel Literature: Islands in the Clouds • Sean & David's Long Drive

CENTRAL AMERICA & THE CARIBBEAN Bahamas and Turks & Caicos • Bermuda • Central America on a shoestring • Costa Rica • Cuba • Eastern Caribbean • Guatemala, Belize & Yucatán: La Ruta Maya • Jamaica • Mexico • Mexico City • Panama
Travel Literature: Green Dreams: Travels in Central America

EUROPE Amsterdam • Andalucia • Austria • Baltic States phrasebook • Berlin • Britain • Central Europe • Central Europe phrasebook • Czech & Slovak Republics • Denmark • Dublin • Eastern Europe • Eastern Europe phrasebook • Estonia, Latvia & Lithuania • Finland • France • French phrasebook • Germany • German phrasebook • Greece • Greek phrasebook • Hungary • Iceland, Greenland & the Faroe Islands • Ireland • Italian phrasebook • Italy • Lisbon • London • Mediterranean Europe • Mediterranean Europe phrasebook • Paris • Poland • Portugal • Portugal travel atlas • Prague • Romania & Moldova • Russia, Ukraine & Belarus • Russian phrasebook • Scandinavian & Baltic Europe • Scandinavian Europe phrasebook • Slovenia • Spain • Spanish phrasebook • St Petersburg • Switzerland • Trekking in Spain • Ukrainian phrasebook • Vienna • Walking in Britain • Walking in Italy • Walking in Switzerland • Western Europe • Western Europe phrasebook
Travel Literature: The Olive Grove: Travels in Greece

INDIAN SUBCONTINENT Bangladesh • Bengali phrasebook • Bhutan • Delhi • Goa • Hindi/Urdu phrasebook • India • India & Bangladesh travel atlas • Indian Himalaya • Karakoram Highway • Nepal • Nepali phrasebook • Pakistan • Rajasthan • South India • Sri Lanka • Sri Lanka phrasebook • Trekking in the Indian Himalaya • Trekking in the Karakoram & Hindukush • Trekking in the Nepal Himalaya
Travel Literature: In Rajasthan • Shopping for Buddhas

LONELY PLANET

Mail Order

Lonely Planet products are distributed worldwide.They are also available by mail order from Lonely Planet, so if you have difficulty finding a title please write to us. North and South American residents should write to 150 Linden St, Oakland CA 94607, USA; European and African residents should write to 10a Spring Place, London NW5 3BH; and residents of other countries to PO Box 617, Hawthorn, Victoria 3122, Australia.

ISLANDS OF THE INDIAN OCEAN Madagascar & Comoros • Maldives • Mauritius, Réunion & Seychelles

MIDDLE EAST & CENTRAL ASIA Arab Gulf States • Central Asia • Central Asia phrasebook • Iran • Israel & the Palestinian Territories • Israel & the Palestinian Territories travel atlas • Istanbul • Jerusalem • Jordan & Syria • Jordan, Syria & Lebanon travel atlas • Lebanon • Middle East on a shoestring • Turkey • Turkish phrasebook • Turkey travel atlas • Yemen
Travel Literature: The Gates of Damascus • Kingdom of the Film Stars: Journey into Jordan

NORTH AMERICA Alaska • Backpacking in Alaska • Baja California • California & Nevada • Canada • Florida • Hawaii • Honolulu • Los Angeles • Miami • New England USA • New Orleans • New York City • New York, New Jersey & Pennsylvania • Pacific Northwest USA • Rocky Mountain States • San Francisco • Seattle • Southwest USA • USA phrasebook • Washington, DC & the Capital Region
Travel Literature: Drive Thru America

NORTH-EAST ASIA Beijing • Cantonese phrasebook • China • Hong Kong • Hong Kong, Macau & Guangzhou • Japan • Japanese phrasebook • Japanese audio pack • Korea • Korean phrasebook • Kyoto • Mandarin phrasebook • Mongolia • Mongolian phrasebook • North-East Asia on a shoestring • Seoul • South West China • Taiwan • Tibet • Tibet phrasebook • Tokyo
Travel Literature: Lost Japan

SOUTH AMERICA Argentina, Uruguay & Paraguay • Bolivia • Brazil • Brazilian phrasebook • Buenos Aires • Chile & Easter Island • Chile & Easter Island travel atlas • Colombia • Ecuador & the Galapagos Islands • Latin American (Spanish) phrasebook • Peru • Quechua phrasebook • Rio de Janeiro • South America on a shoestring • Trekking in the Patagonian Andes • Venezuela
Travel Literature: Full Circle: A South American Journey

SOUTH-EAST ASIA Bali & Lombok • Bangkok • Burmese phrasebook • Cambodia • Hill Tribes phrasebook • Ho Chi Minh City • Indonesia • Indonesian phrasebook • Indonesian audio pack • Jakarta • Java • Laos • Lao phrasebook • Laos travel atlas • Malay phrasebook • Malaysia, Singapore & Brunei • Myanmar (Burma) • Philippines • Pilipino (Tagalog) phrasebook • Singapore • South-East Asia on a shoestring • South-East Asia phrasebook • Thailand • Thailand's Islands & Beaches • Thailand travel atlas • Thai phrasebook • Thai audio pack • Vietnam • Vietnamese phrasebook • Vietnam travel atlas

ALSO AVAILABLE: Antarctica • Brief Encounters: Stories of Love, Sex & Travel • Chasing Rickshaws • Not the Only Planet: Travel Stories from Science Fiction • Travel with Children • Traveller's Tales

LONELY PLANET

Lonely Planet Online
www.lonelyplanet.com *or* **AOL keyword: lp**

Whether you've just begun planning your next trip, or you're chasing down specific info on currency regulations or visa requirements, check out Lonely Planet Online for up-to-the minute travel information.

As well as mini guides to more than 250 destinations, you'll find maps, photos, travel news, health and visa updates, travel advisories, and discussion of the ecological and political issues you need to be aware of as you travel. You'll also find timely upgrades to popular guidebooks which you can print out and stick in the back of your book.

There's also an online travellers' forum where you can share your experience of life on the road, meet travel companions and ask other travellers for their recommendations and advice.

And of course we have a complete and up-to-date list of all Lonely Planet travel products including travel guides, diving and snorkelling guides, phrasebooks, atlases, travel literature and videos, and a simple online ordering facility if you can't find the book you want elsewhere.

Lonely Planet Diving & Snorkelling Guides

Known for indispensible guidebooks to destinations all over the world, Lonely Planet's Pisces Books are the most popular series of diving and snorkelling titles available.

There are three series: **Diving & Snorkelling Guides**, **Shipwreck Diving** series, and **Dive Into History**. Full colour throughout, the **Diving & Snorkelling Guides** combine quality photographs with detailed descriptions of the best dive sites for each location, giving divers a glimpse of what they can expect both on land and in water. The **Dive Into History** series is perfect for the adventure diver or armchair traveller. The **Shipwreck Diving** series provides all the details for exploring the most interesting wrecks in the Atlantic and Pacific oceans. The list also includes underwater nature and technical guides.

LONELY PLANET

FREE Lonely Planet Newsletters

We love hearing from you and think you'd like to hear from us.

Planet Talk

Our FREE quarterly printed newsletter is full of tips from travellers and anecdotes from Lonely Planet guidebook authors. Every issue is packed with up-to-date travel news and advice, and includes:

- a postcard from Lonely Planet co-founder Tony Wheeler
- a swag of mail from travellers
- a look at life on the road through the eyes of a Lonely Planet author
- topical health advice
- prizes for the best travel yarn
- news about forthcoming Lonely Planet events
- a complete list of Lonely Planet books and other titles

To join our mailing list, residents of the UK, Europe and Africa can email us at go@lonelyplanet.co.uk; residents of North and South America can email us at info@lonelyplanet.com; the rest of the world can email us at talk2us@lonelyplanet.com.au, or contact any Lonely Planet office.

Comet

Our FREE monthly email newsletter brings you all the latest travel news, features, interviews, competitions, destination ideas, travellers' tips & tales, Q&As, raging debates and related links. Find out what's new on the Lonely Planet Web site and which books are about to hit the shelves.

Subscribe from your desktop: www.lonelyplanet.com/comet

Index

Text

Bold indicates maps.
Italics indicates boxed text.

Boxed Text

MAP LEGEND

BOUNDARIES

- ▪—▪—▪— ....International
- ▪—▪—▪— ....Provincial
- — — — — ....Local

HYDROGRAPHY

- ~~~~ ....River, Creek
- ⬭ ....Lake
- ———— ....Canal

ROUTES & TRANSPORT

- ═════ ....Motorway
- ═════ ....Highway
- ━━━━ ....Major Road
- ──── ....Minor Road
- ═════ ....City Motorway
- ──── ....City Highway
- ━━━━ ....City Road
- ━━━━ ....City Street, Lane

- ══════ ....Unsealed Road
- ⇒═══ː ....Tunnel
- ⊢—⊢—●—⊢— ......Railway & Station
- ━━—Ⓜ—━ ....Metro & Station
- ⊬—⊬—⊬—⊬— ...Cable Car or Chair Lift
- ·············· ....Bus Route
- — — — — ....Footpath
- ·········· ....Walking Tour

AREA FEATURES

- ✝ ✝ ✗ ✗ ....Cemetery
- .... Forest

- ....Pedestrian Mall
- ....Urban Area

MAP SYMBOLS

- ⊙ **Vienna** ....National Capital
- ⬡ **Graz** ....Large City
- ● **Amstetten** ....City
- ● Kitzbühel ....Town
- ● Zürs ....Village

- ■ ....Place to Stay
- ⚠ ....Camping Ground
- ⛽ ....Caravan Park
- ⌂ ....Chalet
- ⌂ ....Shelter

- ▼ ....Place to Eat
- ☗ ....Pub or Bar

- ✈ ....Airport
- ⌐⊶ ....Ancient or City Wall
- ∴ ....Archaeological Site
- ⊖ ....Bank
- ⬈ ....Beach
- ⚐ ....Bird Sanctuary
- ⌘ ....Castle or Fort
- ⌒ ....Cave
- ▭ ⌂ ....Church
- ⌒⌒⌒ ......Cliff or Escarpment
- ⊘ ....Embassy
- ✿ ....Gardens
- ⚑ ....Golf Course
- ⊕ ....Hospital
- ⚲ ....Monument

- ▲ ....Mountain or Hill
- ⏛ ....Museum
- ← ....One Way Street
- ⓟ ....Parking
-)(................................Pass
- ⛽ ....Petrol Station
- ✉ ....Post Office
- 23 ....Route Number
- ❖ ....Shopping Centre
- ⏛ ....Stately Home
- ⌸ ....Swimming Pool
- ⓘ ...... Tourist Information
- ⊖ ....Transport
- ⟋ı ....Waterfall
- 🐘 ....Zoo

Note: not all symbols displayed above appear in this book

LONELY PLANET OFFICES

Australia
PO Box 617, Hawthorn, Victoria 3122
☎ (03) 9819 1877 fax (03) 9819 6459
email: talk2us@lonelyplanet.com.au

USA
150 Linden St, Oakland, CA 94607
☎ (510) 893 8555 TOLL FREE: 800 275 8555
fax (510) 893 8572
email: info@lonelyplanet.com

UK
10a Spring Place, London, NW5 3BH
☎ (0171) 428 4800 fax (0171) 428 4828
email: go@lonelyplanet.co.uk

France
1 rue du Dahomey, 75011 Paris
☎ 01 55 25 33 00 fax 01 55 25 33 01
email: bip@lonelyplanet.fr
3615 lonelyplanet *(1,29 F TTC/min)*

World Wide Web: www.lonelyplanet.com *or* AOL keyword: lp
Lonely Planet Images: lpi@lonelyplanet.com.au